Ralph Emerson McC

Ralph Emerson McGill

VOICE OF THE SOUTHERN CONSCIENCE

Leonard Ray Teel

THE UNIVERSITY OF TENNESSEE PRESS / KNOXVILLE

The paper used in this book meets the minimum requirements of ANSI/NISO
Z39.48-1992 (R 1997) (Permanence of Paper). The binding materials have been
chosen for strength and durability.

Library of Congress Cataloging-in-Publication Data

Teel, Leonard Ray.
    Ralph Emerson McGill : voice of the southern conscience / Leonard
Ray Teel. — 1st ed.
          p. cm.
Includes bibliographical references (p.   ) and index.
    ISBN 1-57233-133-X (cl. : alk. paper)
    ISBN 1-57233-135-6 (pbk. : alk. paper)
1. McGill, Ralph, 1898–1969. 2. Journalists—United States—Biography.
3. Southern States—Race relations. 4. African Americans—Civil rights—
Southern States. I. Title.
PN4874.M37 T44 2001
070' .92—dc21   00-012738

For

Harold E. Davis

Humanist, scholar, teacher, reporter, editor,
mentor, and friend

Contents

Illustrations

Preface

Historians can be remarkably clear about their intentions. Having settled on a subject, and committed to seeking the truth, they search out numerous routes to the past, starting on the main highways, diverging onto tributary roads and dusty lanes, alert for contexts, settings, milestones, memories, stories, documents, facts. From these sojourns, they return to piece together a narrative, attempting, as the Civil War historian Shelby Foote has said, "to reconcile differences and bring order out of multiplicity." The journey of the biographer may require years—I recall one specific expression of incredulity from a dear friend, JoAnn Sloan: "What's the hold-up?" With the commitment to truth, there is also the need for patience to allow the discoveries piece by piece to come together, eventually, one hopes, revealing a picture. Clearly, Ralph McGill was a great man, as Alabama publisher Malcolm MacDonald once surmised, "but I want to know—what made him tick?"

I never met Ralph Waldo Emerson McGill, but I felt I made acquaintance with his spirit. In July 1969, I went to work as a reporter in the same building where he had worked right up until the day he died five months earlier, at the age of seventy. There was still a McGill aura about the elevators that went to the *Atlanta Constitution* floor. There was a carryover of his legacy of thirty years of daily commentaries, and there was some curiosity about his successors, about who could "fill his shoes." In the city at large, both whites and blacks, freed in the early and mid-1960s from decades of obliging legal segregation, were adjusting to the new order as school desegregation proceeded under the watch of the federal courts and the concept of integration spread deliberately to questions about housing and jobs.

This process was moving along by the time Ralph McGill's friends and associates memorialized him in 1979 on the tenth anniversary of his death. The people who took the microphone to testify to his greatness gave, as a whole, a portrait of a personality bigger than life. Each had witnessed facets of this remarkable man. Listening that evening, it was possible to catch two implicit realities etched by the collective memory. First, that for the white population of "conscience," he had provided a steady, moral searchlight, beaming through the darkness of segregation for an end to the evil manifestations of racism. He could see years ahead. And, second, that this gathering of friends and acquaintances appreciated everything about the great man's feats and foibles such that his presence among them had made them greater. That night they were ennobled in the ensemble act of witnessing.

I carried these impressions of McGill with me as my career in journalism blended into my parallel endeavor to research the roots of human rights grievances in nineteenth- and twentieth-century African history and European colonialism. My interest in these matters was stimulated by the life, death, and philosophy of Martin Luther King Jr., and by living for the first time in a city with a majority African American population. My thesis on the systemic enslavement of Congo natives by the Belgian King Leopold, directed by Professor Duane Koenig of the University of Miami, was followed by a dissertation studying the influence of journalists upon British imperialism, directed by Professor Joseph Baylen of Georgia State University.

These streams of the contemporary and the historical joined in my work on the McGill biography only after I made the transition from daily journalism to teaching media history at Georgia State University. One day at lunch, Professor Harold E. Davis asked me to consider writing McGill's biography. He himself had just completed a biography of Henry Woodfin Grady, the only journalist ever honored by Atlanta with a public statue on a downtown thoroughfare. As the orator-editor of the *Atlanta Constitution* during the 1880s, Grady had championed a "New South," a torch McGill later carried. During the 1960s Harold had known McGill in the newsroom and as a guest in the Davis home, and had intended to write his biography but knew that he did have the time. This book is the result. As is customary, Harold Davis as the assignment editor on this project gets the credit for anything good that came of this work, and I as the writer take the blame for whatever else.

Leonard Ray Teel
Atlanta, Georgia

Acknowledgments

OVER A PERIOD of fourteen years, I have been graced by the talents, assistance, and encouragement of numerous people, for whom I am grateful. They have helped with free time, research assistance, financial grants for travel, mentoring, editing, forums for my early papers, publication of a few formative chapters, permissions, patience, general encouragement, and prodding.

Apart from Harold E. Davis, the originator of this project, the cast of colleagues at Georgia State University who helped me along the way includes the chairs of the Department of Communication, who arranged release time from teaching, especially Marsha Stanback and Carol Winkler, and the Dean of the College of Arts and Sciences, Ahmed Abdelal.

Helping me with the research tasks in the early going was the late Elmo Colburn, a Ph.D. candidate in history, and graduate research assistants Francesca Cesa Bianchi, Zehra Barlas, Zhong Yi, Rachel Ramos, and Miglena Sandmeier, and presidential scholar Stacey Evans. Numerous graduate students contributed pieces of the puzzle, especially Beth Ann Hill, with her sensitive reading of McGill's love letters to Louise Stevens, Drew Dowell, with his analysis of the cyclical recurrence of McGill's main themes, and Hye Kyeong Pae, who helped me to lift the level of discourse.

One of the lessons of historiography is the essential importance of librarians. I hope not to omit anyone who helped. The bulk of the Ralph Emerson McGill Papers today are housed in Special Collections on the top floor of the Robert W. Woodruff Library at Emory University, and for guidance through the indexed boxes I thank all on that staff, especially Linda Mathews and, more recently, Laura Micham. At Georgia State University's Pullen Library, interlibrary loan specialists, especially Jane Hobson and Margie Patterson, secured the entire microfilm of the *Nashville Banner* during the 1920s. The history of McGill's family and his own early years in Chattanooga were fleshed out with inestimable assistance from Holly Hodges of Special Collections and William W. Prince, head of the Reference and Information Services at the T. Cartter and Margaret Rawlings Lupton Library at the University of Tennessee–Chattanooga. For background on McGill's university years, I thank the various staffers at the Jean and Alexander Heard Library at Vanderbilt University. Researchers at the Library of Congress made my day when they handed me the Carl W. Ackerman Papers, including his diary and letters to his wife, Vandy. Also of great value was Bill Brown's staff, which provided access to the William C. Baggs Papers in Special Collections at the Otto G. Richter Library at the University of Miami, Florida. The Baggs Papers had only recently been donated to the university by his widow, Joan, and I thank her especially for the special privilege of letting me ascend into the attic of her house to survey the letters ahead of everyone. At the Atlanta Newspapers Archives, archivist Richard Hallman of the Research Services Division led me directly to the Ralph McGill and Clark Howell files. I am also grateful to the librarians who permitted me, on short notice, to peruse the Martin Luther King Jr. Papers at Boston University, and the Harry S. Truman Papers at the Truman Library, Independence, Missouri.

Certain individuals were particularly helpful. Alan Duke of CNN had already catalogued the Lyndon B. Johnson White House Tapes, indexed so precisely that he could locate McGill's conversations with LBJ. Kittrell Rushing guided me around the Chattanooga courthouse and introduced me to Holly Hodges at the Lupton Library. Douglass Daniel helped me research the Eisenhower-McGill correspondence at the Eisenhower Library. Kathleen L. Endres and archivist John Miller assisted with the John S. Knight Papers.

Financial grants assisted my travels. The National Endowment for the Humanities made possible trips to Boston and to Miami to discover the Baggs Papers in the attic. My home base, the Department of Communication, provided a steady base of support for presenting papers at conferences and doing research while in those cities. Competitive grants from the U.S. Information Agency permitted us to conduct workshops in Africa, South Asia, and the Middle East and North Africa, permitting international travel to sites where McGill lectured and spoke.

No amount of thanks is adequate for those who mentored me and edited my early manuscript as I was trying to find the threads and tell the meaningful stories. Chief among these was the late Professor Harold E. Davis of Georgia State University, who encouraged me in the early research papers presented to the American Journalism Historians Association and was able to read through chapter 14. I am grateful too for the careful reading given the draft manuscript by historians David Garrow of Emory University and David Sumner of Ball State University. Patrick Washburn of Ohio University guided me through the hoops of the Freedom of Information Act as I applied successfully for McGill's FBI files. John Merrill of the University of Missouri directed me to an international venue at the University of Miami, suitable for presenting papers on McGill's overseas adventures. Another helpful forum was provided by the History Division of the Association for Education in Journalism and Mass Communication, at whose Southeast Colloquium at the University of North Carolina–Chapel Hill I presented the paper on McGill and Carl Sandburg.

Authors, literary agents, and publishers moved the project along insightfully. Georgia State University biographer Virginia Spencer Carr gave every encouragement. She also directed me to her New York agent, Roberta Pryor. Miss Pryor, after a careful reading of three early chapters and an evening sharing a bottle of Southern Comfort in her Manhattan apartment, asked me a few poignant questions. She also returned my chapters, edited. In the same vein, Malcolm Call of the University of Georgia raised provocative questions about the early chapters, encouraging me to elevate the level of discourse. While he was at the University of Alabama Press, Malcolm MacDonald showed a keen interest in the book and would have published it, I think, if I had finished it while he was there. It was he who gave me one of his press's t-shirts printed with the prodding message in white letters on crimson: Publish or Perish.

That this biography of a native Tennessean was published by the University of Tennessee Press would have pleased Ralph McGill. It has certainly pleased me to work with so cooperative and professional a team, notably my own editor, Scot Danforth, the senior editorial assistant June Hussey, and the press director Jennifer M. Siler.

Publication of an important segment of McGill's career gave credibility to the subject and a foundation for completion of the whole work. I am indebted to Professor David Sloan of the University of Alabama for overseeing the publication in *American Journalism* of the first article, on McGill's worldwide mission for international freedom of the press.

I worry that I cannot list all the other people who cooperated with me, persuaded as they were that I was doing something of value and would complete the work. They gave me permissions, showed patience with repeated interviews, provided general encouragement and necessary prodding. Among these were the connections to McGill's years in Tennessee, including Frances "Fannie" Cheney and Fred Russell. Some contemporaries of McGill's generation who helped me have since died, among them former governor Ellis Arnall, Jack Tarver, Harry Ashmore, Harold Martin, John Griffin, John Popham, and Harold Davis. Others who continue to be helpful include Eugene Patterson, Jack Spalding, Mary Lynn Morgan, Calvin Kytle, Margaret Tarver, and Jack Tarver Jr.

This book of course would never have been completed without the constant support of my wife, Katie, the daughter of a historian of the South, together with the persistent questions from my two purposeful, Montessori-educated children, Oliver and Elizabeth.

Grateful acknowledgment is made to Mary Lynn Morgan of Atlanta for permission to "cite the various and sundry works in the Ralph Emerson McGill Collection."

Excerpts from *Ralph McGill, Reporter,* by Harold H. Martin, published by Macmillan, Boston, in 1972, are reprinted with permission of Little, Brown and Company (Inc.).

Grateful acknowledgment is made to Calvin McLeod Logue for permission to reprint excerpts from *Ralph McGill, Editor and Publisher,* published by Moore Publishing Company, Durham, N.C. in 1969.

References from *Henry Grady's New South* by Harold E. Davis, published by the University of Alabama Press, Tuscaloosa, in 1990, is granted by Priscilla Davis.

Photographs from the Ralph Emerson McGill Papers, reprinted by permission of Mary Lynn Morgan and the Woodruff Library, Emory University, in Atlanta.

Grateful acknowledgment is made to Charles R. Pugh Jr. for permission to reprint his photographs.

Grateful acknowledgment is made to Robert J. "Jeff" Norrell for sharing his manuscript, "Next Steps to Democracy: The First Fifty Years of the Southern Regional Council."

Introduction

Bury the South together with this man
Bury the bygone South . . .
Bury the whip, bury the branding-bars,
Bury the unjust thing . . .
And with these things, bury the purple dream
Of the America we have not been. . . .
—STEPHEN VINCENT BENÉT,
John Brown's Body

I live my life in growing orbits,
which move out over the things of the world.
Perhaps I can never achieve the last,
but that will be my attempt.
—RAINER MARIA RILKE,
"I Live My Life," 1899

AMERICAN JOURNALISM IS the nation's daily witness to freedom of expression, or its absence. In no other country do the constitution and the laws actually permit a journalist to publish, so freely and so widely, ideas that offend the ruling elite and violate the social conventions of the majority of citizens.[1] Yet in the history of this country there have been subjects considered so taboo that they were rarely mentioned in public. The career of Ralph Emerson McGill became a model for a social reformer willing to risk hostility and isolation to break the "spiral of silence" in public opinion about one particular taboo, often called the greatest moral issue in twentieth-century America.[2] McGill shed the straitjacket that confined conscientious southern journalists from questioning racial segregation.

Beginning in the late 1930s and continuing for thirty years, McGill's daily columns in the *Atlanta Constitution* steadily inserted the issue of racial justice into a southern public agenda that, by a code among whites, excluded consideration of the issue. The power of the press to stimulate public discourse had become a lively subject during the 1920s in the writings of Walter Lippmann and Edward Bernays. The media could reinforce or redirect public opinion by "choosing what to emphasize and what to ignore or suppress—in effect, organizing much of the political world for us."[3] McGill began by emphasizing questions, posed gradually at first, rather than answers. But his questions about the morality and justice of enforced segregation broke open something that would never be put back together again. Long after he had been targeted for vilification, McGill pictured the dilemma of segregation in one of his characteristic ways, by telling a story:

> Back in the days of minstrel shows there was one end-man ballad singer whose specialty was titled: "I'm the Only Man in the World Who Can Take a Biscuit Apart and Put It Back Together Again Just Like It Was."
>
> In a very real sense the inability to do just this is the dilemma of the Southern politicians. . . . They spend much of their time and emotions continually trying to put the biscuit back together again just like it was.
>
> They can't. No matter how much of the molasses of tradition and recrimination they pour on it, it never will go back "just like it was."[4]

With the attitude of a teacher and the aim of a reformer, McGill sought to arouse white southerners of like mind whose consciences lay dormant or anaesthetized. The circulation of the *Constitution* reached some editors in smaller communities who, in time, were emboldened to speak despite segregationist law and politics. In urging a friend and colleague to express his conscience more confidently, McGill confirmed his professional credo: "You can say it in print, you can say it to a million people. That's what you've got to do in the newspaper business."[5]

When McGill's career in journalism began, first in Tennessee and then in Georgia in the 1920s, the South was locked by law into a system of segregation. Apart from laws, the system was regulated by public signs and private vigilantes who punished errant social behavior with nighttime whippings and lynchings. All of this confounded the precepts of Christian ethics, the Declaration of Independence, the spirit of the Constitution, and the Supreme Court's 1896 ruling condoning a "separate but equal" society. "There was never anywhere an effort to make the separateness equal," McGill noted.[6] Southerners, then, generations after the bloodletting of the Civil War, lived separate but unequal lives. Law kept the Negro in place, in his own neighborhood, in his own church, in his own school, in his own job, in his own rest room, in his own place at the back of the bus.

In time, McGill made it his concern to do something about the "sickness" of racism. He saw white southerners living lives of hypocrisy in churches and on the streets as if helpless to do anything about it. Certainly they seemed to have no incentive to change. The politicians of the era vehemently reinforced silence. Those who disagreed with the South's disregard of human rights were more likely to conceal their views rather than express themselves in public for fear of ostracism. In polite white society, the thinking went like this: Segregation was "the situation." You did not talk about the situation, code-named "the sitch." There was nothing you could do about it. It would only stir up trouble. Against the silence, the situation prevailed as the dominant way of life for southerners through most of McGill's life.

McGill's principal contribution in thirty years as editor and publisher of the *Atlanta Constitution* was to break this silence at every opportunity. He had a hound's nose for sniffing prey, and frequently his prey was some unexamined hypocrisy. Time and again, he cast up a subject that had been suppressed from discussion during years of racism—the right to vote, to justice, to equal education, to housing, to jobs.

McGill's philosophical development had been shaped well before he came to Atlanta. Reared in a reverent Presbyterian family, he developed a personal commitment to Christian values that eventually alienated him from formal churchgoing—"the astonishing spectacle of ministers of the gospel angrily defining Christianity as a segregated religion."[7] His high school training honed a debater's skill at finding gaps in others' arguments and a love of public speaking. Tennessee journalism stirred a passion for politics. His Vanderbilt years encouraged a love of

poetry and a respect for the writers of the 1920s who attacked convention, among them H. L. Mencken and Stephen Vincent Benét.

When he first induced readers to think about race, it was with the
gentlest nudging. He simply asked whether the South had fulfilled the
promise of "separate but equal." Was there equality in voting rights? In
the schools? People read this and began to talk, many only to curse
him. He risked and received social approbation, epithets, and threats.
From others, eventually, he earned love, appreciation, and one particular professional honor he felt he deserved—the Pulitzer Prize. Among
newspaper rivals in Atlanta, some said his ego drove him to violate the
code of silence solely to attract attention to himself.

McGill lived his life in expanding orbits. Fulfilling dreams fed by a
lifelong love of reading, he traveled far beyond his isolated rural birth-
place near Soddy, Tennessee, and his boyhood oasis of Chattanooga.
After university life at Vanderbilt, he traveled across the South as a sports
writer, crafting a masterful storytelling style afterward described as "pun-
gent" and "colloquial." He ended his long confinement to sports topics
at the age of forty. Building upon his earned readership, he then flourished
for thirty years as an influential observer of political, social, and economic situations. He never lost his sense of humor, nor his concern for
the South, which he loved "with a fierce protective passion such as parents have for a crippled child[,] . . . crippled by discriminatory rates and
tariffs; an orphan child whose parents of wealth and culture were killed
on the field at Appomattox." Nor did he lose his sting: "Not all the per-
fumes of Araby will wash clean the political hands of Mississippi's Governor Ross Barnett." For all this he disgusted some and gained the respect
of others. "How one saw him," the scholar Calvin Logue surmised, "usually reflected as much the observer as the observed."[8]

He realized his dream of making his work his play, of traveling
the world and sharing in the experiences of other cultures, of making a
difference. In these tumultuous years, his philosophical development
was influenced greatly by his frequent use of travel as method for learning. He was in Vienna to witness the Nazi takeover and Nazi racism
against the Jews, which galvanized his revulsion for "home-grown"
demagogues. He was in England in wartime, and as the war was ending, he circled the globe. In 1946, going directly from the Nuremberg

war criminal trials to see Jewish settlements in Palestine, then under the British Mandate, he was persuaded to support the movement to create a new nation of Israel.

By the early 1940s, McGill's leadership caught the attention of national media. As his views distinguished him from the mass of southern journalists, the press in Boston and New York portrayed him as "the conscience of the South." When reporters needed to know something about the South, time and again they telephoned or visited McGill for a comment, often referring to him as a spokesman for the New South. McGill readily accepted the opportunity to speak for the South, as *Constitution* editor Henry Grady had done in his "New South" speeches of the 1880s. Urged by a Boston publisher to write his autobiography, McGill did so, calling it *The South and the Southerner.* His appreciation of the history, geography, and culture of his region empowered him. Few at that time wrote about the South with more insight and sensitivity.

There is room for debate about McGill's place in the great movement for civil rights in the segregated South. But there is no doubt that his daily columns, focusing frequently on the race issue and an "honest facing up to facts," thrust the issue into the arena of public discourse. When all is considered, he was seldom far ahead of his readers, although it seemed so, given the vehemence with which racists and demagogues called him "Rastus" and "Red Ralph" and "traitor to the South." Against the silence of the majority, the voices of reaction sounded all the greater. Through the 1940s, he was not yet advocating an end to segregation, only acknowledgment of the failure of "separate but equal." He offered that the South had been "dishonest" in its segregation policy: "We wrote our laws to say that while the races were to be separated, we would provide 'separate but equal' educational, travel, recreational and other facilities. This we have not done."[9]

The idea of equitable treatment for Negroes raised the specters of social mixing and intermarriage, fear fanned by political rhetoric. In the 1940s McGill assured readers that he respected the law as it was. "There will be no mixing of races in the schools," he wrote. "There will be no social equality measures." For personal and political reasons, McGill was persuaded by friends and instinct against going too far ahead of his white flock.[10]

Part teacher, part preacher, he tried for thirty years to show southerners a peaceful way out of the Old South and into the new one— a transition he told them was "inevitable." After the Supreme Court's *Brown v. Board of Education* decision in 1954, the issue he had championed was now plainly thrust onto the public agenda across the entire region. The South "became a substantially open forum, which sharply distinguishes this contemporary period from earlier ones." The debate now was joined by more than segregationists and rabble-rousers— there were ordinary people, men and women, blacks and whites.[11] Accordingly, McGill adjusted his course, now asking southerners to disregard frenetic demagogues and white citizens' councils and instead obey the higher law laid down by the U.S. Supreme Court. He warned that the cost of noncompliance could be federal intervention as happened in Little Rock, Arkansas, or a disastrous closing of the public schools. His public and private efforts helped Georgia schools pass from Governor Ernest Vandiver's obstinate "No, not one" to the concession of token desegregation. When those in the civil rights movement demanded speedier desegregation, McGill's advocacy of obedience to law kept him from endorsing illegal acts. Eventually, he conceded that the students' nonviolent lunch-counter sit-ins had speeded the end of segregated public accommodations.

In his final years, McGill was deeply saddened when the Vietnam War widened fissures among social groups and caused friction between him and friends. His lifelong loyalty to the Democratic Party and the U.S. Marines, and his friendship with President Lyndon Johnson, committed him to support the war long after others had sided with the antiwar movement. His support for the war was evidence to some of his inability to evaluate foreign affairs with the same instinctive accuracy he brought to segregation and other problems closer to home.

PART I
The Long Apprenticeship

1

Provincial

*There was a South of slavery and secession—that South is
dead. There is a South of union and freedom—that South,
thank God, is living, breathing, growing every hour.*
—Sen. Benjamin Hill of Georgia, c. 1870

The prospect of revolution in Cuba quickened his spirit. In the
newsroom of the *Atlanta Constitution,* in the summer of 1933, Ralph
McGill hovered over a teletype machine and read the latest story, of
protests against the president, arrests, gunfire, bloodshed, and a secret,
shadowy, outlawed society. The machine's keys clacked the words noisily. News editors would soon come by and, with a deft snap of the
wrist, rip the paper evenly off the roll and send the story to be edited
for page one. A prime benefit of newspaper work was that McGill could
read the news before it was published.

In Atlanta, at a clinical distance of almost a thousand miles, he
could picture the lovely island for which men were dying. His one
visit there had been brief, a stopover in port, long enough to sample
the culture and cuisine and make friends. His first friends were fellow
sportswriters who surprised him with their attention to American baseball. They chatted expertly about the major leagues, spoke glowingly
of the great Babe Ruth and Lou Gehrig, and cited batting averages
and home-run counts. Cubans had entered the American orbit as a
prize from the Spanish-American War. Many more Americans discovered Havana after 1918. During the dozen dry years of American Prohibition the harbor became a beacon for wets, with Havana opening
its arms gladly every night. Nightlife attracted men with wallets into
a variety of intoxicating adventures. Southerners of both races found
an additional sanctuary. Here, off the southern coastline, was a foreign land where one could escape for a time the strictures of strictly
segregated society.

Havana in the 1920s had been buoyed by an economic boom, sweet-ened by its sugar exports. Now, with the deepening of America's Depres-sion, the island's economic euphoria had receded like a flood, revealing a regime, engorged from the good times but unable to answer where much of the nation's wealth had wandered. To many, evidently, it seemed time for Cuba's president to step down. The conflict stimulated McGill's instinct to return.

He trusted his inspirations. McGill thrived on envisioning the possibilities of a situation well before they were obvious to desk-bound editors who habitually relied on the wire service reports for events beyond their normal reach. This reliance, which bred an institutional apathy when it came to news gathering, was fortified by the fact that most newspaper publishers in the South discouraged paying their own reporters to travel beyond the orbit of the paper's circulation. For as long as anyone could remember a key to a story's news value was its *proximity*.

In a parsimonious profession, travel money was spent when there was a clear payback, as when a politically motivated publisher was supporting a candidate and authorized expenses for his reporters to cover the campaign thoroughly, statewide. Newspapers did pay for travel to sporting spectacles, even across state lines, holding back the largest bankroll for the fall cycle of southern college football. In other cases, however, provincial publishers imposed strict limits to largess, usually bounded by the state line. Journalists (except those covering the southern sports leagues) usually did not cross the border. Yet in Tennessee, on one notable day years earlier, McGill's intense curiosity had succeeded in breaking the travel ban. He persuaded reluctant edi-tors to free him from daily duties to the sports pages in order to travel to the next state, to a remote cavern in Kentucky, where frenzied res-cuers were trying to save a young man trapped when a rock fall pinned him below ground. Floyd Collins was only one sad soul, but McGill saw a story in the thousands who gathered at the mouth of Sand Cave watching the attempts. McGill was right. Through newspapers and the mysterious reach of radio, one man held a nation in mourning. Collins had nothing to do with Nashville, Tennessee, but people there read all the details McGill supplied. In such ways McGill slipped past the borders and checkpoints of provincial journalism, each new success encouraging him to more.

For a young newspaperman, disasters and murder trials distinguished a day. They were like gifts, dramatic distractions from daily routine, like the thrill a child feels when a snowfall cancels school. These emotional elevations of newsroom life were ephemeral, the thrill of that day, usually leading nowhere. The conflict in Cuba offered more than an isolated adventure. It might carry him for days or months. It was as though the muse of journalism spoke directly, presenting him with a gift revolution, answering his fervent wish to escape confinement.

On the surface McGill seemed suited to the job of sports editor. Since his days as a cub reporter, in the early 1920s while still at Vanderbilt University, he had matured in the role, rounding out with the body fat that accrued from watching football comfortably rather than playing it strenuously as he had at Vanderbilt. He had found one of those grooves in newspaper work where one might stay for years so long as he remained competent and showed up for work. There was comfort, too, in the foreshortened name by which he was known to the klatch of reporters who traveled from one press box to another: "Mac." A name that did not suit his image of himself as poetic and philosophical, a seed planted by his father when he deliberately christened him Ralph Waldo Emerson McGill. In fact, those few in whom he confided knew he was restless to escape this groove.

At thirty-five, the age at which writers are often said to be *flourishing*, McGill had the feeling of being confined, as in a close room. During his student days at Vanderbilt he relished the sessions of the university's "Fugitive" poets and for a long time labored at verse before compromising by turning to journalistic writing. When he entered his first newsroom in Nashville, he imagined that newspaper work would open to him the world of people seriously engaged in politics and economics, ideas and art, literature and poetry. And frequently this happened, though usually by chance, and never often enough or long enough. He was keen to spend *hours* with people with ideas and engaging stories. In the summer of 1933 even a vivid imagination could not have persuaded him that his circle of friends would eventually include great poets, writers, politicians, and intellectuals. Years would pass before he counted as friends and associates the poet Carl Sandburg, the novelist Carson McCullers, the sociologist Gunnar Myrdal.

Apart from a small cluster of friends, McGill found he was much of the time conversing or making small talk with people who were less interested in his ideas than in the pitcher who might help the Atlanta Crackers win the Southern Association. Many whom he came across in his daily rounds were, if not brain-dead, backward looking, undereducated, racist, or simply uncouth, of the ilk he had come to label as *ginks*.[1]

A decade earlier in Nashville, he fashioned himself as a connoisseur of ginks. As he made the rounds of the city, which in the 1920s was swelling with the largest in-migration in its history, he cataloged, classified, and labeled bores and other offenders, as Linaeus might have done for subhuman species. Ginks were the barbarians one suffered in daily transactions on streets or in trolleys, some of them untutored in simple courtesies. The females of the species he called *ginkettes*. He preserved their obnoxious gestures and habits in brief boxlike paragraphs published daily on the front page of the *Banner*.

McGill's condemnatory tone echoed H. L. Mencken's lament for the South as a whole. In the early 1920s, Mencken rattled southerners by declaring that their once-gallant and intellectual culture had been subsumed by "white trash," which had bubbled to the top of the ooze after the Civil War. Many of the Vanderbilt Fugitives brooded that Mencken was all too correct. Determining to do something about it, McGill appointed himself to hunt down the oozy creatures, whether to reform them or simply to affirm to Mencken that *some* southerners recognized and disdained "trash." Each day, his ginks were castigated prominently. The *Banner* featured his miniatures in a bottom corner of page one, across from the syndicated snippets of western sage Will Rogers. The idea caught on, and McGill, too, soon became syndicated, but without his name. Only insiders knew McGill's role, until *Time* magazine in the 1940s revealed that Ralph had been the brain behind the gink.

In the long run, hunting down bores and belligerents did not liberate McGill. His philosophical barbs, though they supplied an unmet appetite, were not what the *Banner* hired him to do. In that respect the newspaper's hierarchy was authoritarian, not unlike a family in which editors often acted as father figures to their reporters, alternately encouraging and cajoling. From 1922 to 1929 McGill was fundamentally the *Banner*'s star sportswriter, increasingly popular, and eventually their star sports editor. He maintained a routine, attuned to the cycle of seasons. The poet in him thought of autumn's burnished leaves adorning the Tennessee hills, but the sports editor in him addressed the fervent southern male embarking on the *football season.* Day after day, in the role of "Mac," he chronicled life on the fields of play, and sometimes wandered well off the fields for his personal column, "Sports Aerial."

While football and baseball tethered him to the southern conferences, another sport freed him. He loved boxing. Boxing respected no seasonal restrictions or geographical boundaries, giving him license to indulge his craving to travel. Wanderlust had become an irrepressible longing, fed by voracious reading during his boyhood years in the watch-pocket burg of Chattanooga. The *Banner* lavished Mac with tickets for trains in all directions, the only stipulation being that there be a sporting event at the terminus. With good results and increasing frequency, his trains went farther, crossing the Tennessee border, and the farther they went, the better.

After eight years at the *Banner* he may have appeared the model of stability, until he turned thirty. Then, in the spring of 1929, in a burst of decisiveness, he changed dramatically and outwardly, as though Nashville had been his larval stage and he was leaving it in a call of nature. Friends and the prospects of a new life beckoned him, drawing him irresistibly, as to a dawn. Early that year, he seemed to get over a crush on his first real love, who had chosen someone else, and he married his second real love, Mary Elizabeth, a dentist's daughter. He quit his job, which was eagerly taken up by his assistant, who declined to move with him, and went east across the divide of the Appalachians to the biggest city in the Piedmont Plateau, where there were *three* newspapers to Nashville's two. A decade earlier, he had been among the waves of migrants who swelled the roads to Nashville in search of a better life. Now he was leaving for the same reason, certainly for a better salary to support a family, but also for something more personally urgent. At he approached thirty he was confiding a compulsion to get on with doing something more important with his life, something worthy of the ideals imbued by his parents and the education vested in him at Vanderbilt, clearly something more politically potent than sports writing, and to do it in a wider arena, a bigger city, less provincial, more competitive.

His friends at the morning *Constitution* persuaded management that McGill could help beat the two afternoon rivals, one of them bankrolled aggressively by William Randolph Hearst. The *Constitution* had the greater history. It been the city's first newspaper after the Civil War, beginning in 1868 as Atlanta itself was rebuilding from the ashes. It was joined in 1881 by the *Atlanta Journal,* and years later by the *Atlanta Georgian,* now owned by Hearst.

During the 1880s, the *Constitution* articulated the agenda of its politically and economically savvy one-fourth owner, Henry Woodfin Grady. Then in his early thirties, Grady was the most ingenious promoter the city had ever known. He traveled the rebuilt railroad to the triumphant North and assured investors in New York and Boston that a "New South" had emerged, a South where people were putting the Civil War behind them. The New South was eager to rejoin the Union in spirit as well as in law, at the very least for the understandable motive of promoting *economic* development. It was Grady, as financial promoter, who underscored for northern investors the advantages of moving mills to a region where wages for freedmen and poor whites alike were still depressed by the recent devastation of war and the dissolution of the plantation cotton economy. It was Grady, as political kingmaker—employing a secret code in which one word "meant" another—who manipulated statewide politics so his "Atlanta Ring" might elect its favorite sons to office and settle the dispute over the site of the state capital.

Grady's persuasiveness placed Atlanta at the epicenter of a New South, positioned to enjoy the coming surge in economic prosperity. In the service of Atlanta, Grady, the civic booster, orchestrated the region's first exposition in 1881, drawing thousands to Atlanta for what was later recognized as the "inaugural ceremony" of the industrial stage of the New South movement. The best Atlanta families made certain to entertain northern guests in their fine homes, which paid off when the Yankees went back with tales of southern hospitality. It was Grady, again in secret, who persuaded Grover Cleveland, the first Democrat elected president since the Civil War, to forsake invitations from other cities and to visit only Atlanta during his swing to the South in 1887, thereby delivering "such multitudes to meet him here that he can have no reasonable conception of." Many in that crowd of fifty thousand at the Piedmont Exposition in what became the city's Piedmont Park had traveled by train, at a penny-a-mile cut rate negotiated by Grady the businessman.[2]

Atlanta in 1933 was something of an enigma, a sizable city languishing somewhere between hope and despair, a clearinghouse less for New South potential than for Old South politics. Since Grady's death in 1889 at the age of thirty-nine, of pneumonia contracted in wintry Boston while making his last New South speech, the city had grown steadily in population and capital investment. In the 1880s alone, it nearly doubled its population, from thirty-seven thousand to sixty-three thousand, and more than doubled its assessed property values, from $16 million to $47 million.[3]

Apart from its economic stature, Atlanta could not make a serious case for being the center of a "new" South. In so many public manifestations, Atlanta testified to the perseverance of an ancient regime and alien culture. Since the 1890s, white southerners had grown accustomed to the practice of disfranchisement of the African American population and separation of the races by "Jim Crow" laws. An elaborate dual system was to provide everything in duplicate, from water fountains to schools, though most whites and blacks would have agreed that the system never met the Supreme Court's standard of "separate but *equal.*" The dual system required signs, many of them crudely handwritten and sometimes misspelled, herding "colored" and "white" to separate rest rooms and ticket counters.

Although Henry Grady won the political battle to erect the capitol building in Atlanta, his political heirs had lost the fight to gain political ascendancy over the state. Small counties under the "county-unit" system retained as much or more political weight in statewide elections as did the South's great population center. Though some few attorneys would appeal to the courts for the constitutional principal of "one man, one vote," citing statistics that many rural counties had more cows than people, the county-unit system preserved the grip of the rural Old South in the hands of many whom Ralph McGill would classify as "white trash."

Empowered in 1933 in the capitol that Grady built was a state legislature dominated by rural networks, and a newly elected governor, former agriculture commissioner Eugene Talmadge, champion of poor white dirt farmers. In deference to Talmadge's popularity, the legislature did not punish him when, as agriculture commissioner, he helped farmers by improperly buying their hogs and reselling them in Chicago at a loss. Amid allegations that he illegally transferred state fertilizer funds to friends' banks instead of the treasury, Talmadge boldly told a state senate investigating committee, "If I stole, it was for farmers like yourselves." Talmadge, one biographer noted, "emerged a Robin Hood, taking from an unresponsive state to help the poor farmer. The fact that the farmers saw nothing wrong in a public official more or less stealing money from their state said something about their economic plight and their historic attitude toward state government."[4]

Grady's magnificent exaggeration—that Atlanta had put the Civil War behind it, or forgotten it—was myth manufactured in a South in which nearly ever family bore the scars of suffering. Nor was forgetfulness likely so long as Confederate veterans were wheeled along the city streets in parades on Confederate Memorial Day. Memoirs and histories documenting the War between the States were plentiful. One of the first journalists McGill came to know on the *Constitution* staff, Margaret "Peggy" Mitchell, was hard at work in her apartment on Tenth Street, writing a novel.

In most respects Atlanta in the 1930s appeared to share the same apartheid profile as the region around it, as though the apple had fallen not far from its tree. The social terror of the 1890s that ravaged the Negro population and was legitimized in the Jim Crow segregation laws had by the 1930s been accepted as the way people would live for time to come. Legal de jure segregation of the races afflicted the vastness of the South like a plague that infected even the simplest communications between the races, even the way people passed each other on sidewalks. It would be another generation before a few eloquent visionaries could make plain the moral, spiritual, and economic cost to the white population of holding down the Negro race.

Atlanta, however, had saving grace. This was perceptible in the few hearts and consciences concerned with finding a reasonable solution for this pervasive and perverse sickness afflicting the soul of the South. Yet it was to be another decade before such humanistic impulses could begin, slyly at first, to overcome massive, inbred resistance which, in a vicious cycle, was perpetuated by each generation of would-be politicians. In 1933 the oppressive nature of legal segregation so discouraged meetings of whites and Negroes, public or private, that any nascent impulse toward racial justice was stunted, as a plant shrouded from sunshine.

Occasional glimmers slanted through the darkness. Creative initiatives often arose from the class that was most repressed. Along the main street of Atlanta's Negro district, Auburn Avenue, a young entrepreneur, encouraged by the rapid concentration of Negro population in Atlanta, in 1933 began publishing the nation's only daily Negro newspaper, the *Atlanta Daily World*. William Alexander Scott's training in persuasive debate at Atlanta's Morehouse College, and his subsequent successful career in advertising, laid the groundwork for an economically successful newspaper. Begun in 1928 as a family-run weekly, full of advertisements by and for the Negro community, the *World* gradually increased in frequency to semiweekly and thrice-weekly until it dared to go daily in March 1933 under the editorial aegis of an experienced journalist whom Scott had lured south from Chicago.

A thoroughly stubborn spirit, Frank Marshall Davis overcame his fear of the South, lured by the challenge to edit a daily newspaper. Having arrived in Atlanta, Davis rebelled against racial injustices, protesting the persistent pattern of horrific lynchings by insane mobs as well as what he considered legal lynchings by the state through unequal application of capital punishment. His relatively brief tenure as an editor on Auburn Avenue resulted in some of the boldest declarations for racial justice that southerners had ever seen *in print*. Scott appealed to Davis to tone down his stridency, but Davis persisted. In January

1934, Scott was shot as he arrived home one night and died several days later. As the newspaper passed into the hands of a brother, C. A. Scott, Davis returned to Chicago, packing in his trunk a passel of even more poignant poetry soon to be published there, in relative safety.[5]

Against this political picture, there was a note of encouragement in the spring of 1933 for any broad-minded, politically astute journalist. McGill certainly saw the opening of general advantages in the South that had helped elect the first Democratic president since Woodrow Wilson, and specific opportunities in that the new president, Franklin D. Roosevelt, would make his winter White House at the rehabilitation center in Warm Springs, Georgia, a short automobile ride from Atlanta.

Though few in Atlanta paid attention to it, the new president's stance toward Latin America, the "Good Neighbor policy" proclaimed in the first months of his term, triggered a response in McGill. Cuba had quickly become the first challenge in the new president's Caribbean neighborhood. Through spring and early summer McGill gave the news from Havana inordinate attention. The bloodshed fascinated him for what it represented. Leaders of the opposition and their sons were risking life and liberty to oppose the regime of a ruler who had perverted the mechanisms of democracy. Popularly elected, he had altered the Constitution to extend his term. As the island slid desperately during the Depression, he refused to relinquish. The few correspondents already in Havana wrote of alleged government tortures and secret executions and reported the underground's countermeasures— bombings of government buildings and assassinations of officials. Hundreds were imprisoned or fled into exile.

McGill simply had to make a case to go there. In fact, anything to do with Cuba interested many of the *Constitution*'s readers. During Prohibition, southerners in increasing numbers had explored this tropical oasis where fun kept coming and rum, unprohibited, kept running, dolled up pleasantly in the guise of an icy daiquiri, many honeymooners' first legal drink. Like the more famous—Ernest Hemingway in 1933 was writing and fishing there, living in a rented room on the fifth floor of the Hotel Ambos Mundos—they discovered the island's breeze-swept mornings, cool and fresh, even in summer. By day they explored Havana's wide boulevards, and by night found the city's narrow streets aglow with life, bedazzling to almost any eyes fresh off a boat from the Bible belt. For any sense of sin imported from the mainland, one quick immersion in the culture of *Habana* often did wonders. Dance academies featured girls who charged five cents a dance and, as one writer noted, "variable rates for extracurricular services." Under the palms at the Sans Souci, one could drink, dance, and gamble. Casinos welcomed the naïve and the cagey to their felted roulette tables, or to high-stakes poker in sequestered rooms. To suit the likes of more visceral bettors, the island legitimized cockfighting. Despite the surrounding poverty and political insurgency in the spring of 1933, one could still enjoy the gamier aspects of Havana. In fact, the troubles of Cubans were documented in black-and-white that spring by the young photographer Walker Evans. Yet Evans returned to New York in June thinking of Havana as "a grand place, and I'd be sorry not to go there again."[6]

Persuading the *Constitution* to send him to Havana was McGill's preoccupation in the early summer. The fact was that nobody really could do his job as well as he did it. In four years he had established himself as a preeminent sports editor, perhaps the best in the South, although Ed Danforth would certainly have contested him for that title over a bottle of port in a restaurant down the alley from the office.

Danforth, who in 1929 was the *Constitution's* sports editor, had persuaded the publisher, Clark Howell, that hiring Mac was essential if the paper hoped to beat the *Journal* and Hearst's *Georgian* on the new battlefront, the sports pages. Danforth and his wife Betty befriended this moody bachelor on the several occasions he was in Atlanta to report on Tennessee teams. They fed him, housed him, and came to love him like family. The opportunity to hire him opened up when Danforth needed an assistant sports editor who could write voluminously, with charm and style. Nobody but Mac filled that bill. He was thus hired for one reason only: to storm the sports pages with imagination and energy.

In the four years since, Mac had risen by his own abilities. In 1931, Hearst's men, in a characteristic move that echoed their chief's lifelong belief in the power of money, made Danforth an offer he couldn't easily refuse. Would Mac go with him? It was a crucial decision, and Mac decided that if he ever wished to get out of sports reporting, his best chance was in staying with the *Constitution* as its new sports editor. By moving up into Danforth's vacancy, Mac once again became manager of a department, with his own daily column. Although sports fans would expect him to write always about some fascinating aspect of football or baseball or golf, he knew that he could occasionally slip from that strait-jacket and write about stuff fans *ate* (barbecue) or things fans should *support* (charities). Most days, though, considering that many journalists were happy to do *any* work as the Depression deepened and salaries were reduced sometimes by half, Mac kept his eye on this ball or that, as he was paid to do.

His frustration at having to write "drivel" always seemed more troublesome when he was on the road, alone in a hotel room in the early hours of the morning, or when he was in one of his dark Welsh moods, or when he was drinking—or when he was doing all three. These moods had overcome him often during his years writing sports ephemera at the *Banner*. "I wonder, sometimes, at the seriousness with which we take things—golf, for instance," he wrote in August 1926 after the frenzy subsided at the Golf and Country Club. "I do it myself at times but there are moments when I know it is all silly." The letter was to his debutante girlfriend in Nashville, Louise Stevens, with whom he kept a running correspondence on hotel stationery. Two months later from his first fox hunt at Dawson Springs, Kentucky, he scrawled raggedly to "Steve" concerning his worries about work and money: "I'll never get anywhere. . . . You who are so used to things which I perhaps can never give—God, I am such a failure." At two o'clock the next morning he wrote again, explaining, "I was tight when I wrote you last night, but I'm not sorry—Darn it. I must be some kind of weak creature." The next day he confessed that he had been "very very tight" when he wrote *both* letters. "I am quite convinced now that I will never do much with myself."[7]

His blessing or good fortune was an unfailing resiliency in his character that led him to search the shadows for exits. At the *Banner,* he had found temporary relief in other people's unique misfortunes. When in the winter of 1925 the *Louisville Courier-Journal* amplified the plight of young Floyd Collins, trapped in Sand Cave, Mac persuaded the *Banner* to send its own writer to the cave. Mac stood outside the entrance, interviewing anxious friends, loved ones, and crowds of the curious who had to be restrained by barbed-wire and state troopers with bayonets. In his twenties, during Prohibition and the Jazz Age, Mac's blood could be pumped up by testimony in a murder trial as he flipped page after page from his typewriter to the hands of waiting boys who raced on bicycles to deliver his prose to the *Banner* newsroom. Fresh violence sometimes distracted him, though by the age of thirty he expressed his sense of futility in being a reporter of it.[8]

Since his Vanderbilt years, he had been fascinated most by politics. University friend Fannie Cheney always claimed McGill and his circle had been "bitten by the political bug." In the recurrent cycle of the state's political seasons, Tennessee's ward bosses in Nashville and Memphis reprieved him from ball-game boredom. Yet toward the end of his Nashville years, in his darker moods, even Tennessee politics took on in his mind a too-predictable routine of the "usual stuff—speeches—charges—vice—etc."[9]

When he finally left Nashville, he summed up the experiences of eight years of his "kaleidoscopic whirl" at the *Banner* in one succinct farewell. One sporting highlight he mentioned was his trip by train in December 1928 to the Rose Bowl, where he witnessed "Roy Reigels running the wrong way in the game when [Georgia] Tech beat California at Pasadena for the national football title." While in southern California, he detoured for two days and discovered "the bar a block long at Tia Juana, Mexico." Many of these parting vignettes were of scenes away from playing fields: "A woman's face as she turned away from her son, who was to be electrocuted at the state prison. . . . The wild ride with Bill Carr to Sand Cave. . . . Climbing across a ladder over an alley, three stories up, at a fire on Broad Street. . . . Mrs Fiske in a revival of 'The Rivals.' . . . The corner at South Pittsburg where six men were killed. . . . A Negro who was shot 16 times in South Nashville."[10]

In moving to Atlanta, McGill abandoned a lifetime of Tennessee routines, leaving behind most of the people who knew him as Mac. Yet for security he clung to the all-too-familiar job of sports writing, which seldom challenged his intellectual capacity or gave him the satisfaction of doing something vital or mature, and, because of these vacancies, actually dulled his sensibilities. He continued to read widely, yearning for some outlet for discussing the ideas blazing from those books, sharing his passion for poetry.

This desire was met somewhat in 1931 when Danforth went to the *Georgian* and McGill began writing the daily "Break O' Day!" column. For the showdown between boxers Max Baer and Primo Carnera, McGill rode a train to Manhattan. On the way, he served up a column that may have puzzled his sports fans, steeped as it was in sentiment from watching the sun rise outside his window and adorned with a shard of poetry: "And then suddenly there was dawn. The fields became lighted. The houses took on outline. Day was breaking. I thought of one of Oscar Wilde's poems and that line which reads: 'And the dawn, on silver-sandaled feet, crept down the street like a frightened girl.' The dawn came to the world liked that." After Baer knocked Carnera down twice in the eleventh round, McGill "thought then of the line from Kipling's poem of the slaying of Hans, the blue-eyed Dane, who 'came down like cattle drop across the fist-banged boards.' Carnera tonight was like a felled ox. The ring was a shambles with his blood."[11]

Boxing and the possibility of earning one thousand dollars lured McGill into writing a book-length manuscript. When Georgia's heavyweight contender, William Stribling, headed to Cleveland in the summer of 1934 to fight for the heavyweight championship, a press syndicate dangled the prospect of money for a "Life of Young Stribling," the American upstart who was taking on the pride of Nazi Germany, Max Schmeling. Writing furiously, McGill completed fourteen chapters before the first punch. The deal fell apart when on the Fourth of July Max Schmeling won and the syndicate lost interest.[12]

Trips outside the South whetted McGill's latent appetite for distant places. He had been eager to go overseas since his sophomore year at Vanderbilt. He so wanted to go to France that he enlisted to fight the Germans in Gen. John Pershing's American Expeditionary Force. Although he trained as a Marine—an experience of lifelong importance for him—he was still stationed in the United States when the Armistice ended the Great War, and he returned to Vanderbilt with only domestic war stories plus a lifelong pride in being a Marine.[13]

The Rose Bowl took him farther than the Great War. His Bowl reporting for the *Banner* led to that brief excursion in Mexico, and his assignment to write about the Georgia Tech team in the January 1931 Rose Bowl landed him back in southern California, this time with more amenities. On the *Constitution*'s expense account, cleared by Ed Danforth, Ralph traveled with Mary Elizabeth on what after almost two years of marriage was a belated honeymoon. It turned into a working holiday, one of many they would share over the years. In southern California they spent sunny hours enjoying flowers and oranges and a tour of the MGM studios, while, in his automatic habit, McGill thought of work, of how he could shape what they were experiencing into some story around flowers or fauna. Still, he thought, they had a good time. He wrote home to his "Dad and Mam" that "we went to Robert Montgomery's dressing room, and talked with him for thirty minutes. Mary Elizabeth nearly had a fit."[14]

More important for his career was the next Rose Bowl. In January 1932 he enjoyed the return voyage, the "long and delightful trip down the coast and through the [Panama] canal" aboard the SS *Virginia.* In the Caribbean, the ship sailed into Havana Harbor and McGill got his first view of Cuba. During the stopover he sampled Havana's entertainment, food, and drink. In Havana, you ordered rum without mediation of bootleggers, the middlemen with whom a generation of Americans had become chummy. It was a place to which he longed to return.[15]

2

In the Labyrinth

*Ralph McGill: "What if all mediation
fails? Does it mean intervention?"
U.S. Ambassador Sumner Welles: "I am not
permitting myself to think about it failing. I am
thinking about completing it."*
—INTERVIEW, HAVANA, 1933

*Ralph McGill: "Mr. President, your enemies say that you
have organized police bands who have killed defenseless
men and women. Have you ordered this done?"
President Gerardo Machado: "I never have. I never have."*
—INTERVIEW, HAVANA, 1933

CUBA IN 1933 was to be McGill's France of 1917, with opportunity
for patriotism and adventure, if on a smaller scale. He landed with a pen
rather than a bayonet and with considerably more control than a private
in the Great War. To report a revolution in a land where his only contacts
were sportswriters, he had arranged for help. Disembarking at the harbor
in the collar-drenching sauna of late July, he sought the one man whose
assistance he most needed. In his pocket he carried a letter of introduction to the U.S. ambassador, Sumner Welles, who had been quoted in
dozens of stories as the American "mediator" between President Gerardo
Machado and the opposition. Welles had been appointed by President
Roosevelt and immediately thrust into the center of the island's political
maelstrom. As McGill strode from his ship, he quickly found the first
people wanting to help him, a crowd of impoverished taxi drivers who
sized him up as walking dollars.

The revolution was not as obvious as the heat and beauty of this
foreign place. Somewhere, beyond the crescent harbor and Morro Castle
standing guard over it, and the royal palms, and the curvaceous

waterfront boulevard, the Malecón, revolutionaries were fashioning bombs for domestic use. If he were to land his big story, he had to track the trail of blood, hunt these killers as well as the president and his henchmen. McGill trusted that, as before, he could persuade people he had never met to take him into their confidence. He hoped to be invited into homes and hideouts, where the opposition would tell him their side of the story, untold tales from the underground. He could offer in return that their message would be published, sympathetically, in America, on the front page of the *Constitution,* unobscured by bias, either Machado's or his own. Ultimately, he hoped to be led in the *heart* of the underground. He had always possessed the detective's most important skill: the ability to coax one person to lead him to another.

The dictator's story, though he need not mention this journalistic fact to Machado's sworn enemies, was central to McGill's success. An interview with the man at the center of the storm, the elusive one who seemed now as inapproachable as a spirit, would be the crowning achievement. The story had blossomed in McGill's poetic imagination until he conjured an image of a cruel despot now possessed completely in darkness by evil, whose greed for power and domain yielded to no one. The more he imagined Machado, the more he likened him to a soul lost in desperate straits, akin to Joseph Conrad's icon of imperialism gone mad with power—Kurtz, evil personified, enthroned among his subjects' skulls.

Why would Machado grant an interview? McGill's trump card was Welles. Tucked in his coat pocket was the letter of introduction to Welles from the *Constitution*'s publisher. The plan, worked out in Atlanta, was to ask Welles to arrange the interview with the dictator, who by late July was rarely seen or heard from. By then McGill would have seen the opposition, and he hoped Machado would see, as had many reluctant interviewees many times before, the benefit of having *his* side of the story told as well.

On the face of it, McGill was an unlikely foreign correspondent. At thirty-five he had no reputation for foreign reporting. Aside from his previous brief stopover in Havana, he had visited only in Mexico, and only as a tourist sampling the alcoholic drinks then still illegal in his own country. The only bloodshed in his stories dripped from the faces of boxers.

Sports reporting had made him one of Atlanta's best-read writers, and the *Constitution* capitalized on this in the circulation wars against Hearst by advertising his column with his photograph on the sides of delivery trucks. Sports writing, dealing as it did with victory and loss in a world removed in kind from the arena of the real world, had freed him to experiment with style as news writer could not do. He honed a style of storytelling that came easily, was appreciated, and became a niche, distinguishing him from the minions who worked in journalism as laborers in a factory. The flavor of his stories rose from the spice inherent in the characters he sought out or came upon by accident or Welsh luck. He learned to observe and read emotions in the manner of a poet. It was as though his interest in and effort at poetry at Vanderbilt, while in the end delivering the verdict that he was not one of the chosen ones, nevertheless left him with a concession, that of recognizing poetic elements in life, the tragic and pathetic, heroic and cowardly. He also had the gift of communicating sentiment, the magic, as all writers eventually think of the mystical process, of finding the words that precisely matched the emotion he felt and simultaneously touched the sensibilities of his readers. If he could not write poetry, he approximated that precision in his prose. His other gift was speed. Time and again those who watched him work on important stories came away astonished at the accuracy and clarity of his first, quick drafts.

His editors, as a breed ornery and not given to praise of writers, were won over, first in Nashville and now in Atlanta. They in turn gave him more tether from the newsroom, the newspaper's equivalent of a license to specialize. McGill's stories sold newspapers, and what was good for circulation was good for southern journalism. His reward in Nashville and now in Atlanta was a personal column signified by name and photograph. Devoted readers talked about how they turned to the sports pages every morning to see what "Ol' Ralph" had to say. He had their attention, and that in journalism was more than half the battle.

Success paid off in raises, not substantial but remarkable nonetheless in a profession that enriches publishers long before money trickles down to editors and lastly drips to writers. So saddened was one Tennessee mother that her daughter was marrying an improvident Nashville reporter, Brainard Cheney, whose best man was McGill, that the mother and her sister wore black mourning dresses to the wedding. At the *Banner* McGill fared better than Cheney, who eventually left for Washington politics and novel writing. But even for McGill, the biggest raise, to a hefty ninety dollars a week, came when he switched newspapers and in the spring of 1929 entered the circulation war in Atlanta.[1]

By 1933 he was seeking frequent respites from this secure but artificial and isolated universe of football, baseball, and boxing. At mid-career he hungered for the serious subjects, the politics and economics, that had nourished his imagination at Vanderbilt. He wanted the front page of the paper, not the inside pages of sports. Years later he explained, "I liked sports but I never thought it was something I wanted to stay in. I was looking around for something else to do."[2] The "something else" was all the more interesting if it mixed politics and travel.

Little wonder that the drama of the Cuban struggle flamed in his mind from day to day. It had irony. The despot had been a hero of the Spanish-American War. Gerardo Machado, a deliverer in the Generation of 1898, now fostered the despotism he despised under the Spanish. The irony deepened. His enemies called him "butcher." The archetypical "butcher" had been the notorious general during Spanish rule thirty-five years earlier, whose final solution for suppressing nationalism was to herd Cubans from the countryside into towns where starvation and a plague of smallpox and fevers killed them by the thousands.[3]

Cuba's martyrs interested McGill as much as its despots. The great luminary of the Generation of 1898 had been the poet José Martí, the self-styled "apostle of liberty" whose words took on even brighter glow after he was killed fighting the Spanish. Martí's poems evoked in McGill the romanticism of "sword and pen."[4]

A passion to cover the revolution would not have landed McGill in Havana without the support of his publisher. In the *Constitution* newsroom, a journalist's personal wishes seldom guaranteed a choice assignment. Foreign travel was so rare the very idea was alien. A journalist with a passion to travel tried to do it during vacation, at his own expense. In such a frame, it was best to write about Atlanta, a necessity which influenced McGill's friend, the journalist Peggy Mitchell, to write about the city in the Civil War, her only travel being in *time*.

In the early '30s in a city with three competitive newspapers, what counted beyond ambition was a proven usefulness to the management. In four years at the *Constitution,* McGill had proven to be a superb hire. From his view at the top, the publisher, Clark Howell, recognized an ambitious and talented writer worthy of the front page. Howell saw McGill providing an edge in circulation against the two evening papers, the *Atlanta Journal* and William Randolph Hearst's acquisition, the *Atlanta Georgian.* Howell began grooming this outsider from Tennessee, giving him freedom to range far afield in the green, profitable pastures of sports writing and, on occasion, without releasing him from the commitment to competitive sports pages, permitting *additional* work in the serious world of public affairs.

Back in Tennessee, McGill's publisher had let him do the same, so that by the mid-1920s McGill, while still sports editor, had become that city's best-read newspaperman. This was partly because, as envious journalists said, McGill knew how to promote himself in two parallel careers. Not giving up his bread-winning position as a daily sports columnist and storyteller, he became a part-time chronicler of Tennessee crime and politics in the heyday of Prohibition, an age when Nashville was plagued by armed gangs and Memphis was lorded over by Boss Crump. When a lover's triangle murder trial opened in Nashville, McGill was yanked off the sports beat and sent to the courthouse, where he reported testimony as if it were a sporting event, blow by blow, with two copy boys standing ready to bicycle the pages to the *Nashville Banner* office five blocks away.[5] When he wrested free to report from the mouth of Sand Cave the fate of Floyd Collins, his only disappointment was in not getting close enough to the story, in part because he was too large to squeeze into the cave to interview Collins. That honor went to William Burke "Skeets" Miller of the *Louisville-Courier Journal,* who explained how he got an exclusive interview with Collins because he was "small and able to get back" into the cave and "place a bottle of milk to his lips."[6] Still, it was enough for McGill to break out of the provincialism of Tennessee sports and converse with his counterparts from around the nation. In a profession which did not compensate reporters to gather at annual conventions, as publishers and editors did, this was McGill's early ad hoc solution for expanding his orbit from the region to the nation.

In Atlanta, his travel plans now affected a wife. Six months after moving to Atlanta and testing the situation, McGill returned to Nashville to wed the girl he had been dating for about two years. Mary Elizabeth Leonard, called "Red" because of her hair, was the daughter of a dentist and the younger sister of a Vanderbilt football player whose home McGill visited. She was slight and fragile, wracked by two medical handicaps: she was born with one kidney, and she was recovering, after a prolonged rest-cure, from tuberculosis. Still, as Brainard Cheney's bride, Fannie, recalled, "she pursued him. He used to say anyone who pursued him was a weak sister. She was much younger than he. Everybody called him 'Mother McGill.' He didn't care." By 1929 Mary Elizabeth must have known all she needed to know about McGill, including his salary. In an era before the onset of "professionalism" in journalism, when newspapermen were not particularly respectable, his writing had earned him an audience and a better-than-average living. It was evident that he would continue in journalism. He would also continue to travel and, probably, drink. On occasion she could do both with him, though drinking could make her sick in public.[7] Most times, though, she stayed at home.

When McGill arrived in Havana on July 29, a Saturday, with Clark Howell's blessing and letter, he was serving the same two masters—sports and news. As before, he had to balance the requirement of writing a daily sports column, which his readers had a right to expect, with the serious task of tracking the remarkable story he imagined and sensed.

    On Monday morning he set off to see Welles. He walked along the palm-lined driveway of the Hotel Nacional, waving off eager taxicab drivers who "will drive for two blocks along the curb as one walks, giving a sales talk in Spanish." His destination, the U.S. Embassy, was not far, and before his appointment he wanted to see the life on the streets. McGill dodged the vendors who lay in wait. They clustered along the streets, sat on the sidewalks, came out of nowhere like the no- see-um bugs in Georgia's summers, all testifying to the stinging poverty of the island by their urgency to sell him something at any price. They seemed, he told his readers back home, "the most persistent people in the world[,] . . . one of the plagues visited on the people years ago." He was even more impressed by idlers and beggars. "Havana is filled with beggars," he wrote afterward. "There were always beggars there. But now they have grown to small armies of mendicants, large and small, old and young, male and female."[8]

The beauty of the Malecón boulevard near the harbor's seawall contrasted with these stark scenes, ameliorated only when he noticed boys playing a game that looked like baseball. Along the waterfront, near the embassy, he heard the sharp crack of a gun. It seemed to come from a shady park on his left. Next he saw a mounted policeman spurring his horse into a gallop into the park. He followed. "There was a young Cuban with a hole in his head and plenty of blood," he wrote. "He had picked some of the brilliant hibiscus flowers which matched his blood. They lay loosely in the half-opened hand which had picked them." McGill had witnessed a martyr taking his life for the revolution. "He had killed himself," McGill concluded, "as a protest against the dictatorship of Machado; against the closing of the university; against the whole dirty business."[9]

Starkly introduced to the passion of the revolution, McGill arrived at the door of the U.S. Embassy. It was housed near the waterfront on the Avenue of Missions in one of the old buildings of 1830 vintage, reflecting Spanish New World architecture.

Ambassador Welles received him, and McGill handed him the letter. Whatever impression McGill made, he was clearly impressed by the ambassador. Welles was tall and lean, with an amiable face marked by a thin white mustache. McGill, perspiring from the walk, noticed that Welles's shirt collar remained stiff. That seemed a metaphor for a diplomat "so cool that even his stiff collar never had a damp spot while others around him wilted like rags."[10]

After the formalities, McGill felt his way into an interview with his own sense of diplomatic finesse. "I do not wish," he said, "recognizing the diplomatic position you are in, to ask any embarrassing questions."

"Go ahead," Welles replied. "Ask what you wish. I think you will find me willing to answer all questions."

Guarding the most sensitive matters, Welles briefed McGill with what seemed like great candor. The ambassador had been rushed to

Havana on May 8 after the political opposition in April resorted to bullets and bombs. The opposition claimed it "fought terror with terror."

For a time, the bloodshed distorted the picture, temporarily marginalizing democratic alternatives such as negotiation. The regime jailed political prisoners and then, persuaded to show leniency, released them. By July, factions on the Right and Left were planning coups.

McGill knew that Welles had arrived in Havana with the implied threat of U.S. military intervention to protect American citizens and investments. Under the Platt amendment, the United States retained hegemony over the island. Welles became the power broker, using that leverage. The first concern was whether he could resolve the crisis. If Machado had to go, Welles would have a role in selecting a successor.

"What about President Machado?" McGill asked.

"I believe that he was a sincere man," Welles said. "But I know that about him there were a few, only a few, who were sincere patriots. The others were not serving Cuba. When the opposition, hastened by the Depression, grew to serious proportions, Machado listened to much bad advice and was led to measures which he originally would not have considered."

These were the words of a diplomat glossing a situation with a vision of how all this would appear in a newspaper. In May, Welles had been horrified by Machado's excesses. After only five days, he reported secretly to Secretary of State Cordell Hull that if the "present acute bitterness of feeling" against Machado persists, it would "highly desirable that the present chief executive be replaced . . . by some impartial citizen in whom all factions have confidence." By the time McGill visited the embassy, Welles, with State Department support, had quietly given Machado an ultimatum: resign or risk punitive action. U.S. recognition could be withdrawn, leading to economic disaster, or the marines might intervene.[11]

Welles told McGill nothing about the marines, but instead briefed him on the ongoing negotiations between Machado and the opposition. A month earlier, in an act of diplomatic intervention, Welles bestowed legitimacy on the main factions opposing Machado. He summoned the opposing forces for continuing mediation with the Machado regime. Under the influence of implied U.S. power, the "warring factions" sent negotiators to the embassy. In a stroke of diplomacy, Welles persuaded Machado to recognize the validity of the talks by sending his own representatives. The process enabled Welles to calm the revolutionary fever and restore order temporarily, gaining time to search for a possible successor. The room in which McGill now sat was where the talks had been held. McGill counted about twenty chairs where the representatives, including the mayor of Havana, met each day.

"The opposition sits there," Welles told him. "The government sits there. When we first began they glared at each other. They would not speak except through me. Yesterday one of the opposition went out with his arm around the shoulder of a government man. So, you see, we are getting somewhere. But there is much to do."

The talks would have failed at once without government concessions, coaxed and wrenched from Machado's men. There was pressure for constitutional reform, repeal of constitutional changes made to prolong the Machado era, restoration of the vice presidency, freedom of the press, revision of the electoral code. Very important to the opposition factions was an amnesty for all political prisoners jailed in the months of violence.[12] "I suspect," McGill wrote, "that Welles had to bring much pressure to obtain this amnesty. It meant the freeing of hundreds of prisoners, many of them students and young girls from the University."

One who argued vehemently against amnesty was the mayor of Havana, Tirso Mesa. "Why free men who have killed government officials, or tried to kill them?" Mesa later asked McGill. "It means that relatives of those slain will try for revenge. It means, probably, more bloodshed." Among the dead was Mesa's brother-in-law.

The amnesty, Welles told McGill, did not result in revenge killings. So long as the talks continued and seemed fruitful, negotiation replaced bloodshed. What the ambassador did not tell McGill was that he was using the negotiations as a tool for forcing Machado out. On July 17, two weeks after the negotiations began, Welles informed Roosevelt that, with the vice-presidency restored in Cuba, "the suggestion will be made that after a Vice President satisfactory to all parties has been selected and has taken office, the President resign."[13]

McGill had saved for last the potentially "embarrassing questions" that could yield a scoop. He had heard the rumor on the streets that the

U.S. Marines would intervene. Anything concerning the marines touched McGill's pride. Semper Fi. It was the pledge he took when, after dropping out of Vanderbilt in 1917, he enlisted and trained as an officer. He was ready to do his duty in France when the war ended in 1918. Once a marine, always one. McGill asked Welles about intervention.

"It would be the worst move possible from the standpoint of the United States," Welles replied. "It is time we bettered our standing in Latin countries."

"What if all mediation fails? Does it mean intervention?"

"I am not permitting myself to think about it failing. I am thinking about completing it."

The interview ended on this far-from-candid comment. Welles the diplomat was reciting the Roosevelt administration policy, which stressed that the United States would be a "Good Neighbor" to Latin America. Privately, to the State Department, Welles told a different story.

The negotiations were in fact deadlocked. The opposing factions, wielding an economic weapon, the threat of a general strike, demanded Machado's departure. The strike had begun on July 25, four days before McGill arrived, when several unions of bus drivers protested the mayor's new tax on bus fares and his order that bus drivers buy gasoline only at garages with which the mayor had an agreement. By the first week of August, the strike had spread, each day affecting more aspects of daily life.[14] Privately Welles was urging that the only way to restore stability was to set a date for Machado's departure, the sooner the better in Welles's opinion: "If President Machado remains in power he can only continue through the exercise of the most brutal methods of repression. . . . If the present condition is permitted to continue much longer, I am positive that a complete state of anarchy will result which might force the Government of the United States, against its will, to intervene in compliance with its obligation under the Permanent Treaty."[15] To strengthen his hand, Welles urged one or two courses of action. The United States could threaten to withdraw recognition. The stronger step would be to send a contingent of marines, justified as a guard to protect U.S. citizens during the uncertainties of the strike. Once there, the marines would reinforce U.S. resolve.

Before McGill left the embassy, he stressed his need to interview Machado. Both he and Welles knew it would be a journalistic coup. No reporter had interviewed him for a year. As the opposition increased, Machado became more reclusive. Traveling between his farm and the presidential palace, he gave the public little more than a glimpse of his cortege of armed guards. Nonetheless, Welles thought the interview could be arranged.

Welles was probably the only influential figure in Havana with leverage to arrange an interview. He had access to the palace. Two days before McGill arrived, on July 27, Machado had summoned Welles because the president wished to apologize for certain undiplomatic remarks he had made to his legislature. His speech had seemed to discount the effect of Welles's mediation, which so far had resulted in the government amnesty and the opposition's pledge to cease acts of vengeance. At the palace Machado told Welles that "almost invariably when he spoke in public he made statements which he did not intend."[16]

Welles made a lasting impression on McGill. He would remember Welles as "one of the most brilliant diplomats, one of the most brilliant ambassadors and one of the most courageous of men the United States has ever had as a representative." It had been a "wise move" to send Welles to Cuba, wrote McGill, because "another man would have meant intervention."[17]

Welles returned the compliment. Writing to McGill's publisher, Clark Howell, Welles said he enjoyed meeting the journalist and thought his articles in the *Constitution* portrayed the situation in Cuba accurately.[18] The fulsome praise recognized McGill's faithfulness to Welles's version of events, and McGill's complimentary portrait of the diplomat in crisis. While other reporters were more circumspect or "objective," McGill found it easy to look at the situation subjectively from the personal view of the erudite American ambassador who conquered chaos.

The trust McGill placed in the ambassador's insider information led McGill naturally to accept and give legitimacy to U.S. policy. This pattern of gaining access to U.S. government insiders and of demonstrating loyalty to those confidants became a keystone, for better or worse, of McGill's career. Time and again, he would seek to be drawn into the circle of insiders, and, having been admitted, saw the panorama from their points of view. In Havana, McGill's compensation for loyalty was access to the highest counsels. He was soon in the middle of things, with a privileged view.

Buoyed, he emerged from the embassy after noon and set off on foot again, along the Prado, and soon witnessed more evidence of revolution. Suddenly "a crowd came surging out of a side street and collided with police who were swinging clubs very lustily indeed. They knocked down a few and the others dispersed." Many in the crowd were older men "and couldn't stand the punishment very well." They were, he was told, a contingent of Cuban veterans of the 1890s war for independence, protesting because their "pensions had not been paid." This confrontation and the suicide in the park had a lasting effect on McGill's sentiments, inclining him to believe accounts of other events he later heard about but did not witness.

Leaving the Prado, McGill was persuaded to patronize one of the taxis pursuing him. His driver was from the "perfect horde of taxi drivers who are to be found in any part of Havana—at any time. One has but to hesitate and lift one's dogs as if they were paining one . . . and the mob descends." When McGill entered the taxi, the driver, Thomas, joined McGill's own pursuit.[19]

Every day in Havana McGill searched for something to write about that would fill his daily column and keep his expectant readers satisfied. As was his habit, he had written several extra columns to be used daily as he traveled, but now he needed something fresh. The Welles material was for the news pages, probably the front. For his column he needed something chatty, and it didn't have to be about sports. Occasionally he treated readers to a new recipe for barbecue, or to some touching story he told so well that they didn't notice the absence of a football. Some would wonder of course where Mac was leading them or what Ol' Ralph was up to. All the same, they would read on as he told his story, and by the end would forgive any perceived lack of substance because of an abundance of sentiment and style.

Now, in the taxi, he decided Thomas would serve as his guide and take him into an easy column, one he could dispatch quickly, trusting to his talent for listening well and his gifts of memory and speed. Thomas and anybody he met might wind up this week in the obligatory daily columns. The dictum McGill often preached to other journalists—"Don't waste a minute"—was applicable. Thomas was a tall, black Jamaican, speaking English with an Oxford accent—"very few Havana taxi drivers speak English," McGill noted. As readers soon learned, Thomas talked as he drove, speaking "in faultless English, sounding a bit like Clive Brook. One expected him to launch into a lecture on old English china or the murals in the king's palace." The taxi pulled up at the pier where McGill had disembarked on Saturday.

While waiting for a ferry that would carry them, taxi and all, across the harbor, McGill found a tidbit he could toss to his readers as a link to sports, much as Picasso said he tried to include something recognizable in cubist abstracts, a guitar here, a newspaper there, so that people could find a window into his work. Docked in Havana's harbor was the American liner SS *Virginia*. McGill felt a rush of nostalgia and went to greet the crew. From the portholes and decks of the *Virginia* in January 1932 he had first glimpsed the outline of Havana. He was returning from California, taking the long voyage home with the Georgia Tech Rose Bowl football team, via the Panama Canal: "The crew members still recall the Tech team—as who wouldn't. And they asked to be remembered. Several of the waiters declared they were just now getting the humps out of their backs, put there by carrying trays of food to the Tech team on that long and delightful trip down the coast and through the canal."[20]

During the *Virginia*'s stopover in 1932 McGill had sampled the city and its fare, its food and its unsuppressed drink. An island of eager middlemen delivered his rum without delay, reminiscent of the enterprising procurers of Nashville who served McGill's generation, which came of saloon age just as the nation declared drinking illegal. For more than a decade, the Prohibition generation drank anyway—and anything, almost. At Vanderbilt and later at the *Banner,* McGill's bootlegger supplied bottles of the local brew, corn liquor, and, on occasion, bourbon. In the manner of a milkman, he delivered to McGill's apartment on West Side Road, and even made special deliveries. Brainard Cheney's wife Fannie recalled that McGill's bootlegger once smuggled a bottle for Brainard into Vanderbilt hospital. It was just after Brainard crashed his car while driving under the influence and had been forced to toss his unfinished bottle far from the car. In pain and unbearably sober, Brainard was cheered by the visit of this quart of liquor accompanied by a quart of eggnog. Well into her eighties, Fannie maintained that Brainard learned to drink from McGill.[21]

McGill's serious sorties with assorted elixirs began fittingly during Prohibition. He was a man who couldn't stand being prohibited from anything, and he became a legendary drinker about whom many tales were told and retold. The remarkable thing Fannie Cheney noticed was that while she never saw McGill when he wasn't drinking, "he never got drunk. He was an enormously fat man and he seemed to absorb it. He got a bit unsteady on his pins but never really drunk." Fueled by corn liquor or bourbon, he was a great conversationalist when friends gathered for a weekend social occasion outside Nashville at a camp along the curves of the Cumberland River. On these occasions McGill loved to read aloud the new daring works, both poetry and prose, of T. S. Eliot or James Joyce. Fannie recalled the time McGill "stood up and said, 'Somebody's put water in this drink.' Then he fell flat on his face, which made quite a thud because he was fleshy, as they say."[22]

Apart from that flashback to the Tech team, McGill's column resembled a travelogue, tinged with optimism, as though he wished to preserve every portent of pessimism for his special reports. Despite labor protests in the countryside outside Havana, the capital still tried to carry on as "a playground for the world." The city beckoned those looking for a place where "one may do virtually anything one wishes without interference." Day and night, but especially after dark, there was "gaity, pleasure, entertainment, luxury, amusement, drinks, vice and very little crime." The city's physique was "beautiful," and its "inhabitants know how to live." Knowing the inhabitants, as McGill was beginning to do, was to know the city, and the inhabitants were not to be found vacationing. "Only the tourists," he said, "make the dizzy round of the night clubs, the entertainment spots, the bars."[23]

In the role of tourist, McGill followed Thomas across the harbor to Morro Castle. In the heat of the day, McGill on deck felt a sweeping breeze that was "delightfully cool." Off the ferry, the taxi climbed a steep dirt road to the Spanish fortress that "did things to the imagination." He conjured up ghosts who had passed there since 1597. There were Spanish laborers who carried the great stones and placed them by hand, pirates counting loot, soldiers in armor, prisoners known only by bones found behind a wall, English troops besieging for sixty-seven days then storming the castle. "It does something to one again to know that 300 years ago the sweating, begrimed Spanish gunners stood there firing and that finally English soldiers swarmed in at them through a breech in the great walls."[24]

Legends were those ghostly stories he could retell without effort and often did. Sites which embodied battle and bloodshed had appealed to his sentiments since boyhood. When Ralph was five, his father, Benjamin, not much suited to farming, a life to which he had been relegated because of a blight in his past that no one wanted to talk about, moved the family from the acreage near Soddy to the nearest big city, Chattanooga, and took a job in a company that installed furnaces. He bought a white clapboard house in the Highland Park section of the East End, at 1509 Kirby Street, which became the setting for the rest of Ralph's youth. Two blocks west was the great Civil War cemetery, and several blocks east was the site of the Battle of Missionary Ridge. There in the midst of battle sites he stored up tales of Confederates holding the high ground along Missionary Ridge and the Union army charging up the hill until, panicking, the defenders ran. When he was thirteen, he attended the private McCallie School, nestled high on the western slope of Missionary Ridge with a grand view of the city. The campus was a daily reminder of the summer of 1863, where, without much difficulty, a digger could find bullets. People swore that ghosts walked that ridge and the rows down below in the cemetery at the dead end of Kirby Street.[25]

With one column sent, McGill wanted the interview with Machado. Although on Tuesday morning Welles sent word that he had managed to secure McGill an interview, no day or hour was set because in the midst of the crisis Machado had "gone fishing."[26] There was nothing to do but write another column, this one with more sports, and so he took a taxi to visit the sports editor of *El Pais*. Marble steps led up to the newsroom floor, where he followed a hallway adorned with marble busts of former editors and, of more interest to his male readers, "beautiful statues of Diana and other well-known young ladies in the raw." He found the sports writers chattering enthusiastically as they followed the progress of an American baseball game, play by play, as relayed and delayed by cable. In the bunch was the "splendid editor and gentleman" Pepe Conte, conversing with his baseball writer, Vicente Gomez Kemp.

"Isn't it exciting?" Kemp asked McGill. "We are all excited."

"What is it?"

"The Giants, the Giants. The Giants are beginning a difficult series."

The Cubans were buzzing about the *New York* Giants playing the *Boston* Braves in Boston. Inside this room there was no hint of a revolution in the making. McGill knew as certainly as a photographer who comes upon a scene that this was a picture worth preserving. What more did his readers need but the story of Cuban sportswriters in the middle of summer enthralled with American baseball, in part because of a Cuban hero. The Giants' roster of great but distinctly un-Latin stars—Bill Terry, Mel Ott, and Carl Hubbell—was strengthened that summer by a light-skinned Cuban, the veteran Adolfo "Dolf" Luque, "the pride of Havana." He had pitched his way into the National League with Boston in 1914, at the age of twenty-three. He endured twelve seasons with Cincinnati, including his first World Series in 1919, when he threw five scoreless innings against the Chicago White Sox—the "Black Sox" whose key players were paid by gamblers to throw the series. The Cuban sportswriters could recite his accomplishments: In 1923 he won twenty-seven games, most in the National League, and in 1925 had the league's best earned run average. By 1933, now forty-three years old, he was a relief pitcher and destined to pitch that year in his second World Series.[27]

McGill found an Atlanta connection as well. "Mr. Kemp likes Blondy Ryan," McGill mused, reminding his readers that the Giants shortstop had gone to the majors from Atlanta's minor league team, the Crackers. "I told him of Blondy Ryan's failure to play good ball for the Atlanta club. He transmitted the news politely to the others. But it seems they already knew about it. They know everything about baseball."[28]

McGill became the center of attention, a target for trivia that he passed along to his readers.

"How many baseball games did Burleigh Grimes win in 1926?" he was asked.

"Given a record book, I could find out," McGill said.[29]

"What did Ty Cobb hit in 1926?"

"It is not in the old head ready for answer to the questions."[30]

"What year was it that Connie Mack bought all his star players?"[31]

McGill laughed at the onslaught. "While your old partner fumbled around trying to get the old skull to respond, out would come the answer from some little guy sitting in the corner." That man could recite all the leading players' batting averages and knew all the teams they had played for, including minor league Atlanta. "I doubt if there is one on the staff of any American paper who can do that."

It was a perfect setup. "They know baseball," McGill conceded. "Records fascinate them. They put whole books to memory. They recall offhand all Matty's [Christy Mathewson's] old pitching records. They know fight records well also, but baseball amounts to a passion with them."[32]

This revelation led him to mull moodily over whether America had less enthusiasm for its national game than Cuba: "I think we have lost our national game. It is no longer a national game. It is an international game." He worried that American kids were losing their heritage. He had seen Cuban boys playing ball on the sidewalk along the harbor. He ventured that "every kid in Havana thinks that Babe Ruth and Lou Gehrig are the world's greatest heroes." In the United States, when he was coming of age, "all the kids were playing baseball." In just twenty years, he observed, "the American kid had lost most of his sandlots and much of his love for the game. Today in America there are more of them playing golf."[33]

Having diagnosed a malady, he prescribed a workable remedy. "It is necessary," he wrote, "for the American Legion to organize leagues and carry on sandlot baseball." The Cuban frenzy persuaded him that America should institutionalize spontaneous sandlot adventures. It was an opinion shared by others, and during the 1930s other Americans devoted themselves to developing what, in 1939, became Little League baseball.[34]

Conte led McGill in to meet the editor. The newspaper might have exerted political influence because it sold 120,000 copies daily, most of it from street sales, yet the editor (whose name McGill never mentioned) became cautious when discussing politics. On reflection, "the more one talked with him," the more he began to seem "a very wise editor" who "considered the sports pages of a newspaper its greatest asset." Sports was a safer subject.[35]

McGill had enough for a column. He typed it quickly—he could finish the first draft of a column in under an hour—headed it with the dateline "Havana, Cuba, Aug. 1," and sent it by airmail to be published on Wednesday, August 2.

When McGill learned that Machado was still fishing, he turned his attention to the underground as soon as three men of the Abecedarios (literally, "alphabets"), or ABC, showed up at the Hotel Nacional. McGill wanted to talk with its secreted leaders even before Welles confirmed the continuing influence of the ABC against Machado. The secrecy made it all the more appealing. "One wonders," he wrote, "what is this powerful society which can bring about revolution and balk the efforts of the most powerful president Cuba has ever had, a dictator with a large and powerful army of soldiers and national police at his call." The clandestine aspects of the group were reminiscent of the Ku Klux Klan, which McGill had investigated in Tennessee. Both organizations used brutality and murder and both were outlawed and at the same time revered by segments of the community. There the similarities ended, as McGill knew after the briefing by Welles.[36]

The ABC was born in Cuba's political underground in 1931, when Machado had overstayed his presidency by three years and showed no inclination to give up power. In August 1931 Machado's army defeated a band of Cubans intent on overthrowing him by armed force, and the defeat suggested a change in the opposition's strategy. In late 1931 a cell of ten young lawyers and businessmen established the ABC with one aim, the destruction of Machado, agreeing to welcome U.S. intervention if necessary. The Abecedarios multiplied in numbers but for a time maintained secrecy. As a cloaking device members borrowed loosely from Leninism, organizing by cells with each member knowing only the men in his unit. Cells were linked by middle men whom most members never knew.[37]

Infiltration of the cells was inevitable. As McGill learned, Machado's secret police stole records from the ABC and soon rounded up those whom it identified, confining some in the regime's new prison on the Isle of Pines and others in dank Morro Castle, some of whom were rumored to have been fed to the sharks.[38] "The hands of some missing men were found," McGill was told, "in the bellies of sharks by shark fishermen who fished in the vicinity of Morro Castle."[39] Others fled, some to New York, where they joined previous exiles.

By 1932, the ABC, now engaging students, adopted terrorism as its tactic and the bomb as its signature weapon. With experts training amateurs, the ABC detonated devices nightly, killing police and politicians. Police retaliated by killing students, who marked more police for death. The cycle of bloodletting was what attracted McGill and what faced Welles when he arrived in Havana in the spring 1933.

No governor in Havana would have considered negotiating with terrorists and outlaws. This was the surprising turn that Welles introduced. He believed that, despite its violent history, the ABC included reputable people who, although driven underground by circumstances, inclined to a pragmatic political settlement. Among its members were middle-class lawyers and businessmen who could legitimize any government that succeeded Machado.

Now, exploiting the amnesty negotiated by Welles, McGill seized the opportunity of meeting the Abecedarios, inviting them to his hotel room. Two of the group were students, twenty-three years old, who said they had been prisoners at the Isle of Pines for twenty months when released by the amnesty. Under martial law, they had been arrested by Machado's forces and, they told McGill, "were not given a lawyer, were not told of any charges against them, were not permitted to see relatives or friends." One took off his shirt and showed McGill "where the long scars of whips were deep and ugly-red." Another wound, he said, was made by a dagger when criminals in the prison were armed to attack political prisoners. The two young men fared better than ABC's bomb makers. One boy had been shot "while his feet were tied" and another, they said, had been shot "while he prayed for his life." In both cases, police claimed the right to shoot them as fugitives under the *ley de fuega,* the "law of flight."[40]

The visitors agreed to lead McGill into the labyrinth of the ABC. Just a week earlier this would not have been so easily arranged, but his timing was fortunate. The government's release of prisoners and the ABC's agreement to abstain from terrorism had created a temporary truce.[41]

From the hotel McGill followed them from his familiar boulevards to their unfamiliar streets. The car stopped outside a large building—"one of the finest in Cuba and one which compares favorably with any in our own country"—and he was led inside to an office where he was introduced to a man whom he later identified only as someone "who directs a business which grosses several million each year."

McGill mentioned Machado.

The businessman took down an English dictionary and paged through.

"Monster," was the word his finger stopped on.

That was all. "He said never a word about Machado."

Extreme caution was what McGill expected. Access to the ABC had been possible only because of Welles, but even then it took time to persuade the Abecedarios that McGill was not the dictator's tool. Eventually they began talking about the corruption, which had become so rampant that government officials at times did not bother to camouflage it. The capitol building in Havana, which cost $25 million, and the central highway were built under agreements by which the contractor kicked back a percentage to officials' private pockets. The difference now was the size of the percentage, which had grown in greed from the customary 10 percent to an outrageous 50 percent.

Gaining the trust of the ABC, McGill was introduced to other businessmen. "The lottery must go," said one. "Not that it is wrong per se. But it is too powerful a weapon. It brings on graft and misuse of funds. The congressman with lottery tickets controls thousands of votes."

Since the decline of sugar prices, the national lottery had become a symbol of corruption by which politicians covered losses during the Depression. As the government controlled the operation, thousands of tickets were given to congressmen who in turn doled them free to constituents who sold them for 15 cents a "piece" or $7.50 for full ticket. The seller got a cut, and the congressman got the bigger cut. Every Sunday the winning ticket paid more than $30,000, the second ticket

$5,000. With all the skimming, McGill was told, "much of the money paid for the tickets is not repaid in prizes."[42]

His guides escorted McGill to the office of a lawyer, "one of the society's leaders." As a welcome breeze blew from a garden outside, he learned the history of ABC from this unnamed young man who had been educated at the University of Havana and in the United States and now had a thriving practice in international law. McGill, already tilting away from the dictator, felt a positive bond with the purpose and passion of the young man and the society. "He told me one of the most amazing stories of modern times," McGill wrote, "a story of how 10 men began a movement which today occupies the attention of the entire world."[43]

"Our chief requisite was that the members must have no complicity with the past," explained the lawyer, whom McGill agreed not to name. "Sometimes, reviewing Cuba's political history, we were almost ashamed to admit being Cubans." The "past" meant the Generation of 1898, the generation of Machado, in particular.

"It was a cellular organization," the lawyer said. "The first ten men were the 'A' cell. Each of these ten men got ten more. They were the 'B' cells. Each of these got ten more. They were the 'C' cells. And so on. The 'B' men knew only the man who had recruited them. The 'C' men know only the 'B' men who had got them to join. That was the origin. We went on with the 'D,' 'E' and other sections. We have thousands of members all over Cuba. We frankly have done much to stop the flow of tax money to the government. The Cuban government is bankrupt and it cannot endure. The A.B.C. is largely responsible."

Keeping his audience of Georgians in mind, McGill asked basic questions: "Explain to me about Machado's government and the reason back of your movement to remove him."

"Machado is merely an incident. The thing goes deeper. He represents what our system of government produces. He is a tyrant. He has been more corrupt than our past governments and the government of Cuba has always been filled with graft."

"Machado," McGill interrupted, "points to his public works program and says he is the first president to build roads and public buildings; that other presidents appropriated money to build the central highway and a capitol building but did not."

"Yes. But Machado and his men made greater opportunities for public thievery. But we lose sight of the point. Machado is but a political incident. You see, when our government was formed its constitution was a copy of the one of your country. It has been amended since but it is still a copy. It was a great document for the United States. But it was made after 12 years of study. It fitted a particular country. It does not fit ours.

"The A.B.C.," the lawyer continued, "is not aligned with the old political leaders in the opposition. They would merely be other Machados as we have had in the past, not as vicious, not as cruel, not as corrupt but still merely Machados. We are asking your ambassador to help us strike at the deep-rooted and fundamental ills of our government. We must have a new constitution, one which changes radically our form of government, one which takes away the power which the president has."[44]

McGill prodded him. Machado had charged that the ABC was "a group of terrorists."

Mere self-defense, the lawyer argued. "The A.B.C. has fought terror with terror. It was all we could do. Our members are the leading professional and businessmen of Cuba. We include all the youth of importance. We were being murdered by the *porra* (strong-arm thugs) and our families were being insulted and disgraced. You heard of the treatment accorded some of the ladies of Havana who marched to the presidential palace in protest." McGill had been told that prostitutes, freed from jail cells, attacked the marching women and stripped off their clothes.[45]

The lawyer was incensed in recalling that day, and it seemed to McGill that each government affront "put iron into the souls of those fighting the Machado government."

"We knew," said the lawyer, "the only way to halt this terror was to terrify them. We did."

McGill relayed these views without comment, framing them uncritically, and his lack of criticism of the ABC appeared to support the agenda of the rebels, as a sports writer might appreciate the struggle of an underdog. His partisanship showed through when he compared its program with Roosevelt's agenda, noting that the ABC was making determined efforts to bring a "new deal" to Cuba.

McGill's sympathy earned more access to the underground's leadership. Led further into the labyrinth, his guides now introduced him to their charming and articulate spokesman, the man who had been the voice of the ABC in New York before returning triumphantly to Havana.[46] From the first, Dr. Juan Andres Fliteras impressed McGill as "a brilliant attorney and a student of government. I talked with him at length."[47] Fliteras spoke about farmers and the land, in terms McGill could appreciate on an emotional level from his father's experiences trying to make a living on the farm at Soddy until he quit and moved the family to the city. "Cuba," said Fliteras,

> is primarily an agricultural country. Yet since the Spanish War and especially since the collapse of the sugar markets, the Cuban has been slowly losing his land. There are vast, landed estates. Most of the land of Cuba is owned by foreign corporations. They do not have any interests in Cuba beyond their profits.
>
> Foreign banks control most of our sugar mills. About 60 per cent of Cuba's farm lands are foreign owned. And sugar is 80 per cent of Cuba's agriculture.

Fliteras told McGill ABC's remedy for the land problem: "We would buy those lands back, issuing bonds of low interest and long terms. Cuba can never be a nation of free men until Cuba owns her own land. What if 70 per cent of all the arable land in the United States was owned by English or French companies? You can see what we are up against. We want to buy it back."

That would be a beginning. In the post-Machado era, the ABC's "new deal," McGill explained, would depart radically from old ways of doing business. U.S. companies and banks with investments in Cuba might be expected to object to some of the economic measures. The ABC called for transferring control of the sugar-mill towns from private companies to city governments. The society wanted homesteads exempted from debts and foreclosures, and banking reform. It wanted tax reform, an end to regressive, arbitrary taxation, and a new, broadbased levy on incomes. The most radical economic goal was to nationalize public utilities. Other economic measures seemed inspired by U.S.

legislative and labor-union initiatives—social security insurance against old age, disability and unemployment, and an eight-hour work day. The practice of importing cheaper contract labor from the British West Indies had taken jobs from Cubans, and this would be prohibited.[48]

The economic reforms depended upon political change. Welles's mediation was moving the country in that direction, but it must go much further, the lawyer said. "It is not well for us to have a president with the power which your president has. We would change the government to a parliamentary form. The president would have a position similar to that of the king of England or the president of France. The real power would be vested in a premier and a cabinet."

In this lair of saboteurs, McGill sympathized with their motives. He injected his own view that in the topsy-turvy world of Cuba these men labeled outlaws were the only ones acting in accordance with the nation's interests: "The A.B.C. leaders believe this would enable the Latin people to satisfy that rather volatile temperament with changes in government achieved without revolution." McGill presented the society's case that Cuba needed a system of government that was not a U.S.-style democracy. "The A.B.C. rejects communism and fascism," he wrote, "but does not believe that democracy automatically produces advantages."

Cuba's Communists, McGill was told, were aligned with Machado. "As long as he is in office," McGill wrote, "the communists can point to him and his government as an example of the evils of the capitalistic form of government." The Communists supported the ongoing strike, but ABC wanted to stop it because it menaced Welles's intervention and the mediation, which the ABC now considered a likely way to undermine Machado.[49]

The interview with Fliteras was a prelude to the next adventure. His guides now drove McGill to a house in the suburbs, to the home of a former president of the Havana Rotary Club. His hosts led him down some stairs into a wine cellar. They drew out bottles of wine and opened them. There that evening, McGill was treated to a demonstration of bomb making. "One could sit there in the cellar sipping excellent Spanish or French wine," he recalled, "and watch the experts, young and middle-aged, wrap and wire the explosives."[50] While fabricating weapons of terror, the ABC underscored the tactics of their enemies. The Communists were inflaming labor unrest, which was spreading daily, McGill was told. There was a call for a general strike across the island, which aimed to cripple transportation in and around Havana.[51]

The increasing chaos benefited McGill in an unusual way, as the threat of a general strike forced Machado to return from his fishing trip.[52] A message arrived that Machado would see him soon. The president, hated or revered, was still the center of power, the focal point of everything, the key to McGill's success. No matter what came out of the interview, access to question the dictator was good enough to lead off a series of stories.

That morning in the streets McGill witnessed more signs of the increasing chaos. A parade of veterans of the glorious war against Spain was winding along the Prado from the costly new capitol through the center of the city when police broke it up. From rumor and appearances, the strike was spreading. He concluded that the march of the veterans and the labor unrest were evidence of a popular uprising, and he discounted stories that it was a Communist plot. The Communists, he wrote, "are an off-stage noise. The strike is part of a general protest."[53]

The strike had accelerated partly because of clashes between workers and police, but there were non-Communist factions against Machado as well. During the week, strikers were joined by streetcar workers of the Havana Electric Railway Company, whose owner was anti-Machado, followed soon by stevedores at the docks and by newspaper employees. The Communists, however, were not offstage. Machado considered them central enough to summon their leaders to an urgent meeting at the palace, where he dangled legal recognition if they agreed to call off the strike; the leaders agreed, but so strong was the passion for protest that their rank and file accused the leaders of betrayal and refused to quit the strike.[54]

On the morning of his interview, McGill showed up at the palace and waited at the designated entrance. He imagined the helmeted guards with rifles were frowning at him. The palace looked more like Morro Castle—"a fortress." He saw machine guns behind sandbag barriers at each entrance, at the corner, on the roof.[55]

Eventually a messenger came. "This way, please."

His guide now was one of Machado's staff. Martinez Ybor led him away from the reality of the city, from the steel-barred gates and the "gawking tourists" and "the cries of the street vendors, the sounds of ships from the harbor, the rattle of traffic." Ybor was a veteran civil servant who had served three presidents before Machado. He escorted McGill past a guard and up a flight of marble stairs. At the top, another guard saluted. They walked along a corridor. Heavy walls muffed the noises of the city and colorful rugs in the corridor muffled their foot-steps. McGill noticed the quiet. "It was probably my imagination," he wrote, "but one felt that unseen eyes were watching."[56]

They entered the office of Machado's secretary, Dr. Ramon Guerra, who began by asking what McGill had heard. Were they aware of his intrigues with the ABC? Did they consider him a messenger from Welles? Inside this fortress one might hear everything from spies, but know nothing of value. McGill responded cautiously. He said he was sure many of the press reports from Havana had been exaggerated and "do not give a true picture of the situation." Some had been outright false— "reports of revolutionary armies on the outskirts of the city; of thou-sands of men under arms in the outlying districts." McGill said he believed there were only "a few hundred men under arms, mostly guer-rillas who had come out of the mountains and harass the government soldiers."

Guerra nodded. He was an impressive figure who framed his talk with history and economics. Guerra said he knew that public opinion was hostile to the president's government, but he assured McGill that Machado "had not done all of the evil things attributed to him."

"Our troubles are all economic. We must sell more sugar. The United States must give us a larger quota. If things improve the oppo-sition will die out. President Machado is undergoing the same sort of abuse that your President Hoover did. He was a good man. He was a victim of a worldwide crisis which he could not control."

McGill became conscious of the ticking of the clock on the wall. The time for the interview with Machado came and passed. Then a door opened and a soldier motioned.

Volunteering to interpret for Machado, Guerra led the way down a corridor past barricaded stairways to an elevator, the only way up to

Machado's enclave. McGill thought of Macbeth and his soliloquy "when all his kingdom was armed against him." At a door a guard motioned them in.

The room was dim. No windows opened to the street. A large man in a dark suit arose as they entered and shook McGill's hand firmly. Gerardo Machado's face was "pleasant, though a bit heavy. . . . His forehead is high. . . . His eyes are a bit deeply set. They were pleasant though. He wore horn-rimmed glasses. His large shoulders were somewhat stooped."[57]

Sizing up McGill, Machado saw at the very least an emissary from Welles, someone worthy of flattery. The president said it was a pleasure to meet a representative of the *Atlanta Constitution*, "a famous paper." He said he regretted the present circumstances in Cuba. "I am a patriot. I love my country and its people. I am *from* the people. When the wars for liberty began, my father fought for Cuba. When we fought the Spanish in 1898 I was in the army and rose to the rank of general."

His sympathies were with the laborers. "I have always been on the side of the laboring man," he said. "The working people are for me. Many of them are out of work. It is a situation we cannot help. We must work our way out of it." Discontent was understandable. "We have not been able to pay our teachers and some of our veterans, but other nations have had the same difficulty."

McGill realized that he was an audience to a speech rather than a participant in an interview. Machado compared Havana and New York: "We have had communists who attempted parades and demonstrations which were unauthorized. We have broken them up. New York and other American cities have done the same thing, have found it necessary to do this."

Abruptly, McGill seized the moment and squeezed in a question out of context with the president's message: "Mr. President, your enemies say that you have organized police bands who have killed defenseless men and women. Have you ordered this done?"

"I never have. I never have." McGill thought Machado's voice now sounded "a bit hard."

Machado felt it important to distinguish between acts he authorized and acts done on his behalf. "There have been crimes," he conceded. "I cannot control my partisans in these matters because they, too, have been murdered and beaten. But the government has never done this."

McGill was hearing platitudes and time was running out. In the end game, he tried another ploy, asking the dictator about his fishing trip. "His face really lighted up. Some of the weariness left it. He seemed more alive. He told of catching 400 pounds of red snapper, of landing sword fish." On that bright note Guerra and Machado ended the interview and McGill was led out, retracing his steps across the carpet and down the marble steps past the soldiers.

The interview was in the bag, but what had it revealed? In the coolness of time, years later, McGill would conclude that it was "worthless." Machado was so out of touch with reality that it had been "impossible to make an interview."[58] Certainly this is not what he thought in August 1933, nor what his editors thought. McGill went to work as though he had bagged the scoop of the century. He had already framed a newspaper series of four stories. The two about the ABC and Welles could be written later, as numbers three and four. He would lead the series with the big catch, Machado. Within hours he completed the first two articles, one focused on waiting to see Machado in a garrisoned city, the other about the interview itself and his own observations about Machado and revolutionary politics. In the end, what the dictator said mattered less than the fact that McGill, alone among reporters, got the interview. In Atlanta, his editors would headline the front-page story "Machado Receives McGill."

The next day, McGill airmailed the two Machado pieces. The first appeared near the top of page one with the dateline "Havana, Cuba.— (By Air Mail)" and with the lead: "I was waiting to see President Gerardo Machado, head of the Cuban government." To underscore the scoop, an editor's note in italics explained that this was the first of a series of "articles on the Cuban situation" based on McGill's exclusive interviews with Machado and Welles.[59]

In Havana, McGill had lunch one last time at the American Club, punctuated by the noise of a bomb exploding in the mailbox outside, shattering windows in the club. "That night," he recalled, "I complained to my friends who made the bombs, asking them to be more careful."[60]

That day, McGill airmailed his Sunday sports column, concocted from leftovers, and then packed his bags.[61] He was returning to Atlanta when his second Havana dateline appeared in the Sunday editions. Prodded perhaps by Clark Howell, the editors now emphasized McGill's journalistic coup more so than before, underscoring on the front page that the interview with Machado took place in "near-revolution" conditions and "was the first individual interview given to an American newspaperman by Machado in almost a year."[62]

Back in Atlanta, McGill still had to complete the series. The article on the ABC appeared on Monday. On Tuesday, he published the finale, lauding Sumner Welles as "one of the most brilliant diplomats, one of the most intelligent ambassadors and one of the most courageous men the United States has ever had as a representative."[63] In the circulation war against Hearst's *Atlanta Georgian,* the *Constitution* editors trumpeted their enterprising reporter as a modern-day prophet, reminding readers of his astonishingly accurate prediction about the timing of the revolution. "McGill predicted three days ago," they wrote, "that President Machado would be forced to resign. An authoritative source now asserts he will resign this morning."[64]

By that prediction, McGill risked his credibility. Now he hovered anxiously over the Associated Press teletype machine as they clacked the blow-by-blow stories from Havana. It was nerve-wracking when Machado did not resign on schedule. On Monday, even as the *Constitution* editors were bragging about McGill's timely prediction, the Associated Press's John P. McKnight reported from Havana that Machado's government troops occupied Havana and that police had fired on some ten thousand people thronged to celebrate his expected resignation, which had been announced on the radio by the ABC. Thousands had come into the streets near the capitol "yelling, singing, embracing one another, flinging their hats into the air." The shooting began when police fired into the air. Then a policeman was killed. After that, "pistol, rifle and sub-machine gun fire rattled, roared and echoed from around the great white capitol. Dozens fell, dead or wounded." The count later was 26 reported killed, 150 wounded. Machado had used the strike as a reason for declaring an emergency, and the congress granted him authority to suspend the constitution.

Curiously, Machado was reported to have agreed to resign the next day, but the condition he laid down—"he would not quit as the result of any 'foreign intermeddling'"—left him room to renege.[65] Two days later, on August 9, Machado declared a state of war and a curfew. The dictator dared to resist Welles's "meddling" and his threat of U.S. intervention but used the threat as an external challenge to Cuban patriotism and independence.

The turn of events stunned McGill. For his credibility, he felt he must follow with some response. It was a sign of his resilience, one of his lifelong characteristics, that he immediately dashed off a sequel for Thursday's paper which again claimed a spot on the front page. This time he did not make the mistake of focusing on *when* Machado would fall, but he reasserted that the dictator's end was "inevitable" and that he was "playing his last desperate cards." One card, he noted, was Machado's knowledge that "the very idea of intervention in Cuba is distasteful to the United States government." A second card was Machado's effort to rally other Latin American nations to support Cuba as though this were not an internal Cuban dispute but a hemispheric clash with U.S. imperial power.[66]

McGill postulated a basic primer about political power in Latin America. Machado—"ruthless, cruel and fierce" and "calculating and shrewd"—had managed to hang on because "in the Latin American countries the man with the guns is the man who holds power." Machado had loaded the high ranks of government and military with loyal friends and guaranteed the wages of the "fat, lazy soldiers who have become used to shooting civilians in the streets . . . [and] are not at all eager about being mustered out . . . when a new president assumes charge." During the Depression, the army offered the only sure pay-checks. School teachers "are starving because they have not been paid in almost a year," while $25 million has been squandered on a new Cuban capitol building, while "farmers of Cuba are bankrupt" and "existing businesses are taxed beyond endurance." McGill concluded: "BUT THE ARMY HAS NEVER MISSED A PAY DAY." In sum, in back of Machado "stands his army—his foes have none."[67]

What McGill did not know was that officers in Machado's army feared that a successful U.S. intervention could dictate demobilization of the Cuban military. During the Welles-moderated mediation, one Havana newspaper reported a U.S. military attaché's recommendation that Cuba reduce its army from twelve thousand to only three thousand peacekeepers. Army leaders, among others who had supported Machado, were trying in early August, as historian Louis Perez observed, "to seek new arrangements to guarantee their survival in post-Machado Cuba."[68]

Multiple machinations pushed Machado closer to his end. On August 10, the *Constitution* published McGill's exclusive—Machado "Places Last Hopes in Trained, Well-Paid Army"—with the subhead "McGill Believes President's Policy in Regard to Military Was Shrewdly Conceived Against Just Such Crisis as Now Prevails." The army, however, failed Machado. In Washington, Roosevelt advised the Cuban ambassador that Machado should accept Welles's plan to resign. At about the same time, the army's higher officers, collaborating with Welles, told Machado they demanded, unanimously, that he leave by August 12. At 6:00 A.M. on August 12, ABC radical radio announced that Machado had resigned and left Cuba.[69]

The aftermath was violent and chaotic. Some took revenge against Machado's cohorts. Others gathered in plots, one of them headed by an army sergeant, Fulgencio Batista. None of this, however, stirred McGill's publisher to rush him back to the island, or to publish regular stories about it from a distance. McGill's first overseas news assignment was finished. He had garnered a good deal of glory in the newsroom and now returned to what the circulation wars demanded most, superior sports writing. Cuban politics and social life would remain a lifelong interest, however. In 1935, with Batista firmly in control, McGill would return to the island and, after being wined and dined by the Cuban tourism board, write a series of stories about the restoration of stability on the island under Batista's leadership. But it was that first, swashbuckling adventure of August 1933 that he would recall time and again in columns throughout his career. His first venture into foreign correspondence whetted an appetite that would not be long suppressed.

3

Breaking with the Past

He jerked that ball game up by the nape of its neck, did Don Brennan. . . . They tied the game on him in the ninth because of an outfield mistake. But they couldn't beat him. It was a ball game after he went in.
—RALPH McGILL

Tradition is not a kernel carried within the self but the witness of one age lived in the next by a community of individuals sharing a common teleology.
—DON KECK DUPREE, "NEWT AND JEFF SHALL PREVAIL"

McGILL HAD NO sooner unpacked from his adventures in Cuba than he was fully engaged writing about the prospects of college football. Sports columns from around the South, not adventures from overseas, were what his readers expected, and why the *Constitution* had promoted him to sports editor. Since April 2, 1929, when he stepped off the train at Atlanta's Union Station as the new assistant sports editor, his writing had played a key role in the *Constitution*'s high-stakes competition to win readers.

By 1929, the rivalry among Atlanta's three daily newspapers centered on which paper had the best sports pages. A survey made around 1928 confirmed that if the *Constitution* were to maintain its slight circulation lead, it would have to strengthen its sports section and cater to this appetite in its readers. The magical ability of a "name" sports writer to win readers was recognized as early as 1910 in New York. Within the next decade, publishers paid attractive salaries to writers with style. New York became the mecca of sports writers, luring Grantland Rice from Nashville, Ring Lardner from Chicago, and Damon Runyon from Denver. Around the country, the best writers on many newspapers were those writing sports, as Rice observed, with a "personal approach." By the 1920s the fixation with sports was energizing newspaper writing in the South.[1]

In the era after World War I newspapers reflected this national obsession with sports. Writers, McGill among them, would come to think of the 1920s as a golden age of sports. While Americans played these games, millions more got thrills from watching, or from radio commentators who began broadcasting games in 1920. This was the first decade of sports broadcasting, with the voices of Rice and Graham McNamee reporting play-by-play miraculously into the living room. It was the decade of George Herman "Babe" Ruth's home run records, big-money prize fights of giant killer Jack Dempsey, the astonishing golf conquests of Bobby Jones, and college football that drew mobs to see running back Red Grange and coach Knute Rockne's "four horsemen" of Notre Dame.[2]

Hearst sparked the contest between sports departments. Envisioning his chain as a leader in sports coverage, in 1911 he had hired Runyon at the *American* in New York and by 1914 was promoting him as "the greatest baseball writer in the country."[3] In 1912, Hearst bought the *Atlanta Georgian* and *Sunday American,* and his papers soon became notorious for sensational coverage of the murder trial of Leo Frank, who was lynched.[4] Taking cues from Hearst, his editors strengthened the sports department and, in the 1920s, promoted their name columnist, Ed Danforth. This strategy prompted a response from the *Atlanta Journal,* which led the *Georgian* in circulation. By the mid-1920s the *Journal's* O. B. Keeler had became one of the nation's best known writers about golf and about Georgia's greatest golfer, Bobby Jones. Jones's unparalleled triumphs inspired a generation of men just taking up the sport—some two million amateurs around the country at about five thousand golf courses. The *Journal* also featured the musings of its esteemed sports editor, Morgan Blake, and its football guru, Fuzzy Woodruff, who in 1929 published a history of southern football.[5]

The *Constitution,* slightly ahead of the *Journal* in circulation, resisted the rush to sports.[6] In early 1929 it was still publishing comparatively drab sports pages with smaller headlines and graphics and no featured columnists to match Blake and Danforth.[7] Then, spurred by a sense of the competition and a survey of readers, the *Constitution* suddenly joined the race, blatantly borrowing tactics that had made Hearst successful. Thirty-five years earlier, Hearst's weapon, when he generated the heated New York circulation war after buying the *Journal,* had been his disposable fortune. To combat Joseph Pulitzer's *New York World,* Hearst dangled exorbitant salaries in front of Pulitzer's best writers, editors, and his famous cartoonist, Richard Outcault, luring them into his own newsroom. In similar fashion in 1929 the *Constitution*'s publisher, Clark Howell, raided Hearst's paper in Atlanta, enticing Hearst's sports ace, Danforth.

Danforth had come from a Kentucky daily in 1916 at the age of twenty-four. There, he first gained attention as a chronicler of racing ("turf" writing was the vogue term) with a stroke of luck at a Kentucky Derby by picking the win, place, and show horses. In Atlanta through the 1920s he matured, in part because Hearst's editors gave him opportunities and groomed him to be not only a reporter but a personality. Danforth even developed a fictional alter ego named Wayward Boye, an eccentric character of considerable skill and strength.[8] By 1929 Danforth was at the top of his game. But while the Hearst operation appreciated his value, it had grown stingy with the purse, in part because of Hearst's personal extravagances. When the *Constitution* asked Danforth to reshape its coverage at a salary of $175 a week, about twice what anybody else was making in sports, he was ready to move. "But before he ever accepted," recalls Freddie Russell, "he wanted McGill."[9]

The best southern sports writers knew each other. From season to season, sharing press seats and barstools, they had developed a camaraderie on the seasonal circuit that carried them from fall campus football rivalries into the long run of spring and summer professional baseball in the Southern Association cities. McGill and Danforth rendezvoused over corn whisky. As McGill remembered, "Whisky sold for a dollar a quart" but as much as two dollars a pint. Although the Tennessee legislature enacted Prohibition in 1909, officially closing Nashville saloons that summer, a popular backlash led to the election that year of a "wet" mayor. Declaring that "as long as I stay in a free country, I will eat and drink as I please," Hilary Howse carried 75 percent of the vote. As one historian noted, Howse was supported by a "whole underground network of liquor dealers, bootleggers, saloon keepers, and their patrons." Speakeasies and gambling houses operated under cover of back entrances. Some were dumps. The late-night "sour ghostlike smell" in the long room at Charley's speakeasy stenched McGill's memory. "At one end of the bar was a glass-covered clutch of ham sandwiches" so dried that "the corners of each slice of bread curl upward, revealing the think slice of mottled ham beneath." Charley's also had a "grease-incrusted two-burner oil stove for cooking hamburgers." But his "main business was white corn whisky, sold by the drink or the pint." Together in Nashville for the Georgia Tech–Vanderbilt game, McGill and Danforth would go to Billy Baker's Speakeasy with a back entrance on Printers Alley behind the *Banner* office. Both were fond of a good story, funny or otherwise, and both were respected for the fine crafting of language. Both knew and loved their business.[10]

It was a secret among friends when Danforth called McGill in Nashville and confided that he would soon leave Hearst to join the *Constitution* and wanted McGill to join him as his assistant sports editor. Together they could put out a section to whip the competition. Danforth would write the daily column and McGill could unwind with a daily feature story in addition to covering sports news, the football and baseball games, boxing, and some golf. Years later, McGill recalled that he had been weary that day from covering a long murder trial and said yes without hesitation, remembering later that he forgot to ask the salary. It was all the sweeter when he learned the *Constitution* would pay him $90 a week. He had almost no money to his name after seven years at the *Banner*. As he wrote to a Nashville girl two weeks after leaving, "Rather pathetic and condemnatory commentary on my passing from Nashville was that I left in debt after working there that long and with nothing to show for it." He confessed to being "in a terrible rut there in Nashville. I had got to the point where I did a column a day, a theatrical review on Monday that was about all." The *Constitution* was getting its money's worth. "I am working 12 and 14 hours a day down here," he told her, "and learning some things I didn't know. And finding out how little I knew. . . . I don't know how I am going over down here. . . . They have advertised me extensively." Evidence of his success came after he had been on the job a short while. The *Georgian* tried to lure him by offering $150 a week, but McGill declined, whether out of loyalty to Danforth or because McGill wisely regarded the *Constitution* as a more stable operation.[11]

Some regarded McGill as better than Danforth. One *Constitution* reporter noted in his diary that in four months McGill had become the "best writer on the paper. Fine person. Well liked." At the *Journal,* Keeler had become fond of McGill while traveling the circuit in the 1920s. McGill, fleshy at five feet, ten inches, reminded Keeler of "a Buddha[,] . . . calm, reflective, placid and comfortable, and above everything else, giving the impression he knew what it was all about and that it didn't matter. . . . It didn't make much difference."[12]

McGill did not develop his writing style in journalism class. This was in part because Vanderbilt was not among those few universities beginning to offer journalism courses, and in part because McGill more or less *slid* into journalism rather than choosing it. After realizing that he did not have what it took to be a doctor, he followed his interests, playing tackle on the Vanderbilt football squads coached by the great Dan McGugin and majoring in English. He credited the chair of the English department, Edwin Mims, for lessons that "remained with me. . . . He wrestled mightily with young minds out of the small towns of Tennessee and adjoining states, seeking to make them 'see' and 'feel.'" Mims's classes stimulated McGill to read and memorize poetry. Early on, McGill thought of himself as a poet and a romantic.[13]

Outside class, his desire to play football met with astonishing success. On his prep school team at McCallie he had trained hard to play tackle "by doing a lot of hard work and some bicycle riding on Sundays to build up the legs." In the summer of 1916 he cycled the round trip between Chattanooga and Atlanta and that fall became team captain. But as a Vanderbilt freshman he was, at 152 pounds, too light to expect a starting position on the varsity. Then the world war indirectly improved his chances as several upperclassmen left to serve as officers in France. McGill immediately advanced to Coach McGugin's first team. The coach also got him a job as a waiter in the student dining room. Thus began a lasting affection for McGugin, "a kindly gentleman and a former member of Michigan's famous 'point-a-minute' teams." McGill missed the 1918 season because he too joined the U.S. Marines, but he was back on McGugin's reinforced postwar teams in the fall of 1919 and 1920. "But already," he recalled, "there were other interests."[14]

One keen interest was alcohol. Years later, when asked by Vanderbilt to reminisce about teachers who "stimulated" him, McGill happily recalled a graduate chemistry student. From this "patron saint of the Lost Generation," McGill learned to make amber booze with a Bunsen burner and glassware, from dried apricots, water, and alcohol. The brandylike fluid had a "pleasant taste with a proof ranging from 100 to 150," a welcome change of tonic from Prohibition moonshine. "On many of the weekends he kept my mind pleasantly stimulated," McGill recalled. McGill and his cohorts hid gallons of the booze in the old Sigma Chi house on Garland Avenue, making more when needed and selling the surplus.[15]

His passion for poetry led McGill into a bohemian group and to moonshine poetry readings down by the Cumberland River. The bohemians centered around Will Ella (Willa) Johnson, the university librarian, and her husband, English professor Stanley Johnson. Johnson was writing a novel, *The Professor,* which, for its thinly disguised portraits of Mims and another professor, would eventually get him fired. "Willa— and Stanley—introduced him to the Bohemian life," recalled "Fannie" Cheney. "They had a camp outside Nashville at Haysboro where they gathered in the summer, winter too. Because if you drank enough you didn't care." One night McGill "jumped up and went swinging from the rafters, from one to the other. We thought he was going to break his neck." On campus, the Johnsons' apartment was the oasis where McGill and a few others gathered to imbibe corn liquor and poetry. Those nights were even more important than classes, he would recall, in providing "the stimulation to read and think." It was a romantic group which shared a yearning to live the creative life in "the garrets and fleshpots of Greenwich Village."[16]

These were years of remarkable fervor in poetry at Vanderbilt. While the Johnsons' cell quietly nourished its budding poets, Johnson was associated with another group of writers, more audacious and more talented, who inspired the general insurgence of poetry at Vanderbilt. From 1920 to 1922, "the Fugitives" published under pen names as "the campus buzzed with speculation" about their identities. As a marginal insider, McGill knew that the faculty leader was John Crowe Ransom, whose *Poems about God* had been attacked by clergymen; other faculty included Donald Davidson, Walter Clyde Curry, and Johnson. The Fugitives welcomed serious students, and these included Allen Tate, Robert Penn Warren, and McGill's friend, Merrill Moore. In April 1922, the group published the first edition of its magazine, *The Fugitive,* which to their delight was acclaimed as constituting "the entire literature of Tennessee" by the iconoclastic critic of southern culture, H. L. Mencken, the "sage of Baltimore." With his aggressive, satirical essays in *Smart Set* and the *American Mercury,* Mencken inspired a generation of aspiring intellectuals, including McGill: "Henry Mencken, of course, was our knight in shining armor who each month slew the dragons of dullness in the pulpits of Washington, the governor's office, the legislature and in the seats of the mighty generally." Before its demise in 1925 the magazine published contributions from Louis Untermeyer, Christopher Morley, and Robert Graves and bestowed an award on Laura Riding.[17]

McGill soon realized that despite these associations and his fervor for poetry, he was not a poet. His Vanderbilt roommate preserved a fragment he found in McGill's typewriter, written after a night of drinking, perhaps through one of his famous hangovers:

> I am scared and so I run breathlessly
> And sop my bread of pain and fear
> Into the gravy that is God.

Though he always was able to recite lines, frustration with his own verse confirmed his decision to write prose.

His first break in journalism came in 1919, when he suggested an idea for a column to the weekly student newspaper, the *Hustler.* It was accepted, and the first of a lifetime output of more than thirty thousand columns was published on page one. He soon joined the staff and began sharing the rite of producing the paper, staying up all night, "talking and arguing on a variety of subjects."[18] Also in 1919, when it seemed Vanderbilt students wanted a humor magazine, McGill was one of the founders and the second editor-in-chief of a quarterly, the *Jade.* He edited this "thin but sparkling little journal" until 1921, publishing whimsical poetry, very short stories, satire, and jokes.[19]

His transition to daily journalism happened as suddenly as a storm and was just as understandable. As often happened in his career, a friendship drew him into the new situation and an innate sense of opportunity kept him going until he satisfied some ambition. This new situation lasted seven years, beginning that spring day in 1921 when he visited the *Banner* newsroom to see two Sigma Chi fraternity alumni who worked there. The newsroom interested him, and he came back another day and found his opportunity. The young typist who usually took the play-by-play over the phone from the Nashville baseball park had quit. McGill had seen typists doing this, and it seemed easy enough. "The detail came in slowly—'Smith struck out. Jones flied to right. Johnson singled to left.'" The *Banner* put him on the payroll. Soon after, his part-time job expanded to writing police stories. By the summer of 1921 he was earning seventeen dollars a week and feeling "intense excitement. . . . I knew then I had found what I wanted to do."[20]

Captivated by the joy of seeing his words in print, McGill brought to newspaper work the energetic romanticism he had offered to poetry. The paychecks sealed the relationship. He soon had a new circle of acquaintances in the newsroom, notably Brainard "Lon" Cheney. Cheney had migrated to Nashville from rural Georgia and shared McGill's passion to write. "We burned to be writers, authors of books and of magazine articles," McGill recalled. They soon teamed up as roommates and good friends. Cheney remembered how he and McGill reveled in the "romance of journalism, the then new notion of Bohemianism, and our own youth. The corn liquor that we drank had something to do with it, too." Newspaper work stimulated McGill. The thrill he felt transformed him into what another friend later called "perhaps the most willing cub who ever sat down at a typewriter in a city room with his hat on."[21]

McGill had such eclectic interests that he would take any assignment: "I did everything they'd allow. I wrote politics, covered police, reviewed books and plays. I also had a yen to be an actor and carried spears in touring Shakespearean plays" in Nashville's old auditorium. McGill reviewed the early roles of actor Ralph Bellamy in summer stock "before the movies had taken over all the local theatres. . . . Bellamy sweated through his coat but, of course, only cub reporters playing at being critics noted things like that." With unbounded energy, McGill wrote often and well and fast—three permanent characteristics of his career.[22]

Certainly the new job was a blessing when, in the spring of 1922, shortly before McGill was to graduate, Vanderbilt suspended him. Largely because of McGill's inaction, the suspension dragged on until it became a virtual expulsion. The trouble began when he wrote a column in the *Hustler* which, as he put it, "the chancellor did not like." Vanderbilt had not erected a student lounge, as stipulated in the will of a professor who had bequeathed twenty thousand dollars. Was this embezzlement? The column got him suspended, but he got into more trouble when he embarrassed the Beta Theta Pi fraternity with what he later called "a bit of by-play in inter-fraternity rivalry."[23] Fannie Cheney recalled how McGill "sent out invitations to all the whores to attend a fraternity dance. The fraternity didn't like it a bit." McGill might have appealed to return to finish his senior year. "He probably could have come back and re-entered school the next year," said his friend Fred Russell, "if he had wanted to. But he had a fulltime job. The degree didn't mean that much to him."[24]

McGill's quitting school would have meant something more to his father who had for years encouraged the young man's education. In his own boyhood on the farm, Benjamin Franklin McGill had dreamed of a college degree. When Ben McGill came of age, he had little interest in working the family land, which was located in the remote community of Igou's Ferry in East Tennessee, along the west bank of Sale Creek at the Tennessee River, about twenty miles north of Chattanooga. The nearest civilization, down ten miles of dirt road, was the tiny settlement of Soddy, which had grown up in Indian country in the late 1700s around William Soddor's trading post. Some miles to the south was the star in Ben McGill's firmament—Chattanooga—where he wanted to study law. He was inspired by an uncle who was a leading Chattanooga attorney and by a cousin who successfully defended 150 murder defendants in three states.

Like Atlanta to the south, Chattanooga's civic leaders also championed a New South in the 1880s. At the same time Henry Grady and the *Atlanta Constitution* were hoisting Atlanta's banner, the progressive owner of the *Chattanooga Times,* Adolph S. Ochs, heralded his city's economic benefits to industry. "Better come to the cotton fields, cheap water power and the favorable climate of the south," the *Times* advised manufacturers in 1883, "than depend on railroad favor for artificial and unjust advantages that may be lost any hour." Other Tennesseans noticed Chattanooga's resurgence. Editors at the *Knoxville Dispatch* stated in 1880 that under Ochs the *Chattanooga Times* had become "one of the most aggressive and progressive papers of the State," which "steadily and courageously" helped build Chattanooga into "one of the most flourishing and progressive cities in the South." In Augusta, Georgia, one of the cities competing with Atlanta for New South industry, the editor of the *Augusta Chronicle* in 1886 praised Ochs as "ambitious for his city and tireless in his efforts to advance her interests and improve her connection."[25]

In the late 1880s as the South was reestablishing its educational bearings, Ben's father encouraged his son's desire to move away from the land. "Many Southerners of that generation, which had so little chance for schooling, had almost an obsession about educating their children," Ralph understood years later. While in the next generation there would be a romantic attachment to the land as integral to the southern culture, Ralph McGill's father came to reject agrarian sentiments in favor of the newer movements evident in Chattanooga and other cities attracting business and industry.[26]

The founding of Chattanooga University symbolized this movement to a newer way of life. The university opened for its first class in 1886, when the South was only beginning to recover economically from the Civil War. One year later, in 1887, Ben McGill entered, at the age of nineteen. "His great boyhood dream was to be a lawyer," McGill's mother told Ralph many years later. Ben spent some of "the first money he earned" to buy copies of Blackstone's law *Commentaries*. In his freshman year at the university, he was already talked about as a "brilliant scholar."[27]

What happened in the second half of his freshman year was to remain for years a family secret. So terrible was it that Ben withdrew from the university, never returned to college, and became an exile from the city. On February 22, 1888, in a outburst of temper, he killed a fellow student during an argument on the baseball field and was charged with murder. Considering that his trial was pending, the university faculty, recognizing "certain extraordinary peculiarities that render the ordinary disciplinary measures inappropriate and difficulty of application" and noting that "Mr. McGill has voluntarily withdrawn from the University," voted on April 13, 1888, that "the charges against him be laid upon the table" and that "his name be published in the catalogue as having withdrawn under charges." The *Year-Book of Chattanooga University* in May 1888 in fact listed first-year student Benjamin Franklin McGill of Igou's Ferry with the footnote "Withdrawn under charges" and his victim, James Columbus Johnson of Half Moon Island, as "Deceased."[28]

The incident occurred during a baseball game, the northern sport just then becoming popular in the South. Consistent with his passion for the law, Ben was the umpire behind home plate when he was heckled from the sidelines by one of the players, a fellow freshman, James C. Johnson. Johnson objected to a pitch that was thrown before his teammate was in position to hit.

According to witnesses, Johnson shouted at McGill, "Mack, they're bulldozing you."

"You're a damn liar," McGill answered.

"You're another," Johnson said, walking toward McGill and stopping just in front of him. "Here I am. I dare you to hit me."

Johnson was turning away when McGill picked up a bat and "with muscles of both arms bent in the endeavor," hit Johnson on the left side of the head. Stunned, Johnson sank to the ground, holding his head and saying, "Ben, you had no right to hit me." Johnson insisted he was not hurt badly, but friends took him to his room as the game continued. "It was all a joke and I didn't think McGill would strike me," Johnson told friends. Soon after, he began to bleed and lost consciousness. A doctor diagnosed a fractured skull. At 5:00 P.M., Johnson "gave a shudder and died." The death was all the more upsetting to the community because Johnson, the son of a well-to-do farmer, was "considered a social and clever boy," an officer in the Demosthenean Literary Society, and "universally liked by his teachers and schoolmates."[29]

On the field, the game had continued. McGill "sauntered carelessly about the grounds and declared that he was mad at Johnson and had intended it when he struck to fix him up," several students later told a reporter. Privately, McGill may have felt differently. A professor at the field said McGill told him that he did not mean to hit Johnson so hard. In the early afternoon when word spread of Johnson's condition, McGill vanished. Rumors spread that he fled by train. A reward of $250 was posted by Johnson's father, and the sheriff sent deputies to find him. The next day, McGill turned himself in. "I know I am innocent of any purpose to kill Johnson and I could not leave," he said. When Ben met his father, "the young man with tears streaming down his face, threw his arms about the old man's neck and cried, 'Oh, father, I did not intend to kill—I had no idea of killing him.'" The next day, the newspaper reported "the scene in the court room was an affecting one" as Ben, in the company of friends and beside his family attorneys,

> cried as though his heart would break. Surrounding him were students of the university, ranging in ages from ten years to the older scholars.
>
> The venerable Dr. Rust pressed forward and shook the young man's hands, and Bishop Walden, Prof. Lewis and his wife, and others of the faculty did all in their power to comfort him. To all questions he had but one answer—"I did not intend to kill him."[30]

For legal counsel, the McGills turned to the respected family lawyers on the Clift side, Ben's uncle and cousin. The Clifts were as solid a family as any in East Tennessee. The scion of the Clifts was Ben's great uncle, Col. William Clift of Soddy, an avowed opponent of secession and a Union officer during the Civil War. An immigrant from Wales, he welcomed the opportunities of the industrial age and supported the Whig Party policy of national development. In the process he became Hamilton County's first millionaire as owner of coal mines and a gristmill, as an investor in one of the first steamboats on the Tennessee River, and as a promoter of railroads, as well as being one of the largest landholders. When the Civil War began, Colonel Clift at the age of sixty-seven was the militia commander and rebelled against Confederate sympathizers seeking to impress the militia into the Rebel army. He formed his own volunteer unit, the Eighth Tennessee Infantry, outfitted with shotguns, squirrel rifles, knives, pepper-pot pistols, and one flawed cannon made from a part of the *Black Hawk,* one of Clift's steamboats. The unit surrendered just before its first battle, but Clift went north and fought in Kentucky until he was captured by his own son, Captain Moses Clift, in 1863.[31]

Given the family reputation, the Clifts guaranteed the court that Ben would not vanish again. Presenting character witnesses, they got him released on a $5 bond. They managed to postpone the murder trial repeatedly, so that when it occurred in 1889, sixteen months after the killing, passions had subsided. This may have contributed to the jury's inability to agree on a verdict of second degree murder or manslaughter. Ben McGill was allowed to enter a guilty plea to a lesser charge, "assault and battery." Because he had been expelled from the university the previous April, the family attorneys argued that he had already paid a penalty. The court fined him $250, ordered him to pay court costs, and released him. He spent no time in prison.[32]

At the time, the newspaper publicity and the nature of the small community at Soddy meant that almost everyone there should have known of the poor McGill boy who lost his temper and killed a student with a baseball bat. Ben's response was to give up the dream of lawyering. Eight years after the killing of James Johnson, Ben and Mary Louise Skillern married on May 5, 1896, in the Soddy Presbyterian Church. Once, he showed his bride the Blackstone's *Commentaries,* stored in a trunk, but refused her suggestion that he study law in an attorney's office. "I tried to persuade him to find some attorney who would give him some help," she explained to Ralph after Ben's funeral in 1940, "but he shook his head and put them [the lawbooks] away. He would not discuss them again." Instead, he retreated for a time to the six-hundred-acre family farm along the Tennessee River. "My father," Ralph would recall, "had only the inadequate schooling offered in those foothills of the Appalachians, but he had a liking for books and a grief because he had not been able to have more education."[33]

There is no evidence that Ralph's mother ever spoke about the reason for Ben's grief to her son and three daughters, and the family moved away from the farming community when Ralph, the oldest, was seven. If Ralph knew the story, he never discussed it publicly. In fact, he seldom mentioned his father. In his autobiography, Ralph noted that Ben McGill read aloud to him, that he "was a hard-working, kindly man" with "a streak of stubbornness in him, as well as brooding, but these moods were always short. . . . I never had even a light spanking from him, though I deserved many." McGill concluded, "Ours was a happy family largely because of the spirit and faith of my mother."[34]

His mother's family, as well, had a shameful story that Ralph said he never heard until 1948, when he was fifty years old. His mother's father was Anderson Skillern, a newspaperman "with a flowery style" and a love of travel. He had taken his wife, Nancy Isabella "Belle" Clift, to Texas, where Mary Lou and her brother Fred were born, and abandoned them. Skillern was last seen in Idaho and rumored to have died of fever. "I had never heard a word of criticism or malice from my mother," he explained. "None of the Clifts mentioned him to me" until an aunt, Molly Clift Walker, then ninety, revealed the story with compassion for the "newspaper writer" who abandoned his family: "He was not a bad man. Weak and selfish, I guess, but his trouble was that the horizon always lured him."[35]

Ralph was Ben and Mary Lou's second child. Their first son died within weeks. Then, on February 5, 1898, Ralph was born at the farm. Ben so admired the Walker family and their young son, Richard, who delivered his boy—"My father saw in the young college graduate all he had wanted to be"—that he gave the doctor the honor of naming the boy. "Splendid," said Dr. Richard Walker, summoning forth the name of his favorite philosopher. "We'll call him Ralph Waldo Emerson." Ben was sympathetic to naming a boy after a famous American. He had changed his own name from Benjamin *Wallace* to Benjamin *Franklin* after reading about Franklin. But it was "so dangerous a name" in East Tennessee, Ralph later realized: "Presbyterian preachers who came there for services denounced Emerson's Unitarianism and transcendentalism as heresy and worse. . . . So it was that quite early I knew I had a meaningful name." After being hailed as "Waldo! Waldo!" that part of the name was dropped "by something like mutual consent."[36]

That September, Ben's father died and left the farm at Igou's Ferry to him and six brothers and sisters. Ben, at thirty-one, was planning to quit farming. In 1899, he sold his share to his brothers and sisters. As it was explained later to Ralph, the farm, if evenly divided, would not have been big enough for anyone, "so it was decided that the sisters would stay on until they married and then the farm would be sold." Leaving the farm also suited Mary Lou. "She wanted a place of her own," was how Ralph understood it, and "she wanted my father out on his own." A third reason was Ralph's frail health. The boy's sickly nature, aggravated by digestive problems, troubled her all the more because of the death of her first son, who lived only a few weeks. "I suppose some of the attention shown me was because of memories of that infant son, her first child and first intense grief," Ralph wrote years later. Dr. Walker had his office in Soddy, which is where the McGills moved in 1899. Around Soddy, Ben found temporary work in the coal mines while looking for something that would allow him to use his mind above ground. Soon he found a part-time job as a clerk with the Tom Snow Heating and Roofing Company in Chattanooga, to which he commuted by train. In 1904, after winning some sales awards and establishing himself as a full-time salesman, Ben completed the transition to the city, moving the family to Chattanooga. He ended an exile of fifteen years.[37]

Ralph's memories of the family farm derived from summers spent there to improve his health. An early recollection was of floating with his parents on a small skiff on the Tennessee. He recalled buggy rides to church, Bible readings at night, the farm's cornfields and threshers, the big barn and "the pond in which ducks and geese reveled," and steamboats arriving at the farm's river landing with bells ringing and, at night, with lights searching out the shore while men signaled with lanterns.[38]

After leaving Vanderbilt, McGill devoted himself to his work. He discovered in journalism constant opportunity to make his work his play. His sports writing and work-related travels, and his interest in the theater, fox hunts, and Prohibition era corn liquor, were usually enough to satisfy him. In his bachelor years, McGill vowed to Brainard Cheney that he would avoid romantic entanglements. The way Brainard remembered it, McGill declared, "It will be a cold day in July when they get me to the altar." He seemed reluctant to pay the price of reforming his habits. Yet at the same time he expressed disappointment, especially when inebriated, in what he had so far achieved. He suffered from the self-criticism common to the best sports writers of the age, Lardner among them. No matter what literary quality they attained in their chronicles, sports writers were perceived as disreputable types, as well as chronic drinkers (which McGill and Lardner both were). His own repetitive cycle of seasonal sportswriting, drinking bouts, and cursed hangovers stirred McGill's sense of his shortcomings and limitations. In his late twenties, he fell into depressing sloughs of despondency when contemplating his future, all the more so when he contemplated marriage.

His limitations disturbed him even more in the summer of 1926. While covering a political campaign, he met a Nashville debutante who became his first serious love. Over the next two years, this relationship outside his social class haunted him, especially late at night when he was tired and drunk, reminding him that he had a calling beyond sports writing that was unfulfilled. After meeting her, McGill suddenly tired of the Vanderbilt crowd who gathered at the Cumberland River camp. Willa Johnson had just divorced Stanley, and Stanley was hanging out at the camp with a much younger woman. "I am fed up on camp and Stanley [Johnson]," McGill wrote her, "but I couldn't hardly get out of it—I'd give anything if I could be with you tonight— I love you so utterly. . . . I'm coming to love you so much that I'm coming to believe in God."[39]

Louise Stevens lived in a world distant from sports writers. Her well-to-do family nested among the fashionable homes in the new upper-class suburb of Belle Meade on acreage that had been a thoroughbred horse farm and the antebellum "Queen of Tennessee Plantations." Stevens was a few years younger than McGill and she loved formal society events and games of bridge in the country club set in the mid-1920s, the Nashville world reflected in Peter Taylor's fiction, where "any man was expected to have a career of some kind." Newspaper work qualified as a hobby, not a serious career. At the mature age of twenty-eight, McGill associated with gritty athletes and devious politicians, and his closest companions were itinerant newspapermen who boozed. His was a world of sports events, political rallies, and distant news events, and he slept fitfully in hotels as often as in his own bed; his loves were reading, writing, and drinking. Apart from his bleak career prospects, an East Tennessean with no Confederate army grandfathers, was, in Taylor's stories, alien to "the grandeur which Nashvillians claimed for themselves. . . . The world I am speaking of isn't the hard-bitten monkey-trial world of East Tennessee that everybody knows about, but a gentler world in Middle Tennessee."[40]

"Steve" as McGill called her, was already serious about a younger fraternity brother of McGill's. Yet in the summer of 1926 she became a romantic obsession, so much so that he stammered in her presence. "You do something to me, Steve," he wrote that September a few minutes after they parted and he was sitting around with Cheney. "I feel that I must say something—there is something that makes we want to say a poem and I can only clutch at words and fumble them. . . . I do want you to know that because of you life is sweeter." The relationship often seemed like youthful infatuation, with McGill constantly unsure of his worthiness or of her feelings, especially when he was drinking. "You are so sweet that my big hulk trembles—at the fact that you love me—or at least like me. . . . You are all in the world that I am holding to. . . . Please let me love you and hold to you." Considering the time she spent with him and the numerous letters he wrote her, she probably knew him better than any other woman between 1926 and 1928.[41]

On the road McGill revealed to her his sensibilities and deep misgivings. Often fatigued and confessing loneliness, he wrote frequently, usually on hotel stationery with pictures of Memphis's Peabody, the Farragut in Knoxville, the Dinkler in Atlanta, the Battery Park in Asheville, the Latham in Hopkinsville, Kentucky. One night after drinking, his mood turned dark and confessional: "Did you ever feel, Steve, that you were struggling to thrust off a lot of things that were sort of smothering you down? I feel somehow as if I were trying to rid my mind of a lot of broken up ideas, philosophies and that if I could just throw up my hands and run, I might get out from under them." He conceded to "an inferiority complex, a very bad one, I suppose." From Dawson Springs, Kentucky, he continued in the same mood one night after midnight: "I'll never get anywhere. Last night—in the rain—the thought came to me that I was very presumptuous to love you—you who are so used to things I perhaps can never give. God, I'm such a failure. I suppose I'm a weak coward—you don't love me and it is best you don't—. But I do love you." The next night he apologized for seeming so depressed and explained that he "was tight when I wrote you last night." He was still depressed about his career. "I don't guess I'll ever amount to anything," he wrote. A month later, still in the black mood he later attributed to his Welsh blood, he declared, "I am quite convinced now that I will never do much with myself."[42]

When he wasn't berating himself, he was trying to interest Louise in the adventures of his itinerant life. It seemed to help him to purge his depression about being so alien to her social circle. Then he would rejoice in the reality of the visceral world of his characters and situations. "I really feel conceited about knowing so many interesting people," he wrote in August 1926. On the fox hunt circuit in the chill of that October, late at night after telegraphing his story, he introduced her to his latest discovery in the realm of Prohibition era drinks, the houndsman's hot brick. "Few people in Nashville will know what a 'hot brick' is." A tumbler of the blend of boiling water, a pat of butter, and a "finger or so" of whisky "serves simply to warm you up. I intend to take one in the morning— that is about three hours from now." "Honey," he cautioned the following spring, "let's don't ever get set in our ways."[43]

The letters also chronicled his disparate assignments. None was more challenging than the Christmas massacre in South Pittsburg, in southeastern Tennessee. In the midst of union-management warfare, McGill abandoned the role of simply reporting the conflict. In the end he was credited with mediating the settlement that restored peace. "This is funny work, a man near thirty," he wrote of himself, "sitting here at a desk in a small-town hotel lobby a few feet from where six men died. . . . Outside a truck with a machine gun on it goes by." He was courted by both sides:

> Bankers, supporting "law and order" will call me in and say, "Mr. McGill, these damn dirty strikers are at the bottom of this. Will you have a drink? Any decent citizen can see that—"
>
> Union heads will call me in and say, "These damn scabs are at the bottom of this. The damn bankers and the mayor own stock in the plant and they armed the scabs. That's why this damned dirty killing happened."

Plenty of damns. Who is damned? I wonder.

Children imitating soldiers—women strutting—strikers, scabs as they call them, who woke up on Christmas morning cold and hungry and with no toys for their children and then went out shooting and who would have shot the mayor and the bankers if they had found them—all these and more on parade—[44]

Having survived, the mayor praised McGill for "his wisdom, courage, and tact" in mediating a peaceful settlement. According to the mayor, "Only an impartial outsider could have had any dealings whatever with the bitter factions, and Mr. McGill grasped the situation immediately and set to work to iron out the difficulties. He made hundred of friends on both sides. . . . For two days his efforts were strenuous and well directed."[45]

Years before his concern about civil rights, his letters reflect almost nothing about race relations in the segregated South. Once, however, he did relate to Louise a story, heard in Bible class in Nashville, that suggested a stereotype of the Negro as uneducated but nonetheless clever. The teacher "told the story of the Negro boy who was trying to figure out why god had made some of the things that were in the world—flies for instance—'I reckon,' said the negra, 'if he hadn't some fool would have said he couldn't.'"[46]

McGill continued writing to Louise even after she revealed that she was planning to be married to his friend Kirk, who was twenty-one, a couple years younger than she and eight years younger than McGill. He concealed any disappointment and approved of her choice. "Kirk came in yesterday. . . . He is very much in love with you, I think, at least he is hell-bent on making big money quickly—so that he may marry you. I think now, as I have always thought, that he is perhaps the best boy I ever knew—Man, if you choose—he is a man. I love you Steve. Mac." In the same letter he lamented having been one of the "damn fools who have lived in a fool's paradise and at 29 are making barely enough to keep ourselves and let our dreams exist as they may—are in a rather silly state—we can't help but be sentimental." As for her, she deserved something better: "You were made for a very fine love, Steve. Don't ever be careless about that." Just after Christmas 1927, in the thick of the labor war in

South Pittsburg, McGill wanted her to know that his letters were from "one who loves you and who always will and from one who understands how things are, without bitterness."[47]

McGill seemed to understood that their parting was better for him as well. While she had the positive effect of making him feel he needed to do more with his life, he also realized that his outgoing spirit could not be contained as part of a social class that was inherently exclusive and centered on itself. Years later, McGill indicated to his son that it was he who had shied away from Louise. Advising his boy against wasting time on card games, he said, "I liked books, she liked bridge. She never could teach me to play so she gave me up as a bad job. I was glad, for not long after I met your mother."[48]

During this period, McGill met a woman of very different temperament. Mary Elizabeth Leonard was from a middle-class professional family, the daughter of a dentist who had migrated from McMinnville, Tennessee, and did not have birthright among the Nashville social elite. Strong in spirit but fragile in health, Mary Elizabeth had just returned home from a long hospitalization. At the age of three she had suffered the first attack of a kidney ailment that troubled her throughout life. Then, after graduating from Nashville's Peabody College, where she majored in home economics and planned a career as a dietitian, she was diagnosed with tuberculosis and spent two years in a sanitarium in the hills at Ridgetop, thirty miles from Nashville.[49]

McGill was the town's best known sports writer and on occasion he visited the Leonard family's modest brick home to see Mary Elizabeth's older brother, Thomas Leonard Jr. "Mouse" Leonard was the star quarterback for Coach Dan McGugin's Vanderbilt team. Mary Elizabeth, seven years young than McGill, already knew something about this sports writer. The story is told that she first saw him at a hot-dog stand in Nashville. That day he was the hefty man "whaling a bully who had pushed a little fellow around." As Fannie Cheney recalls, "She pursued him."[50]

After being cooped up for two years, Mary Elizabeth was eager to party, and she was attracted to Ralph's bohemian ways fueled by bottles of bootleg liquor. At times her kidneys rebelled and, then, friends recall, Ralph would doctor her. "He mothered her. We used to call him 'Mother McGill,'" remembered Fannie Cheney. "He was not a womanizer, before or after his marriage. But he loved women." Fannie herself adored Ralph, who in the 1920s reminded her of a fleshy boy who had eaten too much candy. Once, at his urging, Ralph and Fannie made a "solemn pact." McGill ground a glowing cigarette into the back of his hand, and she did the same to hers, making a scar she could still discern in her eighties. In 1928, McGill was at her wedding, as best man for the groom, his fellow journalist and drinking companion, Brainard Cheney. The only others present were the bride's mother and aunt; both wore black, Fannie remembered, "because it was a tragedy, marrying Lon Cheney—an indigent reporter, a terrible drunk." Until 1929, when McGill married Mary Elizabeth (in a ceremony on the Vanderbilt campus) and moved to Atlanta, the Cheneys' home became a retreat where he could drink and work. "Ralph used to come see us and write his column there. He would sit down and write 'This is Tuesday,' and then he thought a long time and wrote, 'So this is Tuesday.'"[51]

Leaving Nashville behind, McGill's outlook changed radically. By good fortune and personal contacts, he had landed in a new city and a new life, married to both Mary Elizabeth and to a new job, which was paying better by leaps and bounds. They settled into an apartment near Ponce de Leon Avenue, where he could catch the trolley to the office. By the summer of 1929, his writing about that season's lackluster Atlanta Crackers baseball team was often better than the team's performance.

McGill brought to the pages a talent for storytelling. That and his voracious, studious reading of other writers lifted his pieces above traditional game reports. His baseball players were crafty gladiators, as exciting on the diamond as his boxers were in the ring, as cunning with a curve as a fighter launching a right to the schnozz. In contrast to the bookkeeping style of starting with a head count in the bleachers, McGill looked for a hero and a decisive moment and put the reader in that moment. In a Crackers game in mid-July of the 1929 season, he found his man in the fifth inning when a relief pitcher with a catchy moniker rescued the team. "Stalking from the dugout in the fifth inning yesterday at Spiller Field," so the words came, "Don Brennan, 'The Newark Natural,' brought order out of extreme chaos and defeated the Barons for the second time in as many days. The score was 13–12." Scores placed second to performance. McGill reveled in grand images—hyperbolic, or humorous, or both. The Crackers-Barons struggle was "a fantastic nightmare of a game" and "a jumble of base hits, errors and runs."[52]

Identifying the moment when the tide turned, he spun his story, weaving the theme, developing characters and focusing microscopically on the duel in that middle inning when the visiting Barons were stalking madly around the bases. They scored five runs against the home boys and threatened more. The Barons' ace hitter, Scrappy Moore, came to bat, setting up the showdown against the Crackers' "Newark Natural." McGill wondered if the Natural was too tired, worn out from pitching the day before when he beat the Barons 7 to 2. Why would they pitch him so soon? Because, as McGill discovered later, the Natural asked for it: "The 'Newark Natural' calmly and surely struck him out. He jerked that ball game up by the nape of its neck, did Don Brennan. . . . They tied the game on him in the ninth because of an outfield mistake. But they couldn't beat him. It was a ball game after he went in."[53]

A passion for the intricacies of human nature and the drama of sporting contests distinguished his writing from that of the "hacks." Most early sports writers, patterning their writing after news style, were constrained by rote formulas: news summaries with the score and attendance, followed by chronological development of plays. McGill, with his background in theater and poetry, had a knack for beginning as would a dramatist, en media res, in the middle of things. His writing was of characters and situations caught up in that moment of decision.

While some wondered at his originality, he owed much to his love of literature and recognized the literary potential of journalism. His habit of reading voraciously, two to three books a week, kept him from being isolated from the wider world. Certainly he was familiar with the masterful sportswriting of his day, coming of age as he did during the flourishing of Grantland Rice (who was also a poet), Runyon, and Lardner. In the early 1920s, Fred Russell recalled, "everybody sort of was influenced by Grantland Rice."[54]

Unlike Rice, McGill was not a versifier. Having taken a path away from poetry, he searched for different ways to express the reality of sport. He had more in common with a school of journalists and writers who borrowed techniques from literature. This coincidental flourishing in the 1920s, for which New York was the stage, included Lardner and Runyon, but also Paul Gallico, Frank Graham, Westbrook Pegler, Arch Ward, Aloysius "Tad" Dorgan, and Heywood Broun.

The new breed loathed the cliches leaned on by lame writers and broke from the straightjacket of reporting play-by-play. They were not journalistic slaves shoveling words into a formula as lumps of coal into an engine. With literary intent, they aspired to bring to sport the art of storytelling, crafting tightly woven narratives. Even before the game began, critic Benjamin Rader observed, "they looked for an 'angle,' or a theme to tie together the beginning, the middle, and the end." Writing for Hearst's *New York American,* Runyon got a head start on his competitors by coming early to the ballpark and absorbing the emotional currents of "human interest": "Somewhere in the afternoon—sometimes during warmups, sometimes when the game was done—he decided on an angle, a single line of attack that would yield the best story." The new sports writers loathed predictability. Let someone else recite who won or lost. They took seriously Grantland Rice's message: "He writes not that you won or lost, but how you played the game." Their charm, and their ticket to success, was in how they played the story.

After two years in Atlanta, McGill's knack for storytelling distinguished his column such that people read *him,* regardless of subject. Then, in 1931, he moved up a rung on the executive ladder. Danforth backtracked to rejoin the *Georgian* (McGill had declined an offer), leaving McGill as his successor as sports editor. The promotion gained McGill a pay raise, restoring some wages lost when staff writers twice took pay cuts as preferable to layoffs as the Depression deepened. He was thrilled to inherit Danforth's daily column, which he christened "Break O' Day." Now he managed assignments and travel and could assign others to cover stories, enabling him to slip away occasionally to cover subjects with more substance.

As work expanded to match his energy, McGill traveled as frequently as he had during his bachelor years in Tennessee. Occasionally Mary Elizabeth accompanied him on the travels, and would refer to her in his columns as "the Lady Who Travels with Me." Most trips, however, took him to football games and community meetings in circumstances far from glamorous and social. Usually, she stayed home.

Mary Elizabeth's health was so fragile that she was not expected to have children. They had been married for six years when, in late May 1935, she found she was pregnant. Ralph remembered getting the news the day he returned from a second assignment in Cuba. The Cuban Travel Bureau had invited fifteen editors and publishers from Georgia, Alabama, and Florida, with the hope that their stories would dispel fears of disorder and emphasize that Cuba was once again a peaceful sanctuary. In anticipation of the baby, they wanted to rent a house. The house they settled into in 1935 was a two-bedroom, one-bath brick bungalow at 700 Martina Drive in the small Buckhead subdivision of Peachtree Highlands, some distance from downtown.[55]

McGill's glow from news about the baby dimmed to worry as Mary Elizabeth's health declined. For extra money that summer, she had found a job as director of a new customer relations service for shoppers. As McGill recalled years later, he was busy that autumn traveling with the football teams. If she were in pain, he did not hear her complaints. But pregnancy and the downtown job seem to have aggravated her chronic kidney problems. At first she had backaches, then in December she developed fever and chills and was hospitalized. On January 7, 1936, the baby was born, slightly premature, a daughter. The next day, the baby died.

They were distraught. McGill in his feverish pace at work had never missed a day's column. Even when he underwent tonsil surgery in 1934, he wrote from his hospital bed, complaining that to show off his new scar he would need a tongue depressor. Stunned by the baby's death, however, he wrote nothing. For two days, the *Constitution* noted only that "in the absence of Ralph McGill from the office" his column was being written by staff sports writer Jack Troy. McGill's absence was not explained, and no death notice was published. In time McGill would tell his close friend Harold Martin about his grief that cold, gray January day when he carried a casket in his hands to West View Cemetery. Within days the McGills decided to adopt a child if the agency could find a girl born about the same time as the one they had lost. In two months they received a black-haired, black-eyed girl they named Virginia Colvin McGill and called "Miss Virginia."[56]

Mary Elizabeth was not yet well. That spring she became so ill she was admitted to Emory University Hospital. Surgery was recommended, and doctors found one kidney so damaged they removed it. After the operation, Mary Elizabeth caught pneumonia and hovered near death, then just as suddenly recovered. McGill came to the room and found her "sitting up in bed, a ribbon in her hair, her fever gone, calling for her baby." She was soon discharged, and McGill went back to his work. In 1936 they moved back downtown, to apartment number six at 110 Fifth Street, partly to get a fresh start with the new baby, but certainly to economize and to put Ralph back on the trolley line so he wouldn't need a chauffeur. To help pay doctors, McGill took on a freelance assignment, writing an article about a friend and colleague at the newspaper, Margaret "Peggy" Mitchell, who had just published her first novel, *Gone with the Wind*.[57]

Throughout the 1930s, the Depression that would not go away, extending misery like a plague, became the most engaging story of the decade. Despite all that had been written, the New York stock market "crash" of 1929 and the Depression were understood only feebly by the mass of Americans. The widespread economic disaster, striking in the midst of continuous postwar prosperity, shocked the nation all the more because it struck without warning. A few economic caution lights as early as 1926—the Florida land bust, the decline of housing starts—were recognized only by the few who understood economic cycles. Cautionary lights, however, tended to be ignored as investors risked well-being in search of fortune in the escalating stock market.

Critics of American institutions placed some of the blame on the media. Where were the journalists who might have sounded a warning? Walter Lippmann, America's first popular philosopher in the mass media, said the inability to see the "treacherous conditions" had been a "marvel."[58] Even as stock values began falling, the *Wall Street Journal* branded pessimists as ignoramuses. Its editors interpreted the decline as "a major advance temporarily halted for technical readjustment."[59] Such shortsightedness has since been blamed on editors who conceived their mission narrowly, as not attempting to analyze the market. In the era before "interpretive" reporting, journalists still focused more on events rather than on underlying causes, and even less so on trends.[60] After the crash, some analysts blamed a commercial conspiracy in which newspapers served the interests of big business. The preeminent press critic of the 1930s, George Seldes, contended that press coverage of the U.S. economy "furnished the lies and buncombe of the merchants of securities" and maintained a false sense of security.[61] In a survey of Washington correspondents, 91 of 107 (86.6 per cent) agreed that their newspapers failed to give "significant accounts of our basic economic conflicts."[62]

McGill was among the few journalists who maintained a concern for the plight of farmers. Throughout life, however far from the land, he sympathized with farmers—with their economic setbacks, mechanization, and plagues. In the early 1920s the boll weevil infestation destroyed such quantities of cotton that thousands of sharecroppers abandoned the life-style of generations to find work around railheads (the biggest being in Atlanta), many of them making the long trek north to Detroit, Chicago, and Harlem. Atlanta's population in the 1920s swelled as thousands of men with nothing but farm skills arrived, many hoping to send money home, or to send for their families. By 1933 a fourth of all the nation's farmers had lost their land and between one-fourth and one-third of all American workers were unemployed.

In Georgia, McGill sympathized most with those who lived marginally, at mere subsistence as they farmed other people's lands. In 1930 more than half of all Georgians lived in rural areas, and many were sharecroppers, usually paying half their crops in rent to the landowner and another share to repay the store for seed, fertilizer, and goods bought on credit. As farm prices fell, sharecroppers suffered.

McGill's early stories about farm troubles coincided with the publication of an agrarian credo, a militant argument for a return to the ideals of the South's agrarian way of life. The credo was published by a group headed by some of the Vanderbilt professors whom McGill knew from the disbanded Fugitives. In their book of essays, *I'll Take My Stand: The South and the Agrarian Tradition,* the Vanderbilt group contended that the source of southern character lay in the land. The agrarian way of life had been corrupted by materialistic industrialism and urbanization, which perverted farmers into mere servants of the city populations. These tenets were confirmed as the Depression deepened, and they urged a return to former ways, when farmers' lives were not dictated solely by what they could market. John Crowe Ransom articulated the view that mere work was not the southerner's only distinction, nor material prosperity his only measure: "His business seemed to be rather to envelop both his work and his play with a leisure which permitted the activity of intelligence." Ransom traced the economic disasters of the early 1930s to the industrial revolution and the frantic overproduction of commodities accompanied by destructive rivalries in competition for markets and survival. Now that the market economy had obviously collapsed, Ransom's solution was a return to agriculture, which, he believed, would restore confidence and self-determination.[63]

In February 1931, Ransom visited Atlanta to defend the agrarian credo and tradition in a debate with a Georgia industrial executive. The event at Emory University drew an audience of almost one thousand. McGill, slipping away from the sports desk, reported the event, reflecting his own prejudice against the agrarians and in favor of industry and urbanization, a New South. In the tradition of Henry Grady, McGill embraced Yankee capital as a solution, not a problem. Though he began his article with Ransom's ideas, McGill credited William D. Anderson of Macon, an obscure executive, with articulating the most persuasive argument, and he gave Anderson the last word. Ransom wanted farmers to "turn from industrial farming with its devotion to the money crop." Anderson "declared that Dr. Ransom was living in an age of romanticism that was gone forever." Anderson's greenback statistics seemed to bury Ransom's yeoman farm ideal: The average net income from farming in the south Atlantic states was $635 a year. Cotton farmers did even more poorly: 288 farmers in a county outside Atlanta had average incomes of $287 a year. "Devotion to agriculture has caused this low economic scale," Anderson said. "The south must have more money for schools, hospitals and other facilities. Industry will bring it."[64]

Years later, with more evidence, McGill concluded that the agrarians, driven by myth and sentimentality, "made an error which all but one or two die-hards regret." To McGill, the plea to return to the ways of the Old South seemed linked to restoring the planter class at the expense of others, a view never popular in mountainous East Tennessee, where cotton was not grown and slaveholders were rare. Even in high school he had been inclined toward the excitement of an industrial society. Active in the Interscholastic Discussion League, he represented McCallie at other area schools in a discussion of "The Manufactories of Tennessee." By the 1930s, McGill reasoned, what was left of the Old South was disappearing as fast as its mules. "Ralph, he was a New South man, like Henry Grady," Fannie Cheney noted. "He didn't want any part of that Back to the South. He was not a farm boy." In time, Ransom himself recanted agrarianism as a "childish & unworthy belief."[65]

Although he disputed the agrarians' economic solutions, McGill shared their love of the land. Although he had no desire to farm, beyond having a garden behind his midtown apartment on Myrtle Street, he had come from a bloodline of Scots-Irish farmers. While that line had been broken when his own father abandoned the land for the opportunities of the city, the family experiences bequeathed McGill with a heartfelt sympathy for farmers, particularly sharecroppers. Displaced by circumstances, they were in most cases unprepared by temperament and training for city jobs and assembly lines.

McGill assigned himself to investigate conditions in rural Georgia, while still keeping responsibility for his daily sports column. Around the state, community leaders were conducting discussion groups and welcomed speakers from Emory University and Georgia Tech. McGill, associating with university faculty as well as with football coaches, tagged along with the professors "to spend a day investigating and half a night in argument and in question-and-answer hours." On these trips he met victims of the one-crop cotton system under which the majority of farmers toiled. He heard stories of poor farmers dependent on a feudal system ruled by the baron whose general store controlled seed, feed, and credit.[66]

Occasionally McGill added to the discussion. One subject at these meetings was the Hawley-Smoot Tariff of 1930, which President Herbert Hoover said would benefit U.S. farmers. McGill explained to farmers and mill workers that the tariff dried up the South's foreign markets for cotton. One evening at a community gathering in LaGrange, southwest of Atlanta, his expertise was challenged by a sports fan who worked in the cotton mills. "I enjoyed your story on the game last Saturday," the man said, "but what in the hell do you think you know about tariffs on cotton?" McGill conceded it was "a blow to my pride. . . . I learned more about it." He found statistics showing that U.S. exports of cotton had declined from 65 percent of the crop in 1914 to 59 percent in 1930, and that tobacco and wheat exports had been affected. In 1932, when Franklin Roosevelt as the Democratic nominee for president was at his retreat in Warm Springs, Georgia, McGill visited him and learned that the tariff had so depressed exports that even midwestern farmers were abandoning the Republican Party.[67]

Through the Depression, McGill worked long hours, traveling, writing the daily sports column, and expanding his expertise to economics, politics, and international reporting from Cuba. Far more than when he was in Tennessee, he now focused on his career and what he could make of it. His farm stories articulated despair but also suggested solutions. In May 1937, he wrote a front-page story about a meeting of the board of governors of the Federal Reserve System, after which he interviewed the bankers and coaxed them to elaborate in layman's terms. He spelled out their economic prescriptions. "Once the south solves the problem of farm tenancy and income," McGill wrote, "it will take its proper place in the nation's affairs."[68]

McGill persuaded the bankers to discuss two other issues during the community meetings. One was farm credit, scarce or exorbitant. "The main economic problem of our generation," McGill reported, "is to devise a system wherein the flow of money will be steady and uninterrupted, increasing only in proportion to produce more goods." The other issue was education to improve farming methods. He said the bankers realized that the South "is making great strides in the development of new opportunities for employment from its rich resources. The farmers are organized in a war against practices that waste their soil. That understanding grows upon information and education."[69]

Inspired by the discussion of new farming practices, McGill felt compelled to find a living example of the new breed of farmer. Shortly after the meeting, he went to the land and found John Gunnels, who had gone back to college, to the University of Georgia's Agricultural College, and was now trying new techniques. As an expert, Gunnels now managed the farm for an absentee businessman. McGill sat on the front porch of the farmhouse and chatted with Gunnnels, who had just "come in from the field where the hay had been cut and harvested."[70]

McGill communicated the new faith in soil conservation. "You've got to put back organic matter into the soil," Gunnels told him. "Commercial fertilizer won't do it. The soil has got to be loose. Manure is the best thing to put back into the land. Most farmers waste it. Too much land is getting hard. When it rains it doesn't hold the moisture."

"And don't they refuse new ideas?" McGill asked.

"I work for a man who won't let new ideas be neglected. This year we were planting an acre of beets for cow feed. An Englishman tried it in North Carolina. It made better milk."

"What other ideas?"

"Keeping books and a budget. Too many farmers don't keep books. I know this month about what I'll do next month."[71]

Given his diverse interests and ambition, McGill was despairing that he might never break out of the cycle of sports writing. Despite occasional opportunities to write about other subjects—politics, farm problems, and authors he admired—he was expected to write year in and year out on events which had a numbing predictability, as he confided to a friend, Thomas Chubb. Chubb was a writer of poetry and literary biographies who spent winters at his family plantation and hunting preserve near Thomasville. McGill and he had met in the winter of 1933 at the Southern Amateur Field Trials for bird dogs, where Chubb had brought his best, "Springwood Spider." Inspired, McGill wrote a column based on his interview with the hound. Chubb encouraged McGill to write for literary magazines. When in 1937 one of these magazines rejected McGill's article about Margaret Mitchell and other "new women" of the South, he wrote to Chubb the same sort of confessional he used to send to Louise Stevens: "I'm tired. I haven't been sleeping well, and I've decided I can't write a line and will never be able to do anything but this newspaper drivel."[72]

Just as he was despairing, he was rescued, not by chance but by the recognition of his contribution to understanding the plight of southern tenant farmers, whites and Negroes. By 1937, his articles represented a body of work, demonstrating his compassion for farmers, his stamina, his fluency and grace in storytelling, and his determination to find solutions. His efforts to alter farming practices endeared him to the academic community. During 1937, the Emory University professors with whom McGill had attended community meetings encouraged him to apply for a study fellowship. The Julius Rosenwald Foundation in Chicago was promoting progressive farming and offered money for southern teachers and journalists. With such a grant he could travel, study, and write about innovative farming. "It is all fantastic and impossible, and I know the odds are against me," he wrote to Chubb. Soon after, he was awarded seventeen hundred dollars, and the *Constitution*'s publisher agreed to give him half-pay in exchange for a stream of columns. One ardent supporter on the Rosenwald board was Mark Ethridge, who as editor of the leading newspaper in Macon, the *Telegraph,* admired McGill's work. "It was the feeling of the board, and certainly mine," Ethridge explained, "that McGill was far too intelligent and too socially conscious to be a mere sports editor. If the cycle of sports writing could be broken, Ralph would come into his own." McGill told Harold Martin it was one of the luckiest things that ever happened to him.[73]

4

Scandinavian Studies

Ralph McGill: "Do you think it will work?"
Gunnar Myrdal: "I don't know. It is necessary
to try something."
—Interview, Sweden, 1938

America [unlike Sweden] has not been subjected to . . .
the calm and sane teaching of temperance . . .
[which] teaches the effects of over-indulgence on the
individual and the community.
—Ralph McGill

Having created his own Grand Tour, McGill trekked to Europe, conscious that something he would do there would change his fortune. His escape from the sports desk afforded him the first chance for international reporting since his Cuban adventures. His chronicles of the rise and fall of Machado seemed a sideshow to events in Europe. Europe was where American journalists since the 1920s had whetted a love of travel and intrigue, proving that the America which emerged from the war was not monolithically isolationist. Reporters sent back stories of Europe's politics and wars, and American audiences read them, especially in the big cities: New York, Boston, Baltimore, Washington, Chicago, Los Angeles. Occasionally a great story amplified a reporter's reputation, and some reporters became household names. Dorothy Thompson's star shot across the sky when Hitler, offended by the results of her interview (she found him short and unimpressive), expelled her from Germany. Floyd Gibbons's daring with a microphone for the new radio networks thrilled his audience when one day, in the midst of the Spanish Civil War, he broadcast from beneath a haystack, bursts of gunfire sounding in the background. In 1937 Edward R. Murrow pioneered the CBS overseas network linking New York, London, France,

Rome, Vienna, and Berlin. For his on-air cast he hired former print journalists, among them William Shirer and Eric Sevareid.

McGill wanted to be part of that scene. Apart from his Rosenwald Foundation mission to study farming methods, he determined to write about the chief political distraction of all Europe in late 1937, Adolf Hitler.

Sixteen days at sea aboard the *Samaria* provided a quiet buffer unconnected with the world's anxieties. Behind him were the demands of daily sports writing and ahead were challenges he could only contemplate. Certainly it was a relaxing time for Mary Elizabeth. Their first trip to Europe was something they never could have afforded on a sportswriter's salary, and she was inclined to enjoy it as she had his working vacations to bowl games. The calm of the crossing was a second honeymoon, and they enjoyed it in their snug cabin and along the busy deck and bar.

McGill soon became fidgety to write and stalked the ship hunting for characters and stories to chronicle for his readers, driven to do his part to earn the *Constitution*'s half-pay. He had agreed to mail columns home "more or less regularly." He knew also that a columnist not published regularly is soon forgotten. Passengers and crew and even Mary Elizabeth—"the Lady Who Travels with Me"—became characters to be chronicled for the *Constitution* readers.

McGill by now felt secure in the ranks of the peculiar new breed of journalists, the columnists. Creations of the 1930s, these men and women surfaced to supply the new demand for commentary on the news. Nothing created this desire more than the stock market crash and the ensuing financial collapse, a mysterious force which surged through the economy with a visible impact of joblessness. Audiences wanted explanations. Why were the crash and Depression unforseen? Why did things happen this way? What could be done? In Europe, American commentators explaining world economy and politics focused increasingly on the rising power of Germany. McGill, when he wasn't explaining sports, had ventured to depict the Depression's destruction of farmers and to look for solutions. His realm had been the poor southern sharecropper and the new farmer schooled in modern techniques.

Over the years he had picked up the columnist's habit of mixing work and leisure. By the mid-1930s he might turn into a column almost anything he observed or did. His work had become his play and his leisure a fit topic for the next column. The habit was common among sportswriters, who worked while spectators enjoyed the games. As a young sports columnist, he found it natural and even expected of him to inject personal bias into stories about boxers, baseball players, and football coaches. If readers had not warmed to McGill's homespun storytelling, editors would have discouraged it. But the opposite happened. In a short time he became the rare journalist—one whose private thoughts shot straight into the public vein.

Soon after the *Samaria* sailed, McGill sequestered himself away from deckhounds, fitness fanatics, and gossips. He found "a quiet corner in the smoking room where it was pleasant to peck away at [the] typewriter." Here he typed the first of more than two hundred columns and articles he would write in 193 days of travel. Occasionally some grim English fitness fanatic burst in and dragged his overweight frame to deck tennis. "I must admit that I can take my ping pong or leave it alone," he wrote. He had come to accept his girth, and those who wanted him to diminish it seemed always to be devotees of physical radicalism.[1]

Ensconced in the smoking lounge, he recorded anything profound, annoying, or humorous that crossed his path or plate. Nine meals a day, he felt, were bulging his waistline, but Eccles cake was more tempting than exercise. Dining on the Scottish sheep dish, haggis, became the focus of the first "Break O' Day," mailed with a batch of shipboard musings when he reached Liverpool. His second column retold stories from a group of Irish travelers who were in the smoking lounge arguing about the English. They told him the legend of the Irish spirit who, because he was off dreaming, arrived last in Valhalla when causes were being handed out. The Irish spirit accepted all the causes left, which were only the lost ones.[2]

His journalistic habits urged him to find a routine of work. "It is very difficult, indeed, working on a ship," he noted. It was so comfortable "sitting on a deck chair, well wrapped in blankets, warm and comfortable." His thoughts wandered to the blowing wind, the smell of the sea, the cries of gulls, the "miles of tumbling waters with white caps appearing and disappearing" and "the sound of the water off the bows."

These often induced a nap. His instincts, and Mary Elizabeth as well, persuaded him to relax into the lazy rhythm of the cruise so that "when it comes time to work it always seems a better idea to go look at the gulls following the ship. And when it positively is time to work, there always is a sunset that one must see. Or perhaps there is sun on the left of the ship and rain on the right. And, of course, only a foolish person would miss seeing that. And then, when one gets to work, there is a fishing vessel or another ship passing, and that must be seen. And so," he concluded, "it works out. There is all the time in the world and nothing much to do. But it requires all one's time doing it."[3]

It was a struggle to find individuals with stories worth repeating. He learned to avoid the cliques of "middle-aged females" in deck chairs who gossiped about passengers and tried to waylay him. Their presence gave him ample excuse for not walking eight times around the ship—the exercise recommended for burning off calories.

His love of writing about people who nettled him was a holdover from his Nashville days. Then he had found it fun and profitable to write about social brutes of both genders. At the *Banner* he had originated the daily "I'm the Gink" feature, a one-paragraph commentary on obnoxious personality types. Each day's item, like a script for a skit, focused on one gink or ginkette whose behavior annoyed him and probably most people. Drawing on his thespian experience at the McCallie School, McGill cast himself as the gink explaining his brutishness. In the end every gink justified everything or admitted he didn't care what people thought. The *Banner* featured "I'm the Gink" on page one in the lower right corner. By 1927 the ginks were syndicated by Republic Syndicate, Inc.[4]

The vignettes let McGill express his bachelor biases. In the midst of the Jazz Age, he was socially liberal but not concerning women's behavior in society. His conservative expectations for females matched more or less the steadfast model of his mother, to whom he wrote regularly. He ridiculed the ginkette who is "ashamed" of her parents because they are "hopelessly old-fashioned and a bit peculiar."[5] He was just as disturbed by the mothers of girls he had dated who "find something to criticize or laugh about in all the young men who call on her." He also found tiresome, as he told Fannie Cheney, any woman who wanted to "mother" him with advice in the belief that "all men are helpless and know nothing about taking care of themselves." This evidenced itself anytime a woman told him how to dress or how to get well.[6]

In public, "liberated" females who put on airs to attract attention nettled McGill. It seemed that the women's movement was encouraging public monstrosities. One of the worst was the smoker. This ginkette did her smoking "exclusively in public" and "just for effect. I like to think that those around me are looking at me admirably as a modern girl, unshackled and free." Another ginkette liked "to swagger about in men's shirts and ties." Females in politics, spurred by the Nineteenth Amendment in 1920, had created the political poseur who "talks loudly on the train or interurban" and will "tell you what I think of politics. They are so interesting since women got into them. Of course all I do is display a vast vulgarity and ignorance." He thought the new pulp magazines were nurturing a ginkette "strong on stories of passion and love," who reads at the office and lets work slip because "I'm going to marry as soon as I can." Such violations of the work ethic were common features of ginkettes, those vain, lazy, sloppy, garrulous, and gushing women who "loaf away the hours" and then work by "fits and starts."[7] McGill seethed about insensitive, acquisitive women. The boardinghouse ginkette grabbed "all the white meat when there is chicken on the table" and hung on the telephone "as much as possible" even while "others may be waiting for calls or wanting to make them."[8]

McGill had no problem coming up with ginks, male or female, although toward the end of his *Banner* employment he invited readers' ideas. McGill's everyday peeves were juiced by freeloaders and loafers (especially pool sharks), by hypochondriacs and "robust" men who fell helpless when ill, by spendthrifts who afterward needed to borrow money, and by people who wasted his time or abused his hospitality. As a journalist he was critical of political toadies, sponges, and namedroppers, and of slap-on-the-shoulder "Well, what-do-you-know?" types. At the office he bemoaned customers telling reporters how they'd run the newspaper, and the undereducated who were careless with grammar. As a drinker, he hoped to soften "the hard cop with no mercy especially where moonshine is concerned." And, especially when he was drinking and telling a good story, he was nettled by the gink who "always interrupts your narratives by saying, 'No, that wasn't the way it happened. It happened this way.'"[9]

McGill did not drive a car and some of his peeves were with loutish motorists and inconsiderate streetcar riders. He asked for justice against the careless driver who ran red lights, speeded, parked in restricted zones and, if caught, offered the cop a "cheap bribe." McGill's abstinence from driving, some thought, derived from family and childhood patterns established in Chattanooga. His father, Ben, had come of age before the automobile and, according to the family, never owned a car; he walked, or relied on Chattanooga streetcars. On streetcars, McGill seethed during rush hour when an inconsiderate rider made the conductor change a five-dollar bill as McGill languished in the line waiting to board. McGill was always eager to get seated and start reading. "He never got on a streetcar that he didn't have a book in his pocket to read," Fred Russell recalled. "He used to tell me, 'Don't waste a minute. I read every second I can.'"[10]

McGill's first printed attack on outmoded farming methods, the subject which had won his passage to Europe, was a brief tirade in 1928 against the "shiftless gink on the rundown farm." That gink was an agrarian Neanderthal who could be found at the crossroads country store sitting on a barrel and talking "about the hard times a fellow has on a farm" and at the same time discounting "the new-fangled notions about farming that are taught by the agricultural schools." His feckless ways ran counter to common sense. "I leave my farm machinery out in the field to rust from one season to the next," says the gink, and his livestock has wandered away because "I let my fences gradually fall to pieces."[11]

Given McGill's selectivity, he was delighted to find one person aboard ship worth writing about. The Edinburgh fighter Bob Scally was worth two columns because McGill could link him to the most famous name in boxing, world heavyweight champion Joe Louis. Scally, with "flattened nose and a tin ear," was returning to England after serving as the sparring partner for a British contender whom Louis had beaten.[12]

By the time he got to England McGill was eager to disembark. He had been closeted with too many members of what he called "The League for Health and Beauty." The English had turned fitness into a national fad and had picked up the American zeal for winning, which turned them into grim competitors. "It was a bit sad," he wrote, "quitting the ship which had behaved so well. But it was splendid to escape keeping fit and all the games necessary to keeping fit."[13]

After a stopover in England, the McGills went on to Denmark so Ralph could start his research on Scandinavian farming. They got to Copenhagen before Christmas and checked with American Express for messages and money. They had problems with the language. Amid this strangeness they found things which reminded them of home. McGill spotted the blue and orange colors of Auburn University flying from the mast of a ship in the harbor and was told they were Sweden's colors. One snowy day he was interviewing a Dane named Hamlet Olsen when McGill saw a horse-drawn wagon with the letters "K.K.K.K." painted on its side:

> "Hey," I said to the Melancholy Dane, "do they sell bed sheets over here? When did the boys organize here?"
>
> "All Americans are slightly mad, I think," he [Olsen] said, very moodily. "What do you mean?"
>
> "Why the Ku Klux Klan, of course. But why do they have the extra 'K'? Is it the Kurious Ku Klux Klan?"
>
> "Well," said the Melancholy Dane, "they won't sell you any bed sheets. The letter 'C' isn't used very much in Danish. This is just the Kobenhavn Kul and Koks Kompagni . . . the Kopenhaven Coal and Coke Company."[14]

By late January, Ralph and Mary Elizabeth were trekking around Norway and Sweden. From Oslo, they took a day trip to the museum at Bygdoy to see three Viking ships recovered between 1867 and 1904 from great burial mounds of kings who ruled around 800 A.D. Ralph sized up the Vikings as a suitable subject for a column. Buried in one ship, the skeleton of King Olav Gierstadalv suggested that he had suffered from advanced arthritis, consistent with the lyrics of a ninth-century minstrel song immortalizing the severe pains in the king's left knee and foot. "It's no wonder they suffered from arthritis," McGill mused, because they slept on earth or stone floors. As he had done in Cuba, he engaged in time travel: "More than a thousand years seem to disappear and it is possible to fill the ships with their crews of muscled oarsmen and their furred and armed fighting men."[15]

Back in Oslo, he pressed on to finish the series that would satisfy the requirements of the Rosenwald fellowship. In Oslo, as in Cuba, his interviewed key government insiders and newspaper editors. Norwegian elites seemed eager to meet this pudgy American with double credentials, on one hand an American columnist and on the other a scholar on a fellowship. McGill soon proved to be an enthusiastic student of Norwegian history, back to the Vikings, as well as an investigator of the country's social experiments. He enjoyed easy access to sports writers and the foreign editors of three newspapers, but he also arranged a brief appointment with Norway's prime minister, Johan Nygaardsvold, "big and square of frame and honest of manner," who had worked on railroads in Utah and in lumber camps in Oregon and Canada.

In reading about Norway before the trip, McGill was fascinated with the rise and fall and resurgence of the Norwegian Labor Party. In the revolutionary fervor following the Russian Revolution, the party had nearly destroyed itself during a short-lived affiliation with Moscow and the Communist International, the Comintern, from 1919 to 1923. It was the only Western socialist party to join. For details about the Communist affiliation, the prime minister preferred that McGill speak with the minister of foreign affairs, also a leader of the Labor Party, Halvdan Koht. "It was impossible," Koht told McGill. "They wanted to dominate us. They wanted to use us for their benefit. They interfered too much in our internal affairs. We could not go on. We refused their demands and were expelled. It saved us the trouble of quitting." Before the break, Labor's accession to demands from Moscow caused right-leaning members to quit and form the Social Democrats. Left-leaning members then quit to form the Communist Party. After a decade, the party had recovered the Social Democrats, and by 1936, leading a government coalition with the Agrarian Party, introduced old-age pensions and unemployment insurance.[16]

In addition to his pencil and paper, McGill now carried a camera. He had borrowed one of the expensive new thirty-five-millimeter models in Copenhagen and was somewhat baffled by its knobs and buttons. He worried about losing it and slept with it under his pillow. In Oslo, he remarked that "the half dozen times when a dinner required dress clothes and I could not carry the camera along, I suffered acutely with the camera hidden in the boarding house room." On other occasions, he gained access by ostentatious display. Hung around his neck, it "acts as a sort of admission ticket to places of vantage at sports events where one ordinarily may not go." At ski jumps, the guard "hastened to open the door" and McGill climbed one hundred feet and photographed the event from the top.

A sports writer in Norway must see skiers. "The Swedes and the Finns and the Italians and the Swiss and other nations are good at it," McGill acknowledged. "But it is a Norwegian sport." At the jumps he met the famous Norwegian athlete Birger Ruud, whom McGill compared to Georgia's best, Ty Cobb and Bobby Jones. Ruud had won the jumps in the 1932 and 1936 Olympics and since then had come in first 110 times and set fifty new records. What seemed to onlookers as pure genius, McGill reminded, was actually the work ethic alive and well in Norway. McGill identified with tales of hard work and relished stories of Ruud's dedication and discipline in the early years when "he used to practice until he couldn't take off his skis. His mother used to unhook the harness. I forgot who it was who said that genius was nine-tenths perspiration. It was with [Ty] Cobb and Bobby Jones and Birger Ruud and most every other genius who has come along. They sweated at it for long hours which the crowds that cheered them never thought about."[17]

From Oslo, the McGills took a train to Stockholm. It was early in February and the best women figure skaters were gathering there for the world championship. A warm spell in late January had embarrassed the host country, proud of its subzero cold. To warm-weather Georgians he underscored the Swedes' quirk: "When it snows they say, 'Isn't this magnificent weather?' The tourist attractions are not to warmer climes—but to colder." And he recalled advice from a friend that "the best way to see the sights in a foreign country was to get a seat by the window in some nice, warm pub." McGill soon linked up with Swedish journalists who made sure he walked around the city. They took him to numerous barber shops, each claiming to be the one where Greta Garbo worked before she became an actress. Garbo rubbed lather on the chins of the customers before the barber came along to shave them. McGill walked so much in the cold that the landlady at his pension provided him with a pillow for his feet while he was typing. McGill told her he was the only newspaperman with such a pillow. "Do you mean," she asked, "that the managers of newspapers do not make their journalists comfortable?" McGill added: "They are very smart people, the Swedes."[18]

The Swedish passion for public education fascinated McGill, who saw this as transferable to Georgia. Here was something the legislature could reasonably adopt. He talked with experts about how schooling helped Sweden manage social change. The Swedes had also dealt with temperance in a unique way. Rather than try Prohibition, which had failed in Norway and Denmark, the Swedes resorted to rationing, which was also controversial. McGill found it strange being rationed his refreshment. Indeed, the law's restriction on drinks in restaurants had just triggered a response from the Swedes themselves—a hotel strike.

One of the most important contacts he made in Europe was with a prominent political economist then relatively unknown in America but soon to become legendary. The trail of economic and social reform led McGill directly into the living room of Gunnar Myrdal. Before leaving Atlanta, he read everything he could find about Myrdal, who by then was "regarded in Sweden as the most brilliant young man [he was forty, McGill's age] in the Swedish parliament. He has helped give Sweden a 'New Deal' which experiments even more daringly than our own." In the wake of the worldwide Depression, social scientists with solutions found eager audiences, and Myrdal was among the most recognized in Sweden and abroad. On a bitter February day, with "the feel of cold wind on my face and the crunch of snow underfoot," McGill traveled the seventeen miles from Stockholm to Myrdal's "modernistic, comfortable, roomy house."

Myrdal seemed pleased to detail his schemes, most of which required government subsidies to stimulate economic and social change. His housing plan, intended to reverse Sweden's declining population rate, offered a 10 percent subsidy for each child up to a total of five, or 50 percent. McGill was even more interested in the farm scheme.

Rather than pay farmers to grow less food as a way of lifting farm prices, Myrdal's plan was to use those government subsidies to stimulate farmers to grow *more* food. The goal was humanitarian and economic— to alleviate domestic hunger while paying farmers. As McGill reported, Sweden's farmers "would 'dump' their surplus crop not on the declining world market but instead on the home market." Low-income families could buy food at a reduced price and the government subsidy "would pay the farmer the difference" between the market price and welfare price. To McGill it seemed more sensible than U.S. farm policy, which lifted prices by cutting production. "There would be no burning of wheat," he wrote, "or ploughing under of oats or barley or restrictions on crops of potatoes, milk, pigs or vegetables."

"Do you think it will work?" he asked Myrdal.

"I don't know," Myrdal said. "It is necessary to try something."[19]

Their conversation in Myrdal's living room soon focused on the American South and the race question. The previous summer, the Carnegie Corporation trustees in New York, which had been funding Tuskegee Institute in Alabama, invited Myrdal to direct "a comprehensive study of the Negro in the United States, to be undertaken in a wholly objective and dispassionate way as a social phenomenon." Myrdal was chosen because of his reputation as a social scientist and because the trustees believed a Swede, from a nonimperialistic nation with no Negro population, would approach the subject with an open mind. The study was expected to result in a book.[20]

The timing of McGill's visit was propitious. Myrdal was then planning the trip to the United States to start organizing a team of experts. He was looking to tap the South's new generation of social scientists and visionaries. He wanted men who could study the South's problems from many angles—anthropological, economic, educational, and social. The race question, the legacy of the slaveholding economic system, would thread through the entire study. McGill knew of some of the men being recruited—the cultural anthropologist Guy Benton Johnson and the sociologist Arthur F. Raper. Both belonged to the South's emerging intellectual caste and both had been nurtured in the Rockefeller-funded Institute for Research in Social Science at the University of North Carolina in Chapel Hill. Johnson's scholarly articles in the 1920s about the Klan had been followed by studies of Negro culture and Depression-era economics. Raper's *Tragedy of Lynching* in 1933 provided a scholarly rationale for the NAACP's forceful but failed effort to secure a federal antilynching bill; his *Preface to Peasantry* in 1936 documented the hardships of farm tenants in the South's black belt.[21]

Through Myrdal's eyes, McGill glimpsed what these liberal thinkers considered the South's inevitable political and economic future. Although liberals had virtually no political power and were understandably timid on the race question, they envisioned within reach a New South which put the race problem to rest and lifted standards for all its people. How southerners would actually reach that point was another matter. Myrdal believed that the South was approaching a historic crossroad. As he would write, "Even the ordinary conservative white Southerner has a deeply split personality. . . . In the long run it means that the conservative white Southerner himself can be won over to equalitarian reforms in line with the American Creed." Yet his most optimistic assessment in the '30s was balanced by a note of realism. While he saw the era as one of great potential for positive change, he recognized that southerners would probably pay a great price in "unexpected, tumultuous, haphazard breaks, with mounting discords and anxieties."[22]

Equality for the Negro was a subject which McGill felt comfortable discussing with a Swedish political scientist in the seclusion of snowy northern Europe, but he wrote nothing about it in the *Atlanta Constitution* in the winter of 1938. Among white southerners, the race issue was a social taboo. If the issue did come up in polite white society, men and women referred to it euphemistically. It was "the situation." In polite society, one did not talk about "the situation." McGill's generation lived, however uncomfortably, with the situation they had received as a legacy from their parents and *their* parents before them. After nearly half a century of legislated discrimination in voting, jobs, churches, housing, schools, and society, white southerners were psychologically committed to the system as surely as if they had been chained. Even white liberals felt paralyzed, unable to do anything. Political leaders reflected the general paralysis. The situation had become too awesome, too frightening, too intractable. The politicians who won elections were those who did not advocate change or, at times, adamantly defended the system against those who suggested change. McGill, a son of the South, acutely aware of all this, did not taint his Scandinavian reports with the race issue. What he and Myrdal talked about was, as journalists say, off the record.

At his typewriter in Stockholm, with his feet resting on the landlady's cushion, McGill finished the last of the Rosenwald articles by mid-February. He had written the first piece two weeks earlier in Oslo; now in Stockholm, he produced the final articles focused on the Swedes, making a few comparisons with the Danes and Norwegians and even the Finns, though he did not visit Helsinki. As it turned out, he quit at six pieces (in addition to frequent "Break O' Day" columns), writing swiftly, with more or less the voice of his columns—chatty, thoughtful, informal. The main difference was his posture: he was now the astute, well-traveled commentator.

The first three reports featured organizations grappling with Depression era problems similar to those troubling Americans. He investigated labor organizations, economic opportunities, and social legislation, and stressed the worth of spending tax dollars for more education at all social levels. The first article featured Norway's Labor Party and its misplaced hope in Soviet communism. The *Constitution* started this piece on the front page, partly because if was timely. The Communists were wooing American labor, disheartened by the grinding Depression. McGill considered the impact on his reputation of focusing so much on the iniquities of the Comintern in Norway. Could he be branded a propagandist? He decided to include his concern in his the article. "If I write that," he told an Oslo newspaper editor, "there will be some people who say that McGill has turned propandist or that he is engaged in the process of pulling red herring across trails, or that he has listened to only critics." And he included the editor's response: "Give them your sources. Tell them you talked to the men who led the federation into the affiliation and who led it out."[23]

McGill's second dispatch lauded the Scandinavians' profitable paper-mill industry, with hopeful notes for Georgia. Norway, Sweden, and Finland now harvested trees as a cash crop. They supplied paper to the world. A Georgia businessman, Charles Herty, had been trying to do the same since 1931, by harvesting the state's abundant slash pine.

Fortune magazine in 1937 wrote about Herty's modest success, and Swedes had noticed the article. After dinner at the home of a Swedish newspaper editor, as they sat looking at a birchwood fire, the editor asked McGill about possible competition from Georgia. McGill was pessimistic. Georgia could trade in the same league with Scandinavia, creating thousands of new jobs, if it followed Herty's lead.[24]

But McGill worried about southerners' adherence to old ways. As with farming in general, rural Georgians maintained a "pioneer habit of mind"—"an attitude of mind which seemed to say, 'Let the land wash away, cut down the trees, burn the forests, there is plenty more left.'" He told one Swedish editor "of the flaming forests each fall, of millions of dollars in grown and young pine trees casting a red light against the skies at night[,] . . . of driving in south Georgia and of swirling smoke obscuring the roads by day."[25]

The contrast between Georgia's education system and a resultant lag in other areas of southern life was reflected in McGill's third dispatch. "After more than two months in Scandinavia," McGill concluded, "it is perfectly obvious that practical education has made possible the progress in social legislation, in co-operation and in agricultural aids which distinguish the scene in north Europe." Scandinavians, as one American had briefed McGill back in Atlanta, had "removed the three thorns from the heart of the average man." The northern countries provided for universal education regardless of income, for universal health care, and for care in old age.[26]

The key to all advances, McGill stressed, was education, including schooling for adults. Here, too, he anticipated political resistance. "I can imagine one of our politicians, speaking with great irony and asking what good the knowledge of a book or of his country's history will do a farmer who is hoeing cotton or ploughing corn": "Yet, facts are facts. An educated man with at least some way to rationalize himself with the world about him, is better prepared for making his lot a better one and for making his community an improved one."

McGill's appeal for increased funding of education was undercut by a headline writer in the *Constitution* newsroom. Weeks later, McGill must have cringed when he read the headline. In the article, he conceded that the Scandinavian social system as a whole could not be immediately adopted in the United States. Indeed, he distanced himself from utopian social engineers. The "sincere idealists who have sought to present the entire system as one now fitted for America were dreaming," he said. By that, he meant to focus attention on first adopting *educational* reforms. But the editor who wrote the headline discounted *all* the Scandinavian social reforms as "Not Suitable for Transplanting to U.S."[27]

After completing those three articles, McGill was restless to leave Scandinavia. For some time he knew he must go to Berlin. The big story in Europe was Nazi Germany. It is little wonder that he wrote the last three pieces entirely about one subject—Sweden's curious social legislation on alcoholic beverages. Lawmakers had come to terms with the social problem of drinking by striking a compromise; rather than prohibit access, they restricted it. McGill was amused by the national reaction to the law, including "the strangest strike in all labor history," and by his own difficulty in getting his personal ration.

He justified writing so much about the liquor legislation because it was timely. Then, too, he found humor in the history and lore of liquor and temperance, or the lack of it. After the preachy tone of the first three installments, the mention of booze and hangovers was light relief, the mix of light and heavy he served readers throughout his career. "The Swedes used to be heavy drinkers," he pointed out. But now the government legislated temperance so that "the gentleman with a hangover would be unable to use the prescription of some of the hair of the dog before noon. No liquor is sold, for consumption on the premises, before noon."[28]

When he arrived in Stockholm, all hotels and cafés were closed; they had been shut for two weeks in protest of the liquor laws. Researching whisky regulations had not been easy, he said. He had labored more than a week interviewing all sides about "the whys and the wherefores" and in learning how one went about securing a drink. "The only places open are the beer cafes," he reported. "Beer is regarded as a harmless drink, which it is." It was simply unbelievable by U.S. standards, he wrote, that a city of seven hundred thousand should have all its hotels closed. Even more surprising, editors thought so little of the news that they buried the story "on the inside of the paper alongside the story on the best recipe for puddings." One journalist told McGill the hotel and café closings were based entirely on the employees' demands for higher wages and the owners' insistence that parliament permit higher profits on liquor to pay for the wage increase.[29]

The Swedish law severely restricted liquor taken home. It interested McGill that convicted drunks could not buy liquor, nor could "people whose economic conditions do not meet requirements." If John Doe wanted a bottle of brandy, McGill wrote, he underwent a process like an insurance examination. He must tell what he wanted the brandy for. Only then does he get a ration book good for a maximum of four liters a month. "Yet," McGill wrote, "despite the fact that the government has the monopoly, every effort is made to persuade the customer he does not require that much." Airtight laws, combined with temperance instruction, had reduced yearly consumption from ten gallons a person in 1858 to about five quarts.[30]

McGill's last Scandinavian study concluded with a visit to a liquor-control office. He was there when an American businessman came in seeking paperwork to buy a bottle of Scotch and was made to fill out an application.

"Why do you require spirits?"

"To drink it," the businessman wrote.

Age was a barrier. Applicants under twenty-five were permitted no more than one liter a month, and most Swedes received cards for less than the maximum four liters. When the month was up, they had to reapply. An American might score four liters, McGill found out, "by saying that his wife was along; that she was expecting to entertain friends and members of his firm."

McGill discounted the value of this Swedish system for America. It would no more work in America than Prohibition. "The reason is that America has not been subjected to a system of education[,] . . . the calm and sane teaching of temperance." McGill, who could have written a book on hangovers, touted this education, which "teaches the effects of overindulgence on the individual and the community." Indeed, when he was sober, particularly in the grips of a hangover, as his friends would recall, he could be extremely reform-minded and repentant.[31]

Finished, he mailed the six articles to the *Constitution*, three datelined Oslo, three Stockholm. In Atlanta, the editors gave McGill's commentaries an intellectual lilt, labeling the series "Scandinavian Studies."

5

Witness to Tyranny

Hitler seemed to pull his head into his overcoat collar.
He was in an open car and it was bitter cold. He
looked out without a smile or a change of
expression. It was a perfect mask.
—Ralph McGill, Berlin, 1938

Somewhere in all this, should be a lesson to the
democracies to check up and see to their own houses.
Are there any seeds of terror and horror and despair
being nourished for some strong man to harvest?
—Ralph McGill, Vienna, 1938

As so often happened, travel blessed by fortunate timing expanded McGill's vistas and opportunities. After an arduous train ride, he and Mary Elizabeth arrived in Berlin in time to witness a Nazi spectacle. On February 20, Germans awaited Hitler's speech to the Reichstag. The Nazis were menacing Austria and Czechoslovakia, and Hitler now was coming to explain his pledge to protect the interests of ten million Germans living in those countries.

Events in Germany were building to a climax. Earlier in the month, Hitler had purged the armed forces of argumentative leaders and put himself in supreme command. The pro-Nazi anti-Semitic *Völkischer Beobachter* then proclaimed in headlines, "Strongest Concentration of All Powers in the Führer's Hands." Still secret was that, one week after the purge, Hitler had used a military sham—the threat of invasion—to wring concessions from the Austrian chancellor, Kurt von Schuschnigg. Schuschnigg had formed a new Austrian cabinet with a Nazi minister directing the nation's police. Hitler's *Lebensraum* policy of expanding German borders by first absorbing Austria seemed within grasp.

Stepping into Berlin amid the many Nazi flags, McGill found a "a new morale and new spirit," which he credited to Hitler. "Hitler has done much for Germany," he conceded. "He has few unemployed. He is building great roads, bridges and many buildings." Berliners, so recently enfeebled but now sensing empowerment, seemed manic, amplifying Hitler's shrill megalomania. "He has made them extremely nationalistic, even to the point of being ridiculous in their nationalism." Few things seemed more ludicrous than the ubiquitous greeting, "Heil Hitler!" It was so ridiculous, he wrote to a friend, "I keep thinking they will laugh but they don't. . . . No one laughs. He has given them an arrogant morale." Now, all eyes, including McGill's, waited to see Hitler and hear his speech to the compliant Reichstag in the Kroll Opera House.[1]

Much had been written about the cult of Hitler and the Nazi drama, but the frenzy now threatened Germany's neighbors and thus took on new significance. Seeing the frenzy firsthand, McGill was impressed. Early on February 20 he went out into the freezing cold. He intended to report the event not as news, which news agencies would do far more quickly. His piece would not be published until March, so he focused on impressions, "how it looked and sounded." But he also offered his opinions, which sounded less like the ramblings of a sports writer and more like the insights of a knowledgeable commentator.

That morning, McGill probed beneath the Hitler cult. He started by speaking with Nazi troops. Four hours before Hitler arrived, McGill found "the streets were noisy with the sound of marching feet and martial singing as detachments of troops marched by." These were the SS, or Schutzstaffel, established in 1928 to guard Hitler during speeches. Among them he noted the "Adolf Hitler" troops "committed to his personal care," who were all at least six feet tall and wore his name on their black jackets. He knew of nothing like it. Certainly Machado in Cuba had not commanded the same personal allegiance, even in his heyday of sugar-money graft. In the lull, McGill and the soldiers chatted in broken English. "At ease, without their helmets, these soldiers became just German boys" who knew fragments of American songs ("You are—my lucky star"). "You stay with us," one told him, "and we will point out the famous men. We will move so you may make a picture."[2]

The spectacle was worth detailing. Troops lined both sides of the avenue, from Chancellor Hitler's home, where Bismarck once lived, to the opera house. Loudspeakers, which he had seen used extensively for the first time in Georgia in the Talmadge-Russell slugfest two years earlier, were strung "everywhere," in movie houses, in cafés, even in trees. Despite the bitter cold, crowds jammed the route. Only those who had come hours early and were near the soldiers could see well as cars with officials whizzed by.[3]

"Goebbels," a tall young officer whispered from a corner of his mouth. McGill glimpsed the master of propaganda.

"Goering." A roar of "Heil" could be heard far up the street, "and then came the field marshal's car with Goering—his hand in the Fascist salute—very grim and huge in the car."

"In a moment, now," said the tall soldier.

McGill stared up the street, later reporting, as was the custom of foreign correspondents of that era, his own first impressions of seeing the dictator who had made himself a wonder of the world:

> Then we could hear the uproar, far away, but coming nearer. The Fascist leader was coming. His car swept around the curve. Parents held up their babies. Men shouted and women shrieked, "Heil! Heil! Heil!" with their right hands stiff in salute.
>
> Hitler seemed to pull his head into his overcoat collar. He was in an open car and it was bitter cold. He looked out without a smile or a change of expression. It was a perfect mask.
>
> The car flashed by to meet more "Heils" and then pulled up before the opera house. Amid thunders of applause, Hitler entered.[4]

That day in a speech that went on for three hours and was broadcast throughout Germany and Austria, Hitler asserted Germany was "a world power" that must protect the "political and spiritual freedom" of ten million "racial comrades" or "co-racials"—Germans in Austria and Czechoslovakia. William Shirer, who heard it in Vienna, where he had gone to work for Edward R. Murrow and the CBS network's new European operation, considered it "blunt, public notice" that Nazi Germany would intervene in both countries. McGill's reaction was similar. "To one not even understanding German," he wrote, "the speech sounded full of arrogance and defiance[,] . . . probably his most belligerent." McGill thought it signaled a turning point. "He is stronger now than ever before. He and the Fascist coalition would not hesitate to attempt conquest of any nation they believed they could defeat."[5]

What disturbed McGill as much as anything was the condemnation of press freedom. While insisting on freedoms for Austrian and Czech Germans, "he condemned free speech and particularly a free press." Over the next several years McGill adopted freedom of the press as a steady and profitable theme. That day, McGill reported, Hitler conceded that "he did not understand . . . a government which permits a press to express its opinions. . . . He has come to power through ruthless killing, brutality and a complete disregard for the civilized qualities of mankind. He actually does not understand a free people with free speech and a free press."[6] Disparaging remarks such as those had been cause enough for Hitler to revoke visas, but McGill knew his story would not be published for more than a week and that Hitler likely would not see the *Constitution* nor chase a correspondent who had made one raid and departed.

Before leaving, the McGills visited historic sites worthy of a couple "Break O' Day" columns. Berlin had hosted the 1936 Olympics and it was one of McGill's regrets that he missed them. Now on a cold, bright day he found the Reichssports field empty, with patches of snow in the shadowy corners, "a stark mass of concrete and pillars, beautiful with a cold beauty of line and mass." Their guide said one of the fields was used now for political demonstrations. Nearby was a German war memorial. The bell in the Olympic tower had a huge inscription around its rim: "I Call the Youth of the World." The contrast between the Nazis and the Olympics struck him: "It may have been the kraut and sausage for lunch that day, or it may have been the ironic feeling, but what with war memorials and something else, I kept wondering for what the youth of the world is being called."[7]

Mary Elizabeth persuaded Ralph to pay a "nominal fee" to hire a guide, who took them though the museums. McGill conceded the guide, with his sing-song English, was worth his pay as he translated the museum cards. In the Pergamon Museum, McGill "asked him to become a little more eloquent and at [the] same time wished someone would kick me rather briskly for not having put more time on history." The museum collection had treasures brought back by Germans from excavations Ninevah, Assur, Uruk, and Babylon in the time of Nebuchadnezzar II.

Finally they came to the palace study of the exiled Kaiser Wilhelm II. This was the man whose troops McGill had enlisted to fight twenty years earlier. As a teenager in Chattanooga, he would recall years later, "I had learned to hate the philosophy symbolized by Kaiser Bill." McGill noticed his books, including some by Mark Twain, and his large desk, a gift from the English, made of wood carved from Admiral Lord Nelson's old flagship. At this desk in 1914 the kaiser had signed the mobilization papers sending Germany into what soon became a world war. McGill felt the war wash over him: "I could see all the millions dying and all the nations ruined and all the blood spilled since a pen scratched across the paper there at 5 o'clock on that August afternoon 24 years ago. It is still going on, that spilling of blood. And the sound of marching feet which began that day has never ceased."

"Of course," McGill told the guide, "he was just a puppet in the hands of a destiny, but if he could have looked ahead. . . ."

"I am but a guide, sir, but I think he had to sign. They told him the war would be over in six weeks."[8]

The sound of marching feet still echoed in his mind after he and Mary Elizabeth reached London in early March. Sitting in on sessions of the British Parliament, which he likened to a dignified form of the Georgia legislature, McGill recorded how Britain was receiving news of Hitler's latest audacious acts. On March 12, German troops crossed into Austria, allegedly invited by Austria's leaders. On March 14 Hitler entered Vienna in triumph, greeted by cheering throngs, and declared that he had made Austria part of the German Reich with a new name: "Ostmark." Austrians and Germans would vote on the union in a plebiscite on April 10. That same day Prime Minister Neville Chamberlain told Parliament that nothing short of war could have averted Hitler's seizure of Austria. McGill was impressed by the warnings in Parliament of Winston Churchill, who opposed appeasement of Hitler. "The German war machine," McGill wrote, "is back again, in a more deadly form than before. The dead of that war did not die in vain. Some of our statesmen have lived in vain."[9]

Shortly after, news arrived that McGill's energetic efforts in Europe had paid off handsomely. One day, when Mary Elizabeth was bedridden in London, recuperating from a new attack of her kidney ailment, McGill picked up his mail at American Express and found a letter, dated March 24, from Maj. Clark Howell. The major had become the Constitution's president and publisher after his father's death in 1936. "I know you are having a grand experience," Howell wrote, "and only regret that your happiness has been marred by Mary Elizabeth's illness. I know how trying it is to have a member of one's family sick in a strange place with unfamiliar surroundings and far from home and friends."

Howell congratulated McGill on the latest series of articles on England, which were "most entertaining and highly instructive." Howell took pleasure in every success. His father had groomed McGill both before and after sending him to Cuba. By 1936 it was clear that McGill was the most articulate voice at the *Constitution,* with the widest following of readers in the half-century since Henry Grady.

Now the publisher, who was only five years McGill's senior, revealed a new opportunity to showcase this talented writer. McGill knew that the *Constitution's* executive editor, Francis W. Clarke, had died shortly after McGill sailed for Europe. Howell explained that he was keeping everything as "open and flexible" as possible "until you return to this country. I want to talk the whole situation over with you and believe that we can work out a plan which will be beneficial to the paper and which, I believe, will hold great interest for you." The major was offering everything McGill wanted: an end to the cycle of sportswriting and a voice in politics: "While I haven't thought the matter through to its definite conclusion, my thought is that you would disassociate yourself from the sports department and become editorial director, at the same time handling a daily column on the editorial page. Before you get back, I want you to turn the thing over in your mind so that you will be prepared to give me the benefit of your suggestions and thoughts when you get here."[10]

He would not be returning until early June, but McGill seems to have put on the mantle of editor at once. More than likely he answered

Howell immediately. At the same time he determined that he must go to Vienna, at least in time for the plebiscite on April 10. He was only waiting for a visa. A series of articles written from Vienna could be featured on the *Constitution*'s op-ed page, opposite the editorials, conditioning readers to his presence. This was the space where two years earlier the newspaper had featured Clarke's series on "war preparedness" in Europe, written after talks and tours in England, Germany, and France. The series with his name had been unusual for Clarke, who wrote unsigned editorials, not a daily column.[11] While waiting for the visa, McGill left Mary Elizabeth in bed and crossed the Channel for a short visit to Paris.[12]

Back in London, with his visa approved, McGill prepared for the journey to Vienna. Mary Elizabeth could not go, which was just as well for at least two reasons. The long trip by train was fraught with uncertainties, especially in Austria, now completely occupied by Nazi troops. Also, McGill had a secret agenda. He had accepted a risky mission on behalf of Austrian Jews who had fled to England.

Before leaving Atlanta, a friend had given him a letter to deliver to a friend of his in London. At that man's home in London, McGill met two refugees who had escaped in haste before the Nazis had closed the borders. One was a Viennese lawyer who had been a leading supporter of Schuschnigg; he asked for a vital favor. "They had asked me," McGill wrote, "to see their people, from whom they could not hear, and to bring back, if possible, some of their effects." They also wanted McGill to deliver a message, but said it would be safer if he did not carry anything in writing. They asked him to memorize it. He was to tell them "the location of certain papers which were to be burned lest they fall into Nazi hands."[13] Acceptance of this mission gave McGill a personal way to defy the Nazis, who by now he had come to detest, if not fear. It also permitted him to help a people who had befriended him for years and whose culture he respected. It was also the first of many demonstrations of support for the Jews in the struggles of the next three decades.

McGill left London the first week of April, about the same time Hitler was preparing to return to Austria. McGill found the journey as arduous as expected. Across the Channel at Ostende he rode through Belgium to the German border at Aachen. There for the trek across

Germany and Austria he got a third-class ticket, which did not guarantee a seat. The train was "jammed with Germans and Austrians going back to vote. For three mortal hours after leaving Aachen at the Belgian border, I stood in the corridor of the train." In Cologne he managed to share a compartment with seven others seated on polished planking. The ride lasted twenty-nine hours, getting him to Vienna on Thursday April 7.[14]

The Nazi propaganda machine had been astonishingly absolute. Across Austria the Nazis, now in control, had ordered festive decorations. McGill noted that "even those who did not have a voice in their country had to decorate. Every hamlet tried to outdo the other. . . . Each tiny farmhouse, each church, each barn, had flags and the hooked cross made with garlands and flowers." The railroad engines carried painted signs: Large "Ja" signs at each railroad station and posters declaring "Thank the Fuehrer with Yes," "Bread and Work Comes with the Fuehrer," "One People, One Reich, One Fuehrer," and "Blood Calls to Blood."[15]

This was a foretaste of what McGill found in Vienna. It was as though he were traveling deeper into an abyss of human depravity. It might have been Joseph Conrad's *Heart of Darkness,* but in the middle of European civilization. Gone from his dispatches was the initial awe of his first observations from Berlin. Now McGill focused on the terror. He felt the wave engulfing Austrians would soon roll over nations in Hitler's path eastward. He saw the pattern through non-German eyes, as a sane man in a madhouse. His dispatches were notable for repeating this warning. He seems to have been haunted by immersion in this alien milieu. By repeating the most horrific scenes in detail he helped confirm their reality in the modern world of 1938. Whereas he had written only six articles after weeks in Scandinavia, now a week in Vienna drove him to write nine.

McGill's home base was the Osterreichisherhof Hotel. From there he soon got his bearings so that he would be in the right places at the right time. His most constant guide was a South Carolinian, Robert Best, the son of a Methodist minister. They spent several nights together on streets and in the coffeehouses. Best, briefing McGill on what he had missed, "was then most critical of Hitler and the Germans, although insisting, and quite truthfully, that Austrians were taking him as the better of two evils."[16]

On Saturday April 9, the day before the plebiscite, a now familiar Nazi commotion penetrated McGill's hotel room too early in the morning. Outside, he heard the band and the tramp of marching feet, "the start of the big show, the plebiscite, beloved by the Nazi government, which would show to a world that the people of Austria almost were unanimously in support and approval of the coup which had wiped out the Austrian republic and opened the way for the German dictator to move on toward Bagdad."[17]

Certain themes reverberated through all his Vienna dispatches. There was the frothing hysteria which overwhelmed reason as Hitler, an unsmiling "mask of a face," entered the city. On the eve of the plebiscite, there was Hitler speaking, ecstatic and frenzied, amplified by loudspeakers that McGill began thinking of as "tin throats." The machinery of coercion was so pervasive that Nazis celebrated victory the day before the vote. There was abundant evidence that Austria had been doomed economically since its creation in the Treaty of Versailles when it was severed from Hungary. Clearly Hitler had fed upon the hopes of young men and women who had come of age since the war and were jobless, promising better times through a new partnership. "Do not think Austria did not want him," McGill wrote. "Perhaps 40 per cent of the people did not. But the others did." Civil liberties, free speech and a free press had been traded for bread and jobs. In the bargain, Austria's Jews were being sacrificed to the same cruelty dealt German Jews. "Somewhere in all this," McGill concluded, "should be a lesson to the democracies to check up and see to their own houses. Are there any seeds of terror and horror and despair being nourished for some strong man to harvest?"[18]

The appeal of the strong man fascinated McGill. He got as close as he could to the people and their führer. After Hitler arrived in Vienna, thousands along his route crowded around the Imperial Hotel "where the god of the German nation was resting." It was an hour and a half before McGill wormed a half block through to a spot in front of the hotel, facing police, soldiers and secret service, fifty yards from the balcony. The crowd screamed, chanted, and "heiled."

"We would our leader see. We would our leader see."

"Ein Volk, ein Reich, ein Fuehrer."

"Sieg Heil! Sieg Heil! Sieg Heil!"

An hour passed as afternoon light faded and in the bitter cold, snow began to fall. "At last there was a movement at one of the doors on the balcony. It opened. The crowd sat [*sic*] up a frenzied shout as the man in the brown overcoat stepped out. He walked to the center and saluted. He walked to the other end and saluted, and then returned to his room."[19]

The shrill madness all around provoked McGill to brash acts of defiance. Earlier that day he tried to take photographs. Each time he was stopped as soon as he took the camera out of the case. The first time a trooper grabbed his arm, checked his passport, and warned that photographs were not allowed. Then, as Hitler's car approached and McGill unbuttoned the camera case, two men in plain clothes grabbed the camera and "hustled your reporter to one side" and interrogated him.

"It states that your occupation is a newspaper man," one said. "Is that the same as a journalist? You know that only those on the official car may make pictures. Others are forbidden."

McGill sparred with them. In America, he answered, "a newspaperman was not a journalist." He lied and said he did not know photographs were forbidden. They took his film. "In a nearby coffee house I put in a new film and started with the crowd." Later in Michaeller Platz, he photographed some of the hundreds who placed flowers before an "altar" with a bronze bust of Hitler.[20]

Vienna had been taken over by the Nazis and McGill refused to be polite and conform, as though he felt he must demonstrate that he at least was retaining free will. After seeing Hitler on the balcony, McGill found warmth in a coffeehouse and sat down in a corner. Soon the waiter came over, and lifted his hand in the fascist salute.

"Heil Hitler!" he said.

"Coffee," said McGill.

It was madness, he thought. He had seen it all before, in Berlin. "Vienna learns quickly. All the shopkeepers greet each customer as he enters and leaves with 'Heil Hitler.' I sat there stirring my coffee and wondered what the opponents of Mr. Roosevelt, who think him a dictator, would do if they had to say 'Heil Roosevelt' every time they purchased a collar or a pack of cigarets."

"Heil Hitler!" said the porter back at the Osterreichisherhof.

"Zwei and Zwanzig," answered McGill.

In his room he discovered that someone had gone through his bag. This confirmed warnings he had been given in London. "I had left it unlocked so it could be done easily," he wrote.[21]

For sheer defiance, nothing matched his hidden agenda. He gave every appearance of delighting in having a secret mission, that he was carrying a message to Jews with the intent of thwarting the new Nazi overlords. Amid the madness of Vienna, the Jewish families appear to have been the sanest people McGill met, and the ones he most trusted.

Even in Machado's Cuba he had found a great number of people to speak with. The ambassador had led him to members of the opposition, and on his own he had found a number of journalists with whom he could talk baseball, boxing, and politics. In Vienna Hitler had muted opponents or sent them hiding. He went looking for newspapers and magazines and discovered that they had "disappeared from the stands." In a blitz, the Nazi propaganda machine replaced the city's journalists with toadies answerable to Nazis who swarmed in the newsrooms. "No one there prints an opposition editorial or whispers an opposition word," McGill wrote. "The newspapers cease to be newspapers. They became sheets which record little news of the world. They all hammer, hammer away at the Nazi doctrines." On the air, "there were no radio programs save those sent out by the Germans. There was no information save the information they supplied." The stream of propaganda before the election "was so skillful that few could withstand it." It aimed to document German prosperity under Hitler. "The German Reich is strong on figures and statistics. Few can be checked."[22]

Nazi book burnings were notorious, and now he saw one. "A great pile blazed in the center of the square." Booksellers now stacked their shop windows with Nazi best-sellers by Hitler, Goering, Rosenberg, Goebbels, and Hess. McGill, probably accompanied by Robert Best, managed to have one conversation about newspapers with a Nazi official.

"Why do you not have free newspapers if your government is so popular and so secure?" McGill asked. "Why do you not let the people have news?"

"We don't care about them knowing but one thing. Nothing else matters. The state is the one thing. We don't teach anything else, we don't print anything else."[23]

McGill's refuge from the Nazis was in the parlors of the Jews. On his first day in Vienna, he found the partner of the lawyer who had fled to London. "It makes us feel good," the lawyer said, "to have a visitor. It makes us feel there is, after all, a little liberty left in the world."

McGill delivered the memorized message that certain papers should be destroyed. Even more daring, he offered to smuggle some items. "I brought another message about getting things out of his house and into my possession."

"I cannot go out on the streets except early in the morning and late," the lawyer said, "without being subjected to the chance of being arrested and made to sweep streets or polish automobiles."

Each day life for Jews had become more precarious, a repetition of what had happened in Germany. After the coup and invasion on March 12, German Nazis quickly tapped Austria's wealth. On March 21, with the plebiscite almost three weeks away, a Nazi cabinet minister, Dr. Hjalmar Schacht, arrived in Vienna to take over the Austrian National Bank on behalf of the Reichsbank, with the comment that "not a single person will find a future with us who is not wholeheartedly for Adolf Hitler." The lawyer imagined far worse ahead.[24] He arranged for McGill to meet the mother of the partner who had fled to London. He could have tea at her house at four o'clock that afternoon. When he arrived, he found the elderly woman, an old and loyal servant, and three others. They were in a room with the lights on and curtains drawn for safety. The woman was eighty, but the Nazis had come and pulled her out of bed and interrogated her about her son. Then they had taken valuables, including some old paintings. Even so, the woman said she would rather die than leave Austria. Probably she had no choice now that her son had fled and she, not believing him, had refused to go. "I am sorry," she told McGill. "I cannot let you have tea from a good service. The Nazis have said I cannot use it."

"Nothing may be taken from the house," another explained. The house was being watched, as was McGill himself. "Even a small package will be noticed by the neighbors, some of whom are paid to watch."

"I sat there in the house," McGill wrote, "and tried to believe that this was the world of 1938—that it was a dream. But it was the truth. I had read and heard the Nazi's very effective propaganda that such things are not true. I was seeing them."

The invitation led to another. The next day, Friday, McGill had tea in the home of a Jewish lawyer who had fought in the trenches for Austria in the world war. Now he was ordered not to do business with Christian firms.

"Europe is mad," said the lawyer. "I cannot leave but I want my children to leave. My wife and I will remain. We must."

The lawyer introduced him to a Christian friend, a woman who had been married to a Jew since 1923. The Nazis told them they must be divorced if she wanted to be a Reich citizen. She refused, but she worried about her son.

"My child came home from school today and he sang for me a song. He is only nine and so he did not know what it meant. It is one the Nazis are teaching. Would you like to hear it?"

> Wie schon ist Eisen
> Wie schon ist Stahl
> Wie schon ist der Jud am harterpfhal
>
> How beautiful is iron
> How beautiful is steel
> How beautiful is a Jew at a stake of torture.

"It was, seeing it and being in it, impossible to believe," McGill wrote. In the crucible of Vienna, it seemed that a war must be inevitable, partly because the children "were being taught that torture and burning at the stake are fine things for people who have been set aside as enemies of the state. . . . [If] the Germans persist they will bring up a race which is so terrible and so depraved it cannot do other than produce its own destruction. An aroused world will, even though it does not want war, be forced to go to war."[25]

Nazi power, he concluded, was built on youth. "I keep repeating that. Youth that saw no future, no hope of profession or job, turned to the strong man." Hitler, as he siphoned money for the armed forces, had given Germans "black bread, low wages, a standard of living our relief families would protest," but it was "better than what they had obtained previously."[26]

If war were inevitable, it would not come soon, McGill wrote. Germany itself did not seem ready. "And I know, what is more important, that Hitler will get what he wants without war. England will not fight. Not yet, at any rate. And Hitler, who doesn't want war, will go ahead." McGill agreed with the alarmists who saw Hitler stopping at nothing:

> Soon he will have autonomy for the Sudeten Germans in Czechoslovakia.
>
> And then, one fine day, there will be "disorder" in Sudeten Germany and there will come a "legal" request for German troops to put down the "disorder." . . . [The] technique of the Nazis . . . is to make a loud noise and to get in charge of the police and then to "quell" the "disorder" they themselves have created.

Perhaps the one thing that could stop Hitler, McGill wrote, remembering a line Victor Hugo wrote about Napoleon: "God became bored with him."[27]

On Saturday night, the eve of the plebiscite, new terror ran through the Jewish community. McGill had gone to a small coffeehouse for coffee and Hungarian goulash. Afterward, in a large crowd, he listened to loudspeakers as their tin throats broadcast Hitler's speech. Hitler "played on their emotions as well as any Huey Long ever did and better than our minor 'Fuehrers' who have infested the scene political in America. . . . He had them cheering, weeping, laughing." He saw a torchlight parade and lights piercing the sky, armored cars rushing through the street and lorries of soldiers. Bands, singing, marching, and shouting, went on until midnight. Through it all McGill heard the whispered rumor that "a pogrom was planned for Sunday night or Monday night" because of an alleged plot to kill Hitler. "Thousands of sheets of propaganda carrying rhymed threats that Hitler would not go back to Germany alive were scattered in the streets. They were thickest where the Jews of Vienna live."[28]

The Nazis amassed a plebiscite victory of 99.75 "Ja" by simple intimidation, McGill reported. That Sunday he visited two polling places guarded by Austrians, newly sworn into the Nazi party, who were "not yet, at least, insolent and arrogant." They allowed McGill to look from the door. Only Aryans could vote. Although there were secret booths, "a Nazi would, when handed a pencil, happily and joyfully bless the name of his Fuehrer and then and there mark a cross through the circle opposite 'Ja.' And quite as obviously only those desiring to vote 'nein' would arise and go to the secret booths, knowing full well his name would be jotted down on another list." That night McGill talked with disillusioned Austrians. One woman, twenty-three years old, said she would have voted "nein" but she had already had trouble. She had not objected to Hitler's coup: "But when he took away my country and my nationality, I did not like it. . . . When he had done this I removed the Nazi flag from my window. The police came and made me put it back."[29]

Two nights later, in another coffeehouse encounter, an Austrian insisted that he look over the voter statistics. No more than 1,050,000 of the city's 1,850,000 were eligible to vote, yet 1,219,000 had voted "Ja."

"It is quite impossible," the Austrian told McGill, "to anyone but a Nazi election chief."

"The whole thing," McGill said, "reminded me of our own late Huey Long and his less able imitators in other states." The difference was that Hitler was guilty of overkill. "There was no need to make the election unfair, by putting pressure on the relatively few who wanted to vote against him, and by padding the lists."[30]

During the week he visited others who did not fit the mold of the new Reich. Each person had been systematically eliminated from circulation and degraded. On the Monday after the plebiscite McGill visited a German author whose "books are known to most of the people in the world who study politics and government." He had left Germany because of the Nazis. He taught in England, then in Vienna.

"I was ordered to sweep the streets," he said. "I am not permitted to leave Austria. I hope to go later on. I have hired a Nazi lawyer and bribe him well. I expect to be sent to a concentration camp with my family." As they spoke, a concentration camp for thousands of Austrians was already under construction at Mauthausen on the north bank of the Danube near Enns.[31]

The friendly Aryans and Jews would soon become only memories as McGill lost track of them. The memories served him for a lifetime. The Vienna conversations in parlors and coffeehouses gave him authority to write persuasively about the Nazis and ammunition to combat their likenesses among demagogues in the South. In Vienna he was seared by immersion in human madness. It had revolted him against tyranny in a personal way. What he found there inspired two important crusades in his first years as a new editor. One was a cautious effort to expand civil liberties in America. The other was a gallant effort to extend to other countries the First Amendment's protection of freedom of speech and press.

McGill was on the train out of Vienna, probably on Wednesday April 13. Again he traveled third class, talking much of the time to other riders on the hard wooden benches. He could glance back at the days in Vienna as a signal time in his new career, his first self-styled assignment as a new editor, unleashed from sports and focused on serious issues. The Scandinavian studies paled when compared with the political storms in Vienna, London, and Berlin. Just as he would look back on the Rosenwald fellowship as his great turning point, he could regard that April week in Vienna as the heart of the experience, emotionally and psychologically. In that sense, Nazi aggression had handed him an opportunity. Those who knew him well credited the Nazi experience as one of the formative influences on his philosophical development.[32] During the war he would write, for a national audience, how he could "never forget [the] froth-flecked lips on the faces of shouting men and women. . . . Frenzy, cruelty, hypnotic delirium. . . . I knew I had seen a new cult, the cult of utter social control over the minds of young people who could be trained to think exactly as others wanted them to think by educational processes and the uses of propaganda."[33]

Back in London, he looked after Mary Elizabeth, who was feeling better, wrote most of the series, and mailed the bundle of nine articles to Atlanta. The *Constitution* gave the series a display commensurate with the as-yet-undisclosed plan to elevate him to editor of the editorial page. The "McGill in Vienna" headline and his personal stories focused as much attention on McGill as on Vienna. His defiance of the Nazis gave his adventures a heroic tinge.

By the time the last dispatch was published in early May, he was traveling around England, Ireland, and Scotland and finding new topics for his last "Break O' Day" columns. Some subjects were light and some serious, a combination like a fighter's punches or a pitcher's fastball and change-up that McGill would employ throughout his editorship to avoid being deathly predictable. While he noted the English preparations for war, the stockpiling of gas masks, he and Mary Elizabeth escaped on a pilgrimage to Shakespeare country to see "Ann Hathaway's cottage," and he toured Keats's home in London's Hampstead. In Dublin he wrote about a flower woman who charmed him with the line, "It is not every day ye can buy beauty." In Troon, Scotland, he covered the national sport, golf, in typical Scottish weather, lashing rain, and met another sportswriter destined for other assignments at the *New York Times,* James Reston. In late May, the McGills packed for the trip home. His last dispatch was actually a revised lead for his column on an Atlanta golfer's bad luck in the British Amateur Tournament. He sent that by wireless, datelined "Somewhere at Sea."[34]

PART II
Facing Facts

6

Fleas on the Southern Body-Politic

In addition to tenancy, lack of soil conservation programs
[and] adequate educational facilities, health programs
and other fleas on the southern body-politic, there has
been the political rabble rouser. He was responsible
for most of the other fleas which kept the southern
"dog" flea-bitten, hungry and in poor health.
—Ralph McGill, 1938

[McGill] learned that the organization was being
infiltrated by Communist elements and editorially
denounced and exposed them for their true aims. . . .
He further advised he never associated with any of its
leaders after he learned of its true purpose.
—FBI Special Inquiry, 1951

Nothing was ever to be same for McGill. In going to Europe he had passed through a tunnel in time and emerged in a vastly different world. It was a world he wanted and seemed ready for, but it was strange nonetheless, peopled by a new and tougher crowd. His competitive spirit and faith in what he had already learned "on the job" enabled him to forge ahead into uncharted territory.

When he and Mary Elizabeth got off the train on June 7, friends and co-workers crowded around with the biggest homecoming celebration he would ever receive. The *Constitution*'s photographer snapped a shot of McGill, surrounded by the crowd, smiling shyly and looking straight into the lens while his hand was being shaken in congratulations. At his side, Mary Elizabeth wore a corsage and beamed joyfully. To her, "home" meant rest from fatigue and reunion with their daughter, Virginia, who in the past six months had made an indelible, loving impression on McGill's mother and ailing father. Although Ralph loved his daughter dearly, to him "home" was almost synonymous with office. As soon as possible, he was at work, seeking out his publisher to go over the details—responsibilities, salary, transition—of the promised editorial position. At last there seemed to be no obstacle to his leaving sports.[1]

There was nothing tentative in Clark Howell's proposal. Even though McGill would be setting editorial policy, Howell gave no indication of worry about McGill's politics. The newspaper wanted vigor on its editorial page. Nothing McGill had written during nine years appeared to conflict with policies and traditions established by Howell's father and grandfather or by Henry Grady.

Since 1880, when Grady joined Evan P. Howell in the ownership, the newspaper had established a reputation, North and South, for civic boosterism and public service. In the debris of the Civil War and Reconstruction, Grady used the pages to promote the owners' political and economic agenda. Declaring to the financial centers that the Civil War was forgotten, he boosted Atlanta as the economic center of a "New South" at the expense of rival business interests in Macon and Augusta. Working behind the scenes, exchanging messages in secret code with his political organization, the "Atlanta Ring," Grady girded this economic policy by securing the election of state and national politicians who were favorably disposed toward Atlanta.

After Grady's death from pneumonia in 1889, the same policies were handed down through the Howell family. Added to boosterism, however, was a concern that profitable business and honest government be part of the city's image. Evan P. Howell's son, Clark Howell, was assistant managing editor with Grady and became editor when his father retired in 1897. Under his leadership, the *Constitution* staff won a Pulitzer Prize for uncovering corruption in bidding practices at city hall.[2]

By the 1930s, the *Constitution*'s editorial writers were supporting diverse means of repairing the state's economy, including acceptance of help from the federal government. On economic issues, they urged new uses for cotton and federal efforts to bolster sagging cotton exports. They supported management and denounced strike-minded labor-union "agitators" as Bolsheviks acting on orders from Moscow. They praised positive acts by labor leaders, as when the head of the Georgia Federation of Labor secured New Deal construction money to put men back to work. Under the New Deal, they urged Georgia to join the forty-five states that had already approved Social Security for the aged and infirm.[3]

In supporting some New Deal projects, the *Constitution* sided with other newspapers calling for federal tax cuts to stimulate private economic investment, as when the Southern Railway invested $4 million in new freight cars. They opposed the New Deal's wage-and-hour bill because it would make southern industrialists pay the same "high wage scales" as in the North.[4]

In politics, the editors continued unabashedly Democratic, as in Grady's day. Clark Howell was a blueblood Democrat, a state senator, speaker of the Georgia House of Representatives, and a candidate for governor in 1906, when he was defeated by another Atlanta newspaperman, Hoke Smith, former owner of the *Journal*. In 1936, the year the elder Howell died, the *Constitution* editorialists envisioned the "death rattle" of the republican (with a small *r*) party on the way "to join its progenitor, the whigs." Editorialists scorned the "autocratic" Governor Eugene Talmadge, especially when he dismissed public officials in an evident effort to consolidate power and patronage.[5]

In civic matters, the newspaper deputized itself to fight for honest, businesslike government. After uncovering corruption in city bidding, the editors championed a grand jury's investigation of corrupt police officers. They supported a judge who admonished lawyers for creating a "courtroom circus." Especially after the elder Clark Howell chaired the Federal Aviation Commission and developed a plan for regulating aviation, editorial writers stressed the importance of air traffic to Atlanta; construction of an airport control tower was called "imperative." Now that the automobile had displaced horses and mules in the city, they hailed all road improvements.[6]

Seldom, however, did the *Constitution* address racial issues. Generally, editors maintained white society's polite silence concerning the intractable "situation"—social segregation and political disfranchisement. But in the wake of massive immigration from the farms, they urged the city to ameliorate slum housing, an issue concerning Negroes as well as whites. In opposing lynchings, they defended the region's image, maintaining that critics unjustly "stigmatize the south because of an occasional lynching."[7]

None of these views differed from those McGill had expressed in print by 1938. And if he saw any disparities between his private views and the *Constitution*'s policies, he did not let them get in the way of this opportunity. Yet after talking with the publisher, McGill came away with an assignment different from that which Howell had mentioned in the letter to London. The publisher still wanted McGill to write a daily column for the editorial page. But in March Howell had written that McGill would "become editorial director." Now in June, he decided to give that position to the man who had been doing the job daily for four months since Clarke's death, steadfast chief editorial writer and columnist Ralph T. Jones. As the *Constitution* announced on its front page on June 17, Jones "will have complete control of the editorial page."[8]

Howell, however, offered McGill other responsibilities, ones that at least sounded better and bigger: Howell wanted to promote him to "executive editor." McGill would be "in complete charge of the news, sports and society departments." This was a curious compromise. McGill had risen to prominence as a writer, not as an axe-wielding manager responsible for cutting budgets and firing reporters. Once, as sports editor, his staff had urged him to fire a writer, but the writer prevailed, pleading to McGill that his wife was pregnant. "He had too soft a heart," concluded a colleague. The other aspects of being executive editor were compelling, of course—a promotion, a raise, and a daily column. Over the next four years, he never acquired the facility for management. If he had been frank with Howell, he might have told him that, after six months in Europe, staying around the office and managing the staff seemed uninteresting, if not parochial.[9]

As his first act, McGill chose his successor as sports editor. A year before, he had tried a second time to lure Freddy Russell from Nashville to be his assistant at $47.50 a week. Russell, who had become the *Banner*'s sports editor in 1930 after McGill left, "seriously considered it, but didn't do it." The man who got that job, Jack Troy, had in McGill's absence managed the department well, though he wrote without

McGill's conviction or style. Now McGill put in a good word for him. On June 17, the day Howell announced McGill's promotion, McGill used his last "Break O' Day" to "name Jack Troy as sports editor." McGill realized that, after seven years on the sports pages, he had to sell this substitute. In six months, he reasoned, "readers had an opportunity to become acquainted with Troy. They like him. He and his staff of fine young men will carry on. . . . He brings character to his job, and the willingness to work hard and the ability to tell a story."[10]

The last column lapsed into sentimental rumination. Sports writing had given him "a span of the most pleasant years possible." Newspaper work had given him interesting friends and had spurred him to experiment and to express his opinions. He recalled the day in 1922 when it began. The *Banner*'s owner, Jimmy Stahlman, called him off the Tennessee political beat, saying, "No political writer will be busy Saturday, so I want you to cover the Michigan-Vanderbilt football game." Since coming to Atlanta, he had seen "revolutionists with guns in Cuba; the bullet-splashed walls of Panama; Rose Bowl games and horse races and baseball and track. There were the six months in Europe and a week with Charlie Yates as he won the British amateur golf championship. There were the big fights and the grand fellows who write about them."

In the flush of his success, he saluted his publisher and painted his profession in romantic hue: "Working for the Constitution means a lot. No real newspapaperman works merely for the working. He would not be in a newspaper job if he did not like it and the paper for which he works."[11]

On Monday, June 20, McGill launched the daily opinion column, which, under different headings, would become a staple of the *Constitution*. That first month the audacious, syndicated Westbrook Pegler was on vacation, so McGill's "One Word More" ran in Pegler's long, single column, the sixth column from the left.[12] McGill was in good pontificating company; to his left was Joseph Alsop, syndicated from Washington.

Now on the editorial page every morning, McGill assumed the role of a civic leader. He did this, however, by shifting gears rather than by switching cars. He was still the familiar voice "Break O' Day" readers had come to expect, though now less predictable because his tether extended beyond sports. He was the same storyteller, but with more purpose. Feeling his way at first, he began by framing possible choices, then indicating which choice appeared best. He had begun to demonstrate these characteristics in the Vienna series, after he had received the offer from Howell.

With an understanding of his audience, he alternated drama and light relief. "More" could be serious or preachy one day and lighten up the next. That first week, he recycled some of his serious European adventures, alternating them with tales reflecting his love of fox hunting, sports, kids, and animals. He focused on the humorless Nazi "gangsters" who had made the Viennese afraid to laugh, then the next day he told a long tale of fox hunting and unrequited love. On the third day the Nazis reappeared, this time scheming to take proud Czechoslovakia without war. Next he praised the genius of Gunnar Myrdal's economic experiments in employment and housing. On the fifth day he argued that Atlanta could sensibly combat juvenile delinquency and cut prison costs by investing in recreation programs. He finished the week with a historical tour of Number 10 Downing Street, where "there is a really tremendous battle of the diplomats" as Chamberlain tried to keep England out of war.[13]

The freedom to write about any subject was one of several perquisites that came with being executive editor. He soon discovered other satisfactions. He had, as sports editor, already enjoyed wide popularity. He had spent pleasant hours at the plantations of wealthy men such as Robert Woodruff and Col. Tillinghast Huston. Now, as executive editor, he found himself not only welcome but accepted among elites as a peer. Among the honors that first autumn, he was elected to Francis Clarke's vacancy in a group of business and professional elites, the Ten Club.[14]

Very soon the crosswinds of Democratic infighting buffeted McGill. As the 1938 Democratic primary election for the U.S. Senate neared, he sat at his typewriter pecking out a difficult editorial. President Roosevelt was seeking to purge Georgia's conservative senior senator, Walter F. George, because George wielded too much influence in the Senate, as many as forty votes, enough to defeat New Deal bills George considered radical. At last Roosevelt's Georgia supporters recruited a lawyer who agreed to risk ridicule by denigrating George—

Lawrence Camp, a former Richard Russell campaign manager who had been rewarded with appointment as a U.S. district attorney. Fogging the political air still more was Eugene Talmadge, still anti–New Deal but now emphasizing populism, standing for the little man against big government and big business. He envisioned winning the Senate nomination if the other candidates split the vote and he carried his loyal 100,000 in the small county units.[15]

On this issue, the *Constitution* editors broke with the president and supported George's reelection. It was an uncomfortable position for McGill and Howell. McGill was expected to make it clear that the newspaper supported the New Deal. They admired Roosevelt, all the more because his frequent visits to his southern White House at Warm Springs, Georgia, made him a neighbor. But, as McGill unraveled the puzzle, Roosevelt could be an even bigger loser if Talmadge won. First, Camp was weak and had little chance of winning, mainly because of "lack of time" for his political machinery to work. Meanwhile, votes Camp took from George could swing the victory to Talmadge, who was "gaining strength." In a fight with Roosevelt, Talmadge expanded his rural base of support to include city bankers and businessmen who were also anti–New Deal.[16]

With Talmadge in mind, McGill defined the "political rabble rouser" and described the southern *variant* by its dominant characteristics, as Charles Darwin had done with species: "The 'rabble rouser' could tell a few jokes, compare his opponent with a jackass, call up the ghosts of Ben Hill and Bob Toombs and Tom Watson and wind up with a few screams of the eagle and win an election. The fact that he had no issue at all seemed to make no difference." Farmers and others mesmerized by this style

> could be told that the tuberculin test for cattle was bunk; that all the schooling any community needed was the old one-room school of the past with one teacher striving to instruct a half-dozen different classes and ages; that soil conservation was just politics and that Georgia had the greatest history of any state in the union. All this the farmers seemed to take to their hearts with great glee. . . .

If the candidate spoke informally of having gone bare-
footed as a country boy so long he never got used to shoes
this alone was worth 500 votes.[17]

Drawing a metaphor from his East Tennessee upbringing, McGill likened the rabble-rouser and his cronies to "fleas on the southern body-
politic." The fleas kept the unhealthy southerner scratching at the bite,
distracting him from regarding the future with vision: "A candidate
with a sound, intelligent platform which provided real education, pay
for teachers, more money for health and a plan which actually would
aid the farmer to market his crops, had a difficult time making his
voice heard." Denigrating intelligent solutions, the rabble-rouser compounded misery. "In addition to tenancy, lack of soil conservation
programs [and] adequate educational facilities, health programs and
other fleas on the southern body-politic," McGill wrote, "the political
rabble rouser . . . was responsible for most of the other fleas which
kept the southern 'dog' flea-bitten, hungry and in poor health."[18]

As for loyalty to Roosevelt, McGill in his first year outside the sports
department was learning to walk the tightrope between national politics
and states' rights. "This is a queer campaign," he wrote, citing the case of
political insider Edgar Dunlap, both a Roosevelt supporter and a friend of
Senator George, who "was told to give up Senator George or give up his
[federal] job." McGill noted that "regardless of one's political affiliations,
that was not a pretty story from Washington." Dunlap's case was "but
one example of federal pressure. . . . Various government officials are
actively engaged in politics." Dunlap himself complained about conflict
of interest—that candidate Camp "still was United States district attorney and all his assistants actively engaged in the campaign were government employees." While agreeing that the president had a right to insist
on loyalty, McGill, a witness to Nazi tactics, declared that Georgia was
not Germany or Italy. He amplified the argument of Senator George's
supporters—that "the voters of Georgia have a right to choose their own
representatives." In August, Roosevelt campaigned in Georgia, embarrassing George, calling the South "right now the nation's No. 1 economic
problem" and backing Camp as the man who could do the most for

Georgia. In September, however, George defeated both Camp and Talmadge for the Democratic nomination, which assured his reelection in November.[19]

In his high-profile position, McGill quickly became a magnet for issues and causes. He found himself popular for the influence he could wield. During his first few months as executive editor he learned to be wary of organizations seeking him as a member. He soon learned a lesson that would stay with him, a mark on his record, for the rest of his life.

Ironically, his belligerence toward the Nazis' suppression of human rights suggested to some that he was as willing to lead a crusade against the suppression of civil rights in his own country. This was a misconception. Anyone who has ever written editorials knows the phenomenon of Afghanistanism, that it takes less courage to criticize a foreign government than to fight city hall; a distant government cares little, but local officials read every word. On certain issues begging reform, including matters of racial justice and labor standards, there were, as John Kneebone has noted, unwritten "limits of permissible public discussion."[20]

Given McGill's high profile on human rights, he was soon contacted by the new Southern Conference on Human Welfare. The SCHW was established in 1938 by a group of Birmingham, Alabama, liberals as a forum to advocate the "human welfare" of economically and politically disfranchised southerners. The roster of delegates, guests, and organizations, one historian noted, "could have formed the nucleus for a who's who in Southern liberalism . . . and Southern liberal organizations."[21]

McGill and other newspapers editors were among numerous elites the SCHW asked to be sponsors for the first conference, set for November 21–23 in Birmingham. The other editors were associated with leading newspapers. The list included George Fort Milton of the *Chattanooga News*, who chaired the Southern Commission on the Study of Lynching; Virginius Dabney of the *Richmond Times-Dispatch*, who served with Milton on the Southern Policy Committee created in 1935 to foster and guide New Deal economic development; Mark Ethridge of Georgia's *Macon Telegraph* and later of the *Louisville Courier-Journal;* Jonathan Daniels of the *Raleigh News and Observer,* and John Temple Graves, whose columns the *Constitution* was reprinting. McGill agreed to sponsor the organization, and on October 27, three weeks before the sessions, he was listed as a sponsor in a story in the *Birmingham Post.* He gave his initial support, as he explained to the FBI a decade later, because he felt the conference's "purposes were sound."[22]

On the surface the SCHW seemed worthy of McGill's support. It was a child of New Deal economics, which the *Constitution* for the most part endorsed. The SCHW had been created as "the south's answer" to a White House–inspired economic report promoting New Deal solutions for the region. In the report Roosevelt affirmed what he had said earlier, that the South was "the Nation's No. 1 economic problem." Eleanor Roosevelt's presence indicated White House support. Delegates were expected to address a wide range of issues, including one of McGill's special concerns, the plight of poor tenant croppers, who were largely unhelped by New Deal economics.[23]

The conference's purposes may have been sound, but its tactics soon alienated allies and compromised its usefulness. The broad reach and aggressiveness of the SCHW exposed the first session to criticism. Its delegates, Negroes and whites, joined in condemning Birmingham's Jim Crow segregation laws. They approved a resolution instructing the SCHW leadership to hold future meetings in cities "where such laws are not in effect."[24]

The organization's zeal and urgency distanced moderates. Delegates urged repeal of the poll tax, opposed "wage differentials for Negroes in both public and private industry," endorsed unity in organized labor, supported investigation of civil liberties violations, and encouraged southeastern governors in the fight against discriminatory freight rates. Unfortunately for the conferees, they got the wrong kind of attention when they gave their highest honor to Supreme Court Justice Hugo Black, who had been a Ku Kluxer. Black's membership in the Klan had been publicized a year earlier, after Roosevelt nominated him in an effort to pack the Supreme Court with supporters of the New Deal. Told in advance about the award, Dabney in Richmond decided not to attend the conference. To liberal journalists, the award to a former Klansman seemed "an irresponsible declaration that loyalty to the New Deal was enough to wash away any sins."[25]

The taint of communism did still more to distance liberals. The SCHW naturally attracted labor organizers of various backgrounds, including some the *Constitution* editorials had labeled as "agitators" taking orders from Moscow. In fact, some Communists did attend. What influence they had is disputed. Kneebone argued that the Communists had "little influence." A scholar of American communism, Harvey Klehr, contended that a small number of Communists not only participated but also were appointed to staff positions.[26]

McGill, with his political savvy, undoubtedly sensed a gathering storm. At some point before the first conference, he distanced himself from the group and avoided the Birmingham sessions. When queried later by the FBI, McGill told an agent that "he never joined the SCHW nor had he ever attended any of their meetings. Upon learning of the CP [Communist Party] infiltration and true aims he denounced and exposed the organization."[27]

That week, McGill obeyed his political hunches and stayed home. It was typical of two career-long penchants—avoiding participation in advocacy groups over which he had no control and ducking when others tried to pin him with a label. That Monday, while the conference was disturbing the peace of Birmingham, McGill devoted his column to support for Roosevelt's push for rearmament because the Germans "can understand force." Monday night, an anonymous man called to ask why McGill was so critical of the Germans, so on Tuesday he reminded readers of his indelible experiences in Vienna: Nazis, sieg heils, censorship, book burnings. Thursday, Thanksgiving Day, he was awakened at 5:30 A.M. by a caller who wanted to argue about the New Deal, and later that morning had a nontraditional Thanksgiving breakfast of sausage flavored with sage and pepper at the Saddle and Sirloin Club's annual breakfast. On Friday, when Mrs. Roosevelt returned from the Birmingham conference, McGill reported her talk to Atlanta's League of Women Voters, not her participation at the conference. He concluded that her social welfare work made her "the greatest foe Communism has in this country."[28]

Neither McGill nor the *Constitution* opposed the conference in 1938. But one week after it adjourned, an unsigned editorial that could have been written by McGill questioned the undertone of the president's

declaration that the southern economy was the nation's "No. 1 problem." That White House report had met with "more or less unfavor-
able reaction," the editorial noted, because it "conveys the impression
that little or no progress has been made; that the south was blissfully,
or otherwise, dozing over its economic opportunities." The editorial
writer disagreed. The South was "very much awake" in the areas of
crop diversification and livestock. Referring undoubtedly to the urgent
proposals at the Birmingham sessions, the editorial also questioned
the wisdom of haste: "The south feels that a quickly fueled prescription for all southern ills might prove to be a more incurable affliction
than the alleged disease."[29]

McGill's identification with the SCHW troubled him for years. As
he recalled, he never attended any of the conferences, and after the second, in April 1940 in Chattanooga, he formally broke any connection
with the organization. His eventual repudiation of the SCHW did not
expunge his name from the list of sponsors. When the House Special
Committee on Un-American Activities in 1944 cited the SCHW as a Com-
munist-front organization, McGill's connection resurfaced. His sponsorship and his repudiation became part of his permanent record at the
Federal Bureau of Investigation. An FBI agent who interviewed McGill
reported that when the editor "learned that the organization was being
infiltrated by Communist elements," he withdrew his sponsorship and
"editorially denounced and exposed them for their true aims. . . . He
further advised he never associated with any of its leaders after he learned
of its true purpose."[30]

Although McGill became wary of organizations that attempted to enlist
his name, he relished supporting politicians he liked. Since his Nashville
days, politics flowed as an undercurrent in all his journalism. Political
allies and great causes roused his passion. Given that Atlanta was far more
liberal than the rest of the state, it was easier to find allies among local
politicians. Since his victory over an aging incumbent in 1936, Atlanta
mayor William Berry Hartsfield seemed progressive and honest enough,
inheriting and nurturing a Depression-riddled, debt-ridden city government without any noticeable scandal or corruption. Before defeating
Mayor James L. Key, Hartsfield had been elected a city alderman and a

state legislator and had demonstrated his civic progressivism by championing the purchase of land that was to become the city's airport.[31]

Finding political allies outside Atlanta, in the state, was far less likely. But a few emerged. The most notable was a former high school quarterback named Ellis Arnall. Arnall was from Newnan, southwest of Atlanta, had played football at Newnan High, and in the late 1920s had attended the University of the South in Sewanee, Tennessee. There he read the *Banner* and McGill's sports columns and occasional political stories. On trips to Nashville, he struck up a personal relationship with McGill. They would find a restaurant and talk sports and politics. Arnall went on to the University of Georgia Law School, where he graduated first in his class in 1931. He went home to Newnan, got into politics, and asked a favor of McGill, then *Constitution* sports editor. "I came to Atlanta," Arnall recalled, "and told him I wanted him to say some nice things about my running for the legislature." McGill printed a visionary compliment: "Keep your eye on Ellis Arnall." It mattered little that the blurb was on the sports pages, Arnall said. "One department had a lot to do with another."[32]

In 1932, on Roosevelt's coattails, Arnall was elected by a landslide to the state house of representatives. He was then only twenty-five years old, but he aimed to become speaker pro-tempore. He drove his "old jalopy" around the state to visit house members in every district and defeated eight other candidates. He was reelected in 1934 and 1936 and served a while as Governor Talmadge's floor leader. Arnall's friendship with Talmadge ruptured in 1935, when the governor at the start of his second term turned against Roosevelt and repudiated New Deal legislation. Talmadge contended that Georgia was "better off than any other state in the Union" and nothing more was needed to relieve the state's economy. Arnall and Speaker of the House Eurith D. Rivers met with Talmadge to stress that federal work-relief programs would bring in millions, including federal administrative positions that could be filled by Georgians. Rivers said Talmadge was at first silent, then dazed them by declaring there wasn't going to be any New Deal giveaway legislation passed in Georgia, that it would destroy the country, and that they must choose "Roosevelt or Talmadge."[33]

Arnall, however, made other friends. As speaker pro-tempore, he allied with Rivers. After Rivers was elected governor in 1936 as an ardent New Dealer, Arnall got a political appointment as the state's assistant attorney general, in line to become attorney general in 1939. By then, Arnall and McGill agreed that the key issues were, at heart, economic. "Scratch a Communist," McGill wrote, "and you will find scar tissue of bitterness inspired by some economic maladjustment."[34]

Arnall and McGill saw each other frequently in 1939 as McGill covered the legislative session from January into March. Unlike editorialists who wrote about matters from afar, McGill would always trust most what he saw and heard. Of newspaper "leg men" who walked the beats, he romanticized, "More than anyone else on newspapers they get to know human nature—to see people in the raw—they grow wise eyes and keen minds." The capitol building was only a few blocks from the *Constitution,* so he went there frequently, spying from the galleries, chatting with members at their seats on the floor, sitting in on committee meetings.[35]

In 1939 McGill was most interested in how the legislators would solve "dismal" economic dislocations aggravated by the Depression. Hard times had altered the South's demographics. A study of high school students in a small Georgia town showed that 86 percent left immediately after graduation to find jobs in cities of ten thousand or more. Small towns accused the cities of "draining away their people." Yet in crowded cities, McGill noted, "jobs have run out." Cities demanded "more and more relief." Governor Rivers's spending pumped out so much money during 1937 and 1938 that the state faced a deficit and cutbacks. Teachers and other state employees feared they wouldn't be paid. McGill saw a legislature unable to agree on "a tax system which is sound and fair." He was among the few who believed "Georgia is not too poor to pay for the program."[36]

There was now the likelihood that Georgians, having tried the New Deal and fallen into debt, might again succumb to Talmadge's simplistic self-help rhetoric and oppose federal programs already benefiting other states. "Those who so blindly and bitterly oppose the President," McGill wrote, "destroy their own perspective."[37]

From his capitol vantage point, McGill could see through the rhetoric and knew he spotted Talmadge's shadow. Progress was deterred, he wrote, because certain politicians, Talmadge among them, were posturing for the 1940 governor's race. Rivers could not run again because state law forbade a third consecutive two-year term. Nobody wanted to be associated with a tax increase. Talmadge, McGill chided, postured as the "original Economy Kid." Though not a legislator, Talmadge was busy doing "plenty of talking in private." But Talmadge's public stance reminded McGill of the Tar Baby in the Uncle Remus tales. As readers would recall, the Tar Baby "sat in the middle of the road and said nothing at all."[38]

In this vacuum, there was clearly an absence of capable leadership. A leader was needed to frame all possible options, and then to champion by persuasion the one that seemed best. McGill mused on leadership when he heard the question raised at a meeting of Georgia's disillusioned vegetable growers. "What are leaders?" one man asked. "A leader may expound, may insist, may teach, yet if the people will not follow he is powerless." McGill wrote, "That, of course, is true." For the next several years, he could picture for himself that role, or burden, of leader, seeking to frame the possible options for a New South while people all around chose the familiar comfort of the status quo or, worse, reverted to irrational options to restore some rear-view vision of an Old South.[39]

McGill's interest in economic solutions drew him to wherever problems surfaced. It was because of his special interest in agriculture that he went to the vegetable growers' meeting in Griffin, finding someone to chauffeur him. There, he heard not only the "warning" to growers but also solutions. Georgia lagged behind other states in sales. The reason seemed to be that other states' farmers and legislators had "worked out advertising, co-operation and grading standards." Growers had been overlooked by the Georgia legislature, but McGill urged consideration. Would their recovery also pump more money into the state? "Industry has outstripped agriculture," he conceded. "Yet industry would be trebled in its output if the farmers could buy. Not until there is a better balance between the two industries, of manufacture and agriculture, will there be a real forging ahead."[40]

The framing of domestic alternatives now preoccupied McGill. In his columns, local issues displaced events in Europe. When the German army occupied and extinguished Czechoslovakia, McGill reminded readers that he had foretold it. He had written from Vienna that Hitler would try to take the country without a war. He had predicted that other countries in Hitler's path would be occupied. He had urged support for Roosevelt's war preparedness. And he had said England eventually must fight, which is what, by summer's end, happened.

In 1939, buoyed by higher income, Ralph and Mary Elizabeth moved into a house. After bouncing around apartments (in 1938 they stayed briefly at 659 Peachtree Street), they found a tree-shaded house at 843 Myrtle Street, N.E. That summer, Virginia became ill. Preliminary tests revealed that the three year old suffered from numerous food allergies. Then she came down with scarlet fever. Each day McGill would bring home a new book, sit by her bed, and read to her. After the fever was gone, a new problem appeared. While playing outside, she fell and hurt her knee. When the knee did not heal, more tests revealed that Virginia had leukemia. The next few months were filled with fear and hope as doctors at Henrietta Egleston Hospital tried various treatments. One procedure involved transfusing "a constant flow of new blood." McGill was grateful when *Constitution* reporters, Jack Spalding and Luke Green among them, volunteered several times as blood donors. After giving blood, Spalding recalled, "McGill would buy us lunch at Herron's. That was his only child. It was great devotion, a great love." McGill wrote to his friend Tom Chubb, "They gave her a really tremendous amount of blood. . . . We do not yet know the result. . . . We are clinging to hope."[41]

At the *Constitution* McGill did not miss a day writing his column. He ridiculed the American Communist Party leader for rationalizing that Stalin's nonaggression pact with the Communists' sworn enemies, the Nazis, "is a natural one." Similarly, he mocked Hitler's tribute to Russia as an "eternal friend." Hitler, McGill scoffed, "changes 'friends' as readily as a prostitute changes beds." McGill could not understand Hitler's allies. "Japan is one. Italy is sure to leave him. Spain has withdrawn. The chancellor must know that Russia will not help him with men. Guns, yes. Food, perhaps. Raw materials, yes."[42]

When on September 1 Hitler launched the military invasion into Poland, McGill tried to make sense of the nightmare. That morning, as he often did, he rode the bus to work, eavesdropping and probing. Although "the town talked of war," the thought which inspired his day's column came from an "old negro man who sat near me asked the most pertinent question of all." The man had said, "They tell me them German people don't want no war. Now this heah man has done give it to 'em. How do he do it?"[43]

McGill thought the man's question summed up so much of what he had been writing for a year and a half about the Nazis' suppression of freedom. Hitler could not have gone to war if the press and radio had been allowed free expression. This notion that a free press could somehow inoculate a society against war had become an article of faith. "A free press belongs not to the publishers but to the people," he wrote, "and they ought jealously to guard that right."[44]

He went to the office Sunday and stood watch. The staff worked on "Extra" editions, and England and France declared war. A wire photo from London pictured Prime Minister Chamberlain taking a gas mask to the House of Commons. News arrived that Germans had torpedoed a British liner, the *Athenia,* carrying 1,400, including 246 Americans. McGill stalked the wire service room as "bells jangled, the keys of a dozen machines clattered, copy boys went from machine to machine taking the copy. . . . The telephones were busy. Great pots of coffee were brought up from a restaurant across the street. Unshaved, sleepy desk men, printers, reporters and copy readers sipped the coffee and cursed Hitler, the treaty of Versailles and hoped for an early end to Hitler." He wrote his column as dusk was coming on Atlanta and it was late evening in Paris and London. "War had come," he wrote, "to a world not nearly recovered from the world war of a few years ago."[45]

Now that war had started, McGill struggled to understand the situation. At first he adopted the newsroom's hope for "an early end to Hitler." He had thought all along that intervention by England and France would stop him. As days passed and Germany did not bomb England, there was the possibility that Hitler might bargain for peace. "I think we are seeing the beginning of the end of Hitler," he wrote on September 5. "He cannot win this war."[46]

In any case, it was not America's war. On this McGill and the editorial board agreed with Roosevelt and Congress, who were committed to neutrality. Although the sinking of the *Athenia* caused many Atlantans to telephone the newspaper offices to express "horror and indignation," McGill stated, "We can wait and see. There is no need for us to rush, or be rushed, into war. And we can remain neutral, selling to those who have ships to come and get it." Similarly, the editorial board urged that, for the present, "we must exert every effort to keep out. We have not been provoked. It is not yet our fight."[47]

That fall, as news from the war dominated the front pages of the city's three competing newspapers, deals were struck to sell both afternoon papers to a Yankee publisher. The Hearst corporation, which bought the afternoon *Atlanta Georgian* in 1912, had by 1936 extended its holdings to include twenty-eight newspapers with a daily circulation of six million, reaching about one-seventh of the readers in the country. Since 1936, largely to increase his cash flow, Hearst had reluctantly disposed of seven newspapers through mergers, sales, consolidations, and one outright closing. So it was only a mild surprise in December when it was announced that Hearst had sold his Atlanta paper, which in recent years had appeared to be struggling. Perhaps the Hearst negotiators were glad to recoup anything. They settled for a mere $180,000 and an agreement that the buyer pay off a loan balance of $80,000 on the *Georgian*'s four-story building, which was valued at $186,000.[48]

The buyer was James M. Cox, sixty-nine, publisher of newspapers in Dayton, Ohio, and Miami, Florida. Cox was a true Democrat, a former governor of Ohio, and the 1920 Democratic nominee for president with Franklin Roosevelt as his running mate. Thus, the absentee media mogul–politician from the West had been replaced by another absentee, a Yankee. Instead of Hearst, a leader among Roosevelt-bashers in 1936, the new owner was a Roosevelt New Dealer. The substitution was to have important consequences for Atlanta journalism and for McGill.

The stunning news was that Cox at the same time had also bought the more important, locally owned *Atlanta Journal* and its fifty-thousand-watt radio station, WSB. The news broke when Cox filed to buy WSB; a day later the whole deal was detailed. The story warranted a bold banner headline on the *Constitution*'s front page. Among newsmen at least, the sale upstaged the story displayed beneath it—the scheduled arrival of Vivian "Miss Scarlett" Leigh and other Hollywood stars for a parade on Peachtree Street, a Junior League ball, and the world premiere of *Gone with the Wind*.[49]

The *Journal* had been owned by Atlantans since its founding in 1881, and the latest owners, the Grays, had managed it since 1900, when lawyer James R. Gray Sr. bought it for $300,000. In 1923, Cox acquired the Miami newspaper and "hoped for a long time to get into the Atlanta field, but there were persistent difficulties." Regarding the Grays, Cox noted that there were many to deal with and "they were not newspaper-minded." At last, they accepted his offer of slightly more than $5 million for the package: $3,156,350 for the *Journal* and $1,943,685 for WSB. As a reason for selling, James R. Gray Jr. cited the "difficulties inherent in" division of control since his father's death in 1917. This would be even more difficult in the next generation when grandchildren with a stake in management "would have been scattered from Atlanta to as far away as the Pacific coast."[50]

Gray made no mention of the legal, financial, and ethical problems that beset the Gray family and made Cox's offer welcome. Many problems were linked to a sensational murder case involving a grandson of James Gray Sr., Richard Gray Gallogly. Gallogly was a student at Atlanta's Oglethorpe University when in October 1928 he drove the getaway car after two armed robberies during which another Oglethorpe student, George Harsh, shot and killed a grocery clerk and a pharmacist. The pharmacist shot Harsh in the hip. Bloody clothing found in Peachtree Creek was traced by a laundry mark. Gallogly and Harsh said they were drunk at the time. Eventually they pleaded guilty. In 1929, the gunman and driver were sentenced to life in prison.[51]

For a decade, the Grays experienced personal and public anguish. At one point they hired Ellis Arnall as a private attorney to appeal the severity of Gallogly's sentence. In 1939 Gallogly escaped to Texas, and Arnall, then attorney general and realizing his political integrity was at stake, demanded extradition. Arnall told the Texas sheriff, "If I can't have this fellow legally I'm going to kidnap him." The entire episode drained the family's finances and, some readers felt, compromised journalistic objectivity. "Everything they did," recalled Jack Spalding, "was taken as something to get Dick Gallogly out of jail. And that is why the Grays sold."[52]

The sale to a Yankee publisher further diminished the *Journal's* reputation. Cox's first statement assured readers that the *Journal* would "remain a free newspaper, above coercion by any interest." There was ample evidence, however, of the newspaper's tilt on national issues such as the New Deal. President Roosevelt telegrammed Cox with "hearty congratulations as you enlarge your activities and broaden the field of your influence." In an editorial, the *Constitution* noted the *Journal's* contributions since 1881 in building Atlanta and welcomed Cox as a good omen: "It is reason for self-congratulation by all Georgians that a man of his business acumen had been so impressed by the opportunities within the state." In a house advertisement that week, the *Constitution* underscored that it was now the only locally owned daily. "From editor to copy-boy," it read, "the morning paper always has been and always will be southern as a platter of hot biscuit [*sic*]." A few days later another advertisement featured McGill, who wrote a tribute to his hardworking news staff. A strip at the bottom emphasized local ownership: the *Constitution* was "An Independent Georgia Newspaper, Georgia Owned and Georgia Edited."[53]

Within days of the deal, Cox announced without elaboration that he was closing the *Georgian* and its Sunday *Georgian-American* beginning December 18. The *Georgian's* comics, features, news, and services, as well as its subscription and advertiser lists would be transferred to the *Journal*. Consolidation was a shrewd business move. In one stroke, Cox eliminated his evening competition and strengthened the *Journal*. The closing was consistent with a trend in the newspaper industry that had been thinning out competition in major cities. That same day in Chattanooga, editor John Fort Milton told the city and his 149 employees that the *News* was closing, leaving Chattanooga with one morning and one afternoon paper.[54]

The *Georgian's* closing displaced most of its 450 employees a week before Christmas. To ease the shock, Cox paid a "dismissal bonus," severance pay that varied according to years of service. Some workers found jobs on the other papers. The *Journal* hired Ed Danforth, the popular sports editor. At the *Constitution,* McGill used his influence to hire Harold Martin, who since graduation from the University of Georgia in 1933 had been writing sports and features for the *Georgian.* Martin quickly became a star reporter, and during the next thirty years he and McGill, twelve years older, became the best of friends.[55]

It was fitting that Cox shared the headlines that week with *Gone with the Wind.* The publisher and the movie stars were all celebrities, though of a different cut. Cox's arrival symbolized the opportunities of a New South every bit as much as the film romanticized the Old South. The movie, McGill wrote, would make people weep. He concluded that it was a "mistake" to think the Old South was "gone with the wind. There is something left of that old South." It was "a strength" derived from development apart from the rest of the nation, "having escaped large foreign populations; having been treated by the government of the United States as a colonial possession." The truth about slaveholding in the South had been distorted, McGill said, quoting some statistics in a new book by Raleigh editor Josephus Daniels. Although there were 3.8 million slaves in 1850, the great plantation owners holding more than 200 slaves numbered fewer than 300. The largest slave-owning class was comprised of the 77,000 southerners who owned only 1 each.[56]

There was praise for everyone associated with *Gone with the Wind.* A *Constitution* editorial contended that Margaret "Peggy" Mitchell, a friend of McGill's, had done something for her city, "surpassed by none of the great citizens who came before her." For personal reasons, McGill wrote his thanks to the movie stars who helped make a success of the Junior League charity ball. One of the benefiting charities was Henrietta Egleston Hospital, where three-year-old Virginia was born and now lay gravely ill. "Those who knew Ralph," Harold Martin wrote, "realized how much of his own private suffering went into these lines." McGill wrote:

> I wish the Junior League might have an *annual* ball with movie stars in attendance, so that the sound of dancing and of music might resound every year and be translated into bandages and medicines, and the care of nurses and the relief of pain and

suffering by little children. The real charities after all are those
which touch the lives of the very young, and the old who are
helpless and cannot do for themselves.

It is difficult to discuss them without becoming, perhaps,
a bit too emotional. Yet we may know that in the years ahead
there will be mothers and fathers . . . who will thank God for
those merry dancing feet.[57]

At Egleston, doctors staving off the leukemia had done all they could for
Virginia. On December 19, she died not yet four years old. The next day
Ralph and Mary Elizabeth buried her in Westview Cemetery near their
first daughter. After months of strain, they both came near a breaking
point, where everything—dolls, toys, photographs—reminded them of
her. Martin recalled that Ralph in his grief worried more for Mary Elizabeth, who "took the form not of withdrawal from life, but an almost
reckless gaity." McGill wrote to Tom Chubb, "It was a ghastly six months
which produced a breakdown for Mary Elizabeth and a near one for me."
When friends in later years referred to her "bad drinking problem," they
associated it with the loss of her two children and to "many miscarriages,"
about which almost nothing was said outside the home.[58]

Ralph was so distraught he could not write. Other staffers, Jack
Spalding among them, each contributed a "One Word More" column
during what the editors explained was McGill's "absence from the
office." Ralph and Mary Elizabeth left town for Christmas, hoping a
change of scenery would help. Somehow they made it to the Mississippi, then went south into Louisiana's Cajun country. Soon his compulsion forced him to write a column. His emotions were raw, and he
wept easily, as when he viewed the halls and galleries and gardens of
an antebellum mansion near Nachez and thought of that lost civilization. "You will stand there," he said, "and inexplicable tears will run
down your cheeks." The nostalgia and sorrow, he said, are "not for a
system which was based on the production of one crop with slave
labor, but for a time and civilization which was, in some aspects, the
finest this nation ever knew."

Now writing every day, his columns traced their journey into
Louisiana's bayous and Cajun country. There McGill found solace in

St. Martinsville's crayfish bisque and in the bronze statue to Emmeline Labiche, the Acadian girl of Longfellow's "Evangeline." On Christmas Eve they were in New Iberia, sitting by a window in a hotel dining room. Outside, Acadian children amused him as they ran along the sidewalks tossing firecrackers, laughing shrilly, and shouting in their French patois. This other world seemed to sooth him and give him something new to think about. Travel had always done this for him, confirming his lifelong instinct for wanderlust. "There are so many countries in America," he wrote. "One must travel to find them."[59]

7

Taking on the Talmadge Machine

Ralph and I were very close friends. We were together.
We agreed on 90 percent of everything. I conferred
with him a lot about what to do and what not to do,
about positions. He was very effective. He helped me
in projecting on a lot of the speeches that I made.
—Ellis Arnall, 1987

From such conditions dictators are created.
—*Constitution* editorial likening Talmadge
to Hitler and Mussolini, 1942

Throughout his life McGill found solace and comfort in his work. Often he stayed in his office well into the morning, until there was nothing on the radio and he could think with only the sound of a "purring fan going and an occasional truck rattling down the street." One engaging aspect of journalism was its capacity for distraction. Having taken on the world as his concern, there was always something imminent and important to diminish personal problems. At night McGill would read the late news that would be in the morning paper and write a column that responded immediately. In the night, too, he kept up with increasing correspondence and wrote ahead to create an inventory of columns that would appear daily despite his travels. He liked this stillness, "when the presses have stopped, when the streets are quiet, when the only bright spot to be seen from the fourth floor window is George and Angelo's all-night restaurant across the street."[1]

For some time he had been worrying about his father. Ben McGill's health had been failing, but he kept working as the heating company's secretary-treasurer until 1936, when at age sixty-eight he retired after more than thirty years' service. Ralph went home as often as possible to visit him, his mother, and sisters, but he regretted that he could not be closer. "I never did know much of my father's dream, hopes and disappointments," he later wrote. "I was, I guess, too much occupied with my own." In 1940 Ben suffered double attacks of pneumonia. Ralph got there before he sank into a coma and died in August. He was seventy-two. Ralph felt the loss of the one who "early encouraged me to read books" and was "borrowing the money for my tuition each year and somehow managing to pay it back." Ralph recalled his father as "inclined to be dogmatic in his views" with a "streak of stubbornness in him, as well as brooding, but these moods were always short."[2]

The day after the funeral, he learned the "sad" story of "one of my father's defeated dreams." In a storage chest he found the copies of Blackstone's *Commentaries,* each with his father's signature on the flyleaf.

"What about these?" he asked his mother.

When she finished telling him, they both wept. "Your father bought them with the first money he earned," she said, "long before we were married. He told me he had read them there at the farm, but it was no use. One had to be in a lawyer's office for some instruction. . . . I tried to persuade him to find some attorney who would give him some help, but he shook his head and put them away. He would not discuss them again."[3] If she told him also about the tragedy at Chattanooga University, Ralph never mentioned it.

In journalism he found none of the heartache that wracked his personal life. As a writer he could address grievances, mobilize the community to help the helpless. If anyone offended Georgia or the South or the New Deal he could take to his typewriter and, come morning, his retort would be on doorsteps and at breakfast tables and echo through the day in corporate board rooms and county courthouses and the capitol cloakrooms. More often than not, he was articulating what people had on their minds but had not yet said.

By 1940 his newspaper readership had grown substantially. The faithful who followed him from the sports pages had been joined by new readers, among them the community's business and political elite, attracted by his range and repertoire. As before, he mixed his offerings, changing pace or shifting levels. He would write a few columns about state politics, about the failure to deal with the state's $40 million deficit or Gene Talmadge's apparent lead early in the 1940 governor's race. For variety he turned to national politics, which in 1940 meant the debate over a third term for Roosevelt, the next steps for the New Deal, advocacy of military preparedness, and denunciation of "appeasers." Across the oceans, there was always the war. During 1940 it grew nasty as the German army flanked the Maginot line, trampled France, began months of bombing England, and now seemed clearly to threaten America.

McGill's approach to subjects and his style of persuasion evidenced deep convictions. Far from being random in attacking issues, his editorial columns as a whole reveal, as rhetoric scholar Calvin Logue concluded, "stock values that guided his choices and actions. These were honor, integrity, intellectual honesty, decency, human dignity, common justice, civil liberties, opportunity, and promise." His experience as a southerner in the Bible belt, in both Unionist East Tennessee and the secessionist South, informed his sense of morality and his awareness of what was worth keeping and what needed to be changed. On the subject of race relations, he sympathized with southerners who were still angry and suffering from the aftereffects of their history: from slavery, the Civil War, and Reconstruction, from political suppression and economic deprivation. Logue identified six basic beliefs that influenced the advice McGill as editor offered on race relations over three decades, beginning in the late 1930s: (1) individuals and governments should pursue policies that are feasible, (2) laws should be obeyed, (3) free individuals have a moral responsibility to oppose wrong, (4) education is requisite to individual and community progress, (5) all persons should be granted the rights and privileges of full citizenship, and (6) southern states should ensure the rights and privileges of their own citizens.[4]

Added to this was another appealing characteristic of his writing—his voice, the sound of his words and phrases. He had not become the poet he once aspired to be, but as a sports writer he had found a prose rhythm in the alternation of long and short sentences. His cadences also evoked the mood of oral storytelling. At other times his prose was prayerful. In most columns he practiced a "reasoned, low-key pleading," said his friend Harold Martin, who in 1940 was writing his own wistful column for the editorial pages, aptly titled "Dreams and Dust." On occasion, however, McGill would raise his voice and unmercifully attack his prey, notably anti–New Dealers and shortsighted politicians, Talmadge in particular. Martin, who came to understand his friend as well as anyone, said McGill's occasional outbursts sprang from "a sense of outrage. . . . [His] voice became harsh and angry, and his words were like fire and heavy hammers." On such occasions, McGill's philosophy was pugilism. "Sometimes," he told Martin, "you have to step out in the center of the ring and hit them in the nose." Martin believed the key to understanding McGill was that he was "a man of good and decent instincts and stubborn courage speaking with the voice of reason in a violent time."[5]

Few people angered him more in 1940 than "appeasers" in Congress who practiced "Chamberlainism here at home." "Hitler laughs," he wrote after the Germans had taken France. "Don't they see," he asked, that Germany, Italy, Russia, and Japan "would like to loot us? They will, if they can." When opponents of preparedness claimed Thomas Jefferson would have agreed with them, McGill said the country should give Senator Arthur Vandenberg, Senator Burton K. Wheeler, and others of their camp "coonskin cap and flintlock muskets and send them out against tanks and flame-throwers. . . . Especially do I object to those who are so intimately in touch with the ectoplasm of Jefferson's mind."[6]

McGill remembered that it took eighteen months to get ready after war was declared in 1917. His own marine unit was still in training near Washington and he was still enjoying the thrill of being around the wartime capital when the war ended. Of course, American units had been rushed into battle and some of these had met catastrophe. He retold a story about a night battle at Château-Thierry in which a unit of New Englanders were found dead in groups because they "didn't know what to do when caught in shell fire." There was another story about a unit of twenty young Americans in which eighteen perished because they had not enough training in using gas masks. What harm then could there be in accelerating military training? "As an old Marine," he wrote in August during the German bombing of London, "I can think of nothing finer for the young man than a period of training at Parris Island with an old-time marine corps top sergeant in charge."[7]

To those in Congress and elsewhere who criticized the press, he warned that they played into the hands of dictators. In Vienna he had seen Hitler's press strategy. Had no one else learned the lesson? "I wish some of the critics of newspapers would recall," he instructed, "that the first thing any dictator does when he takes a country is to take over its press and begin to use it." Far from being a nuisance or a danger, the press was "the greatest protector of freedom and liberty the people possess."[8]

In July, preparedness was one of the major issues when McGill went to Chicago to report on his first Democratic National Convention. Two months earlier, Roosevelt had asked Congress for $2.5 billion to expand the army and navy and proposed building fifty thousand airplanes a year. In June Congress complied by passing a National Defense Tax Bill providing almost $1 billion a year. The Georgia delegation, McGill reported, supported the move toward preparedness, as well as a third term for Roosevelt and the New Deal. A month earlier in Philadelphia McGill had covered the Republican anti–New Dealers when they nominated Wendell L. Willkie. The battle lines seemed clearly drawn. "It is to be the New Deal principles against the anti–New Deal principles."[9]

As the Democratic platform was being drafted, an effort was made to declare support for a federal antilynching law. Congress had twice suppressed antilynching bills in 1919 and 1934 because of opposition by southern senators. The issue now threatened the solidarity of the Democratic Party, as McGill saw it. He congratulated the "excellent work" of Roy Harris, the political kingmaker from Augusta and head of the Georgia delegation. Harris's backroom maneuvers kept an antilynch plank out of the platform. "Such a plank," McGill declared, "would swing many Southern states to Willkie."[10]

Lynching haunted the soul. It drove McGill to become a southern apologist and defender. He could agree with the National Association for the Advancement of Colored People (NAACP) that lynching was an abomination, murder. But he was inclined to see it in larger scope, as a scourge upon the South. Here was a sickness that must be remedied, yet without subjecting the patient to unnecessary processes, such as federal intervention. He reasoned that by 1940 so few southerners resorted to lynching that one could say the practice was "disappearing." He credited the "pressure of public opinion on law enforcement." When a sheriff stood up to a lynch mob or a grand jury indicted members of their own community, they elicited rejoicing from McGill's typewriter. The South, he would say, could eliminate this scourge on its own. But when a mob struck with fresh, heinous vengeance, it caused McGill to lament anew, not only for the victims but because "our northern critics have new weapons."[11]

A few weeks after the Chicago convention, a Gallup Poll showed Willkie leading Roosevelt in electoral votes, 304 to 227. The same day, McGill assuaged Democrats' fears. It was not that he distrusted George Gallup's pollsters. On the contrary, Gallup had correctly predicted Senator George's victory over Talmadge and Camp in 1938 "with a very small percentage of error." In 1939, McGill met Gallup when he attended the annual Georgia Press Institute in Athens and explained new polling techniques.[12]

One key was that Gallup understood Georgia's county-unit system. The state's election law tilted power to the rural areas despite the growing population of the medium-sized and large cities. The county-unit rule awarded victory to the candidate who won the most counties, not the most votes statewide. A bloc of 3 sparsely settled counties—and there were many among the 159—counted the same as booming Fulton County. Also, Gallup's pollsters sought opinions from a "cross-section" of voters, "not just those with automobiles," McGill noted. Gallup kept his workers busy up to the eve of the election, having learned from the mistake *Literary Digest* made in 1936, when it quit too soon and predicted that Alf Landon would beat Roosevelt. The *Constitution* published the Gallup Poll with confidence, said McGill, because it represents "what America is thinking."[13]

The latest poll showing Willkie with more electoral votes might be accurate for July, but McGill reminded readers that, four years earlier, Landon had led in electoral votes at the same time but "lost it by September." Besides, the same poll showed Roosevelt ahead in the popular vote 51 to 49 percent. The anti-Roosevelt forces, he assured, still consisted of the same old anti–New Dealers joined by the "bolters" opposed to a third term. "The same thing is true in Georgia," he wrote. "Their voices mean nothing."[14]

In Georgia that summer, the chief anti–New Dealer returned to the race. Though he had lost his runs for the U.S. Senate in 1936 and 1938, Talmadge was determined to win a third term as governor. In 1939 he organized fifteen of his close friends to promote his candidacy and set up speeches. Judging the race in the summer of 1940, McGill observed that "at the quarter pole Mr. Talmadge seems to be out in front."[15]

Talmadge had several advantages. Three lesser-knowns running for the Democratic nomination would splinter the vote among them. Talmadge was the known candidate. He projected the strength people might be seeking in a world menaced by war and in a state endangered by Rivers's deficit. Then, too, Talmadge usually commanded a loyal bloc of about one hundred thousand votes. "In his hey-dey," said his son, Herman, "one third of the people of his state would have followed him to the Gates of Hell." In July McGill wrote that Talmadge "with the usual supply of human faults and virtues, remains one of the outstanding characters in Georgia's political history, carrying on in the old manner of the late Tom Watson, with a personal following . . . intact through the years." Some Georgia politicians, sensing a likely Talmadge victory, negotiated through Herman to soften Gene and liberalize his platform. On July 11 a group of prominent New Dealers announced support for Talmadge, telling the *Atlanta Journal* that "Gene was on the wrong side of the fence . . . but he's okay now."[16]

Two weeks later, McGill interviewed Talmadge. They met in a downtown hotel, probably the Henry Grady, the "Talmadge hotel." The interview was in the lobby and it was brief.

Talmadge had had an operation for hemorrhoids and his foes speculated about his health. At a riotous rally at Warm Springs the previous weekend he had arrived late and left early on doctor's orders. To McGill, the former governor looked "OK," though he seemed weak from the operation. "He never suffers from an excess of acids, since he pours them over his foes in the accepted Talmadge manner."[17]

What about the accusation that Talmadge was flirting with Willkie? Had his bitterness toward New Deal politics driven him to "Republicanism"? Back in the '36 campaign Richard Russell had talked about "Old Republican Gene." Talmadge denied it. He was, he said, a "party man"— Democratic Party. Who was the prisoner whom Talmadge said he planned to pardon? Was the Gray family asking for Dick Gallogly? No identification now, said Talmadge. Not even his closest aides knew the name.[18]

McGill learned little from Talmadge. Not that he expected anything. That summer, all four candidates spoke in generalities. They
promised to maintain education and pay teachers, pay off the debt
(Talmadge opposed a sales tax), control highway extravagances, and
continue some of Rivers's social programs which had become popular.
Talmadge also promised to protect counties against a consolidation
bill, to encourage the development of natural resources, and to advocate a single motor vehicle license plate for each family.[19]

McGill accused them all of avoiding specifics and ducking tough
issues. What about the national defense plan? Talmadge said only that
the state should cooperate with the federal government as war approached.
McGill asked: What about Washington? What of Willkie? National
affairs? "Surely Georgia, as one of the states, must participate." The provincialism seemed related to "a national complacency" that reminded
him of France's Maginot line. The French had been satisfied with a static
defense, and that spring the Germans had simply gone around it. In Georgia, McGill believed the issues would never be discussed because the candidates had "developed a cynicism about the sincerity of the people
themselves and their interest in government."[20]

A fistfight at the Warm Springs rally on July 27 clobbered any possibility of a debate. The candidates had fervent supporters, some of whom
had come from other cities. The fight broke out when Talmadge arrived
and his faithful shouted, drowning out a speech by Abit Nix. On stage,
Talmadge cried, "That's a Nix man that started that fight. That's the type
of people he brought over." After they had "swapped punches and
scrambled a few noses," McGill said, the loser was the voters. "Heckling
and skull and fist engagements will break up the custom" of debating
and invites critics to "ridicule" Georgia politics. As the Democratic primary neared, McGill continued to lament that the candidates "still have
not yet clearly told the people how they will wipe out the more than
$40,000,000 indebtedness," nor about plans for promoting public health,
paying for a seven-month school term, and providing social services.[21]

Details did not seem to trouble the voters. Talmadge was "getting
the crowds," McGill noted. "He always has got them and likely always
will." In September Talmadge triumphed easily, with 179,882 popular
votes and 320 county-unit votes. His nearest opponent, Columbus

Roberts, polled 124,858 and 78 unit votes. Nix got only 42,534 votes and 12 units. What could McGill say? Well, Talmadge "is always . . . Talmadge," whose "direct honesty" men appreciate. Any analysis of the governor's success, McGill wrote, had to credit him with "that quality that makes men want to follow him, to fight for him, to defend him." He didn't say so, but he had seen similar devotion in the zeal of Nazi storm troopers willing to die for the Führer. The spectacle of the Nazis, their blind allegiance to Hitler, and their trampling of civil rights had given him a look into the darkest side of human nature, never to be forgotten.[22]

The 1940 election so disturbed McGill that he now defended the state poll tax as a protection against tyrants. Georgia was among eight states from Virginia to Texas that still taxed the right to vote. Repeal had become a liberal cause, spurred by the Southern Conference on Human Welfare. In November, the Georgia League of Women Voters invited an advocate of repeal to speak at its Atlanta conference. The ensuing debate put the sessions an hour behind schedule. McGill scoffed in horror. Abolishing the poll tax was no democratic panacea: "It won't cure the ills of government. It will exaggerate them." McGill reminded that "idealists" were always talking about "the large number of those whom they term apathetic boobs who vote like sheep" or don't vote. "I never quite understood why there should be such a whooping up of a crusade to bring more such boobs into the balloting booths. The cold fact is that it would not assist democracy one whit but would exaggerate the evils we have by putting more persons into them."[23]

After witnessing Talmadge's resurgence, McGill thought Georgia was unprepared for more of the same. Insisting that "there is no more ardent Democrat than I" and "no one believes more in the wisdom of the people than I," he nevertheless argued for a limited electorate. Repeal "would plunge the state into more woes than one can imagine." North Carolina's "poll-taxless voters," he said, helped elect an arch isolationist senator, Robert R. Reynolds. "The worst political machines in the nation exist in states where there is no poll tax," he noted. "There is no improvement in government or democracy or interest in the ballot in the states which have removed the poll tax." Conveniently, he overlooked exceptions. In

1937 Florida repealed the poll tax because local gambling and racing interests in Miami manipulated the system, frustrating state officials.[24]

McGill also assailed the repealers, making them seem as noxious as his Tennessee ginks. They were impractical "idealists" who "toss off some nice phrases about trusting government to the masses and accepting their verdict." Repealers were "the boys" who "keep talking about something which may be true in the good year 2980." They were "ambitious and inexperienced crusaders." They were "medicine men" selling "Poll Tax Abolishment Bitters hawked from the back of a theorist's wagon." Or they were able, well-meaning, but dangerous editorial writers rightfully bemoaning voter apathy but "breast-beating" so loud for the wrong remedy that they could substitute in the Ringling circus "if Gargantua ever becomes ill."[25]

McGill justified the tax as a citizenship fee. Voting was not a right but a "privilege," he said, which "ought to carry with it some direct contribution to government." The poll tax was such a contribution. The tax in Georgia was one dollar a year. This was small enough, he reasoned, "and if there be those who are unwilling to contribute less than a third of a cent per day for the privilege of casting a ballot, I am not at all interested in fighting for their privilege to vote." Again, conveniently, he disregarded the repealers' argument that the tax was doubly punitive because it was *cumulative*. An older person voting for the first time had to pay the accumulated tax for each year, up to fifteen dollars.[26]

As McGill portrayed it, the tax was not a racial issue. Its original purpose, however, had been to disfranchise blacks. The cumulative tax became, as one scholar noted, "the most effective remedy for preventing blacks from voting." Thus in 1940 anyone seeking to abolish the poll tax was construed to be pro-Negro. Yet, liberals argued, the poll tax was not racial in that it also screened out poor whites.[27]

Liberals saw poll tax repeal as the key to political and social reform. Extension of the vote had already proven effective in swamping old ways of doing politics. In 1934 Huey Long defeated Louisiana's poll tax to break the hold of local sheriffs. In Tennessee, the "Boss" Crump machine lined up against repeal, which was advocated by the *Nashville Tennessean,* the rival to the conservative *Banner*. In Alabama, the *Montgomery Advertiser* stated the conservative case bluntly: Repeal "would arm the dispossessed with a political power that the responsible citizens cannot afford to grant. [It] would invest the pauperized thousands of our people with the balance of power in Alabama politics." McGill raised the same specter, that repeal would open flood gates, enfranchising masses of unqualified voters; they would make Georgia prey to manipulative demagogues and bosses straight out of "the black pages of corruption." The ship of state was already in flames. "My position," wrote McGill, "is somewhat akin to that of the boy who stood on the burning deck from whence all but he had fled."[28]

Although McGill would years later lament the use of the "states' rights" phrase by segregationists, in 1939 he found it useful and justified in opposing a federal voting law. That year, despairing of any action by the states," the SCHW persuaded a California Democrat to sponsor a *federal* repeal bill. While the bill lay in a House committee, McGill argued the conservative line on states' rights. Voting rights "must be a state matter." Simply put, "Georgia is not ready for it." Any action now, particularly an unpopular federal law, would "exaggerate the evils we have." He then articulated the view which in essence guided his thinking for the coming decade on all matters of civil rights: "Never forget this one fundamental fact—legislation cannot go ahead of the capacity of the people to absorb and execute it. If it does, it fails. That is the one infallible rule of history."[29]

There was a similarity between this position and his opposition to a federal antilynching law. In both cases, federal action reeked of a return to the Reconstruction era. Those egregious acts of radical Republican lawmakers in Washington who dictated the political life of the defeated and war-ravaged South—saying who could vote and who was banned from running for office—horrified generations of southern whites. Georgia had not been ready to extend the vote to newly freed slaves, so federal law and federal troops in 1867 forced it. After the first election, as one native historian put it, "well might the hearts of Georgians have been sickened at the sight of those elected."[30]

For decades, the "ominous shadow of negro domination" dominated southern politics. In the 1890s this "bugaboo" doomed Tom Watson's radical democratic populism. Watson much later enjoyed a political resurrection only after he "abandoned his old dream of uniting both races against the enemy" and instead advocated means to "perpetuate white supremacy in Georgia." Whether advocating a grass-roots electorate or, later, disfranchisement of the Negro, Watson and other southern political leaders found authority by quoting the great, enigmatic southern democrat who had been a slave owner, Thomas Jefferson. Eugene Talmadge continued the tradition of using Jefferson's antifederalist rhetoric, in his case as ammunition against the New Deal.[31]

The voters' choice of Talmadge soon proved fateful for McGill's career. Talmadge had built his political base on the strength of his personality and voice. In the midst of trouble and doubt he exuded a fierce, gutsy courage. When his personal instincts clashed with others' personalities or views, Talmadge trusted himself. He seldom compromised, whether the foe was an old friend, Clark Howell Jr., or the president of the United States. This instinct for combat had helped make him governor again in 1940, but it soon drove him to a collide with social and political forces headed in an opposite direction. His dirt farmer habit of wielding power like an ax made him a target for McGill and an increasing number of editorialists.

Ostensibly Talmadge in 1940 buried the ax he had used to menace the New Deal. He sent his son Herman to give that pledge to Roosevelt. Yet privately the governor still begrudged Roosevelt. His anti-Roosevelt feelings festered as the president diverted loans to Britain, a policy Talmadge knew made no sense to poor and hungry farmers. Isolationist, from a white-America-first perspective, Talmadge warned that "America cannot take the stand of being permanent guard for Europe." He argued that the United States shouldn't fear attack from Hitler. "If you lead a bulldog around with you nobody is likely to jump on you."[32]

McGill easily found a moral high ground from which to battle Talmadge. He fused two causes into one, equating party loyalty with national security. Indelible memories of Germany and Austria turned McGill away from isolationists. In the last war he had voted with his feet by leaving school to train with the marines. Now, proud memories stiffened him to fight for Roosevelt. From this patriotic high ground, he sniped at the enemy. He castigated any "selfish forces" who were "seeking to beat Roosevelt because they know he must have unity. . . . They seek to create disunity. We will beat them. Never forget that we are fighting to make it a better world for all the people." The escalation of war in 1941 proved that the president (and McGill) understood the challenge and proper response.[33]

The most contentious battle in Georgia that year was over control of the state's universities. Georgia had chartered the country's first state university and, ever since, its governors had played a role in guiding policy. In the late 1930s, Rivers's reforms aimed to slow down the exodus of Georgia high school graduates bound for better colleges. To upgrade, the board of regents approved hiring more educators from out of state. New teachers and administrators with different outlooks soon advanced progressive ideas.

By 1941 the newcomers breached the silence about segregation, the "situation." At the regents' request, the new dean of the University of Georgia's College of Education, Walter D. Cocking, studied Negro college education. Cocking recommended that Negro students be permitted to use some of the better facilities reserved for white students, at separate times. This proposal soon became distorted. As McGill unraveled it, a teacher who had been dismissed from the university charged that Cocking "advocated a campus where graduate white and colored students would study the state's educational problems. More than thirty others, attending the same meeting, did not hear the statement. The dean had denied it." Rumors sparked a wildfire of fear. Soon the whole state was confronting the monster specter, race mixing.[34]

Talmadge seized the moment and fanned the race issue, casting himself as defender of segregation, as decreed by the state constitution. His supporters would fight the "furriners" to defend Georgia. McGill accused him of manufacturing the issue with a eye on beating Russell for the Senate in 1942. "He stoops to it, when the going is hard," McGill wrote. He had "cooked up" the Negro issue in the 1936 Senate race against Russell. "He used then to say, privately, that he knew it was not an issue but that there were enough 'backwoods' people in Georgia who would believe it." In his pitch to poor whites, Talmadge, as one biographer noted, "would allude to the black in the most patronizing or derisive terms. Racism had been a part of his career, but it was far from crucial prior to the 1940s." In 1941 and 1942, McGill concluded, racism "got out of hand."[35]

The issue flared in 1941 when Talmadge used his leverage as a member of the board of regents to fire two educators. The first was Cocking; the second was Dr. Marvin S. Pittman, the progressive president of the Georgia Teachers College at Statesboro, who was accused by one teacher of engaging in "local partisan politics." McGill called Talmadge's allegations "a lot of palm readings or stuff dreamed up out of an angry mind." The regents approved the action, but the president of the University of Georgia objected, calling the charges false. After a hearing for Cocking at which witnesses supported him, enough regents changed their votes to reinstate him, eight to seven. It was a reversal Talmadge would not accept. "When Gene Talmadge got excited about something," his son Herman recalled, "no force in heaven or earth, short of death itself, could quiet him down."[36]

Talmadge immediately escalated the confrontation. Roosevelt in the 1930s had failed to pack the Supreme Court with cronies favorable to New Deal legislation, but now Talmadge felt he could get away with the same tactic on the board of regents. He demanded the resignations of two regents. One was an old friend. The other, however, was the publisher of the *Constitution,* Clark Howell Jr. Wasting no time, Talmadge barged into the newspaper office and made his demand. Howell agreed to write a letter. Talmadge wanted it at once. "Get your secretary," he ordered. Within hours Talmadge had packed the regents.[37]

Talmadge's advisers, including his wife, would claim they cautioned him that dismissing the regents would backfire. His closest adviser, Jim Peters, warned that intervention risked loss of accreditation for the universities and the lifelong animosity of a newspaperman: "You can fire Lucian [Goodrich] 'cause he's your classmate, and he won't get mad or do anything, but if you fire Clark Howell he will be your political enemy as long as he lives." Talmadge proceeded, undeterred. "This accreditation you're talking about is just an incident," he told Peters. "It'll be one hell of an incident before you get through with it!" Peters said.[38]

Talmadge framed the issue as a test of the governor's powers. Rather than back off, he raised the stakes. Seeking a victory with visibility, he arranged a public hearing in the state house of representatives, where the galleries were packed with his supporters hooting approval. It seemed to one historian like "an athletic event with a noisy crowd on the sidelines." Public opinion, however, seemed lined up against Talmadge.[39]

The confrontation exposed and confirmed Georgia's embrace of racism. The chancellor of the university system and the president of the University of Georgia denied any efforts to violate the state constitution by mingling whites and Negroes. Despite his dislike of Talmadge, McGill publicly conceded that segregation was the will of the people as well as the law. "It is simply fantastic," he wrote, "to think that anyone would, in Georgia or any other southern state, attempt to have racial co-education. The Negroes themselves don't want it. White people don't." The newly constituted board of regents gave Talmadge what he wanted. They voted ten to five to fire Cocking and Pittman. The event became a defining moment for everyone involved.[40]

Rather than gaining ground, the governor lost it. The news triggered a chain of events and the "hell of an incident" Peters envisioned. The confrontation escalated to the national level, where Georgia's governor looked like an outlaw. Accrediting agencies and educational associations investigated. The Southern Association of College and Schools concluded in 1941 that the governor had tampered improperly with academic freedom and educational integrity. Until the situation was remedied, Georgia's colleges would lose accreditation and its students could not transfer credits, forcing Georgia's brightest students to start college out of state. Parents complained to Talmadge. He answered defensively, "We credit our own schools down here." Refusing to budge, Talmadge carried the issue into an election year. In 1942, rather than challenge Russell for the Senate, Talmadge decided to seek a fourth term as governor.

The Democrat who emerged as Talmadge's rival for governor was the young attorney general, Ellis Arnall. Talmadge had helped Arnall along in politics, but the two men clashed visibly in 1941 when Arnall refused to justify Talmadge's packing of the board of regents. Arnall, only thirty-five in 1942, easily won backing from key power brokers, not the least of whom was Clark Howell Jr. and other newspaper publishers eager to settle the university mess. Equally crucial to his political ambitions, Arnall developed a discreet friendship with the new publisher of the *Atlanta Journal,* James M. Cox. After 1939 the two men met during Cox's frequent visits to Atlanta. Their friendship took on the trappings of a conspiracy. Arnall would slip away to see the publisher in his suite in the Biltmore Hotel on West Peachtree Street. Both men agreed their meetings had to be secret, Arnall said, because in the South Cox was an "outsider" from Ohio, a meddler.[41]

Not surprisingly, Arnall's most articulate advocate and closest confidante in the 1942 campaign was McGill. The two had been friends since Tennessee days and now, with Howell's blessing, McGill set out to make Arnall governor. The strategy came straight from Henry Grady's political playbook. In the 1880s Grady played the role of kingmaker, securing the election of governors and U.S. senators who favored Atlanta's interests and secreting messages to his candidates in a now-revealed secret code by which words stood for other words. McGill, preferring the telephone to a code, differed in one significant way: while Grady remained a kingmaker behind the scenes, McGill relished the spotlight, championing his candidate and castigating the opponent in the full glare of his signed column. "Ralph and I were very close friends," Arnall said. "We agreed on 90 percent of everything." Their meetings continued, but they also talked frequently by phone. "I conferred with him a lot about what to do and what not to do, about positions. He was very effective. He helped me in projecting on a lot of the speeches that I made."[42]

Together they set strategy and tactics. The main spike, which McGill and Arnall pounded relentlessly, was the salvation of the university system. Talmadge had held his ground, insisting he was protecting the universities from the threat of racial coeducation. McGill and Arnall made that issue stick to him like an Uncle Remus tar baby. "He stuck himself with a fake issue in this campaign and it is embarrassing," McGill wrote. "He doesn't believe in it himself, but he is stuck with it." The bottom line was whether Talmadge's use of power had devalued every diploma. "That was the whole issue," Arnall said. "Now, Talmadge tried to get into the *race* issue but the university issue overshadowed it—whether we were going to leave the educators free to teach or whether the politicians were going to tell them what to teach and how to teach."[43]

They could heap on other issues. Talmadge had pardoned so many prisoners under questionable circumstances that it might be called a racket. The governor was also suspected of playing too freely with the state's $60 million budget. The charge that he created hundreds of jobs for political supporters carried weight as well. Beyond that, McGill planned to remind voters of Talmadge's opposition to Social Security and his vetoes over the years—the old-age pension bill, the free-school-books law, and the seven-months school law.

McGill and Arnall agreed to portray Talmadge as a dictator. The analogy between Hitler's Aryan supremacy and Talmadge's "Hitlerian" racial politics had been drawn earlier in the national press. McGill had saved a 1941 editorial headlined "Hitler in Georgia," written for a Catholic review. The editorialist observed that the "Governor will tolerate no teacher in its State University who dissents from the proposition that the white man is by nature the superior of the black man." Referring to "the Governor of Georgia and his local petty Fuehrers," the writer observed that what Americans may denounce abroad, they may tolerate at home: "Sometimes it seems to us that the chief difference between bigots in the South and bigots in the North, is that the Southern bigots are more vocal. We protest Hitler's theory of race supremacy with poor grace when we reduce it to practice in the United States."[44]

In a decade of dictators, dictatorship seemed the apt yoke to throw around Talmadge's neck. "We were at war then," Arnall recalled, "and I used it right down to the line. Talmadge said I talked so much about dictatorship, why didn't I join the army." On the stump Arnall answered, "I said if they want me to fight home-grown dictators, then elect me governor." As the label stuck, they repeated it: "We don't want a home-grown dictator." A *Constitution* editorial referring to Talmadge's use of state police powers and free spending noted that "from such conditions dictators are created." Newspaper political cartoons portrayed Talmadge resembling Hitler, and even some photographs managed to convey the same image. "The way his [Talmadge's] hair hung down," Arnall mused, "he looked like him." The comparison was assisted by Talmadge's earlier misguided admiration for Japan and Nazi Germany (he admitted he had read Hitler's *Mein Kampf* seven times). And he did not wholly disagree with the comparison. "I'm what you call a minor dictator," he reflected in later years. "But did you ever see anybody that was much good who didn't have a little dictator in him?"[45]

McGill had learned pugilistic politics early on in Tennessee. Knockdown battles there were a carryover from the dueling days of Andrew Jackson and the shoot-the-editor-through-the-window era chronicled by Mark Twain. As a cub reporter McGill discovered that "all but the more timorous reporters kept loaded pistols in their scarred old desks, along with a bottle of bourbon whiskey." In 1922 the *Banner*'s publisher, Maj. Edward Bushrod Stahlman, assigned McGill to butcher the U.S. Senate candidate endorsed by Luke Lea, publisher of the morning paper, the *Tennessean*. Stahlman, McGill discovered, was "fierce in his support of a candidate[,] . . . ruthless and merciless in his opposition." During World War I, Lea had advocated interning Stahlman because he had been born in Germany, but the effort was blocked by U.S. senator Kenneth D. "Kaydee" McKellar. Now Lea wanted McKellar defeated. Stahlman tossed McGill into the fray, sending him on the trains to track McKellar's challenger, a Memphis lawyer named Gus Fitzhugh.[46]

The rules of political reporting were laid out when Stahlman called him in for a meeting. "The Major's style was to walk right out of his corner when the bell rang and throw his Sunday punch," McGill learned. Write about everything negative—every catcall, small crowds. "In brief, I was to do a hatchet job on Mr. Fitzhugh. I went at it with great enthusiasm and succeeded rather well." The stories appeared every day on the front page, underscoring that "local leaders everywhere predicted Fitzhugh's defeat, that he frequently had been jeered, and that his speeches were flat." "This," said McGill, "was all true." Fitzhugh may have seen some truth, too. While he complained in his speeches about the biased press, he never spoke harshly to McGill when they saw each other in railroad breakfast rooms.[47]

In the end, Fitzhugh lost, partly because the Boss Crump machine in Memphis also backed McKellar, and McGill learned how publishers influence politics. "I realize," he said years later, "there is something of the Major in me. I do not hold with his extreme almost compulsive partisanship. But I believe in being strongly partisan on issues which require a choice."[48]

There was clearly "something of the Major" in the *Constitution's* coverage of the 1942 governor's race. Voters had a choice, and McGill wanted them to see clearly which was the correct choice. He and publisher Howell were as solidly behind Arnall as they were set against Talmadge. The newspaper led its readers not only in McGill's personal columns and its editorials but also, as Stahlman (a ghost since 1930) would have ordered, on its news pages.

The *Constitution* assigned one reporter to write most of the front-page campaign stories. For this task they chose Lamar Ball. Lamar Q. Ball was a wizened veteran of southern journalism. He had come from the *New Orleans Times-Picayune,* where he distinguished himself and owned stock in the paper. His colorful, satiric style landed him a job on Hearst's *Georgian;* he made a timely switch to the *Constitution* and by 1938 was a city editor. Ball had a penchant for practical jokes—he once scared a young obituary writer with a Hollywood movie-style ultimatum: "Get out to that house and get a picture and if you can't get a picture just don't come back." He had a reputation for being unreliable, mainly because of whiskey. "He was a very smart man," recalled Jack Spalding. "If it hadn't been for booze he could gone to the top of the ladder. . . . One Saturday evening he passed out cold on the city room floor." Writing was his strong suit, especially satire. "A lot of his writing was making fun of people and things."[49]

With or without instructions from his publisher, Ball's stories did to Talmadge what McGill's in Tennessee had done to Fitzhugh. Ball's front-page dispatches day after day reported the hardening feelings about the universities' loss of accreditation, the governor's handling of the $60 million state budget, the alleged racket by which the governor granted forty-five hundred pardons, and declining support from local political bosses. Stories usually quoted any official's disparaging remarks. There was no effort to be objective. "That was perfectly all right then," Spalding recalled. "Papers were very partisan."[50]

Talmadge supporters, on the other hand, were often labeled "henchmen," in part because they were suspected of shady campaign tricks. Five weeks before the election, a *Constitution* story linked Talmadge henchmen to a "tear gas plot." The story, reprinted in other newspapers, alleged that Talmadge wanted disgruntled college students blamed for releasing tear gas during his campaign appearance in Statesboro, in southern Georgia. A week later, a Talmadge henchman, Robert F. "Cowboy" Wood, who had been under surveillance, reportedly admitted to the local sheriff that he was "paid" to stage the tear gas plot. "Who paid him and why?" asked an editorial in the local *Statesboro News*. "It was not a supporter of Arnall who went among the crowd spreading chemicals to do bodily harm to unsuspecting bystanders, but it was a Talmadge man."[51]

The university crisis persuaded some politicians to abandon Talmadge. Each new defection confirmed the *Constitution's* wisdom. The biggest page-one story on August 28 was the resignation of the chairman of the board of regents, whose letter to Talmadge warned that "your actions are depriving our Georgia children of a college education." When two north Georgia political leaders defected, Ball's story underscored that they had been "former Talmadge stalwarts." McGill's comparison of Talmadge with Hitler seemed verified by one of the politicians, who stated, "Talmadge and his Gestapo gang of cutthroats are hell-bent on wrecking our public school system and setting up a pardon-racketeering dictatorship in Georgia." The other former supporter worried about his two nephews at the University of Georgia because "their diploma will not be worth a thing unless we get rid of Talmadge." Talmadge, said the stalwart, "is a beat man today. . . . He does not sound like the Talmadge of old."[52]

The emphasis on accreditation was underscored because Talmadge insisted in 1942 that it was "meaningless." On August 1, the president of the University of Georgia entered the fray, denouncing the governor's charges of racial coeducation as false and insisting that accreditation was "a badge of academic worthiness." A week before the election, McGill explained accreditation so any Georgian could understand it, and at the same time stuck Talmadge with another allegation. McGill came up with a barnyard analogy, referring to "a bull from one of the enormous herds the Governor has accumulated since he became Governor. . . . Governor Talmadge and Regent [John] Cummings, just to mention a couple, are very careful to see that their bulls meet the standard and are accredited by the proper accrediting agency. . . . Apparently the Governor and his regents don't think as much of the students of Georgia as they do their accredited bulls."[53]

In mid-August, the *Constitution* publicized two new scandals involving Talmadge's campaign. Ball loved scandalizing the opposition. He wrote that Talmadge was accused of "selling" or promising state jobs for votes and contributions. This was not an uncommon practice, but the difference, Ball reported, was in the degree: "The job sale this year, the present jobholders revealed, has reached hysterical proportions unheard of in past years." Ball cited as his sources unnamed civil service employees who said some contributors to previous Talmadge campaigns had later been denied jobs. Ball said five-thousand-dollar-a-year "sinecures" were being auctioned "at a $3,000 cash starting price." The state jobs included purchasing agent, tag bureau chief, state auditor, and state revenue commissioner. For gifts of three thousand dollars, you could buy a job with the state highway board. Buyers were coming forth, and more than five hundred new employees had been added to various state departments since summer, Ball wrote.

The other scandal alleged that Talmadge and his "Palace Guard" had conducted a "shakedown" of state textbook publishers to raise campaign funds. The charge, made by Arnall in a speech and reported without rebuttal from the governor, accused Talmadge of promising a post-election "pay-off" to publishers by permitting them to raise prices to the state by as much as 40 percent, despite existing contracts at lower prices.[54]

Ball's coverage of Arnall was as positive as his coverage of Talmadge was negative. Wherever Arnall went, he was well received, according to Ball's stories. "Up here in the industrial and agricultural center of northwest Georgia," Ball wrote from Summerville, "Ellis Arnall was cheered by more than a thousand citizens of Chattooga county late today when he warned against the rosy promises of Talmadge's bushbeaters to build roads Talmadge has neglected for years." In Statesboro, Ball noted that Arnall "was acclaimed in a monster ovation as the peoples' candidate for the restoration of democratic rule." He quoted local residents' estimate that Arnall's audience was "twice the size of the crowd that heard Talmadge speak from the same platform last Tuesday."[55]

The *Constitution* also put Ball to work writing feature stories which pumped up Arnall's image. A series of five articles detailed the candidate's life and career and were featured prominently in the paper's *Sunday Magazine* section. The public learned how Arnall was the son and grandson of successful merchants, that Arnall "knew and understood the problems of the mercantile business," had friends all over the state and early on "acquired a passionate devotion for the study of law." As attorney general, only 3 of his 4,816 opinions were reversed—an "unmatched record." Ball recalled how Arnall embarrassed the Talmadge forces on the last night of the 1941 legislature. The pro-Talmadge Senator Hell-Bent Edwards tried to censure Arnall, saying he was "a crook and a rascal, and he ought to be run out of Georgia." Rejecting that notion, the legislature, despite being packed with "ardent disciples" of Talmadge, voted to support Arnall. "Many of them," Ball wrote, "are with Ellis Arnall and the people of Georgia today—against this 1942 Talmadge and this 1940–1942 Talmadgeism."[56]

The tide appeared to be running against Talmadge, as evidenced by endorsements and polling. Even in the governor's strongholds, the rural areas, weekly newspaper editors were endorsing his opponent. By mid-August, McGill counted seventy-four weeklies for Arnall and ten for Talmadge. "We had at least 90 per cent of the newspapers, weeklies and dailies," recalled Arnall. He greeted each endorsement as an extension of his energy, noting that "newspapers print when you sleep." Including dailies, the papers opposing Talmadge's reelection numbered almost one hundred.

Two weeks before the election, the *Constitution* publicized the "unbiased poll" of Georgia's justices of the peace. The poll gave Arnall a "more than 2-to-1" lead over Talmadge, and, wrote the reporter, "the Arnall strength is increasing daily." The poll, begun in 1936, had always been right. In 1940, when the poll showed Talmadge leading, it had been praised in print for its independence and accuracy by Talmadge himself.[57]

Talmadge's confidence in the 1940 poll had been printed in the *Statesman,* a newspaper he bought in 1934 and was still publishing in 1942 in Hapeville, a suburb south of Atlanta. Talmadge's "house organ" was what the *Constitution* called the *Statesman.* Eugene's son, Herman, who by 1940 wrote for the paper, said "it looked to be the perfect

vehicle for Papa to get his message across to the people of Georgia."
As Herman saw it, the *Statesman* under his dad "took a populist line,
defending the little man against big business, big government and
big everything else that took no mind of the individual." McGill wrote
that the *Statesman* was where Talmadge "slanders and smears and
libels anyone who opposes him." McGill searched the paper for material and occasionally discovered live ammunition. In a copy from July
1940 he found reprinted a campaign speech in which candidate
Talmadge declared that "any doctrine that preaches class hatred in
Georgia is a sin of the deepest dye. Any doctrine that preaches prejudice is merely the doctrine of a hypocrite who is trying to hide under
a shadow for the purpose of stealing. No religious or racial prejudice
has any place in a Christian heart."

McGill happily turned Talmadge's 1940 declaration against him
in 1942. "Once again," wrote McGill, "I am gratified to find the Governor in complete agreement with me. . . . He said a man who would
make such charges was a hypocrite hiding under a shadow for the
purpose of stealing. Well, I don't use such strong language. It's pleasant to have the Governor say it."[58]

The race issue must be disposed of, McGill and Arnall agreed.
Georgia had no "nigger" problem, McGill declared. The walls of segregation were solid. Talmadge "wanted to make it a race issue," Arnall
said, "but I wouldn't join issue with him on that." It was clear as day:
"The blacks would not go to school with the whites." In the battle of
words, Arnall kept the focus on the crisis in education. "I made it a
school issue," he said.[59]

By the eve of the election, Arnall's campaign had persuaded more
politicians to abandon Talmadge. The Justices of the Peace poll now
increased Arnall's lead to three to one. It was front-page news when the
state agriculture commissioner, Tom Linder, endorsed Arnall and told
farmers, the backbone of Talmadge's support, that Arnall was "safe in this
race." McGill crowed on election eve that Linder was "a smart politician"
who . . . would not, even if he felt Mr. Arnall was the best man for the
agricultural future of Georgia, urge the support of Ellis Arnall if he did
not think him the winner." Linder's defection, said McGill, debunked

the Talmadge "propaganda" that he was a friend of farmers who work the land. "He has been the friend of huge landowners." The governor "never farmed and now farms only when the photographers are around." He quoted a farmer who said of Talmadge, "The people were just sick of him." It was true, McGill said, clanging the dictator-in-wartime symbols: "In time of war, with young men going off to fight against dictators, it didn't seem sensible to nurse a small one at home." In the news columns, Lamar Ball editorialized, too, characterizing the electorate as "favoring plain, straight-talking Ellis Arnall over a Talmadge dipped in barbecue sauce."[60]

Behind the media onslaught, however, was an equally energetic political maneuver to beat Talmadge at his own machine game. Roy Harris, who in 1940 had kept the divisive antilynching plank out of the Democratic platform, now worked behind the scenes on county political bosses. By Harris's reckoning, forty small counties were dominated by a courthouse ring and could be bought up until the day of the election. Another forty counties were what McGill called "venal" counties—they couldn't be bought for cash but could be had by an expert agent like Harris, who knew those who could bargain. "I used to watch Roy Harris get on the phone and call a dozen men in a dozen undecided counties," McGill recalled five years later. "When the returns came in, those counties went for Arnall."[61]

The election ratified McGill's hopes. It was a landslide, even though Talmadge refused to concede for a week. Arnall received 174,198 votes, or 57.7 percent, to Talmadge's 127,488 votes. More important were the county-unit votes. Here Arnall stunned Talmadge, getting 63.6 percent. Arnall led in 89 counties with 261 unit votes—55 more than a majority. Talmadge got 69 counties with 149 votes. Almost half of those 69 Talmadge counties were barely won, by fewer than 100 votes.[62]

McGill was jubilant. After sharing the thrill with Arnall at the governor-elect's suite in the Biltmore Hotel, McGill hastened to write a victory column. "Georgia won a great victory Wednesday," he wrote, citing Old Andy Jackson's plainspoken advice to politicians: "Never get far away from the people. They rarely are wrong." Arnall's unit-vote victory was "one of the greatest in the state's history—because none has won against odds so great." Finances and organization had been on the governor's side. But the people had voted for good schools, for happy teachers, against "reckless pardoning of criminals," for a professional, not a political, state patrol, and not least for freedom from a home-grown dictatorship—all things Arnall represented. Talmadge would be mistaken to contest the election as he had in 1938, McGill concluded. First, the people didn't like a sore loser who "can't take a defeat without squawking," and second, a recount probably would increase Arnall's total, not Talmadge's.[63]

McGill crowed about the power of the press, incidentally slapping himself on the back. He was "tremendously proud" of the newspaper editors who "entered vigorously" into the campaign and "patiently and courageously stuck to the issues." Some had supported Talmadge, but "it so happened, quite inevitably, that Mr. Arnall had the support of those newspapers sincerely interested in the state; those which believed the school system and the other functions of the state were important and worth as much attention as the budget. . . . It demonstrated that the counties and the communities of the state will react to vigorous 'here-are-the-issues' journalism." As for himself, McGill said, "I had a swell time. . . . It was fun. But winning was important. Let's all go forward together. The election is behind us."[64]

Winning was the triumph of a humanistic morality Arnall and McGill shared. McGill had identified and denounced the excesses of the culture of segregation. While not discrediting segregation as a way of life and the law of the state, his columns focused attention on some foul tumors which threatened the well-being of the general popula-tion. Segregation as a political crop had yielded a harvest of hate and aberrant behavior. Behind a fabricated curtain of irrationality, the Talmadge gang cloaked systematic malfeasance and corruption, most of it unindictable, condoned, or protected by the governor's office.

The combination of blatant racism and abuse of power affronted everything in McGill's upbringing, education, and training. While smiling and saying he had nothing against Gene Talmadge as a per-son, McGill cleverly identified the governor as a local monstrosity, a man run amok, a "home-grown dictator," and jousted Talmadge as the symbol of a system that catered to gangsters. "Mac went for the soul and the mind," observed Jack Spalding. For those who didn't recognize a dictator when one appeared in their midst, McGill had the splendid current examples of Mussolini and Hitler, with whom the country was now at war. This historic tidal wave McGill and Arnall rode deftly, turning attention away from where Talmadge wanted it, on segregation forever, to where they wanted it, on the damaging, and costly, abuse of power. Against the background of a war Talmadge did not support, the governor was transformed within a year from a populist champion to an enemy of the people. With such great stakes at risk, any poker player would have shared McGill's sense that the campaign had been "fun."[65]

8

The National Arena

*Newspapers have got to come down and be close
to the people—not merely interested in informing them
and in interpreting for them, but interested in their
health, their housing, their living conditions, their
children, and their whole panorama of interests.*
—RALPH McGILL, 1944

*"You want me to be another McGill,"
Jack Tarver guessed.
"Tarver, you can out-McGill McGill," George Biggers said.
"No. I don't have that much conviction
about the things he does."*
—JACK TARVER, INTERVIEW

TALMADGE'S DEFEAT IN the race for governor eclipsed other political news coming from the South that season. Framed for a national audience, Georgia presented the picture of a racist, chain-gang state of the Deep South overthrowing the rural, race-baiting machine politicians. Contrary to tradition and image, Georgians had installed an enlightened governor who spoke a language the North could understand. Had Georgia rejoined the Union? Defeat of the Talmadge gang sent signals to the North that a new breed of southerners was redeeming the South. Perhaps Henry Grady's New South had been born again. Perhaps this was a younger South responding to Mencken's lament about the submergence of political and cultural life in "white trash."

For a change, and for that moment, Georgia gained *positive* national publicity. It was a heady time for McGill. The national press gave him much of the credit for the political miracle, cued in part by the dispatches of McGill's old friend, William Howland, southern correspondent for

Henry Luce's *Time*. With input from Howland, *Time* said McGill, at forty-three and 230 pounds, was "the South's fastest-rising new editor[,] . . . the new blood the *Constitution* needed" in the tradition of Henry Grady. "Like Grady, he loves political slugging matches, especially with Governor Eugene Talmadge." At times it was as though Goliath had been slain anew and the one with the slingshot was now a national figure, an unlikely hero, this pudgy southern newspaper writer with bushy eyebrows and double chin.[1]

The image of a "newer" South was punctuated by news reports about Arnall's reforms. The 1943 legislative session, with Talmadge delegates in the minority, readily passed so much of Arnall's reform package that McGill was prompted to declare that it "was not a rubber stamp legislature." Rather, he wrote, the lawmakers were adopting measures "on which the people had spoken." The legislature, which included "the fewest incompetents the capitol has seen in years," left "a record which revives faith in the democratic form of government. It came through in time of a national and state crisis with the legislation required to meet all known problems."[2]

Arnall's reforms included extending the vote to eighteen year olds. With young men fighting and dying, passion persuaded the legislature to allow a popular referendum. Old-line politicians fought extension of the vote, McGill reasoned, because they "fear the wholesome effect of the young people's vote in their counties." To the "old gang's" argument that the young were unprepared, McGill observed the "tremendous advances in education" and, in the golden age of radio, "the greatly improved methods of disseminating information." After one witness contended that extending the vote was a Communist plot, McGill said the comment was shameful and added that he had "fought the Communistic party in everything I have written about it and this country."[3]

Many reforms aimed to protect state resources. The governor's highway bill also passed, thwarting Talmadge jobbers who had been awarded "vast expenditures" in the last days of Ol' Gene's administration. The bill made it impossible to sue the state without the governor's permission. Talmadge forces countered that Arnall had become a "dictator." Also successful was the bill to abolish the governor's private influence over the state patrol. One reform failed. Arnall wanted to regulate the lucrative purchase of state school textbooks, a perennial source of political payoffs. The bill passed the house but was buried in the senate after what McGill called "shameful" pressure on school officials by the "school textbook trust[,] . . . the most powerful and iniquitous lobby that has for years infested the state and corrupted its dealings."[4]

Much of the success of the new politics McGill credited to an old-style politician. After manipulating buyable counties in Arnall's ranks, Roy V. Harris was rewarded by being elected speaker of the state house, unanimously. Political insiders knew that Harris hoped to be governor after Arnall, and in 1943 he emerged as Arnall's right-hand man, ramming through electoral and fiscal reforms. McGill was so elated with "the wonderful job" of the legislature that he declared "the boys deserve a raise" from their seven-dollar-a-day hotel and food allowances—as soon as the wartime freeze on raises was lifted. "An honest man," McGill reasoned, "cannot live on $7 a day."[5]

The national media singled out Arnall and McGill as spokesmen for Georgia's new political direction. While McGill retained the pulpit as editor, Arnall starred in media coverage of governors' conferences, making speeches often crafted by McGill. In their respective roles, Arnall and McGill sometimes were the only southerners and, as such, became identified with the "voice" of the South, or of what one newly elected antimachine Florida congressman, Claude Pepper, was calling the "newer South."[6]

McGill's first opportunity to speak as a voice of the South was over radio. He was invited to the University of Chicago's popular *Sunday Afternoon Round Table.* He would be on the show with a University of Chicago historian and a sociologist. It sank in that he would be in the spotlight. The focus would be on him as the purveyor of news from the South. People would want more than news. He would probably need to say what Arnall's victory over Talmadge meant. What about the race issue and segregation? Where was the South headed politically?

As he thought about it, the broadcast seemed awesome. The thought that he might blunder intimidated him. Aside from debating and acting at the McCallie School he had little experience with impromptu discussion. Now he would be speaking as a representative of the South to a great audience, perhaps twelve million listeners. What if he couldn't find the right words? "There is no script," he noted. He felt "a bit of awe and some fear."[7]

When he mentioned such misgivings to Mary Elizabeth, she propped up his ego. There was nothing to worry about, she would tell him: This Chicago show gave him a chance to use this new medium to speak to the nation, and he'd do fine. Friends saw her as a font of optimism and encouragement. "She gave Ralph a great feeling of backing, especially in the early years," recalled Margaret Tarver, whose husband, Jack Tarver, was editor of the *Macon Telegraph*. "She was solid and behind him before Ralph made his name." She could chase his attacks of gloom, his chronic, brooding moodiness which McGill attributed to the Welsh nature and blend of Scottish-Welsh parentage. Despite Mary Elizabeth's chronic kidney problems and a bout with tuberculosis, she remained optimistic and unintimidated by new situations and important people. Rather than shrink from important opportunities, she thrust herself forward. "There wasn't anybody she wouldn't hug," said Margaret Tarver, "including Mr. Woodruff," the Coca-Cola tycoon whom McGill occasionally joined for lunch at the Coke offices. During the war, when the aviation ace Eddie Rickenbacker was hospitalized in Atlanta after an air crash, Mary Elizabeth cooked beef broth he could sip through his wired jaw. She volunteered for war work at St. Philip's Cathedral and spent hours there feeding and consoling young, homesick soldiers. When she was moved by a situation, she dipped into her purse to help them take the train home, or sent money to help their wives.[8]

The consolation she received from helping others gave her escape from her own problems. She had suffered another miscarriage, the latest of several disappointments in trying to have a child. Escaping by drinking was no answer because it compounded her misfortune. Her kidney was barely able to handle alcohol, and her friends, among them Margaret "Peggy" Mitchell, had seen "Red" lose her composure quickly, one drink unbalancing her talk and walk. They worried about her drinking every time they went to lunch. Ralph took precautions to protect her, trying not to drink in front of her. As editor, he was now entertaining more—in 1943 they bought the house at 3399 Piedmont Avenue in Buckhead—but Ralph usually kept no liquor at home. Friends would bring it when they came to see him or attend one of Mary Elizabeth's parties, and take the booze home when they left. A family friend often carted away the bottles after Christmas parties. Ralph began doing most of his drinking away from home, when out to dinner or away on travel. He got to where "he never drank at home," one friend recalled. "But away, he would overdo it."[9]

Shortly after the Georgia legislature went home in March, Mary Elizabeth saw Ralph off on the train to Chicago. On the long ride, thoughts of the war distracted him. Eight of every ten men aboard were in uniform. And from his window he noticed the "towns look lonely," the "new war plants . . . with heavy steel fences around them," the "highways . . . empty." Just the opposite was happening in Atlanta and other railroad centers, wartime boom towns. A war town, he had written a few days earlier, "had to watch its step or it soon will find itself all run down at the heel: unpainted, drab, its streets dirty, and its whole aspect that of a slattern among cities." He complained that owners of rundown property had friends on the city council who kept the police from closing disorderly joints that attracted drunks, bums, and prostitutes. Other lamentable signs of the war boom were the "cheap wiener and hamburger stands" that "ventilate their little rooms on the sidewalk" and have sanitation that "would horrify a cannibal."[10]

In Chicago, the *Round Table* staff eased him into the show. The evening before, he met the other panelists for a relaxing dinner during which they talked about issues for more than two hours. The next day they taped a rehearsal and heard the playback. McGill resolved not to make the same mistakes on the real broadcast, but he was sure he would make new ones.

By the time the program aired, McGill was focused on his message about the South. He planned to defend the South against accusers and make a pitch for economic assistance. He would talk about the region's immediate plight and, indirectly, the plight of minorities. He would steer the discussion toward *economics,* away from race, as he and Arnall had done against Talmadge. Arnall contended that the "race issue resolves itself in my judgment down to an economic issue. It always will be economics. As long as in the South there were not enough jobs to go around, we keep the black man in the ditch and we stayed in the ditch with him. There was only a half a loaf to go around." In a speech at Tallahassee, Florida, Arnall had declared that the New South must use its clout in the Democratic Party—not in a new third party— to win economic reforms, leading off with equalization of freight rates that discriminated against shippers in the South.[11]

On the air, McGill portrayed the "entire South" as "a minority." The South had been a minority "since a political structure, or third and fourth and fifth-term Republican administrations put it in the economic position of a tributary section." Without prompting, he raised the race issue. What of the Negro? If the South was a minority, then "the Negro might be said to be the minority's minority. As such he has suffered, and is suffering, from unworthy and unnecessary discriminations. Many of them have grown out of the pinch of poverty in a section which is short on money. We have never had enough hospitals, schools, jobs and so on."[12]

After the broadcast, he got telephone calls which buoyed him. Some thanked him for focusing the dialogue on economics and "the economic bonds which have kept the south poor, nervous and fearful." On the train home he wrote about his own fear that Democrats unhappy with Roosevelt might split off into a third party and give Republicans "another four or five or six" terms to call the shots in the South. Under the strain of the broadcast, he felt he had not delivered the message well. Back home, he confided to Harold Martin how he had fumbled for words and come up with inept phrases. "I'd like to have a try at it again some day," he said, "but I know the strain would be as great."[13]

He worried far more about the war. Immediately after Pearl Harbor, he accepted an appointment as chairman of the local draft board. Martin said this job left McGill "restless and fretting" about sending soldiers to war. Another associate recalled that McGill fretted most because mothers called him at night and pleaded with him not to take their sons. As chair, he sometimes decided the fate of men he knew. Edwin A. Peebles was a towering eighteen year old whom McGill had met at the exclusive Piedmont Driving Club. Was Peebles too tall for the service? McGill got a ruler, stood on a chair and measured him. "The man is 6-foot-8, just like he said. You are 4-F, go forth and be happy!" The incessant pressure was so disturbing that McGill got himself transferred to handle only draft-board matters involving inmates in Atlanta's federal penitentiary. This helped, he said, because "they don't let them use the phone after 9 o'clock."[14]

McGill himself wanted to go near the war to write about it. In the summer of 1943, the government granted his wish. A few American editors were invited by the British government in the expectation they would write sympathetic articles about how the British were countering the enemy. The U.S. War Department issued him an identification card as a civilian assigned to the military with the "assimilated" rank of second lieutenant. This was to be a secret mission. McGill met the editors at a small Baltimore hotel from which they moved at night to a blacked-out dock, then onto a stripped-down flying boat crammed with forty passengers, mostly British officers. As they roared off on the twelve-hour flight to Ireland, the man in the next seat asked, "What the hell are you grinning at?" McGill said he was happy because he finally was going to the war.[15]

The stories he sent home connected his readers with the air war. Now joined by American pilots, the Allies were regularly launching bombers against German cities as well as fending off Nazi attacks on London. He listened in awe to the "incessant din" of British antiaircraft guns, some shooting down German planes four to seven miles high, many of the guns fired by women. He was impressed with the courage and daring of young Americans in Flying Fortresses who risked German antiaircraft. "One thing I wish," he wrote, "is that all Americans could see once and hear once the Forts go over. You can't turn over and go to sleep when you hear them. You have to start thinking." The war gave him stories he would repeat for years.[16]

McGill and the other editors were treated well. Their host was the British minister of information, Brendan Bracken, whose enlightened wartime news policy contrasted with that of the Nazi propaganda machine. While the Germans feared the foreign press, censored it ruthlessly, and expelled correspondents, the British ministry engaged journalists, gave them plenty to write about, and, when necessary, sought to censor through moral suasion rather than force. In the war of words, the battle for minds, the British hoped that their policy would win through credibility.

The ministry courted McGill and his colleagues. The British made their visit fruitful and, despite the war, comfortable. As important guests they saw the king and queen, although not at a palace. The occasion in Edinburgh was the awarding of prizes in a Scottish contest for wartime cooks who had made creative dishes from oatmeal and potatoes.

McGill and two of the editors formed a lasting friendship. McGill's outgoing personality quickly broke down the New England reserve of Lawrence Winship of the *Boston Globe* and Edward "Ted" Weeks of the *Atlantic Monthly*. Winship was so amused by McGill's good humor that he sent the *Constitution* a story about how the delegation lost McGill in Hull while they were touring a bomb shelter in a schoolhouse. Eventually the group found the "ample figure of the Atlanta editor" in the school's large basement, surrounded by children, and with a nine-year-old girl on his lap, spelling out for McGill the words of a song called "Doing the Hokey-Pokey." To other children gathered around his feet, McGill explained that he came from America, from Atlanta, where the lady who wrote *Gone with the Wind* lives. McGill said he wished all Americans could see how brave the British were. Winship said a dock worker with a baby on his shoulders cried out, "Three cheers for the man from America." The children joined, "Hip, hip, hooray." Later that evening in another bomb shelter, Weeks and Winship told people McGill came from the land of Uncle Remus stories, and McGill wound up telling, in Negro dialect, little children tales of Brer Rabbit. After that night, Weeks and Winship let McGill be their spokesmen whenever the three editors were called on to make a statement.[17]

After he returned to Atlanta, McGill persuaded Governor Arnall to grant both men the courtesy rank of lieutenant colonel on his staff, and afterward always addressed them as "colonel." Arnall readily saw the value of McGill's new media friends. "For many years everything written about the South was critical," Arnall recalled. "So, now, we have an editor who speaks out with the support of the governor, saying the days of racism and bigotry must be eradicated." That new message should be delivered to a national audience, Arnall and McGill agreed. And what better forum than the *Atlantic Monthly*?[18]

That same year, McGill finally persuaded Jack Tarver to leave Macon and work with him as an associate editor. Tarver had made a mark as a small-town publisher and a social critic with a caustic sense of humor. In 1939 he created a stir when he wrote a satirical column panning the movie version of *Gone with the Wind* at a time when Georgians were generally praising the film and basking in the glow brought to the state by Clark Gable and Vivian Leigh. Tarver boiled down the long movie into four paragraphs laced with puns and double meanings. "Anyway, The South lost the war again in the picture (what could you expect with a lot of Yankee producers) and Scarlett married Rhett to get even with him. . . . However, Rhett had had enough of her foolishness and when she told him [that she really loved him], he says, 'Frankly, my dear, I don't give a damn.' Neither, by this time, did the audience. They were glad to see the end, their own having become number than somewhat." The review was published first in the small paper he had established in 1938 in Lyons, the *Tombs County Democrat*. The *Macon Telegraph and News* reprinted the review, as did the *Chicago Tribune* and some four hundred newspapers across the nation.[19]

Tarver soon quit publishing the *Democrat*. He was frustrated in that "one-dentist town," partly because the officials were not cooperating in their agreement to make his paper the newspaper of record. In 1940 he left Lyons for Macon to cover the legislature for the *Telegraph and News*.

Tarver and McGill shared a love of dessert. The first time they met, McGill dragged him to an ice cream parlor in Savannah famous for giant malted milkshakes. Finishing off the shake at last, Tarver was ready to leave when McGill said, "Let's have another!" McGill told Tarver he had lost one thousand pounds at one time or another. Dieting had unexpected effects on McGill. Tarver's wife, Margaret, never forgot his lettuce regimen. At the Capital City Club in Atlanta, McGill once ordered only a head of lettuce. Having eaten it, he ordered two more.[20]

McGill watched Tarver's career take off in Macon. In three years, through a series of events, he advanced to become editor. His first break came when the publisher went to Orlando to run another newspaper in the chain, asking Tarver to write editorials. Eighteen months later, when the publisher asked for a progress report, Tarver told him it was "terrible" working for three bosses. "I can't please over two of them any given day," said Tarver. "Well," said the publisher, Morton Andersen, "go back to the office and put your name down as 'Editor' and tell them go fuck!"[21]

During the 1942 campaign, Tarver thought his endorsement of Arnall helped swing Macon and Bibb County away from Talmadge. About a year later, Talmadge visited the newspaper office, and the publisher, W. T. Andersen, brought him around to see Tarver. "This is the fellow that carried Bibb County for Arnall," Andersen told Talmadge. "Hell," said Talmadge, "I can walk out of his circulation in 10 minutes." The disparaging remark sunk in: Tarver had to admit that Macon was an isolated bastion which counted for little in the county-unit system. "Talmadge always said he didn't want to carry a county that had streetcars," Tarver recalled. Tarver had had enough. "That night, I called McGill!" They agreed on the job—associate editor, writing editorials, handling the mechanics of putting out the editorial pages, correcting proofs.

The tougher question was salary. The rival *Atlanta Journal* had already tried to hire Tarver earlier that year. Governor Cox's business manager, George Biggers, had offered Tarver $150 a week to write a daily column for the *Journal*. Tarver quickly sized up that proposition.

"You want me to be another McGill."

"Tarver, you can out-McGill McGill," Biggers told him.

"No," Tarver told him, "I don't have that much *conviction* about the things he does."

The *Journal*'s offer of $150 became Tarver's bargaining chip for discussing salary with the *Constitution*. McGill talked it over with Clark Howell Jr. and told Tarver they could give him five bucks more than the *Journal*. Tarver took it, having already decided it was better to work with McGill than compete against him.[22]

The dickering over five dollars was symbolic of the *Constitution*'s financial problems in the 1940s. "I didn't realize how bad it was or I might have gone to the *Journal*," Tarver said. He was surprised to find in the rest room a razor blade dangling by a string from the ceiling, with an index card explaining, "For wrist-slashing purposes only." Almost all financial matters, including raises and new hires, had to be cleared by the bank, which held the numerous loans made to the paper, mostly during old Clark Howell Sr.'s last years in the early 1930s. This was the situation inherited in 1936 by Clark Howell Jr., who confided that "the bank really owns the *Constitution* now." In order to keep it, he would visit the bank almost every morning before going to the newspaper. "Clark never was a newspaperman," Tarver thought. "That's one reason he let McGill have a free hand."[23]

By early 1944 McGill was writing about the war as won. With the increasing success of the Allied effort, McGill coaxed readers to think about what the war's end would mean for the South. His alma mater, Vanderbilt, convened a regional conference on postwar planning which McGill reported. One Georgian, wealthy retired cotton-mill industrialist Cason Callaway, hoped for an end to one-crop agriculture, but to accomplish that, he said, farmers must get long-term credit "to improve their soil, buy machinery and establish perennial crops." An Atlanta banker, Robert Strickland of Trust Company, well connected with Coca-Cola and other enterprises, also envisioned a postwar expansion of new industries which would become "the backbone of the towns and small cities." Both men emphasized the first source of assistance to boost the South along these lines should come from private resources. "If business and industry don't," McGill concluded, "the government will have to do it."[24]

Others of McGill's circle urged a revitalized New Deal. With $110 billion a year being spent on the war, some envisioned a host of postwar government programs, despite Roosevelt's indication that a majority of Americans wanted the New Deal to die. One of the brightest of the latter-day New Dealers among McGill's acquaintances was Mark Ethridge, a native Mississippian who had worked as a newspaper editor in Macon and as editor of the *Richmond Times-Dispatch* before being lured in 1936 by publisher Robert Worth Bingham's offer of $2,000 a month to become general manager of the *Louisville Courier-Journal*. Bingham, Roosevelt's ambassador to England until his death in 1937, was an ardent New Dealer and made the *Courier-Journal* into the South's foremost liberal newspaper. By 1944 Ethridge hoped that Roosevelt would turn postwar attention to efforts as varied as job and health insurance, rural electrification, rural housing, education, tax revision, foreign trade, old-age pensions, and planning.[25]

Some also shared Ethridge's optimism about political reform in the South. From his vantage point in a border state, he was buoyed by the election victories of liberals and New Dealers across the South. "The swing of the post-war world *will* be to the left," Ethridge assured McGill. "It is hardly conceivable that people who have been so long under petty tyrants and their fascist brutality will have any patience, after the liberation, with authoritarian methods." Following the lead of Arnall's victory in 1942, other states in 1944 were swinging toward New Deal politics. "Roosevelt haters," "revolters," and "obstructionists" had been defeated in North Carolina, South Carolina, Tennessee, Alabama, Arkansas, Texas, and Oklahoma. Ethridge was delighted that Florida's liberal Claude Pepper won his U.S. Senate race "with all the odds against him, with all the money against him, with all the hatred of both Mr. and Mrs. Roosevelt as his liability." And in Virginia, the political leaders "are rushing in with the statement that they favor abolishing the poll tax[,] . . . certainly a retreat from the reaction which has characterized that machine."[26]

The poll tax, which existed nowhere outside the South, was also losing political support in Georgia. Arnall favored repeal and worked at persuading McGill, who clung to his fear of the unenlightened mob and his belief that the legislature would not permit further extension of the vote. The electorate, only five hundred thousand when Arnall was elected, had already been increased by lowering the voting age to eighteen and allowing soldiers at war to vote. By Arnall's calculation, repeal would boost the electorate to nearly one million, almost *double* what it had been in 1942. "We talked it out," recalled Arnall, who during this time was consulting almost daily with McGill either by telephone or over sandwiches at the Capitol or at the newspaper. "I said I'm going to do away with it. I want you with me, because we'll never have broad democracy unless we have more voting. My whole concept was that we don't have a democracy in this country. . . . We are run by a minority."[27]

McGill had supported extending the vote to eighteen year olds. He framed it as an act of equity: if youth could die to defend the country, they should be permitted to vote. It had not become a race issue, as repeal of the poll tax seemed to be. With no poll tax, critics asked, what was to prevent hordes of Negroes from voting together to defeat the white political machines? McGill worried that Talmadge forces would have a field day arguing that Arnall wished to turn the state over to a bogey that haunted white supremacists: "nigger rule."

Arnall worked on a political rationale for putting the poll tax on the political agenda and minimizing opposition. At the very least, he reasoned, the tax law must be revised because it now applied only to voters aged twenty-one to sixty; the new, younger electorate was exempt. After the poll tax was open for discussion, Arnall believed he could persuade whites that repeal would actually strengthen white supremacy. True, repeal would extend the vote to Negroes as well as whites, but only whites could vote in the white Democratic primary. Besides, Georgia would retain its literacy test, a further screen against the Negro vote. "A requirement to read, speak, and understand [English]," Arnall stated, "is reasonable."[28]

McGill came around. "After a lot of persuading, he agreed it was the thing to do," Arnall said. "He changed his views because I talked to him." However, McGill urged Arnall to back off immediate repeal by executive order. Arnall had received an opinion from the attorney general that the governor "had the right to suspend the payment of any tax by executive order until the next meeting of the Legislature." News of this leaked to the legislature. "They could have lynched me, they were so angry," Arnall recalled. Repeal threatened every elected politician. McGill believed that if Arnall suspended the tax by executive order he jeopardized the reelection in 1944 of legislators who supported other reforms. The 1944 election would become a referendum on Arnall, a rallying point for Talmadge, who was waiting to run again in 1946. As McGill saw it, suspension of the tax would be political disaster for the rest of Arnall's reform program. "The people would have voted against it," Arnall recalled, "because at that time only the whites could vote in the white Democratic primary." In the end, Arnall settled for delay. He decided to wait for the recommendations of a constitutional revision commission, which was scheduled to report in 1945.[29]

Meanwhile, the whites-only primary came under attack in the federal courts. On April 3, 1944, the Supreme Court ruled eight to one against the Texas whites-only primary. The decision shocked the South, as reflected in front-page news stories about the *Smith v. Allright* case. The *Constitution* also reported "Southern reaction," noting that some southerners pledged "stubborn determination to preserve traditional white control of election machinery." With primary elections only three months away, political leaders across the South conspired to defeat the intent of the court.[30]

There was no rationalizing this issue as anything but a race question. Careful to assess the mood of Georgians, neither McGill nor Arnall rushed to support the ruling. McGill held off a month, until the first flush of passion had subsided, before writing about the case. Even then he mentioned it only as part of an overview on recent elections in the South. In breaking silence, he offered moderate southerners a new interpretation of the importance of the ruling. The court, he said, gave Georgians an *opportunity,* a period of time in which to change election laws on their own before Congress might do it by force. He thus evoked latent southern fears of a recurrence of Reconstruction, of northern colonial rule by decree. The Supreme Court, he wrote, "has brought to the fore the question of the right to vote. . . . Voting is a question the people of Georgia must decide." On the other hand, if Georgia did not act, there was the possibility of "Eastern influence" (substitute: Yankee imperialism), which McGill urged "must be kept out of the problem." He asserted a faith that "the common sense of the south must solve it." On the other hand, failure to act invited Yankee intervention. In this way, he was also stressing urgency.[31]

Could southerners abolish the whites-only primary without abandoning social segregation or inviting race mixing? McGill reasoned that electoral reform should not raise the specter of social equality. "As I have often said before," he wrote, as though he could hear the taunts of Gene Talmadge, "I know no one who asks for social equality. I know no one who wants to mix the races. It is not desirable from the viewpoint of either race. That is not the issue."[32]

Language such as this was earning him a reputation in the northern media as a leader among southern moderates. Two weeks after the column appeared, *Life* magazine ran a portrait of him at his typewriter and declared he was "famous for his tolerance and depth of

understanding of southern problems." Informed by Luce's correspondent in Atlanta, McGill's friend Howland, *Life* described McGill's
uneasy position as located in a hopeful South slowly coming to terms
with the racism of its entire history but resisting any forced federal
intervention: "He feels that the South must gradually change its attitude toward the Negroes, but realizes that any change cannot be arbi-
trarily imposed. He has always been a supporter of minority groups."
In the same *Life* article McGill was identified as the true architect of
the anti-Talmadge force, the one who "led the fight in 1942 to defeat
Governor Talmadge, a militant 'white supremacy' man."[33]

McGill by 1944 was trying to rationalize his zone of moderated
segregation. He knew he couldn't persuade white supremacists and
older whites for whom generations of segregation had made moderation unimaginable. Segregation "is not an argument in the South,"
wrote Birmingham journalist John Temple Graves. "It is a major
premise." So long as segregation held the high, legal ground in the
South, the territory for moderate, progressive thought would be marginal, a beachhead. But moderates, so long as they kept up a dialogue
and encouraged participation, could expand their numbers.[34]

McGill seemed settled in for a long period of attrition. He and
others who considered the dilemma of segregation had begun to identify with modernist thinking on the race issue. Though he would not
have called himself one, McGill qualified as a modernist intellectual.
He had long had a habit of reading and by the 1940s was reading two
or three books a week. "Here of late," he would write, "I seem to be
receiving books." And then he would launch into a review of ideas
presented in the best ones. His daily column often became the conduit through which readers learned about books that discussed southern problems, including race. Here McGill could interpret the essence
of Gunnar Myrdal's *American Dilemma: The Negro Problem in Modern
Democracy,* which came out in 1944, and books by the school of soci-
ologists publishing steadily since the 1930s at the University of North
Carolina Press at Chapel Hill.[35]

McGill found intellectual compatriots in a new nongovernmental organization established with his encouragement in Atlanta, the Southern

Regional Council (SRC). Atlanta had long been the scene for biracial cooperation. Immediately after the First World War, racial tensions caused by the return of Negro soldiers led to creation of an emergency agency, the Commission on Interracial Cooperation. In more than twenty years the CIC expanded across the South to deal with interracial concerns as diverse as lynching and voting.

In 1942, rising racial tensions generated wild rumors of Negro resistance to segregation. As Negroes sought the vote, the more the rumors flew. What would they want next? Would they insist on breaking the color barrier in buses? Would Negro cooks threaten white domestic tranquility by staging a work stoppage? Southern leaders, McGill among them, now regarded the CIC as too moribund to handle the new crisis. After meetings in Durham, North Carolina, Atlanta, Richmond, and Atlanta again, southern whites and Negroes replaced the CIC with the Southern Regional Council, the brainchild of Howard Odum of Chapel Hill, who became its first president. It would have greater scope in planning regional development, with separate commissions for race relations, economic affairs, community life and welfare, cultural development, and public affairs. Soon the SRC endorsed a program for equal employment opportunity, Negro policemen and firemen, equalization in education and public transportation, and Negro voting.[36]

The SRC had McGill's wholehearted support. On February 16, 1944, despite concern from some executives at the newspaper, McGill joined thirteen other southerners in signing the SRC's founding charter. In political circles this confirmed McGill as a "known liberal." But in an era when he saw the need for institutional support to advance reforms in education, he weathered the criticism. He continued to build his rings of loyalists. Soon he was referring like-minded people to work at the SRC and defending the SRC as he would a wartime ally. "The fact that so obviously worthy an organization . . . should need defending," observed McGill's friend Harold Martin, "was a reflection of the masterly demagoguery of Eugene Talmadge in creating a climate of fear and suspicion in all matters dealing with race."[37]

With McGill's assistance, the SRC began planning a new magazine about the South. During 1944 McGill and Arnall tapped a number of people for contributions to a "southern magazine" to be published at

Newnan, Arnall's hometown. McGill asked Cason Callaway to elaborate on the Vanderbilt conference presentation; Callaway sent an article on the welfare of southern farmers titled "Our Roots Are in the Soil." Mark Ethridge mailed a column on "the rebirth of the New Deal." It was twice as long as one he had written for John Temple Graves's *Birmingham Age-Herald.* "I don't think there will be any conflict," Ethridge wrote, "as his paper has very little circulation." Florida's newly elected U.S. senator, Claude Pepper, endorsed Arnall's bid to "get the Nation's freight rate structure revised so as to have fair access to the Nation's great markets." Pepper congratulated Arnall, McGill, and "all those who have had a part in the good venture of establishing this magazine." The SRC finally named the magazine *New South,* publishing the first issue in 1945.[38]

The audience McGill hoped to develop for his dialogue on southern problems was increasingly biracial and progressive. In Georgia, they included a growing number of younger whites who either believed in the creed of equality or expected that racial harmony would be good for Atlanta's expanding business. In this trade group none was more prominent than Robert Woodruff, who envisioned a postwar multiracial world as the growth market for Coca-Cola. In the Negro community, McGill's readers included leaders with courage enough not to be intimidated by whites, hooded or otherwise. "We never did a reader survey on McGill's column," Tarver recalled, "but we knew he was well read. There were as many who hated him as liked him."[39]

The racial tensions triggered in April 1944 by the Supreme Court ruling and agitated by the Talmadge crowd, began to be directed personally at McGill. From this time on McGill received anonymous calls from white supremacists who sometimes addressed him as "Rastus" or "nigger-lover." McGill developed a style for answering these calls at home. He named a schnauzer puppy Rastus, and when he got a call for Rastus, he'd tell the caller, "Wait a minute, I'll call him." Other times, in an effort to shield Mary Elizabeth, he would simply talk idly into the receiver, "Yes, yes, uh-huh, well, that's interesting."[40]

McGill kept a vigil on Talmadge's maneuvers. On one occasion, he criticized Talmadge for making an anti-Roosevelt speech at an annual banquet of the Ku Klux Klan at Covington, Georgia. Since the 1920s in

Tennessee, McGill had discounted the Klan as an organization of suckers who paid a surcharge for sheets, and of swindlers who kept the money. Now in two columns he castigated Talmadge for waltzing with the Klan.[41]

Talmadge went on the attack, questioning McGill's loyalty to his own race. "I heard some years ago that one of the tenets of the Ku Klux Klan was WHITE SUPREMACY," he replied in a typed, four-page letter. "I believe in white supremacy, Ralph. Your compromising position would say that you do not." McGill's attendance at the conferences which led to creation of the SRC made him suspect. "This Inter-Urban League," Talmadge went on,

> has a very deceptive name.
>
> No one would guess . . . that it really means Interracial League, where Negroes and white people are members of the same club, and meet together and talk about social equality and equal rights together.
>
> You attend those meetings, Ralph. I expect you allow negroes to call you "Ralph," and say "Yes" and "No" to you. That is *social equality,* you know, Ralph.[42]

Talmadge traced McGill's pro-Negro stance back to 1937. He dredged up the matter of the fellowship McGill had accepted from the liberal Rosenwald Foundation in Chicago. Had McGill been forever bribed? When the Southern Railroad rejected a federal directive to give equal employment opportunities to Negroes, Talmadge commended the railroad. McGill, however, had written nothing:

> ARE YOU IN FAVOR OF IT, OR AGAINST IT, RALPH? Watch out how you answer, Ralph. You might lose some of that Rosenwald Fund if you say you are against it.
>
> But here is the pitiful part of it, Ralph.
>
> In your heart, you are against it, but you have accepted some of that Rosenwald Fund, and you have joined the Inter-Urban League, which is the Interracial League.
>
> You are in a very compromising position, Ralph, and can't exactly be yourself.[43]

Actually, Talmadge's scattergun attack had hit one point squarely. The Rosenwald grant *was* related to McGill's positions on race, especially as it related to the development of human potential regardless of color. But it was wrong to think that the money had *changed* his views; if anything, witnessing the rise of Nazism had the cathartic effect of underscoring the multiple evils of that creed: not only racism, but the liquidation of diverse voices, of whatever race, whether spoken or in print. McGill had seen it happen, the demise of liberty, even while the Viennese shouted "Heil Hitler" with "froth-specked lips." It had a been a living nightmare. The specter stayed with him through the maelstrom of the war, and it had been natural to see the aura of a homegrown Hitler in Talmadge's demagoguery. Talmadge was right on one thing, the Rosenwald grant was a key to McGill, but it was not the money itself or the hope of more of it, but rather the experience of seeing totalitarianism in a crucible.

McGill carried this reverence for freedom of expression throughout the war. By 1944 he was expressing these views in a national forum, the American Society of Newspapers Editors. As it happened, the new ASNE president, John S. "Jack" Knight, had his own memorable experiences with suppression of news and was looking for someone to do a project for him. At the spring conference, Knight chose McGill to chair the ASNE's Committee on Freedom of the Press.

Knight had just served nine months representing the U.S. Office of Censorship in wartime London. Since the First World War, it had been U.S. and British policy to recruit highly respected journalists to persuade editors of the importance of "voluntary censorship" of wartime news. Few American journalists were more respected than Knight, who in 1943 was editor and publisher of newspapers in Miami, Detroit, and Akron, Ohio. In the late summer of 1943, Knight undertook the government censorship mission, to mingle and "maintain friendly relations at the top" of the British government.[44]

Knight was too much a publisher to cow to government suppression. Earlier in the war he had protested after the Office of Censorship asked him to hold back for a full day a story about a submarine which sank a U.S. destroyer near Key West; Knight complied, but censors released the story in time for James Cox's rival *Miami News* to publish a scoop. "We have no quarrel about withholding information in wartime,"

Knight wrote to Price, "but it hardly seems fair to release to afternoon newspapers a story that broke on morning time."[45]

Now in London, Knight battled constantly with military and civilian censors. In a speech in Manchester, England, Knight declared that "the right of worldwide news agencies to gather and report honest, unbiased and truthful news must be protected." In the spring of 1944, he resigned. Back home, he was elected ASNE president and in an acceptance speech declared that "when peace returns, worldwide freedom of information is essential to preserving the very things for which we are fighting. The people are entitled to the truth." Looking toward the postwar world, Knight developed a battle plan that would not only defeat censorship but open the world for news. He found McGill passionately interested in leading the campaign.[46]

McGill made the most of his appointment. He contacted his wartime friend, Ted Weeks, editor of *Atlantic Monthly,* and arranged to write an article about the eclipse of liberty in prewar Vienna. Weeks published McGill's essay in September 1944 in an issue that included contributions by other liberal voices, among them Richard Wright and Gerald W. Johnson. It was good company. The editor's note flattered him as a southerner "known for his fearless and liberal views" who has "maintained the tradition of the *Atlanta Constitution* and made it one of the most influential newspapers on the Atlantic seaboard. . . . McGill is today an editor who honestly upholds the freedom of the press." It was at this time that McGill began writing for a national audience in terms he never used for his readers at home.[47]

McGill's article underscored how easily American publishers could lose the guarantee of the First Amendment. He recalled the Vienna nightmare. The suddenness with which newspapers, magazines, free radio, and books had been banned or burned was a phenomenon which, he said, "I shall never forget. . . . I have worked for newspapers for almost a quarter of a century. I suppose I always felt that behind me was the great guarantee of a free press. But never until I saw there in Austria the physical disappearance of that freedom, along with others, did it become something vital."

He took American publishers to task for assuming that press freedom was their personal property as much as their building, typewriters, and phones. The First Amendment was "merely one of the guarantees to the people. It is their property. . . . I know it can be taken away casually. . . . The press is free only so long as it exists in that status in the minds and affections of the people."

Why was he writing about this now? Wartime censorship forced the issue. "One may detect this fact in all the ringing speeches made at meetings of editors and publishers." He claimed to have examined "hundreds of speeches on the subject." To characterize what disturbed journalists, he used a curious metaphor: "The mouse of fear gnaws at the minds of many persons whose daily job is newspapering." In his own state, the harangues of demagogues had turned many against a free press. McGill recalled when evangelist J. Frank Norris, making a "hellfire" speech for Gene Talmadge, said, "'All those who think we ought to nail to the fence the hides of the newspaper editors who don't support these things, stand up.' They all stood."

What had happened to American journalism? "The newspapers have failed in the past, and I think they have failed miserably, to interpret America to the people." Publishers in the pursuit of "other ventures and enterprises" were "watering out their newspaper interest." With haphazard hiring practices and the lowest possible salaries, publishers failed to find enough "men and women who know history, economics, and the facts of life, and who can write of them so that newspaper readers can understand." The information gap was a major reason why Americans were unprepared for the stock market crash of 1929 and the Depression. "I do not say they should have foreseen it," McGill wrote. "But when it came they did nothing but flounder and attempt to see, with the gentlemen in the White House, around the corner. They were not living with the people."

What could be done? Shouting and haranguing in editorials and filling the paper with "learned discussion" was not the answer. What publishers and editors must do, he insisted, was "regain, if they have lost it, the vision of serving the people of their state and community." He presented his own credo for editors and publishers: "Newspapers have got to come down and be close to the people—not merely interested in informing them and in interpreting for them, but interested in their health, their housing, their living conditions, their children, and their whole panorama of interests. They must recapture for themselves the American Dream. And in turn they must give it back to the people. . . . There is time yet."[48]

With the war nearing an end, Knight stressed press freedom with new urgency. He persuaded both political parties of the wisdom of committing to freedom of the press in their 1944 party platforms. It was also agreed that ASNE's Committee on Freedom of the Press would write the proposed statements for both the Republican and Democratic national conventions. In a hurry to meet the deadline, McGill attacked the task alone. He felt "it did not seem practical to attempt a meeting then." Unfortunately, at least one prestigious committee member, the dean of the Columbia School of Journalism, Carl W. Ackerman, felt snubbed. "I assure you with complete sincerity," McGill wrote Ackerman, "there was no idea of ignoring the committee. I simply got busy in Washington and later on in Chicago. . . . I deeply regret it was not possible to have a meeting before the final convention in Chicago, but talks with Mr. Knight and Kent Cooper [general manager of the Associated Press] convinced me that too much time would be lost and time was of essence [*sic*]."[49] Ackerman had visited Atlanta and may have felt that McGill was avoiding him. "Nothing distressed me more," McGill explained, "than the fact that I was able to see so little of you when you were in Atlanta. My wife and I were leaving that afternoon to be gone in the country for the weekend and I felt very guilty that we were not able to do something for you."[50]

Knight had even grander plans for the committee. "Mr. Knight," McGill informed Ackerman, "said that he wants us to be the continuing committee." Knight hoped they would extend their mission from domestic concerns to the world arena. By 1944, postwar planning envisioned a United Nations, an improved version of the League of Nations, which might have more authority to prevent wars. Far from withdrawing from such a scheme as after the First World War, the United States, as President Roosevelt indicated, would take a leadership role and host the negotiations. Knight wanted the new world organization to become a guardian for freedom of information globally.[51]

Publishers were motivated by profit as well as principle. Access to information across national boundaries promoted national freedom and international business, the information equivalent of a land rush. U.S. and European publishers and news agencies, with international communication infrastructures and technologies, would stake out the globe. Knight insisted that the ultimate aim of world press freedom was the protection of human rights and the prevention of war. "True journalism—and I emphasize that word true—is the lamplight of our modern society," he wrote in 1944. The suppression of press freedom in Italy and Germany had facilitated the triumphs of Mussolini and Hitler. Knight and others reasoned that a pledge by all nations to guarantee freedom of information would frustrate the schemes of would-be dictators who, with even greater weapons of destruction, might become more terrible than Hitler. International press freedom could become a preventive moral force, inoculating against the scourge of dictators. All that was required was the inclusion in all peace treaties and in the UN treaty of a carefully worded promise, a "pledge of governments not to censor news at the source; not to use the press as an instrument of national policy, and to permit a free flow of news in an out of signatory countries."[52]

By September, Knight was pressing the committee to undertake an ambitious mission to persuade countries to adopt that promise in postwar treaties. The ASNE now regarded the mission "as one of the major projects of the Society," said its executive secretary, Dwight Young of the *Dayton (Ohio) Herald and Journal.* Knight wanted a team of three to start as soon as possible on a whirlwind trip around the world. To head the mission, he chose Wilbur Forrest, ASNE vice president and assistant editor of the *New York Herald Tribune.* McGill was thrilled to be asked. Ackerman was eager to go to China, in particular, where Columbia sponsored a journalism program at the University of Chungking. The three agreed to go as soon as they got wartime travel clearance from the State Department and assurance that they could fly on U.S. military aircraft.[53]

9

The World in Flux

*In the end the peoples of all nations will know each
other better and the problems of nations may be readily
understood through a truer and freer flow of news.*
—Ralph McGill and Wilbur Forrest, 1945

*[I announced] I was resigning from the committee;
that I consider McGill's behavior a disgrace
to American journalism and as this had
happened in every capital we had visited I
would continue on the journey independently.*
—Carl W. Ackerman, 1945

THE ENTERPRISING JOURNALIST from rural Tennessee knew that going around the world was as important to his career as his sojourn in Hitler's Reich. His experiences among the Nazis and the triumph over Talmadge had given McGill some small prominence among journalists nationally. Now he had been asked by the American Society of Newspaper Editors to travel widely and report on the world emerging from war. Finding the profession opening to him, he was exuberant. He imagined no barriers.

During the last months of 1944, as the Allies advanced toward Germany and Japan, McGill and his associates prepared for their ambitious globetrotting. Their wartime mission depended upon cooperation from the State Department, U.S. military, and Allies. Timing was crucial for the ASNE's objectives, and Knight expected McGill to make all arrangements before November 27, when the ASNE board of directors held its annual meeting in Washington, D.C. Knight believed the project must be undertaken quickly, and he was disturbed that McGill did not keep him informed between September and November. "I have heard nothing from Ralph McGill since I asked him to call a meeting of his committee," Knight complained to ASNE executive secretary Dwight Young. "I assume he has done so but he has certainly failed to give me a fill-in on his program."[1] It was the first note of discord associated with this assignment.

McGill had decided to handle arrangements alone, relying on his own contacts in the Roosevelt administration. His progress was slow, but he evidently did not ask for help. Through the first week of November, the 1944 presidential election campaign distracted him, as did the demand of writing his daily column, which he refused to vacate for any reason.

Then there had been a surprise distraction at home. Mary Elizabeth was pregnant. This was something of a miracle. They thought that during surgery on her kidneys the doctors had performed a hysterectomy to protect against a pregnancy. Now, after years of frustration, a child was due in April. With each week, all became more hopeful of her health and the baby's. McGill was reconsidering the mission. As he explained to Harold Martin years later, Mary Elizabeth would not let him turn down the opportunity. "She was going to have this baby," Martin related, "and he was going wherever his job called him."[2]

McGill had run into delays at the State Department. The ailing secretary of state, Cordell Hull, was planning to resign, and with his bureaucracy in transition, the staff seemed sluggish about new requests, especially one as ambitious as this mission to circle the world while the war was still on. After Roosevelt's victory in November, a new secretary, Edward R. Stettinius Jr., had to approve the mission.

Stettinius seemed to sympathize with the ASNE plan to lobby foreign governments for freedom of the press to be included in the peace treaties. Since August, he had been negotiating with Britain and the Soviet Union to shape a "United Nations" whose aim would be the preservation of world peace and security. He was also preparing for Three-Power talks at Yalta and was engaged in efforts to bring about a Latin American accord intended to heal the rift with Argentina's Fascist government. But Stettinius's penchant for secret negotiation carried over to journalists. He did not seem to be a champion of freedom of information, and it appeared that he was trying to delay the mission on grounds of poor timing.[3]

In November Knight summoned McGill and his committee to Washington to meet with the ASNE directors. The bureaucratic delays did not surprise Knight. "The administration suffers from hardening of the arteries," he concluded, "its bureaucrats bickering like small boys, all wanting to be pitcher." With the board's approval, Knight used his considerable influence with Byron Price of the Office of Censorship and others in the Roosevelt administration. In December, the Germans' last military offensive in the Battle of the Bulge delayed arrangements again, but eventually the three journalists were cleared to leave in early January. By then, Mary Elizabeth was in the sixth month of her pregnancy. McGill assured himself that she was in good hands and that his being in Atlanta was not vital. Assuming no delays, he planned to be home by March, a month before the baby was due.[4]

The itinerary was set by early January 1945. The agenda suited McGill's private agenda. As a working journalist with a daily column always in mind, he wanted to speak with politicians and ordinary people. From the first he wanted inside information about the shape of politics and economics of the postwar world. From the second, he wanted stories of war and peace that would interest the average reader. He, Wilbur Forrest, and Dean Carl Ackerman would visit journalists and government officials in twenty-two cities in eleven countries in Europe, the Middle East, and Asia. With treks into Russia, India, and China, it would be a journey of forty-three thousand miles. They canceled the plan to visit Latin America when twenty countries, including Argentina, agreed on a hemispheric peace agreement providing for "the lifting of war-time press controls and peace-time interchange of information." They also excluded Africa, except for Egypt, and the ongoing war barred them from Eastern Europe. By arrangement, they agreed to keep notes. Forrest and Ackerman were pleased that McGill readily agreed to write the final report to the ASNE, subject to their approval.[5]

Military planes carried them most of the way. They took off from New York on January 10, riding "without priority" in a plane assigned to the Air Transport Command. At the first stop in London, British publishers and press societies received them warmly. Brenden Bracken, still minister of information, assured them that Britain expected to close the ministry at the end of the war. "We think that is a very fine idea," Forrest told the Associated Press, which was following the mission's progress. There was ample evidence to support Winston Churchill's political axiom that "war kills liberalism." During the bitter early years of the German bombing, British publishers cooperated with strict wartime censorship. By early 1945, controls were being relaxed. Eager for expansion into the postwar world media market, British publishers naturally supported global news flow.[6]

London had become a center for political refugees from totalitarianism, some of them eager to promote press freedom. "I recall talking with Eduard Benes, president of Czechoslovakia, shortly before he left London to return to his liberated country," McGill wrote. From the lengthy statement Beneš gave the committee, McGill extracted what seemed the most important message. "A free press," said Beneš, "is the best friend a small country can have. . . . There must be healthy opposition. Newspapers help supply it when they are free." On a global scale, Beneš told them he believed that a free press enables a small country to get its views before the world. "I hope when peace comes," he implored the committee, "that the small nations will not be neglected by the news agencies and by newspapers which maintain foreign staffs. It is important that our voices be heard." Beneš told them that in Hitler's storm of propaganda the Czechs had been "flooded and drowned out by the German claims in the appeasement." Beneš later wrote to Forrest that "during the Munich crisis the sympathy which we enjoyed in the free world despite the overwhelming mass of German propaganda was due only to the freedom of the press."[7]

The Americans accumulated enough testimony to prove the global need for a free press. McGill revived the Jeffersonian political philosophy that it was better to have newspapers without a government than to have a government without newspapers. The Americans concluded, "Had not Fascist and Nazi forces in Italy and Germany seized and dominated the press and all communications facilities at the start, the growth of these poisonous dictatorships might well have been prevented and the indoctrination of national thought in the direction of hatred and mistrust might have been impossible."[8]

McGill loved London. Despite the new threat of German V-2 rocket bombs, Londoners were happier than when he had visited the bomb shelters in 1943. There was plenty of beer, but McGill found it miserably weak. The booze that was "fit to drink is so costly . . . that the average person cannot begin to pay for it." Away from home and having a good time, he gave in to his tendency to drink to excess. His intemperance offended Ackerman, who believed that professional conduct demanded sobriety. To Ackerman, the three were always "on the job" and should act as though they were "representatives of an American idea." Later, in Paris, Ackerman wrote to his wife, Vandy, that McGill was drinking to excess again, and did so again in Rome.[9]

Drinking reflected McGill's zest for life, cultivated since Prohibition. On this trip he made it part of his research. In answer to one of his Atlanta drinking buddies, McGill devoted a column to the "drinking habits, opportunities and so on in the newly liberated countries. This is a task which takes me somewhat out of the course laid down for this journey, but I am happy to comply." In France, he observed that "the Germans took about everything there was to drink. They left behind several warehouses filled with bottled stuff labeled 'Cognac.' It was for distribution to the Wehrmacht. . . . [The] bars of France were selling canned heat and anti-freeze liquids and a number of the Allied soldiers had been killed by drinking some of it. . . . [If] you wish to cure someone of the drink habit, send them abroad."[10]

McGill's public demeanor grated on Ackerman. While Ackerman and Forrest were quoted occasionally, McGill got more attention, overshadowing his senior companions. He never quit being the working daily journalist looking for a story, keeping up the daily column, which he sent home usually by mail. With an innate ability to speak in public, he readily accepted invitations to broadcast to American audiences from London and Paris. His affability and accessibility inclined newspapermen to turn to him as a spokesman and newsmaker.

McGill's zest for meeting strangers daunted Ackerman and amazed Forrest. Some were southerners who had read McGill's column. He noted that Forrest and Ackerman did not understand that "in the more provincial journalism of the South a byline that had been appearing in the *Atlanta Constitution* for sixteen years would have become known to a great many Georgians and Southerners." Soldiers sought McGill for news from home. "And, truthfully, there was a run of Georgians," McGill recalled, noting that one duty officer from Georgia had "warmed us with hospitality and Scotch." Forrest found McGill's popularity humorous, alleging that McGill had "rigged" these coincidental meetings. On the way to see Gen. Dwight Eisenhower, Forrest told Ackerman, "Well, Carl, at least Ike is a Middle West Dutchman with no Georgia connections." McGill, however, had news for Eisenhower about his son, John, who was in the army at Fort Benning, Georgia. John had been visiting Atlanta and "having dates with the attractive daughter of one of my neighbors." Eisenhower showed McGill a newspaper photograph of his son and several young women and asked McGill to point out the neighbor's daughter. "This I did," McGill said, rubbing it in, "not failing to pass it on to my associates for a look."[11]

Paris in January was still in the euphoria of liberation. At a Paris bar McGill met Ernest Hemingway and Mary Welch and they had drinks and "a good visit." The U.S. Office of War Information briefed them that the press situation was promising. The "new French press was eager not to return to the old corrupt system of before the war" and that the new government had pledged cooperation "in keeping the press free." One new paper, serious, independent, and owned by the reporters and editors, was *Le Monde,* founded in December, just four months after the liberation. French editors soon wined and dined the Americans. As McGill wrote in the final ASNE report, the French insisted that they were "in no way a governmental press. [The new French press] is the heir of the underground press which was freely established in the resistance movements."[12]

In quick succession, the Americans flew to Brussels and Rome. They found the Italian press in a trancelike state. Subservience to Mussolini for more than twenty years made the newspaper editors appear "to be like persons coming out of an anaesthetic. . . . They had taken orders so long they didn't know how to use freedom from orders." McGill focused a column on Italy, observing that the country now had a new set of ruins that "still ask a question of future. Will we be able to rid ourselves of the German sickness?"[13]

McGill was clearly having a good time. He loved Italian food and red wine and being a center of attention. As they were being driven to the Vatican to visit Pope Pius XII, Forrest observed, "Ike let us down. But one thing is sure. The Holy Father hasn't got a son who has dates with the daughter of McGill's neighbors." Even McGill was surprised when the Pope greeted him. "Mr. McGill," he said, "we have had a nice letter about you from Bishop O'Hara in Atlanta." McGill and Forrest could hardly keep a straight face. Ackerman, who was becoming ill with an infection, was not amused. As they left, two young priests from Atlanta asked them all to dinner. "Georgia's triumph," wrote McGill, "was complete."[14]

Next they flew to liberated Greece. On February 8, the committee began recording the horrors of Nazi occupation. The travel, the hurried pace, the constant interviews, and the cold of winter wore on Ackerman's health, and he was confined to bed with a cold and an ear infection while McGill and Forrest met with editors who had survived the Nazis. McGill kept up his own spirits with glasses of retsina, which he found in abundant supply. "This is a delicacy which the Germans didn't appreciate," he wrote. "At any rate, the Germans didn't drink it up."[15]

Greek editors had revived more quickly the Italians. The Greeks readily agreed to promote international mechanisms to support a free press. As the Americans later reported to ASNE, "The Greeks explained that they, and other small nations, would be stronger in their use of a free press if the larger nations would join with them in providing some sort of council to hear complaints." McGill was told how Nazi institutions had subdued decent citizens proud of their democratic traditions. When intimidated by systematic terror, he explained, "their minds, of course, protest. But they do nothing." The resultant silence licensed the Nazis with the appearance that they had a majority behind them. McGill could make connections with totalitarian tendencies in the South's past, with the Klan and demagogues whose social and political noise enforced racial segregation, silencing decent people who in good conscience disagreed.[16]

The newest obstacle to establishing a free press in Greece was the fear of Communist subversion through propaganda. With the German withdrawal, a small but well organized Communist party supplied with arms through Yugoslavia was igniting a civil war. "When liberation came," McGill explained in his daily column, "the Communists came up out of the underground with the only efficient organization. . . . That is why, in many of the liberated countries, we heard so much about Communist activities."[17]

In the Middle East, government officials cited this fear of Communist subversion as the reason for not permitting a free press which could be subverted. In Cairo, the Americans sensed no commitment to a free press from either the British or King Farouk. The Egyptians seemed to dread free expression. The king's French-educated prime minister, Dr. Ahmed Pasha, told the Americans their mission was "idealistic but impossible." A free flow of information, he said, would not permit the government to suppress propaganda, which infiltrated in "every way," particularly from the Communists. The next day, the committee was puzzled to hear King Farouk blame censorship on the British and announce himself "entirely" in favor of a free press and a free flow of news. Otherwise, Arab editors were preoccupied with contesting the Jewish Free Palestine movement and with trying to gain the Americans' condemnation of it. The committee ducked the Jewish issue "on the ground that editors cannot be advocates and must be objective."[18]

Justifications for controlling the press did not persuade McGill. Rather than modify his Western ideal, McGill discounted the fear of Soviet propaganda. Unfortunately, as he later explained, the committee's solution for the Egyptians was a Western democratic concept alien to their culture and perhaps unworkable—John Milton's "marketplace of ideas": "Let your papers discuss it fully. If it isn't true, the people will know it. If it is true in any sense it would force your government to bring about needed reforms." McGill said the Egyptian rulers just "shook their heads." He concluded that "fear of Soviet propaganda leads some nations to queer lengths."[19]

McGill's overall demeanor and behavior had alienated Ackerman. This was certainly in part because McGill's drinking offended him but also because the dean's health did not improve. McGill's lack of sympathy also irritated Ackerman. "Ever since the beginning of my cold McGill has found it very difficult to control his temper," he wrote to Vandy. "Yesterday morning, in conference when I was running a temperature and feeling almost too weak to sit up he said to the assembled U.S. government officials: 'Dean, you should be ashamed yourself [*sic*] for being ill. I never felt better in my life' and he thumped his chest with obvious pride and satisfaction."[20] McGill, the workhorse, suffered mainly from hangovers, but he worked through even the worst of those. He had "the constitution of a rhinoceros" and "was anxious to press on."[21] Delays frustrated him most when he thought of Mary Elizabeth at home without him, or the miscarriages, or their first infant who died after birth, or sweet Virginia. Ackerman, succumbing to a cold, gained lifetime membership in McGill's gallery of ginks. More than a decade later he treated his colleagues to "talk about that trip and how much he liked Wilbur Forrest. But Ackerman—he thought he was a solemn, pompous ass. What a pill, what an ass. He wondered, 'How can a man rise so high and have so little judgment.'"[22]

McGill couldn't resist needling the dean. On the day when he felt himself "almost too weak to sit up," Ackerman was cheered by a "nest with two young birds being fed by a parent 'kite.' It was so close to the [hotel] window that we had an unusual view of the family." While Ackerman thought the scene touching, McGill made light of it. When U.S. officials arrived for a meeting, McGill showed the nest and announced, as Ackerman recalled, "I have just witnessed the love life of the Kites and Mrs. Kite, smoothing out her feathers, said: 'Nature is grand.'" In saying this, McGill "strutted across the room as if he had personally participated in the affair. I never knew a man who derives such obvious satisfaction from another man's misfortune."[23]

The next day, Ackerman checked into a hospital for diagnosis and treatment. "Ward 33 is a friendly place," he wrote his wife. Meanwhile, McGill and Forrest kept on schedule, flying to Turkey for a few days. Ackerman felt abandoned. "My colleagues have decided evidently to move on without consulting me," he wrote Vandy, "which is disappointing but not unusual."[24] The entire episode, detailed in his letters and diary, created a personal animosity that would only intensify. Whatever McGill thought of the dean, Ackerman's opinion carried more weight. He had had a distinguished career as a journalist and a respected public relations counselor before becoming dean of the Columbia University Graduate School of Journalism and secretary to the Advisory Board for the Pulitzer Prizes.

In Turkey, the government, in line with its wartime neutrality, had closed both anti-Russian and pro-Russian newspapers. Despite Turkey's late entry into the war on the Allied side, the Americans sensed that censorship would continue and concluded, "Governments, once they have a taste of censorship, like the idea." McGill got further evidence of Turkish censorship from a young journalist in Istanbul. When they met in a newsroom, McGill encouraged him to send dispatches to U.S. newspapers. The next day, the young man replied in a letter, "Please don't mention this letter to my boss Paul Foley. I was scolded enough yesterday for my questions to you. . . . And you talk of freedom of press!"[25]

Management of news and information seemed to have deep roots in the Middle East. In several countries regulation of the press was still guided by laws laid down during five hundred years of domination by the Ottoman Empire. In concluding that Turkey was *not* an "eager exponent of a free press," the committee noted the manner in which the country filtered and obstructed news flow through the Agence Anatole, "a theoretically independent, but actually government-controlled agency." Agence Anatole exemplified an authoritarian philosophy of message control which completely contradicted the libertarian credo of free flow promoted by the ASNE missionaries. Vulnerable nations, as the Turks explained, could advance their national self-interest best by managing, filtering, and even diverting news and information which might harm national security.[26]

The Soviet news agency Tass was actively staffing offices in the Middle East. Back in Cairo, as the Americans waited for visas for Russia, McGill met the Egyptian correspondent for Tass at a reception. As McGill told his readers, this affable, sturdy, and intelligent Russian, Nikolai Kossolowsky, did not fit the Western model for a journalist. He was modeled for diplomacy and intrigue. As "an Egyptologist, one of the best in Russia. . . . Egypt had been his life study. I can imagine what excellent and thorough reports go back to Moscow in the Moscow pouch." The Tass agent seemed to outclass any American diplomats assigned to the region, and McGill worried that the United States underestimated the stakes in the Middle East.[27]

The Americans waited in Cairo on the hope of flying to Moscow. In February, visas arrived, secured by Secretary of State Stettinius, who was attending the Three-Power talks at Yalta. Hastily, McGill, Forrest, and Ackerman packed aboard an army transport which would take them as far as Tehran.

The mission in Moscow, critical for postwar cooperation, seemed unreasonable. They would be asking a totalitarian state to permit freedom of expression. Only the fact that the Russians were wartime Allies gave them any hope. The flight itself tested their resolve. Stories about the helter-skelter Soviet air force were legendary. McGill would never forget the takeoff from Iran in a U.S. DC-3 sold to the Russians for the war. "There were no safety belts and the baggage was not lashed down"—an important detail when the Soviet pilot handled the DC-3 like a fighter plane, tilting it in "tight climbing banks while your hair curls." They got a good view of the Caspian Sea because the pilot flew low over it. He did well to guide them through a winter storm, but, with no lights or radio, he had to make a stopover in Stalingrad.[28]

The flight was rough on Ackerman. As soon as the plane landed, he hastened to quench his thirst with two glasses of cold water handed him by a waitress. Within hours he had diarrhea. In midwinter, he told his wife, he made "pilgrimages to the toilet about one hundred yards across the snow covered field. . . . The dirt and stench of the toilet were sickening." The layover in Stalingrad lasted three days. When the storm cleared, they boarded another plane, which soon became engulfed in a blizzard that shook the fuselage. To calm himself, Ackerman played cards, and was nettled when "McGill made some wisecrack which caused us to stop playing."[29]

In the frigid north, Moscow became their oasis. The Associated Press correspondents met the plane and took the Americans to the Metropole Hotel for lunch: American whiskey or Russian vodka with broiled chicken. Afterward they met with the U.S. ambassador, Averell Harriman, who briefed them about what to expect from the Russians.[30]

As often as not, the Americans found themselves on the defensive, explaining U.S. press practices. Here, as in the Middle East, they were questioned about how they could allow their own newspapers to print negative—and false—criticism of their own government and allies. The committee later acknowledged the gulf between the two systems: "It was difficult for an American to keep in mind, or to rationalize the fact, that the Soviet newspapers are not merely owned by the government, they are an integral part of it." To Ackerman's astonishment, McGill at times sympathized with the Soviets, seeming to agree that they had been treated poorly in the American press. When the Russians complained about negative coverage of their country in America's chain-owned newspapers, he could identify with their complaints when he thought of his own South being denigrated by northern-dominated chains. McGill worked for what was still a family-owned newspaper, independent of chains, priding itself on supporting the interests of the South, most recently Governor Arnall's crusade to equalize railroad freight rates discriminatory against the South. In this crusade, McGill saw no sympathy coming from the national newspaper moguls. He had the least liking for the Hearst papers, the McCormick-Patterson, chain and the Scripps-Howard group.[31]

McGill respected the Russian people for resisting Hitler. Like the British, they experienced suffering, only more ghastly and with many more fatalities. Wishfully and naïvely, he felt that after the war these courageous people ultimately would demand civil liberties and prevail against Stalin's dictatorship. In search of the true Russian character, McGill went out with a translator to talk with ordinary Moscovites on the street. From this minimal sampling of public opinion, McGill concluded that subservient people spoke with a powerful voice, distinct from the government's Marxist rhetoric. The Russian people, he told southerners back home, "are not so much Marxists as they are Russians, with the temperaments and reactions developed, as have been our own and those of any other peoples, by events and by their economy and history." By nature, he reasoned, the long-suffering Russian people would be receptive to a world declaration of freedoms that guaranteed no more wars, together with a proviso for freedom of information.[32]

This intuitive bond with a suffering and courageous people guided his perspective on Soviet government in the postwar era. Before America entered the war, he had written his share of anti-Stalinist rhetoric. While Russia and Nazi Germany were allies, McGill condemned "Joe" Stalin for the murder of millions of peasants in the communization of farms. In 1940 he mocked Russia's rationale for bombing Finland. "All that remains in Russia and all that has been there for some years," he wrote in 1940, "is one of the bloodiest, cruelest tyrannies in the long history of the world. No Tzar of Russia ever spilled more blood than has this tyranny of Stalin." In 1942, in line with U.S. wartime alliances, McGill expressed his thankfulness for the new ally against Hitler and became predisposed to envision postwar cooperation. He excoriated those men "high in business and political circles, who think that once the war is done we ought to break off with Russia and build up a wall to keep her out."[33]

His amiability toward the Russians arose not merely from the vodka he drank with them at *Pravda*. In a column written from Egypt, he advised readers that the "Soviet Union is a young nation. The ideas of its people are new. Yet there is within them an ancient tradition and century-old impulses and reaction." If the postwar world presented a new set of rules, he hoped that the Soviets would come out of isolation and drop what McGill deemed to be their understandable suspicion of the West: "Russia, I am convinced, will make agreements. She will drive hard bargains. They will not be idealistic or ephemeral. They will be tough and they will be supported by good reasoning." Of course, McGill was as yet unaware of the hard bargains Stalin had already driven past the Allies for "good reasoning"—Russian hegemony in Eastern Europe.[34]

Despite Soviet ideology and practice, the missionaries chose to be optimistic about the postwar Soviet Union. In drafting the committee's report, McGill gave the Soviets the benefit of doubt, concluding that they were sincere in pledging a freer press. The report gave credibility to the view that "a more liberal press policy is in the making in Russia." Ackerman tended to disagree, and was not easily persuaded, especially by McGill. To Ackerman the world since the early 1930s had been "black with prohibitions upon freedom of speech, freedom of the press, freedom of assembly, of petition, or of religion." In an address in 1934, Ackerman had advocated to President Roosevelt a new foreign policy of "international realism" which cited Russia, Japan and Nazi Germany as "the chief nations threatening world peace. . . . In each of these countries the press is controlled by government officials or militarists."[35]

The issues of colonialism and national independence movements which had surfaced in Egypt presented themselves again in Asia. The stop in India underscored the Americans' dilemma in promoting freedom of communication while they could not freely address the ramifications of press freedom for emergent nationalist movements in the colonial empires. How could they advocate freedom of expression which the British in India did not grant? Certainly the Americans did not want to stir latent hostilities, least of all while Britain, an ally, was fighting Germany and Japan.

Their aloofness from the aspirations of nationalists was visible in India. There, McGill and Forrest stepped into the whirlwind of Mahatma Gandhi's independence movement. During his wartime "Quit India" campaign, Gandhi had welcomed a Japanese invasion as an expedient to oust the British. British censorship had been severe, and many Indian editors were eager to complain in a world forum.

The Americans spent only three days in India. They met Indian editors who attended a day-long newspaper conference in New Delhi. Other Indian journalists who missed that session criticized the Americans for not traveling widely to hear more complaints about British suppression of the press. Writing in the prestigious English-language *Hindustan Times,* the president of the All-India Newspaper Editors Conference, S. A. Brelvi, said his members "wished to draw their attention to the misuse of war-time emergency powers for the suppression of inconvenient news and views and to some of the extremely ridiculous orders passed under the Defence of India rules." Without visiting "at least some of the more important newspaper centres," Brelvi argued, "they could hardly be expected to have learnt the truth about the 'freedom' of the Press in India, nor to have realized how strongly newspapermen in India feel that there can be no freedom of the Press without national freedom."[36]

Disturbed by this criticism, the U.S. general representative in India, Ralph Block, answered for the United States. Block apologized only for the brevity of the visit, explaining that the committee's trip to Moscow had put them behind schedule and shortened the visit.[37]

Amid the tension of wartime China, battered by a new sweeping Japanese offensive aimed at the American air bases, the delegation's facade of unity came unglued. The rift between McGill and Ackerman widened dramatically and was close to becoming a public scandal. After the committee reached Chungking, Chiang Kai-shek's wartime capital in western

China, Ackerman threatened to quit the mission. The break was triggered by McGill's drinking during the day when the committee, in the dean's view, was representing the image of American journalism. Although McGill later denied it, enough witnesses substantiated that he was drinking by midday.

Certainly McGill was tense and tired, worrying privately about Mary Elizabeth. Everyone had been too optimistic about how quickly they could circle the world in wartime and winter. Now it was April and he was dreadfully certain that he would be somewhere in Asia when the baby arrived. The demands of globetrotting and the condescension from the "pompous" teetotaling academic had eroded McGill's early enthusiasm. Could the time zones have also altered his biological clock? Was he really drinking by noon if where he came from it was the middle of the night?

McGill infuriated Ackerman and disturbed Forrest. On April 2, before their interview with Generalissimo Chiang, the Americans addressed a luncheon hosted by students of the Chinese branch of Columbia University's Graduate School of Journalism. While addressing the students, Ackerman was astonished when he overheard an insult from McGill. "McGill became intoxicated and while I was speaking to the students, he shouted 'Liar' on two occasions," Ackerman wrote. "Such behavior is unbecoming for an official representative of the ASNE." After the luncheon, Forrest called McGill aside and "lambasted" him. "I thought the students were well aware of his condition so I made no reply."[38]

Still more deplorable to Ackerman was McGill's conduct during the interview with the Generalissimo. McGill sat on a sofa, slumping, Ackerman told his wife. To Knight, Ackerman said that during the interview, McGill occasionally "pounded the table, made critical remarks in an undertone when others were speaking and was otherwise not in a condition to represent the ASNE in a honorable fashion."[39] McGill, Ackerman elaborated for Vandy, "was intoxicated . . . half of the time with his eyes closed, mumbling incoherent words. Forrest and I were very uneasy and we decided to terminate the interview so we got up; Forrest thanked the Generalissimo for his cordial reception. . . . I wished we could have stayed longer but both Forrest and I, in his words, 'never spent a more uncomfortable hour in the presence of any important personage.'"[40]

McGill's disrespect was prompted in part by his distaste for what he understood to be Chiang's corrupt, autocratic regime. McGill knew the reports of widespread political and economic corruption, and in Chungking he believed he saw supporting evidence. To him, Chiang embodied the familiar attributes of a demagogue, a false leader with a retinue, a gang of sycophants and toadies, looting the war chest supplied by the United States. This view was consistent with the privately expressed conclusion of Gen. Joseph W. "Vinegar Joe" Stilwell, U.S. commander of Chinese forces in China, that "nothing can be done in China until we get rid of Chiang Kai-shek." Stilwell's biographer noted that he "was persuaded that the Communists, as the 'agricultural liberals' of China, might offer the United States a base to build on."[41] This was also McGill's conclusion. So corrupt did Chiang seem that the Communists' social reforms looked attractive, especially the Communists' vows to redistribute land to farmers and abolish loan sharking.

The more he saw, the more McGill was appalled. Emotionally, he sympathized with the landless peasants. How much did they differ from the pitiful Georgia sharecroppers whose cycle of poverty he had been publicizing for a decade? To McGill it did not seem extreme to embrace the admirable goals of the Maoists. McGill recognized in Mao Tse-tung's promises some of the economic reforms he himself championed for southern tenant farmers: He had sought ways to make it easier for sharecroppers to buy small farms and become private landowners. In this mood, McGill saw agrarian reform as more the issue than communism. He concluded that Mao's government, which by 1945 held as much territory as Chiang, was "not Marxist Communist, being almost entirely an agrarian movement. It has given the farmers land and it manages to hold to their affections and loyalty. It rid them of the money-lenders who were, by all accounts, enough to make our loan sharks appear beneficent philanthropists. It rid them of the sharecropper system. So, it has strength; but it is almost all agrarian strength. It is based on land ownership, not communal farming."[42]

Certainly McGill could have been expected to mute his personal philosophy, given the diplomatic nature of their mission. Chungking gin, however, likely lowered the barriers and freed him to express seething hostility for not only Chiang but also Ackerman. To McGill, the dean seemed to fawn over Chiang, who was the principal patron of Ackerman's journalism program in Chungking. The dean, McGill thought, was blind to politics, a naïf. At lunch McGill had been rankled when the dean, addressing his constituency of Chinese students, ascended the ivory tower. As the day wore on, Ackerman and his patron Chiang became insufferable. The dean and the warlord reeked of officiousness and insincerity. Although McGill did not believe the pledge, Chiang, as the committee ultimately reported, "pledged he would abolish censorship when the war ended and he would support with all his power the ASNE plan for a pledge by nations in treaties that would permit a free flow of information between nations." As they left the Generalissimo, McGill said, Ackerman announced that he felt he had been in the presence of deity. McGill insisted that he had not started drinking until *after* he heard that from Ackerman. As Harold Martin retold the story, "This run-in with Ackerman made him [McGill] feel so unhappy that he went out and got morosely drunk on Chungking gin, which made him feel even worse."[43]

The committee disbanded shortly afterward. Back at the hotel, Ackerman, McGill, and Forrest argued vehemently. McGill exploded like a firecracker, saying things he later regretted. The exchange cleared the air but ended the collaboration and came close to negating the value of their journey. As soon as he entered the hotel, Ackerman announced to "both of my colleagues that I was resigning from the committee; that I consider McGill's behavior a disgrace to American journalism and as this had happened in every capital we had visited I would continue on the journey independently." Forrest pleaded with him to reconsider. "McGill wanted to talk it over," Ackerman wrote in a lengthy letter to his wife.[44]

The situation had the potential for scandal. The Americans had made the trip in the glare of publicity and were scheduled to leave the next day for Australia. Forrest cautioned Ackerman to be reasonable and consider that his resignation "would raise a 'stink.'" "But," wrote Ackerman, "I made no reply. Before saying 'goodbye' to him tonight I said that I did not intend to make public anything that I might do but that I would no longer have anything whatsoever to do with this fellow from Georgia." Ackerman felt justified in taking drastic action.

It was not as though his imagination had conjured up this drunken buffoon. Others shared his astonishment, he noted. One U.S. official "came in to ask how the ASNE selected a man like that to represent American journalism in world capitals. I could give no answer. I don't know."[45]

Two days later, Ackerman wrote his official letter of resignation to Knight, marking it "Confidential and NOT for publication." He was planning to stay and work at the university in Chungking and he noted that the resignation was effective upon his arrival in the United States. To minimize publicity, he assured Knight, "I do not intend to make an issue of this matter while any members of your committee are outside of the United States."[46]

Ackerman told Knight that McGill's "conduct has been a disgrace to journalism. . . . In every city McGill has been drunk on the job. . . . I feel that American journalism has been disgraced by his conduct." While "under the influence of liquor," Ackerman said, McGill had made "irresponsible remarks concerning American journalism."[47]

Ackerman believed McGill had undermined the credibility of leading American newspaper publishers. In Russia and again in China, McGill astonished him by agreeing when critics complained about coverage of their countries in the chain-owned newspapers. "He has described the Hearst, McCormick-Patterson and Scripps-Howard newspapers, according to one Chungking newspaper report as being 'either hysterically pessimistic or optimistic to the point of being ludicrous. . . . They do not carry much weight with the people in general.'" Ackerman added a personal insult about Knight: "On other occasions he has said that you ruined the best newspaper in Chicago [the *Daily News*]. . . . He has attacked newspapers whose editors are members of the ASNE." For all these reasons, Ackerman said, he would "not be associated with the Committee in any report to the Society." He promised to keep silent about McGill. "I will submit my own report. . . . I shall make no reference to the matters presented in this letter."[48]

The Americans' last scheduled stop was in Australia, a bastion of the free press. Forrest persuaded Ackerman that it would be good to accompany him and McGill, to present a facade of unity. Ackerman spoke to McGill only when necessary for business. One American who saw them together very briefly was Calvin Kytle, a soldier from the South, stationed in Australia. Kytle, one of McGill's far-flung readers, made a point of visiting the columnist in his hotel room in Brisbane. He found McGill seemingly very relaxed, seated with his shirt open, exposing his navel, into which he had poured salt for dipping his celery. Referring to his navel, McGill noted, "This is the only use I've found for this thing." Kytle also got a glimpse of Ackerman: "At one point while I was there Ackerman came into McGill's hotel room to remind him of an appointment. I can confirm there was bad feeling between them. McGill muttered something under his breath after Ackerman left that was hardly complimentary—the only word I truly remember was 'pompous'—and he certainly conveyed the idea that he was glad the trip would soon be over and he would be free of Ackerman's stuffy presence."[49]

McGill had more important matters in mind. The world's most important business, the war, was ending. In Europe, American forces in April were well inside Germany and the Russians had entered Berlin. While McGill was in the Pacific in April, his marines had invaded Okinawa, 325 miles from Japanese cities. In San Francisco, delegates from fifty nations gathered to complete a charter for the United Nations. And of course in Atlanta, God willing, Mary Elizabeth was about to have their baby at Emory University Hospital. On April 25, she felt the first pains of labor as McGill was leaving Brisbane at 4:27 A.M. aboard an old converted Liberator bomber for a two-day flight via New Caledonia, Fiji, Canton Island, and Christmas Island to Hickham Field, Honolulu. There, as he recalled years later, a young naval officer from Georgia, Frank Wells, brought him a message from Jack Tarver: "Baby boy, weight six pounds seven ounces, born Caesarian, 8:42 A.M., Wednesday, April 25. Looks like you but is healthy." Two days later after a stopover in San Francisco, he was home, gazing upon Ralph Emerson McGill Jr.[50]

During May McGill with some help from Forrest wrote the committee's preliminary report. The timing was urgent because the UN conferees were making decisions about the charter in San Francisco. In June, the official report, written mostly by McGill, was presented to the ASNE board in Washington. On the record, the Americans projected a guarded optimism, as if they could build a tower of freedom, eventually, by starting now with a few bricks. Their efforts had secured a good number of pledges of cooperation, including promising statements from Soviet officials. While underscoring these vague successes, McGill knew they had failed to win anything near agreement on a policy implementing the practice of press freedom. Nonetheless, they understated the negative comments, saying only that "there are others who have given it [a free press] mere lip service and will seek to avoid it." Ending on an idealistic note, Forrest and McGill hoped that the idea of universal press freedom would still "grow and flourish" so that "in the end the peoples of all nations will know each other better and the problems of nations may be readily understood through a truer and freer flow of news."[51]

The personal differences had been hushed up. Ackerman acquiesced and permitted his name to be associated with McGill's on the final report. Both men saw the wisdom of keeping their rift private. Ackerman carried his images of McGill's grossness and drunkenness back to Columbia University. In catching up with office mail, he looked through a passel of press clippings sent from the *Atlanta Constitution,* which had played up McGill's role: "McGill Leaves London for Paris Parley," "'Feeling Pulse of Europe,' Touring McGill Asserts," and "Brussels Indorses [*sic*] Press Freedom of McGill Mission." In Atlanta, McGill would seem testy whenever the dean's name came up. At times he mentioned Ackerman, telling friends and colleagues in the newsroom that Ackerman had kept him from winning a Pulitzer Prize.[52]

Before marrying, Benjamin Franklin McGill, Ralph's father, had aspired to become a lawyer. In 1889, an outburst of violence leading to tragic results forced him to withdraw in disgrace from the University of Chattanooga, another of the McGill family's closed subjects. Ben McGill returned to Chattanooga in 1904 to work for a heating and roofing company, giving Ralph a chance for superior schooling. Courtesy of Ralph McGill Papers, Special Collections Department, Robert W. Woodruff Library, Emory University.

Until he was five, Ralph lived at Soddy, Tennessee. He is pictured here with his paternal grandmother, Mary Elizabeth Wallace McGill, known as "Mammy," and his mother, Mary Louise "Lou" McGill. Mary Lou was the daughter of newspaperman Anderson Skillern, whose abandonment of his wife and two children in Texas was one of the family's closed subjects. Courtesy of Ralph McGill Papers, Special Collections Department, Robert W. Woodruff Library, Emory University.

A school photograph taken around the time of McGill's graduation in 1917 from the private McCallie School in Chattanooga. During those high school years he captained the football team, edited the school newspaper, published short stories in the school's literary magazine, won an orator's gold medal, and was proclaimed "best actor" in the title role of *What Happened to Jones?* Courtesy of Ralph Emerson McGill Papers, Special Collections Department, Robert W. Woodruff Library, Emory University.

Leaving Vanderbilt University in 1922 without a degree, McGill quickly blended into the *Nashville Banner* newsroom as a sports writer always eager to cover politics, tragedies, or murder trials. Years later his friend Johnny Popham sent him this photograph of the *Banner* newsroom in the mid-1920s, with McGill *(center)* typing with his hat on. Courtesy of Ralph McGill Papers, Special Collections Department, Robert W. Woodruff Library, Emory University.

In Havana for the Pan American Press Conference in June 1933, McGill, still a sports editor, mixed with editor Lee Hills *(left)* and executive J. T. Waters *(center)*, both of the *Miami Herald.* Two months after the conference, McGill returned to report on the Cuban revolution. Courtesy of Ralph McGill Papers, Special Collections Department, Robert W. Woodruff Library, Emory University.

Edward "Ted" Weeks, editor of the *Atlantic Monthly*, began a lifelong friendship with McGill in 1943, when a delegation of editors visited wartime England. At Weeks's urging, McGill wrote his autobiography, *The South and the Southerner*, published by Atlantic Monthly Press. Courtesy of Ralph McGill Papers, Special Collections Department, Robert W. Woodruff Library, Emory University.

McGill poses in Chiang Kai-shek's China in April 1945 during the Committee on Freedom of the Press's mission, with Carl W. Ackerman of Columbia University *(second from left)* and Wilbur Forrest of the *New York Herald Tribune* *(center)*. By this time, Ackerman, secretary to the Pulitzer Prize Advisory Board, considered McGill "a disgrace to American journalism" and preferred to pose beside Forrest. Courtesy of Ralph McGill Papers, Special Collections Department, Robert W. Woodruff Library, Emory University.

Mixing business and pleasure was McGill's lifelong pattern. Seen here in the early 1950s, McGill socializes with *(left to right)* Coca-Cola president ("The Boss") Robert W. Woodruff, the new owner of the *Atlanta Constitution,* James M. Cox Sr. of Ohio, and Atlanta's great golfer, Bobby Jones. Courtesy of Ralph McGill Papers, Special Collections Department, Robert W. Woodruff Library, Emory University.

McGill shares a laugh with his dear friend Jack Tarver *(right)* and his frequent adversary, George C. Biggers. Biggers ran the newspapers for James Cox and worried that McGill's civil rights advocacy alienated advertisers. Tarver countered with surveys showing that people read McGill even if they hated him. In 1957, Biggers retired, and Tarver became president of Atlanta Newspapers, Inc. Courtesy of Ralph McGill Papers, Special Collections Department, Robert W. Woodruff Library, Emory University.

McGill sought out Carl Sandburg shortly after the poet moved to Flat Rock, North Carolina, in the early 1950s. For more than a decade, they exchanged visits, gifts, and conversation. Sandburg called McGill a brother and regarded him as a prophet. A frequent messenger from McGill was the *Atlanta Journal and Constitution* photographer Charles R. Pugh Jr. Courtesy Charles R. Pugh Jr., *Atlanta Journal and Constitution.*

McGill relished opportunities to speak for the South on national radio and television. In April 1959, Dave Garroway *(left)* hosted McGill, with *New York Times* managing editor Turner Catledge and *Denver Post* editor and publisher Palmer Hoyt, on NBC's morning *Today Show*. Three weeks later McGill won the Pulitzer Prize for editorial writing. Courtesy of Ralph McGill Papers, Special Collections Department, Robert W. Woodruff Library, Emory University.

The McGills' longtime cook, maid, and housekeeper, Julia Crawford, helps Mary Elizabeth bottle basil and garlic in vinegar. The garden at the house on Piedmont Road was a source of strength and sharing. At the Episcopal Cathedral of St. Philip, Mary Elizabeth lectured on herbs of the Bible and supplied flowers for the children's chapel. Courtesy of Ralph McGill Papers, Special Collections Department, Robert W. Woodruff Library, Emory University.

McGill's columns became one of the most popular features of the newspaper—read by those who respected him and those who hated him. Here in December 1960, Ku Klux Klansmen picket in front of the *Atlanta Journal and Constitution*. Courtesy Charles R. Pugh Jr., *Atlanta Journal and Constitution*.

No nationally syndicated columnist in 1960 supported the election of John F. Kennedy more than McGill. After Kennedy's victory, McGill visited him at the Kennedy winter home at Palm Beach, Florida, with Mary Elizabeth and Ralph Jr. The Kennedy administration appointed McGill as a goodwill ambassador to newly independent African nations. Courtesy of Ralph McGill Papers, Special Collections Department, Robert W. Woodruff Library, Emory University.

In July 1962, shortly after his wife's death, McGill took his son to a publishers' conference in Japan and shared with him the adventure of climbing Mount Fuji. At the summit, McGill poses with Ralph Jr., fifteen, and Kimiko Kawato. A graduate of the University of Tokyo, Kawato later translated McGill's autobiography into Japanese (1966). Courtesy of Ralph McGill Papers, Special Collections Department, Robert W. Woodruff Library, Emory University.

During his African ambassadorial trip in 1963, McGill's record of advocacy of civil rights secured interviews with Africa's nationalist leaders and won over audiences of young Africans. Here in February 1963, he signs autographs for students in Dakar, Senegal. Courtesy of Ralph McGill Papers, Special Collections Department, Robert W. Woodruff Library, Emory University.

Eugene Patterson regarded McGill as "the best friend I ever had." In 1960, when McGill was promoted to publisher, Patterson became editor. He credited McGill with encouraging him to say "out loud, in print" what he had felt for years, that "the racial positions of the South were wrong." In 1967 Patterson's editorials won the Pulitzer Prize. Courtesy of Ralph McGill Papers, Special Collections Department, Robert W. Woodruff Library, Emory University.

Opposite page

On his tour of combat zones in Vietnam in September 1966, McGill spent time with his godson, PFC John Martin of the First Cavalry. He told John's father, Harold Martin, that they plied "the platoon's pet monkey with beer." A year earlier McGill's son had graduated from basic training and entered the Marine Corps Reserve. Courtesy of Ralph McGill Papers, Special Collections Department, Robert W. Woodruff Library, Emory University.

McGill at his desk at the *Constitution.* This is the last known photograph before his death on February 3, 1969, two days before his seventy-first birthday. Courtesy of Ralph McGill Papers, Special Collections Department, Robert W. Woodruff Library, Emory University.

10

A Portable Typewriter

Capitalism and Communism can live in the same world.
It is that problem that has to be worked out.
—Ralph McGill, 1946

I felt the spiritual impact of the Sea of Galilee
and the stalls below the old Crusader Church at
Bethlehem. From Scopus and the old city of Jerusalem
I looked toward the Dead Sea and remembered the old
Prophets and the patient Nazarene. There were
soldiers and there was strife in His time.
—Ralph McGill, 1950

During the spring and summer of 1945 McGill watched from a distance as the long war ended. Even those who had planned for a postwar era were swept along in the rush of events. McGill struggled to understand the consequences of all that was happening. In rapid succession, he noted the transfer of leadership to President Truman, the destruction of Nazi Germany, the dropping of atomic bombs on civilians at Hiroshima and Nagasaki, Japan's surrender. Each event altered the way Americans had oriented their lives for years and raised questions about life beyond the abyss of war. These were profound questions, which McGill was eager to examine and discuss. Having joined that select club of men who had circumnavigated the globe, he claimed the world as his journalistic beat.

For the present, however, his overseas bags were unpacked. For the first time in his marriage he had a family life revolving around a child, this pink son in diapers. Rather than stay late at the office, McGill hurried his pace in the afternoons and took an early bus home. At the house on Peachtree Road in Buckhead, friends watched as he doted on Ralph Jr. For hours at a time the globetrotter would play on the floor in a baby's world with his miraculous, healthy son. Harold Martin, home from serving with the marines in the Pacific and now writing for the *Saturday Evening Post,* watched McGill "lie on the floor and let the little fellow bounce happily upon his ample stomach; he read to him long before he could understand, and he walked out at night to show him the stars." McGill's sensibilities seemed to range between playful joy and awesome responsibility. He told friends he wanted to raise the boy to "love books and dogs and the hunting field" and poetry. "None of these things ever brought me any material gain, but life would have been barren without them."[1]

Tranquil domestic life, however blissful, paled in contrast to the thunder of geopolitics that throbbed mind, heart and soul. McGill could not resist commenting on every global phenomenon that affected the United States, yet he felt uncomfortable pontificating from a chair in Atlanta thousands of miles distant. His frequent drinking companion, Martin, talked with him over red wine or martinis about war brewing in Palestine, about the coming Nazi war criminal trials, about Russia developing its own atomic bomb. "Ralph, in his dark mood," Martin recalled, would try to get at the cause of international hostilities. McGill thought it was the old bugaboo that Roosevelt had articulated as the underlying cause of the Great Depression—fear, which at times McGill imagined as "mice through an attic" or the "black wing of fear." Then there was the question about his own role. Martin listened week after week as McGill worried about "which should have ultimate dominion over his life—his family or his profession? On the one hand was his boy, whom he yearned to guide and shape through his formative years, on other hand was his own need to go wherever the news led him anywhere, anytime."[2]

Ever since his experience in Nazi Austria, he trusted information he personally gathered overseas. The wartime trips to England and the 'round-the-world journey confirmed his reporter's instinct to go to the scene of the news, to talk with people in the streets and decide for himself. If others' views were at odds with his, he trusted his instincts.

When pundits began criticizing the Russians, McGill recalled the brave people he had met there and defended them and their motivations. In the months after he returned from Moscow, he preached moderation in

Soviet-American relations. His self-styled role was as one who had been to the Soviet Union and thus had insights which could make Soviet actions more understandable, if not acceptable. In August, when Russia declared war on Japan two days after the atomic bomb devastated Hiroshima, McGill discounted the critics' outrage: "Yesterday, Joseph Stalin led his war-weary, still hungry masses into a war with Japan. The cynical and thoughtless will say the atomic bomb blew him in."[3]

His sense of himself and of his own research undergirded this pugilistic stance that opponents must be "cynical and thoughtless." He believed Americans should see Stalin's declaration of war not as mere opportunism but as the unfolding of the Three-Power agreements at Yalta and Potsdam. Stalin's act demonstrated "the value of unity and planning—damning those who would frustrate and prevent international co-operation." He shared a "confidence" given him by Gen. George C. Marshall when the directors of the American Society of Newspaper Editors met in Washington in June. Marshall "declared the military leaders of this country believed Russia would enter the war and that they would welcome such entry when it came." With Russia's entry, McGill could hear the "death rattle" of Japan's military government and he proclaimed, "Peace for generations is ahead."[4]

When Gen. Dwight Eisenhower went to Moscow to confer with Stalin, McGill ridiculed the "thoughtless" who criticized Eisenhower's public appearance with Stalin reviewing a Soviet demonstration of military might: "As 'they' can tell you, he has had his leg pulled. He believes, poor demented fellow, that Russia genuinely wants to be friends with this country. And of course 'they' know that can't be true. Pretty soon now you will be hearing from 'them' that Gen. Eisenhower is all right as a general, but what a pity he is too far to the left; too much of a liberal; little on the pink side."[5]

The decision to halt the U.S. Army at the Elbe aroused suspicion about the Soviet high command, which was accused of not cooperating with the U.S. armies. Eisenhower had denied that. McGill defended the Soviets, repeating almost verbatim the Russians' complaints about the U.S. media, which they had expressed to him in Moscow. Referring mainly to the Hearst and McCormick papers, McGill lamented that "we have heard so much from the clique in this country which will not agree that anything in Russia is good; which distorts that country's actions; which libels it freely[;] . . . which never corrects, or apologizes when the contrary facts are revealed—we have had so much of their propaganda."[6]

The war had been over only three months when he got another invitation to witness history in the making. The offer came from the director of the Overseas News Agency in New York, Herbert Bayard Swope, one of American journalism's elder statesmen. After becoming the first winner of the Pulitzer Prize in 1917 for international reporting, Swope guided the Pulitzer family's "new journalism" crusades at the *New York World* in the 1920s, exposing the prison labor system in Georgia and the Ku Klux Klan, and in the process gaining three more Pulitzer Prizes. He was by 1946 a dedicated Zionist.[7] McGill's conquest of Talmadge, as well as his seeming support of a homeland for Jews oppressed by Hitler, caught Swope's attention.[8] McGill looked to be the brightest light in the rising generation of crusading journalists. There is, Swope wrote McGill, "no newspaperman in America with a finer sense of fairness than you. There is none freer from motivation; there is none, because of your independence, whose words would carry further than yours."[9]

The Overseas News Agency, which had a special interest in a Jewish homeland, would pay McGill's expenses and an honorarium to write "the real story" of Palestine.[10] "It has not been done," Swope insisted. Why had Britain abandoned its commitment to an independent state for the Jews? Why the sudden limitation of immigration of Jews from ravaged Central Europe? Who rightfully owns title to the land? "The British may be justified in their policies, and that justification should be brought out, if existent." McGill would not refuse the opportunity. The invitation, Martin recalled, rang like "the fire bell," and McGill hastened to accept. He could take this trip and return in time to fight Gene Talmadge's campaign for governor. "We . . . are delighted you can go to Palestine," Swope replied, adding that, as on his old *New York World,* "there ain't no instructions, except to get the story."[11]

In mid-January McGill kissed wife and infant son goodbye without knowing exactly when he would be home. On his way to Palestine, he justified a stopover, a return to Germany, to Nuremberg, to witness the trials of Nazi war criminals. The story of Jewish aspirations in Palestine was clearly linked to Nazi racism, epitomized by the Nuremberg Laws of September 15, 1935, which deprived Jews of citizenship and confined them as "subjects."[12]

McGill by now knew almost as many insiders in the Democratic administration in Washington as he did in the national journalistic establishment. Nudging his contacts in the State Department, he succeeded in being appointed a paid consultant to the Nuremberg trials. To make travel easier, William Benton, assistant secretary of state, provided a letter of introduction, explaining that he had asked McGill "to gather whatever independent evidence he can on the effectiveness and needs of our international information program, including the information control services in Germany . . . valuable for the Department's budget hearings." McGill took on the added government assignment with no evident perception of any conflict of interest or any sense that it restricted his freedom to publish. On this mission, official status permitted him to move with diplomatic ease across Europe; in Paris he caught a night military train from Paris to Frankfurt, where he rode in a jeep to Nuremberg.[13]

For McGill, the trials served as vindication. Since his journey to Berlin and Vienna in 1938 he had despised the Nazi operatives right down to the coercive "Sieg heil." Readers of the *Atlanta Constitution* might have felt his pulse rising in every sentence sent home from the trials. In the brightly lit courtroom, he examined the twenty-two defendants through a pair of field glasses "to bring their second-rate faces up so close they seem to be staring right into your own eyes." When Hermann Goering, second to Hitler in the Nazi Party, appeared, McGill stared at "Goering's porcine face with its pair of shrewd, greedy eyes." He considered the next in line to power, Rudolf Hess: "Hess' strained countenance with its careful mask." Through the glasses he studied the financial wizard, Dr. Hjalmar Horace Greeley Schacht ("stolid Schacht"), and the Nazi foreign minister who had issued declarations of war against the Soviet Union and the United States, the "dapper [Joachim] von Ribbentrop." "How in God's name, your mind asks, did this ordinary bunch ever rise so high they threatened the world?"[14]

The chaos created by Nazi terror could be witnessed firsthand outside the courtroom. "The trail," he wrote, "leads to the 'DP,' or Displaced Persons, camps." McGill kept hearing tales of the DPs. There were as many as 750,000 in 1946, and Germans regularly denigrated them as trouble-makers, "poor devils," black marketeers, idlers, agitators, Communists, and Jews who created problems by insisting on going to Palestine. He visited a camp, and the first DP he saw was a girl with a blue tattoo on her arm, which indicated she had been sent to Auschwitz concentration camp, and another Auschwitz tattoo at the base on her breastbone, marking her as a "prostitute for officers only." For the first time in his career, he found it impossible to interview these people because "the ugly horror of that degradation is always in the mind. But if a little bit of it has dimmed I did not want to bring it back again."[15]

The Germans also had been reduced to poverty. In the devastated cities, McGill saw them, hungry and poorly clothed, the picture of sickness. Thinking how the Nazis had treated others, he wrote, "you try to harden your heart. But you cannot." His compassion went out to children. "When he looked at them," his friend Martin said, "you could tell he was thinking of his own small son at home—warm and strong and well fed." As McGill told Martin, one Sunday afternoon he was walking through Heidelberg with three other journalists when he met a young girl who reminded him of a girl he had been fond of as a young reporter covering foxhound trials in Tennessee. She was ten years old, named Else Bender. He took her address and later checked with army intelligence and found out her father had been drafted and killed in the war, but that the family had probably not been Nazis. Then he asked Mary Elizabeth to send her skirts, sweaters, stockings, and saddle shoes. McGill hoped readers still bitter toward anyone German would share his view: "It was our responsibility that the children of postwar Germany should not grow up to become the monsters their parents had become after growing up in a defeated Germany after World War I."[16]

The sight of thousands of displaced persons in Germany touched McGill's emotional core. In a rather sudden conversion, he now accepted Zionism as a solution for the dispersed Jews. In Atlanta his editorials had supported repatriation of Jews to their prewar homelands, "to enable them to go back to their countries and again become a part of the life of those countries." Now, he told his readers, "I was wrong. Persons who are not survivors, or who have not seen these survivors, cannot know how haunted by the past are these people; how unbearable life would be if these people were forced to go back to live, among the graves of their people, awaiting God knows what." He thought of anti-Semitism as "the German sickness" that "remains in the minds of Europeans like mustard gas in old shell holes . . . after a battle has ended."[17]

When he left Germany for Palestine, McGill thought of himself as "no Zionist." That stance seems to have been a mere political precaution, because his sympathies had been with the homeland movement as early as 1938. When he witnessed the Nazi seizure of Austria, he had became "convinced . . . that the idea of a Jewish homeland in Palestine was one which had to be translated into fact." Years before the revelations of Nazi death camps, his "witnessing human beings reduced and destroyed by the constant pressure of fear and uncertainty was enough to convince me then of the necessity for Palestine." In America his only concern had been that "the Zionist story and proposals were a little too flawlessly and easily put; . . . that the Arabs were being pushed around too strongly." After visiting Cairo in 1945 and while still on the global mission, he had noted that the fervor of Jews "has made the Palestinian settlement unique, and, indeed, one of the most remarkable colonization projects of our epoch." He thought a Jewish "commonwealth" could be good for the Arabs as well. Rather idealistically, he wrote, "Leaving national passions aside, the Jewish colonization of Palestine has been an immense uplift for the Arabian world." The war had "radically changed the Jewish situation in the world," he concluded, forecasting that "if a true United Nations world emerges, many things that seem incapable of settlement now should have another and more co-operative aspect only a few years hence." Less than a year later, the death camps and displaced completed McGill's conversion.[18]

A stopover in Cairo gave him a sense of the postwar Arab opposition to a Jewish homeland in Palestine. He talked with Arabs he had met the year before during the ASNE free-press mission. Those surrounding the king still spoke about a movement for a pan-Arab league headed by King Farouk. But McGill surmised that the greatest enthusiasm belonged not to the pan-Arab movement but to nationalism and to the independence movement whose leaders were in the younger generation, better educated, articulating reforms which were beginning to appeal to the masses. These new leaders were unawed by the king and rich landowners, the "antiquated, corrupt, feudal leadership which has held on for centuries."[19]

McGill discounted Arab opposition to a Jewish homeland. Aside from his view that no one voice spoke for Egypt, McGill could not acquit the Arabs' role in the war. "Nor can the Arab insist he was on the side of the democratic forces," he wrote, "or in the present struggle for democratic stability." On the contrary, "Egypt and the others, believing Germany would win, remained unhappily neutral." The nation and individual Egyptians enriched themselves from war profiteering, he noted, amassing "something like one billion dollars" in London and New York. "In the greatest of all wars, Arab sympathies generally were with the Nazis and the Japanese. They overshadowed the exceptions."[20]

In Palestine McGill lost any objectivity he may have had about the Jews' settlements. They soon impressed him by their ingenuity and innovation in farming. McGill had never met a farmer he didn't empathize with or admire. On his second day, he dropped in at the Jewish Agency and found two helpful guides—Harry Beilen of the Jewish Agency and Harry Levin of the Jewish National Fund, who "arranged for me to see what I wanted to see."[21] Just outside Jerusalem, he saw the way farmers tilled the hills. In the South, he had seen "small farmers break their backs on poor, eroded land. Not one I know would tackle a hill near Jerusalem." There was good soil here, but "not too much of it any one place."[22]

Yet these settlers had tamed their hills. McGill noted their chief produce, the apples, plums, peaches, grapes, milk, and eggs, and the 150 cattle and 3,000 white leghorn chickens. The farmers said they had learned the Arab system of terracing and hill plowing but had modernized with machinery, new crops, and new methods. It seemed that the small Palestinian farms were doing even better than those plots McGill had praised in 1938 in Denmark.[23]

His estimate was confirmed at the Agricultural Research Institute south of Tel Aviv. Here was the source of the new methods being tried by the Jews. McGill was reminded of the University of Georgia's research efforts to transform poor Georgia farms, resisted mainly by farmers who wouldn't change old habits. There seemed to be few enemies of change here. The institute's head, Dr. I. Volcani, assured McGill that "six good acres here are equal to 25 in Denmark or Holland." The longer growing season of course helped, but the land was also better, yielding two and a half to three crops a year. Given that all the farms had to be small, Volcani had developed a plan for intensive farming to fit any hill or valley, centered on dairying, poultry, fruits, vegetables, small grains, and, more recently, mangoes and avocado pears. Dr. Volcani, McGill thought, was "a great man." Volcani's Czech assistant was also impressive; she had developed a new "rich, warm-looking orange" and a larger olive with higher oil content "which will replace the olive of Biblical days."[24]

The biblical dimension thrilled McGill. Daily he remarked on the dreamlike reality of traveling in the land of the Old and New Testaments. The names were threaded through his memories from the time his Presbyterian grandmother in Tennessee had spoken of such places as "the river of Jordan." Now he had arrived, merely the most recent pilgrim in the Holy Land. As he made his "first sentimental journey," he "tried to picture the dust and the noises along the trail as the tribes set out from Nazareth to be taxed in Bethlehem, with others joining them in the Valley of Jesreel along the Plains of Armageddon. I felt the spiritual impact of the Sea of Galilee and the stalls below the old Crusader Church at Bethlehem. From Scopus and the old city of Jerusalem I looked toward the Dead Sea and remembered the old Prophets and the patient Nazarene. There were soldiers and there was strife in His time." Now on this ancient stage he was meeting the new inhabitants, Jewish farmers and small industrialists "all up and down Palestine."[25]

Small factories seemed to be everywhere, manned by Jewish refugees. "You realized that what Nazi and world persecution had done was to funnel into Palestine some of the best minds, creative and directive, from almost every country of the world," he noted. "You could see the impact of those minds on the country." At Haifa he met Austrian Jews who had started a glass factory. Others from Antwerp had built thirty-five plants cutting diamonds for industry. The Palestine Electric Company was a "Jewish triumph over the 'it-can't-be-done-school.'"[26]

McGill was impressed by statistics about the growth of Jewish industry. "Today, in less than 30 years," McGill wrote, "there are 1,864 Jewish factories and plants, in addition to more than 10,000 small workshops." These, he reported, employed about 25 percent of the Jewish population and produced goods worth more than $100 million. Jews now paid about two-thirds of all taxes levied for Palestine. In thirty years of British occupation, Jewish industries and trade had flourished amid a predominantly agricultural Arab economy. He accepted the conclusion that the two divergent economies "rather than competing" were complementary.[27]

The Overseas News Agency got its money's worth from McGill. Seven articles he wrote for the Agency were sent to 120 papers in the United States and Canada with publication beginning on March 31, followed in August by a condensed version of all seven articles in *Pageant* magazine. The timing was important for the Zionist cause: "Appearing just before the Anglo-American Commission report was issued, McGill's findings were cited by various sources in answer to certain negative conclusions of that report. In particular, McGill's call for the establishment of a Jewish state, with the Arabs as part of it, proved to be influential for his readership in the American population."[28]

When McGill returned to the office, the governor's race seemed all but settled. Arnall lost his attempt to lift the constitutional limit of one four-year term and could not succeed himself. The *Constitution* endorsed a businessman, James Carmichael. Because Negroes had fought in the war, McGill "had hoped, had even prophesied," he told Martin, "that the race issue would lose its power to terrify." However, the strongest contender was Talmadge, who in April 1946 announced he was seeking his fourth term as governor. After four years in the political wilderness, the "wild man from Sugar Creek" was resurrecting the cause of white supremacy.[29]

The ability of whites to exclude Negroes from the political system had been undermined by the U.S. Supreme Court ruling in April 1944. The Court's declaration—that "the great privilege of choosing his rulers may not be denied a man by the state because of his color"— led to abolition of Georgia's whites-only primary. Governor Arnall opposed the passionate efforts to defy the Court and weathered abusive epithets and threats. Ultimately, legislators maintained some control by allowing only "literate" Negroes to vote in the primary. "The number of Georgians who think that the Negro, if he is literate enough to understand the issues presented to the electorate, is unfit to be a voter was surprisingly small," Arnall concluded. By 1946, Negroes who passed a literacy test could register to vote in Georgia's Democratic primary on July 17.[30]

Talmadge declared he did not want the Negro vote. Further, he pledged that if he were elected, no Negro would vote in Georgia for the next four years. Roy Harris, the former Arnall ally who now pledged allegiance to Talmadge, busied himself drafting a plan to resurrect the white primary.[31]

Talmadge's race baiting reached a national audience, contradicting as it did Arnall's liberalism and the liberal tilt of the Court. The racial rhetoric attracted two out-of-state neo-Hitler organizers, Emory Burke, an Alabamian, and Homer L. Loomis Jr., the son of a wealthy Wall Street lawyer. Burke and Loomis got a state charter for "the Columbians" and set up a business as a brown-shirted, goose-stepping hate group competing for dues with the Ku Klux Klan. Infiltrators soon divulged the Columbians' schemes. One *Constitution* reporter, Keeler McCartney, smuggled notes to McGill, who wrote about the Columbians' plan to imitate Nazi-style violence by intimidating "innocent and terrified Negroes and saying the Jews were next." The hate group's life was cut short when its leaders were jailed for assault and incitement to riot, convicted, and sent to prison.[32]

Loomis and Burke were disappointed that Talmadge did not embrace them. But Talmadge, McGill noted, "has never been anti-Jewish, and he is not in favor of sending the Negroes to Africa, not with farm labor needed as it is." The real significance of the Columbians, McGill believed, was "to expose the real threat—the existence of poor, inarticulate, and uneducated people with legitimate grievances and no agency or person to whom to go. . . . Until something is done about all of this, there will always be, not merely in Georgia, but the whole country, a field for the hate racketeers to harvest." McGill hammered that nail time and again: Hate groups were rackets, their leaders racketeers, and their success could be traced to swindlers and dupes, not to a legitimate agenda. Ever since his journalism in Tennessee, he had contended that the Klan's central purpose was "to make money for its promoters, as the Klan made millionaires in the twenties."[33]

The resurgence of Talmadgism spurred dissent from Georgians who did not want to regress to prewar politics as usual. Centered in Atlanta, individuals, groups, and the press condemned the Columbians and Klan and advocated racial tolerance. In the process of breaking silence, they discovered in their numbers a solidarity of commitment to racial justice. In politics, Governor Arnall was joined by Atlanta mayor William B. Hartsfield, a former Talmadge supporter turned reformer who could imagine the positive impact of the Negro vote in the Democratic primary. Bonded in opposition to the hate groups, the Southern Regional Council opened new bridges to the NAACP and the Urban League, the American Veterans Committee, and the Congress of Industrial Organizations. On their own, university professors and church leaders added their voices against the excesses. Though they were still in a minuscule minority, "each new voice emboldened others," historian John Egerton observed. The protestation against violence, however, in no way dispelled the issue of white supremacy. Nor did the general public, McGill included, retreat from the principle of segregation, which was still embedded in hard concrete of state law.[34]

One saving grace for McGill was that Talmadge kept him from being bored in the journalistic sense that bad news is better than no news. The dark forces active in the summer of '46 roused McGill. Talmadge, the Columbians, and the Klan fed him something to write about. "I was in there with my coat off swinging as hard as I could," McGill wrote the day after the election. He resurrected all the ghosts that surrounded Talmadge. Citing confessions of former Klansmen, McGill castigated the Klan as "a dangerous, vicious, evil organization" that bilks money from its members and dupes them into carrying out "jobs" ordered by an elite secret committee. He posed questions as he had in 1942 about what kind of state Georgians wanted, what sort of message they wished to send the nation.[35]

Lynching-style murders in Georgia during the summer sent the wrong message, which the northern and black press amplified. By the 1940s recorded lynchings were infrequent compared with the 1930s, giving McGill and other apologists argument for progress; this stance set them up for embarrassment with each new outbreak of savagery. On July 25, six men and women were lynched; four of these—two black men and their wives—died in Walton County, Georgia. Compounding the murders was the fact that nobody was arrested. This multiplied the embarrassment, which in McGill matured into anger. A year later, he castigated the citizenry who "actually refuse to assist in running down the guilty." On the other hand, he praised southerners when they practiced restraint or, better yet, intervened to frustrate a mob.[36]

As McGill mentioned Talmadge in the same breath as the Klan, Talmadge smeared McGill again as "Rosenwald Ralph," linking him with monied northern conspiracies that Talmadgites called traitorous to the southern way of life. McGill's associate editor, Tarver, fired back, "Gene Talmadge is dead."[37]

Voters settled the score. On election night, Arnall and McGill brooded together in McGill's steamy office as the results came in. The *Constitution*'s candidate appealed to the cities and built up a popular-vote lead of about ten thousand; but Talmadge prevailed in the rural areas, carrying far more of Georgia's 159 counties. Under the county-unit system of counting votes, Talmadge was clearly about to win. That night, savoring sweet revenge, the old politician poked his head into the newspaper office where McGill and Governor Arnall were lamenting the outcome. As McGill recalled, Talmadge pulled out his cigar and said, "Ralph, I give you a good whuppin' this time, didn't I?" A WGST radio reporter thrust a microphone between them and Talmadge declared himself the winner as McGill listened. The photograph of them shows McGill in suspenders with head downcast, emphasizing his second chin, face shadowy with the day's whiskers and hair tousled; Talmadge, gaunt and stern, looks through thick lenses at the mike. As Talmadge left, he confessed his weariness. "This has been a rough 'un Ralph. The way I feel now it took about 15 years off my life." Some of that feeling was attributable to a grave illness, as yet undiagnosed.[38]

Between the primary election in July and the November general election in which he had no Republican opponent, Talmadge's declining health alarmed his inner circle. On October 19, while on vacation, Talmadge hemorrhaged from a vein in his esophagus and was hospitalized in Atlanta. Very few beyond his son, Herman, knew that the governor-elect was gravely ill. The *Constitution* assigned a young reporter, Celestine Sibley, to sweet-talk her way into Talmadge's room in Piedmont Hospital. "He was lying up in bed with a ten-gallon hat on and some loud pajamas," Sibley wrote. "When I asked what was wrong with him,

he shrugged and said, 'Aw, it ain't nothin' but a little ole bleedin' vein.'"
As McGill later noted, people said Talmadge was "the first man who ever
had everyone in the state praying—half that he'd get well and half that
he'd die."[39]

Insiders ruminated over the political consequences. Should Talmadge
die before taking office, the pro-Arnall lieutenant governor, M. E.
Thompson, would claim the governorship. When Talmadge finally conceded that he might not recover, he summoned supporters to Piedmont
Hospital and, in the manner of monarchs, designated his own successor.
"Boys, I'm dying. . . . I need somebody to pick up after I'm gone, and it
oughta be Hummon." Thus was Herman Talmadge dubbed the successor, and Talmadgites schemed to elect him. Talmadge supporters discovered an old law that permitted the candidate with the second most
votes in the general election to become governor if the top vote-getter
died before inauguration. Going on that, and with only days left, they
forces organized a hush-hush campaign to write in Herman's name on
the November ballot.[40]

The matter of succession depended on which law was operable. As
people later said, "That was for the lawyers." McGill tried to explain the
tangle to the nation. "You see," he wrote, Governor Arnall had pushed
through numerous revisions to the state constitution, but "much of the
old text remained": "One paragraph of the new part said that the governor should serve four years and until his successor was elected and
qualified. Another, lifted from the constitution of the old days when the
legislature and not the people elected the governor, said that, in the event
no person had a majority of the whole vote, the legislature should elect
from the two men having the highest number."[41]

In the November general election the unusual write-in vote was so
small and so close that both candidates disputed the count. By one count,
Herman received 106 more write-in votes than Carmichael—775 to 669.
Herman recalled years later, "As it turned out Carmichael got a little over
five hundred votes, and I got a little over five hundred, only it was a
handful more than he got."[42]

The drama played out as the Talmadge team envisioned. On
December 21, Eugene died of cancer and lay in state in the capitol
building, dressed in a blue suit, as thousands came by to pay respect. On

January 15, with Thompson claiming the governorship, the weary legislature during an all-night session, relying on the old text of the state constitution, chose Herman Talmadge. As McGill tutored his national audience, "The legislature was going to elect Herman governor in his papa's place. And that was, they argued, right and proper. They had voted for old Gene, but since the Lord, in his infinite wisdom, had called him to glory, Herman would do."[43]

The situation intensified when Arnall refused to turn over the governor's office. "I never had any idea that he would try to hold onto the office," Herman said. "Both that night and the next day I had to quiet the crowd down and plead for order." Talmadge left Arnall there and ordered his staff to change the locks during the night. Arnall was literally locked out and took his fight to the courts. It was, as McGill concluded, "a coup d'etat out of a fiction-writer's plot." "It's a wonder nobody was killed," Talmadge said. On that first morning as interim governor, Talmadge came armed, "a .38 Smith and Wesson in my belt."[44]

McGill seemed to tilt in sentiment toward Herman. When "Old Gene" lay dying, McGill visited his bedside and wrote a sympathetic obituary out of "pity for an old sick man," as Harold Martin characterized it. The obituary, Martin explained, disturbed Jack Tarver because it seemed to canonize Talmadge. When it appeared that McGill might legitimize Herman, Tarver told Martin,

> I was ready to quit. The idea of Herman just sort of inheriting the governorship was anathema to me. I went into McGill's office, and I got so worked up I got to crying, and I said, "Look, dammit, just take me off editorials. I'll make up the page, but I don't want to write any more editorials."
>
> Then *he* got to crying and said no, dammit, if I felt that way, we'd come out for M.E. Thompson. And I said no, I wasn't that much for Thompson, but I couldn't stand the idea of supporting Herman after fighting him all these years.[45]

Herman held office for more than two months before the state court decided against him. Although McGill did not endorse Herman in the *Constitution,* he did write supportively about him for a national audience, calling Talmadge the "heir apparent" with a "good, moral sort of record.

. . . A good boy, his mother says," who "learned to shoot and ride and swim," a young Georgia-educated lawyer. McGill noted that Herman was the only candidate with a "war record," having served in the navy at the invasion of Guadalcanal and the Battle of Okinawa. His vices, as his first wife vowed in divorce documents, were that "he smoked smelly cigars in the house and went away to political meetings when she didn't want him to go[,] . . . nagged her about money and was 'cold and indifferent' and fond of sitting at home reading the newspaper." In March 1947, Talmadge reluctantly surrendered the governorship after the court ruled five to two that Thompson was the legal heir. "Herman got drunk within two hours after the court decision," McGill told an interviewer, "and stayed drunk for four days." Whatever Herman's personal habits, he had established a foothold in the Democratic Party and had gained a group of powerful allies, including Carmichael men. McGill was convinced that Herman would carry the special election ordered by the court for the summer of 1948.[46]

McGill was seldom so focused on Georgia politics that he took his mind off geopolitics. Unlike the isolationists of the 1920s, McGill never lost interest in the fortunes of postwar Europe. In spring 1947 he was increasingly disturbed by the clamor over relations with the Soviet Union. While McGill continued to advocate sympathy for the position of the great wartime ally, he sensed that coexistence and cooperation were increasingly treacherous subjects. Yet he refused to cave in to hardliners who seemed to want war.

McGill continued advocating peaceful cooperation after that position became, for many, politically untenable. In November 1945, the government of Yugoslavia and then of Albania declared themselves socialist republics. That, together with a civil war against the Communists in Greece and unsettled postwar politics in Eastern Europe, was enough to alarm Winston Churchill. On March 5, 1946, while touring the United States after he had been defeated for reelection as prime minister, he gave a notable speech at Westminster College in Fulton, Missouri, minting the term "iron curtain" to describe the barrier the Soviets had wrought from the Baltic to the Adriatic. McGill, just back from his trip to Germany and Palestine, responded by placing Churchill in the camp of right-wing extremists, along with "the irresponsible spokesmen in this country" who were making it almost impossible to conduct "a reasonable discussion of Russia's position in world affairs, as related to our own."[47]

McGill acknowledged that the Russians meant to maintain their political influence, but he saw it not as an iron curtain but as a politically friendly zone of "buffer nations." Unlike Churchill, he did not express alarm, which seems surprising. For a champion of freedom of expression, McGill was complacent about a hegemony in Eastern Europe orchestrated by a totalitarian government with a political philosophy hostile to democracy. The war, he reasoned, had created new realities and a new balance of power to which the West must adjust. Five days after Churchill's iron curtain speech, McGill explained that Russia "has replaced Britain as the dominant nation in arranging spheres of influence in Europe." The Soviets' show of force in Europe was in the natural order of "the great power scramble for position—seeking security according to their ideas of security." To McGill, as to Churchill, the deed was already done; but while Churchill protested vehemently because his empire had been tread upon, McGill strained dispassionately to explicate the Soviets' rationale. The Soviets, he reasoned, were acting "correctly" by the rules of the power scramble to assure friendly "buffer nations," considering that "these nations were hostile [to Russia] in the past."[48]

McGill now deemphasized the notion of peaceful cooperation but held to the possibility of tolerance, of peaceful coexistence. In March 1946, he articulated the fear that some wanted war with Russia. "Russia doesn't want war," he declared. "There isn't going to be a war any time soon. There won't ever be one with Russia unless this country, as Secretary [of State James F.] Byrnes said, permits an inexcusable series of blunders and errors to bring on war."[49]

Four days later, McGill again sought to muffle cries for war. The focus now was Czechoslovakia. McGill admired the country's president, Eduard Beneš, whom he had met in exile in wartime London. Beneš' ideas about the Soviet need for security matched McGill's own notions of geopolitical reality. Touting him as "the man with the most experience in European politics," McGill quoted from a recent, published interview in which Beneš had explained that "in eastern Austria and Hungary, Russia's chief aim, as it is here, is to assure herself that elements hostile to her do not again get the upper hand. I am convinced that when she has satisfied herself of this she will be ready to retire. Russia's whole foreign policy, as I see it, is founded on a desire for security. She wants time to develop her own territory and friendly countries on her border."[50]

Beneš was proved tragically in error about Hungary and Czechoslovakia. He had already conceded Czechoslovakia's cession of Ruthenia to the Soviet Union on June 29, 1945. Two months after McGill's column, elections in Czechoslovakia gave the Communists a chance to form a new coalition cabinet. In September 1946, Bulgaria joined the Soviet "buffer states," officially announcing its peoples' republic, followed by general elections in which the Communists received a majority.

In fall 1946 the Truman administration toughened its stance against Soviet intervention in Eastern Europe, but McGill held firm against military options. He criticized "our hotheads who think we have got to fight Russia." Holding fast to his vision of coexistence, he insisted that "capitalism and Communism can live in the same world."[51]

In March 1947, he still argued that the West needed to understand Russia's situation. To achieve international cooperation, he wrote, the West had a responsibility "to allay Russian fears" for its national security. The Soviet Union's meddling in Eastern Europe was "defensive" because "the attack on her by Germany was launched from the countries in which she is now so active politically. There is certainly some justification for such an attitude."[52] Two weeks later, he applauded the mission to Moscow of Gen. George C. Marshall, the new secretary of state, and said he hoped Marshall would "work out a peaceful relationship with Russia."[53]

Events in the spring of 1947, however, shoved McGill into company with the hawks. Suddenly his position as a champion of coexistence was indefensible. Churchill and his U.S. sympathizers had won, if only because their anti-Soviet rhetoric had polarized the two camps, eliminating the middle ground on which McGill stood. He had placed great value on insights gained from talking with Russians in their land; how could it be that pundits who had not gone to Moscow were more correct than he? He had tried to understand the Russian character but had run out of time. After he had criticized so many others for taking the hard line against the Russians, he knew he would have to concede he had been wrong on a grand issue where he prided himself on knowing the facts. In the spring of 1947, he struggled with how to do that honorably but without losing credibility generally.

That spring was a troubling time. Added to his dilemma over the Russian developments was the distance he felt from Georgia's channels of power. For four years he had been accustomed to conspiring with the governor to advance their causes. Arnall's departure and the succession of a governor he had not helped elect left a conspicuous vacuum. At the same time, statehouse politics seemed to be reverting to "politics as usual." At least in an election year he could rouse himself for a good fight. If campaigns for governor created, as he said, "social seasons for the poorest ones in the state," complete with barbecue and perhaps a fistfight, the same campaigns fired up McGill's psyche, addicted as he was to conflict. Compounding the boredom in 1947, he had no foreign travel to distract him, no exotic people, no intriguing situations. At home, Mary Elizabeth was as usual not well, and he had lost sleep looking after little Ralph, who was just two years old.

To make matters worse, he was harassed by the Rev. Frank Norris, who on May 20 filed a libel suit against McGill and the *Constitution*. Gene Talmadge had brought Norris down from Detroit in 1941 to help his reelection campaign by preaching against vile newspaper editors. In each district, so wrote McGill, "the governor sat on the pulpit platform and listened while the laborer in the Lord's vineyard told the crowd they'd nail the hides of newspaper editors to the fence; assured them they must defend their heritages." McGill slipped in a gratuitous line: "Dr. Norris denies any pro-KKK connection."[54]

Visitors to McGill's office on May 20 found him "nervous and distraught." Calvin Kytle of Emory's class of 1941 had been one of the students in McGill's one-time course, "Personalities in Politics." In 1947 Kytle visited with James Mackay to interview McGill as part of a study of Georgia leaders who controlled state politics. "We were embarrassed to see him like this. Mr. McGill had for many years been somebody special to us, and to see him as he was this afternoon was like watching a fine old race horse agonizing over a broken leg." During the interview, McGill "kept taking off his glasses and putting them on again, rocking in his swivel chair, running his fingers through his hair; his speech sometimes faltered, as if he had lost track of what he was saying in mid-sentence. He looked terribly tired, almost to the point of hysteria, and his body looked to be sagging under the weight of the world."[55]

Between numerous interruptions, McGill shared his "disgust, sorrow, and intense frustration at the corruption in Georgia politics." The whole democratic process had disappointed him. They asked McGill if he thought there was a conspiracy at work. He shook his head. The problem, he knew, was that the leaders with insight had been unable to reach the people, unable to connect, as the demagogues had, with the great mass of Georgians and southerners. While McGill read books greedily, the great mass he hoped to influence didn't read one a *year*, and if they did it was something strictly practical, as W. J. Cash had observed in 1941, something like advice from Dale Carnegie. It was the old cursed cycle of poverty breeding poor education and vice versa. As he had drilled time and again, the average Georgia child leaves school in the fourth grade. "By God," McGill concluded, "somehow we've got to reach the people."[56]

During the interview, McGill was interrupted by telephone calls, messengers with galley proofs of his column, and by the arrival of Milton Caniff. He was McGill's favorite cartoonist, famous for *Terry and the Pirates* and *Steve Canyon.* Caniff was visiting to accept an honorary law degree from Emory University and drew McGill away from his desk.[57] Half an hour later the editor returned, and the telephone rang.

"Okay," McGill answered. It was about the Rev. Frank Norris. "He's going to sue?"

McGill took off his glasses and put them on his desk, leaned back in his chair, and ran his fingers through his hair. "What can I do about it?" he asked. "All right, Ray. All right." As he started to hang up, he remembered his manners and pulled the mouthpiece back in time to say, "Thanks, Ray." He looked beyond Kytle and Mackay, then noticed them. "You boys come back again, will you?"[58]

Three weeks later, on June 11, McGill reversed his stance on the Soviet Union. The reversal in his public stance occurred six days after Secretary Marshall called for a European Recovery Program to send economic aid to European nations in political crisis. McGill also was set off by the latest Soviet intervention in Hungary, where anti-Communists, including the premier, were being purged. That contradicted what the Soviets had told McGill in 1945, that they would let European Communist parties stand on their own. Certainly McGill was also illuminated by some State Department briefings which evidently persuaded him of the importance of military force as a tool of persuasion.

No longer distancing himself from military options, McGill stepped deftly into the rank and file of the cold warriors. He did so, however, without acknowledging earlier miscalculation, falling back on the wisdom of the sporting life: the best defense is a strong offense. He tried to make retreat resemble a full-tilt charge. Most of his column on June 11 could be characterized as the declaration of a man who has been rudely disillusioned. The ideals of free expression and open borders, requiring international cooperation rather than hostility, now seemed fleeting in the face of a flood of animosity.

McGill began with a sentence of transition so his readers could cross over the gap from the Same Old Ralph to the New McGill. Shuffling backward, he mentioned his refrain of the past two years—the need "to understand Russia." In the next breath, he quietly raised a new caution: "But it is even more important that we not misunderstand her." Then he warned that "no one can misunderstand what happened in Hungary." Without conceding that he had misunderstood Russia, he sounded alarms, sirens, and bells to mobilize Americans.[59]

It was an extraordinary piece of writing in which McGill scrapped his passion for peaceful cooperation with the Soviet Union and reached for guns, if only in self-defense. The outrage and fervor of the column are reminiscent of his style nine years earlier after he witnessed the Nazi takeover. "Russia is following an expansionist plan, which disregards agreements and protests," he declared. "In Hungary it did not win the election. But it used its military pressure to unseat what opposition there was and to create its own idea of what it wanted in and from Hungary."[60]

In two sentences, he expressed his personal disappointment. "All those who hoped that Russia would go along in full participation in working agreements with the Western countries, now know Russia will not." He had been one of the hopeful, but he did not say so. Similarly, he had been a "friend" of Russia, but he said so only indirectly: "The Russians have refused to sit on the trusteeship council, have blocked efforts to make the Security Council work, and have dismayed every friend who believed them really eager to work out a plan for world peace."[61]

He recommended two courses. First, he urged Americans to consider war, if necessary, if only to induce the Russians to make binding agreements. "The Soviet actions," as he saw it, "make it impossible not to be prepared for war." Second, he exhorted Americans to tell Congress to appropriate the money for Marshall's plan, the Foreign Assistance Act for Europe, including Germany. Adopting cold war terminology, which so recently he had scorned, he warned that France and Italy were endangered by Communist Parties and could be taken into the "Soviet orbit." Rounding out the images, McGill resorted to using creatures, the amoeba and the platypus. Russia was the amoeba; the unbelievers were political platypuses. "Like the amoeba," he explained, "the Russian influence flows along, enveloping what it can, flowing around walls too high to cross, or moving along them and creeping around the ends." Those Americans who didn't believe that a minority of Communists could "take over a country which is in an unhealthy, hungry and wretched condition," were either "talking through their hats or politically are ready for the Platypusary in the Bronx Zoo." By those guidelines, McGill was squirming away from the Platypusary.[62]

From that day forward, McGill's role in the cold war increased dramatically. His columns zeroed in on Communist propagandists in France and Italy, and on the economic flaws in Communist nations.[63] He cooperated with Truman administration lobbyists seeking congressional passage of the Marshall Plan for massive foreign aid to assist postwar Europe. In line with this, he readily accepted the invitation of the State Department to travel through Europe with a delegation of influential journalists on a fact-finding tour intended to justify the Marshall Plan, then priced at $5.3 billion. Along on the mission was *New York Herald Tribune* editor Whitelaw Reid, *Saturday Evening Post* foreign editor Martin Sommers, and *St. Louis Post-Dispatch* editorial writer Ernest Kirschten.[64]

Shortly after the editors returned, Communists in February 1948 engineered a coup in Czechoslovakia. Fear intensified for other nations, particularly for Italy, which was about to hold elections. A group of distinguished Americans, including Dean Acheson, had banded together in the Committee for the Marshall Plan to Aid European Recovery. On March 15, 1948, as Congress began debate, the committee chairman telegrammed McGill for urgent editorial support. Given the forthcoming Italian elections and the "distinct possibility that Italy may go the way of Czechoslovakia, the key to prompt action is in the House of Representatives," chairman Robert P. Patterson wired McGill. Delay would be a "historic blunder," Patterson warned. The committee was "urging immediate action reporting bill out without a deletion of Chinese, Greek or Turkish Aid measures. . . . Count on you to help in this crisis."[65]

McGill helped at once. Typical of the anti-Communist stance he would take ever afterward, whether in Europe or China or Korea or Vietnam, McGill drafted a telegram of his own to be sent to influential political leaders and editors. In it, he urged "swift passage of the European Recovery Plan" in order to "defeat of the Communist coalition" in Italy.[66]

11

Political Storms

*We have had too much of the false and wicked
demagogic writing and shouting which talks about
mongrelizing the races, mingling the races, and so on,
every time an effort is made to be just and fair.*
—Ralph McGill, 1949

McGill's political loyalty was about to be tested. Supporting the Democrat in the White House had seldom posed a problem. That changed on February 2, 1948, when President Truman stunned southern politicians by asking Congress for a package of civil rights legislation. In McGill's view, Truman's message "blew the leadership of the Southern Democrats into the air."[1]

McGill could understand the roots of southern reaction. He preferred that the southern states, not Congress, take the lead in extending, first, voting rights and then, gradually, other civil rights. While he disagreed with Truman's wholesale approach, he regarded the reactionaries' remedy as destructive: They sought to ditch Truman or, failing that, to sink the Democratic Party by voting for a third or fourth party, or, God forbid, by voting Republican. McGill resolved the dilemma for himself, criticizing the Truman program for its faults while not abandoning the Democratic Party. McGill called the reactionary movement the "Southern revolt." He judged the revolt to be out of step with the course of the nation and as uncompromising as the southern fire-eaters of 1856–60. Like the fire-eaters' movement toward southern secession, the revolt was either politically naïve or serving narrow self-interests or both. Their strategy of revolt could heap yet another political burden on the backs of southerners.

Turning against Truman was never an option for McGill. In 1945, he had quickly joined ranks behind Roosevelt's successor and had so far been blessed with recognition. McGill enjoyed the reward of loyalty, the feeling of being an insider in the councils of power. Publicly, two months before the national convention, he warned Democrats to settle with Truman because the destructive "revolt really has no place to go."[2]

Truman's civil rights message struck the South like a tornado, sudden and volatile. The president did not consult with congressional leaders but urged adoption of the findings of his biracial committee on civil rights. He endorsed the committee's recommendations to establish the Commission on Civil Rights, pass federal laws against lynching and poll taxes, abolish segregation in all its forms, and create a commission on fair employment practices to abolish job discrimination.[3]

McGill gauged the sentiment of the revolt. Southern Democrats were "of a temper to offer to lick any Truman man in the house, in the manner of the late John L. Sullivan, even though they don't have his punch." The emotional reaction in the South, ranging from "the profane to the exaggerated," threatened to wreck at least Truman and probably the party. Yet, McGill reasoned, even if the president lacked the political savvy of Roosevelt, he had heart and courage. Given a fighting chance, he might prevail at the Philadelphia convention. If they obeyed reason, southern Democrats must remain loyal to Truman; defection would deliver victory to a Republican president and a Republican Congress "committed to even more substantial civil rights legislation than offered by Mr. Truman." Other southern Democrats shared this view, among them Senator William Fulbright of Arkansas, who stated privately that the southern governors' defection "can only result in the disintegration of our party and that we would be in for a long Republican rule of from ten to twenty years. The South has never had fair treatment under such a regime."[4]

To a national audience, McGill pictured the dilemma of southern Democrats. He chose to tell the story of

> old Ely Lanier, rural undertaker in South Georgia, the time a tornado blew him, his house and small stock of caskets into the air.
>
> "It sure didn't comfort me none," he said later, when he had been picked up in a nearby field and his battered frame placed upon a neighbor's feather bed, "to have them three coffins flyin' along with me."

> . . . But even as these Southerners whirl about in their
> political tornado, they can see flying with them certain seem-
> ingly inescapable facts which cast shadows on the revolt
> and that resemble old man Lanier's caskets and are no more
> comforting.[5]

To McGill the abysmal lack of visionary political leadership across the
South seemed comparable to the 1860s, when the Republicans first came
to power in Washington. In this vacuum, McGill styled himself as a voice
of reason, rising above the clamor to defend the Democrats, if not Truman,
against often profane critics. Yet he knew his voice alone was not enough.

For that reason McGill continued to support the activities of nongovernmental organizations, especially the Southern Regional Council.
Working outside government restrictions, with independent though
meager funding, the council grew in importance in the interracial *society*
McGill was fostering in the midst of a segregated community. The relationship was reciprocal. The council "relied on liberal editors like Ralph
McGill," wrote its historian, "as a means to influence public opinion." Its
leadership believed that blacks "suffered because of unfair, even vicious,
images" in newspapers. Its executive director from 1947 to 1957, George
Mitchell, contended that "your every day white Southerner in his casual
conduct with Negroes has it in the back of his mind that before him is a
representative of savagery."

McGill helped direct talent to the SRC. In 1947 he sent Harold
Fleming there. A graduate of Atlanta's Boys' High, Fleming was twenty-
five when he returned to Atlanta in 1947 and went to see McGill. He had
graduated summa cum laude from Harvard; during the war he had been
the lieutenant in charge of a black unit and had developed sympathy for
the black community. At the SRC, Fleming began his long career there as
director of information, focusing the council's media efforts on helping
the national press cover race problems.[6]

The new media strategy succeeded almost immediately. Historian
Robert Norrell attributed the success in part to a policy decision at the
New York Times. In 1947, the *Times* assigned its first full-time southern
correspondent, John Popham, whose featured stories became regular reading for elites in Washington and elsewhere. He was read and quoted by

Russians as evidence of racial oppression in the United States. Popham boosted the SRC's reputation, referring to it as "the South's leading interracial organization." Fleming later noted that "it became impossible for the Atlanta papers and other Southern papers to ignore our statements and other publications when they were appearing on the front page of *The New York Times*."[7]

Popham immediately identified McGill as a "voice of sanity" who could help him report southern politics. Popham recalled that McGill "gave me clues. He'd tip me off—who to see—who to talk to." To Popham, McGill was a Godsend: "You gave thanks to God you found that child!" In turn, McGill began depending on Popham's legs, eyes, and ears. "I would range around the South," Popham said, "and then he'd have me up to his office and ask me what was going on."[8] As McGill devoted even more attention to Washington politics and international affairs, he relied all the more on the astute and energetic *Times* man.

Popham's eyes and ears served McGill well. Younger and freer, Popham traveled the two-lane byways and dirt roads of the South, eating in mom-and-pop diners, absorbing grass-roots ideologies and platitudes. McGill needed this regional outlook, and Popham appreciated McGill's perspective about southerners and their responses to the revolt against Truman. The president's assailants included third-party Progressives led by FDR's former vice president, Henry A. Wallace; the Progressives' insistence on civil rights and a closer relationship with Russia alienated southerners on both domestic and foreign policy. On the right, a fourth party of the revolt-minded southern Democrats, calling themselves Dixiecrats, gathered noisily for a cause—states' rights. It was the same rationale that had been championed by South Carolina's John C. Calhoun a hundred years earlier. The fourth party found for its leader another South Carolinian, Governor Strom Thurmond.[9]

Dixiecrats posed the greater threat to Truman, particularly because Wallace Progressives in the South had been compromised, smeared Red, or at least pink, in the political palate of the postwar era. In Georgia, Gene Talmadge during his last hurrah in 1946 branded Wallace as a Communist sympathizer. Both new parties stood little chance of winning, but they could lure enough voters to defeat Truman and position themselves to bargain with a Republican president less likely to force desegregation. Behind the states' rights banner, Dixiecrats claimed to have the South's best interests at heart. They worked through existing political bosses at the statehouse level. "Almost every Southern state," McGill noted, "will go to Philadelphia with a favorite son to nominate or with uninstructed delegates to employ in the most effective anti-Truman strategy that can be devised."[10] Georgia would have a favorite son in Senator Richard Russell.

While defending the party for practical reasons, McGill distanced himself from Truman's divisive civil rights package. "My position is not pro-Truman," he explained. "It is against the fourth-party Dixiecrats." For perhaps the only time in his career as a government insider, McGill turned down a presidential appointment. When Truman wanted him to join the advisory Commission on Civil Rights, McGill declined, explaining politely what Truman no doubt understood, that it would be radically unpopular for him to associate with a desegregation-minded commission while the South was segregated by law. Abandoning segregation was out of the question in 1948, as was any vigorous prosecution of civil rights in employment, voting, or criminal justice. Even a federally enforced antilynching bill was hopelessly unpopular; while southern sentiment opposed lynching, the South, by declining to indict lynchers, remained the only region which still condoned mob terror as a tool for social control.[11]

The president's biracial committee had found that systematic terrorism continued to disfranchise blacks. In agreement, Truman sought to make lynching a federal crime, a move which southern Democrats had smothered in 1919 and 1934. A wave of lynchings in 1933 had convinced President Roosevelt to condemn lynch law as "that vile form of collective murder," and in 1934 he urged Congress to make it a federal crime. He backed off, however, when southern Democrats—among them Senator Kenneth McKellar, whom McGill knew as a "messenger boy" for Memphis's Boss Crump—held crucial New Deal legislation hostage.[12] In 1948, Senate Democrats were no less opposed.

As in 1940, McGill regarded federal antilynching legislation as wrongheaded. Though he abhorred mob terror and regularly denounced the Klan as mindless and cowardly, he adopted the argument of Senator Russell that the decline in lynchings made an intrusive federal law unnecessary: southern states were capable of enforcing existing laws and abolishing the terror. To the nation, of course, the South lacked credibility. From 1882, when record keeping began, to 1939, 4,697 lynchings were recorded for the nation. More than half (2,598, or 55 percent) were in eight southern states: Florida, Georgia, South Carolina, North Carolina, Tennessee, Alabama, Mississippi, and Louisiana. In those states, 90 percent of the victims were black. Since 1882, Georgia was second only to Mississippi in the number of lynchings; each state had more than 500. In 1942, the Atlanta leader of the Association of Southern Women for the Prevention of Lynching noted that in 1940 "Mississippi dropped out of the regular lynching states, leaving only Georgia and Florida as 'regulars.'"[13]

Each new lynching embarrassed McGill and undermined his position. The 1946 mob killings of two black men and their wives in Walton County, Georgia, indicated the changing nature of lynching, a new level of bestiality.[14] As long as the guilty went free, terror reigned.[15] Declining statistics did not comfort those who felt terrorized, but McGill clung to his argument that only a fragment of southerners condoned mob violence and that lynchings were thwarted in most attempts. In 1947, the toll fell to one, and he congratulated the South for a "fine job in preventing most of the lynchings that have been attempted this year. Both Georgia and Alabama have offered splendid examples of forthright action."[16] Yet it was another seven years before McGill could proclaim an end to lynching as an index of racism—but by then, he lamented, lynching was replaced by "other extra-legal means of control such as bombings, incendiarism (in housing disputes), threats, and intimidations."[17]

Indictments of accused lynchers were rare, and convictions were rarer. In early 1948, a mob near Lyons, Georgia, lynched a Negro as he left church with his wife and children. McGill was outraged that none of the "murdering morons" was arrested. Harold Martin recalled that McGill's criticism led the county grand jury to summon him to testify. McGill went, accompanied by Jack Tarver, who once owned that county's second newspaper. The United Press sent young Eugene Patterson, who always remembered that first encounter with the man who later hired him. McGill advised the grand jurors that if the South failed to do justice, the federal government would intervene. If readers did not appreciate political strategy, McGill employed a labor-management argument. Georgia could not afford to let lynchers scare off the Negro farm labor. This was not a matter of social equality, he made clear. Within the context of Georgia's legal segregation, he pleaded for Christian and constitutional justice: "I see no reason why this grand jury cannot assist the good Christian people in this community in setting pattern which would allow the two races to live and work together in a community, separated socially but united in the rights which our Constitution guarantees to all citizens." The grand jury did indict one white man, but a trial jury acquitted him. McGill's attitude toward that county exemplified his attitude toward the South. As Patterson later put it, "He loved the South like a delinquent child."[18]

On the subject of lynching, McGill held the moral high ground, and the political ground as well. While other white southerners sniped at his stance for abolishing the poll tax and his advocacy of reforms in education and employment opportunities, they found common ground when McGill battled the Klan and masked mobs. Politicians' encouragement of the Klan and juries' refusals to indict or convict killers were morally repugnant and politically self-defeating: akin to shooting yourself in the foot. Nothing was more certain to invite federal intervention, signaling Congress that the South could not solve its civil rights problem. In this respect McGill portrayed the Klan as unwitting dupes: their threats and violence smeared the region's reputation. "The Ku Klux Klan and their sort of people are damning the South and assuring us of continued Federal pressure," he wrote.[19] An antilynching law specifically for the South would represent a return to the punitive legislation Republicans enacted after the Civil War: "We in the South are in for a period of reconstruction—1948 style."[20]

Remembrance of Reconstruction and, as a result, a fear of Republicans ran deep in the South. McGill shared that fear. "If we don't clean our own house," he cautioned in 1947, "it is going to get cleaned in a manner we don't like." He envisioned the Republicans' 1948 election agenda and forecast something foul: they would pay lip service to civil rights by whipping the South. Republican-sponsored legislation would be "aimed at the South with the indirect purpose of winning votes in the industrial key States of the East."[21] Anti-Truman Democrats had no place better to go: "Seeking comfort from the Republican Party is folly. That Party, cynically, will pass an antilynch bill. . . . I trust the hotheads will realize the Republican party is fully committed in all phases of the civil rights bill."[22]

In 1948 alarms sounded as Republicans, in control of Congress, seized the initiative on civil rights. On March 4, 1948, a month after Truman's message, liberal Republicans spearheaded an antilynching bill through the House Judiciary Committee. Smelling danger and hypocrisy, McGill spun into high gear, motivated alternately by a fusion of emotion and logic that often produced his best work. This one he called "They Simply Do Not Trust Us." It was both a manifesto and a position paper; it was a defense of southern progress but an apology for failings; it looked backward with regret and forward in foreboding. "What the South has got to learn is that the rest of the nation regards the Southern position as wrong," he asserted. It was as yet his clearest declaration—he called it "a sort of primer for Southern thinking." Time was running out for segregation as it had for slavery: "The plain truth is that national public opinion is against us. . . . The South, by its failure to correct the injustices within the segregation pattern, while our laws said that the education, travel and the courthouse justice should be equal within that system, has created the state of mind in the rest of the country which makes our predicament one with which they have no sympathy." What accommodations and progress the South had made since the Civil War, he said, were now jeopardized because "we have allowed enough evil to make the rest of the nation look upon us without sympathy. We have plenty of laws against violence, such as lynching. We have not enforced them well in Georgia. We have allowed local pride to cover up the most ghastly crimes. Therefore most of the nation regards an antilynching law as proper, and even necessary, despite the fact that lynching has about disappeared."[23]

Republicans, he warned, were pushing a package of radical legislation. Months earlier he forecast that Republicans were committed to abolishing poll taxes and segregation in interstate travel and might support economic intervention in the South through restoration of Roosevelt's Fair Employment Practices Committee. The motive power behind all this legislation, he said, was "a national complex which accepts the fact of local law failure and regards the steady encroachment of Federal law apathetically."[24]

While the antilynching bill gave McGill a chance to voice his sentiments, the threat was short-lived. One week later, on March 11, the bill
was killed in the Senate by a revived coalition of Republicans and southern Democrats.

If time was indeed running out for segregation, southerners were joining
ranks to prolong that time. McGill argued that "enormous progress" had
been made in eighty years. "It is almost entirely overlooked that the problem is one no other people in history have had to face."[25] In its darkest
shade, southern history could be read as tragedy.

In bargaining for gradual change, southern moderates invoked an
economic rationale. Spokesmen from Henry Grady to Ellis Arnall articulated variations of this economic interpretation of race relations: the South
(meaning the white South) must have *economic development* before civil
rights for the Negro. The South would resist imposition of northern culture. This was nowhere clearer than in the filibuster that stifled revival
of the Fair Employment Practices Act. Senator J. William Fulbright of
Arkansas, a liberal on international issues, defended the South against
what he perceived as imposition of the North's social theories. "Do you
think," he wrote in notes for the Senate debate, "that you can make people
hire those whom they regard as unfit for any reason?"[26]

McGill blamed economic stagnation for many of the South's
entrenched problems and pathologies. The remedy for lynching was
not so simple as legislation nor so mystical as a moral awakening, but
involved attacking poverty and ignorance.[27] Racial hatred, McGill reasoned, would be relieved with the creation of adequate employment for
all, whites and blacks.

No matter how reasonable, this economic ideal implied serious
adjustments for a legally segregated society. A straightforward defense of
justice for the Negro made McGill a target, not just for fringe Klansmen
but for the greater population. For most white southerners, segregation
was the only way of life, had been the only way for generations; most
avoided thinking about the issue and, when they did, imagined no alternative that was livable.

Throughout the 1940s McGill never dared to denounce segregation or advocate integration, two positions he knew were alien to the

southern mind mired in generations of segregation and conditioned by states' rights demagogues. Until *Brown v. Board of Education* McGill's strongest argument was that Negroes were not getting a fair deal promised them since *Plessy v. Ferguson.* As Harold Martin explained, "The separate-but-equal doctrine which he believed had been best for the South and its people had failed because the South itself had failed. It had not been honest enough to provide the equal facilities it had promised." McGill clarified his position repeatedly, insisting that support of legal justice did not mean favoring *social and educational* integration. Such accusations—together with the specter of intermarriage—were conjured by demagogues seeking votes. Talmadge and his kind, McGill lamented, had made it "difficult for us to think straight." The South "has been poisoned by leadership through the years which has tried to say that if we give the Negro a fair trial, prevent police brutality, allow him an opportunity to work and draw the wages paid anyone else for the same work, that this constitutes social equality. We have had too much of the false and wicked demagogic writing and shouting which talks about mongrelizing the races, mingling the races, and so on, every time an effort is made to be just and fair."[28]

Occupying the middle ground on race in the 1940s exposed McGill as a target for all sides. Certainly the segregationists targeted him loudest. To them he was clearly a traitor to the South at a time when segregation was law. Much subtler was the expression of dissatisfaction by blacks in the South and white liberals in the North, who viewed him as too compromising. In the middle, McGill daily charted his course as though through a minefield. If in one column he ranged too far ahead of the readers he wanted to lead, there was Jack Tarver to caution him about lecturing from a "soap box." To his credit, McGill could mix his pitches. He had a remarkable sense for the change of pace, derived in part from his understanding of baseball and the way a pitcher adjusts to the batter by changing the ball's speed and location. After delivering a column about wicked demagoguery, he could follow the next morning with one about real southern barbecue, and the next day with one about a hunting dog he knew, before heading back in a few days to social and political issues that weighed heavily on his mind.

Rival journalists also criticized him, but for other reasons. At the afternoon *Atlanta Journal*, McGill's earnest pleading was dismissed as posturing to save his hide. The *Journal*'s editor, Wright Bryan Sr., pegged McGill as an opportunist, riding the Negro issue to get ahead. Bryan believed McGill set out to attract attention by choosing an issue that was "unusual . . . out of the mainstream." None was more taboo in white society than the race issue. The more attention McGill attracted for airing the race issue in public, the more his rivals resented him. Anything McGill wrote on the issue Bryan interpreted as self-serving. Bryan's wife, Ellen, saw McGill as "a showman and an actor" who "knew how to promote himself." He had "chosen the Negroes. He knew he'd get ahead if he championed the blacks." She thought McGill revealed his true motive once while jesting with her husband about what causes to champion. "Now, Wright Bryan, we want to get rich," McGill had said, advising his rival. "You champion soil erosion."[29]

At the *Journal*, however, Bryan had little choice. He couldn't have crusaded as McGill did for civil rights if he had wanted to. The newspaper's owner discouraged crusades, especially on sensational issues. James M. Cox preferred a newspaper somewhere between the old *Journal*, which "was a little too conservative," and Hearst's *Georgian*, which "most people think . . . was yellow." Shortly after he bought the *Journal* in 1939, Cox directed Bryan that he wanted the paper to be "a thing of stability[,] . . . having a mind that is open to new things, but resolutely opposed to any adventures either in news or editorial policy that might be followed for the sheer purpose of circulation. . . . We don't want crusades to be made for the mere purpose of crusading."[30] The avoidance of controversy proved profitable. A decade later, the *Journal* was the dominant newspaper in town, with a circulation as high as 275,000, compared to the *Constitution*'s 200,000.[31]

Under Bryan, *Journal* policy on racial relations was no less humane than that of the *Constitution*. Bryan advocated "justice for the blacks, but they must be separate facilities." He was offended if anyone thought him racist. Yet the *Journal* stance was expressed less frequently than McGill's repetition of the race issue in its diverse political, economic, electoral, legal, and educational manifestations. Restrained by the ban on crusades, Bryan appeared the more complacent. In coming back to the issue, McGill took more risks, questioning the execution of "separate but equal" while approving the basic bargain. The *Journal* also lacked the highly visible column McGill wrote daily, not to mention McGill's command of the language and his ability to communicate on a personal level. Taken together, these factors left the *Journal* behind on the most profound and interwoven problem of the era.[32]

Even the *Journal's* cautious discussion of justice outraged some whites. Ellen Bryan recalled a threatening "poison pen letter" in 1942 that asked, "Do you want to keep your husband?" George Biggers, the newspaper's general manager, assigned plainclothes detectives to guard the Bryans. She thought it was unnecessary. "Hell's bells," Mrs. Bryan recalled, "we just used them for babysitters."[33] By contrast, McGill more so than Bryan needed protection. His occasional explorations of the South's Negro problem provided enough tinder to torch the ire of Ku Kluxers and like-minded segregationists. "We never took a readership survey," Tarver recalled. "He was the most-liked columnist, but he also the most disliked—the public was badly split. Even those who disliked him *read* him."[34]

While polite society rebuked him gently or behind his back, others of a lawless or brutish stripe unleashed hostility on him. Nasty ones dumped garbage on the lawn of his house along Piedmont Road. More violent ones drove by the house and shot buckshot through his windows. Kluxers wrote letters, invariably misspelling some words or spinning curious metaphors. "We believe in separation of Church and State and White Supremacy for you can not mix oil and water, if you do you get the Mule of Civilization."[35]

The mottled metaphors or plain illiteracy of white supremacists often amused McGill, more so than their offensive telephone calls. When at home, he usually tried to answer the phone. To a vilifier, he would reply in a bittersweet tone, "It was so thoughtful of you to call." His own salvo of sarcasm helped him cope, but it also shielded Mary Elizabeth, who worried for both Ralph and their son. Those who knew she had a drinking problem attributed it in part to the tension of being a target of hatemongers. "Ralph had the ability to handle the tension," recalled a political associate, James Mackay. "But she didn't."[36]

Despite all the venom spewed at McGill locally, he seldom leveled his criticism at local targets. Whether by coincidence or plan, he never criticized any of the practices of major advertisers in the *Constitution*. It was as though he had inherited the city boosterism of Henry Grady. Jack Spalding, a later editor of the *Journal*, contended that McGill understood that his targets were outside the city—in New York, Boston, Washington, and the nation generally. The practice of writing for a distant audience is well known among American editorial opinion writers as "Afghanistanism" because of the tendency to be harshest when discussing faraway places. A corollary of Afghanistanism is the practice of writing about home but for a distant audience, which is what Spalding referred to. It has been understood since colonial times that the farther from home your target, the more critical you can be. However, Patterson, who worked closely with McGill years later during the 1960s, insisted that McGill spoke to all southerners, including those in Atlanta, when he "questioned the way we were living."[37]

McGill was now beginning in earnest to write for national audiences. Harold Martin, who wrote for *Saturday Evening Post,* and Edward Weeks at *Atlantic Monthly,* persuaded him that magazine editors wanted reasonable commentary about the South. All he had to do was recast topics he had been writing for a newspaper audience that was largely unappreciative and frequently offended. This new audience of course had different sets of traditions and principles, and many had distorted ideas about the South, which he had an opportunity to rectify.

National magazines frequently published stories which portrayed the South as a land apart. This was William Faulkner's South, a Gothic landscape where since Emancipation whites had reinvented slavery, terribly policed by lynch mobs. Often these articles were written by correspondents who had been in the South briefly on assignment. Southerners of course also wrote for national audiences, but many lacked credibility. Those with high visibility were often politicians whose motives were suspect and whose language was stained with rhetoric. The problem lay in the writers' point of view. What was required was a southerner with something to say, in a moderate, dispassionate voice, that made sense about the South. For a national audience, it was required that he not be an outright segregationist. Also, it would be helpful if he were both critical of the South and offered solutions to the central dilemma, the race question. Editors, having been offered more heat than light, now wanted cool illumination.

The eastern established press considered McGill a valuable asset at a time when few southerners were represented in the national media. In a timely and apt manner, he filled a void. Here was a southerner who could write entertainingly about a full range of subjects from the region's politicians and businessmen to its cooking and shark research.

For national audiences, McGill shifted his literary approach, style, and content. He elevated his vocabulary and resorted less to the technique of repetition, possibly because he assumed his new readers needed it less. To this audience he could discuss the race issue more freely. For the *Saturday Evening Post* he ranged across serious terrain, advocating voting rights for Negroes. He liked lighter topics as well, and character studies. People whom he admired he extolled in lengthy profiles. His lifelong habit of reading extensively led him naturally to review books, and he made a point to review books about the South that gave him a forum for his own insights.[38]

Once, he tried fiction. In October 1947 *Harper's Magazine* published his short story, "She'll Talk Later," about racism in the police force, using the word "nigger" repeatedly. Accolades came from South and North. The director of the Birmingham Public Library wrote that such a piece "by a Southerner, it is a document of significance." A black publisher in Philadelphia said it was "one of the most moving pieces on the Negro I've read for some time." Others urged him to write more fiction, but he demurred, explaining that his calling was not fiction, but reality. A student in West Virginia elicited a prophetic answer when she asked about the title: "When I chose the title for the story, I thought of it in a symbolic sort of fashion, meaning that all such injustices will be heard from in years to come with a loud voice."[39]

McGill relished the national attention. "Ralph played to the New York juries," said Jack Spalding. McGill would look back on 1948 as a bench mark in southern politics, a turning point. It was also the year of his emergence as a spokesman for the South. In the political crisis of 1948, magazine editors found in his reasonable approach a valuable and convenient voice, someone who could explain southern events in terms of politics, economics, society, and history. Their habit of quoting him repeatedly and printing his byline prominently cast him as a national figure.

He seized the opportunity, expanding his circle of acquaintances. His correspondence with national leaders increased notably in 1948, as his secretary, Dixon Preston, could attest. He was becoming the most noted southern journalist of his generation. Indeed, none had been looked to as a spokesman for the region in the sixty-two years since Henry Grady declaration that the New South had put the Civil War behind and was eager for economic union with the nation.

The Democratic convention in July justified McGill's assertion that the South "really has no place to go" except to Truman. The call for a massive exodus of southerners from the convention did not generate a regionwide secession, though it led to a split in the so-called solid South. In the balloting, the convention nominated Truman over Georgia's favorite son, Russell. Truman's nomination, in effect, underscored the party's commitment to civil rights, a legitimate middle course between extreme options offered by Wallace and Thurmond. Men with wider vision saw great stakes in the civil rights issue as it related to postwar U.S.-Soviet politics. Truman Democrats and Republicans in 1948, observed historian John Egerton, supported civil rights at least "to negate the effect of [the Soviet Union's] Cold War propaganda exposing segregation and white supremacy."[40]

As November neared, McGill had all but given up on the president's chances. Nine weeks before the election, McGill calculated that the Dixiecrats' drive to hold 100 electoral votes would defeat Truman. It was clear to "more and more persons, willing to add" that "Thomas E. Dewey's necessary 266 votes are in the bag right now—with plenty more to spare. . . . My position is not pro-Truman. It is against the fourth-party Dixiecrats." In that context, the *Constitution* endorsed Truman.[41]

The election results surprised nearly all politicians and pundits. The *Chicago Tribune*'s "Dewey Wins" headline was the most conspicuous testament to miscalculation. Truman won twenty-eight states (303 electoral votes), including Georgia. In the South, Democratic Party regulars revolted effectively in four states, giving Thurmond's Dixiecrats the 39 electoral votes of Alabama, Mississippi, Louisiana, and his home state, South Carolina. Dewey won sixteen states (189 electoral votes).

Georgia chose Truman, despite his insistence upon civil rights. On that issue, Republicans were no better and indeed were more threatening because they had controlled both House and Senate. In the end the national Democratic platform meant little in Georgia, where Democrats did not give it "even lip service." Most southerners decided "the safest course seemed to be to stay in the party." In McGill's review of V. O. Key's *Southern Politics*, he agreed with Key's conclusion that southern state politics "have no regional unity per se but are factional, each state conforming to its own folkways and mores." For this reason, McGill concluded that the four states went Dixiecrat "not for any real belief in states' rights by those who led the movement, but because to do so would enable them to seize control of the party machinery within the state." Many Georgians would have joined the Dixiecrats, but "there was no rival group seeking to take over the party machinery."[42]

The day after the election, McGill telegrammed congratulations and a confession to the White House: "We will not be dishonest and say we thought you could do it. The truth is we didn't think you could, conditions being what they were." Sounding pro-Truman now, McGill took a share of credit because he and publisher Clark Howell "were for you and we are very happy over the victory and proud that we helped give you the majority in Georgia." Truman replied, thanking him for the *Constitution*'s support, adding in his handwriting that he hoped McGill would be at the Washington Gridiron show where journalists annually poked fun at politicians. "It will be in reverse this time!"[43]

Because McGill lacked the prescience to envision Truman's victory, it was all the more remarkable that he had held his ground courageously if fearfully in what seemed like a losing cause. He had seen the gathering for a second Reconstruction of the South. But he had rejected the solutions of the far Right and far Left. By staying the course with the national Democratic party, he believed the South had bought itself more time to reform on its own terms.

Drastic reform now seemed inevitable. From 1949 onward McGill sounded more and more like a prophet. Reform, of course, meant justice for the Negro. Writing to his national audience, McGill's voice was direct and secular: the Negro must have equal opportunity, beginning not with federal legislation, but with the ballot box. The vote would be the vehicle for further change—equal justice before the law, improved educational opportunities, and ultimately economic reform: more and better jobs.[44]

When writing this same message for his southern readers, he girded his moral authority by quoting the good book, harmonizing his argument with the voice of the prophets. All modern dilemmas had been presaged by Old Testament prophets who were better known and revered in the Bible belt than any secular sages. More than any other book the Bible was the common text of the South. Racists had used its passages as justification for segregation. McGill now voiced his interpretation, moving freely between the Old and New Testaments. On the one hand he could smite enemies with Isaiah and on the other with the parables of Jesus. If anyone knew how to "get to" these readers, McGill did. Tuning biblical references to an agricultural South, he especially liked the parables that bespoke of seeds and harvests, underscoring that the South would reap what it sowed. It was this voice, touching as it did the southerners' sense of moral righteousness, that helped create some sense of mental balance. Tarver always believed that McGill's voice of reason was the "primary factor that Georgia didn't sink to the depths that Alabama, Mississippi, and Arkansas did."[45]

There was evidence that McGill was "getting to" the readers of the *Constitution*. Like him or not, readers' letters proved their lack of indifference. Merchants who advertised in the *Constitution* often felt uncomfortable about being associated with a newspaper in which McGill undermined the legal system of segregation. In McGill's defense there was no more powerful voice than Tarver's. The publisher, Clark Howell Jr., desperate to get the *Constitution* out of the red—it was losing more than a hundred thousand dollars a year—reassigned Tarver to the business office. Tarver turned the trick within a few months, showing a profit of fourteen thousand dollars. Tarver now carried weight when he defended McGill's column, noting that the editor's notoriety was a major reason people read the *Constitution*. Reader polls supported him. Being "the most liked" and "the most disliked" columnist suggested wide readership. In this way, Harold Martin noted, Tarver was "steadying McGill's soapbox."[46]

McGill also knew how to calm the waters by changing the subject. His regular readers knew his change of pace. Doris Lockerman, an associate editor of the *Constitution* who began working with McGill in 1948, thought McGill "recognized that if he hit one serious, painful wound all the time, that he would lose much of his usefulness and effectiveness. I think surely that was in his mind. So he tempered all these things with just charming columns that everybody liked." After a column that pitched hard for reform, he wrote columns that showed his respect for the South and southern institutions, for the everlasting virtue of bird hunting with fine Georgia hounds, for small-town life, for the sad decline in southern arts, or for the mouth-watering best recipe for down-home Georgia barbecue. All this came naturally, mused his friend John Griffin. "He had all the Southern characteristics. He liked . . . fatback and he liked barbecue, and he could write about hound dogs and piney woods and some of the things that some of these folks liked too." There were periods, Tarver recalled, when McGill digressed too many days. Then Tarver would pop into McGill's office and tell him people had now read enough about barbecue. If McGill went on too long about racial justice, Tarver called him on that, too. As Eugene Patterson noted, "Once he told Mr. McGill, 'You only got one string on your bow? Can't you write about something but civil rights?' Tarver was just trying to help him survive."[47]

Just as McGill settled into his self-styled role as the independent voice of a locally owned southern newspaper, there came the shocking news in 1950 that Clark Howell had sold the paper. There had been a willing buyer for more than a decade. Since 1939, the *Journal*'s owner, Governor Cox, had regarded the *Constitution* as an attractive property, even more so after the farsighted Howell had added a television franchise to his radio station. The deal would give control of both newspapers and access to the medium of the future: forecasters put no limits on the possibilities for television and its advertising revenues. Howell's investment in television, however, had drained the *Constitution*'s resources, and the paper which had been earning up to $60,000 a year now was only barely in the black, and that was thanks to Tarver's business acumen. Cox's sweet deal would give Howell shares in a new Atlanta Newspapers, Inc. worth $4 million in two years, while keeping him on as publisher. Tarver recalled the night Howell told him the rumors were more or less accurate. McGill was in London, and Tarver telephoned him. As Harold Martin told the story, McGill's first response was, "Ohhhhh shit!"[48]

The new relationships soon became clearer through official and unofficial meetings. In the board room in Atlanta, Cox met officially with the key personnel. Clark Howell Jr., though still publisher of the *Constitution,* would have an office, but mostly to keep the southern image of the paper. Cox's business director at the *Journal,* the aging George Biggers, would direct business matters at both papers, assisted by Tarver at the *Constitution.* McGill would continue as *Constitution* editor, and Wright Bryan as editor of the *Journal.* Apart from these formal proceedings, Cox summoned Tarver and McGill to visit him in Miami. "I know how you feel," Cox began. "You feel sold out. . . . Go ahead and do what you're doing. I won't set foot in the newsroom." To Tarver, Cox made it clear that he wanted him for his business acumen. Indeed, Tarver succeeded Biggers after Cox's death and Biggers's retirement, both in 1957. True to his word, Cox stayed out of the *Constitution* newsroom. "But," recalled Tarver, "he did *call.*" More often than not, Cox called Tarver to talk business. Cox wanted Tarver to do for the *Miami News* what he had done so well for the *Constitution.* For the next decade, Tarver spent at least six weeks a year in Miami and a good deal of time talking about Miami on the phone. Any worries McGill had about his security disappeared with time. As Cox had urged him, McGill went ahead and did what he was doing.[49]

PART III
To the Summit

12

One Day It Will Be Monday

*My father, I'm sure, would have preferred
vigorous controversy to dull acceptance.*
—JOSEPH PULITZER II, 1947

*Segregation has been on its way out
for a good long time.*
—RALPH MCGILL, 1953

MCGILL WAS SELDOM happier than when writing from overseas.
Travel had launched him from the sports department, and now it fed
his increasing need to maintain his status as provider of information
and insight. Journeys gave him the vantage point he required to keep
a competitive edge. Foreign lands served as his preferred venue, as
once the sporting fields of the South had been his beat. Often he had
no news, but then he used the country as a loom on which to weave
some exotic tale or some story about a wayward Georgian abroad. Since
his first overseas reporting from Cuba he had linked himself and his
readers to the lives of people he met in councils of power and in the
city streets. His mind easily found commonalities among people more
readily than differences. "What does it mean to you and me?" he would
ask as a transition to his answer: Read and learn. Sometimes he made
a connection to his readers by finding the emotional keys—a sentimental pang of the heart or a visceral twang of the palate and stomach. Other times his appeal was cerebral: he would talk about politics
on the world stage, about whether children in the next generation in
some far-off place would choose to be pro-American or the opposite.
In rare moments, he touched a funny bone, sharing humor he found
in some peculiar but understandable local custom.[1]

His instinct to travel to countries in dramatic moments was matched by his ability to find diverse sponsors outside the newspaper office. The *Constitution* sent him to Cuba and to England in midwar, the Rosenwald Foundation shipped him to Nazi Germany and Vienna, the ASNE supported his circumnavigation of the globe, the Overseas Press Club sponsored his postwar inspection of Jewish settlements in Palestine, and the U.S. Army flew him to postwar Europe to ferret out the threat of Communist takeovers and to lend support for the Marshall Plan. In 1950, the call came from Israel to come back and write about their new nation.

By spring, McGill had returned to the Middle East. It was not only admiration for the Zionist state that lured him back, although like many other western journalists he had sided with the survival of the Jews against Arabs on all sides. Beyond this, he had a sense of history and recognized in the story of latter-day Israel a fusion of the political and biblical. He yearned to tell the story of this Old Testament nation revived in the twentieth century. In his mind the Israeli victory in the 1948 war settled the question of Palestine. In 1946 McGill had insisted he was no Zionist, but by 1950 he championed the victors as manifestations of the Book.

Evidence of the Arab-Israeli War and its aftermath was everywhere. Riding from the airport to Jerusalem, he saw wrecked tanks, noting how well the Jews had fought and how they now guarded a fragile peace. From his window in the King David Hotel, he could see the walls of the Old City, under Arab control. Beyond were the "dark masses of brooding cypresses about the Garden of Gethsemane" and, nearer, "the hills where the Crucifixion and Resurrection had taken place."

McGill set up his typewriter on a table and started writing the first of several columns. He had gone "to see in Israel the nation restored to life after 2,000 years, and witnessed every human and social problem being met with a mixture of mystic exaltation, sweaty toil and realism. . . . I came away feeling as if I had left old friends with whom, in some distant past, I had worked and played and hoped."[2]

He passed along the Israelis' message: They worried that Americans who supported them earlier would forget them with the end of the Arab war. McGill portrayed the Arabs as a constant threat, whether as trained Arab Legion soldiers with rifles ready on the walls of the Old City or as thieves rustling cattle from Israeli settlements. The Israelis could not have hoped for a better advocate.[3]

Each mission offered a kaleidoscope of characters and situations—the heart of storytelling. But the foreign assignments also carried the potential for journalistic prizes, none of which he coveted more than the Pulitzer Prize. In 1951, he accepted a U.S. government offer to visit newly independent India, which had been ruled by England more or less from the end of the Seven Years' War in 1763 until 1948. He had gone there briefly in 1945 when India was under British rule. Now his mission was to assess a U.S. government project to assist Indian agriculture, to boost the nation toward self-sufficiency in food production. The project fit into a grander geopolitical struggle. The Truman administration hoped to keep the most populous nation in south Asia from aligning with the Soviet Union, or going Communist, as China had done. McGill's foreign travel was again funded by the U.S. government, a factor he never regarded as a conflict of interest.

The reliance on government funding was practically the only way McGill could attempt such a journey. The *Constitution* made scant provision for foreign reporting, certainly not for stories about farming in peacetime. When it came to funding travel outside Georgia for other than sports events, the business-side parsimony of the *Constitution*'s management was a common complaint among journalists. "The management simply never put the money and attention into the news operation the papers' resources permitted, and their position demanded," Harry Ashmore wrote years later. "I can't remember any period when either [the *Constitution* or the *Journal*] could be said to be doing a distinguished job of covering Atlanta, or Georgia, much less the Southern region— which both papers traditionally claimed as their domain."[4]

The invitation to India was extensive and generous. McGill's friends in the Truman administration invited him for six weeks to study and write about the agricultural experiment which was the result of a citizen exchange. The previous year the U.S. government had sponsored the trip of an Indian farmer to Carroll County, Georgia, west of Atlanta, to see the operation of a small farm. Now, McGill accompanied a Georgia soil conservationist to visit the farmer's land in north-central India.

The series of articles that ensued deserved the 1952 Pulitzer Prize for international reporting, from McGill's point of view. Aside from the sheer geopolitical importance of India, McGill thought his writing reflected soul and spirit: a knowledge of the problems of farming and sympathy for the farmer, together with a sensitivity to international politics and an identification with India's newly won independence.

The Pulitzers, awarded since 1916, were the highest order of recognition in journalism. Each spring, journalists anticipated the announcement of these professional knighthoods. Winners were automatically exemplars of excellence, men (and a few women) officially regarded as models to emulate. Far greater than the prize (five hundred dollars at mid-century) was this national recognition, which McGill desired.

On the domestic scene, McGill had by 1951 become a national figure. Stories about him in national magazines presented him as a spokesman for the New South of moderate to liberal southerners. Each national article that quoted him on behalf of the New South further reinforced his image as representative of the region's sensible people. To one friend McGill characterized himself as "a modern day Henry Grady," battling the South's provincialism. He cultivated his national audience by frequent articles in the *Atlantic Monthly* and *Saturday Evening Post*. Editors who needed a moderate comment on southern politics and race customarily called on McGill. In part thanks to his friend Bill Howland, the *Time* correspondent in Atlanta, McGill's photograph became familiar to readers of *Time*'s "Press" section.[5] The photographs revealed a somewhat benevolent face softened by chubbiness; perhaps because his weight was visible nationally, McGill attempted to slim down. Margaret Tarver recalled one of his diets: "He would go to the Capital City Club and just order a half head of lettuce. The only problem was he would drown it in dressing. Then he would order another half."[6]

However deserving, McGill had little hope he would win the Pulitzer, given what he perceived were the politics of the selection board. The year before, he had broken his silence and joined the critics of the Pulitzer board. Just after the 1951 awards had been announced, a *Constitution* editorial written by McGill or with his approval questioned the selection criteria.

The editorial did not reveal McGill's private bitterness. He wrote in the pseudo-objective style of the observer rather than in the pained, subjective first-person voice of the bereaved loser. Since 1945, he believed he had been being blacklisted each year because of Carl Ackerman's scathing report on his conduct during the ASNE trip. Ackerman, dean of the Columbia School of Journalism, had served since 1933 as secretary of the Pulitzer board. Then, too, there was the possibility that McGill was also on the blacklist of the influential publisher John S. Knight, the former ASNE president to whom Ackerman had complained about McGill's disgraceful conduct.[7]

The India series was only the latest candidate for the prize. During the late 1940s, McGill believed he deserved the Pulitzer for editorial writing, for placing racial moderation on the South's political agenda. He felt he had distinguished himself from most southern editors, who from fear or custom respected the conspiracy of silence on racial matters.

When in 1951 a southerner *was* awarded a Pulitzer for editorial writing, McGill and others questioned the board's criteria. In McGill's mind, William Harry Fitzpatrick of the *New Orleans States-Item* lacked exemplary qualities of vigor and courage. The Louisianan avoided the volatile issue of race, wrote in a lackluster style, and did little to stir men to change the course of southern history.

Fitzpatrick's competitive advantage, however, was boosted by an influential member of the Pulitzer board. Arthur Krock, Washington bureau chief of the *New York Times,* had twice won the prize. At a routinely secret board meeting, Krock contended that Fitzpatrick deserved the award for his "series of editorials analyzing and clarifying a very important constitutional issue, which is described by the general heading of the series—'Government by Treaty.'" Krock's motion was seconded by Knight.[8]

On the matter of selections, Pulitzer officials at Columbia University maintained secrecy, guarding the identities of the Pulitzer board members. That information was known only to an inner circle around Ackerman and the trustees of Columbia University. Despite occasional criticism of the board and the process, Pulitzer officials declined comment. In 1947, the second Joseph Pulitzer maintained that he was "almost indifferent" to controversy over the prizes. "My father, I'm sure, would have preferred vigorous controversy to dull acceptance."[9]

In May 1951, complaints became more numerous, articulate, and widespread. Syndicated columnists and broadcast critics questioned the integrity of the officials and the process. Some editors urged the Pulitzer board to take a more active course to deflate criticism, perhaps issue a statement by the president of Columbia University, Gen. Dwight Eisenhower. One highly placed journalist wrote to Ackerman, advising that some criticism was "not only untrue but the entire wordage of the reference is quite libelous" and required a response to protect the reputation of the Pulitzer Prizes and of Columbia University.[10]

The loudest critic in May and June 1951 was the nationally syndicated columnist and broadcast personality Walter Winchell. After the awards were announced, Winchell made "repeated slurring comments on the Pulitzer Prize awards set-up." Winchell's main criticism was that awards frequently were made to journalists whose publishers were on the Pulitzer board. "The answer, of course," one editor wrote to Ackerman, "is that Columbia has been able to get the top publishers and editors in America to serve on the board and organizations such as *The New York Times, St. Louis Post-Dispatch,* The Associated Press, *Chicago Daily News,* and a few others are bound to come up with frequent winners. I thought Winchell's blast at [name deleted] was particularly unfair and under the belt."[11]

In his broadcasts, Winchell was amplifying the salvo fired May 9 from the *Constitution*'s editorial page. That editorial stated that with the 1951 prizes "there comes the disquieting feeling that the Pulitzer awards are, in some degree, at least, annually coming to have less & less meaning." In its prize for history, the Pulitzer board had "ignored one of the greatest contributions to American history, the scholarly and magnificently written, *The Emergence of Lincoln,* by Allan Nevins. In other fields, the board followed the line of least resistance by splitting up the prizes in many sections. . . . We respectfully submit that the Pulitzer awards are being too often watered down, and are losing meaning and prestige."[12] *Time* magazine sympathized with McGill's view. Days later, its Press section reported that the *Constitution* "teed off" on the Pulitzer Prize board.

"There were plenty of signs that the *Constitution* was right. Many U.S. newsmen had reacted to the 1950 awards with a 'ho-hum.'"[13]

McGill evidently hoped that the frontal attack might incline the Pulitzer board to change its ways and recognize his achievement. After his series on India, he tried again. In May 1952, he was again passed over.

Ackerman's disgust served to sober McGill somewhat. By 1952 he was still drinking, but less so. In the early 1950s he evidently realized he had to get control of the problem. This is what his friends and business associates confided when FBI agents came around to question them after McGill was nominated for a presidential appointment. Judging from the FBI files, McGill's drinking had become legendary, and the agents invariably discussed it in their reports. One acquaintance who had known McGill for years conceded that McGill once had a habit of drinking "to excess" but insisted that by 1952 intoxicants were no longer a problem. A friend since his Nashville days swore that although McGill "drank rather heavily several years ago, he does know that [McGill] seldom drinks at all now." Most of those interviewed traced the end of excessive drinking to around 1950, the year when Cox bought the *Constitution* and became McGill's new boss.[14]

McGill now tried to limit his drinking to certain occasions. Certainly he imbibed less at home, where he might trigger Mary Elizabeth's habit. He preferred the company of friends. Away from home he was an eager drinker. At one national political convention in Chicago, recalled the Arkansas publisher Harry Ashmore, McGill showed up at Ashmore's hotel room with a bottle of vodka and proposed to make mix a drink with whatever mixer Ashmore had around. They swilled the resultant concoction, a sort of purple screwdriver made with grape juice.[15]

At home he tried to confine his intake to red wine with meals, or purposeful cocktails at the Capital City Club. At least once, a few stiff drinks softened his relationship with the hard-edged business manager, George Biggers. Biggers came over from the *Journal* when Governor Cox bought the *Constitution* and soon Biggers was trying to control McGill's voice in the name of improving revenue. When advertisers believed McGill's fixation with race was bad for business, they complained to

Biggers. Once, Biggers gave McGill such a hard time that McGill thought about bailing out and told Tarver he might accept Robert Woodruff's offer of a job at Coca-Cola. Tarver calmed McGill, reminding him that McGill and Biggers had something in common: Both had been sportswriters. Two days later McGill wrote Tarver, "It's a shame you weren't here yesterday. Two gentlemen were seen staggering out of the Capital City Club arm in arm[,] . . . two hearts that beat as one in the great brotherhood of sportswriters."[16]

After the transition, McGill began to enjoy the new relationship with Governor Cox. Cox continually assured McGill of his support, which the publisher underscored during each visit to Atlanta when they met in Cox's suite in the Biltmore Hotel. McGill needed reassurance, given the newspaper's traditional resistance to discussing taboo subjects such as voting rights and segregated schools.

Certainly McGill's columns on racial questions were not radical. Before 1954, McGill did not oppose segregation, which was law in Georgia. His main contributions lay in breaking the silence about "the situation" and in stimulating public discussion where before there had been almost none. His main point before 1954 was that southerners needed to solve the problem before the nation did it for them. Knowing that serious questioning of segregation raised eyebrows among the elite and attracted epithets from the random masses, he usually constrained his advocacy to what he considered cautious and reasonable topics. Since the early 1940s, he had advocated equal voting rights, and since the late 1940s equal educational opportunities—with increasing focus on the "equal" in "separate but equal" education. In this stance, McGill had company. As Ashmore explained, "I would not have in 1945 come out editorially and demanded an end to segregation. What I did, and what McGill was doing, was demand the vote for blacks. And demand equal treatment in all public facilities. Equalization of the schools, that kind of thing—end the poll tax. See, that was within the separate-but-equal framework."[17]

Even this discussion flagged him and the *Constitution* as targets for steadfast segregationists. Biggers remained persuaded that McGill was bad for advertisers and, more generally, for the newspaper business.

Discovering the middle ground and holding it was an everyday task. When McGill wrote gently about racial inequalities, he disturbed both friend and foe. While some whites felt that in saying anything he had said too much, other liberals and most progressive blacks thought his sermonizing columns lacked commitment. "It was not a pretty time, and Mr. McGill said so," concluded Eugene Patterson, who followed McGill's columns long before his own career in journalism brought him to write for the Constitution. "In the process of course he outraged the bourbons [power structure], the politicians and the masses alike, which left him a pretty lonely man."[18] McGill's friend Bill Howland, who wrote for *Time* magazine, observed that McGill "has long steered an enlightened but discreet course."[19]

In this "discreet" manner, McGill before 1954 certainly did not advocate breaking legal race barriers and on occasion stressed that he was not advocating an end to segregation. While staying within the bounds of "separate but equal" he could argue effectively, as Ashmore noted, about the need to emphasize more the "equal" aspect of the formula. In this way, he was in the vanguard of the few southern editors who recognized the need to discuss the gross inequities of segregation at a time when most editors—and Christian preachers, as McGill noted—participated in perpetuating the racial "situation" by reticence and silence.

By 1953, McGill began to prepare his readers for the "inevitable"—the day *when*, not *if*, segregation would end. Just mentioning the subject broke with the practice of keeping silence on what was referred to as "the situation," or, in short, "the sitch."[20] McGill acknowledged the silence but disputed the wisdom of stifling discourse. "It is a subject which, because of its emotional content, usually is put aside with the remark, 'Let's don't talk about it. If people wouldn't talk about these things, they would solve themselves.'" Borrowing from *Gone with the Wind,* he said southerners should not emulate Scarlett O'Hara, who, "when confronted with a distasteful decision, pushed it away with the remark, 'We'll talk about it tomorrow.' But 'tomorrow' has an ugly habit of coming around."[21]

The inevitability concerned challenges to segregated schools being carried to the U.S. Supreme Court. Referring to the Court's practice of issuing rulings on Mondays, he wrote in April 1953 that "one of these

Mondays the Supreme Court of the United States is going to hand down a ruling which may, although it is considered by some unlikely, outlaw the South's dual school system, wholly or in part." This was more than a year before the Court ruled on *Brown v. Board,* but McGill thought it did not take much common sense to envision the provisions of such a ruling. The Court would decree that separate-but-equal education, legitimized in 1896 by the Supreme Court in *Plessy v. Ferguson,* served the political, economic, and social needs of one race at the expense of another. That December, six months before the ruling, McGill sensed that the emotional backlash in the South was already being focused on the Court's legitimacy and that "hotheads" and demagogues could quickly polarize opposition, diminishing the sphere of rational discourse. In breaking silence with "another piece about segregation," he justified the column as being "written out of a sense of duty . . . as a newspaperman believing newspapers exist to inform—not to inflame or deceive. Also, it is no good sweeping things under the rug. Someone later on always lifts the corner." It was not true, he insisted, that the Court was forcing desegregation on the South. It was simply "required only to interpret the Constitution. . . . If politicians and hotheads will stop talking violence, we can meet this issue as a civilized people."[22]

During the months before the Court ruling, his discussion of justice often referred to Christian as well as political precepts. He had long thought of the segregated churches as hypocritical social clubs for white folks and had become what Harold Martin called a "fallen-away churchgoer." In part for the benefit of his son's Christian education, McGill took instructions in the Episcopal faith, and on November 15, 1953, he, Mary Elizabeth, and Ralph Jr. were confirmed at the Cathedral of St. Philip. With membership in a church which seemed progressive, he might now speak to Christians as a whole that "segregation by color based on law simply does not fit the concepts of our world today, neither political nor Christian. Indeed," as he told the commencement audience at the University of Arkansas in January 1954, the Christian's responsibility makes him "the most heavily beset of all."[23]

Whatever the Court did, McGill argued, no one should fear immediate or sudden change to the school system. The Court would give the

South time, and southern politicians would present "evasive action and legal tests." McGill envisioned years of delay. "The court can rule segregation unconstitutional—but allow the states affected a period of years in which to work our procedures satisfying the court's decision. Whatever happens, for some years the majority of Southern Negro children will continue to go to separate schools. . . . The vital point is—there is no reason for violence, whatever the decision. Leadership everywhere in the South must talk about this and make it clear. Anger and violence will solve nothing."[24]

McGill drew measurable support from a small elite of his own shaping. He continued to value the counsel of his friends Robert Woodruff and Jack Tarver, but during the early and mid-1950s he developed a wider circle of associates in whom he confided and shared ideas and strategies. He referred to these men, ultimately, as the "brethren," other southerners who shared a vision of the South and some of the same growing pains. During the early 1950s the brethren included Harry Ashmore at the *Arkansas Gazette* in Little Rock and Carl Sandburg.

Late in 1951 McGill visited Sandburg to write an article for the *Constitution*'s weekly magazine. Sandburg had moved in 1945 from Michigan to Flat Rock, North Carolina, bringing with him his wife, three daughters, his family's goat herd, and his reputation as an American sage. The Sandburgs settled into an antebellum summer house on 240 acres, named Connemara Farms. In the fall of 1951, McGill arranged to visit Sandburg with the idea of writing a magazine article about the transplanted poet. Himself a latent poet who at Vanderbilt had chosen another path, McGill stood in awe of Sandburg's achievement.

At Connemara he found the great man a paragon of wisdom and understanding, and this admiration energized the portrait he wrote on his return. "This man Sandburg with his Swedish ancestry, was so in tune with the country of his birth, that he was drawn to become the greatest scholar and researcher into the life of perhaps the greatest American— Abraham Lincoln." With his Georgia audience in mind, McGill did not mention Sandburg's politics, that before World War I he had been a Socialist in the party of Eugene V. Debs. Instead, the article noted that

Sandburg had been "one of the Wisconsin progressives."[25] But McGill did stress Sandburg's biography of Lincoln and the respect for Lincoln the two men shared.

After the article appeared, Sandburg wrote that McGill could "come along here anytime and I will knock off from what I am doing to see you and talk with you. I think you represent civilization." Though he remained devoted to a schedule of writing in his retreat, the upstairs study, Sandburg insisted on taking time to welcome southerners who were "good for me."[26]

Sandburg was good for McGill as well. On that first visit McGill felt a healing power in the ancient poet. Sandburg was then seventy-three and white-haired. McGill idled on the wide porch, swaying in a rocker. He nodded in agreement and in awe at how deeply Sandburg's words touched him, as balm.

At his typewriter, McGill started the article with Sandburg's plain message, a message that had spoken directly to his own needs: "A man must find time for himself. Time is what we spend our lives with. If we are not careful we find others spending it for us." McGill passed along the sage's appreciation of solitude: "It is necessary now and then for a man to go away by himself and experience loneliness; to sit on a rock in the forest and to ask of himself, 'Who am I, and where have I been, and where am I going?'"[27]

The two found they had much in common. A generation older than McGill, Sandburg had started as a journalist in Chicago, seeking to make a difference in society. In McGill he recognized a kindred spirit trying to lead a later generation into social change.

In the fall of 1953, Sandburg coaxed McGill into writing about the anniversary of Thomas Wolfe's fifty-third birthday in nearby Asheville. The trip would yield not only a column; Sandburg promised "interesting fellowship" and slopes and mountains "in their rare autumn garb." McGill decided to make it a family trip and towed along his son, who was then eight.[28]

Connemara, near Flat Rock, was within easy reach of Asheville, and McGill and Ralph Jr. were soon settled with Sandburg on the farmhouse porch. A photograph taken during that visit shows the three at the fringe of the woods, with the boy eyeing the poet's scarf. "I have always wanted him to remember he knew Sandburg," McGill wrote a few years later to

Harry Golden, the author and journalist whom he came to know better during visits to Connemara. "He and Ralph [Jr.] hit it off just fine." This was especially so when Sandburg learned that the boy was beginning to write poems.[29] Soon after, McGill published a profile of Sandburg in *Reader's Digest*. Sandburg's editor at Harcourt, Brace alerted him about the forthcoming *Digest* article. Sandburg told McGill, "I said [to the editor], 'I haven't a single misgiving. The man can write and he is a warm-hearted friend.'"[30] Three weeks later, while in New York on business, Sandburg found a twenty-five-cent Civil War script issued by Georgia and mailed it to McGill, noting that his "indebtedness to you runs beyond the amount of this remittance of money issued by the State of Georgia & if you find it is not legal tender then you and your boy might keep it as an odd token of bygone days."[31]

The *Digest* article amplified McGill's preoccupation with Sandburg's twin themes of loneliness and spending time wisely. A few years later McGill shared with Ann Landers that, "This business of being alone is a very complex thing. . . . Carl has a theory I have tried to put into practice with some success. He thinks that only those persons who have learned how to 'use' loneliness are able to compete with the pressures and forces loose in the world."[32] In the *Digest* article, McGill quoted Sandburg as saying, "Time is the coin of our lives. Only those who learn how to live with loneliness can come to know themselves and life. . . . A man must discover his own life, and how to spend time, the stuff of which existence is made."[33]

McGill's article had a therapeutic effect on a national audience. A woman in Leesburg, Virginia, thanked Sandburg "for helping me when I was ill with a heart attack last May." After reading the insight about time "I seemed to understand myself better. I have that splendid quotation of yours, here on my desk now."[34] Sandburg forwarded the letter to McGill, adding, "No telling where idle words sent on a vagrant wind may strike seed. . . . Whensoever you chance to be hereabouts remember the front porch chair you used and that you have irrevocable license to occupy it."[35]

Two who became frequent guests were McGill and Golden. Golden was a son of immigrants and had been a Socialist since his youth. Four years younger than McGill, Golden had moved to Charlotte from

Brooklyn and added an urbane Yiddish viewpoint to their shared experiences and storytelling.

On the columned porch, enthroned in rocking chairs and soothed by the vista of the mountains, they enjoyed the wit, wisdom, and tomfoolery for which Sandburg was legendary. As they sipped tea, or milk from Sandburg's goats, or something stronger, no subject was too small or large to be examined, from the news of the day to literature, and the fate of Adlai Stevenson and his famous predecessor from Illinois, Abraham Lincoln.

Lincoln's spirit seemed to run free here. Together the three at times seemed to constitute a suspect, unsouthern cult honoring Lincoln. Sandburg, while famous for his poetry, had won a Pulitzer Prize for his history of the Civil War years, centered on Lincoln. Beyond conventional historical research in documents and newspapers, Sandburg plumbed the memories of old-timers, some of whom had known Lincoln, gathering anecdotes, legends, tales, and hearsay. He also tracked Lincoln's paths during the prairie years, following the curves in the Sangamon River which Lincoln canoed to his first job as a store clerk. This mass of detail, said one biographer, gave Sandburg "the materials for reaching his full height as storyteller, poet, and artist." Sandburg managed "to communicate the point of view that Lincoln himself thought of his task as being beyond the power of mere man to achieve."[36]

Apart from their appreciation of Lincoln, their visions for the South and the country would have branded them as radicals anywhere but in Connemara. When McGill and Golden could be there together, they shared experiences, stories, private visions, and beliefs. They could sound out the options for the ever-burning race fires. They would part, encouraged and fortified against hostile critics. During this time McGill was encouraged to begin work on his second book, a collection of his columns linked with a recurring theme: hope, opportunity, growth, and accompanying problems.

Very consciously, McGill was cultivating his *national* audience. During this period, his most effective tool was the book review. Reviewing books gave him a lavish opportunity to break silence on already published themes and taboos, including race issues and demagoguery. He was conscious that his national audience regarded him as an unelected southern spokesman unlike any they heard elsewhere. In 1949, in the *New York Times,* McGill criticized as hasty the book of articles written by a Pittsburgh journalist who disguised himself as a Negro and traveled the South for four weeks—"a sort of journalistic quickie in blackface." The journalist emphasized the fear he felt among blacks. McGill countered that "one of the most significant facts about the Negro in the South today is that he has lost his fear." The abolition of the all-white primary had helped in this, McGill argued: "Even an election-day killing in one of the more remote of the old-plantation regions of Georgia served not to intimidate but to make Negroes more determined than ever to vote."[37]

Often he was tilling soil and planting ideas about a new South. Praising V. O. Key's *Southern Politics,* McGill forecast that the dramatic increase in Negro voters would force a grass-roots revolution in civil rights. Between 1940 and 1948, with the movement to abolish poll taxes and white primaries in the South, Negro voter registration increased 600 percent. McGill believed that blacks voting as a bloc for enlightened whites would "bring civil rights long before legislative fiat can do it." The old ways would not fall away easily. "The political chorus of shibboleths is the same in every state, racial superiority being the loudest and most frequent."[38]

In reviews he also tried to forge solidarity among disparate southerners who dared to write honestly about taboos. In 1950, writing in the *Saturday Evening Post,* he welcomed the refreshing honesty of a fellow southern editor in Greenville, Mississippi, Hodding Carter. In a review of Carter's *Southern Legacy,* McGill recognized "a very human, clear-seeing, wise, courageous scholar and reporter." He declared that Carter was "the first" to "do so clear a job" of showing how "the race problem is so interwoven with all that is the South that it may not be dissected out and examined as one may examine an inflamed appendix." The book would offend the southern ruling class and the "hypocritical and dishonest states' rights leaders," McGill noted. Carter argued that the South was not asking the nation for a "let-us-alone period." What Carter "and others who stand with him" are asking for, McGill declared, is "that we must not be set apart."[39]

For the first time in his political life, McGill was attracted to a Republican candidate for president. He admired Gen. Dwight Eisenhower for the same reasons as many Americans. "Ike" was the war hero who had rallied the Allied forces in the "crusade" against the Nazis. "The invasion of Europe across the channel," McGill reflected in 1952, "will remain as one of the Herculean masterpieces of military history."[40]

Back in 1948, in the dark days preceding the Philadelphia convention, some Democrats had looked seriously at Eisenhower as a viable alternative to Truman. The military hero was particularly interesting to the extremist southern Democrats. Republicans had eyed him, too, then. He declined "at this time," leaving the door open. When liberal Democrats urged him to reconsider, the general flatly refused any party nomination in a reply drafted by Truman's White House. Instead, he served as president of Columbia University and, two years later, as a general again in Europe, building an army for the North Atlantic Treaty Organization.[41]

By 1951, both parties again courted Eisenhower. Which he would choose became a high-stakes political riddle. McGill's positive opinion of the public man was shaped partly by his access to him. Ike's appeal suited McGill's political appetite—here was an American hero who had the ability to win the big prize, and here also was a man McGill could talk with, and perhaps influence. The two first met in 1945 during McGill's wartime globetrotting. In the late autumn of 1951 Woodruff invited both as guests at Ichauway Plantation in southern Georgia, where the Coca-Cola magnate hosted quail hunts. Woodruff favored Eisenhower and hoped McGill and the *Constitution* would support him. In the quail hunt, McGill found himself paired with Eisenhower. Between shots, Ike confided in him. "My decision is to become a Republican," he said. "This is based on a belief that the Democratic party has been in for a number of years. . . . I think changes are needed."[42] That same month, Arthur Krock, Washington Bureau Chief of the *New York Times,* reported that Truman offered to support Ike as the Democratic candidate, but Ike replied, "You can't join a party just to run for office. . . . You know I have been a Republican all my life."[43]

After Ike announced, McGill's decision was made as well. Woodruff aside, more powerful countervailing forces persuaded McGill. The dominant voice belonged to Cox, who was as much politician as owner. The crusty old Democrat had been his party's nominee in 1920, when McGill, at the age of twenty-two, broke a promise to his father to vote Republican, choosing instead to vote for this Ohioan who was an early political hero. Now, as McGill recalled, Cox summoned him to his Dayton, Ohio, office. "Now and then, over the years," Cox told him, "you may find yourself leaning toward a Republican. But don't be deceived. There are some good Republicans. But in the long run, the Republican party is no damn good for the country."[44]

McGill's admiration for Eisenhower was tarnished during the campaign when Ike declined to defend loyal Americans caught up in the hunt for Communists in the federal government, led by the Republican senator from Wisconsin, Joseph McCarthy. McGill had earlier assailed McCarthy's pattern of unfounded accusations as "this malignant episode in Washington. No one is safe from that sort of perjury. . . . It has created fear in this country which matches the intangible and real fears produced by Communism's propaganda."[45]

A staunch supporter of Gen. George C. Marshall, now secretary of state, McGill was among the first to come to his defense when McCarthy vilified Marshall with charges of treason and espionage. In December 1950 McGill defended Marshall's choice of Anna Rosenberg as a defense aide for the Korean conflict. "There was not a shred of evidence—just a charge," McGill declared. Despite Rosenberg's "responsible, fine and able" service with the Mobilization Advisory Board in World War II, this "loyal American . . . has been put to embarrassment and trouble and, worse, is open to smearing by any eccentric who wishes to get on the floor of the House or Senate and do so. Despite the proved perjury, there will always be some who will doubt her." McGill called this and other instances of McCarthy's attacks "not Americanism and while it may please those who thrive on half-truths and abuse, distortion and character assassination, it is a dangerous lion to be lose in our streets. It can attack others who now consider themselves its masters." Speculation on the general menace, McGill noted that there "probably isn't a citizen in America who could prove he was not a member of the Communist Party if the charges were made by one of these sinister psychopaths."[46]

McGill blamed the media for promoting McCarthy's ravages. Along with political witch hunters and the crazies, McGill castigated "the little group of men in radio and news whose following thrives on picturesque abuse, daily given like shots of a narcotic drug." He understood how easily the media spread defamation, true or false, and the irreparable nature of damage to reputation. A decade earlier he had written about a downtown Atlanta pitch man who sold "a marvelous glue that will repair all things (save cracked reputations).'"[47]

During the presidential campaign, McGill expected Eisenhower to come to the defense of Marshall, one of Eisenhower's friends and benefactors. During the war, Marshall had urged President Roosevelt to advance Eisenhower several grades, putting him in line to command. In September 1951, on the U.S. Senate floor, McCarthy had called Marshall "mysterious and powerful" and accused him of participating in a immense Communist conspiracy that had led to the loss of China and the disaster of the Korean War, which had been raging for more than a year. McCarthy declared that a "larger conspiracy, the world-wide web of which has been spun in Moscow" was now guiding Truman. So long as few criticized him for preying on innocent persons, he continued in the spotlight of televised Senate hearings.[48]

When Eisenhower campaigned in McCarthy's home state, McCarthy joined the campaign train. At a stop in Milwaukee, where they appeared together, journalists following Eisenhower expected him to break with McCarthy by delivering a prepared tribute to Marshall. But Eisenhower's political advisers persuaded him to cut the tribute and avoid a confrontation with a fellow Republican in his home state over a publicly volatile issue.

In the public talk Eisenhower said he agreed with McCarthy's goals, but not his methods. Because the prepared tribute had been leaked to the press, its deletion made news. Eisenhower's caving into McCarthy made the publisher of the *New York Times,* Arthur Hays Sulzburger, "sick at heart." McGill wrote, "Some of his party associates blushed . . . as he struck out the praise of General Marshall." For McGill, the Milwaukee stroke darkened Ike's image, reflected in his column "Death of a Hero." But the column was so intemperate that he couldn't publish it; he ordered it killed, he told Harold Martin. From then on, McGill thought of the political Eisenhower as weak, compromising, even two-faced: "On political issues,

Eisenhower has taken the side most pleasing to that section of the country in which, on that particular day, he happened to be speaking."[49]

After Stevenson won the Democratic nomination, McGill was pleased when Harry Ashmore drew him into the candidate's inner circle. Ashmore was one of Stevenson's early and astute advocates. When Stevenson asked Ashmore to join the campaign, he took a leave of absence from the *Arkansas Gazette*. On his advice, Stevenson summoned other southern journalists to his home in Libertyville, Illinois. The task was to write policy papers for Stevenson on "what [we] thought on a variety of subjects, all of which concerned the South." In the evening, Stevenson and his brain trust of journalists dined together. Another member of this small group was Harry Golden, editor and publisher of the *Carolina Israelite* and one of Sandburg's circle of friends.[50]

McGill, now an insider, wrote fervently and eloquently about Stevenson. Here was a presidential candidate from Abraham Lincoln's Sangamon Valley. McGill blended poetry and history, with tones of Sandburg's *Lincoln*, romanticizing the valley where "the green corn has slowly turned brown and the prairie winds have come to make elfin music with the sawing and swaying of its dried spear-like blades, while the old ghosts of the Sangamon who gathered there with Abraham Lincoln to receive the returns of 1860 have waited patiently for another night like that one when they sat with their friend, feeling the foundations of the Union trembling beneath them."[51]

He wrote fervently despite evidence that Eisenhower seemed to be ahead. Waiting on election day, McGill concluded that the better man—a man of candor, plain ways, and hard work—might not win. Though he had a "fighting chance" against the war hero, "the odds are against the man who waits by the Sangamon. But, win or lose, he will remain in the public eye for generations to come as the most refreshing candidate in our time and one of the most able."[52] The outcome was a landslide for Eisenhower, with the biggest percentage of popular votes since Roosevelt defeated Alf Landon in 1936. Stevenson won nine of the 48 states; Ike, 39.

When Stevenson visited Georgia a year later, McGill touted his chances for another run at Eisenhower in 1956. True, Stevenson had defended the Democratic Party's pro–civil rights platform, which caused rancor among Georgians. But a year after the election, in the harsh light of the Republican victory, Georgia Democrats greeted him "all without their hatchets." Party unity was Stevenson's theme. In a speech which was broadcast he defended the party against Republican charges that the Democrats were the party of disloyalty, that Democrats either harbored Communists or were soft on Reds. After the Civil War, Republicans had divided the opposition by waving the "Bloody Shirt." Now they were using the same tactic, waving the "Red Shirt." "It was a magnificent speech, enthusiastically received," enough so, McGill wrote, that Stevenson left "everyone wondering if in 1956 the Democratic nominee ought not to be Adlai Stevenson."[53]

McGill could identify with attacks on loyalty. By 1953, the epidemic of Red-baiting which Stevenson decried had spread to infect politics at all levels—national, regional, state, and local. Almost no political figure was immune from the range of attacks—ungrounded allegations or a proper investigation or a subpoena to testify, or in some cases a criminal indictment.

Communist name-calling troubled McGill personally. He withstood being labeled "traitor" by discredited Klan members. In 1951, however, he was stunned that the FBI took seriously other reports from informants. That year McGill underwent another FBI inquiry after the Truman administration nominated him and four others to serve on the Atomic Plant Construction Advisory Panel of the Joint Congressional Committee on Atomic Energy.

The power of atomic energy fascinated and horrified McGill months before Hiroshima, well before the public became aware of it. In January 1945, as he was in New York preparing to depart on the global free press mission, he published a column repeating rumors that "Atomic energy bombs are just around the corner. God help us if Germany comes up with this one. If she really should be first with controlled atomic energy she can conquer the world in two weeks." The column alarmed the directors of the U.S. Office of Censorship, who said it violated the office's request in 1943 "not to publish or broadcast any information whatsoever" regarding wartime atomic experiments. "The Germans may well assume that so informed a person as Mr. McGill was speaking from knowledge of our own progress when he said that atomic energy bombs were 'just around the corner.'" Further McGill's reference to "if she really should be first," assistant director Jack Lockhart noted, "clearly indicates that a race is on and that we, too, are engaged in a driving effort to beat the Germans in this special field of research. . . . Certainly we do not want them to learn, if it is indeed true, that we have progressed to the point where it can be said that the achievement is close at hand." Lockhart asked the *Constitution* managing editor to "re-alert your associates, please, to the dangers inherent in any discussion" of atomic experiments.[54]

By 1951, the United States was racing the Soviet Union to stockpile atomic weapons, and the FBI was instructed to make a rigorous background investigation. An FBI agent visited McGill and asked him about two old relationships, with the Southern Conference for Human Welfare in 1938 and with the Southern Negro Youth Congress in 1944.

Both groups had since been targeted as Communist by McCarthy's Red-hunting campaign. On March 29, 1944, the SCHW was declared a "Communist front" by the Special Committee on Un-American Activities. Again, on June 12, 1947, as the cold war was beginning, the House Committee on Un-American Activities cited the SCHW as a Communist front and declared that the organization "seeks to attract Southern liberals on the basis of its seeming interest in the problems of the South," although its "professed interest in Southern welfare is simply an expedient for larger aims serving the Soviet Union and its subservient Communist Party in the United States." The committee had cited the Southern Negro Youth Congress as a Communist front even earlier, on January 3, 1940; in 1947, the U.S. attorney general agreed.[55]

McGill was interviewed in his office. Special Agent John P. Slayden visited him on November 8, 1951, to discuss these two touchy matters, which in FBI jargon were "derogatory." Suppressing his astonishment and some anger, McGill answered directly. As Slayden later noted, the editor "volunteered that about 1940 when the Southern Conference for Human Welfare first came to his attention, he permitted the use of his name as a sponsor of this organization, but was never active in same." McGill explained that "at the time he agreed with the high sounding principles of the organization, but after the first conference was held and he became convinced that it was infiltrated and dominated by Communists he thereafter fought the organization both privately and through the press."[56]

His reply seemed reasonable and credible. In 1938, McGill had just moved to the editorial page from the sports department. His political savvy steered him away from radical views, whether antisegregationist or Communist-tinged, that could impair his credibility and threaten his career. There was no trace of anything McGill may have written for or against the SCHW, during that first conference in Birmingham in 1938.

His involvement with the Southern Negro Youth Congress had been in public. About 150 delegates attended the four-day conference beginning November 30, 1944, when Arnall was governor. A "confidential informant" told the FBI that McGill "was seated on the stage during one of these conferences." He "was one of several Atlanta civic leaders who made a short welcoming address." The FBI confirmed that McGill's name "appeared on the roster of conference leaders." McGill could explain this involvement as well. He told the FBI that "he was called upon to extend some sort of welcome" to the Southern Negro Youth Conference. In this case, he "did not know anything about the organization but merely went along with some other public figures in Atlanta to welcome the group."[57]

McGill's explanations satisfied the FBI. The agents did not remove the questionable relationships from his FBI files, but they discounted them with McGill's responses. The final report in 1951 ended on three notes of advocacy by the bureau, making a case in favor of McGill's appointment to the Atomic Plant Construction Advisory Panel.

The bureau offered McGill's anti-Communist articles as evidence. "It should be noted," wrote the FBI, "that Mr. McGill has written considerable articles for many years attacking the Communist Party and its policies." The bureau made a qualitative judgment about McGill's writing, noting that he "has exhibited a definite anti-Communist attitude in all of these articles." A man could be judged by his enemies as well. The FBI agents indicated that, to McGill's credit, his avowed critics included the Communist Party newspaper, the *Daily Worker.* In one article, discussing "Negro racial segregation problems in Detroit," James W. Ford, identified as a Communist Party section organizer, "attacked McGill indicating that

McGill advocated racial segregation in the South." If a man may be judged by his enemies, the FBI implied, McGill was no Communist sympathizer.[58]

Third, and perhaps most important, the FBI appreciated the editor's continued service, in his own way, as a reliable source of valuable information. He was also a friendly source. "McGill has always cooperated with the various agencies of the United States Government," the bureau stated. The FBI credited him with "furnishing them any information of value whether it be matters dealing with smuggling, security, or general criminal data."[59]

While this cooperation was inspired as often as not by his desire to serve his country, McGill undoubtedly appreciated by 1951 that his anti-Communist columns and his ongoing cooperation with the FBI shielded him from McCarthyites. Indeed, the FBI appreciated his stand against the Wisconsin senator, who claimed so many Communists had eluded the eyes of the FBI and had, in a sense, taken the luster from Hoover. "Mr. McGill has been severely critical of Senator Joseph McCarthy over a considerable period of time," one FBI media researcher wrote in a memo to Hoover's attention. "Prior to, during, and, for a while subsequent to the so-called 'Army-McCarthy Hearings,' Mr. McGill repeatedly wrote caustic articles concerning McCarthy." While his anti-Communist, pro-America stance neutralized aspersions arising from his FBI files, they also deflected day-to-day carpers who by now commonly referred to him as a dupe, or a pinko, or "Red Ralph."[60]

13

The Brethren

A companionable book, brings you,
R. McG., into the room.
—CARL SANDBURG TO RALPH MCGILL, 1954

The Southern newspaper editor or writer of any
sensitivity, who knows his people, will not, though
he disagree with them, mock or denounce them. It is
part of his duty personally and professionally, since
he knows the path his region has taken, to seek
in every way to ameliorate the problem.
—RALPH MCGILL, 1956

THE "INEVITABLE" MONDAY McGill had forecast arrived on May 17, 1954, when his journeys had taken him to London. He had become such an icon for the South that journalists immediately sought his instant commentary on the Supreme Court ruling striking down segregation in public schools. Eugene Patterson, then bureau chief in London for United Press International, learned from his New York office that McGill was in London. He reached him by phone at his hotel and "told him what the unanimous ruling was."

At first McGill was almost speechless, as though he had said it all before and was struggling to find something new that he hadn't said, something that would not offend the South in the manner of "I told you so." Now that the supreme law of the land outlawed segregation in the schools, speculation would turn to the reaction of southern political leaders who until now could avoid discussion of "hypotheticals." The Court had ushered in a new era for both blacks and whites. Much that had been suppressed over generations, ugly and otherwise, might now surface. Now "the situation" was publicly outlawed and would be openly discussed.

"Do you have any comment?"

"Well, my only comment really is that I'm surprised that it was unanimous."

"Do you want to say anything more?"

"I don't think so. I think I better not."

McGill had responded only to an obvious fact that an seasoned sportswriter would notice: the score.

"I understood fully that he had to be very careful," Patterson said years later. "He had to be very careful. In 1954 there wasn't much liberal journalism. Mr. McGill was trying to hang onto his job. He kept writing columns that he didn't agree with the prevailing attitude on race."[1]

It was the most cautious remark McGill ever made to Patterson, who had come to revere him as a sage. Two years later, the *Constitution*'s business manager, George Biggers, while visiting London, lured Patterson to Atlanta to work for the *Constitution*. Patterson eventually joined McGill—McGill "became the best friend I ever had"—in shaping the *Constitution*'s editorial stances.[2]

The Supreme Court, McGill's "nine black-robed justices in the Greek temple on the Potomac," had done as he predicted and as many southern elites, liberals, conservatives, and agile racists, anticipated, hoped, or feared. The present Court had closed the book on the earlier Court's now obviously flawed constitutional reasoning in *Plessy v. Ferguson* that separate could be equal. That ruling legitimizing segregation since 1896 now was history. That had been the last of the nineteenth century's great "compromises" on race questions; it satisfied the demands of white southerners for separatism from their former slaves while promising opportunities for the emancipated. As with previous compromises over slavery, this intended to heal the rift between the South and the rest of the nation at the price of perpetuating racial institutions peculiar to the South.

Now the new Court articulated an affirmation of simple justice, regardless of the political, economic, and social consequences that always concerned legislatures. It overturned the Court ruling of 1896, which legitimized "separate but equal" schooling. Even if facilities were "equal," would segregation "deprive the children of equal educational opportunities? We believe that it does. . . . To separate them from others of similar age and qualifications solely because of their race generates a feeling of inferiority as to their status in the community that may affect their hearts and minds in a way unlikely ever to be undone."

The Court's unanimity, which surprised McGill and which almost no one expected, was considered critical because it commanded more respect than a divided Court. The vote was orchestrated by Eisenhower's new appointee as chief justice, former California governor Earl Warren, a career politician. Warren inherited a Court on which four justices were willing to overturn "separate but equal" but the other four worried about the enormous political impact across the South. Three justices were from the South. Overturning the practice of school segregation meant ignoring the doctrine of "states' rights," which had guided federal policies concerning the South since the end of Reconstruction in 1877. All laws which perpetuated dual systems for whites and blacks would come under attack. One of the four anxious justices was Felix Frankfurter. His colleague, Justice William O. Douglas, who was committed to desegregation, said Frankfurter eventually reasoned that "if a practical politician like Warren thought we should overrule the 1896 opinion, why should a professor object?"[3]

In breaking legal silence, the Court had found that, in fact, there had been no "equal" schooling for Negro children. Mounting evidence pointed to the conclusion that McGill had been articulating, that "separate but equal" had failed; it was simply not equal, nor could equalization be afforded, nor could segregation be justified as anything but discriminatory.

Nor was the South the only site of segregation. The North matched the South's segregation by law (de jure) with its own segregation in fact (de facto). "The delusion that segregation was a peculiarly Southern institution," Harry Ashmore wrote, "blinded most Americans to the fact that the United States as a whole was, by any institutional test, a racist society."[4] The great migration of Negro laborers from the rural South to black ghettoes of northern and midwestern industrial cities was a theme McGill sounded years before. The Court undoubtedly considered this widespread discrimination against blacks in housing, employment, and education.

McGill told himself there was profound justification for the unanimous decision. The nature of the ruling—"a decision about children"—

had required unanimity. "That's what the wise and moderate, long-overdue words of the nine justices were all about—the rights and opportunities of American children. This is one reason why it was so easy for the court to be unanimous—the Constitution of the United States is as concerned with the rights of children as with those of their parents."[5]

The deeper question that troubled McGill in May 1954 had been laying in wait for at least two years while the Court was considering the case. Long before *Brown v. Board of Education* outlawed segregation, McGill had tried to imagine the ramifications. Though few southerners wanted to discuss it, McGill articulated some of the options. In 1953, he anticipated that the Court could "allow the states affected a period of years" to work out procedures. The South's "dual school system" thus would continue to exist. "Whatever happens, the majority of Southern Negro children will continue to go to separate schools."[6]

Southerners themselves, he thought, would force this delay in implementing the Court's ruling. He knew the pattern of southern demagogues well enough: they would march against the Court. He envisioned "evasive actions and legal tests" as well as delays "by gerrymandering, by abolition of school systems and other methods." In some communities, "the wiser Negro leadership, with segregation no longer sanctioned by law, will be content to maintain separate schools until public opinion accepts it."[7]

For weeks between the ruling and the hostile southern reaction there was an interlude of quiet suspense. Those who supported the *Brown* decision looked to President Eisenhower for leadership. In Little Rock, Harry Ashmore hoped that leadership from the war hero would stimulate "effective local leadership to rally support for the school officials who would have to carry out the Court's mandate." To the contrary, Eisenhower quietly insisted that his Justice Department remain noncommittal. A few years later, the president confided to publisher Virginius Dabney, "I think it makes no difference whether or not I endorse it [*Brown*]." Ike added, "The worst damn fool mistake I ever made was appointing Earl Warren chief justice."[8]

In the vacuum of leadership, demagogues in particular counter-attacked, calling the Court ruling illegal. McGill spent much of 1954 worrying about *Brown* and defending the Court in diverse forums. In November, on an ABC radio network "town meeting" broadcast from Tampa, McGill contested Mississippi congressman John Bell Williams, who told the audience the Court "took it upon themselves to legislate into law, illegally, that which the Congress had down through the years refused to do. And that is to destroy our states' segregated public school system." Not so, McGill countered. "All the Supreme Court has done is lay down a principle[,] . . an American principle that we have had all along—that we can't discriminate. . . . The Supreme Court has done nothing except lay down a principle. It hasn't destroyed a thing."[9]

McGill had imagined the reaction that would follow. Until the Court ruled on *Brown,* there had been only speculation and occasional warnings and stirrings about what might happen. In the meantime segregation was legal, and the South could conduct business as usual.

For generations of white southerners who had lived with segregation for more than half a century, *Brown* was confounding. It was as if the Bomb had been dropped, this time on the conquered South. In the aftermath, there was general shock, confusion, outrage. Southerners could not overlook this as something else that would pass. They saw and shared their neighbors' confusion, pain, and anger.

With ample prompting, people began to express themselves and take sides. McGill girded for the reaction. As he knew, there was "no place to hide." In the days and months that followed, people felt compelled to speak up and choose sides. Those who had honored the taboo now articulated their feelings, however vague and confused.

Polite society, proud of a historic tolerance toward blacks, raised questions about what to do next. Others, more angry than thoughtful, mouthed the rhetoric remembered from Gene Talmadge's time or articulated now in the U.S. Senate by his son, Herman, who warned against "mongrelization" of the races. Some vowed that not one Negro child would ever mix with white schoolchildren. In conversation, faces could become distorted by raging hatred, fed by fear.

The plight of the southern liberal was articulated by Hodding Carter. Before *Brown,* when the race issue was taboo and there was no comfort level for conversation, a conspiracy of silence afforded scarce opportunity for dialogue. The liberal customarily did not know if any neighbor shared his view.

Breaking silence and stimulating discourse had been McGill's increasing burden since becoming editor of the editorial page in 1938. For sixteen years, as his own views on race matured, he tried to break the deafening silence. He crafted each message carefully, sometimes poetically, sometimes with the images of the serpent and prophets of the Bible— thoughts served to his readers' breakfast tables. The *Constitution*'s reader surveys showed that McGill as "the most read but also the most hated of the columnists that we carried" gave him ample evidence that he was shattering the silence on race, making people hear the message, whether or not they liked the messenger.[10]

Brown lifted the cloak of invisibility. Now a southern liberal could see into his neighbors' minds as they spoke about the case. Hate, seething and feeding in a dark region of the mind, often burst into view and expression. As soon as McGill did the expected, siding with the Court, asking obedience to the law of the land, he became along with the Court a target for scurrility, damning notes, threatening telephone calls at the office and at home, placards and pickets. When words failed, the anonymous articulated with garbage, strewn on his lawn. Fear and hate drove some to target his home on Piedmont Road; they punctured his mailbox with bullet holes.

At first McGill responded with compassion and understanding that might have been confused with sympathy. Persuaded that "there is more good than evil in the people of the South," he believed his role was not to condemn or try to "solve" the race question, as northern editors had been doing since abolitionism. Rather, "the Southern newspaper editor or writer of any sensitivity, who knows his people, will not, though he disagree with them, mock or denounce them. It is part of his duty personally and professionally, since he knows the path his region has taken, to seek in every way to ameliorate the problem."[11]

He seldom confused the hearts and minds of most southerners with the venom of the "serpents" and "rats" of the Klan. He had been plain in denouncing the "yellow rats" of the KKK. Worse that the rats, because they were cleverer, were the serpentine politicians. McGill imagined them slithering in the shadows, rattling, spreading fear and confusion. This relatively small group of demagogues held the power to block change, to delay the inevitable: first political justice, then economic progress. In the days and months and years after *Brown v. Board of Education,* segregationist politicians enlisted lawyers as "constitutional authorities" to dispute the legality of the Court. McGill considered this "one of the saddest aspects of the Southern race problem," when governors, reinforced by lawyers, "deceived the people." This conspiracy of demagogues and lawyers was "publicly and slanderously denouncing the federal judiciary and assuring a troubled and indecisive public" that the Court's school decision "was not legal, did not have the force of law, and was Communistically inspired. That this stoked the fires of violence is unquestioned."[12]

The opposition triggered a war of words, which reached a pitch of irrationality and scurrility not witnessed since the Civil War. In counterattack, McGill developed his own litany of epithets to describe those inimical to justice, reason, and law. They were the "jackals, the cowards, the haters, the failures who hate achievers, the yapping feist pack that tries to drown out truth; those who dislike Jews, Negroes, Catholics, 'liberals'; the bitter and evil persons who organize themselves and send out hate literature; the Klan types, the 'States Rights' diehards. . . . They are the abscesses in America's society."[13]

McGill likened demagogues' devices to Doctor Frankenstein's creation. Their monster fanned the flames of fear about "race mixing" in schools and organized counterattacks in public, political forums. The new wave of reactionaries, mostly from the upper and middle classes, needed an organization more politic and public than the discredited, faceless Ku Klux Klan. Yet the Klan's same source of power—"pack courage," as McGill termed it—could energize the new segregationist resistance. On the day of the *Brown* decision, community leaders in Indianola, Mississippi, established the first group which spawned the white citizens councils, organizations that eventually claimed more than a half million members.[14]

In the beginning, founders of the citizens council sought respectability. "The leaders apparently felt that success depended on the support of the white middle class. In this assumption they were undoubtedly correct," observed one scholar of the rhetoric of white supremacy, "for most historians agree that the Council failed in the peripheral South, and even in Georgia, because it could not enlist large-scale middle class support." They tried to distance themselves from the excesses of the Ku Klux Klan and others who used outlaw means. They pledged to fight through legal means in the courts, and with economic clout in the community. Blacks who petitioned for school desegregation could expect economic consequences: employers could fire them, landlords could evict them, and merchants could refuse to sell to them.[15]

Despite the gathering storm, McGill defended the souls of southerners. He argued that most southerners would accept the moral "American principle" articulated in *Brown*. The two profound problems, he believed, were, first, that white southerners were psychologically unprepared and unequipped to break with entrenched segregation, and, second, they lacked the politicians with the moral courage needed to lead the transition to a truly New South. Indeed the politicians, misreading history, had retrenched, summoning images of the "states' rights" appeals of John Calhoun's Old South. McGill articulated this message most effectively to a national audience. Here again his habit of devouring books about southern problems provided him with an intellectual forum in national publications that published book reviews. "It would be interesting to know how many Christians there are who would accept the Court's decision as to schools if it were not for the mores of the community and the fear they and their families might not then be accepted as before," he wrote in a review of Robert Penn Warren's book *Segregation*. He lamented the curse of the demagogues. "One would like to know what will happen when the politicians get through, and what would have happened had they not created a Frankenstein they must continually feed with the raw meat of agitation to prevent it from devouring them politically."[16]

From 1954 onward, McGill devoted more attention to the South, at the expense of his foreign travels. At times he felt the South as a yoke, as surely as if he were a mule in the rows. Despite his love of travel and other cultures and his ambition to escape provincialism, to write about world-shaking geopolitics, he had been called to interpret the South that surrounded him. It seemed a crying need. In the violence that erupted in the years after *Brown*, he found himself increasingly quoted as a voice of reason, ever more frequently referred to as the "conscience of the South."

Publication of his first book helped raise McGill's stature in the spring of 1954. *The Fleas Come with the Dog* testified to his bona fide southern credentials, containing a selection of his southern columns. Written over a sixteen-year period, they were linked by a recurring theme: problems, or fleas, accompanied growth in the South. McGill's credited his Uncle Cade Worley for the concept of fleas. One summer's day in the Blue Ridge Mountains of Appalachia, McGill had been sitting in a rocking chair under an oak, when Uncle Cade, then ninety, said, "You never get the dog without the fleas. Big dog, more fleas."[17] Carl Sandburg congratulated him on the metaphor and read some of the stories aloud to his wife and daughters. "A companionable book," he wrote to McGill, "brings you, R. McG., into the room." The essay from 1945 about the rise of America to an atomic power ("Nations, Too, Often Strut a Brief Hour") was to Sandburg "a contemplative poem of history." The poet felt that McGill had expressed "what I have seen and didn't know was coming. The next span [of history] is harder yet to read." Nothing in the note cheered McGill more than Sandburg's reference to McGill's poetic quality.[18]

For as many as revered McGill, legions loathed him. His foes barked the epithets "Traitor" and "Red Ralph" and painted them on posters so often that the names became as common as clichés, and as predictable. McGill reasoned that no one played into the hands of the Communists' claim that America was an unjust society more than did the white citizens councils and Klan sympathizers.

Unknown to those who tarred him as "Red Ralph" or as a "pinko," McGill was carefully nurturing a personal rapport with America's number one anti-Communist, FBI director J. Edgar Hoover. In May 1954, days before he left for London, McGill mailed Hoover a copy of *The Fleas Come with the Dog* with the inscription, "To J. Edgar Hoover, with the wish that he accept this modest collection of columns as a memento of his 30th Anniversary with the FBI. Sincerely, Ralph McGill." Hoover thanked him and added a personal note: "It was most kind and generous of you to remember me in this manner on my Thirtieth Anniversary as Director of the FBI. I am sure I do not have to tell you how much your support and encouragement have meant to me during the years. They have greatly enhanced whatever success I have achieved."[19]

Fleas contained McGill's attack on McCarthyism and his affirmation of Americanism. In "What Is Loyalty, Anyhow?" he had counterattacked those who "smear" well-meaning, innocent persons who take courageous stands. Targets of these loose cannons included even the conservative Senator Robert Taft of Ohio. National officers of the realtors' association called Taft a Communist follower "for introducing a public-housing bill." Referring to his personal experiences, McGill declared, "Those who try to do something for the several million Americans who have no skills and are almost unemployable are denounced as Communists for mentioning the poor and wretched. Those who seek common justice for the Negro are accused of being Communists seeking social equality."

Loyalty was a very subjective term "because every American thinks of his country in terms of himself and his own background." In the midst of rapid social and political currents, some, including those in his own South, have "antique" concepts of their country and its place in the world. It is easy for them to misread the Americanism of another. McGill flavored the medicine with rural humor. The "antique" American possessed a certainty of his own solutions even though they mirrored a clear lack of alternatives. The antique thinker was "almost as bad off in perspective as the farmer in the mountains who wondered, during World War II, why someone didn't kill Hitler." "It ought to be easy," he argued. "Just hide in the bushes close by his house, and when he comes out on the back porch in the morning to wash his face and hands before breakfast, let him have it." McGill concluded that Americans "must maintain security without surrendering our rights, without losing faith in one another." This "essential dilemma" is made more difficult by "Americans, with their diverse concepts, their hysterical denunciation of one another as Communists in the ignorant manner of the realtors."[20]

The gift book and the exchange of compliments were the latest developments in a relationship McGill had been cultivating with the FBI chief since 1940. McGill and Hoover first met in Atlanta that year when the director was touring field offices with his close associate, Clyde Tolson. In July 1945, the FBI invited McGill to speak at its National Academy. McGill had just returned from a three-month absence during his around-the-world trip, and he was obliged to decline the FBI opportunity "because of a personnel shortage" at the *Constitution*.

During the McCarthy era, McGill made a point of visiting Hoover. On January 19, 1953, according to agency records, he "called at the Bureau . . . and visited with the Director."[21] During their chat, McGill noted that Hoover, like himself, carried too much weight. A year later, in a column about the FBI chief, McGill mentioned Hoover's other war, against excess pounds. One of Hoover's female admirers wrote to Hoover that McGill "mentioned your weight problem" and boldly proposed that Hoover try her high protein, low fat and carbohydrate diet.[22] In June, McGill praised Hoover in a column about mistaken identity, when the name of a corpse was revealed through FBI fingerprints. "Mr. Hoover was the only fellow in the whole wide world who knew him."[23]

McGill visited the FBI whenever possible. Before the year ended, on December 29, 1954, he dropped in again, this time towing his wife and nine-year-old son, Ralph Jr. McGill had promised Ralph Jr. a trip to Washington, and he felt good that he could introduce him to important people. The director was not there, but his associates welcomed the McGills warmly. One associate dutifully noted that McGill's son "was allowed to sit in the Director's chair and an autographed photograph was forwarded to him."[24] Two weeks later, asking Hoover to "pardon my tardiness in expressing our appreciation" because of a hectic schedule of speeches and travel, McGill thanked the director repeatedly for this

> wonderful hospitality and the many courtesies shown us. . . . We will never forget it. I had promised the boy, who is not quite ten, a trip to Washington, and we really saw everything and ended up with about two inches walked off our legs. Mr. Nichols arranged for him to sit for a second or so in your chair, and he will, of course, never forget that. . . .
>
> After he got home his teacher asked him to make a report of his Washington trip, and I noticed that he listed things seen in their order of importance. The FBI was easily in the first place, with the Smithsonian Institute second, and Mount Vernon third.

> He was, of course, deeply thrilled to receive your autographed picture. May I add my own sincere appreciation for your thoughtfulness in doing this? His mother is having it framed to put up in his room and, of course, he took it to school. All of us are really grateful.

McGill added to this message his sincere wish to cooperate with the bureau: "And if there is ever a chore I can run down this way for you, please let me know."[25] Hoover replied that "it was a great pleasure to have your wife and son and you call upon us here" and that he was gratified to hear that McGill's son was "so favorably impressed." Hoover acknowledged McGill's contributions to the FBI: "It was a welcome opportunity for us to repay you in small part for the many generous comments made in your editorials concerning our organization. . . . Your expression of continued cooperation is most heartening. With warmest regards."[26]

The day after this reply, on January 17, 1955, Hoover approved special FBI status to McGill. Henceforth, McGill would be an official and confidential "SAC contact"—a Hoover-certified, trusted cooperative for the special agent in charge in Atlanta. In a memo to the FBI's Training and Inspection Division, the special agent in charge (SAC) in Atlanta claimed that McGill agreed to help the FBI by monitoring news and editorial content before publication in the *Constitution* or *Journal* and broadcast on WSB radio and television. "He has assured the writer that before printing any news or editorial comment which can be interpreted as adverse to the Bureau he will check with the writer or the Bureau direct to assure himself that the facts are correct, and that the contents of the item are justified." The agent added that "except for spot news which might make one appearance he could give the same assurance for the other newspaper and radio and television outlets." The confidential appointment remained a secret to almost everyone, although McGill was proud of his assistance to the FBI and in 1953 confided to the editor of *U.S. News and World Report,* David Lawrence, that he had been providing information to the FBI for years. As with his previous government appointments, he saw no conflict of interest in a newspaper editor assisting the government, even to the extent of becoming a de facto aide. Specifically the FBI link was a patriotic duty. In addition, it gave him more inside sources in high places, while providing the highest possible refutation that he was red or pink.[27]

Hoover thus brought McGill officially into the bureau network for future confidential projects, while recognizing his previous contributions. That McGill had been friendly to the bureau was supported by the FBI agents in Atlanta who nominated him for the "SAC contact" status. Their nomination letter declared that McGill "has an extremely high regard for the Director and the Bureau generally." By early 1955, it was also no overstatement to say that the bureau's files contained "many communications from and to him demonstrating his high regard for the Director and the Bureau."[28]

The timing was propitious. McGill was being branded "Red" in the streets of Atlanta and a "traitor" at breakfast tables and cafés across the South. At the FBI, Hoover warned of a Communist conspiracy and of Communists planted in society and government. Now McGill was admitted to Hoover's inner circle of specially helpful journalists.

The taint of being associated with identified Communist fronts was neutralized, though never erased, in McGill's file. Indeed, his file still reflected his short-lived role as a "sponsor" of the Southern Conference on Human Welfare in 1938. And the file still noted his appearance on stage in 1944 at the Southern Negro Youth Conference. While the FBI never deleted those associations from McGill's file, agents after 1955 gave a favorable interpretation which tended to cancel the negative impact. When its agents next conducted a security check of McGill for a federal appointment, the FBI reported to the State Department that McGill "has explained those participations stating he did not know the purpose of [sic] organizations, which he denounced after he determined they were communist fronts."[29]

While special status satisfied McGill's continuing desire to be part of the inner political circle, the designation also served the timely interests of the FBI. In 1954, the bureau was in the midst of an intensive campaign to publicize its merits and to quiet criticism. The publicity campaign in the 1950s was as extensive as the bureau's network itself. Hoover's agents actually led double lives as public relations agents. Hoover's number three man at the FBI, William C. Sullivan, years later described Hoover's system by which the eight thousand agents in the fifty-nine field offices were "at the heart of Hoover's massive public relations operation." Sullivan asserted that "the real job of the special agent in charge (SAC) of each of these field offices was public relations. The SAC was out of the office a lot, visiting the 'right' people, those who molded public opinion in his territory: newspaper publishers and editors, owners and managers of radio and television stations, corporate executives, and church official, to name a few."

The campaign improved the effectiveness of the bureau. As Sullivan portrayed it, each SAC was able to "place 'news' stories—invented and written in the bureau, really nothing more than press releases, puff pieces for the FBI—in newspapers all over the country." The customary outlets for these stories were not the large metropolitan dailies but the hundreds of small dailies and weeklies, where editors were grateful for news.[30]

Any negative publicity was countered by positive articles, some ghost-written for the director, others written by friendly columnists such as McGill. Many other articles appeared in magazines. Hoover himself was credited with writing at least 178 articles from the 1930s through the 1970s. In that same period, magazines published a total of at least 964 articles by Hoover, about Hoover, or about the FBI.[31] In 1953–54, for example, Hoover was credited with writing "B-r-e-a-k-i-n-g the Communist Spell" and was featured in "Hoover Speaks Out on Spies After Years Chasing Them."

Others—government officers and magazine free-lancers and journalists—also contributed to this flow of public relations stories in magazines. President Eisenhower's new U.S. attorney general, Herbert Brownell Jr., lauded the FBI in two media interviews and one speech, "Success of the FBI Is Outstanding." Journalists, the most effective promoters because they were not so obviously self-serving, focused on the FBI's need for citizens to help in catching spies, on obstacles posed by unnecessary government restrictions on the FBI, and on new crime laboratory procedures which protect the innocent.[32]

Hoover favored certain journalists. These included anyone such as McGill with the confidential status of an official FBI "contact." To the favored ones, Hoover leaked "previously approved" information. Sometimes this was intended to embarrass foes in Congress or in competitive bureaucracies, including the Central Intelligence Agency.[33]

McGill kept quiet about his official linkage with the FBI. His friend Harold Martin knew about it, as did Jack Tarver. Tarver believed that Hoover had set up the arrangement by assigning a relative of Mrs. McGill to the Atlanta FBI office. Martin never mentioned that McGill had official FBI status, but he conceded that McGill benefited from the insider connection. When writing his columns, the editor was privileged to tap into "FBI data."[34]

The Supreme Court ruling cast McGill into the fray ever more prominently, draining his time and energy. Segregationists targeted him more than ever as an ally of the Court, and their strategies and tactics demanded attention. At the same time, he worked the equivalent of a second job explaining the southern reaction to northern audiences who looked to him as a bastion of southern good sense, if not an icon of moderation.

The pressure of these daily demands never completely suited McGill, who yearned for some restorative quiet where he could think, perhaps profoundly. He was always seeking a way to wander from the tether of journalism, to flee any semblance of stark drudgery, ideally to escape to joyful subjects, literature and poetry. Instinctively he knew that readers wanted to escape as well, and so he felt he was doing them a favor to find and share a respite from ephemera.

In the midst of this activity, he accepted invitations that came out of the blue, especially if they took him out of the ordinary. In the fall of 1954, one of these carried him back to Vanderbilt University for Homecoming Day, that time in "the melancholy days of autumn when universities . . . lure the old grad back to the old scenes." Of course, he was not just any Old Grad. By now he had distinguished himself, but at the expense of bastions of segregation such as Vanderbilt. What did it matter that he had not graduated? He had spent his youth there and now the sights and sounds triggered old memories. Easily he slipped into the role of the universal "Old Grad," overweight, bifocaled, weary, ailing, faded, and puffing uphill. He "wanders along the old paths, his memory of happy days when he strolled one of the paths with a co-ed beside him becomes an ache and a pain. He can smell the perfume she wore and recall the lilting sound of laughter, and smell again the aroma of autumn-fallen leaves, the wine of cool air, and the nostalgia of wood-smoke which blows through all the winds of fall."

The old poet's reverie fuses with the present moment as he suddenly encounters "a couple of undergraduates, faces alight, holding hands and talking happily as they come along, oblivious of him, or throwing him the most fleeting and casual of glances, such as they would give a tethered goat." At such times for the Old Grad, "bitterness comes over him and the taste of time is like unripe persimmons in his mouth." Old classmates are hardly any more satisfying: "Too often, unless he hails them, they pass him by." Those who do speak soon exhaust the topics of conversation. It is worse, says the Old Grad in his mid-fifties, on the old football player sitting in the stadium "remembering the tense moment before the ball was snapped; the churning of straining feet, the rasp of the canvas pants; the smell and feel of hot, wet woolen sleeves against his face. He remembers the desperate, panting breath; the long runs on the kick-offs; the hard jolting tackles; the breakthrough; the desperate agony of goal line stands." But now it is all gone. "No matter how often a man goes back to the scenes of his youth and strength they can never be recaptured again."[35]

In his escapes he found sanctuary in the sporting life. Its crowds and heroes took him in, refreshed him, and reminded him of days before journalism had turned hard and cutting. Spring days in May meant, for some, Supreme Court rulings or announcements of the Pulitzer Prizes, but for sportsmen the return of the Kentucky Derby. There, late in the afternoon, "they will spring the gate and the gay and gaudy carousel will spin. . . . You get very giddy riding the whirl of this merry-go-round." Here was a monumental chapel of faith in horse racing, gambling and drinking, "full of history, juleps, romance and rubbish." He embraced this congregation who "contribute 50 cents a week to their church budgets" but who now "crowd into lines at the $2 windows, waving fresh money, crying 'take mine.'" During the race, for a little more than sixty seconds, "life's familiar pattern is shattered" and one can focus with mind, heart, and soul: "When the starting gate springs, the horses surge into a gallop, the quickening drumbeat of steel-shod hooves begins to echo down the track, and the bunched entries come by the stands with tiny, silken-clad figures crouched over the bobbing, silken necks of the magnificent animals they ride . . . the heart constricts."[36]

The difference for the writer over the gambler was that winning was not as crucial as remembrance. Returning to the Kentucky Derby offered a physical bridge to his past, which more and more often he was seeking and sharing. He could write about the '55 derby and connect to beautiful horses whose names were history and two feisty Lilliputian jockeys who gave him the best derby story ever in '33. Nose-to-nose toward the finish the two "were swinging bats at each other between licks at the rumps of their laboring mounts. There was a pull or so at saddle blankets," and the jockey on the favorite fell behind. In the dressing room, McGill witnessed the loser, stripped naked, cursing. When the winner arrived, the loser "went for him as the arrow is released from the bow." They "clinched and flailed there, the small, naked man sobbing and crying out his choked, angry wrath, and the calm, hard-faced little man in his gay, silken shirt, white riding pants and boots." After they had been separated, the winner explained, "Well, he tried to do it to me and I did it to him."[37]

Treks to homecoming and the derby distracted McGill from the hardball of politics, but it did little for his family life. Working longer hours, he had less time than before to share with his wife and son, who in 1955 turned ten. Family vacations became shorter and busier, accompanied by McGill's portable Olivetti typewriter. Mary Elizabeth and Ralph Jr. would drive to the newspaper to pick up McGill and go upstairs to find him often "in the middle of something," as Ralph Jr. recalled. "It was hard to get him to quit. In the car he would still have his tie on. Going on vacation. The second day he would take off his tie. The third day he would take off his jacket. It would take him a week to get into his swimming trunks." For one vacation, the Atlanta department store magnate Richard Rich offered them his secluded place near Fernandina Beach, Florida. "There was no phone there—Mom thought that was great, but dad didn't like it. He would say he was going for a walk, and he would go a mile and a half to the nearest pay phone and call the *Constitution* for an update."[38]

Holidays summoned the family to visit Ralph's mother in Chattanooga. After her husband's death in 1940, Mary Lou Skillern McGill had stayed on in the frame house where McGill had grown up at 1509 Kirby

Avenue in Highland Park. She lived there with one of her three daughters, Sarah Irene McGill. She also had a housekeeper and companion, Nancy Sneed, who attended her when guests came. Sneed recalled that Mrs. McGill praised her son but seldom said anything about the daughters. The other two daughters had married, Bessie living nearby in Signal Mountain, Tennessee, and Lucille in Indianapolis, where she moved with her husband during the war.[39]

In the Kirby Avenue house at Christmas, McGill, Mary Elizabeth and Ralph Jr. warmed themselves around the fireplace in the kitchen or living room and Ralph launched into stories that the old house evoked. In his fifties, he shared these Christmas memories with readers. His own room had become a sanctuary and a launching pad. He remembered being a "scared, scrawny boy recently moved to town from a river farm, big-eyed with wonder of the city and its streets, excited by the tempo of it, and walking to the strange school." In that room he dreamed and wept, "sorrowing over some young grief," listened to train whistles, and imagined "riding off to some faraway place and of doing great deeds." Saturday nights, sore and tired from football, he relived the games, "remembering each play and feeling again the rasping contact and panting breath of play in the line." In that room, too, he had almost died from illness, and remembered leaving it first to go to college and later to join recruits at the train station.[40]

One Christmas, when Ralph Jr. was eight, McGill gave the boy a guided tour of the room:

> "This was your room when you were a boy?"
>
> "Yes. This was it. This very room. And so many of us have come to your grandmother's house for Christmas you will have to sleep with me."
>
> "I don't mind. How long ago was it when this was your room?"
>
> "A long time ago. A long time ago."
>
> "Did you sleep in pajamas then?"
>
> "No, nightgowns. And in winter when we wore long underwear against the Tennessee winters we slept in it if we could get into bed without getting caught."

"Did you do home work for school?"

"Yes. I did some of it in this room. That was when I was in prep school and trying to learn Latin as great Caesar himself wrote it. I used to dream about you, too."

"Me?"

"Yes, I dreamed of some day coming back here with a boy like you and telling him all about the old days when I was a boy here, but that would be pretty tiresome wouldn't it?"

"Yes, I guess it would. You've told me a lot of times about how you walked to school and about going on the train for the first time. I've heard all that. Was it far to your grandmother's?"

"Not so far. Just about 30 miles to the river from here. Some times we went on a steamboat. . . . Well, it's late for a boy not quite 8 to be awake. What about turning out the light and both of us piping down?"[41]

As often as possible, McGill included Ralph Jr. in his travels. The most satisfying trip was to Sandburg's farm. McGill had been delighted when his son met the poet in 1953. Being a bosom friend of Carl Sandburg, McGill learned, meant that your concerns were his. This extended to Ralph Jr. as well. When the boy was grappling with mathematics, Sandburg asked McGill to "tell young Ralph I had mean rassling with arithmetic. Tell him to read the piece Arithmetic in my Complete Poems page 655 and have a laugh at the doggone numbers."[42]

Even as the coming 1956 presidential election demanded attention, McGill accepted invitations which got him out close to the soul of real people. In early June he gave one of his many commencement addresses. He loved graduates because of their persistence, dedication, intensity, and commitment. He also felt it was a moment when he had the attention of the future. Like his friend Robert Woodruff, he loved axioms. He could urge the graduates, as one woman who heard him in 1938 remembered, "Don't stare at the steps. Step up the stairs." This June he was at a small north Georgia college in the Appalachian mountain town of Young Harris. In that gymnasium, he confirmed "an authentic bit of Americana, a look at the real heart of a people."[43]

The Democrats' chance to recapture the presidency in 1956 seemed unlikely at the outset. Only President Eisenhower's heart attack in September 1955 raised any question about his ability to serve a second term. McGill attributed Eisenhower's popularity to the fact that "we are not in a shooting war" and because on domestic issues "the people somehow disassociate him from the failure of his administrators." There was plenty for Democrats to complain about, and McGill noted that some southerners had defected from the Eisenhower camp, including "many of the textile tycoons." Southern farmers disliked Eisenhower's agricultural program and suffered from lower prices, but they blamed the secretary of agriculture rather than the president.[44]

McGill's friend Harry Ashmore explained how Eisenhower escaped blame. His "hands-off, board chairman style of administration distanced him from the controversies engendered by the cabinet officers who actually ran the government." Ashmore noted that Eisenhower had dodged any direct hits on the school desegregation issue simply by maintaining neutrality. "His reaction to the turmoil in the South," Ashmore lamented, "was to dismiss it as the work of radicals on both sides." Undaunted, Ashmore envisioned Stevenson as the "national leader who would assume the role Eisenhower rejected, that of a conciliator who would use the great moral prestige of the presidency to encourage white and black leaders to seek solutions within the area of practical compromise left open by the Court." To help Stevenson, Ashmore took leave from the *Arkansas Gazette* and advised Stevenson on issues through the primary elections and the convention.[45]

McGill, less involved, was never so optimistic about Stevenson's chances. In 1952, Eisenhower had seized upon southerners' discontent with the White House and the federal government. The "Democrats for Eisenhower" liked Ike's pitch to states' rights, his "frequent statements that he believed in allowing the states to have as much latitude in government as possible and in withdrawing the federal government from participation in state affairs." In response to this and to Ashmore's influence, Stevenson presented himself in 1956 as a moderate. But it was no use. Eisenhower campaigned as though he never heard any challenge from Stevenson. "As it turned out, he didn't need to," Ashmore conceded, because Eisenhower could be marketed directly to voters on television:

> By 1956 the revolution in mass communication had begun to transform the political process. Television now reached into the great majority of American homes, and coaxial cable linked the stations together. The networks provided direct, nationwide coverage of the campaign, and candidates could control segments of airtime through paid advertising. . . .
>
> Madison Avenue merchandising techniques could be employed to substitute images for substance—a practice ideally suited to the smiling general.[46]

If Stevenson did nothing else that year, his candidacy acted as a bonding agent for two believers, McGill and Carl Sandburg. Sandburg was never far from McGill's thoughts, and McGill kept him in the minds of the *Constitution's* readers. When the poet turned seventy-eight in January 1956, McGill wrote a birthday editorial and sent a copy to Connemara. Sandburg thanked him for "an act of fellowship and of a kind that lingers deep."[47]

They grew closer that year through several visits. One bright Saturday in March, McGill visited the porch at Connemara, with Ralph Jr., eleven, and Mary Elizabeth driving.[48] Three months later, in July, they visited again. "So good of the three of you to stop here of a Sunday afternoon," Sandburg added in a note to McGill about politics in the presidential election year.[49]

Sandburg visited the McGills twice that year. In January he saw them during a hurried stopover in Atlanta. Mary Elizabeth chauffeured as Ralph pointed out spots of interest. Sandburg said he enjoyed their company for "an hour or two with you hither and yon around the old town. You are good for me."[50] During the fall, Sandburg came to Atlanta to lecture. This time he luxuriated, spending a couple of days and nights at McGill's house and treating Ralph Jr.'s school to an impromptu concert of music and poetry. McGill glowed when he recounted that day: "My boy, at that time, went to school just about five houses up from ours. I had borrowed a Spanish guitar for Carl, and the next morning when my boy went to school Carl took the guitar and walked on up with him. He then got all the Seventh grades together—I think there were three of them—and put on a tremendous show, singing, reciting poetry and lecturing. I think this was the first free show he ever gave, except, of course, it is always a show to those who are lucky enough to be with him."[51]

With the students paying attention, Sandburg demonstrated his instinct to challenge the status quo. He surprised the teachers, advising seventh graders that when grammar boxed them in, they might rebel against it. Afterward, one of Ralph Jr.'s teachers wrote forgivingly to Sandburg. Sandburg told McGill she "was sure I did not do them wrong by telling them to sometimes be ungrammatical rather than to struggle and haul and hew in order to be nicely grammatical. . . . I have a feeling I have been sort of adopted."[52]

"Isn't he wonderful?" McGill wrote to Harry Golden. "He is a continuing inspiration to me."[53] McGill was pleased that Sandburg's friendship had deepened his bond with Golden, who wrote his books while being editor and publisher of the *Carolina Israelite* in Charlotte, North Carolina. Like Sandburg, Golden was the son of immigrants, had been a Socialist since his youth, and was a transplanted Yankee. Golden referred to himself and McGill as the embattled "integrationists." Sandburg too appreciated their interchange and expressed his thanks for having Golden in Charlotte and McGill in Atlanta.[54] Sandburg acknowledged the younger mens' fellowship. Golden, twenty-four years younger, was like a son to him, and he thought of McGill, twenty years younger, as a "brother psalmist."[55] Six years after he met Golden, McGill told him, "I have long been entranced by your wonderful writing style and your ability to keep it fresh and strong."[56]

The klatch of like-minded and supportive souls had grown in adversity. McGill could now count on the wisdom, intelligence, support, and good humor of Tarver, Ashmore, Sandburg, and Golden. This inner circle, anchored by Tarver's daily presence as a political and business adviser, had become essential to McGill, as a bonding of spirits. It was natural then that he thought of them as the Brethren.

14

Harvest of Hate

*There is time yet. The great bulk of the Southern
people are as decent and law abiding as any in the
land. They know that in the years ahead change is
inevitable. They do not want to meet that change
with dynamite and mobs.*
—RALPH McGILL, 1957

*Let us face the facts. This is a harvest.
It is the crop of things sown.*
—RALPH McGILL, 1958

WHEN THE PULITZER board announced its awards in May 1957, McGill
could not argue with their judgment. The board looked South and
honored an editorial crusader who confronted a public outbreak of racial
rhetoric and mob violence in Alabama. In contrast to segregationists'
relatively small public demonstrations in Atlanta, the mob's ugliness in
Tuscaloosa attracted national attention in the press. In naming key
protagonists, journalists gave a personal dimension to the struggle over
desegregation.

Tuscaloosa, with a segregated population of fifty thousand, prided
itself as the home of the all-white University of Alabama. But the city's
civility cloaked a bloodstained past. Since the Reconstruction era,
Tuscaloosa had been a staging ground for terror against Negroes and a
sanctuary for lynchers. During this latest outbreak of violence in February 1956, the editor of the *Tuscaloosa News,* Buford Boone, broke the code
of silence about "the situation" and wrote what the Pulitzer board judged
as "fearless and reasoned editorials in a community inflamed by a segregation issue."[1]

The admission of one Negro student triggered the crisis, attracting national attention to racism in southern universities. The student, Autherine Lucy, roused segregationists as if to a latter-day defense of the Confederacy. Newspapers reported days of rioting. "She was a symbol," Boone said, "and the white attitude was that we've absolutely got to keep this girl out of the University because if she stays another one is coming."[2]

It was the first outbreak of its kind, demonstrating the depth of anxiety, fear, and hatred smoldering since the *Brown v. Board of Education* decision. Astonished by the savagery latent in normally civil people, Boone focused on the irrationality of citizens swept along in mobs. "We had nice cultured ladies who said that this girl [Lucy] ought to be dragged through the streets of Tuscaloosa," he wrote. Segregationists vilified Boone as a lover of Negroes, and of Communists, despite his wartime service as an FBI agent. While not an Alabamian by birth, he claimed impeccable southern credentials: his great-grandfather had been killed at the Battle of Bull Run and his grandfather on the other side of the family had been wounded. While the controversy disturbed Boone, circulation increased. Certainly many readers despised him, and some threats now targeted him. But his message also reached reasonable people who had kept silent because of community pressures. In any case, people continued to read him to see what he would say next. He had stimulated a public community dialogue.[3]

In practice, Boone followed McGill's Atlanta model in departing from the pattern of southern editors who honored the code of silence and in ignoring most racial news, especially in their own communities. "They were printing news on the front pages that occurred in Tuscaloosa and burying it if it occurred in their own hometown," Boone noted. He put the Lucy story on page one. He had authority as publisher and as a southerner, a career journalist's ability to write, and an FBI-bred fearlessness and respect for law. Boone urged simple obedience to law and order. He sided with the Supreme Court. "We were consistent all along," Boone stated, "in taking the position that, number one, we had to abide by the court decision whether we liked it or not and number two, we had to live within the law." At that point he stopped: Like McGill, Boone did not advocate integration: "I knew that it was coming and I knew that we had to accept it, and I was ready to accept it, but I was not promoting it." On February 6, 1956, three days after Lucy started classes, the crisis ended when the university board of trustees overruled her admission and barred her from classes.[4] The outcome aside, the crisis tested Boone's courage, and he had held his ground.

The Pulitzer jurors functioned as archetypal journalists with a heightened sense of news value. The 1957 awards demonstrated that the board preferred honoring someone who proved his mettle *in combat.* "He had the guts to support the law against the mob," wrote John Hohenberg, whom Carl Ackerman chose in 1954 to succeed him as secretary of the Pulitzer board.[5]

By contrast, McGill, untested in combat, might build a national reputation spanning an entire career, as the "conscience of the South," and not win the prize. McGill could, as he appeared to be doing, encourage younger southern editors to preach law and order and compliance with *Brown.* Yet without a dramatic test in Atlanta, the glory that heroes achieved in the heat of battle eluded him. There was also the fact that his nemesis, Ackerman, might still blacklist him in remembrance of the drunken journalist who in 1945 offended American and Ackerman's interests in China. Although Ackerman resigned as secretary of the Pulitzer board in 1954 and retired in 1957 after a generation as dean of the Columbia University Graduate School of Journalism, he still wielded influence. Since 1945, McGill had been certain that Ackerman's intervention denied him the prize. "I have no doubt," Harry Ashmore reflected, "that he felt some frustration at being passed over year after year."[6]

Certainly Boone and a younger generation, fighting the same battles with courage, deserved the spotlight. Yet McGill, nearing sixty, coveted the prize. Certainly he felt he deserved it for bearing the brunt of the wars against Talmadgism, for suffering the consequences of speaking to his people about racial justice, about voting rights and education opportunities. His ego might be tempered by "a generosity of spirit," as Ashmore noted, but McGill required the balm of recognition, entrance to the circle of elites on the national scene. He was not unlike the warrior for whom fame is the only thing worth having because it transcends all else, even death. McGill saw the Pulitzer not as an end in itself. The prize would raise the stakes, grant him and "the South's Standard Newspaper" greater prestige and, with that, authority and latitude. He could escape the helpful but confining labels—southern spokesman and "conscience of the South"—in exchange for the role he had been hoping for through the ASNE in 1944, as a *national* figure. He had "made up my mind that—if a national issue came up—I was going to try to approach it as an American citizen and not as a regional citizen." Segregation and racism were *national* problems as well as southern ones, and his voice spoke as surely to the national conscience. He had no intention of retiring, and the prize could launch his career to a new level, as the Rosenwald grant had done in the '30s. The prize would place him in the lineage of great Americans whose voices were sought out, heard, and repeated—not ignored or put to pasture.[7]

Since the early '30s this had become the goal toward which he labored with unflagging zeal—to gain *enough* political influence to make a difference. At Vanderbilt and the *Banner,* as Fannie Cheney noticed, he and Brainard Cheney had been "bitten by the political bug." Through journalism, McGill had at last found avenues of influence outside of elected office. He had risen by the sheer energy of his ego and through service to the will of one autocratic publisher after another. Although he dealt with a hostile public, they could not vote him out of office for speaking his mind. By contrast, political office in the South carried with it the baggage of generations, the burden of maintaining a system of injustice, corruption, and racial demagoguery. Arnall's triumph over Talmadge in '42 proved to be a rare exception, a confirmation of the self over the system. The four years of the Arnall administration confirmed McGill's belief that through journalism he could wield political influence. He had made a difference.

Although he was passed over for the Pulitzer again in 1957, he did manage to achieve one of his goals, a daily *national* audience. As in 1938, a death created the situation and a publisher supported his advance. That summer, on July 15, Governor James M. Cox Sr. died in Dayton, Ohio, at the age of eighty-seven. The loss shocked McGill: Gone was his principal ally, the politician-publisher who for seven years had supported him against the clamor of bigots, demagogues, and weak-kneed business-office personnel.

McGill in turn had defended Cox against those who maligned him as a Yankee carpetbagger and absentee publisher. Only two months earlier a candidate for mayor of Atlanta, Archie Lindsey, declared on television that both the *Constitution* and *Journal* editors wished to support him, but Cox, "a carpetbagger dictator in Ohio," had ordered them to endorse the longtime incumbent, William Hartsfield. The *Constitution* editors denied the accusation in a boxed, unsigned editorial on page one, and McGill did the same. Replying to one Atlantan's letter, McGill declared that Lindsey's statement "was a complete falsehood. It was made up out of the whole cloth [and] . . . had to be answered."[8]

McGill confided to Harold Martin that the governor's death left him feeling forlorn and vulnerable. Martin understood how Cox's support had "saved McGill's career in a precarious and shaky time." McGill's uneasiness heightened when the Cox family turned the management of the *Constitution* over to its business manager, George Biggers Sr., who for years believed that McGill's repertoire on race stampeded subscribers and advertisers into white flight.[9]

To McGill's surprise, he benefited from the transition, largely because of Jack Tarver's intervention. During the 1950s, at the governor's insistence, Tarver switched gradually from the editorial side to management. The aging governor, who had once enjoyed traveling the circuit to his chain's southernmost newspaper, the *Miami News,* now stayed near his headquarters in Dayton, Ohio. In his stead, he delegated Tarver as his envoy to Miami, especially when editors had business problems. The governor called Tarver from Dayton, and each time Tarver heard his voice he knew immediately whether something was amiss in Miami: "If he'd start by saying 'Jasper' or 'Jason, how's everything?' I'd know it was good news. But if he said, 'Tarver,' then it was *bad* news—go to Miami."[10]

Tarver leaned on his relationship with Cox to protect McGill and advance the notion of syndicating his columns nationally. Tarver reasoned that the column would win national attention for the *Constitution* and the Cox chain and help McGill financially. Cox disagreed and would not take the risk with McGill as a Cox property. Tarver reported to McGill that the governor believed that McGill's strength and niche was only in writing about the South for southerners and that such a column would not appeal to readers around the country. McGill's occasional essays and book reviews for national magazines—the *Saturday Review,* the *Survey Graphic,* the *New Republic,* the *Atlantic Monthly,* and the *Saturday Evening Post*—did not persuade Cox that a national *newspaper* column would succeed. Two concessions, however, helped McGill. Cox had approved of giving McGill a higher profile. In the spring of 1950 the paper moved his column and photograph from the opinion pages to where it could not be overlooked, on the far left side of the front, page one. Cox also expanded McGill's readership on a limited basis, making the columns available to newspapers in his chain in Miami and in Ohio, in Dayton and Springfield. One Florida newspaper outside the chain, the *Jacksonville Journal,* also reprinted the columns.[11]

Shortly after the funeral, which was a national event, Tarver mentioned syndication to Biggers. The North American Newspaper Alliance offered to syndicate McGill's column daily with a credit line to the *Atlanta Constitution.* At the outset McGill would be printed in sixty newspapers. Where Cox had refused to budge, Biggers approved with surprising speed. As a local businessman Biggers had thought for years that Yankees were more likely than southerners to accept McGill. Atlantans had been complaining to him for nearly a decade. Biggers had grown to like McGill personally since that evening when they shared sportswriters' stories over drinks at the Capital City Club. McGill continued to charm him, sometimes with invitations. In February 1957, five months before Cox died, McGill sent a memo inviting Biggers to a private "informal stag dinner" at the Capital City Club. The classy guest was President Eisenhower's press secretary, James Hagerty, who came to Georgia on one of Eisenhower's golfing and hunting trips. "I very much hope you can be present," McGill wrote.[12]

From 1957 onward, McGill wrote daily for his national audience. For the first time in his career, he began each day from a position of exalted authority. Newspapers in the syndicate usually published his views on their "op-ed" pages—the opinion pages opposite their editorials.

Syndication influenced his choice of subjects. While continuing to write about issues of interest to this wider audience—civil rights at home, the cold war abroad—he never abandoned his lifelong practice of exploring his personal, emotional responses to events, travels, and new experiences. However common the happening, McGill's poetic impulses and sense of history and myth led him to discover universality in everyday life.

He was gifted with a rich memory which retained with remarkable accuracy an enormous storehouse of associations. His experiences in journalism and politics spanned two world wars, Prohibition, the Great Depression, and the atomic age. He had grown up with the motor car, traveled around the globe, and kept in touch with people on most continents. He read the new books, often three a week, and recalled the classics.

In his maturity he trusted his instincts and experiences as flowing springs. More so than ever, he followed them wherever they led. "Everything turned him on, mentally or emotionally," Harold Martin observed. "Some of his best-remembered columns were born of some trivial incident that to most men would have gone unnoticed." One morning while McGill was sitting down to coffee and the morning paper, a yard man came by McGill's house on Piedmont Road, soliciting work. The itinerant presented an unusual sight with his wagon drawn by a *horse*. McGill had no need for yard work, but hired the man anyway. As the man labored in the back yard, McGill thought about the horse. He reached for a yellow pad as thoughts streamed one to another, from that bony horse to horses across time: to its biblical ancestors, to Alfred Lord Tennyson's poem about the "Light Brigade," to McGill's boyhood when he rode in the saddle to a mill with some corn, to Xerxes' chariots, Ben Hur, the Spanish Conquistadores, the Sioux, the Civil War cavalry generals, the War of 1812 when Gen. Andrew Jackson stampeded horses into the British lines, to horses that carried knights and horses that towed fire engines, to the great thoroughbred racehorse Citation. The writing frenzy had created a time warp. Although McGill finished before the handyman and horse had gone, he suddenly realized that "somehow my coffee had lost its savor and the morning its bright charm."[13]

The "reader over the shoulder," as poet Robert Graves described a writer's audience, became for McGill less provincial and colloquial, more urbane and philosophical. This elevated attitude lifted his aim, purpose, and style. From the late 1940s on, he wrote more than one hundred articles and book reviews for national publications, somewhat more formal, with an elevated vocabulary, and allusions to ideas, history, and literature. McGill believed the dictum that every writer needs an editor, and he encouraged editors to make improvements when necessary, thanking them when they did. He was, like any sensitive writer, conscious of his audience. His book reviews especially were, as one reader put it, "free of colloquialisms or Southern flavor. . . . This literate national audience did not demand that McGill qualify himself as a Southerner."[14]

McGill never surrendered the South as his subject. In writing for a national audience, he sought to break the stereotype of the southerner as a backward product straight out of H. L. Mencken's caustic 1920s article "The Sahara of the Bozart." To understand the South, he insisted, was to know it was in transition. In his columns, McGill no longer dwelled on southerners "lubricated by whiskey" or southern newspapermen keeping bottles in their desks, although he did testify to the nation the benefits of the "hot brick," or toddy, as salubrious for "man or beast."

Nor did he ever abandon his embattled southern constituency, which he hoped would grow. He realized that syndication carried him to thousands more southerners whom he hoped would turn from the ranting of demagogues after hearing the courageous reasoning of a political "moderate."

This was the difficult political middle ground in the late 1950s. Speaking of his plight in the third person, he told readers of the *New York Times Magazine* that in the Deep South, "the moderate, like the liberal, learns that there is an immediacy of reaction, often violent, to anything he may say or write. From this he learns patience and acceptance of the fact that frustration is not defeat, though it can be almost as bitter." The "moderate and the practical man" would steady the South "through this period which is to many one of agonizing readjustment." The southern moderate had kept faith in the *inevitability* of law and moral justice although southern demagogues "asserted over and over that the Supreme Court's decision was not legal or binding and was entirely unconstitutional." Editors wielded great influence, McGill believed, but he identified those southerners he wished to join the moderates—church vestries, bishops, clergymen, executives of great corporations, attorneys, public figures. Together, such practical, dedicated moderates "with the sense of inevitability can . . . influence others in economic and professional positions to attain that image and to comprehend it and the ultimate meaning to the community."

George Biggers, who suffered a stroke in the fall of 1957 and retired, would have been surprised at how young southerners looked forward to reading McGill. One young admirer in Kentucky was inspired by how McGill "sounded on the printed page." McGill at sixty came across as "well-mannered and charming, tough and tender, easygoing but serious, a good storyteller and a good listener, sentimental and soft-hearted but capable of indignant outrage, a gentle man with a sense of humor and a distant air of melancholy." To this sensitive southerner, John Egerton, McGill's columns on the race issue witnessed the "capacity of white Southerners to change, to repudiate racism and rise up to the standard of justice and quality so courageously sought by their black fellow citizens in the freedom movement sparked by *Brown* and Montgomery. . . . If he could change, if he could do the right thing, maybe the rest of us could too."[15]

If some began to think of McGill as an elder sage, Carl Sandburg regarded him as "a brother psalmist" who "instigated" poetry. In his 1957 anthology, *The Carl Sandburg Range,* the poet dedicated "For Ralph McGill" the poem "Shenandoah Journey," which had been published in 1953 in the *Constitution.* Its twenty-one lines glory in the power of nature to heal the wounds of the Civil War:

> At Cherry Run or Harpers Ferry or Round Hill
> I shall hear a veery thrush in an oak or chestnut
> Some rainy April morning when the earth has
>   sacraments
> And the red scars are lost under a blue rain flute.

"You instigated it," Sandburg wrote him. "I rate it as one of the best I have ever done for music and color." He added, "The implication is clear that you are a friend & cherished." McGill reviewed the anthology in his column, and on reading the review, Sandburg said, "tears came. I think we are brother psalmists. Then comes your sublime exhortation and inquiry into sacrifice." His daughters felt the review was "a blend of poem and love letter."[16]

Resistance to the inevitability of *Brown v. Board* erupted again in the fall of 1957. The previous year a mob had defeated desegregation on a university campus in the Deep South, but in Louisville, Kentucky, the border South, token desegregation began with "deliberate speed." Now the focus shifted closer to the Deep South. In September, while McGill was touring Europe and recording the lethargy of communism, mob resistance erupted over the court-approved desegregation plan for Central High School in Little Rock, Arkansas. Segregationists would try to test local and national will, reasoning that if Arkansas succumbed, the Deep South would fall next. The gathering crisis required emergency strategies.

By summer's end Harry Ashmore realized that Little Rock would become the next southern battlefield. After campaigning for Stevenson in 1956, Ashmore had returned to editing the *Arkansas Gazette* in Little Rock. By the spring of 1957, he observed, segregationists had laid a foundation for levels of massive resistance—from elites to citizens councils to the mob. Richmond editor James Kilpatrick revived John C. Calhoun's antebellum cry that each of the "sovereign states" in the union had the right of nullification. In Arkansas, the general assembly agreed that a state had the "right of interposition," or nullification, and set up a State Sovereignty Commission. This act, Ashmore wrote, was "an expression of pique." In fact, Ashmore underestimated the growing resistance, especially when Arkansas governor Orval Faubus "did not appear to encourage the tide of sentiment that swept the Arkansas general assembly." Faubus in July seemed to honor the *Brown* decision and reject state efforts to stop desegregation of Central High. "Everyone knows," Faubus stated, "no state's laws supercede a federal law."[17]

Behind the scenes, however, Faubus met secretly with segregationist leaders of the Capital Citizens Council, who were encouraged by polls showing that 85 percent of the state's whites opposed school integration. One council leader came away with the "thorough understanding" that Faubus "was going to stop it, the integration of Central High School." Another council member recalled Faubus's disgust with dictates from the national Republican Party and told them, "I will do something. I'm not going to let the Republicans dictate to me."[18]

During August, other southern politicians pressured Faubus to forestall desegregation. Mississippi senator John Eastland warned that without the resistance of governors the southern states would be "picked off one by one under the damnable doctrine of gradualism." Georgia's governor, Marvin Griffin, flew to Little Rock to fuel the flames. Griffin, accompanied by Roy Harris, president of the Citizens Councils of America, told a citizens council rally that southern governors should bring out the National Guard to stop integration. Griffin pledged that he would never permit Georgia schools to accept the Supreme Court order. At least one political leader close to the situation believed Griffin's goal-line stand caused Faubus to "think twice" about supporting desegregation. Faubus invited Griffin to stay at the Governor's Mansion, and that visit was later seen as a turning point.[19]

Within days Faubus changed his position from support to evasiveness to resistance. "Faubus's increasingly inflammatory public statements," Ashmore recalled, "now constituted a virtual invitation for segregationist extremists to fulfill his prophecy of mob action." While the federal court in Little Rock ordered the school board to proceed on schedule, community leaders, unwilling to stand against the governor and the segregationists, "were heading for the storm cellars."[20]

The *Gazette* stood alone. On the weekend before the showdown, Ashmore met in the deserted downtown with his publisher, J. N. Heiskell, and the publisher's son-in-law, Hugh B. Patterson Jr., who was to succeed Heiskell. Should they hold their ground? They faced the wrath of the mob and the economic pressures of the citizens council. As Ashmore recalled, "Mr. J. N. turned his chair to look out across the quiet streets and said, 'I'm an old man, and I've lived too long to let people like that take over my city.'" Hugh Patterson agreed. "It's a silly question. I don't see why the hell you even thought you had to raise it."[21]

None of this gathering storm was reflected in McGill's front-page columns in early September. The travel bug had bit and he had gone to Europe again, this time with his national audience in mind. Travel would offer them a change of pace from the at-home-in-the-South columns. He also took the opportunity to establish with this wider audience his authority as a sophisticated internationalist with depth of experience. Other journalists had reported the postwar rebuilding of West Berlin, but McGill also reminisced about his first visit to Hitler's Germany in 1938 and his next visits in 1946 and 1947, when the city lay in ruin and rubble, "a world each time greatly changed." He crossed into East Germany through Checkpoint Charlie and witnessed the Brandenberg Gate "with the huge red flag of Communism flapping over it." In East Berlin, the building that had been the Nazi Ministry of Information reminded him that in 1938 he had "gone there three times, seeking an interview with various notables." The place was now a center for Russian propaganda. Nearby, the headquarters of the Nazi Third Reich, which Hitler proclaimed would last a thousand years, had been reduced to "only the two massive chunks of manmade stone." Poetry sprang to mind. The Nazi pride and fall had been foretold in Shelley's "Ozymandias."[22] A day later, he mused on the perennial grass around the ruins and "thought of one of Carl Sandburg's poems: 'I am the grass, leave it to me.'"[23]

McGill's columns seemed to his Georgia readers out of touch with reality, or an intentional diversion. During the following week, as mobs formed to sabotage desegregation attempts in Little Rock, Birmingham, and Nashville, McGill was publishing more columns that chronicled his adventures and interviews in Germany and England. Even after he returned, he did not interrupt the series, but let it play out to the end. He did not publish his first column on the resistance to segregation until September 12.

In his absence the *Constitution* editorial board broke the silence. On September 4, an editorial played the old McGill theme that the South by not acting responsibly risked more of the federal intervention they detested. The editorial criticized Faubus's state intervention into local politics, without endorsing the Supreme Court or desegregation and while coyly defending those who supported segregation nonviolently. The *Constitution* declared that local communities "can best handle their own peculiar problems. Those who would preserve segregation had best remember that." The Little Rock School Board had "anticipated no trouble" before Faubus's defiance. His action would set back efforts elsewhere to preserve segregation. The *Constitution* argued that "whatever opinions individuals may have on this subject," Faubus "has precipitated a situation which certainly will accelerate clamor for stronger civil rights legislation."[24]

Southern Democrats had just fought off a package of Republican civil rights legislation that survived as mainly a pledge to protect voting rights and a general statement against racial discrimination. In the congressional compromise, the law specifically protected "the rights of all qualified voters" by empowering the federal government to sue in court. On September 9, President Eisenhower added no comment as he signed the bill into law. He had opposed one section that southerners insisted upon—that all persons accused must be granted a jury trial—on the grounds that it weakened the authority of federal judges. Politically, Democrats claimed the Republicans were trying to win the Negro vote in the North and East. Southern Democrats perceived that the law hurt Republicans in the South more than it helped them elsewhere. Georgia's senators, Richard Russell and Herman Talmadge, both former governors, had helped trim the impact to voting rights. They succeeded, the *Constitution* noted in praise, "in removing the features of the bill most objectionable to the South." Talmadge postured that, "We were able to take a monster and tame him down to a mad dog." As McGill put it, the southern leadership aroused sympathy for the southern dilemma and "succeeded, to a great extent, in persuading the nation their region would take a legal approach; that life and property and human rights were safe."[25]

By September mobs threatening southern schools shattered the social truce salvaged by southerners in Congress. In Tennessee, Alabama, and Arkansas, clamorous crowds formed with tacit encouragement from segregationist politicians and white citizens councils. In Arkansas, long after the Little Rock School Board agreed in court to admit twelve Negro students to Central High, Faubus withdrew his support and defied the federal authorities, declaring that public reaction to integration would endanger students. He also became combative, accusing federal marshals of tapping his telephone conversations and of planning to arrest him. President Eisenhower appealed to him to comply with the court ruling. Caught between the mob and the court, and with the governor sympathetic to the mob, school board members flinched and asked the court to "suspend integration temporarily."[26]

While Eastland and Griffin had urged Faubus to defy the order and thus defend segregation, other southerners were far less sanguine about the outcome, fearing a strategic blunder akin to firing on Fort Sumter. On one hand, the *Constitution* editorial board reasoned from afar, Faubus "could speed all-out effort on the part of the Justice Department to force the issue throughout the South." On the other hand, they reasoned, the Little Rock case "may be the best thing that could have happened because eventually the Supreme Court decision must be resolved." McGill would later examine some southerners' suspicions that Faubus secretly intended to precipitate federal intervention as a means of forcing deseg-regation. "Why else would he say he was for integration and then block it?" the *Constitution* editorial asked. But in Arkansas, McGill added, insid-ers say, "No, Orval ain't that smart. He got in on a political accident and he was just trying to assure himself of re-election." This latter assessment is supported by witnesses who said Faubus's go-between with the white citizens council had initiated the first talks by asking, "would you all support Orval Faubus for a third term if he would stop the integration of Central High School?" Speaking at Emory University that autumn, McGill seemed to side with the "Orval ain't that smart" set. "I know a lawyer over there who is a good friend of Governor Faubus'. . . . He said Orville had been listening to some fellows who said, 'Go ahead—bluff him, bluff him, bluff him.' So we reached the unhappy point where it was Governor Faubus who was trying to ram something down the President's throat, so to speak."[27]

Mob resistance became epidemic during the second week of Sep-tember. In Alabama, a Birmingham "crowd" beat a black minister who tried to enroll black students at all-white Phillips Junior High School. The next day a bomb scare forced evacuation of the school. In Tennessee, whites boycotted seven Nashville schools scheduled for desegregation. Some protesters threw bricks. Agitation engendered greater violence. Segre-gationist John Kasper was arrested for "disorderly and offensive con-duct" after he publicly threatened to use "the shotgun, dynamite and the rope" if integration continued. On the following day, dynamite wrecked Nashville's Hattie Cotton Elementary School where one black student was enrolled. The same page carried McGill's completely unrelated column from London, his interview with a banker. To the many who didn't understand his diversification strategy it seemed a strange juxtaposition.[28]

The introduction of dynamite triggered indignation from the *Constitution* editorial page which targeted the "fanatical extremists." McGill, now home, shaped the appeal to sensible southerners. The mob in Nashville was destroying not just a school but "all it seeks to protect," including, of course, segregation itself. The next day's editorial looked at the broader problem. Resistance across the South "has raised the old fundamental issue of which is supreme—state or federal law." Whatever southerners answered, "no law condones violence."[29]

That day, McGill interrupted his series of European columns. In the heat of the moment, he dashed out an impromptu message about "the face of the South." He wrote as a southerner who realized the nation was now judging the region by its worst elements—the contorted faces in the mobs and the deeds of lawless, dangerous men. "The South has suffered an irreparable blow," he declared. "All the sympathy, all the respectable attention focused on the problem by the Southern Senate leadership in the civil rights debate, now has been blow down by the dynamite, the violence and the demonstrations of the mobs." He warned Governor Faubus and all other leaders to heed "the old proverb: 'Oh, great and wise, "be ill at ease when your words and deeds please the mob."

He repudiated the violence. In doing so, he blamed itinerant "criminals" who were not from the cities they agitated: "The fact is that millions of Southerners who strongly support segregation and who would do all that is possible to retain it, are not willing to tear down the government with violence and anarchy." He wrote this in faith and hope that it was fundamentally true, speaking about the best qualities of character. Certainly he was conscious of the dark side of human nature—the quickness toward violence—the "trigger-quick dander" which W. A. Cash portrayed in *The Mind of the South*. McGill refused to concede more losses to this dark force. He hoped to appeal to the admirable characteristics in the mind and face of the South. McGill's preferred *face of the South*—not shown in the news photographs—would portray a "civilized, Christian people" who "cannot live by the rule of dynamite. . . . The face of the South must not be that of the mob."[30]

McGill certainly had in mind Georgia's governor. Griffin had incited Faubus. McGill saw Griffin at the Southern Governor's Conference in the oasis of Sea Island, Georgia. There, Griffin told the assemblage that any southern politician who did not support segregation—such as one who aspired to be president—was akin to one who "knifes his own people in the back. And if he does that the people back home are going to pull the rug from under him." Thus, Griffin concluded, "no Southerner these days can be elected president."[31]

The "eloquent" rebuttal to Griffin came from the governor of Florida, LeRoy Collins. As McGill heard him, Collins "presented the problem of the Southern governor, or for that matter, of any other person in position of leadership who seeks to stand firmly on law and not run with either the hounds of hate or the hare of fear and despair." Indeed, Collins might have been articulating McGill's dilemma as an editor for the past twenty years. A leader in the South, Collins observed, "must have the discretion and judgment to raise a standard out front, but not so far that it is beyond the horizon of the people and, therefore, cannot be seen and understood and followed by them."[32]

The politicians perched at Sea Island led McGill to focus on demagoguery. "One of the more dangerous things which the more extreme politicians have done is to create the myth of a judicial tyranny created by enemies of the South," he wrote. What was Faubus's role? After an urgent meeting with President Eisenhower at his vacation White House on September 15, Faubus acknowledged that the Supreme Court decision was the law of the land, and that he and the people of Arkansas were law-abiding. McGill praised him for that and thought the Little Rock issue settled.[33]

Back home, Faubus resorted again to obstructing the desegregation plan. Had he relapsed into the dangerous scenario? "It was a commonplace experience of newspapermen to talk with a Southern political leader and hear him say, privately, he knew integration to be inevitable, and then, minutes later, hear the same man say to a whooping audience that the 'left-wing Supreme Court' had acted unconstitutionally and that states' rights would emerge triumphant." Whatever Faubus's role, Eisenhower changed the scene decisively. He federalized the Arkansas National Guard and sent one thousand paratroopers into Little Rock to protect the black students from "crowds of pro-segregationists still gathered in the vicinity of Central High School."[34]

The conflict at Little Rock sent shock waves across the South. McGill sensed a showdown with the "never-never segregationists"—and significant ramifications. Rather than get the news secondhand, he went to the battlefield where "Ashmore manned the journalistic ramparts" amid a "horde" of newspaper, magazine, and TV reporters. Ashmore and McGill renewed their friendship in the city's "only drinking oasis," the private Little Rock Club. Drinks were poured from lunchtime onward. "The Negro waiters, quiet and scholarly in manner, cast covert looks of love and admiration in Mr. Ashmore's direction." Ashmore was also the hero of many a journalist, not only because he bought drinks. In three weeks the *Gazette* treated so many journalists that Ashmore and Hugh Patterson "legitimately became known as 'the battle and bottle scarred' heroes of Little Rock."[35]

The *Gazette* was already suffering financially from the expected white citizens council boycott, and some boycotting white businessmen—"fat cats of the red-neck anarchy"—lunched at the Club. "When the big men came to lunch and saw Ashmore and his publisher standing at the bar with visiting journalists, their appetites went to the wind," McGill recalled. "They dribbled soup on their chins and merely nibbled at the chef's salad or peas and croquettes. Mostly, they fingered their martinis and muttered." These were the silent faces of the South, the ones who acted quietly but treacherously. The showdown had further polarized the position of the races, thinning the ranks of rational men. As some white businessmen would later acknowledge, they realized that desegregation was inevitable but they fought fiercely. They fought because of tradition, as though in a second civil war, or because the social terror that had so long kept the freed blacks in place now pressured the whites to stay in *their* place.[36]

Men and women on both sides acted with passion, as if in battle. In news photographs, McGill witnessed that "face of the South" he abhorred. Near the doors to Central High School he heard "the wailing shriek of a segregationist lady." The paratroops and national guard had arrived, but the crowd still seemed hopeful of blocking the black students. The troops moved the students through a side door. After a while, the crowd found out, and the segregationist lady wailed her shriek, "Oh, Lordy, the niggers is already *in* the school!" As time went on, McGill thought back on that moment as an epiphany: "Ever since 1957 it has been my belief that [it was] one of the most revealing, and perhaps significant sentences in the history of the move to admit the Negro to the First and Fourteenth Amendment clubs." The segregationists, ill-informed and poorly prepared by their leader had lost the battle in another losing cause.[37]

Across the South, moderates suspected Faubus. Had Faubus staged every scene to dramatize himself? What had he actually promised Eisenhower? "Did he have any real intention of acceptance?" McGill asked. It now seemed clear that his direct dealings with Eisenhower had an impact on not only Arkansas but also the whole South: "It suddenly has dawned upon them [the moderates] that before Gov. Faubus made his move there was no great pressure on the South. Integration was proceeding slowly and was entirely confined to the border states." By challenging the power of the presidency, in a showdown of federal law against state interposition, Faubus had forced the president to act, forcefully, to support the Supreme Court decision, a position he had resisted since *Brown*. In the end, the president acted as commander-in-chief. This is what Vice President Richard Nixon was saying: "Gov. Faubus must bear the responsibility for the disgraceful state of affairs in Little Rock." In response, the federal court ordered immediate compliance and federal troops enforced it. If Faubus's goal had been to accelerate the process of "deliberate speed," he succeeded. "For the time being, at least, Gov. Faubus is not quite trusted or understood by anyone."[38]

There was still time. That was the refrain McGill had been reciting for a decade: southerners must act on their own before the federal government acted upon them. "There was still time," he said now, three years after *Brown,* for the border and Deep South states to address the court-ordered end of compulsory segregation in a sensible fashion. The remedy was simple: governors must accept the law of the land, abstain from demagoguery and interference at the local level, and "give local school boards complete authority" to work out agreements for gradual desegregation over a period of years. "Law is our real foundation," he wrote, and with homage to Lincoln and to Sandburg, he let the central issue echo across time: "We cannot exist half lawless and half lawful—

anymore than we could be half free and half slave." He was certain he spoke for the soul of the South, for the mute majority in the South of his hopes, the South of law and order and decency: "The great bulk of the Southern people are as decent and law abiding as any in the land. They know that in the years ahead change is inevitable. They do not want to meet that change with dynamite and mobs."[39]

Once again, however, McGill spoke to the nation about fundamental values of human nature—the reasonable route he hoped for but did not actually see. Even as he cajoled southern politicians to lead, insisting that surely *enough was enough,* many southern politicians after Little Rock viewed compromise as another Appomattox. They preferred resistance, thus encouraging white citizens councils. Local school boards, which McGill said should be left alone, were stripped of autonomy. As a last stand, southern leaders declared they would close their schools rather than submit to federal dictates.

Moderates looking hard for rays of hope found some even in the reelection of Faubus in 1958. Though he won easily, there were almost 120,000 votes against him. These, McGill reasoned, were moderates, driven by political rhetoric and social castigation into silence—except in secret ballot. "In a superheated, almost hysterical campaign," McGill wrote, "about a third of the white voters stood for moderation and due process of law." In Virginia, two months after Little Rock, voters elected a governor pledged to "massive resistance" against desegregation. Once again McGill recognized hope in the minority—one third of the whites voted for the Republican who pledged "limited integration." The moderates, in retreat since 1954 and the subsequent eruption of violence, "are still there," though still anonymous.[40]

Within months, McGill returned to Little Rock to celebrate a special occasion. For the second year in a row, the Pulitzer Prize Board honored a southern newspaper, this time the *Arkansas Gazette,* and its editor Ashmore and publisher Hugh Patterson. The choice surprised neither Ashmore nor McGill—and probably not Buford Boone of the *Tuscaloosa News,* who in 1958 was helping to select the winners. The *Gazette* won for "meritorious public service" and Ashmore specifically for his editorials on school desegregation. When community leaders arranged a recognition dinner in the Marion Hotel, the *Gazette* found it still had numerous friends. On June 3, "the largest crowd ever assembled" there—925—filled the ballroom and overflowed into the annex, the coffee shop, and the dining room, at which point 125 people were turned away.

McGill, invited to give the main speech, avoided rekindling smoldering hostilities. "It is very likely that we here tonight are of many minds about the great issues of our time," he said. "But deep in the subconscious or secret heart of each of us is agreement that we respect and admire integrity and the facing of responsibility by individuals and institutions." As he danced around the hot issues, his speech could have put the great crowd to sleep. He surveyed the history of American journalism from 1864 when Joseph Pulitzer arrived as a Union recruit from Hungary. He capsuled his own thirty-five years in journalism which began in "a different world . . . before the great depression, before the New Deal, before the development of what we call suburbia with all its political and social potentials . . . before atomic and nuclear energy . . . before jets and television."[41]

Only then did he launch what he wanted to say—that what the *Gazette* had done stood far above the accomplishments of most weak-minded newspaper editors. For economic or other reasons, most editors were cowed into silence on controversial issues at home. "Too many newspapers sit like fat cats on the hills of political corruption in their states and cities, sunning themselves in contentment." Borrowing the vocabulary of mental illness, he diagnosed editors as victims of an epidemic *neurosis:* "So many newspapers today are almost neurotically sensitive to criticism. Can it be that this reflects some guilt, or inadequacy? And if this be true, as I believe it to be, does it not lie in the fact that too many newspapers have become unwilling to pay the cost which might ensue from engaging in controversy and debate." Spineless or complacent editors defeat the purpose of the First Amendment "to provide a great and continuing debate, with the people hearing all sides." McGill said he believed the newspaper could doctor the national neurosis by being "something like a teacher. . . . A newspaper cannot assume, any more than can a teacher, that the reader is possessed of all the facts or information. It is the unknown of which we are afraid. And as the nation's population grows, as the industrial society expands, the crowded areas react more readily to fear, to rumor and distortion of fact. Prejudice and ignorance flourish in such soil."[42]

His speech that night had another purpose—to heal his rift with the Pulitzer Prize Board. Here stood the editor who since 1945 understandably assumed he had been blacklisted by Ackerman, and who in the early 1950s publicly questioned the integrity of the Pulitzer selection process. The board's choice of Ashmore elevated them in his eyes. Then, too, he likely saw that Ashmore might now influence the board. He himself could hope to get the prize he had sought for two decades almost, at least since 1942, when he and Ellis Arnall upset Georgia politics by beating Gene Talmadge. The selection of Ashmore demonstrated that "the awards are the product of serious scrutiny and study and there is, to my knowledge, *nothing of caprice or favoritism* in them. And assuredly there is *no outside influence* [emphasis added]." He shared his intimate understanding of the careful selection process that he now believed sacrosanct:

> They are arrived at by juries of newspaper judges assembled at Columbia University each March. Each jury works in private quarters and is, in a sense, locked up in that there are no visitors or no conversations. The task of judging and giving careful attention to each entry, requires usually about two days. Because of the great tradition of these prizes, and the national interest in them, scrupulous care is taken. I do not know of any instance when the honor system has been broken and there has been any leak or violation of the strict code of honor prevailing.

After the juries went home, he explained, the judicious nature of the process was maintained by the final arbiters—the insiders he had held a grievance with, the advisory board which for a dozen years Ackerman had influenced: "The juries make usually a recommended list of three in each category. This is not final. The actual awards are determined later by an advisory board which sees not merely the recommendations, but the exhibits involved. The board can change the order of the jury's listing, but this rarely occurs because of the careful, collective judgments arrived at by the juries."[43]

Such encouragement to champions of civil rights and common sense encouraged fighters like McGill, who still had strength, determination, and dry ammunition. Through 1958, the option of closing schools called into question the fundamental values of the middle class. It was such a questionable tactic—not unlike shooting yourself in the foot to make a point—that the very desperation of the idea gave moderates a glimmer of hope. The same opening had appeared in 1942, when old Eugene Talmadge interfered with the hallowed University of Georgia. In losing the university's accreditation, Gene had also lost the votes of everyone who realized that their diplomas, and their childrens' diplomas, were devalued.

Faced with this specter of closing all schools, McGill sought a way through the impasse. In the spring and summer of 1958, he was cultivating an off-the-record relationship in Washington with Attorney General William P. Rogers. In March, McGill told Rogers, "On my visits to Washington, I like to obtain background rather than seek for what might be called 'stories.'" Unattributed "background," which he could afterwards present as his own ideas, were "much more helpful to me in my job of trying to evalue [sic] and, I hope, influence a little bit, public opinion." By April, Rogers encouraged the relationship, telling him that his columns stated matters "very thoughtfully and accurately. . . . I hope you make a point of stopping in to see me from time to time."[44]

In July, McGill took a direct approach and tried to influence Rogers on how best to use—or refrain from using—the federal government's muscle in the South. McGill despaired that progress toward civil rights in the southern border states "will be stopped unless there is a firm policy by the federal government." Civil rights court cases seemed a fruitful venue for the attorney general. McGill said he had been "hopeful that the Department of Justice would find some way to intervene" in cases testing civil rights. This seemed a responsible use of federal brain power. McGill advised against resorting to brawn. "For example, I think it would be very wise for the Civil Rights Commission not to try to set up committees in the deep South states." Such actions gave ammunition to white citizens councils and demagogues. "There isn't going to be any giving in on the part of those state governments who have put themselves so far out on a limb they can't retreat." Rogers replied in understandably noncommittal language that he "appreciated very much your giving me the information" and suggested that McGill "drop in for a talk."[45]

At home, McGill used whatever influence he had to reason with those still open to reason. He began to stress the only argument which seemed plausible. With the right approach he thought it was possible to herd the barons of business into a coalition where they might admit, as a group, despite public pressure, that closing schools spelled disaster for a public deceived by demagogues. Thinking it through, what incentive would business and industry have to locate in a community without schools? Indeed, how could a major industry keep its talented workforce living in a school-less community? It was almost as ludicrous as the notion that a community could survive without housemaids!

Of course people would have to create new schools, but how long would it take to develop an adequate private system that excluded blacks? How many apart from the elites could afford the cost? These were all issues which, when investigated and explained, could lead enough people back from the polarized extremes into the temperate climate where they might, in the end, accept that desegregation was the law of the land and was, despite what their political leaders said, inevitable. The problem demanded rational exploration. Georgia, for example, could appoint a committee of respected men who would listen to everyone's opinion and at the same time have everyone listen to each other—in public hearings. The *process* of analyzing the consequences of school closings might convert enough people to support the conclusion that closings would hurt everyone far more than desegregation. It was a game plan an old football player could imagine. But against the segregationist lineup of 1958, the opening had not yet occurred through which the moderates could run.

The leading candidates to succeed Governor Griffin all pledged to uphold segregation. This was all the more important in 1958 because North Carolina, Tennessee, Kentucky, and Texas had agreed to proceed with desegregation with "deliberate speed" as decreed by the Court in 1955. Now when McGill addressed his national audience, he wrote with the hope of influencing the next governor to join the border states and separate Georgia from the diehard pack that now included only South Carolina, Alabama, Mississippi, and, for the time being, Virginia. He felt that the governor-elect, Ernest Vandiver, could be nudged toward moderation. In the 1958 campaign, Vandiver focused on reform of state government. He presented himself as an experienced leader who would deep-clean abuses most often traced to nepotism and patronage. Systemic corruption had become a way of life well before Eugene Talmadge, but had become a stark embarrassment during the Griffin administration. Vandiver focused on reform, but when his opponent, a white supremacist state representative, claimed that the lieutenant governor had gone "weak on segregation," Vandiver decided to affirm his opposition to the Supreme Court unequivocally. In the 1958 campaign, he pledged that, "As long as Ernest Vandiver is your governor, there will be no mixed schools or college classrooms in this state—no, not a single one!" In 1958 Vandiver won the Democratic nomination easily and, in the absence of a viable Republican Party, prepared to govern. Reform might be on his agenda, but others were telling him to defy the Court and close the schools.[46]

The crisis Atlanta had so far avoided literally exploded on October 12. Segregationists and demagogues who defied the law had in time bred a band of fanatics who merged into lunacy; these acted out a diehard segregationist scenario, falling into step with the Klan's style of terror—nocturnal, clandestine, violent. Their weapons of choice were bunched sticks of dynamite, homemade bombs, suitcases filled with gunpowder. From 1956 through 1958 they targeted dozens of homes, schools, community centers, auditoriums, and houses of worship. The scourge struck across the South: the home of the Rev. Martin Luther King Jr. in Montgomery, a white elementary school in Nashville, the municipal auditorium in Knoxville during a Louis Armstrong concert, a black school and a synagogue in Jacksonville, a black drive-in theater in Charlotte, and on October 5, 1958, the desegregated high school in Clinton, Tennessee. At 3:37 A.M. on a Sunday, October 12, 1958, the epidemic touched the oasis of liberalism, Atlanta.

McGill received the news later that Sunday when he returned from a speaking trip. He told Harold Martin that Mary Elizabeth greeted him with the news at the door. The Jewish Temple had been bombed. His office had been trying to reach him all day and the company driver took him immediately. There, in an energized state of moral clarity, he dashed out the column for Monday's editions. He set the fresh act of violence in the context of a vocabulary of conscience and compassion which he had been developing for almost two decades. Onto three pages, the words flowed fluently as if automatically. His secretary, Grace Lundy, said he composed the piece in less than twenty minutes.[47]

The first sentence framed the contest between evil and good. "Dynamite in great quantity ripped a beautiful temple of worship in Atlanta." He then traced separate acts of violence to the same diseased minds. "It followed hard on the heels of a like destruction of a handsome high school in Clinton, Tennessee. The same rabid, mad-dog minds were, without question, behind both. They are also the source of previous bombings in Florida, Alabama, and South Carolina. The schoolhouse and the church were the targets of diseased, hate-filled minds."[48]

The perpetrators used a bomb equivalent to fifty sticks of dynamite. The blast woke Marvin Griffin a mile away in the old Governor's Mansion atop a hill in Ansley Park. A subsequent member of the temple congregation, Melissa Fay Greene, described the impact at the southern side wall, where the dynamite went off:

> The brick walls flapped upward like sheets on a line. Offices and Sunday school classrooms burst out of the building; the stairwell came unmoored and hung like a rope ladder; bronze plaques commemorating the war dead from the two world wars spun out like saucers; the stained-glass windows snapped outward, like tablecloths shaken after dinner; and all as momentarily red-hot, white-lit, and moving like lava. Then the strangely animate flying rooms and objects stood still . . . leaving erratic silhouettes and capricious statues of rubble, burst pipes, ashes, and mud, the whole of it colorfully twinkling in the quiet night from the bright bits of stained glass sprinkled over the scene.[49]

As the news spread, hundreds—sympathizers and segregationists—drove along Peachtree Street to gawk at the temple, although the view from down on the street did not reveal interior damage. The *Constitution* photographed Mayor Hartsfield with the temple's rabbi, Jacob M. Rothschild, squatting amid the rubble of bricks. Rothschild presumed that his temple was targeted because of his stand for civil rights. Now, however, he said little to inquiring newspapermen and broadcasters. He declined to go on national television, explaining later that he worried about exploiting the situation. "I was interested in making something valuable come out of this experience. And I felt very strongly that public exposure for personal reasons was not the way to do it."[50]

Others, however, seized the moment. Hartsfield, radio microphone in hand, blamed the bombing on those in high places and low who defied the law: "Every political rabble-rouser is the godfather of these cross-burners and dynamiters who sneak about in the dark and give a bad name to the South." He said the bombing had called the question. It was now time for "decent people" to end their years of silence and join him in speaking up, upholding the law. That, of course, meant the law of land, the federal law, and the Supreme Court. The alternative—silence—was an inadequate response to a historic challenge. Silence now condoned mob rule, encouraging the dynamiters, spreading the epidemic of lawlessness.[51]

In linking the dynamiters to the "political rabble-rousers," Hartsfield affirmed a central theme of the outspoken moderates. In this, he borrowed from fellow moderate McGill, who throughout the '40s and '50s developed the vocabulary and rhetoric to indict hatemongers and their patrons—the demagogues and the silent ones. As Hartsfield seized the moment to speak on behalf of politicians and "decent" people, McGill now seized it as a journalist of conscience addressing sham and hypocrisy.

To begin with he had nothing but loathing for the perpetrators—these were the "mad-dog minds," the "diseased, hate-filled minds," "the yellow rats," "the wolves of hate." But they alone were not to blame. You could trail the jackals back to the houses of southern demagogues whose words encouraged lawlessness: "This is the harvest of defiance of courts and the encouragement of citizens to defy law on the part of many Southern politicians." The freshest bombings proved, if more proof was needed, that "it is not possible to preach lawlessness and restrict it. . . . When leadership in high places in any degree fails to support constituted authority, it opens the gates to all those who wish to take law into their hands."[52]

McGill knew the refrain that would follow, chapter and verse. Among the hundreds of telegrams were messages from segregationists seeking to distance themselves from this particular bombing. Vandiver, soon to be governor, did the same distancing act, stating that he regretted that the bombing occurred in Georgia. "It is a tragedy," he added, "that would seem to be an attempt to violate the Constitution."[53]

Sympathy from segregationists posturing for political gain touched in McGill a core of molten outrage. How dare they advocate defiance and lawlessness, then wash their hands when the lunatics they encouraged carry out their will. This was an hour of shame. Words had become dynamite. Rather than lead their people courageously into the inevitable new era, the southern demagogues had chosen to perpetuate the dying old order—at any cost: "To be sure, none said go bomb a Jewish temple or a school. But let it be understood that when leadership in high places in any degree fails to support constituted authority, it opens the gates to all those who wish to take law into their hands." The political leaders, he charged, had "in terms violent and inflammatory have repudiated their oaths and stood against due process of law." That was the root cause. That was what had "helped unloose this flood of hate and bombing."[54]

Now he had placed the crimes in the hands of the oath-breakers. He had laid the bombs at *their* doors. Like any good editorialist, he anticipated their rebuttal and cut them off in advance. "There will be, to be sure, the customary act of the careful drawing aside of skirts on the part of those in high places. 'How awful,' they will exclaim. 'How terrible. Something must be done.'" But this was also an occasion to cast a spotlight on a generation of weak or backward-looking lawyers, journalists, and clergy who articulated segregation-forever by eroding compliance with the authority of the Court. Without naming names, he thought it would be "the acme of irony . . . if any one of four or five Southern governors deplore this bombing. It will be grimly humorous if certain state attorneys general issue statements of regret. And it will be quite a job for some editors, columnists, and commentators, who have been saying that our courts have no jurisdiction and that the people should refuse to accept their authority, now to deplore."[55]

For the Christian ministers he returned a sermon of his own: "This too is a harvest of those so-called Christian ministers who have chosen to preach hate instead of compassion. Let them now find pious words and raise their hands in deploring the bombing of a synagogue." For the pulpit he had the same message he had brought back from Nazi Germany before and after the war. "You do not preach and encourage hatred for the Negro and hope to restrict it to that field," he wrote. "It is an old, old story. It is one repeated over and over again in history. When the wolves of hate are loosed on one people, then no one is safe." This was not the time to praise the small minority of ministers who courageously addressed the discrepancy between Christianity and racial segregation; most had been driven from their pulpits. He had praised them before, and had even comforted those ministers who, while not outspoken against segregation, did not speak for it. Silence, at least in this situation, had been preferable.[56]

The temple bombing tolled for southern society, the temple's blasted wall testifying that the time for silence has passed. Like Hartsfield, he used the bombing as a clarion for action: "For a long time now it has been needful for all Americans to stand up and be counted on the side of law and the due process of law—even when to do so goes against personal beliefs and emotions." Those who had been doing this for years now welcomed the great silent majority. "It is late," he said, repeating his refrain from the '40s. "But there is yet time."[57]

The power of the writing was not in its novelty or singular style. It was just the opposite. It was as though he had rehearsed a speech for years and now, only now, did he have his audience's attention. What they read on October 13—the rhetorical devices, the rationales, the incantation of rural, agricultural seed-and-harvest metaphors—he had used them all before, as is habitual when one writes daily and focuses on one subject for a great many years. He had been rehearsing, as it were, every time a bomb shattered someone's home, school, or church. After the Jacksonville bomb, he blamed "crackpots" and "dangerous fringe criminals" but traced the monsters to their creators, "those who so violently denounced the federal government for its insistence on upholding the decree of a federal court. This certainly gave encouragement to those who are described as the lunatic or crackpot fringe. . . . For persons and organizations in high places to give support to defiance of the court encourages all criminals."[58]

The next day, McGill changed pace and took readers inside the temple to see what they could not see from the street. The concrete detail of the column contrasted with the rhetoric and metaphor of the previous day. Now he evoked sympathy by mention of "the little sky-blue robes of the children's choir under glass and plaster dust." People could imagine the difference if the bomb had gone off hours later when children were there.[59]

The Atlanta police, collaborating with the FBI, wasted little time in identifying a list of six suspects and making arrests. Three—including George Bright, an engineer, scientist, mathematician, and inventor—had been arrested that summer for anti-Semitic picketing of the *Constitution*. The FBI added three more, two of whom had records of working with explosives and one who had kept company with extremists. As it developed, five were indicted but none was convicted. As Melissa Fay Greene noted, "The conclusion of the jurors and of court watchers was that the state had proved two things: Bright was an anti-Semite, and the Temple had been bombed." Three months after the bombing, all defendants were released.[60]

Despite that outcome, there were those who believed the temple bombing was significant for energizing the civil rights movement in Atlanta, if not elsewhere. Rabbi Rothschild's temple had become a proving ground. "The hatred Rothschild had said existed *did* exist," Melissa Fay Green observed. The bombing hurt, but it vindicated the rabbi. McGill, too, benefited. During January, the *Constitution* submitted his editorials to the Pulitzer Prize board. Surely, he thought, with Ackerman retired, and with attention riveted on violence in Atlanta, he would not be passed over.

He was right. He was expecting the news, and he got it first from his old, dear friend Reb Gershon, who knew as well as anyone how much it meant to him. She had just heard it on the radio. He had won for his column on the temple bombing. "You're kidding!" he said. Moments later, his secretary, Grace Lundy, bolted in with the official telegram from Grayson Kirk, president of Columbia University:

I HAVE THE HONOR TO ADVISE THAT COLUMBIA UNIVERSITY TRUSTEES HAVE AWARDED YOU THE PULITZER PRIZE FOR EDITORIAL WRITING.

The actual citation, dated May 4, 1959, read, "For distinguished editorial writing in a United States newspaper . . . , the test of excellence being clearness of style, moral purpose, sound reasoning and power to influence public opinion in what the writer conceives to be the right direction, due account being taken of the whole volume of the editorial writer's work during the year. One thousand dollars ($1,000)." Lundy recalled that McGill sighed so heavily he rustled papers cluttered on his desk, then sat down, reached for his coffee cup and remarked, "I never thought I'd make it."[61]

15

With All Deliberate Speed

Castro can't last.
—Ralph McGill, 1961

The conscience of even those Southerners
whose identity has been with the old landmarks
is beginning to show signs of uneasiness.
—Ralph McGill, 1963

Admitted into the circle of the nation's elite journalists, McGill achieved the status he had labored for since Nashville days. Far behind him were the nights of intoxicated self-flagellation in the inky letters to Louise Stevens, and although Fannie Cheney and others cherished memories of him, his life now busied him so that he seldom saw the old crowd. The Pulitzer accentuated his growing influence with a new audience that numbered millions. His reputation was grounded firmly, across states and regions. He had reached a national league, having survived in his own region. He had passed the FBI loyalty test and had been adopted into the bureau by Hoover himself. Outside the South, through syndication and now the prize, he had become in some minds "the region's most distinguished journalist." He was busy writing seven days a week and was soon reprinted by three hundred newspapers.[1]

He had now isolated his chief critics, diehard segregationists and evangelical anti-Communists. Some of the latter never forgot McGill's gullibility concerning Mao and Stalin. As for the race bigots, their diminishing numbers seemed to stimulate their anger. They frothed threats by phone and, when they attempted letters, seldom were able to write a sentence without a misspelling. The segregationists' transparent blend of ignorance and naïveté occasionally provided McGill with profound amusement that distracted him from their venom. To his Brethren friends

Ashmore and Golden he sent a newspaper photographer's shot of a segregated outhouse with the painted words: "This Tolit Is for Whites Onley." He also sent it to two others—the rising young journalist Sander Vanocur and William C. "Bill" Baggs, the maverick columnist whom Tarver in 1957 had named editor of the *Miami News* and who had become McGill's protégé.[2]

McGill's new fame came at a price, although he was clearly eager to pay it. If he was looked to by so many over such an expanse of territory, he must extend his range of subjects well beyond the South and quicken his responses to events. Though in Atlanta, he must match the pace of the national press pundits, most of whom worked in Washington, feeding on insider information. If they opined within a day or two, he could not lag far behind. This new deadline pressure carried with it the hazard that, without access to privileged information, he might misspeak. Error was especially possible as McGill ranged afield from the South, into international waters. The misjudgments of praising Mao and hoping for too much from Stalin had, in his mind, never canceled out all the credit due for his prewar prescience about Hitler. Though foreign affairs were not his strong suit—the Pulitzer Prize Committee made no mention of his international travels and writings—he did not resist commenting along with the Washington pundits.

Certainly the challenge increased when the foreign country involved was the one where since 1933 he held a proprietary interest, where he had scored his first international scoop. On New Year's Day 1959, the world woke to learn about the newest Cuban revolution. The persistent challenger, Fidel Castro, whose revolutionaries had eluded Batista's soldiers for years, now strode out of the mountains of the eastern Oriente Province and rode victoriously through the streets of Havana. The dictator since the early '30s, Fulgencio Batista, alerted with probably his most accurate intelligence in years, flew safely from the island with his family and valuables.

From his perch in Atlanta, McGill thought he saw the news at least as clearly as anyone in Washington. Immediately, he welcomed the conqueror. McGill's distaste for despotism and sympathy for those who resisted it predisposed him to brand the fleeing Batista as "the Beast." The

transfer of power, though violent, so pleased McGill that he wrote
Castro a political blank check. Delaying only one day to verify the takeover, McGill interrupted his regularly scheduled column—he routinely
wrote several in advance—and boldly asserted that "whatever Castro is,
he has courage and a dream. For Cuba's sake we can hope neither is corrupted."[3] How could he do worse than Batista? By admission, then, he
wrote from hope.

Hope, in Batista, had been betrayed before. Over the years, Batista
had few more vocal supporters in the American press than the hopeful
McGill. After the revolution of 1933 chased the "butcher" Machado,
McGill looked hopefully at those who followed and tried to restore peace
and order to the island. He praised Sergeant Batista when he rose cleverly
from obscurity. For a generation, McGill appreciated Batista's firmness, a
reign of law and order (not to mention kickbacks) that benefited American and Cuban businessmen and investors. In the early '50s, when the
dictator seemed committed to relinquishing power to an elected president, McGill applauded. In 1952, Batista's chosen successor lost the election, precipitating a crisis. Batista backpedaled, abrogated the new
constitution, nullified the election, and kept power.

McGill the democrat was strangely reluctant to condemn the dictator. Although the editorial board of the *Constitution* labeled Batista a "Fascist strong-man" who had set back the cause of democracy,[4] McGill
reasoned that Cuba was a special case. He pleaded that the world not
rush to judgment. Having shared a wealth of experiences with friends on
the island, McGill felt he possessed peculiar insight about what was best
for Cuba. Blushing somewhat, he conceded that "[it] confuses me a little
that I should have an ill-conceived admiration for Fulgencio Batista"—
this soldier "who has so summarily and without regard for constitutional
law, taken over the Cuban Republic. But I have—and the reason for it
dates back, as they say."[5] To appreciate Batista's value, he reasoned, you
had to compare him to Machado in 1933: "Batista, a young sergeant with
a liking for chicken fights and a head for intrigue, brought off the revolution. I was cheering for Batista then. I knew he was better than Machado,
who was a fiend fit to sit beside Hitler or Stalin and the worst of their
murderers."[6]

This love of "chicken fights," McGill recalled in 1959, made Batista seem a man of the people. McGill himself loved a cockfight. He recalled the first time he had seen Batista "at a cockfight in a suburban pit in the outskirts of Havana. He was in uniform and there was a crowd of young officers with him. They had bets up on the gamecocks even then battling in the pit, and they were leaning over, rooting and calling on their favorites. Batista's face was happy and young looking."[7] Judging Batista's political credits and debits in 1952 had defied McGill's arithmetic:

> I don't know how to add up the chips on Batista. He did give them more democracy than they ever had before. And more schools. And when he bowed out he gave the beautiful island Republic the first really honest election it ever had. It was so honest Batista's man got beat—a most unusual state of affairs.
>
> It was a bit shocking—the way he came back.
>
> But, in this one I am waiting around for a while. I remember Machado, "The Butcher" and Cuba as it was under him. And I recall how I cheered when Batista broke his bloody grip on the Republic. Since then I've had a liking for him.[8]

Indeed, McGill delayed a verdict on Batista until Castro settled the question. By 1959, Batista seemed to McGill as inhumane as his predecessor. "Power has corrupted more able men than Batista," McGill wrote the day after Castro ascended. "But it still puzzles me that this man whom I first saw in the joy and promise of success should have become the butcher of his own people and as great and evil a tyrant as the beast Machado whom he drove out."[9] By comparison with his personal familiarity with Batista and Machado, then, McGill found it easy to be sympathetic to Castro.

With proprietary interest in Georgia's closest foreign country, the editor resolved to visit the revolution. He also felt a sense of guilt that the press had reported unfairly on Castro's struggle against Batista's corrupt regime. "The reporting of the Castro revolution embarrassed most of us," he said in May 1959 in his Pulitzer Memorial Address at Columbia University on the occasion of accepting the Pulitzer Prize. "I must, in candor, make clear my own plea of *Mea Culpa* and move on." An oppor-tunity to visit Cuba occurred in late June, while he was still basking in the glory of accepting the Pulitzer in May. He was a welcome guest, as he had been in the past. And as was his habit he checked in immediately with his newspaper friends, the sports writers and editors, and visited favorite haunts, meanwhile lining up meetings with officials in the strange new regime. In the process, these revolutionaries honored him with a keep-sake of the revolution—an armband.[10]

Reform was in the air, the cafés, and the saloons. McGill soaked up the ideas and enthusiasm, which reminded him of the excitement of the '30s. The island's problems were much the same—among them poverty and a maldistribution of land—but had accumulated through the decades of corrupt dictatorships with formulas for awarding graft. The revolutionary government wasted little time in proposing remedies. In the first months they drafted a plan for agrarian reform, beginning with the redistribution of land.[11]

McGill used his column to appeal for U.S. understanding of Cuba's massive problems. He sympathized with the desire for land reform, though he worried about the landed class and American business interests. With them in mind, he cautioned Americans not to fall into a "common human error of comparing everything with their present situation, laws, customs and comforts." One must sympathize with a people who suf-fered long while their problems mounted. The task struck McGill as gar-gantuan, a challenge even if Castro were *Hercules*. "This why the odds are heavily against Castro. The labors of Hercules are less in comparison."[12]

With precious irony, he haunted readers with the alternative to Castro—the specter of communism. This alone might be reason enough to support him. McGill had no idea how land reform might play out on the island, but he saw it as an issue in the cold war. To a landless peasant class, Castro appeared as a savior. If he failed, would they turn to Com-munists promising land?

How poor were the peasants? Giving a brief discourse about the economy, he noted that most Cubans depended on farming. Many earned less than one hundred dollars a year. Few apart from the wealthy owned land. These facts, he said, were vital to understand in order to stop com-munism. Cuba's economic illness could infect its nearest neighbor and the rest of the Americas. "The long-term issue is not Castro but the stability of Latin America," McGill said, noting optimistically but with an undisguised sense of foreboding, that, so far in Latin America, "there is no head of a government who is Communist."[13]

Within months of his return to Atlanta, McGill converted to the opposition, another instance in international politics when he had to concede error and change course. His initial enthusiasm and hope in January turned to caution in July, and then degraded into suspicion and distrust. In revoking support, he cited Castro's "curious instability." There was also his preference for "bad advice." And there was Castro's insult to capitalist investors. So long as Castro sought to seize land *without compensation,* he doomed any support for agrarian reforms. What stymied McGill most was Castro's arrogance and intransigence. How could he expect to attract tourists and American dollars while he denounced the United States?[14] The ideas so commendable in July when McGill accepted the revolutionaries' armband now hung as dead weight around the neck of any columnist who supported them.

McGill shifted his blessing to anti-Castro exiles whose exodus to Miami created a community growing each month by the hundreds. Certainly these included the rich and landed classes who McGill knew opposed land reform. But they also included the cream of Cuba's professionals, among them doctors, lawyers, and journalists. He expressed his respect for these who had given up much, who voted with their feet by leaving the island. Though his errors of judgment, more common in international affairs, embarrassed him, McGill possessed a philosophical approach to error. In May 1960, well after realizing his misjudgment about Castro, he revealed a wellspring of his philosophy in a speech at Ohio State University to the Institute for Education by Radio and Television. "Like you, I am a seeker. Perhaps I was conditioned for this in my youth. As a boy of 12 [in 1910] I was taken by my father from our home in Tennessee to Louisville, Kentucky, to see Marse Henry Watterson, the then famous editor of the *Courier-Journal.* We got in and I recall listening to the talk. But what I remember best is the motto on Watterson's desk. It read thusly: 'Lord, give me this day my daily idea and forgive me the one I had yesterday.'" By 1961, McGill welcomed anti-Castro plots hatched in the Miami exile community. After the sudden collapse of the exiles' invasion at the Bay of Pigs in April 1961, McGill mourned for the anti-Castro Cubans in Miami and on the island. "It is likely the people would have welcomed the invasion had they been permitted to do so. But Cuban troops, with automatic carbines at the ready, discouraged any show of welcome."[15] McGill hoped for a new Cuban underground, a popular rising like the one that chased Machado. After the Bay of Pigs, he believed this underground resistance would "continue in various forms of sabotage and guerilla raids." Because Castro was isolated in the hemisphere with few friends outside the Soviet Union, McGill though he saw clearly that "Castro can't last."[16]

The summer of 1959 was busy with travel. McGill had hardly settled in from Cuba than he was packing for the Soviet Union. One of the first perquisites of the Pulitzer had been an invitation to dinner in June at the White House. Vice President Nixon was there, lining up the press for his 1960 campaign to succeed Ike. When McGill learned that Nixon was going to Russia, he asked to go along.

Looking for fresh material in Moscow, McGill shunned much of the staged political summit where the international press clustered for more or less the same story. Beside the fact that the summit would be well covered, he was reminded, after Castro, that the intricacies of cold war politics were not his strong suit.

Leaving the pack, he hired an interpreter and headed off searching for human interest columns. This had been his lifelong method, an adaptation of the ancient creed: seek and ye shall find. McGill believed that by knocking on doors they would be opened unto him. From the people of the country he would find livelier and more truthful stories. Loosed in Moscow, as Martin pictured him, he was "like a wide-ranging bird dog casting for quail." Ranging the city, he talked to almost anyone who would talk with him in the streets, restaurants, subways, a school. He attended a Russian wedding. And in this capital of atheistic communism where hundreds of churches had been confiscated, he was delighted to find a Baptist church. He went inside for sanctuary, to sit and reflect.[17]

With his instinctive sense of story, he rejoined the press corps in time for Nixon's visit to the American Exhibition. There the vice president upheld the American way of life in the highly publicized "Kitchen Cabinet Debate" with Soviet premier Nikita Khrushchev. McGill was amused after he "shook hands vigorously with Mr. Khrushchev, who thought I was on Mr. Nixon's staff." Back home, his offbeat, personal approach was well received. His secretary, Grace Lundy, cabled him that his friend, *Boston Globe* editor Lawrence Winship, sent this clipped message: "If anyone communicating with McGill, tell him we think he is doing a hell of a job."[18]

Winship was one of many fans in New England. Generations after Henry Grady had lit up a Boston audience with visions of a New South, McGill's columns were making him a hero in the same lineage. Despite his gaffes in analyzing international politics, he struck at the central questions of domestic issues. Here his reputation was secure. Indeed, some friends urged him to write a book, not another compilation of his newspaper columns, but a full expression of ideas and philosophy. The book idea had lain dormant, but in 1959 friends fired him up again because of his new national prominence and stature.

His chief stimulator was Edward "Ted" Weeks, the editor of *Atlantic Monthly*. Weeks had admired McGill since meeting him in 1943, when the British Ministry of Information sponsored their wartime tour of England and Scotland. For more than a decade Weeks published McGill's articles and came to regard him as "the spearpoint of a group of Southern journalists, each conspicuous in the fight for civil rights for the negro." He cited McGill's "allies"—Ashmore, of course, and Mark Ethridge, publisher of the *Louisville Courier-Journal*, Virginius Dabney of the *Richmond Times-Dispatch*, Jonathan Daniels of the *Raleigh News and Observer*, and Hodding Carter in Greenville, Mississippi. Because he saw McGill as the dean of these courageous southerners, he urged him to write an autobiographical book. This became Weeks's "twelve-year pursuit." It took him that long to persuade McGill to write something more lasting than a column or an article, to claim a true place among authors.[19]

McGill balked in part because he lacked confidence. Weeks wanted something holistic and sustained. "It was not to be a collection of articles," he insisted. He was certain Ralph should write a book about his coming of age in the South and grappling with the difficult issues that made the region unique and which would help explain this special place.

After the Pulitzer, Weeks seized the moment. He asked writer and poet Peter Davison, then associate editor of Atlantic books, to visit McGill in Atlanta. Davison dutifully called on Ralph, who was flattered and appreciative, and led Davison to lunch two blocks away at the exclusive Commerce Club, where the principal fare was prime rib. McGill thought nothing of ordering a drink beforehand, but it impressed upon his biographically minded guest, a generation younger, that journalists of McGill's era drank during the day. Years later he remembered being impressed with McGill's capacity for lunchtime alcohol.[20]

Softened by refreshment and appreciative of the attention from Boston, McGill listened carefully as Davison explained Weeks's idea: "it should be a blend of autobiography, the evils of racism, disfranchisement, educational and economic peonage, and the changes for which he [McGill] had pleaded." By the end of the long lunch McGill seemed almost persuaded, but in a letter to Weeks conceded that he was "beset by doubts and fears."[21]

The publisher's ploy was to yank Ralph out of his comfortable surroundings and rout his final resistance. He lured him to Boston for, as Weeks termed it, a "skull session." Although there is no record of what troubled McGill about revealing his life, there are likely possibilities. For one thing, McGill felt he would setting himself up as a target if he tried to speak on behalf of the South and southerners. To Weeks, that would have seemed a needless worry. He could state out the outset that there are *many Souths,* and this is one. This, in fact, was what McGill believed. He recalled that he had once, during his around-the-world trip in 1945, satisfied the curiosity of a bookseller in Rome. He told him that "there were many Souths, not one, and that they were changing long before the Second World War began and that this process would be more accelerated when peace came." For the bookseller, who had read of the South in Erskine Caldwell's *Tobacco Road,* McGill elaborated:

The American South was a regional abstraction with a capital S. It possessed, like his own Naples and Sicily, a stubborn, often unjustified, pride; it was easygoing and yet violent when it chose to be; it shared, as did southern Italy, a common mystique in which there is grandeur, and pathos, and a note of falseness too. It was something, I said, that I had been born in and to which I had given all my years, but the complexities of it were often too much for me. Now fluid as quicksilver, now rigid and cruel in its adamant injustice and wrongs, now soft and merry, it was difficult to put in words.[22]

More troubling to McGill would have been Weeks's insistence upon autobiography. With the insight of an outsider, Weeks saw plainly that the public, southerners and others, wanted to know more about this enigmatic man. Those who regarded him highly wanted to know what shaped him. A British reader would later remark, "My interest [was] most quickened by the autobiographical parts."[23]

However dramatic his life might be, there were aspects he did not feel comfortable parading in print. In his daily columns it was easy enough to mention his personal life because he revealed only the fragments he wished. Autobiography compelled revelation. Weeks was interested, of course, in McGill's Scottish-Irish-Welsh ancestry and in his father, who had, with broad-minded vision, named his son for the Yankee sage Ralph Waldo Emerson. Ralph could write about his father's aspirations for himself and for his son. But if Ralph knew the family secrets about his father—the violent temper, the killing of the student, the retreat from college to the farm—he would not expose it. Whatever he knew about that bitter episode, he could still mention that his father had given up his dream of becoming a lawyer for some unspecified reasons. And Ralph could emphasize how Ben McGill maintained a reverence for the classics and formal learning, which he passed on in great measure to Ralph by first naming him after a revered philosopher and then reading to the young child.

Nor could Ralph write with complete candor about some of his own difficulties. He had survived the scourge of professional "disgrace" with which Ackerman had cursed him. He had controlled his drinking, for the most part. Why should he mention the sticking points that troubled the FBI or his cross-over compromise to help the bureau's agents as a

Hoover-approved special contact? Only insiders knew that the FBI sent one of his wife's first cousins to Atlanta as an agent.[24]

There were other private matters, smaller perhaps, though people were occasionally curious and suspicious. He knew people speculated about why he did not drive a car. Perhaps the answer was as simple as McGill suggested: riding the trolleys in Nashville and the buses in Atlanta, and being chauffeured by his wife and employees, gave him more time to read, think, and compose. He practiced precisely the advice he once gave a fellow journalist: never go anywhere without a book. Any other answer to the puzzle was not forthcoming. As Ralph McGill Jr. recalled, "It was a closed topic at our house."[25]

Ted Weeks knew little about any of this, nor did he disclose whether McGill now shared any details about his concerns. In the end, they settled on a topical outline that permitted McGill to skip over other topics. They agreed, as Weeks explained, "that it was to begin affectionately with his boyhood, his grounding in the Southern tradition, his years at Vanderbilt, the sports writing and travel which preceded his outreach in Atlanta, where he came to know the black leaders and to entertain them in his home."[26] The book would proceed thematically, skipping over regions of his life he could keep conveniently private.

Once he agreed, McGill impressed Weeks as a man possessed. "The book became possessive," Weeks recalled. It was as though he led two lives: McGill the columnist now searched each journalistic mission for something of enduring value for the book, as a miner panned the day's stream for glimmers of gold. Weeks kept after him, almost haunting him to work faster, that people were eager to read the manuscript. McGill seemed even more persuaded after Harvard University awarded him an honorary degree of Doctor of Laws with the citation: "In a troubled time his steady voice of reason champions a New South." After that, Weeks noted, "the writing quickened."[27] Nonetheless, the book suffered from neglect in the wake of current events.

At home, the white citizens councils' massive resistance was coming to a head in a devious but unimaginative last-ditch effort to delay desegregation if not defeat it. Georgia's two senators were at the heart of the resistance, and in February 1959 McGill "felt a sort of urge to write" to President Eisenhower to explain the "confusing, often contradictory, actions" of Georgia's senior senator Richard Russell—"a sick and somewhat broken man" who "is politically vulnerable"—and the junior senator, Herman Talmadge, "who has become to Georgians, THE senator." Both followed the "political truth" that "a politician's real concern must be with being 'politically right' at the time when he must run for election." As the outgoing governor in 1954 Talmadge acknowledged "the path" laid down by *Brown vs. Board* but pledged, "My position will be to delay as long as possible putting our feet in that path." On the one hand, Talmadge could make an "eloquent defense of education . . . but he would, at this period in the evolution of acceptance of the Supreme Court decision, go along with abolishing the public school system." The demagogues had created a living monster. "This Frankenstein which the Deep South politicians have created is now devouring them, or threatening to." McGill closed with his weary outlook on the South from his promontory: "I don't know when it is going to happen, but one of these days the Deep South has got make up its mind to join the Union. There are evidences, even in Georgia, of change in opinion. The tide has not turned. But it is slowing down. It must reach a slack period and then change."[28]

The president replied only three days later with a three-page letter that laid out his own views for America. He felt confirmed in his support of "moderation in the race question" and his conviction that "coercive law is, by itself, powerless to bring about complete compliance with its own terms when in any extensive region the great mass of public opinion is in bitter opposition." Eisenhower agreed with McGill's "observations about the Southern Senatorial Group" except that he placed South Carolina's Strom Thurmond and Olin Johnston and Mississippi's James Eastland "in a special group" who "seem so entrenched in their prejudices and racial antagonisms that they never show so much as a glimmer of a readiness to see the other side of the problem." By contrast, Eisenhower noted that Talmadge was in a group of senators—with William Fulbright of Arkansas—whom many considered to have "real ability. . . . I was particularly interested in your evaluation of Senator Talmadge. With the equipment he has, it would be a pity if he allows it to be dissipated by a too great anxiety to be 'right'—to pick the expression out of your letter."[29]

At least for the present, Talmadge did not betray any change of direction as political leaders and white citizens councils proceeded with a passion. There were two basic strategies, one of them destructive, or as McGill regarded it, self-destructive. If whites could not have their own schools, they would close all public schools. They had state law on their side. During the Marvin Griffin administration, in 1956, and during Governor Ernest Vandiver's first year, 1959, the legislature passed statutes "providing for school closing when integrated."[30]

The second strategy was deviously constructive. Persuaded they could maintain the outlawed "separate but equal" dual system, the Griffin administration rushed to accelerate spending for Negro schools, to offset the most noticeable inequalities. Ironically, this is what McGill had urged ten years earlier in a completely different context. In the years of legal segregation before *Brown*, McGill advised upgrading Negro schools to live up to the promise of *equal* in the "separate but *equal*" bargain. The incentive in the late 1940s was clear to any reasonable politician: the South's abysmal provision for Negro education eroded support for "separate but equal." In fact, by 1950 the thoughtful segregationists in Georgia also realized that the state needed to go on record as committed to Negro education. To fund this initiative, Herman Talmadge, then governor and gaining a reputation as a great spender, approved using money from Georgia's new state sales tax. After *Brown*, the legislature, a half-century late, intensified the desperate effort to respect the segregationists' compact of 1896.[31]

Whites and Negroes alike joined in the Griffin administration's extraordinary spending spree. The binge was fueled by a strange brew of hope and anger, hypocrisy and guilt. In two years, Georgia built dozens of new Negro schools, adding to and remodeling others. The state multiplied Negro classrooms by *six times* and virtually eliminated the one-room schoolhouse where generations of blacks, sitting in the cold in winter, had read from books worn and outdated.

The spending made the governor proud. Between 1955 and 1957, Griffin reported, "169 new schools and 3,447 classrooms have been constructed for Negroes. Plans are now completed for 86 more schools and 1,379 classrooms for Negroes by the end of 1958. Fifty-four percent of the outlay for building has been used for Negro schools, although Negroes constitute only 30% of the school population." In 1957, the state equalized salaries for twenty-five thousand white and nine thousand Negro teachers at a minimum twenty-four hundred dollars and a maximum thirty-eight hundred dollars. Segregationists looked to Griffin's successor, Vandiver, to fulfill his campaign declaration against integrated schools—"no, not a single one." In his State of the State address in January 1960, Vandiver pledged to continue segregation by "every legal means and remedy," including cutting funding to desegregated schools.[32]

Certainly Vandiver had captured the segregationist vote with that simple, absolute phrase. Yet at some point, as governor, he realized that Georgia's two primary strategies, the offense and the defense, were weak, discredited, and likely doomed. The offense—the educational buildup—had provided too little, too late, coming as it did *after* the Supreme Court ruling against dual systems. The defense, shaped by lawyers who now earned thousands of dollars fighting the U.S. Constitution, could hope for no better than General Lee at Appomattox. Federal courts had struck down other states' segregationist laws identical to Georgia's.

Vandiver's move to the middle of the road owed much to the plotting of one Talmadge segregationist who foresaw clearly the political repercussions of closing the schools, and dared to articulate them. James S. Peters of Manchester was by 1960 an elderly banker, the patriarch of the Talmadge political machine with a hand in everything. He was dedicated to Herman and the preservation of the existing political order. In addition to his political weight, earned by long and loyal service, Peters chaired the State Board of Education and had chaired the Georgia Democratic Committee; he was still vice chair. He concluded that segregationists were traveling blindly down a road that would lead to their political end.[33]

Peters now broke with the segregationists who advocated resistance to the last ditch. By late 1959, he had come to accept that defiance of federal law to the point of closing the schools would damage the state economically and socially. Politically, school closings would result in political suicide for those who shut down education. Further, he now dared to express these views despite the fact that they converged with the positions of the anti-Talmadge crowd—the Atlanta power structure, a grow-ing group of Georgia businessmen, and the liberal camp, including Ellis Arnall and Ralph McGill. To surrender on the threat to close schools, however, was political heresy for a Talmadge Democrat.

As 1959 came to a close and the state General Assembly was prepar-ing to consider legislation in early 1960, Peters expressed his views in a private letter that became public. He wrote to Roy Harris of Augusta, a political ally of the Talmadge faction and, in the eyes of the *Atlanta Con-stitution,* "probably the most die-hard segregationist in the state." It was unlikely that Peters intended to convert Harris, but the letter read as though Peters were trying to persuade *someone.* Such a bombshell from the politi-cally connected chairman of the State Board of Education was not likely to remain "private," and Peters seems to have directed his views to a wider audience. To begin with, he sent copies to Talmadge and to a few trusted Talmadge stalwarts, and at least one copy found its way into the hands of a *Constitution* reporter in Washington.[34]

In the letter, dated December 30, 1959, Peters asked Harris to imag-ine the worst possible outcome for Talmadge Democrats. Voters were fickle and public attitudes could change fast, particularly when politics inter-fered with peoples' daily lives and concerns. Supposing the state did close schools because of the impasse over segregation. Peters imagined wide-spread social discontent. He pictured mothers with children out of school, pulling their skirts all day, and fathers coming home to furious wives. "Unless Herman Talmadge and his friends find a better answer to this problem than closing down the public school system," he told Harris, the present Democratic regime "will be swept aside for decades to come."[35]

Peters was looking ahead to the election of 1962. If the state closed the schools, the overbearing issue in the election would "not be whether people favor or oppose integration." Simply put, the dominant issue would be "are you in favor of reopening the schools with Ellis [Arnall]" promising to do just that. Arnall would "be difficult indeed to defeat and Herman could very well go down with him." Political power would swing wildly to Arnall and the liberals who were insisting the schools must remain open.[36]

Arnall had been waiting in the wings since Herman succeeded him as governor in 1948. Arnall could run on the school closing issue, as he had run in 1942 on the loss of accreditation to the University of Georgia. The Talmadge machine that Herman inherited from Eugene could "lose control of the government and entrench" Arnall. With that loss would go thousands upon thousands of state jobs.[37]

Having made his case, Peters broke with the die-hards. More than five years after *Brown v. Board,* he accepted the end of segregated schools. He reasoned that "some form of integration is inevitable, and the only question left unanswered today is whether this integration will be under the control of the friends of segregation or the proponents of integration." The Talmadge machine, he concluded, must choose a course away from massive resistance and at the same time avert the sweeping changes promoted by integrationists. Peters gave his authoritative nod to what became known as *token* desegregation.[38]

The potential for lost employment went well beyond politicians' concern for lost patronage jobs. McGill and the *Constitution* argued that closing schools would spell general economic disaster. By the 1950s, industries were coming to South, welcomed by cheaper non-union labor and legislated tax incentives. But if the state had no schools, McGill insisted, Georgia's economic sweeteners would sour. The state would lose thousands of potential jobs. "Closed schools do not go well with a new industry," he reasoned. Harold Fleming, who directed the Southern Regional Council, thought McGill reached the business power structure with the main point that "if you close the schools you are going to wreck your economy."[39] This view gained converts first among the Atlanta power structure, then gradually among leaders in other Georgia cities.

The Peters letter turned the issue around. On January 15, 1960, about two weeks after the letter was dated, it was leaked to the press in cloak-and-dagger fashion. Late on that Friday afternoon, a Talmadge press aide in Washington called the *Atlanta Journal's* political reporter and they met for coffee in the Senate dining room. The reporter, Harold Davis, recorded precisely how William H. Burson "showed me a flimsy brown copy" of the Peters letter. "Burson didn't need to tell me that if it were known he leaked the letter it would cost him his job. It would also cost me my best news source in Washington. . . . I called the *Journal* and got the new city editor, Pat Watters, and Charlie Pou, our political editor. All pledged to protect the source and Charlie wrote the piece in Atlanta after I dictated the letter over the phone."[40]

As Peters could have expected, the newspaper article had an explosive effect. It appeared on Sunday, January 17, in 514,000 copies of the combined *Atlanta Journal–Constitution* under a four-column headline: "Integration Sure, Peters Predicts." The shock waves were reported for weeks as politicians condemned the messenger as well as his message. Davis, Washington correspondent for the *Journal,* noted, "In Augusta, Roy Harris announced that the usefulness of Peters was over and said he should resign from all state positions. He didn't. The next day in the State House of Representatives, Rep. Joe Underwood of Mount Vernon denounced Peters to some handclapping and cheers."[41]

Noisy denunciations did not silence Peters's message. His authority and credentials could not be so easily dismissed. "Talmadge politicians everywhere were thinking," Davis observed. "They had been exhorted before by people of various stripes, but this was the first time an elder of great reputation had told them they stood to lose their jobs. Slowly, they began to get it." In Washington, Georgia's senators and representatives in Congress seemed stunned, waiting to see what would happen. "Although they could talk of little else," Davis said, "none had anything to say."[42]

Talmadge himself signaled the proper course. When Peters visited Washington for a banking conference, he sat in the Senate gallery as Talmadge's guest. Peters was also a guest in the Talmadge home. "Slowly in Georgia, members of the business community were speaking out," Davis noted. "The first was W. R. Bowdoin, senior vice president of the Trust Company of Georgia, the Coca-Cola bank. In what became a kind of ritual as he and others spoke, he said he preferred segregation but that Peters had told the truth. The Peters letter has entered the history books as a pivotal moment."[43]

In this context, Vandiver also retreated from a collision course with the federal courts. Like Peters, he conceded that time had run out more quickly than expected for Marvin Griffin's brand of segregationist posturing. Vandiver had been caught in the middle of the school issue, when reasonable southern sentiment, faced with a clear choice, seemed to be turning away from drastic alternatives. While the post-*Brown* legislature had spoken defiantly for *no* schools rather than integrated ones, Vandiver now abrogated his own "no, not a single one" pledge. In light of recent developments, he wanted a plebiscite of sorts: Was closing the schools the choice of a majority of Georgians?

If Georgians needed evidence of the impact of school closings, they needed only to regard Virginia, where the most powerful political leaders had supported massive resistance and confronted the courts. When court-ordered integration of the Norfolk secondary schools appeared inevitable in September 1958, Governor J. Lindsay Almond Jr. ordered the city's white junior and senior high schools closed. Of the 9,950 students turned away, fewer than half were included in informal tutoring groups while segregationists tried to establish private schools for whites. For five months, the closing pitted resisters against pro-school forces. In February 1959, Governor Almond conceded to the supremacy of the federal courts, and on February 2 of that year, Norfolk reopened its secondary schools.[44]

Georgians now doubted the wisdom of closing the schools, if only for economic reasons. When moral arguments failed, rational southerners of both races targeted southerners' financial interests. Earlier, in 1942, McGill and Ellis Arnall had toppled Gene Talmadge primarily because of the economic ramifications of the University of Georgia's loss of accreditation. In the Virginia closing, the Norfolk business community organized to urge reopening the schools. Later, in Richmond, an assembly of leading businessmen and industrialists feared that Virginia had to resolve the school crisis if it hoped to attract businesses.[45]

Vandiver's new strategy of *lawful resistance* bought him time and deflected the political heat. In shifting state politics away from *unlawful* resistance, he remained sympathetic to segregation, but now argued that segregation's best defense lay not in declarations of nullification, or denial of federal authority. Looking down that path he saw only "blind destruction" of children's education and the state's economic potential. Rather than fight as a mob in the streets, he reasoned, the best hope for those who valued racial segregation was to defend it with imagination and creativity in the state legislature. Addressing the general assembly, he said, "I reject as I know you and the people of Georgia do, any thought, suggestion, hint, or encouragement of defiance of lawful processes or the subjecting of the children of Georgia to the bodily hazard of violence and mob rule. Our course is lawful resistance—not defiance—not violence." For his stunned and disheartened white supporters, Vandiver borrowed a strategy from Virginia governor Almond. In a face-saving buffer against total capitulation, Vandiver appointed a School Study Commission, to be headed not by a legislator, as in Virginia, but by a civic leader, John A. Sibley. The commission was to hold public hearings in communities around the state at which citizens could declare publicly what course they preferred, and to report back to the legislature.[46]

The Sibley Commission's town meetings in 1960 attracted at least as many people as had Gene Talmadge's free barbecue rallies. Hundreds of witnesses vented the extremes of sentiment. At one hearing for fourteen south Georgia counties, attendees voted overwhelmingly to close all public schools rather than integrate any. In contrast, the largest urban system in Atlanta strongly favored open schools, led by School Superintendent John Letson, whom the *Atlanta Constitution* editors praised for his graceful acceptance of federal authority: "The goal of all must be to accomplish peacefully and with dignity what we are required to do." In the end, Vandiver concluded that the people had given their message: "There is no—NO—sentiment in this state for a blind destruction of public education without offering an effective alternative."[47]

With the commission's contradictory findings, but with a legislative caution that continuing segregation would require additional state and *local* funding, the 1961 legislature approved a "local-option" plan. The state left the fate of the local school systems up to local school boards in the 159 counties. To soothe parents who feared for their children, the Georgia legislature adopted a package of safeguards—the "Freedom of Association Child Protection Package"—aimed to slow the pace of desegregation and lighten its impact. The plan permitted children to withdraw from public schools and receive a share of public funding. Georgia thus bridged the chasm, crossing over from "massive resistance" to comply at least minimally with desegregation orders, without closing its public schools. The stage was set for integration of Atlanta's public schools in the fall of 1961. McGill believed that a real impetus to legislative action appeared to have been a timely court ruling, ordering the desegregation of the University of Georgia in the winter of 1961 with the admission of two Atlanta high school graduates.[48]

The university desegregation order caught the governor and legislature off guard. As McGill later recounted the story for an oral historian, Vandiver was quoted on a Sunday in January 1961 as saying "nothing was expected to come up," when "Bang! Early Monday, the order had come in to submit these people's classes that morning. And so they were in classes at 8 o'clock, these two people, Charlayne Hunter and Mr. [Hamilton E.] Holmes. Well, by the time the legislature could meet, the University of Georgia was integrated. It was a *fait accompli.*" Protests poured through the telephone lines, but when parents learned that the governor could not close the University of Georgia without closing all the public colleges, public opinion gave way. A small number of Ku Klux Klan members and some students staged a small riot on the Athens campus—"largely, if not entirely, actively created by the White Citizens Council element"— and then the integration "went off really rather well."[49]

The Montgomery bus boycott had lit the imagination of southern blacks to see the efficacy of their own collective action—a reply to the whites' massive resistance. Although the Montgomery boycott was arranged hastily by an impromptu association, it became a national and international issue. Its ultimate success crowned the minister who had emerged as the articulate leader in the crisis, the Rev. Dr. Martin Luther King Jr., and inspired bus boycotts in other cities. As McGill feared, the blacks' revolutionary success stimulated the white counter-revolt. The aftermath—bombings of black churches and homes in Montgomery— tested King and other blacks. In choosing to continue the boycott, they increased the stakes. With King at the helm, the black clergy's new regional organization founded in 1957, eventually named the Southern Christian Leadership Conference (SCLC), sought to build a wide-ranging resistance. In awe and apprehension of the confrontation, McGill envisioned shock waves of violent lawlessness from both blacks and whites.[50]

King's momentum took on the dynamics of a *movement.* Although McGill confided that he held "the highest esteem for the reverend," he also dreaded King's persuasive powers. In mid-December 1959, when he learned that King was returning to the pulpit at Atlanta's Ebenezer Baptist Church and moving the SCLC headquarters to Atlanta, McGill worried that King's self-styled nonviolent protests might provoke Atlanta's segregationist whites to violence or fuel the movement to close the schools. He wrote to Ashmore, "I view this in much the same manner as the citizens of medieval cities who heard that the great plague was coming." There had been a fear of violence in 1957. After King's successful boycott, Atlanta's Rev. William Holmes Borders conducted his own nonviolent demonstration against Jim Crow buses, provoking Governor Griffin to alert the state militia. Now King's presence and possible intervention could not have been more ill-timed, McGill told Ashmore, if it aggravated what little progress had been made in the school situation. The legislature would begin its annual session in three weeks, and the U.S. district court, he noted, "yesterday notified city officials that what the legislature did with the school placement plan will determine whether or not they had schools."[51]

The efforts of King, who in 1960 was only thirty-one, seemed to be inspiring black college students to a daring test of segregated public places. Direct action against the barriers of segregation appealed to younger blacks impatient with the delayed implementation of *Brown v. Board* and anxious for desegregation without more multiyear lawsuits in the courts. "To them," said the Rev. Martin Luther King Sr., "this was a long enough time to wait for general action to bring about all the changes America had been promising." As a key member of the coalition of Atlanta leaders, the senior Reverend King, known as Daddy King, warned Mayor William Hartsfield that "it was increasingly difficult to convince younger people to wait any longer for the rights of their Constitution guaranteed them just weren't being heard. The storm kept brewing."[52]

This impatience was evident as Daddy King's son, Martin Jr., was leaving Montgomery to make his headquarters in Atlanta. What became known as the "sit-in" movement started in Greensboro, North Carolina, as black college students took the lead, more or less spontaneously with no evident long-range plan. On February 1, 1960, four freshmen at North Carolina A&T entered a Woolworth's department store and, at the segregated lunch counter, started a "sit-down protest." They simply sat at the counter, were refused service, and refused to leave. The result was surprising—no one ejected them all afternoon. When they left, they said they intended to return the next day. Although there was little media attention the first day, reports spread by word of mouth among college students interested in joining the Greensboro four. On the second day there were nineteen students, and on the third day, joined by some white students, the number rose to eighty-five. Some brought homework and took turns in the seats while others went to class. In these first days, news photographers captured a relatively peaceful, quiet situation. At last, the *Atlanta Constitution* took notice with an Associated Press story buried on page twelve.[53]

News of the Greensboro students' protest spread immediately through the city and across state lines. "It is hard to overestimate the electrical effect of the first sit-in in Greensboro," one participant said. In Nashville, black college students disregarded warnings of danger from older blacks and marched, neatly dressed, to lunch counters. In Atlanta, the southern city with the greatest number of Negro colleges, black students "couldn't let Greensboro and Nashville outdo them," recalled Lonnie C. King Jr., who at the age of twenty-four in 1960 was an instigator of the Atlanta protest. On February 5, Lonnie King and other students met at a drugstore near the campus. An Atlanta sit-in, King thought, could "let the power structure know just how we felt." The first planned demonstration was postponed because too few students were available.[54]

At this point, the elders in the black community intervened, reflecting the generational divide. The older generation had favored deliberation in the courts that did not directly threaten their delicate biracial cooperation with moderates in the white community. The president of Morehouse College, Dr. Benjamin Mays, gained another delay by persuading students that a protest now would adversely influence the imminent trial of Martin Luther King Jr. in Montgomery. Then the president of Spelman College, Alvin E. Manley, and the president of Atlanta University, Dr. Rufus Clement, urged the students to write a statement of their goals. The students agreed, but with the understanding, Lonnie King recalled, that they would afterward carry their protest into the segregated restaurants. Julian Bond, who with fellow student Roslyn Pope, wrote the draft of the statement, thought years later that this step "was a delaying move. . . . What Dr. Clement really wanted to do was have us put off the initial demonstrations believing if we ever did begin we couldn't be stopped."[55]

Meanwhile, as the movement spread in February and March to more than seventy cities, whites' reactions changed from surprise and confusion to outrage and anger. By the end of the first week, police in Raleigh, North Carolina, had arrested forty-one students, who soon were released on bail. In downtown Montgomery, white vigilantes wielding baseball bats attacked black shoppers. In Nashville, police arrested more than seventy Negroes and five white sympathizers as white onlookers shouted epithets. Some store managers temporarily closed their lunch counters. Police in Orangeburg, South Carolina, used water hoses and tear gas to disperse students marching to a sit-in.[56]

If students did demonstrate in Atlanta, it was hoped that any arrests would be peaceful, without gas and hoses. Perhaps unique in all the South was the working relationship between the police and the Negro community. Black leaders had begun petitioning officially for Negro police officers in 1934, and on December 1, 1947, secured city council approval to hire eight. On April 3, 1948, some four hundred people lined the street to witness the eight uniformed officers walking in pairs out of the Butler Street YMCA (they were not permitted to change in the police station), followed by two key figures in the transformation, Mayor Hartsfield and Police Chief Herbert Jenkins.[57]

In the mayor's "Atlanta style" of governance, City Hall could avert more problems by taking a leading role in desegregation matters. Jenkins developed a working relationship with the Negro community, particularly with Daddy King. When Martin Luther King Jr. was making the move from Montgomery to Atlanta, Daddy King came to see Jenkins:

> "They gon' kill my boy," he told Jenkins.
> "I think you're right, with the other things I've seen and heard."
> "Well, he'll be over here tomorrow, and I'm gon' bring him by here. Will you see him?"
> "Yeah."

The next day they came together to see Jenkins. "I think you're a marked man," Jenkins told Martin Jr. "I think if you don't leave Montgomery and come back to Atlanta, they gon' *bury* you over there." Jenkins recalled the young King agreeing: "You're probably right and I appreciate it. But I want you to know that this is my job, and if that's the way it ends, well, that's the way it'll have to end."[58]

When the sit-ins appeared imminent, the police chief, Daddy King, and other leaders of the black community coordinated to avert violence. "I talked to him [Daddy King] about a lot of things," Jenkins said. "I sought his advice, because there was times I wanted to know what the blacks was plannin', what they were gonna do next. And I had respect for him and had his cooperation."[59]

By the first week of March, the Atlanta students' statement was approved by the black college presidents and set to be published, paid for by donations. On March 9 it was printed in the *Atlanta Constitution,* the *Atlanta Journal,* and the black-owned *Atlanta Daily World* as a full-page advertisement entitled "An Appeal for Human Rights."[60]

The measured protest of the Atlanta students, though coming a month after the spontaneity in Greensboro, was passionate with "unqualified support" for students engaging in sit-ins. The "Appeal" characterized students of the early 1960s as "dissatisfied, not only with the existing conditions, but with the snail-like speed at which they are being ameliorated." The Atlanta students referred to democratic ideals and Christian virtues: "We want to state clearly and unequivocal that we cannot tolerate, in a nation professing democracy and among people professing Christianity, the discriminatory conditions under which the Negro is living today in Atlanta, Georgia—supposedly one of the most progressive cities in the South." The statement advised whites to "stop believing those who tell us that everything is fine and equal, and that the Negro is happy and satisfied." And it contained what whites soon took as a threat: "We must say in all candor that we plan to use every legal and nonviolent means at our disposal to secure full citizenship rights as members of this great democracy of ours."[61]

In Atlanta, politicians reacted immediately. Governor Vandiver predictably attacked the appeal, saying it was "not written by students" and that it resembled "anti-American propaganda . . . calculated to breed dis-satisfaction, discontent, discord and evil." Just as predictably, Mayor Hartsfield, while praising the appeal as expressing "the legitimate aspirations of young people throughout the nation and the entire world," at the same time urged patience and deliberation. He met the day of publication with President Clement and the student leaders, counseling against immediate demonstrations. He and others promised to set up talks with the white business community regarding segregated facilities.[62]

After weeks of delay, the Atlanta students readied the first sit-in. Persuaded again by their elders who hoped at best the sit-ins would lead to litigation in federal courts, the students targeted public buildings linked to interstate commerce. On March 15, from 11:00 A.M. onward, almost two hundred black students staged, as the *Constitution* charitably reported, "orderly sit-down demonstrations . . . aimed at erasing the customary ban on integrated eating facilities in public places of business." In all, seventy-seven were arrested at city hall, the state capitol, the Fulton County Courthouse, two office buildings where federal employees lunched, two railroad stations, and the lunch counters at the Trailways and Greyhound bus depots. Welcoming the students' statement that no more sit-ins were planned for the near future, the *Constitution*'s editorial said the demonstration "blurs and damages the reception accorded" to grievances in the students' published appeal.[63]

The second series of sit-ins began after classes resumed in the fall semester. Elsewhere, progress had been dramatic. Four national chain stores reported their lunch counters had been integrated in 112 towns. Integration at lunch counters occurred in Nashville on May 10, and in Greensboro, North Carolina, where the protest had begun, on July 25. In Atlanta, students targeted lunch counters in the downtown shopping district for the second wave of sit-ins, beginning October 19. At least six stores responded by closing, the same reaction segregationists had prescribed for schools. At Rich's department store, more than fifty blacks were arrested, including Martin Luther King Jr. King, who was on probation for a misdemeanor traffic violation, was sentenced to four months at the state's maximum security prison at Reidsville; he served several days before being released on bond. Atlanta's students and business establishments had locked horns in protests, boycotts, closings, arrests, interventions, and frustrating negotiations and delays that went on for a year.[64]

The deadlock was broken in private negotiations arranged by influential members of Atlanta's Chamber of Commerce. The Chamber in 1960 had already thrown its weight in favor of desegregating the Atlanta schools by "local option" to prevent school closings. Now its new president, Ivan Allen Jr., agreed to host negotiations in the plush rooms of the downtown Commerce Club. Allen wanted confidentiality and openness and little media attention. Seeking maximum secrecy for the negotiators, he secured a pledge from the Atlanta newspaper editors to keep as quiet as possible about the talks while in progress.[65]

The breakthrough came in part because the business establishment had grown weary from the protest. On March 7, 1961, Allen announced that the black leaders, among them Lonnie King and Daddy King, agreed to stop sit-ins and boycotts, and the downtown merchants pledged to desegregate lunch counters and rest rooms, but not immediately. They would comply after the desegregation of the city schools in the fall, but no later than October 15. The *Constitution* immediately endorsed the compact as "magnificent testimony to the reason and common sense that distinguishes both races in Atlanta," and praised Ivan Allen's role. Delighted, Mayor Hartsfield was quoted by the national press as saying, "This is the city too busy to hate." But opposition was also immediate and articulate, especially from students who, after a year of protests and jailings, expected that Atlanta would comply as other cities had already done. The final agreement reflected "very nearly what the management of Rich's had been urging since June 1960. . . . Those who had been parties to the agreement were the objects of ugly, abusive assaults and charges that they had 'sold out' to the white merchants." At a tumultuous public meeting on March 10, an audience of some two thousand booed the compromisers until Martin Luther King Jr. made his statement. He had won the students' allegiance as both strategist and jailed demonstrator, and now he persuaded them to accept the compromise. "We must move out now on the road of calm reasonableness," he declared. "We must come to a mood of mutual trust and mutual confidence. No greater disease exists for the Negro community than to be afflicted with the cancerous disease of disunity. Disagreements and differences there will be, but unity there must be!"[66]

The student sit-ins clearly contradicted McGill's well-worn public philosophy of obedience to the law. During the 1940s he could chide the South for reneging on "separate but equal." Since 1954 he had taken as his bedrock stance that the South must obey the law of the land as interpreted by the Supreme Court. As much as he was repulsed by political hypocrisy and racial bigotry, McGill's insistence upon obedience to law placed him to the right of the students, made him at least as conservative as the black elders of the biracial coalition. While he could sympathize with the students' appeal and their courage to back it up, he could not bring himself initially to sanction lawlessness. In response to the March 15 sit-ins, McGill's editorial board at the *Constitution* was diametrically opposed to the concept that civil disobedience was justified if laws were unjust: "We are a nation which must continue to live by law and this is a good time to remember it."[67]

Moreover, McGill thought student protests would set back peaceful change. He worried about the precarious position of the biracial coalition that he had helped build since the 1940s. In the best of possible outcomes, McGill still wanted whites, not blacks, to initiate the change. He saw hope in the rising profile of white chambers of commerce that were "increasingly aware that segregation no longer is economically practical."[68]

The violent reaction of self-styled white vigilantes shamed and angered McGill. Race hatred which the Klan had acted out by night now showed itself in daytime, with apparent public support. White youths assaulted the demonstrators at lunch counters, hitting them and splattering them with mustard and ketchup. The violence woke McGill from his legalistic, trusting posture. Searching for a new rationale, he suggested that the students were resorting to a "higher moral law." "Whatever the lawyers may say of them," he wrote, "they have an honored place in history and literature." He suggested the sit-ins were consistent with biblical and historical precedent—with the refusal of Shadrach, Meshach, and Abednego to obey the laws of Nebuchadnezzar, Henry David Thoreau's civil disobedience, and Mahatma Gandhi's victory for Indian independence.[69]

The sit-ins called attention to the "preposterous" system of segregation. A department store could sell a Negro a suit of clothes, but not permit him to try them on, nor permit him to eat lunch. Because of the sit-ins, "a hot dog or a hamburger and a cup of coffee have become the symbols of freedom." The sit-ins, he agreed, "dramatized the immorality and the irrationality of such a custom. . . . No force brought change as quickly as they."[70]

The sit-ins and the activities directed by King thrust the race issue into the 1960 presidential campaigns. Neither party could afford to ignore the new pressure from Negroes for civil rights. By April, Congress passed a new civil rights bill after a filibuster by southern Democrats, who claimed victory by confining the bill largely to *voting* rights, which, McGill noted, "no Southern leader opposed." That in a sense was a landmark, he proclaimed: "It is simply not any longer possible to deny the right to vote." Yet he wondered if white southerners would find new technicalities to deny voting rights. If so, he prophesied that "there will be more civil rights legislation introduced in the sessions of the next two or three Congresses. It will be less and less possible to oppose such legislation if the new laws are defied or frustrated."[71]

This sudden turn toward civil rights surprised McGill. Despite the obvious delaying tactics, Georgia's politicians at the highest level were persuaded that secession from the Union and the closing of schools were not viable options. The governor's renunciation of violence and advocacy of lawful resistance constituted a major victory for moderates. Further, the political leaders now seemed willing to face the electorate and say so.

McGill admitted that the advocates of civil rights at the lunch counters and in the streets had speeded change. His own arguments for gradualism now made him feel out of step with the intensified pace. Where for so long he had been a step ahead, he had fallen behind, especially in the esteem of civil rights liberals. In his own rational argumentation, he had worried that public demonstrations for civil rights would backfire. The white South, he believed, would accept only moderate change. The Negro activists' insistence on disobedience to segregation undermined their cause and polarized even their white supporters.

Liberals and moderates—he was both on some days—had felt stranded because they could scarcely defend a civil rights movement that violated the law. This very insistence on obedience to the law had been his central argument when governors and mobs alike flagrantly disregarded *Brown v. Board.* Having cast his lot with the law, he could not condone civil disobedience among Negroes.

The dramatic sweep of events, however satisfying, also shamed McGill. Each victory by the advocates of civil rights seemed proof again that his approach in avoiding many local racial issues had been too tame. One day, after rereading a batch of his earlier columns, he remarked to Eugene Patterson, "They're pretty pale tea."[72]

Patterson during the 1960s became McGill's colleague, friend, and confidante. McGill saw in Patterson "that quality which Ralph admired above all else—courage, both physical and moral," Martin thought. "He could not be bullied or bought and he wrote like an angel." Tarver appreciated those qualities as well, and in 1960 intervened to arrange a major shift of responsibilities. After Governor Cox's death in 1957 and Biggers's retirement, James M. Cox Jr. appointed Tarver president of Atlanta Newspapers, Inc. Now, in 1960, the former owner, Clark Howell Jr., stepped down as publisher to become vice chairman of the ANI board, and McGill was promoted to publisher. Tarver, who in 1957 had made Patterson the executive editor of both newspapers, now appointed him to succeed McGill as editor of the *Constitution* with a column to write on the editorial page. "I'm doing you no favors," Patterson recalls Tarver saying. "I'm asking you to play right field after Babe Ruth." A key reason for the shift was that, as publisher, McGill escaped ANI's policy of mandatory retirement at age 65, which he dreaded. Tarver was continuing to shelter this elder statesman of journalism who had brought him to Atlanta.[73]

From 1960, Patterson did the work of running the editorial page, freeing McGill from conducting editorial board meetings or any other daily editorial concerns, permitting him to travel and focus on national issues. Generally, McGill from 1960 dealt with civil rights "as a national story. I wrote it as a local story." During the sit-ins, Patterson, in his late thirties, developed close ties with the downtown business community and the Chamber of Commerce, and especially with Ivan Allen Jr. They became particularly close as Allen was elected mayor in 1961 with 64 percent of the votes, defeating Lester Maddox, the segregationist restaurant owner vocally defying the federal government. In this way, Patterson succeeded McGill not only in title but in developing close ties with the inner circle of decision-makers.[74]

In their daily talks at the newspaper, Patterson came to regard McGill as the "best friend I ever had." For years he had admired McGill from afar. He was a high school journalist in Adel, Georgia, in the late 1930s when he first saw McGill at a Georgia Press Association gathering at the University of Georgia. McGill had recently been named executive editor and was on the stage with W. T. Anderson of the *Macon Telegraph*—"both great portly fellows. I thought, hey, I didn't know newspaper editors were so fat. Mr. McGill was rather corpulent." In 1948 he was assigned by the United Press to cover McGill's appearance before the grand jury in Lyons, Georgia. "I was so glad to have a chance to see him up close," he recalled. "Mr. McGill had simply written a couple of columns" against lynch mobs and "the grand jury was empaneled to whitewash it. They called Mr. McGill to rough him up. That's the way justice used to work in Georgia." Over the years, Patterson was fascinated with "the great range of his mind, the depth of his understanding, the utter charity in his heart."[75]

McGill addressed Patterson's weakness, a certain timidity. "Before you had the guts to declare yourself," Patterson told one interviewer, "there was a long period where you did things, said things, that you wished you hadn't. . . . If you were in journalism, like McGill and me, through this period each day was a new page in your life and you learned something." McGill coached him to write his heartfelt thoughts. "For years I had known that the racial positions of the South were wrong," Patterson said. "I didn't know you could say that out loud. And he taught me, yeah, you can say that out loud, you can say it in print, you can say it to a million people. That's what you got to do in the newspaper business." McGill stressed that boldness encouraged others to break their silence. "Small papers all over Georgia were reading this," Patterson said, "and saying, 'Look what they're saying in Atlanta. Maybe we can say it.'"[76]

In this context, it seemed strange to hear McGill conclude that he had been wrong to be so "pale" in defense of civil rights. Patterson reminded him that, given the constraints of newspaper ownership, community standards, and segregation—which until the early 1960s was still the law in Georgia—McGill's earlier columns represented as much as an editor could have published *at that time.*

"Yes," McGill conceded, "but I'm ashamed of them."[77]

No amount of defense swayed McGill from that conclusion, although other friends sympathized with his instinct for moderation. In the thick of the fight in Little Rock, Harry Ashmore understood the pressures toward self-censorship and self-preservation. "Our cautionary stance," Ashmore said, "frequently fell short of the demands of those who dealt in moral terms with the central issue posed by the Supreme Court's desegregation rulings." Ashmore argued that McGill—"situated . . . in the eye of the political hurricane that enveloped the region"—"was particularly vulnerable to criticism by those who equated compromise with lack of conviction." Ashmore had met McGill in 1948, when as editor of the *Charlotte News* he visited Atlanta to witness the showdown at the state capitol between Ellis Arnall and Herman Talmadge. Ashmore came to regard McGill as "more a preacher than anything else. Through the long season of the South's travail, his eloquent appeal to the conscience of his readers, well larded with hell-fire-and-brimstone denunciation of their prejudice, has provided one of the noblest chapters in the history of American journalism."[78]

Ashmore agreed with Patterson that the compromises—McGill's "pale tea"—had been a courageous path in the dark age of the late 1930s in the reign of Eugene Talmadge. "In the beginning," Ashmore said, "McGill's writing on racial issues frequently reflected the conflict between the demands of his quixotic nature and the restraints imposed upon the spokesman for an economically vulnerable publishing enterprise." It was true that, after 1950, the *Constitution*'s new owner, Governor Cox, "insulated McGill against the conformist pressures" of the conservative business manager, George Biggers. From 1954 on, McGill's courage showed in his defense of law as articulated in *Brown v. Board.*[79] If his columns had been "pale" they nevertheless stood out starkly in the 1940s and 1950s against the social landscape where polite society honored silence on "the situation." McGill's persistence in discussing racial justice in voting and education clearly had stimulated discourse in the public sphere, provoking many to begin to think and to break that silence.

This tide of civil disobedience that swept over the moderates and gradualists in the early 1960s and forced the issue of civil rights would taint McGill's self-image and confidence. Where for so long he had voiced the "conscience" of the South, a self-respecting defender of freedom, he now seemed, almost overnight, to have lost his moral leadership. Contrasted with the new generation of articulate and activist Negro leaders, McGill seemed almost an apologist for maintaining the status quo of the Old South for a little longer, for the sake of its own laws, or for transition, or for harmony. Despite his achievements, his reluctance to support nonviolent civil disobedience to legal segregation shamed him despite the profuse defenses offered by Patterson and Ashmore.

McGill worried for the Democrats' chances of retaking the White House. In the spring of 1960, Harold Martin attributed McGill's "blue mood" to Vice President Nixon's rising popularity. "He felt," Martin wrote, "that only an act of God could keep Nixon from the presidency." McGill told Martin he still distrusted Nixon for his part in fanning the frenzy in Congress over alleged Communists in government. Then, McGill had written to a friend that "Mr. Nixon is the type who would like to jail anybody who does not agree with him." In 1960 McGill asked Adlai Stevenson, "Do you think the Lord has decided we deserve to have Nixon, much as he sent Attila the Hun and other well-known scourges?"[80]

McGill's friends coaxed him out of his brooding. Carl Sandburg stopped over briefly in mid-July en route to Hollywood, where he had been hired as an adviser on a movie, *The Greatest Story Ever Told*. Gene Patterson, the new *Constitution* editor, drove Ralph to meet Sandburg's plane, which had a short layover in Atlanta. "Sandburg rode his wheelchair off the plane," Patterson recalled. "He'd hung something like saddlebags on the chair, and crammed them with books and newspapers, goat's milk and brandy. He'd brought his guitar, too." They drove him downtown to the Capital City Club, where they had reserved a small private room for lunch. "For most of a memorable afternoon we listened to that marvelous man talk in his Scandinavian singsong lilt, or else we heard him strum his guitar and sing folk melodies which I expect he made up. He was a happy and open man who readily displayed his admiration and affection for Mr. McGill. . . . He seemed immensely pleased with himself and eager to share his music, his stories and snorts of his brandy mixed with goat's milk, which we all declined with thanks."[81]

The summer's national conventions increased McGill's anxiety. He went to the Democratic convention in Los Angeles as a devotee of Adlai Stevenson and left stunned by the victory of the forty-three-year-old senator from Massachusetts, John F. Kennedy. "It is almost impossible to accept the fact of Kennedy's age." He rationalized that the Democrats had gambled on making a blatant "appeal to the feminine voters. The older ones wish to mother him. The young ones think in terms of the ads for convertible cars and imagine how nice it would be to be riding along the beach with the reddish-thatched young man." For his national readers he tried to fathom the nature of this young man, so rich, so bold, so well educated, intensely ambitious, mentally tough. Kennedy closed his acceptance speech with "a Biblical quotation which should please the Bible-loving South."[82]

The Republican convention of course had a different appeal for a Democrat. "We had a great time at the Republican convention," he wrote to Carl Sandburg, who was in Hollywood. "It was good, clean fun for a Democrat to watch the great agony of the Republicans as they kicked and screamed. . . . Otherwise it was fairly dull." Twice he and Harry Golden saw Stevenson, once in Stevenson's Chicago apartment to discuss gossip about Kennedy family politics as it affected Stevenson's possible role in a Kennedy administration. McGill told Sandburg that Golden, "with some time on his hands," accepted an invitation to address some Republican Jewish delegates. "He talked with them briefly, closing with a ringing appeal to write in the name of Adlai Stevenson on their ballots."[83]

The conventions in Los Angeles and Chicago provided reunions of McGill's circle of Brethren, men of decency and good conscience. Harry Ashmore had finally left daily journalism in 1959 after the *Gazette* restored its lost circulation and advertising and the Little Rock schools reopened. That year he acceded to his scholarly impulses and accepted appointment as a senior fellow in the "salubrious surroundings" of the Center for the Study of Democratic Institutions in Santa Barbara, California. They were joined in their rambling around Los Angeles by the young new editor, Bill Baggs, whom McGill had championed to lead Cox's *Miami News,* and McGill's own protégé at the *Constitution,* editor Gene

Patterson. While they could confide their hearts to one another, all the Brethren—Harry Golden, Jack Tarver, Johnny Popham, who had become editor of the *Chattanooga Times,* and the Atlanta civil rights activist John Griffin—were also fond of corralling one another's egos. McGill delighted in the banter they carried on in correspondence and in person. They chided each other on their "solemn admonitions to give up drink, to practice Christian charity, to lose weight, to adopt sounder political views, all couched in jesting terms."[84]

Away at conventions, they tended to forget restraints. Ashmore mocked McGill's "scabrous conduct" at both conventions. As a mere spectator among the Republicans, McGill, like Golden, had "time on his hands." One story Ashmore told on McGill was so outrageous that Harold Martin, in retelling it, used the journalist's protective word, "allegedly":

> McGill allegedly had to be restrained during an evening of merriment at the 606 Club from punching a surly Mafioso type who had refused to allow his date to dance with him. McGill had fallen into a crouch, fists extended, announcing to the surrounding company that he had learned from Jack Dempsey himself that it was always best to fight from a crouch. He had also gained a certain renown for gallantry when the club's stripper, who finished her act lighting the tassels attached to her breasts and revolving them in a clockwise direction, had trouble getting them to ignite. McGill, borrowing a cigarette lighter, leaped to her assistance and lit them for her.[85]

Patterson, a junior partner among the Brethren, focused instead on the wit and wisdom of his elders. Thirty years later he would recall, "sitting up late in Mr. McGill's hotel room in Chicago at the 1960 Republican convention, listening to Harry Golden, who sat in a straight chair in the center of the room, grinning like a Buddha and telling uncomplimentary stories about Richard Nixon."[86]

The South was up for grabs, McGill feared. Although the Democrats chose a southerner, Lyndon Johnson of Texas, as the vice presidential candidate, McGill still worried that the civil rights issue might push the

South to risk voting Republican for the first time since Reconstruction. On civil rights, Republicans in nominating Vice President Nixon cautiously followed his advice and tracked the Democrats' platform—with the object of winning the large Negro vote in the northern cities without alienating the white South.[87]

McGill did not doubt Nixon's popularity. The freshly nominated candidate was greeted warmly in Greensboro, North Carolina, where the sit-ins had started. He then entered Atlanta on August 26 to a tumultuous reception. Thousands "blotted the sidewalks" and gave Nixon an "unbelievable welcome" wrote the astonished journalist-author Theodore H. White. Without mentioning the race issue, Nixon championed states' rights and declared that the Democratic Party had deserted southerners. The crowd that listened, about 150,000, amazed McGill. "This has been the greatest thing in Atlanta," he mused, "since the premiere of *Gone with the Wind*." The day was all the more puzzling in November when Georgia voters chose Kennedy-Johnson by a greater margin (62.5 percent to 37.4 percent) than any other state except Rhode Island.[88]

After eight years of a Republican administration, McGill was eager to see Democrats restored to the White House for personal as well as party reasons. Despite being in the opposition party during Eisenhower years, McGill had done well. As he had hoped, he earned a national audience and added to his column's luster of the Pulitzer Prize. If the Democrats won the White House, McGill envisioned opportunities for national service as he had enjoyed during the Roosevelt and Truman administrations.

Early on, he decided to cover the national political campaigns more closely than he had done in the two Eisenhower-Stevenson races. Focusing more intently on presidential politics, he gave greater priority to his national audience and hoped the *Constitution* readers at home would read his columns all the same. Armed with the stature of syndication, McGill easily endeared himself to Kennedy campaign. Down the stretch toward November, he toured with Kennedy day and night in the South, Midwest and New York, each day cementing a relationship with the insiders who, come January, could consider McGill himself one of them.

The campaign invigorated McGill. Though sixty-two, he poured himself into the politicking more energetically than at anytime since

1942, when he and Ellis defeated Ol' Gene. Now of course he was addressing a national audience when he explained his enthusiasm: "I have been covering presidential candidates since Franklin Roosevelt's second term. They are all interesting. But, none has come along like this intense young man who believes."[89]

Untrammeled by reporters' restraints of "objectivity," McGill told his national audience that Kennedy, viewed by many Democratic officials as a loser, could actually win. "The only way McGill could have supported Nixon," Harold Martin would later note, "was for him to have been running against Count Dracula." Across the South, McGill noted that Democratic leaders "long-silent" since Los Angeles, had healed any rift with Kennedy, as witnessed by Georgia Sen. Talmadge's appearance with the candidate at Warm Springs, Georgia. McGill picked apart Nixon's weaknesses in the televised debates. In Ohio, McGill lauded the Kennedy organization's "belief that hard work will win and that genius, in politics as in art, is 90 per cent sweat."[90]

Kennedy's artistry in politics fascinated McGill and stimulated him from day to day. Not since the Truman campaign in '48 had he been so energized by a political fight. Over the years he conceded what Fannie Cheney and others knew, that he was addicted to politics. Politics, he wrote, was "a fascination that is almost narcotic." As one interviewer found, he was drawn to "the give and take," the "maneuverings, the organizing, the methods of bringing in the sheaves. . . . Mostly I go along with the policy of getting in there and firing both barrels—after you have something to fire."[91]

Whatever it took to beat Kennedy, McGill concluded, the Republicans didn't have. If Nixon loses, he said, "it will be because of party failure and an inability to match Kennedy's astonishing personal appeal." In Florida, McGill declared that the religious attack, on Kennedy's Catholicism and his alleged allegiance to the pope, had been "so scurrilous as to awaken the opposition of all those who believe in fair play. . . . The people could see that Pope John was not, as some of the preachers have been saying, right behind Sen. Kennedy." A day later, on October 20, he praised Kennedy as a man of beliefs, honesty, and courage. "Quite oblivious to thousands before him, cheering and beating their hands together, his mind runs fast. It is too swift to be other than honest. He does not calculate. . . . He forgot texts and talked at length about what he believes." In New York, McGill declared that "confidence and hope grow stronger in the Democratic camp. It sees a very real chance to win." On October 24, McGill noted that "nervous" Republicans wanted Nixon to "take off the gloves" and become "the old Nixon." But, McGill said, "so far, he has been neither the old nor the new but a combination unsatisfactory and unconvincing to himself or his supporters."[92]

McGill entered political frays with the intention of winning because, as he once said, losing was "awfully hard." The night Kennedy won, McGill was at his celebratory best. He and Patterson and other jubilants got out the newspaper's "little brass cannon, which Henry Grady had first fired in 1884 to celebrate the victory of Democrat Grover Cleveland." They lugged it a half-block to the pedestaled statue of Henry Grady in the middle of Marietta Street, where Patterson loaded the cannon with black powder. McGill applied a match to the touchhole. There was "a thunderous roar, a flash of flame, a billowing of smoke. The little cannon kicked back, climbing halfway up McGill's leg and peeling the skin from his shins and singeing his eyebrows. Bruised and triumphant, he returned to the office to start firing off a congratulatory telegram to President-elect Kennedy and a consoling message to Nixon."[93]

In a column, he said farewell to Stevenson, who, McGill said, had had the misfortune to run at the wrong time. "Kennedy," McGill noted, "is a happy combination of the intellectual and the politician." McGill hoped that Kennedy, now choosing his Cabinet, would nominate Stevenson. There was pressure for and against appointing Stevenson. McGill had heard through publisher John S. Knight and *New York Times* political writer Arthur Krock that Joe Kennedy, the president-elect's father, thought Stevenson "didn't deserve it and hadn't worked for it." Persuasive support for Stevenson, however, came particularly from Democrats in New York's Liberal Party, who had sought Kennedy's pledge to name him secretary of state in exchange for the 600,000 votes the party controlled in that state.[94] Kennedy compromised and appointed Stevenson U.S. ambassador to the United Nations.

The continuous travel on the campaign made McGill feel a toll on his health. After the election, he confided to Helga Sandburg, "I have not been taking proper care of myself but I hope to begin to do so now, at least reasonably so." The travels also caused him to miss his son's high school football games. Now fifteen, Ralph Jr. had made the varsity squad but "has been unhappy about getting in only a few games." In his absence, McGill had not been around to console "my youngin.'" McGill rationalized, "At his age, they rarely let you know what they are thinking." In November Ralph Jr. announced that the school magazine would publish some of his poems, which surprised dad and mom. "Lo and behold, it turns out that he has been working on his own in that exquisite Japanese-Cameo-Cut form of three line, seventeen syllable poems which seek to create either a precise image or mood. Also, without our knowing it, it develops he has been picked in the school choir to sing base."[95]

In December, McGill took the family on a two-week vacation, his first in two years, which as before turned out to have an element of serious work. Ralph headed his family to South Florida, where Kennedy was consulting with his aides and interviewing candidates for his administration. The McGills visited the president-elect at his winter home in Palm Beach. It is probable that Kennedy at this time mentioned that Ralph himself might wish to serve his country in an official capacity. A photograph of the occasion shows Kennedy in long white shirtsleeves, standing outside the house with Ralph, in a suit, Ralph Jr., and Mary Elizabeth. She held her hands clasped in front as she talked with the president-elect, showing no sign of the increasing pain caused by her chronic kidney condition. It was one of the last trips the family would take together. Within a month, Ralph would be busier than ever. He made plans to attend the inauguration, proud of his role in the Kennedy victory and expectant of some *official* role in a Democratic administration. To him, a government appointment was another step in the direction he had longed for since his Nashville years when he and Brainard Cheney were "bitten by the political bug." While Brainard had gone off to work for politicians in Washington and subsequently turned to writing novels, Ralph had stayed with journalism as a path to political influence. Now, journalism was satisfying that need for influence handsomely.[96]

16

Ambassador to Africa

The old Buddhists who said that climbing
Fuji was a cleansing experience were right.
—RALPH MCGILL, 1962

There is no mystery about the
instability of African politics.
—RALPH MCGILL, 1963

WITH KENNEDY'S VICTORY McGill expected to return to the arena of national politics, as both politician and editor. There was never any doubt that he would accept a position from which he could influence politics and government. He had thus far lived out his and Brainard Cheney's dream. In Tennessee, the best he had done was prejudice some voters for his publisher's candidate, a tame preview to his triumph with Ellis Arnall. Wartime and postwar assignments from Presidents Roosevelt and Truman and party loyalty through the Stevenson years now led to this expectation of reward as he waited to hear from the Kennedy team. Fannie Cheney always thought it ironic that her husband had gone to Washington to break into national politics and failed while Ralph worked his way into Washington politics by going to Atlanta.

While he meditated on Washington, McGill worried over the gathering storm at home. By early 1961, Negro leaders' demands for civil rights had quickly exhausted the ready supply. As black activists responded to the call, they soon outnumbered and overshadowed the white moderates in the ranks, McGill among them. The moderates had tried to interpret what was taking place. McGill had foreseen this swelling up of social unrest. "As McGill and a few others had long prophesied," Harry Ashmore wrote, "the mass of Southern Negroes simply rejected the institutions of segregation."[1]

As civil rights protesters walked in greater numbers into minefields of racial intolerance, McGill found it difficult to rationalize the value of *nonviolent* resistance that was clearly provoking predictable *violence*. Segregationists, aroused as if to war, countered with ugly reprisals, epithets, and physical attacks. Their lawlessness in defense of the law of segregation troubled McGill, who tried to calm irrational forces with doses of reason. He worried that the civil disobedience and resultant civic disturbances were damaging to the climate surrounding the issue of school desegregation. In an editorial which, if not written by McGill at least reflected his views, the *Constitution* noted that the student sit-ins were untimely: "At a time when Georgia is struggling toward a decision on the future of public schools, we trust the students will recognize they have established their protest and will refrain from unnecessary and unproductive repetitions."[2]

At the same time, the surge of reinforcements and enthusiasm into the civil rights movement guaranteed that the Negro protest would not be quelled until it had achieved reform. That May, McGill foresaw disaster for the new civil rights initiative—an integrated group of "freedom riders" who were challenging segregated seating in interstate commerce by riding across the South from Washington, D.C., to New Orleans. Sponsored by the Congress on Racial Equality (CORE), the riders arrived in Atlanta on May 13, where they dined with Martin Luther King Jr. before heading off in two buses into Alabama. The next day, outside Anniston, Alabama, a mob attacked one of the two buses, smashing windows and fire-bombing it; the nine freedom riders fled the bus. Some suffered from smoke inhalation; some were beaten before the Alabama state troopers arrived. Photographs of the Greyhound bus with black smoke billowing upward from its windows and open doors appeared on newspaper front pages across the nation. Freedom riders on the other bus, the Trailways, made it to the Birmingham station, where a mob waited for them. As a CBS radio correspondent reported, "Toughs grabbed the passengers into alleys and corridors, pounding them with pipes, with key rings, and with fists." While some had gaping wounds and broken teeth, one rider's injuries resulted in permanent brain damage and a paralyzing stroke. The first freedom ride confirmed McGill's fears but satisfied the goals to test civil rights in the South and to draw national public attention to blatant racism. "We were counting on the bigots in the South to do our work for us," CORE's new national director, James Farmer, said afterward. "We figured that the government would have to respond if we created a situation that was headline news all over the world."[3]

In contrast to Alabama, Atlanta seemed all the more an oasis of sanity. Its business and civic leaders, some of them grudgingly, had kept the schools. In response to court orders and the "inevitable," political leaders had made difficult compromises, risking the backlash of segregationists and hoping to carry the majority. So it was that Atlanta in 1961 desegregated its public schools and Georgia its state university, if only with a token number of blacks. Having crossed the threshold from "no, not one" to "yes, some," the stage was set for a generation of younger, transitional politicians who could carry the city, if not the state, toward fuller compliance with desegregation. By such a slim margin, Atlanta would gain the reputation as the "city too busy to hate" and secure a lead in the South's postsegregation sweepstakes for economic growth. To the segregation-forever factions, some politicians stressed how the state still controlled the process and could stall integration through lawful resistance, minimizing the effect. It was not unlike what southern Democrats had done for years in the Senate with the filibuster.

Outside Atlanta, the nonviolent movement besieged other bastions of segregation. In Nashville, the black student "stand-ins" by May 1961 had also desegregated theaters. Even amid the white backlash, Nashville had a cluster of whites who understood the inevitability and urgency of the civil rights movement and made practical concessions. At Nashville's Vanderbilt University, editors on the student newspaper, the *Hustler,* for which McGill had written his first journalism forty years earlier, were reading his syndicated columns on civil rights. In the spring of 1962, the editor of the *Hustler* was Lamar Alexander, later to become governor of Tennessee. "We talked about Ralph McGill," Alexander recalled. "We admired his views." By the spring of 1960, he said, some Nashville citizens had become embarrassed by the violent reaction to the black students, among them John Lewis, who became one of Martin Luther King's ardent disciples, a leader of the Student Nonviolent Coordinating Committee (SNCC) and eventually a congressman from Georgia. At Vanderbilt, Alexander thought the newspaper staff "made a difference," if not with the students perhaps with the trustees. "We provoked a debate in the undergraduate school." In a referendum on whether to admit Negroes, the Vanderbilt students voted no. "But the Board of Trustees the next month voted Yes."[4]

At this point in his career, McGill functioned on many levels. The newsman in him sensed the big stories, and the historian understood that he was making history. But he was also part preacher, as Harold Martin often observed, and the preacher in him cast his messages into near-sermons for the faithful and the damned. And the politician oversaw the whole crowd, trying to maintain balance between idealism and realism. The journalist, historian, and preacher dominated his columns, crowding out other voices. As he made the nation's and the world's troubles his own, readers found less buoyancy from McGill, less of the humorist and almost nothing of the intimate man who for years had made a habit of publicizing his personal life.

McGill's service to the Democratic presidents soon would constitute almost a second career in government, a dramatic increase in his national political connections. In the early 1940s, he had been a relative neophyte, his only national post being institutional membership in the low-profile politics of the American Society of Newspaper Editors. The trip around the world on behalf of press freedom provided his first national press exposure. Then and later on his mission to document the need for foreign aid to postwar Europe, he was a junior member of teams, almost a token southerner. Politically, he remained on the fringe without benefit of substantial personal or party prestige. In 1948, he collected some honor by demonstrating his loyalty to the Democratic Party and condemning Wallace's supporters and the Dixiecrats. After his stunning victory in November, Truman, smiling broadly and rousing laughter from his audience, thanked all Democrats, including those who came late to his campaign—the "September Democrats, the October Democrats, the Monday Democrats, the Tuesday Democrats," and those who flocked to him the day after victory—the "Wednesday Democrats." McGill escaped that stigma. His political reward in 1951 had been the modest appointment to the advisory panel for Atomic Energy Plant Construction, after he cleared his first FBI loyalty investigation. In the wilderness of the '50s, McGill's loyalty to Stevenson solidified his party credentials while, professionally, he outlasted or subdued his detractors, gained favor with the FBI, and won the Pulitzer Prize. A survivor, he now offered the Kennedy administration his unique voice, loyalty, stature as a southern spokesman, and a national audience.

McGill had been expecting an appointment since his amiable audience with the president-elect at Palm Beach. Kennedy had made him feel a part of his team of loyalists. As a start, the president soon appointed him to another advisory committee, the President's Advisory Committee on Labor and Management Policy, which met during the first week of March. Its national security designation was so low that the appointment required no FBI investigation. McGill was one of five "public" members, and he soon learned that the key members were some of America's business and labor union leaders—Henry Ford of Ford Motors, Walter Reuther, president of the United Automobile Workers, George Meany, president of the AFL-CIO, and Richard S. Reynolds Jr. of Reynolds Metals. Although he was more or less an observer, McGill saw this as a great opportunity to expand his Washington contacts. Indeed, on March 1 he was on the White House calendar and met briefly with the president.[5]

From this point on, he was firmly planted in two worlds, as a syndicated columnist and a Washington insider. The closer he got to the inside, the more he had to write about. This was the realization of his lifelong strategy at which Fannie Cheney marveled—how he infiltrated and influenced Washington politics from the outpost of Atlanta.

There is no evidence that McGill ever worried about a conflict of interest between journalism and politics. In all his career in the South he had never tried to be an "objective" reporter. He was instructed and guided by his *subjective* nature—his passions and his sense of right and wrong and whatever it was that drew him to poetry and the Bible. His sensibilities favored the new brands introduced by the *New York Times,* interpretive and in-depth reporting. Years before he had rejected the trend toward "objectivity" encouraged as professionalism by the American Society of Newspaper Editors and the Associated Press. "One of the curses of newspapering was, and is, the cult of objectivity," he had declared in 1959 in his Pulitzer Memorial Address. "Objectivity, of course, was a formula invented for escaping from the recklessly slanted news of the good old days. Print both sides, we said, and let the people make up their minds. But we overdid it." He blamed objectivity for its own host of sins, including the regrettable success of demagogues, among them Sen. Joseph McCarthy. "If a senator . . . spoke falsely, we didn't say so, even though we knew it, save maybe on the editorial page. And not always there. We waited for someone else to say the senator had lied and we then printed that. Both might have been false. But there was almost never any background or bracketed clarification of what the facts were. The trouble with American journalism's objectivity was that it wasn't really objective since it usually obscured the facts. . . ."[6] He had found journalism more practical than poetry and a somewhat indirect road to politics. He had formed an amalgam of two essential metals, journalism and politics, and had become a political journalist. It would have been impossible to separate the two without killing the patient.

With the Democrats now in charge, McGill felt remarkably welcome in making the rounds in Washington. On March 6, he was in Washington again. On his way to visit Attorney General Robert Kennedy, he stopped in at the FBI to "pay his respects to the Director." Hoover was out and McGill went on his way, but the momentary visit at 12:49 P.M. triggered three more pieces of paper by the record-conscious FBI— a memo and request for background, a background memo, and a letter of regret to McGill from Hoover: "I wish that I had been in my office at the time of your visit yesterday for I would have enjoyed very much being with you." An attached background memo documented the FBI's cozy relationship with the publisher: "We have had very cordial relations with McGill and he is on the Special Correspondents' List. He is also an SAC contact in our Atlanta Office. Largely due to McGill's influence, we have had very cordial relations with The Atlanta Constitution which has published favorable articles and editorials concerning the Bureau. On each of these occasions we have written a cordial note of gratitude to McGill." The memo reveals that, among the many FBI contacts, McGill had been raised to the decidedly higher status on the "Special Correspondents' List."[7]

At the moment of his visit McGill was past deadline on an article he had promised the FBI. In July 1960, Hoover's top assistant, Clyde Tolson, had directed Atlanta agents to ask McGill to write for the FBI's *Law Enforcement Bulletin*. The subject was sensitive: "Cooperation Between Law Enforcement and the Press." One of the FBI's publicity monitors, Milton A. Jones, noted, "Years ago we realized we could not put out an article on this subject under the Bureau by-line."[8] McGill was chosen for his stature—he had been appointed publisher of the *Constitution* on June 1— and because he was deemed "ardently in support of the Bureau." Tolson, however, wanted the "all-important" theme written to specifications— he wanted six specific points covered. More than a year later, in October 1961, McGill finally sent an article about law enforcement and teenage lawlessness, but it was "not by any means the type which we desired and expected from Mr. McGill," Jones's memo concluded. It was "controversial," and Jones recommended against publishing it: "This is a serious indictment of the liquor industry, however true it may be considered in many circles, it is not believed that we can afford to take on the liquor industry in the *LEB*." Tolson overruled Jones, not because he liked the article but because they had asked for it and got it and "we are stuck with it now and therefore it will have to be published. Henceforth we should use better judgment in soliciting articles." Likewise, Hoover wrote, "I agree with Tolson. We are stuck with it and will have 'to bear and suffer.'" The article was published in the February 1962 issue, and Hoover's office wrote McGill that "it was indeed a pleasure to publish this interesting and informative article."[9]

Late that year McGill got word that he was being considered for an appointment that required yet another security clearance. In late November 1961, about a month before Mary Elizabeth's hospitalization for her debilitating kidney ailment, the FBI's Washington office advised McGill that he was being investigated again. State Department officials made the request by letter on November 16, asking for a report in two weeks. On the twentieth, the FBI teletyped its Atlanta agents that McGill was "being considered for presidential appointment, exact position not stated" and ordered the agent in charge of the Atlanta bureau to assign "mature, experienced agents" to make a "thorough investigation covering character, loyalty, general standing and ability, accounting for entire adult life." As a concession to McGill's status in the community and in the FBI—as an official source sanctioned by Hoover—the FBI directive to Atlanta stipulated that agents "conduct no neighborhood investigation unless reason for doing so arises, at which time Bureau approval must be secured."[10]

For the rush assignment the FBI in Georgia and Tennessee assigned more than a dozen agents. From the tenor of their reports it was clear they were assuming nothing. They searched for any weakness of character or loyalty that might compromise McGill in, as they put it, "a sensitive position . . . of trust and confidence." Ironically, McGill's sympathy with the civil rights movement that made him attractive to the Kennedy administration made him suspect at the Hooverized FBI.[11]

Agents, as ordered, investigated McGill's financial status. The credit bureau had no McGill file. One interviewee noted that McGill was "not a businessman." But two banking officials agreed that the publisher was "financially sound." The agents made "no inquiries as to the source of his income." By 1961 McGill had fared better than he could have imagined, by trusting Jack Tarver's financial acumen. "Knowing McGill's ineptitude with money, Tarver had, in effect, taken over the management of his income," Harold Martin wrote. A single investment in a Cox enterprise, a paper mill, earned a profit of ninety-six thousand dollars. His daily column earned more after Tarver urged McGill to change to a syndicate that promoted him better. Even more impressive to bankers, however, was the value of McGill's stock-option arrangement with the Cox company. Harold Martin thought it curious that McGill worried about providing for his family when the value of his Cox stock was then approaching a million dollars. He had achieve status, fame, *and* wealth.[12]

Agents in Tennessee probed back to McGill's high school years at McCallie. They verified his marine service in 1918–19 and the credit records and whereabouts of his mother and three sisters. Two sisters lived around Chattanooga. Bessie was at Signal Mountain, and the police there told the agents that Bessie and her husband Paul Lewis were "known as persons of good character, reputation, and loyalty." Ralph's unmarried sister, Sarah Irene McGill, looked after their eighty-three-year-old mother, Mary Lou, in the modest family home on Kirby Street where the Ralph had grown up. Indiana agents made a character check on Ralph's third sister, Lucille. Her husband, Arthur Staley, had died in 1960 and Lucille was working and living in the St. Regis Apartments on Fourteenth Street, where she had resided for almost twenty years. Someone there told the agent that "he has never questioned her character or loyalty to the United States." Neither Arthur nor Lucille had a police record.[13]

Agents in Tennessee and Georgia interviewed sixty-five people who knew McGill socially and professionally. Their reports indicated the FBI's concerns—McGill's general reputation, his political philosophy, accounts of his drinking problems—contained in previous FBI reports in 1951 and 1952, and noted his current reputation for integrity and good character. Most of the people were asked whether they could recommend him "for a position of trust and confidence." It took agents several days longer than expected to finish the interviewing, but in the end McGill cleared. On December 12, about two weeks after their deadline, W. V. Cleveland at FBI headquarters reported, "All persons reported favorable information concerning Mr. McGill and recommended him for a position of trust and confidence."[14]

The shadow raised by tales of McGill's alcoholic adventures was lifted. "It was stated, however, several years ago he had a 'drinking problem,'" Cleveland added, "but is not known to use alcoholic beverages to excess in recent years." Neutralized again were the other two suspicions— his involvement with the Southern Conference for Human Welfare and the Southern Negro Youth Conference, both still branded as Communist. Cleveland noted that McGill "explained his participation in these organizations to the Bureau and State Department stating he did not know their purpose and denounced them after determining they were communist fronts."[15]

The people contacted by the FBI neither condoned nor condemned McGill's philosophy on racial relations. "Persons interviewed," wrote Cleveland, "stated Mr. McGill in his editorials spoke out forcefully concerning his convictions for desegregation in the South and advocates a change in the South in its attitude toward the minority race." There followed a notable suggestion of FBI sympathy for a man beleaguered by illegal reprisals. Once, McGill had reported to the FBI that vandals had shot up the mailbox at his home. "Because of his editorials he has been subjected to nuisance and obscene telephone calls." The FBI had decided "because of the prominence of Mr. McGill" not to conduct "neighbor-hood investigations." Cleveland reminded that McGill was indeed a friend of the FBI. "Bureau files indicate we have had cordial relations with Mr. McGill and his newspaper. He is on the special correspondent's mailing list." McGill by now was well versed about what the FBI wanted to know. Often, agencies asking him to participate in executive or military func-tions simply requested existing files rather than asking for new investiga-tions. In the Washington press corps, McGill might have had the most actively consulted FBI dossier.[16]

That same month, as he waited for the next White House assignment, he worried with a sadness he could not share with the public or con-ceal from friends. On Christmas Day 1961 Mary Elizabeth became des-perately ill. Her pain and his son's suffering haunted McGill. Over the years, during Ralph's constant travels, Mary Elizabeth and Ralph Jr. had grown close. In that sense it seemed to him that her death would be a greater loss to the boy than if he died. Ralph's letters reveal that he was not sure he fathomed his son's feelings. Now, suddenly, the sixty-four-year-old traveler and the sixteen-year-old high school senior were left alone, together, to wait, week in and week out, in hospital rooms. While the young man did his homework for his final classes at the Westminster School or thumbed through magazines, the old man duti-fully met the demands of his daily deadlines. Jack Tarver had urged him to change syndicates, and his column now appeared in fifty-four newspapers and he was earning more for it. When that was done, he agonized over the last chapters of the memoir Ted Weeks was urging him to complete. The Atlantic Monthly Press wanted to publish it in the spring. He had always had the ability to work wherever and how-ever, and now he wrote from a bedside chair, using his lap for a desk, spilling his words onto the lines of a yellow legal pad.

The long period of waiting ended in March. On the first day of spring, at eight o'clock in the morning, "she went serenely," as Eugene Patterson wrote, "undefeated but overcome by months of supremely gal-lant struggle." At her bedside, "a fine son of 16, bearing himself like a man, kept vigil bravely and read a prayer for her in the last hour." While news headlines on page one of the *Constitution* and on page thirty-five of the *New York Times* categorized her as an appendage, the wife of the publisher, Patterson chose as his focus something special to her: the backyard herb garden that gave her solace and the sun dial in the midst of it. "Around the pedestal of the little sun dial grow the sprigs of tarragon and marjoram, oregano and chives, which she planted for her vinegars and spices. . . . And on the face of the sun dial . . . an inscription in the iron gleamed in the sunshine. She had read it many times as she worked among her herbs and flowers. It said: 'Count none but Sunny Hours.'" That was how Patterson explained her "remarkable resistance and defiance" of the illness that had lived with her many of her fifty-seven years.[17]

During those weeks of waiting, McGill resolved to spend more time with his son in the months before he went off to college in the fall. Harold Martin sensed that McGill "felt a sense of guilt at having so often left his family alone as he made his long journeys overseas." Immediately after the funeral, father and son flew to Miami, where as guests of Ralph's friend Bill Baggs, who was editor of the *Miami News*, they spent time together, walking the beaches and fishing. During the spring, they spent far less time together than McGill hoped. He had imagined that Ralph Jr. would need more of his companionship, but as it developed he found himself more in need of his son. Ralph Jr. began dating a girl who lived twenty miles away and often came home well after midnight. Over martinis at his house, McGill confided to Harold Martin that the worst times for him were the weekends when the boy sometimes telephoned to explain he was staying with a friend. "Look, I know I'm behaving like an old hen with one chick," he told Martin, "but what do you do?"[18]

That spring, McGill asked Julia to help. She had become much more than a cook to them during Ralph's absences and Mary Elizabeth's illnesses. The boy thought of her "like a second mother to me. She was there before I was born; she looked after me all during my growing up," he later told Harold Martin. "She'd say, as if it were her own idea, that I ought to stay home with him more. And I would try. But I was seventeen, and much in love." Some nights after a quiet dinner they both settled down, McGill to read and write and Ralph to study. But that spring especially, despite their worries about whether Ralph would flunk Latin and fail to graduate, the young man seemed uninspired by his schoolbooks. McGill tried something else, asking Julia to prepare special dinners for

Ralph and his girlfriend and on weekends bigger dinners for them and their friends. "But nothing did much good. Except for a few evenings my dad and I, then and for a few years thereafter, were strangers. No matter how we tried, we could not break through that barrier of years, of shyness, whatever it was, that kept us apart."[19]

McGill determined to bridge that gap. He was invited to travel to Japan to speak with newspaper publishers, and the sponsors arranged the expenses so he could bring Ralph for a month. In the meantime, commencement at Westminster School turned out to be happy occasion, with Ralph, now set to attend Wesleyan University in Connecticut, among the graduates listening to his father giving the commencement address. By the spring of 1962, McGill was being asked to attend numerous commencements, some of which he had to decline. Two days later he spoke in a drizzle at the stadium commencement at the University of North Carolina at Chapel Hill. After a few hours sleep he flew back to Atlanta's Morehouse College to share the commencement platform with President Nathan Pusey of Harvard University. Morehouse president Benjamin Mays, who had been a mentor to Martin Luther King Jr., revered McGill and now presented him an honorary doctor of humanities degree of which McGill was extremely proud. The citation read: "You told the people the truth . . . at the risk of losing social prestige, friends and even life."[20]

By July father and son were far from home, doing together what was unimagined six months earlier. In Japan McGill was told of the natural wonder of witnessing the sunrise from the peak of Mount Fuji, up 12,388 feet, and he determined to make the ascent. With two guides, they set out the day before, camping below the peak until early the next morning. "Those who are determined to see the sunrise . . . begin their climb from the eighth way-station not later than 2 A.M." The cold numbed their gloved hands and Ralph's eyes wept from "the whipping gusts of biting wind." Along the way, up the rocks and across loose lava stones, they passed some who rested, exhausted, and others turning back. The last five hundred feet up a "dark, bare rocky slope" were "agony for those who come to the climb without young legs." A photograph taken at the top pictured the exhausted father staring at the lens and his slightly taller son, his chilled hands sunk into the pockets of his windbreaker, both wearing scarves and hiking boots. Standing between them was a beaming young Japanese woman, Kimiko "Kim" Kawato, a translator of haiku poems, whom McGill claimed was "sent along by the Japanese newspaper publishers and editors association to summon medical aid in case I should collapse." McGill said Kim pushed him from behind on the last few steps to the top. He wrote eloquently about the adventure as a cathartic, religious experience:

> One stands there, legs trembling, lungs laboring and turns to wait for the sun. The dark awesome slopes of the old mountain already are softening in the growing light. . . . The flaming edge of the sun appears, causing the whole sky to turn rosy, then a deeper vermillion, as the round disc of day rises above the horizon. . . . Those who dwell on the earth below have not yet seen the sun. It seems to throb with flame and to have being only for those who have earned it with their climb. Shouts go up. Tired, grimy faces, streaked with the dark volcanic dust, are rapt. . . . The old Buddhists who said that climbing Fuji was a cleansing experience were right.[21]

What he didn't write, but what Harold Martin surmised, was that this Japanese adventure with Ralph Jr. ended his period of mourning. Over the years of Mary Elizabeth's chronic illness he had adapted to worry and finally grief. Now suddenly he was freed. Other friends sensed that the month in Japan revived Ralph's spirit from morbid depths. Could he, at sixty-four, be interested again in entertaining women? The journalist Sander Vanocur had seen McGill in Tokyo and reported to McGill's friends that the widower climbed Fuji with a woman and suggested McGill had adventures with other Japanese ladies. Harry Golden at the *Carolina Israelite* amplified Vanocur's story when in August he wrote to Adlai Stevenson, now President Kennedy's ambassador to the United Nations, sending copies to Harry Ashmore and Baggs. "He [Vanocur] told me that Ralph McGill went wild in Tokyo—with women," Golden said. "The report is that Ralph was seen with two or three at a time and as if that wasn't enough he spent every following morning at those Sanno steam baths." Ribbed by all of them, McGill wrote to Stevenson denying the womanizing rumors and contending that Golden, Ashmore, and Baggs "seem disturbed because my son and I climbed Mt. Fuji. This is very easy for me to understand. These critics could never do better than lift one foot as high as a barroom rail. Naturally it disturbs them to read about someone climbing Mt. Fuji." At home, he confided to Harold Martin that he was so charmed by Kimiko that he told her, "If I were thirty years younger, I would ask you to marry me." To which she answered, "I would say yes."[22]

In the fall of 1962, with Ralph gone to Wesleyan, McGill plunged into his work. Alone, his career became his refuge and preoccupation. He discarded the trappings of family life as if they were old clothes. With no one at home but the cook Julia, he seemed to lose interest in meals and experimented with dieting, eating so little that his weight sank from 225 to 187, worrying Harold Martin by his "drawn and bony" look. He further astounded his friends with his refusal to drink, a temporary abstinence as it turned out, claiming that even a small drink made him ill for a day. His habitual pastimes lost appeal and he looked to become absorbed in what was now most interesting—his assignments from the White House.

The FBI report to the State Department cleared McGill for an exhausting challenge. The Kennedy coterie appointed him to the President's Advisory Committee of the Arms Control and Disarmament Agency, which drew upon Ralph's background with the atomic energy planning. Because it was a high-security assignment, dealing in classified information, he could not use the information as grist for his columns. Recently approved by Congress, the agency's mission was to develop a global nuclear nonproliferation treaty by which nuclear nations would limit their weapons and other countries would agreed not to build them. The nuclear arms race of the 1950s made it evident to the United States and the Soviet Union that each could destroy other several times over. Nuclear terror had led to a balance of terror. Whoever attacked first, intentionally or by accident, faced certain retaliation. Both faced the certainty that a massive effort must be made to protect against mutual destruction. At the same time, politicians now questioned the practice of testing nuclear bombs by detonating them in the atmosphere. Scientists measuring atmospheric effects reported alarming levels of radiation circling the earth. For the first time, the public became concerned that radiation from distant tests could be carried through the atmosphere and contaminate food on the other side of the world.

McGill's committee worked with their counterparts from several nations. Over the months, the work gave him dark insights into the political attraction of "nuclear status"—the prestige accruing to a nation with nuclear reactors and the Bomb. The dynamics of nationalism, an almost irrational drive to serve *national* interests, seemed to overpower the threat of *global* destruction. He discovered that the two superpowers could more easily agree on the main points of a nonproliferation treaty, but France and other nations expressed a right to do what was necessary in their national interest to attain nuclear status. As he explained to his lifelong friend Reb Gershon, "The small nations take the highly nationalistic but somewhat understandable attitude of why should the small nations be excluded from something the big ones have? This indicates a complete lack of awareness of the real and terrible meaning of nuclear energy."[23]

The frequent trips to Washington whet his appetite for wider travel. Late in 1962 he got his wish as the White House decided he was uniquely qualified to undertake a goodwill mission to nations in West Africa newly freed from centuries of colonial rule. His briefings in Washington added little to what he already knew: The new African leaders looked suspiciously at relationships with the United States, allied as it was with the European nations which in 1885 had partitioned the continent so each would have a share. Along this former "slave coast" America's credibility was vulnerable to racial propaganda. America had been the last major importer of West African slaves, and the last Western nation to abolish slavery. America still suppressed the rights of its freed blacks, especially in the segregated South. In competition for influence, the Soviet Union, not having existed in the age of slavery, could put forth a clean record on race. It was easy enough to amplify horrors about the plantation South, lynchings, the Klan, and day-to-day civil repression. Long before the Soviets arrived, stories of ancestors sold in chains to America had become legends, repeated generation after generation in the rich oral tradition of West Africa.

From his Western viewpoint, McGill believed he understood the contemporary concerns as well. After breaking the bonds of colonialism and achieving *political* independence, West Africans now guarded against Western "neocolonialism," an *economic* hegemony. In the flush of independence, the West African nations opened to Communist assistance, as when Guinea accepted large financial credits from the Soviet Union and opened links with China. All of West Africa could tilt to the Socialist/ Communist sphere with long-range geopolitical implications. In a worst-case scenario, the Republicans might ask, "Who lost Africa?"

Few Americans were better postured to defuse the race issue than this ardent southern editor and political ally who exuded goodwill. For a quarter century McGill had written reasonably in support of justice for the Negro. His career as a civil rights advocate made him a symbol of an enlightened breed of American. As a citizen ambassador, he hoped to lift the debate to the realm of *human* rights. It seemed a mission for which he had been preparing a lifetime. Apart from his mission to persuade doubters, McGill would be acquiring information useful to the White House. He was scheduled to report to President Kennedy by late March. As a State Department envoy, he was to have exceptional access, including an appointment with one leader of special interest to the Kennedy administration.

Kennedy needed to know more about the intentions of Ghana's charismatic president, Kwame Nkrumah. Since independence in 1958, Nkrumah had united Africans in former French West Africa into an economic and military power bloc, a "union of independent African states" with a free trade zone and financial institutions. In 1961, with Morocco, he aligned with Egypt's Socialist leader, Gamal Abdel Nasser, in proclaiming the "charter of Casablanca" for a military alliance. In 1962 the "Casablanca bloc" created an African Development Bank and a "high military command" with headquarters in Ghana under an Egyptian general.

McGill set off in January to speak at universities and visit leaders in six nations, starting in Senegal. The itinerary of twenty-five thousand miles in a little over two months would carry him from Senegal to Guinea, Ghana, Togo, Dahomey, Nigeria, and the Congo. It was his longest trip abroad since the editors' mission for freedom of the press in 1945. They had bypassed black Africa; now, he steeped himself in African history and culture and politics, which he soon passed on to his readers. In his column datelined "Dakar, Senegal—'Afrique Occidental Francaise,'" he traced the French influence back to 1659, when Norman adventurers with "great expectations" came in search of gold. Now, three hundred years later, the French had released their grip. McGill sympathized with a four-year-old nation struggling with a stunted, undiversified economy (based on peanuts and phosphates), no educational system, and too many *immediate* needs. Now it was the Africans who had great expectations: "There is so much to be done . . . and there is understandable impatience. Yesterday is gone. It is today and tomorrow in Africa."[24] He could sympathize readily as he likened their plight to that of the conquered southern states which "were for generations in a colonial status."[25]

His pieces drew readers into the politics of West Africa by charming them first, with a tour of the old city. He walked the streets of the coastal settlement of Saint Louis, "the intellectual and cultural center of Senegal." He recognized a familiarity, a link from Old World to New World, "something like the older sections of the New Orleans French quarter . . . the same narrow streets, wrought-iron balconies, and shuttered doors." The mood changed from enlightened tourist to American ambassador when at the upper school he was presented as the featured speaker. Students crowded into a dining hall, heard his prepared remarks, and then probed him about racism. "Their newspapers and radios had told them the worst," McGill reported. "They know about Little Rock, even though that was a story of six years ago. And they most assuredly have on their tongues questions about James Meredith and Mississippi. One tall, young Senegalese asked, beating his chest with a clenched fist, 'Tell us about it. It hurts us in here.'" It was a tough audience. He conceded the first round. "One begins by admitting the problem," he wrote. He followed up with a few defensive strokes: "The progress made far outweighs the incidents of violence." He thought he scored points for America, with his impression that the students "are cheered by reports of what has been done voluntarily in other Southern states."[26]

The slave coast in Guinea brought him face-to-face with reminders of *the trade*. A collector of antiquities wanted him to have a string of porcelain beads. In his hand they felt cool. The beads had been currency, exchanged to buy a slave. "It shook one, somehow . . . to know that more than a century ago they had been a part of the price paid to sell some man or woman into chattel slavery." In reverie he imagined "the hour was early morning. The sea was in sight, looming against some of the masses of red-black iron-ore rocks which ring the Guinean coast. When the long lines of captives, brought from the inland, came to the beaches and for the first time saw the always curling, foaming sea, they must have known then the acid taste of bitter, hopeless despair and deep, unbounded terror."[27]

Obligatory speaking duties paled in comparison to his favorite pastime, interviews with men of power and influence. Africa's charismatic political leaders fascinated him, these men whose political ideologies seemed mysteries to the West. They were less mysterious when met face to face. "As one looks, listens and learns one comes to know that while there are of course Marxist Socialists in Africa, few of the Socialists really have any ideology." McGill saw the blazing light of West Africa through the prism of economics. "They have little capital. They have resources but are unable to mobilize them" while their people, "who had believed that independence was a sort of panacea, are impatient. There is no mystery about the instability of African politics."[28] In Senegal he sang the praises of that country's poet-president, Leopold Senghor, the "brilliant . . . poet, philosopher, teacher and prophet." In Ghana, a visit with the American expatriate W. E. B. DuBois left McGill with "a feeling of having emerged from a place far back in time as we came out of the high-ceilinged home. There was a lot of history in the slender, sick and slowly dying man."[29] Most "puzzling" was Ghana's premier Kwame Nkrumah.

McGill considered it good luck to have forty-five minutes with Nkrumah. As McGill afterward recounted the story for an oral history interviewer, he made careful notes, anticipating Kennedy's compelling interest in this ruler. McGill knew Nkrumah had spent twelve years in the United States, part of the time as a student at Lincoln University. "He told me at one time of being desperate, broke, out of money, and sleeping on park benches." It had been an "embittering experience," McGill later advised Kennedy, and Nkrumah as premier was "no friend of this country." McGill was right up to a point. If he distrusted America, Nkrumah at least admired some Americans. The African leader in 1957 put Martin

Luther King Jr. into the *international* spotlight. Recognizing the impact of the Montgomery bus boycott, Nkrumah promptly invited King to Ghana's independence day ceremonies. McGill tried, as he had with the students in Senegal, to draw him into a discussion about his feelings about race, but he would not take the bait. It was a closed subject. "I thought then," he said, "that this was because at that time he had had a shock in that some of his students in Moscow had been physically attacked and had suffered beatings, including some head wounds that had to be bandaged. And, indeed, some of these had arrived in Ghana while I was there. I've had the feeling that this led to a turn by Nkrumah toward the Chinese."[30]

The ambassadorial mission ended officially with McGill's report to Kennedy. McGill met with Kennedy for their longest interview. Kennedy sat in a rocking chair and rocked gently as McGill talked. After McGill delivered his impressions and advice about American relations with black Africa, the question of civil rights led Kennedy to ask about his political problems with Georgia's Senator Richard Russell. Kennedy was "troubled with civil rights legislation and with other domestic legislation" over which Russell had leverage. Russell blocked Kennedy's legislative objectives in civil rights, and Kennedy wanted to avoid an "open break" with this senator who influenced so many votes. "I admire Dick Russell very much," Kennedy said, "and I wonder if you could explain to me a man like him. . . . The whole world is changing, and the whole nation is changing. And yet this gifted man remains adamant and defiant in the matters of any measures which tend to enter the field of race—civil rights." Was Russell ill? Kennedy told McGill he had heard that Russell "was more and more withdrawing" and his "friends were concerned that he was becoming lonely, that he was not well, that he tended to withdraw more and more from contact with fellow senators." The questions and pondering about Russell went on for about twenty minutes, and it seemed to McGill as if Kennedy regarded Russell as "a man of great gifts and potential who had yet found it in his mind to carry on what really seemed to be a petty, personal . . . oh, what shall we say? Not a vindictive feeling because I don't think the president felt there was any of that in it. But he wondered why a man of such gifts would have this sort of attitude when all the world was changing, when his own state was changing, when his fellow senator was changing."[31]

Kennedy was clearly puzzled how Senator Herman Talmadge, steeped more deeply in the tradition of race-baiting demagoguery, now seemed far more amenable to civil rights than Russell, who was "clearly adamant." Kennedy didn't know whether Senator Talmadge had changed any of his person opinions, but Talmadge "knew realistically that it was no longer possible to deny the qualified Negro the vote, to have jobs, to participate equally in all of the gifts of our Constitution and citizenship in a pluralistic society."[32]

McGill, for his part, was reading into Kennedy's intentions his own developed arguments for civil rights and for the role government should play in assuring those rights, all of which had been confirmed by the African journey. McGill shared his reasoning in an interview with a professor of speech communication, who classified McGill's "six premises from which he refracted public arguments." First, the pragmatic McGill believed in pursuing "policies that are feasible." Second, as he had insisted after *Brown v. Board of Education,* "laws should be obeyed." He practiced the third as much as he preached it: "Free individuals have a moral responsibility to oppose wrong." The white code of keeping silence about "the situation" had compounded the sin of racism. Fourth was his rock-bound belief, derived from his upbringing and confirmed in every stage of his career, in the promise of education as "requisite to individual and community progress." The fifth, one he had risked most to express in print, was his commitment to the spirit of the Constitution, that "all persons should be granted the rights and privileges of full citizenship." Lastly, he held that the southern states which had blocked civil rights had violated their mandate to "ensure the rights and privileges of their own citizens."[33]

On that evening in the White House as the clock neared 7:00 P.M., both the president and editor could see from a high place the tide that would overcome the resistance of all who marched with Russell. It was as if Russell were playing a role expected of him, a southern archetype making a last stand in a wasteful war he could not win. It would take time to wear down the resistance. Certainly they could have expected from the dark pit of racism more political eruptions and public upheavals.

17

Law of Compensation

All things are double one against another,
said Solomon. The whole of what we know is a
system of compensations. Every defect in one manner
is made up in another. Every suffering is rewarded;
every sacrifice is made up; every debt is paid.
—Ralph Waldo Emerson

To see the self-consciousness of most of those
who boarded a bus and sat at the front or center,
after a lifetime of going to the rear, was both an
accusation and a compensation.
—Ralph McGill

The violence unleashed upon civil rights activists in the spring of 1963 astounded and disappointed McGill, but also stoked his fighting spirit. During May, when the Rev. Martin Luther King Jr. staged sit-ins and demonstrations in Birmingham, extremists and police retaliated with customary weapons, the one with dynamite bombs, the other with official instruments, hoses, cattle prods, and trained police dogs. The fact that news photographs and television footage showed it all to the nation surely would have some impact.

McGill, in New York at the Carnegie Foundation for discussions about international tensions, took breaks to phone home for news. As he told Harold Martin, there was supreme irony in his being there to consider the world's problems while situations at home, in his own South, were as flammable, if not more so. Another irony was that his own newspaper did not send a reporter to cover the Birmingham confrontations, relying instead on "objective" wire service reports. Nor was he or his associate editor Eugene Patterson cleared to go. The *Constitution* had decided against giving the story major attention in its pages. As Harold Martin knew, Jack Tarver made these coverage decisions based on advice of the *Constitution*'s lawyers. In New York, far from the action, McGill wrote in the *Herald Tribune* that the Birmingham situation made him feel "an occasional, near compulsive wish to break suddenly into loud, despairing laughter. Birmingham was smoking with hate." Given that city's "long and ugly history of violence," he wrote later in the *Constitution,* any act of hate was conceivable.[1]

Through the summer, tension escalated between demonstrators and police and extremists. Official violence endorsed by Birmingham police commissioner Eugene "Bull" Connor provoked Negro resolve and white resistance. Activists now seemed attuned to the need to risk physical injury and imprisonment. The resistance, both legal and outlaw, seemed willing to dispense both. In Jackson, Mississippi, Negro students took cues from Birmingham and in late May staged sit-ins and demonstrations. Two weeks later, an assassin in Jackson shot the acknowledged NAACP leader, field secretary Medgar Evers, as he was entering his home. The ambush was a flashpoint in the midst of a period of rising protest, as statistics later proved. At the Southern Regional Council in Atlanta, Harold Fleming later noted that during the ten weeks after Birmingham there were 758 racial demonstrations in 186 cities and 14,733 arrests. Birmingham had become a model for subduing demonstrators. Two weeks later in Danville, Virginia, more than forty blacks were hospitalized after confronting authorities who were armed with fire hoses and nightsticks.[2]

By summer's end, extremists in Birmingham raised violence to a new level. On Sunday morning September 15, Negro children were attending Sunday school in Birmingham's Sixteenth Street Baptist Church when a deafening explosion tore the room apart. When the smoke settled, four girls ages eleven to fourteen had been killed. Twenty-two more children were injured. Searching the rubble, investigators found the cause—dynamite.

Dynamite had become the signature weapon of racists. Now it was obviously being aimed to take lives, where previously it seemed targeted to destroy buildings—schools and churches and the homes of targeted civil rights activists and blacks moving into all-white neighborhoods. In Birmingham alone more than forty bombings had gone "unsolved,"

McGill noted. Now the dynamiters deliberately targeted innocent children "at the Sunday school hour, with the full knowledge that it would be crowded with children and that some would be killed and wounded." McGill was touched to the quick. This new twist on lynching—the bomb had displaced the noose—sacrificed innocents. It spewed from a new depth of hatred. Not only had the perpetrators gone beyond the bounds of law. They had stepped outside the human fold. Others later acknowledged this deed as the nadir of depravity.[3]

McGill traced the blame higher than the anonymous beasts who murdered children. The killers had received their cue, he said, from the demagogic rhetoric of Alabama's "segregation forever" governor. Whether George Wallace intended the murders of innocent children was not the point. He had unleashed the mad dogs. To McGill, Wallace's announcement of a five-thousand-dollar reward for the arrest of the men responsible was a pitiful effort to distract the public from his culpability. As he had explained after the 1958 Atlanta temple bombing, McGill now told his national audience that the "extremists in high and low places—who inflame by word and example—have for a long time been sowing the seeds now come to harvest." Could Alabama's demagogue weasel away from the commonsense cause-and-effect relationship between his fiery rabble and these demonic deeds? "Governor Wallace, for all his urgings that there be no violence, cannot escape the widely held opinion that he has, by his closing of school doors against court orders and his appeals to the people 'to keep up the fight,' contributed to the climate of general resistance by those whose only concept of 'fighting on,' is dynamite and rifle and pistol fire."[4]

The publication of his book on the South lifted McGill's spirits and his stature. Appearing in the spring shortly after his return from Africa, *The South and the Southerner* was his third book, but the first that was more than a compilation of his columns. Much of it had been written in the same impromptu manner as some of his columns, as some of its brighter epiphanies came to him while he was traveling and scribbling on yellow legal pads. Toward the end, the task wore on him, but Ted Weeks kept in touch and monitored McGill's pace. "It was slowed down by the fatal illness of his wife," Weeks noted, "and by a plaintive warning from McGill's dedicated secretary, Grace Lundy, asking for an extension of the delivery date." Lundy told Weeks, "I can tell Mr. McGill is getting very tired." Delivered at last of the manuscript, McGill confided to Harold Martin that he hoped the book "would not fall on its face." In fact, it sold modestly well, including more than four thousand copies in Atlanta. When autographing his books, McGill sometimes inscribed his deep sentiments. In signing the title page of *A Church, A School* for Ralph Jr.'s friend and schoolmate Bill Schwartz, McGill shared his sense of the South's triumph and his wish for a longer tenure in it: "To Bill Schwartz III—who had the great luck to be a young Southerner at a time when the South was required by history and events to make great decisions."[5]

The South and the Southerner won McGill respect and appreciation, especially from those who already admired him. Weeks hailed it as "the most telling and noble book I have read about the South in my time. . . . True and searching and compassionate." As soon as the book came off the press, Weeks recommended it for the five-thousand-dollar Atlantic Nonfiction Prize, which McGill won. "No award I have ever had a hand in has given me more pleasure than this," Weeks wrote McGill. Other friends in publishing chimed in. Harry Golden wrote to Weeks that some credit belonged to McGill's *editors,* including the persistent Peter Davison: *Atlantic Monthly*'s "handling of Ralph McGill's great book has produced one of the outstanding bit of journalism I have seen in a long time." In a larger sense, the book explained McGill's rather complicated divided loyalties to the South and to humanity, as well as his place in journalism history. It was autobiography with a purpose, and that purpose, as Harry Ashmore eloquently put it that summer, was a mixture of moral preaching and practical politics.[6]

During the summer, Ashmore published his review, in the tone of a tribute to the author with characteristic eloquence. In the *Virginia Quarterly Review,* he ruminated on the political importance of McGill's origins in Unionist East Tennessee, "where race had not become an obsession," and his quarter century as an editorial page columnist who was essentially "more a preacher than anything else" but who was also, "when the occasion demands, a political fixer. . . . Through the long season of the South's travail, his eloquent appeal to the conscience of his readers . . . has provided one of the noblest chapters in the history of American journalism." McGill had held to his convictions against a cast of demagogues, embittered segregationists, and spineless, silent "businessmen and ministers and lawyers and professional men" who "acquiesced in the senseless last-ditch tactics of men like Orval Faubus and Bull Connor— and did so knowing that these maneuvers would fail and leave behind them a new heritage of bitterness."[7]

McGill declared the battle for civil rights nearly won by the summer of 1963. Martin Luther King's nonviolence movement had gone on "to victory after victory." In a period of eighteen months, more than two hundred southern cities had "altered in some degree their pattern of segregation." Ashmore concluded that the segregationists had run their course, their arsenals were empty, their arguments bankrupt. Nine years after *Brown v. Board of Education,* it "was no longer logical to rationalize the failure of senators, congressmen, governors, mayors, editors, clergymen, businessmen and publishers who in 1954 had let the golden moment slip and failed in leadership by silence or, worse, by inciting mobs and riots."[8]

In retrospect, McGill acknowledged that the turning point in the civil rights movement had come long before anyone realized it. He referred to the lunch-counter sit-ins and other demonstrations, the front-line actions that directly confronted de jure segregation. Certainly he had been among the cautious, rational ones, an defender of law and order, who at first questioned the wisdom of going *outside* the law to confront Jim Crow. As a gradualist who preached obedience to law, he thought it wise to avoid confrontations that provoked the hatemongers and alienated the silent majority. "Those who had been demanding that the processes of law be honored in the school cases were impaled on the hook of this dilemma," he noted. To advocate lawlessness now gave the dark side ammunition. "Mobs, which engaged in vicious violence in which men and women were brutally beaten, insisted their 'demonstrations' were no more illegal than those of peaceful sit-ins or bus riders."[9]

Certainly he was not alone on that "hook." NAACP officials had criticized the sit-ins for strategic and political reasons, arguing that public disobedience jeopardized the outcome of their pending lawsuits against segregation. Those cases were moving through the court systems, admittedly slowed or obstructed by segregationist judges unwilling or unable to concede the existence of unjust laws and restrained by judicial philosophy from "making new law." Politically, NAACP leaders worried that Martin Luther King's Southern Christian Leadership Conference was usurping the role of the NAACP, which from its founding in 1909 had gradually become the Negroes' leading advocate for civil rights. At the NAACP convention in Atlanta in July 1962 King recognized the importance of the NAACP court strategy but declared that "legislation and court orders can only declare rights. They can never thoroughly deliver them. Only when the people themselves begin to act are rights on paper given life blood." McGill was impressed by King's ingenious application of the concepts of Thoreau's *Civil Disobedience* and the nonviolent techniques Mahatma Gandhi used against the British in India, and he quoted King's own written acceptance of the consequences of resistance: "It may mean going to jail. If such is the case the resister must be willing to fill the jail houses of the South. It may even mean physical death. But if physical death is the price that a man must pay to free his children and his white brethren from a permanent death of the spirit, then nothing could be more redemptive."[10]

Reason, passion, and historical precedent, together with the surprising courage of students in the face of physical reprisals, persuaded McGill. Long before many other whites, he converted to the support of the sit-in demonstrators, placing them *above* state and community law. He broke ranks with many southern editors. He thought it ironic that among the first to condemn the illegal sit-ins and demonstrations were many who were quite willing to defy federal law, the "Southern newspapers and segregationist leaders who had been urging defiance of the federal court orders." Negroes had dared to do what he and other liberal whites could not easily do or even say. Students had defied the segregation of public accommodations as unjust and then made a public commitment to change. Between the demonstrators and the militant segregationists stood the silent society, and McGill thought many of them privately agreed with the students, especially after segregationists began assaulting them: "Rare . . . was the person who did not admire the courage and vitality of the ideals made visible by the sit-in students," he concluded. "Many angry, ugly things were said of them and their techniques.

But that they symbolized a really inspiring surge of the human spirit could not be argued away."[11]

When the walls of segregation did fall, many asserted that it happened not as much for moral reasons as for economic pressures. McGill concluded that, at last, prodded by federal action, the hibernating South had experienced an awakening of conscience and an accession to the necessity of the new day. To white southerners "one fact became clear to all but the most hopelessly obtuse," McGill wrote. "It was that the South could not win. It was again on the wrong side of another morally discredited 'peculiar institution.' . . . Without question, morality has been one of the many factors that moved to end segregation or make a beginning." However, most of these who understood the moral obligation were nonetheless tongue-tied into silence by tradition, peer pressure, and economic influences.[12]

Recognition of immorality and inevitable defeat was not enough to alter deeply rooted patterns of people who had known no other way but segregation for generations. As Senator Herman Talmadge would explain in southerners' defense, "Their parents had lived that way and their parents' parents before them and their parents' grandparents." McGill conceded that it "would be comforting to say that moral right had shown effective power in the swift changes taking place in the South." But, he quickly added, "it cannot be said. . . . There is no blinking the fact that in general the Christian church has been either in retreat or standing afar off wringing its hands in an agony of spirit and guilt." Aloof or ineffective or driven out by reactionary congregations, ministers followed rather than led. After *Brown v. Board of Education,* a few ministers thought that their congregations might now consider the southern race problem in light of Christian principles and doctrine. One Georgia minister who risked discussing the race issue was the Rev. Robert B. McNeill of Columbus. After consenting to be featured in a *Look* magazine article about conscientious southern ministers, McNeill was subjected to a hostile campaign of gossip and malicious phone calls. The fact that he defended McGill's right to speak in Columbus about the school situation only added to McNeill's problems. The congregation dismissed him and he left the community.[13]

By 1963 all but the "most hopelessly obtuse" saw the power of the economic boycotts. McGill reminded that Martin Luther King Jr. had put his crusade in perspective "with characteristic candor" when King said, "The one thing a business community understands is the sound of the cash registers." The "obtuse" and the demagogues, thinking dimly, miscalculated, relying on trespass laws to defeat desegregation:

> When Negroes decided not to trade where they were unwelcome, the trespass laws, of course, ceased to have meaning. Merchants and operators of bus lines who were saying, "The trespass laws give me the right to insult you, but I expect you to trade with me anyhow," actually became enraged when Negroes did withhold patronage. (In Mississippi Negroes were arrested for encouraging refusal to trade under such segregated conditions.)
>
> Communities that saw how immature their position was, and that the legal trespass status was untenable because of the moral issue involved, went ahead and ended discriminations.[14]

The moral awakening, quickened by economic pressures, hastened changes that had been brewing since before the war. As McGill surmised earlier, segregation had become bad for business. "And so," Ashmore forecast in his review of *The South and the Southerner,* "the cash register will prevail where the conscience has not."[15]

If most of the South's ministers and demagogues were morally in error, so too were most lawyers and most in McGill's own profession, journalism. McGill indicted the "segregationist press," which facilitated and vented the vilification of the Supreme Court. Southern newspaper editors and publishers had contributed to public resistance by describing the Court's vilifiers as "constitutional authorities" when they were usually no more than local attorneys "publicly and slanderously denouncing the federal judiciary and assuring a troubled and indecisive public that the U.S. Supreme Court's school decision was not legal, did not have the force of law, and was Communistically inspired. That this stoked the fires of violence is unquestioned."[16]

Not infrequently, these lawyers were hired hands, paid by southern governors to "join with them in public pronouncements which deceived the people." McGill branded this "one of the saddest aspects of the Southern race problem. . . . One reluctantly concludes all concerned know better, because they, as lawyers, could hardly have been ignorant of the meaning of the Supreme Court decisions. . . . And some, in private, are men deeply ashamed of themselves." Together, the governors and their lawyers were "the best illustrations I know, in our time, of Frankenstein and his monster."[17]

These lawyers, "peddlers of defiance," had free rein in the absence of any declarations by southern bar associations. The bar associations remained silent, reflecting the private stance of powerful clients who sought to avoid controversy. "As late as January 1962, not a single Southern state bar association had gone on record with a resolution of court support and an analysis of the processes of law which would have provided the people with an alternative to the peddlers of defiance," McGill wrote. Only one *city* bar association, in Atlanta, affirmed the validity of court orders on the schools.[18]

While claiming victory, McGill worried now that advocates of desegregation would become impatient for rapid change. While some two hundred southern cities had "altered in some degree their pattern of segregation," as he noted, many had only changed the letter of the Jim Crow laws, not the spirit of segregation. He worried now that civil rights radicals would endanger hard-fought gains in favor of immediate, grand-scale desegregation. He could cite the Reconstruction era and the rule of former slaves as evidence of a policy of *too-far, too-fast.*

He was especially sensitive to civil rights spokesmen who denounced tokenism. "Use of this word has cast a shadow over some of the school integrations," McGill noted. "I do not agree that small beginnings were unwise or that they were in any sense tokens." Desegregation of schools and colleges by small numbers of black students was a deliberate effort to select "carefully screened" students "who would not fail." The alternative was fraught with dangers, he said:

> Had there been larger, unscreened admissions there inevitably
> would have been a number of failures. There would have been

unavoidable charges of discrimination. Therefore, it seemed
to me that it was the better part of wisdom to select students
for precedent-breaking changes who would be able to hold
their own. In all southern states where such admission policies were used the results have been good. It was possible then
to build on this and to admit a larger number in the next year's
classes.[19]

By 1963, a political dilemma inside his own newspaper troubled and
embarrassed McGill. As McGill's friends knew, the business managers of
the two Cox newspapers, on advice from company lawyers, decided against
sending newspaper staff to cover civil rights demonstrations. This was
why they did not cover the Birmingham sit-ins and the ensuing violence.
McGill and the newspapers had been sued for libel because of earlier
coverage of the civil rights movement, including comments and names
in some of McGill's columns about armed hate-group resistance to James
Meredith at the University of Mississippi. In court, justly or unjustly, the
newspapers stood to lose. "For some reason this seemed to spook Tarver,"
Eugene Patterson recalled. "And it certainly spooked Mr. McGill. He told
me, 'I'm not sure that Mr. Cox and Jack are going to back me up. I don't
have enough money to pay off a multimillion dollar law suit.' Mr. McGill
got the feeling that the paper was going to abandon him. That he was
going to be ruined. I don't know where he got that idea."[20]

Beginning in 1962 the Atlanta newspapers had a practice, if not a
policy, of depending on wire service stories rather than sending staff to
civil rights protests out of state. "I never ever saw anything [in writing]
about travel restrictions," Patterson said. "The practice was that the news
side was not covering these matters that needed covering." This contrasted with Patterson's practice in the late 1950s, when he was executive
editor of both newspapers and sent reporters into the crucible of the civil
rights movement. "In 1957 John Pennington and Jack Nelson went to
Little Rock, to Central High School," Patterson noted. "They wrote some
great stories." Harold Martin said that Jack Tarver reluctantly agreed to
the earlier ban: "Tarver usually rode with a loose rein, but in his decisions
regarding coverage of civil rights stories, he was largely guided by the
Constitution's lawyers. These, a cautious lot by nature, were counseling

that, in view of the libel suits McGill had already gotten them into, the papers should keep a very low profile when black and white were confronting each other on the streets." Martin explained that "after the Meredith incident at Oxford gave rise to the libel suits," neither McGill nor Patterson "was allowed to take the forty-minute flight to Birmingham" or anywhere else where protesters faced police. This ban was in force as long as the newspapers were being sued.[21]

The ban frustrated and embarrassed McGill and Patterson. "The lawsuits were piled up against us for a reason, to try to silence us," Patterson said. The ban achieved that result. For as much as McGill and Patterson were free on the editorial pages to rage against racists or praise the civil rights movements, they could not travel to where the deeds were being done. "Mr. McGill and I just had sense enough to know that if Tarver was not approving travel for reporters, we would look bad if we did too much of it," Patterson said. Nor could they easily explain in public why they did not go. Moreover, week in and week out, they seemed to be writing themselves out onto a limb, unsupported by the trunk of the news pages. As Harold Martin noted, the news editors routinely

> chose to play down the news of the great confrontations, leaving the coverage of such events . . . to the wire services and the national press. It pointed up the fact that, though McGill had the title of publisher and had held the title of editor, neither rank carried with it command of the coverage or play of the news. The chain of command here ran from Tarver through his assistants, William H. Fields and William I. Ray, both dour and solid men, not give to taking stands that might cost the papers money or circulation.[22]

McGill resorted all the more to his practice of "picking the brains" of friends who could travel the South. No reporter was wiser or more informative than Johnny "Pop" Popham. None was more sober, either; Popham's abstinence from drink was so remarkable that journalists accused him of "saving your liver for your golden years." Popham made the new southern beat pay off for the *New York Times*. Rather than cover crises only, he traveled the highways and back roads from day to day, more than seventy thousand miles in thirteen years, from 1947 to 1957. He could "sit on the porch and talk" with the common people or hasten as needed to a big story. He could be found listening to grass roots gossip while eating at Widener's in Meridian, Mississippi, or covering the jailing of Martin Luther King. "I've sat up all night with people," he said, explaining how he got some of his stories. "In Texas it was 114 degrees— you could hardly breathe—no air conditioning. And when I wrote they would say, 'Pop understands.'"[23] During the 1960s, McGill and Patterson found others to bring word from the civil rights showdowns across the South. As Patterson recalled, "Mr. McGill and I would talk to Jack Nelson and Claude Sitton [Popham's successor on the *Times* southern beat] and then Gene Roberts. They would come to our office and fill us in on what they'd seen. The big stories were over in Selma, and over in Mississippi and we didn't cover them."[24]

The frustration of traveling only to meetings struck a sensitive nerve in McGill. "We did make trips to Washington for civil rights meetings," Patterson recalled, "but when it got down to the state level we didn't want to embarrass Jack or grandstand. Mr. McGill was infuriated that we had no reporter driving over to Selma to report the headbusting that was about to occur over there. He came in one day and said,

"Why don't we go over to the bus station and take the bus to Selma?"

I told him, "Pappy we can't do that. It would humiliate Tarver if we do that. Now do you want to do that? I don't. It's going to look like grandstanding."

He agreed.

We should have gone. Mr. McGill had great instincts about that. We should have gotten on the damn bus. Here I was, the guy trying to protect Tarver.[25]

Atlanta by 1963 was already experiencing positive results from desegregation. Borrowing from his namesake, philosopher Ralph Waldo Emerson, McGill called these results "compensations." Some compensations were personal. Frequently in restaurants, a Negro waiting his table would whisper, "Thank you, sir, for what you write." Public compensations were visible on the bus and trolley lines. "To see the self-consciousness of most of those who boarded a bus and sat at the front or center, after a lifetime of going to the rear, was both an accusation and a compensation." One black college professor told him, "I was angry with myself for being self-conscious when I took a seat midway up a bus. But unless you have lived all, or most of your life, on a strictly segregated, separate basis, you simply cannot comprehend what it means suddenly to be able to sit in the middle of a bus."[26]

Many whites also felt self-conscious. Mingling with Negroes on buses or in libraries or at department store restaurants and on golf courses, "one could not avoid the feeling of guilt that came with the knowledge that fellow human beings had for so long been denied." On the buses, at first, some whites preferred to stand rather than sit with a Negro. McGill, who often rode the bus to work, noticed that whites eventually sat, if only because of "tired feet and weary legs. The sight of Negro and white persons sitting together ceased to be a novelty on my route. This, too, was a compensation." But the "greatest of all compensations," he wrote, "was to be one of the many who worked long and patiently at the arduous job of seeing to it that the people of Atlanta knew the facts and the alternatives."[27]

By 1963 McGill savored the "greatest of all compensations." After twenty-five years of personal enlightenment and growth, which he shared steadily with his Atlanta public, he took pride in the fact that he had been "one of the many who worked long and patiently." The visage before him was unblemished: "To see the golf courses, transportation, eating places, libraries and schools desegregated without an incident but rather with understanding and good manners was a warm and rewarding experience. There is almost an ecstasy which is quite indescribable, in seeing, and feeling, a city slowly but surely reach a decision and act on it. For a time, one lives a shared existence which is deeply rewarding."[28]

Witness to such progress, McGill thanked his good fortune. "To have been, and to be, a Southerner in all these years is the finest sort of luck," he wrote in the opening chapter of *The South and the Southerner*. He affirmed the "many Souths"—Appalachian, plantation, urban, rural—and said he had been luckier still to have been born in the Appalachian region of East

Tennessee, where racial superiority was not an obsession, and to have grown up the cities where people from all Souths came together and confronted and resolved the region's moral problems.[29] Ashmore felt McGill wanted something more life-affirming from his white South than grudging acquiescence to racial justice. "The South's need," Ashmore concluded, "is not for order but for love."[30]

McGill did want one thing more. Youth. "I know from being with them that to be young Southerners is the most delightful, mystical and wonderful agony of all." In his sixties as he surveyed progress and envisioned what seemed a Promised Land, he envied young people just starting their careers, and whenever possible shared their energies and their quests, helping them along with his vast network of acquaintances. "Once McGill decided that a young person was worthy of his help," Martin noted, "nothing could stop him from putting forth the utmost effort." McGill wrote letters of recommendation laced with history and reason that resounded in the halls of officialdom. In helping a gifted young black graduate of Atlanta's Spelman College, Judy Tillman, to get into Columbia University's Graduate School of Journalism, he urged the dean to consider that the "great need is to make a breakthrough . . . which would train young Negroes for various occupations and professions." After Tillman was accepted, McGill asked the Pulitzer Prize Committee chair, John Hohenberg of Columbia University, to "be a sort of counselor for her" and asked the same of two staffers at the *New Yorker,* Charlayne Hunter Stovall, the black woman who had integrated the University of Georgia, and Mary Painter.[31]

Though McGill could envision the beginning of a new era, he stressed that there was still a great gap between southern and northern education. In his letters to Stovall and Painter he reminded both women that although "Spelman is a good college in the context of southern education, neither it nor any other southern school prepares a young woman, or young man, for the sort of competition you get in the north, especially in graduate school."[32]

18

To the Summit

*Politics is being nationalized. Thought is being liberal-
ized. And industry, as it comes, is largely responsible.*
—RALPH McGILL, 1964

*Optimism would be greater if it were not for the harsh
realities of the Asian problem presented by Viet Nam.*
—RALPH McGILL, 1964

THE ASSASSINATION OF President Kennedy so shocked Americans that
they would retell for years the exact circumstances in which they received
the news and how others near them reacted. On the afternoon of
November 22, 1963, McGill was boarding a jet in New York bound for
Nashville when the news spread among the passengers. "Someone said
that a man carrying a small transistor radio had heard the President had
been shot in Texas," he recalled. "There were concerned faces and a buzz
of conversation, as the huge craft, its engines screaming like the Furies of
Greek mythology, lifted into flight."

Over the intercom the captain's voice sounded strained.

"I regret to inform you," he said in a tense, flat voice, "that our
President was shot at Dallas and that he lived only about an hour thereafter. He is dead."

McGill the reporter noted that this confirmation was followed by
"gasps and exclamations of grief and horror. One woman began to
weep. Several passengers leaned forward, putting the hands over their
faces, and sat silently in grief and thought."

Then from the back of the forward cabin came an unexpected
response.

"Whee!" someone cheered impulsively.

Against the hush, the cheer sounded loud. Eyes turned to see a slender man wearing a matching shirt and tie "and his hair worn long in theatrical fashion. . . . The cheerer picked up a book and tried to read."

McGill watched as a tall man with a gray shock of hair unbuckled his seat belt and walked to stand beside the cheerer. He said something that McGill could not hear. "The man," McGill added, "did not look up from his book."[1]

In the fury of the moment the journalist started working in midair, writing with pencil on a yellow legal pad drawn from his underarm briefcase. The man who cheered triggered McGill's anger toward hatemongers. Those who cheered violence welcomed the killings of Medgar Evers and the four innocents in Sunday school. In the heat of the moment he blamed right-wing maniacs for the president's assassination and dispatched the column to the *Constitution* as soon as he reached Nashville. As Harold Martin was told, Gene Patterson called McGill at his hotel room in Nashville with the latest news indicating that the crime was *not* committed by right-wing crazies. The suspect in custody was Lee Harvey Oswald, who had been to Russia and may have been Communist-inspired. Patterson persuaded McGill to kill the original column.[2]

But McGill could be budged only so far from a moral position. Whether left-wing or right, the sniper who killed the president lived in a culture progressively afflicted by hate. Again, McGill assigned ultimate responsibility to the South's wrong-headed politicians. What more evidence was needed of a "harvest of hate"? Kennedy, in conversation with McGill at the White House, had been unable to fathom the South's irrational obstinance, the willingness to bend laws or break them, to rationalize injustice, to delay change that seemed to the rest of the country inevitable. "What he could not understand was that segment of the Southern *leadership* in the Congress and in the states by encouraging hate and by deceiving the less informed, also inspired many to violence, and worse, to hatred of their country."[3] As McGill expected, demagogues expressed regrets. In Alabama, Wallace called it an "unbelievable crime." In Mississippi, where a sniper had so recently killed Evers, Governor Ross Barnett called the killing "a cowardly act."[4]

The killing shocked McGill profoundly. It was as if in the midst of battle the general leading the charge had been shot off his horse, leaving the troops to fend for themselves until the new leader took charge. Momentum for the civil rights legislation which Kennedy sent to Congress on June 17 had built steadily through the year and some would now think that the legislation was as dead as its prime sponsor.

McGill soon found consolation in the new president's words and deeds. Lyndon Johnson announced immediately that he would retain the Kennedy Cabinet. He soon confirmed support for Kennedy administration initiatives, domestic and foreign. This included Kennedy's proclaimed commitment to the civil rights legislation. Before the civil rights bill had been unveiled, Johnson, as vice president, seemed to waver, worrying over the reaction to integration of public accommodations. Kennedy then entrusted him with the tricky task of shepherding the bill through the southern bloc in the Senate. Now, having achieved the presidency at last, it was as if Johnson could dispense with the cautious approach to civil rights he adopted in the mid-1950s, when he had presidential ambitions. In the Civil Rights Act of 1957 he had supported the compromise that limited federal action to protecting the basic right to vote. Johnson had ducked the more flammable issues of desegregation of schools and public accommodations, seeking, as one of his veteran political counselors said, "all the credit for . . . a compromise [bill] . . . with the emphasis in the South on compromise, and emphasis in the North on getting a bill."[5] Now as president, Johnson seemed to have made the transition from a regional voice to a *national* leader, willing at last to risk antagonizing the southern bloc, if not the South.[6]

So intrigued was McGill with domestic politics in early 1964 that he barely mentioned Vietnam, although he *worried* about it "daily" as a fisherman might worry about his line snagging. Vietnam appeared to him as a drag on the "cautious optimism" he felt for world affairs generally. In his customary state-of-the-world column on New Year's Day he cheered the warming of the cold war, especially the U.S.-Soviet agreement on nuclear weapons testing, and the estrangement of the Chinese Communists from the Soviets. "Optimism would be greater," he added, "if it were not for the harsh realities of the Asian problem presented by Viet Nam."[7]

A morass of political, religious, and economic problems loomed over the region. Without criticizing the legacy of European colonialism, McGill thought the lack of democratic processes made the problems intractable. Diem and other Vietnam rulers doomed themselves, McGill wrote, because they "failed to establish any support with the average people." At the same time, the religious tradition—"the Buddhist tradition makes for apathy"—stymied progress. In a jungle of autocracy, demoralization, and economic depression, "the communist promise of land and participation has a strong appeal."[8]

As long as Vietnam figured so prominently in the cold war and sought U.S. help, America had little choice but to back up its pledge, at least for now. "We will continue to oppose Communist aggression there," McGill said, nevertheless showing a way out, "until, and unless, the government and the people fail utterly to respond."[9]

So far, the cold war formula of U.S. economic aid had failed to do for Asia what the Marshall Plan had done for Western Europe. With the Soviets now aiding newly independent countries, McGill thought Johnson wise to ask for a comprehensive study of foreign aid. "Viet Nam reminds us daily—as do Laos, Pakistan and South Korea, to name only four—that economic aid and trade do not necessarily make for stable political alliance." He saw a repeating cycle of economic and political chaos: "The 'new' or 'developing' countries will never attain political stability until their internal economies are stronger." What had been Kennedy's dilemma now passed on. "How to help them with this is the central issue and a comprehensive study is part of the Johnson plan."[10]

What intrigued McGill more than Vietnam was the transition in White House politics from the Kennedys to Johnson. The new president acted as though he were thoroughly prepared, without the "period of adjustment" needed by Truman after Roosevelt and Calvin Coolidge after Warren Harding. "President Johnson's instant acceptance and his decisive actions since are a story unique in our history," he noted. Having enjoyed an insider's track in the Kennedy years, McGill tried to surmise

Johnson's style and where he could play a role. After the shock of November, McGill, loyally devoted to what the Kennedys did or represented, was himself in a "period of adjustment."[11]

For McGill, the Kennedys had been an *acquired* taste. Palm Beach and Hyannisport were as far as one could get from Soddy, Tennessee, and still be in America. The president had been a man of wealth, glamour, and New England wit, refined in Europe, who in only a short time cast a spell over politics, expelling the Old Guard. After his loyalty to Adlai, McGill had been charmed quickly enough by Kennedy and his wife and brother. Over time, the Kennedys solicited his views as a window on the South, confirming McGill's status as a White House insider. Access to the Kennedys brought him just inside the circle. The insights he gleaned from the Kennedys and their people benefited him and, to the extent that he shared them in print, enlightened his readers while serving the administration's purposes. He viewed the Kennedy experience as a capital advantage, a reward for loyalty to the party. The Kennedys had recognized his national status and gave him entree to the administration. Washington was his town. All he had to do was knock on doors.

With Johnson, McGill strived to maintain his access to the White House and the administration. Since coming to the Senate in 1949, Johnson had made it his business to win the support of the southerners. Since coming to the House in 1937, Johnson and his wife, Lady Bird, had courted the favor of Senator Russell. Johnson regarded Russell as a superior and mentor and through Russell built strong working relationships with about a dozen aging southern Democratic senators who teamed to block civil rights legislation as an interference with states' rights. As president Johnson was relying on these relationships to move along his legislative agenda in the spring of 1964. In this context, McGill waited, ready to help as needed.[12]

Symptomatic of McGill's initial distance from the Johnson White House was the way he misread the new president's wishes early in the political season. Still enamored of the Kennedys, McGill in January asked his readers to consider seriously the talk of a Lyndon Johnson–Robert Kennedy ticket in 1964. To sweep the Republicans, Democrats needed an "excitement beyond mere party loyalty . . . to produce that extra percentage of voters" in the big electoral states. A Johnson-Kennedy ticket would boost Democrats for senate and governor as well. McGill calculated that "the presence of Robert Kennedy on the ticket would produce excitement in the big cities of the East and in the industrial giants of Detroit and Chicago." Kennedy himself was said to be interested. Johnson in early February believed Kennedy had organized a campaign for vice president in the New Hampshire primary election. "Bobby is running for Vice President up in New Hampshire and that is causing a lot of embarrassment," Johnson told the Speaker of the House, John McCormack, on March 7. Outside the loop, McGill continued to be charmed by the Johnson-Kennedy ticket in March, long after White House insiders knew the president loathed Kennedy as conspiring for the presidency. "Not only was that personally irritating," Secretary of State Dean Rusk later explained, "but Johnson didn't think that Bobby Kennedy was qualified for the job." The political reality may not have dawned on McGill until Johnson announced that he would not invite any of his Cabinet to be his vice presidential nominee. McGill's second choice turned out to be more realistic: Hubert Humphrey.[13]

Meanwhile, Johnson seemed secure, with approval polls "astonishingly high," as McGill noted, as high as 80 percent. Yet it was reasonable to expect that Johnson's advocacy of desegregation would have, in the nuclear jargon of the day, certain political *fallout*. The agitation in Congress for civil rights kept southerners' attention.

To McGill the civil rights movement resulted in the domestic triumph of the century, not only for the South but for the nation. It was a mythic battle with heroes and demons—arraying the forces of good and evil, of love and charity against hatred and intolerance. One hundred years after Lincoln emancipated the slaves and Congress imposed Reconstruction, and seventy years after the devious "separate but equal," the nation was moving toward another historic legislative adjudication of the role of the American Negro within the context of the Constitution. Having gone to the courts and won landmark decisions, having gone to the streets and into the jails and witnessed to the nation via television, having secured the support of the president, the Negro leaders, followers and sympathizers now looked to the last holdout: Congress. In fact, the House on February 10 passed the bill 290 to 130, outlawing racial and sexual discrimination in employment and segregation in schools, public accommodations, and federally assisted programs.

In early 1964 it was difficult to predict the fate of the bill. McGill campaigned steadily for its passage. He estimated that while most Senate opposition would come from the Old South, segregated de jure, there was also opposition in the de facto segregated North and Midwest. In the South, demagogues targeted the public accommodations provision as the end of a way of life, invalidating generations of Jim Crow laws, legitimizing the gains of the illegal sit-ins. As the bill welcomed Negroes to integrate the public sphere, whites South *and* North wondered about the effect on housing and jobs. In Chicago, which had convulsed with riots after mass Negro immigration from the South early in the century, whites worried about desegregation of the suburban neighborhoods to which they had fled from the inner city.

Citizens of suburbia could not flee far enough to escape what McGill saw as the explosive consequences of justice suppressed. Central cities and their ghettos had become "social dynamite," a clear and present danger "when the heat generated by its friction with the society about it touches off an explosion." He counted several cities in the Northeast, Midwest, and South—St. Louis, New York, Chicago, Cleveland, Jackson and Hattiesburg in Mississippi, Birmingham, his own Atlanta—where "the tension grows out of some injustice—voting rights, housing, schools, jobs." If the dynamite metaphor did not work, he tried others. The slums grew "like glaciers. And the social impact of them is like the movement of a glacier—slow, relentless." Then, too, he saw the slum as biological, "like an amoeba, flowing out, and surrounding an object in its path."[14]

McGill's columns in early 1964 elevated civil rights to a cold war issue, as a fundamental necessity in the worldwide struggle against communism. If the United States hoped to defeat the Soviet Union in competition for allies among newly independent nations in Africa and others in Latin America, America must improve its image. "The image of us as democratic government and a land of opportunity open to all citizens is at stake," he wrote in mid-January. "President Johnson recognizes the objectives and is hard at work seeking to find support for his program."[15]

McGill's assessments were wishful. In January, he discounted any strong Senate opposition to the bill. "There is no real reason why Southerners should now wish to filibuster civil rights legislation," he wrote. Support for irrational opposition to civil rights had melted, layer by layer. On a practical, economic level, corporations and city and state governments now had a record of hiring "qualified Negro applicants," although there were not enough "technically skilled Negroes" to fill the openings. This last fact sounded a *moral* note that "underscores the injustices and discriminations of a segregated school system."[16]

Time and again he sounded the themes that America must do justice to the Negro for moral *and* practical reasons. In the role of teacher, he recited phrases that most Americans knew by heart from their Declaration of Independence. He reminded them of the Bill of Rights "in which the 'inalienable rights' were specified and protected." Turning rationalist, he argued that "this vast country of 180 millions of people cannot longer refuse to some 19 million citizens the day to day rights as set forth in the Constitution's Bill of Rights." Rising to his pulpit, he sermonized that the "nation cannot be made weaker by doing what is morally right." For those resisting a Communist plot, he asked, "Is it communistic to do what is right?" For unbelievers haunted by the specter of race mixing, who often read his column despite themselves, he offered solace: "There is no social 'mixing' involved in voting, attending classes and holding jobs. The personal choice of association is not disturbed." In any case, the struggle for civil rights was both inevitable and enduring. "It should be obvious that neither brutality, violence nor filibuster will halt demonstrations so long as undenied inequity and discrimination exist."[17]

Whatever was happening in the rest of the country, the South was changing, dramatically, historically. By spring, McGill proclaimed the dawning of the New South prophesied by Henry Grady and others after him. In April he dug up and dusted off a New South oration made in 1906 by the president of the University of Virginia, Edwin Alderman. "Our real problem," Alderman had said, "is to try to industrialize our society without commercializing its soul. I wonder if the thing is possible?" After long travail in darkness and Depression, McGill thought the South "has begun to replace the old patriarchal attitudes of race and industry with those based on equality of law. Politics is being nationalized. Thought is being liberalized. And industry, as it comes, is largely responsible. Perhaps, with this new South will come the Jeffersonian ideal of the civilized man that he and Dr. Alderman saw emerging from our schools and universities."[18]

McGill's hopefulness wavered from week to week. That same month, he was less sanguine about the sensibilities of the white South when he joined some of his like-minded "Brethren" in Tallahassee to tape a radio program on the subject "Is There a New South?" The show was hosted a former Atlantan, John Griffin, who was then doing educational programs at Florida State University. Griffin assembled an esteemed group of talkers. Harry Ashmore arrived from Santa Barbara, California, where he had moved, after Little Rock, to head the Center for the Study of Democratic Institutions. Other panelists were Harold Fleming, then head of the Southern Regional Council in Atlanta, Johnny Popham, then editor of the *Chattanooga Times,* Claude Sitton of the *New York Times* and Bill Emerson of *Newsweek.* McGill, the last to speak, disagreed with them all. Griffin never forgot how McGill proclaimed that his friends' talk of a New South was "pious hedging." McGill wanted the educational audience, mainly younger people, to know that hatred and bigotry still held the field. None of them could deny it, of course, but, for the show, they had spoken their hopes rather than their fears. Ashmore concluded that McGill's "old black Welsh mood was upon him." They all gathered at Griffin's house that night, drinking and talking. Griffin remembered that McGill raised a hearty laugh telling his story about a rural southerner unaccustomed to hotel stationery. The man asked room service for a brown paper bag "so he could leave a message." The next morning when they came for breakfast McGill was gone, but left a note, on a brown paper bag: "Dearly Beloved, at the dawning of a new day in the New South, I leave these greetings and apologies. I regret that a feeling of malmania, weakness and sweating came over me. I do not think it was caused by the conversation. Perhaps by my own frustrations. It was fine weekend, and I feel blood brother to you, an improvement for the time being in the human condition. I lean on each of you. Affectionately, R.M."[19] Some of his moodiness his friends attributed to his own condition, his declining health. Early in 1964 he was diagnosed with an irregular heartbeat, and his condition cast a pall over his work. He confided to Harold Martin that he had asked his doctor, Joe Wilber, who had attended Mary Elizabeth, how much time he had.

"Ralph," said Wilber, "nobody can ever be sure about these things. But I think I can promise you ten more good years."

"I'll settle for that," McGill said.[20]

The civil rights bill of 1964 monopolized national political attention as the spring blossomed into summer. McGill, believing the bill would go far to answer the question of race, focused much of his energy on explaining the issue to readers, many of whom were understandably anxious about the stalled the bill that was poised to outlaw racial segregation. In the belief that southerners understood the Communist menace, he pounded away at the theme that Communists around the world gained from exploiting the South's race problems. This approach gained credibility in the spring after J. Edgar Hoover testified before Congress. McGill, still an FBI Special Correspondent, quickly amplified the warnings of the FBI boss. "It is not at all facetious or inaccurate," McGill wrote, "to say the Communists have been helped enormously by the various excesses of the Klans, White Citizens Councils, Birch-type societies, and so on. The Communists could not have organized the Birmingham and Oxford riots, or the murder of Medgar Evers. All these things and others like them have been helpful to communism's efforts to do precisely what Edgar Hoover was talking about—to cause large masses to lose their perspective." Racists, operating in dim light, completely missed the point when they labeled desegregation a Communist plot. "The racist, who has a stereotype image of the Communist party, thinks that only Communists believe the aspirations of the Negro to be legitimate."[21]

All that spring, McGill kept his lines open to the White House and to the Senate office of Richard Russell, seeking to make himself useful and to keep an insider's edge on the shifting political landscape. The civil rights bill, now pushed forward valiantly by Johnson, provoked the greatest passion in the South. Russell and the bloc of southern Democrats entrenched and strengthened their defenses, relying on the Senate filibuster to prevent a vote. Viewing their numbers now as ever-diminishing, with desertions by prominent one-time sectionalists like Johnson himself, they lauded the filibuster, which dragged on for more than three months, as a vital instrument of democracy, protecting the minority from the tyranny of the majority.

While the Senators evoked the spirit of the Founding Fathers, McGill focused on three "unnecessary errors" in the strategy of obstruction. The flaws stood out starkly in June as the Senate ended the filibuster with a two-thirds vote for cloture, assuring imminent passage of the bill. The South had lost a chance for compromise. In retrospect, McGill considered how the southern bloc had acted in ignorance of reality, or in defiance of it. The first error, he noted, was denial, their "refusal to admit there was any racial discrimination in the Southern states. The fact that there were daily evidences of it and that in some states violence was inflicted on persons seeking the fundamental right to register to vote made no dent in this facade of opposition." Hoodlums had called more attention to the situation by attacking newsmen covering the violence. The senators' second error was to "attack the clergymen and the church leaders who urged passage of the rights bill as being as hypocritical and as mixing in politics. It so happened that the religious pressure was bipartisan." A third error was "angrily to insist the civil rights bill was merely politics and was in no sense associated with a moral issue of human beings." In essence, the filibuster displayed the bankruptcy of southern political ideas in the national marketplace.[22]

With passage assured, there loomed the question of acceptance. McGill knew from the bitter aftermath of *Brown v. Board of Education* that southern politicians at all levels would be inclined, if not committed, to cater to segregationist blocs. Though the forces arrayed against them now included the Congress as well as the Supreme Court, they could continue, officially and unofficially, the policies of obstruction. To McGill, a national civil rights act offered these same politicians a way to obey without losing face, as Governor Vandiver had conceded in Georgia. At best, the act presented an opportunity for real leadership. "There is now the opportunity," he stressed, "for those who fought the fight, which they believed they had to make, to lead in acceptance of the news laws." Not to do so would be pathetic and self-defeating to the South, politically and economically.[23]

The imminent legislative triumph was tempered by the challenge to the executive. The question of enforcement that had plagued the South during Reconstruction and troubled the Supreme Court in *Brown* now passed to Johnson and devolved to governors and mayors. On this question, Johnson looked for advice from friendly southerners. In mid-June, Johnson sought McGill's counsel. During the morning of June 17, two days before the Senate vote on the act, he telephoned Atlanta to ask McGill's advice on two matters. The first concerned a background check on an Atlantan, Harold Walker, whom Johnson was considering for a federal civil rights position. The delicate subject of enforcement of the act was the second matter. How and when should he address southern political leaders? Johnson said he would call back later that day or the next morning, but McGill had a prompt answer on Walker by day's end. Relying on his own association with the man, McGill reported that Walker was "married, has a family and is highly regarded by his neighbors." He was the son of a former governor of Georgia in the 1920s. Moreover Walker was "the soul of honor, honest and able. Lockheed thinks most highly of him. He has had considerable success for Lockheed in negotiating labor and race problems. He is of quiet disposition but this might helpful in the sort of situations in which he would have to operate. He is not a table pounder but his ability to get people to listen and negotiate has been very well demonstrated." He dictated this in a "personal and confidential" letter to Johnson's secretary Juanita Roberts "so he can have it on his return," and added, "I am thinking over the other problem we discussed and will try to have some ideas on it."[24]

It was another five days before McGill called back about "the other problem." Concerning the need for "reaching the governors," McGill said, dictating again to Juanita Roberts, the "only thing I have been able to think of is for you to make a nationally televised talk at the time you sign the bill, or shortly thereafter directed toward governors, mayors and local officials." Before the televised talk, however, Johnson should use his legendary personal appeal to speak to the governors privately about his intentions and determination, making it clear that he solicited their help and wanted to avoid use of federal force. "I also think a personal call to each governor *ahead* of the signing of the bill in which you would say that the federal government certainly does not wish to intervene in any local situation, that the way to avoid the necessity of this is to have local cooperation, to ask for it."[25]

McGill also urged Johnson to work through local businessmen as a channel to civic compliance. That very day, June 22, three days after the Senate passed the Civil Rights Act of 1964, seventy-three to twenty-seven, McGill's political sensibilities were inspired by a public pledge of twenty-six businessmen in St. Augustine, Florida. The businessmen, some undoubtedly leaders in the community, vowed to accept the act's requirements "when and if they become law." The pledge carried political significance because St. Augustine had been a violent racial battlefield since 1960 when student lunch-counter demonstrators, inspired by the Greensboro, North Carolina, precedent, were run off by a mob. In June 1964 police there jailed Martin Luther King Jr., and Florida governor Farris Bryant interceded to seek a negotiated settlement. Now the businessmen, acting independently from the political negotiations, joined to deter further militancy, concerned for the city's tourist trade and conceding the certainty of a civil rights act. Their pledge justified McGill's confidence that economic realities could shape political agendas. As in Atlanta, he regarded the business community there as leverage to civic acceptance. As businessmen played to a different and fluctuating constituency, responsible principally to investors, they often proved to be more flexible than elected politicians, and sometimes more visionary. He urged Johnson to exploit the situation: "If there is some way national attention can be called to this pledge of acceptance there might be an opportunity to create a snowball effect. I have an idea that a number of businessmen in the larger Southern cities will accept the law when it is signed and put into effect. It might be then a good idea if today or tomorrow some national attention could be called to this pledge in St. Augustine."[26]

A week later, McGill's column, citing the St. Augustine businessmen's pledge as "common sense," expanded on the need for compliance and obedience. People now must choose between progress or paralysis. Citizens must now either accept the law or join "in defiance and disorders that paralyze business and create cities of fear rather than of proud progress." He recognized progress made so far, in that "all major Southern cities" except those in Mississippi and Alabama "are well along with programs of eliminating the discriminations the new legislation makes unlawful." Those cities, he argued, "demonstrated that removal of discriminations in the public sector of a Southern city's life passes largely unnoticed." From an economic viewpoint, the threat came from "deliberate actions by inflammatory person or organizations to foment resistance or disorders that bring about loss of business." McGill worried about the politicians who opposed the bill during the long filibuster. "If the men who led the fight against it should in any sense encourage lawless and fanatic elements in the nation, then there will be trouble and grief."[27]

Passage in the Senate stirred a new wave of defiance and suggestions that the South might not comply. Governor Wallace called the vote a setback "for individual freedom." A survey of southern leaders in the *New York Times* on June 22 found "mixed forecasts about their areas may comply. . . . Indications Sunday were that many more legal means of resistance would be explored." Wallace, in Raleigh opening a drive to get onto the ballot as an independent candidate for president, raised the specter of the president deploying the army, as during Reconstruction. "It's not up to me as governor of Alabama to enforce that law. It'll be up to the Justice Department, the executive wing—and the Army, probably. They needn't call on me. . . . I'm not going to help enforce the law that will put a barber in jail when he refuses to shave a man. I don't ask disobedience of law, but it is not my responsibility to enforce the civil rights bill. My attitude will be to leave it alone. It will take a police state to enforce it."[28]

Then the Supreme Court on June 23 disposed of five sit-in cases in favor of the demonstrators, reversing their convictions. The reversals were based on narrow questions of procedures the prosecutors used in gaining the convictions. With the civil rights bill needing only the president's signature, the Court "sidestepped the most sweeping constitutional controversy on whether states could use trespass and breach-of-peace laws to maintain segregation at privately owned restaurants." This was already decided in the public accommodations section of the bill.[29]

The violence McGill anticipated erupted that month across the South. In Philadelphia, Mississippi, three civil rights workers (referred to as "integrationists" in a United Press International story) disappeared. On June 23, their station wagon was found burned. Trying to head off a racial confrontation, President Johnson sent the former director of the

CIA, Allen Dulles, to confer with Governor Paul Johnson Jr., who clarified that Dulles was "here for the purpose of doing good and not destroying the state." J. Edgar Hoover dispatched FBI agents to work with state troopers while the NAACP planned a two-thousand-man demonstration outside the Justice Department. "So," McGill wrote, "as the search goes on for the bodies of three young students, presumed dead, the nation waits. There is need to think rationally, calmly, and try to answer the 'why?'"[30]

Mississippi provided a case study in the consequences of racism. Here, McGill agreed with the arguments of a history professor at the University of Mississippi. The state embodied the distortions of a "closed society." McGill adopted the phrase from the new book *Mississippi: A Closed Society,* by James Silver. "The strongest preservative of the closed society," Silver wrote, "is the closed mind":

> Hostility to authority and disrespect for law are commonplace in Mississippi. . . . Mississippi's spiritual secession from modern America has never ended. For more than a century, Mississippians have refused to be bound by the will of the national society. Mississippi has erected a totalitarian society which to the present moment has eliminated the ordinary processes through which change may be channeled. Through its police power, coercion and force prevail instead of accommodation, and the result is social paralysis.

Professor Silver's considered view, coming as it did from a Mississippian, supported McGill's views and his particular disgust for the comments by senators and congressman who said that the three civil rights workers had "asked for it" by going into Mississippi, as if the territory itself were off limits to outsiders and the trespass justified violence. Such comments were "enough to make all but the more callous stop and reconsider the facts of life—and the values of life."[31]

The nation's highest values were affirmed for McGill on Thursday, July 2, when President Johnson ceremoniously signed the Civil Rights Act. By contrast with the Supreme Court's *Brown* decision a decade earlier, the South was less surprised by the news, if only because of months of filibuster and delay. The same day of the signing, the *Constitution* published a story allaying fears of federal intervention. Enforcement would be "strictly a low-key operation," the story stressed. No "crackdown" was planned. There would be no repeat of the Reconstruction era. "No armies of federal officials are mobilizing to enforce the new statute. In short there really seems to be no 'master plan' for enforcing the Civil Rights Act of 1964." The government, through meetings with public officials, had been preparing for months for "massive voluntary compliance." To no one's surprise, as the article noted, the "bulk of the enforcement problems on one of the most controversial of the sections—covering nondiscrimination in business places—is expected to arise in the South."[32]

The very next day a pistol-toting segregationist angrily challenged the right of blacks to eat in his restaurant. While Atlanta mayor Ivan Allen urged all citizens to obey the law and even Senator Herman Talmadge conceded "there is no alternative but compliance," pockets of "closed society" meant to demonstrate resistance. The restaurant owner, Lester Maddox, pistol in hand, threatened three out-of-state ministers who attempted to integrate his Pickrick restaurant downtown. "Get out of here and don't ever come back," Maddox said as he intercepted the ministers before two of them could emerge from their car at the curb. Behind him was a crowd composed mostly of his customers, some carrying axe handles as a badge of solidarity. Maddox, having lost the mayor's election to Allen in 1961, and a run for lieutenant governor in 1962, at some point became encouraged to carry the segregationist revolt statewide in the 1966 governor's race. The axe handle would be his symbol of resistance. Meanwhile, segregationists could still hope that, despite the liberal Warren Supreme Court, the Civil Rights Act would be found unconstitutional. That the Maddox incident erupted not in the "closed society" of Mississippi but in the seemingly less intolerant oasis of Atlanta confounded McGill's hopes for reasonable acceptance and signaled that the summit just reached had revealed another yet to climb.[33]

The peak McGill had already reached was remarkably high. In September, President Johnson presented McGill the highest honor a president can give a civilian, the Medal of Freedom. On September 14 he was in the East Room of the White House with twenty-nine other recipients, among them his dear friend Carl Sandburg, Walter Lippmann, Edward R. Murrow, John Steinbeck, and Walt Disney. The occasion was awash in emotion, and he had been permitted to bring four guests. He took old friends: Jack and Margaret Tarver, his devoted secretary, Grace Lundy, and Reb Gershon, the sweetheart of his teenage years who had listened to him reading "poetry by the ream" and helped him open up a wider world beyond Chattanooga. After the ceremony, she recalled, "I was so proud I just couldn't quite hold it. And he was just so calm about it." The medal was placed around McGill's neck, but very soon, as Gershon recalled, he took it off. That night at a reception held by George Ball, assistant secretary of state, McGill was asked to comment on behalf of the honorees. Gershon considered it "pretty much of an honor when you looked around at all the other people. I think he was pleased, but he didn't do any showing off about it, bragging."[34]

The Civil Rights Act represented a pinnacle as well for Martin Luther King Jr. A month after McGill received the Medal of Freedom came the news that King had been awarded the 1964 Nobel Prize for Peace. Not since the sit-ins of 1960 and 1961 were Atlanta's whites more dumbfounded about how to respond. This award of the highest prestige had been given to a man who had done so much to disrupt the political, economic, and social order and, in the process, anger the white business community. During a press conference, Mayor Allen led the way, stressing the positive. He praised King for having "displayed remarkable leadership at both a national and international level to the 20 million Negro citizens and has been instrumental in bringing full citizenship to them." McGill also coached the city how to respond. He ventured that the Nobel Committee understood King's value better than southerners whose view "has become befogged by emotions and prejudices." He predicted that the South would "one day be grateful when it realizes what the alternative would have been had Dr. King, with his capacity to stir and inspire, come preaching violence, hate and aggression."[35]

The idea for a highly visible public event to honor King gained favor with blacks and some whites. One of the whites was the civic activist Helen Bullard, who conceded she failed to get support from either the chamber of commerce or Mayor Allen. "Oh, no, nobody would come," she said Allen told her. As Allen wrote later, there was such "resentment in the Atlanta business community" that "I was angry at some people who had been my friends; for a long time." By December, McGill and three community leaders took the lead. They put out the word that there was to be a dinner in the ballroom of the downtown Dinkler Plaza Hotel on January 27. In inviting more than one hundred civic leaders to be sponsors, the four—McGill, Rabbi Jacob Rothschild, Morehouse College president Benjamin Mays, and Roman Catholic archbishop Paul Hallinan—aimed to demonstrate that all Atlantans recognized the magnitude of King's honor were progressive enough to honor him. At the same time, they would be sending a message to the nation that Atlanta was transformed beyond racism.[36]

The plan, however, appeared be backfiring on its creators. "Several days went by and the tickets were not going very well," McGill's colleague Eugene Patterson recalled. "There was no great civic or business community rally behind this event, and it was clear that the hall was going to be largely empty. I remember Mr. McGill expressing serious concern that it was going to be a bad mark for the city if this happened." McGill's fears were underscored when a *New York Times* reporter heard gossip about the resistance and wrote a story highlighting the "behind-the-scenes controversy" among Atlanta's leadership. "Most of those receiving letters have not replied." Quoting sources who obviously did not want to be identified, he reported that some whites opposed honoring King because of a fresh insult to the business community. Soon after returning from accepting the Nobel Prize in Oslo, King had joined the picket line at Atlanta's Scripto pen and pencil factory. Sensing trouble, Mayor Allen and former Mayor Hartsfield, according to the story, "have moved in forcefully but quietly to prevent any incident that would become a snub to Dr. King." The *Constitution* published its own account of the city's "mixed comment." Allen said he was "not involved in any controversy" and pledged to "extend all courtesy, consideration and cooperation in recognizing Dr. King." McGill was asked but said he had no comment. The *Atlanta Journal* focused on hopeful statements by Archbishop Hallinan and Rabbi Rothschild.[37]

To confound the plans still further, the FBI intervened. News of the Nobel award intensified FBI director Hoover's effort to discredit King as immoral. In December and January, bureau agents contacted both McGill and Patterson, seeking to sabotage King's reputation. One wanted Patterson to send a photographer to Florida to snap King with a woman at an airport, presumably set to fly off for an extramarital sexual affair. "He said, 'Gene, . . . here you on this paper have raised Dr. King up to be some kind of model American, some kind of saint, some kind of moralist.' He said, 'Now here's the information, and why don't you print it?' And I had to explain to him, 'Look, we're not a peephole journal. . . . Furthermore, I'm shocked that you would be spying on an American citizen.' But he was highly offended at me, seeing us as an immoral newspaper for not printing back-alley gossip that the secret police of the United States were trying to ruin this man with."[38]

McGill, Hoover's special contact and with a vested interest in the success of the dinner, deserved special handling. The task went to Assistant Director Sullivan, who

> contacted . . . McGill in mid-December, and on January 20, 1965, the two men spoke again and at length. Sullivan's immediate purpose was not only to persuade the *Constitution* to "expose" King, but also to enlist McGill in a Bureau effort to undercut [the] testimonial dinner. . . .
>
> The two available versions of Sullivan's conversation with McGill differ greatly. Sullivan reported to his Bureau superiors . . . that McGill "believes that the very best thing that could happen would be to have King step completely out of the civil rights movement and public life." . . . Sullivan stated that "McGill believes that an exposure of King will do irreparable harm to the civil rights movement."

The suggestion that McGill and Patterson derail the movement they so highly regarded, or the dinner they supported, did not make sense. Patterson afterward stated both he and McGill had been outraged.[39]

The King family was kept informed of FBI smear tactics. Since the early 1960s, Police Chief Jenkins had communicated with Daddy King about law enforcement agents' inquiries, no matter how bizarre. Once he had "two captains for the Birmingham state police come to see me and shut the door. Great secrecy. They had 'confidential information' that young King was not the Kings' child. He'd been smuggled out of the

Mideast when he was three weeks old." Jenkins said he tried to stay clear of the FBI's "dirty" tactics:

> Along there at the last, you know, he was under severe investigation by the FBI after he and Mr. Hoover had an open break. And on several occasions I had a detective come to me and say, "My friend who is an FBI agent just called me and said, 'Dr. King is in hotel room so-and-so in such-and-such a hotel with a white woman. Didn't I wanna go out there and raid that hotel?' And he said, "I told him I didn't think so." But that he'd come and ask me, and he come asked me.
>
> And I said, "Well, I have great admiration and respect for the FBI, and they have our full cooperation, but don't let 'em push us into doin' any dirty work they wanna do. And obviously this is some dirty work they want done, but they don't wanna do it themselves. So tell 'em if they've got to make a raid, you'll go with them. Let them make the raid and you'll go to assist 'em if they want you to."

Once, Jenkins said, FBI agents persuaded one city investigator to make an immediate raid on a hotel room where King was seen with a white woman. "So he went out there and knocked on the door, and they opened the door, and there was Dr. King, and there was a white lady, and there was five other people in there having a meeting, see. And he [the city investigator] told them what it was and what had happened."[40]

Given these obstacles, it was a wonder that the organizers succeeded in staging the tribute to King in a packed ballroom. On the night of January 27, as *Time* magazine reported, it was "remarkable even for Atlanta that some 750 whites, including most civic and business leaders, should gather with about the same number of Negroes to honor the man whose name is synonymous with progress in the U.S. civil rights movement." Hartsfield took credit for "a little selling job" to Atlanta's whites. "Dr. King, I told them, was being honored as a Nobel prizewinner, not because he sat down at a lunch counter or picketed over in Selma." While Hartsfield had done a selling job, there was another plausible explanation for the mass conversion.[41]

The most persuasive argument perhaps had been communicated from a rural hunting field to the Piedmont Driving Club, the gathering place for the city's elite. Mayor Allen recalled that in December he sought advice from his longtime mentor, Robert Woodruff, at Woodruff's plantation, Ichauway. Allen recalled that he was hunting when J. Paul Austin, Coca-Cola's president, "came up to me in the field . . . and said, 'You're right. Dr. King has won the Nobel Prize, and the city should properly acknowledge it.'" Austin, speaking for the Boss, said, "We feel that the city must move ahead as you suggested." A day or so later, in the comfort of the Driving Club, Austin delivered a message to several of Atlanta's influential leaders in business and finance. As McGill recounted the story to Patterson, Austin walked into this gathering and got right to the point: "Fellows, the Boss thinks we ought to go to the dinner."[42]

The aftermath was stunning. "Dramatically, and almost overnight," Patterson recalled, "the big banks and businesses in the city began ordering tickets for the dinner. We can never be thankful enough that we had that man there because he understood the world. He understood that Coca-Cola had to be sold to every region and every race. We can thank his good heart and also his good business judgment." "The story I heard," Rabbi Rothchild's widow, Janice, recalled twenty years later, "was that Mr. Woodruff let it be known that if the hometown of Coca-Cola proved to be an embarrassment in relations with Third World Countries, then he would reluctantly have to move its headquarters to another city."[43]

The sponsors finally numbered 134, and tickets sold out so fast that some major players were disappointed. One telephone order came personally from Richard Rich, at whose department store Martin Luther King Jr. had been arrested. "Mr. Dick Rich himself called and said how was I," recalled Helen Bullard, who was selling tickets. "And he said, 'I want 20 tickets.'. . . 'Now,' I said, 'Sir Richard, I'm sorry as I can be, but. . . .' He said, 'Now, Helen, don't tell me, there's always tickets around.' I said, 'Yeah, and I've sold 'em. . . . And he said . . . he wanted a whole table. And I said, 'Look, Sir Richard, ain't nobody gonna have a table.'"[44]

For McGill the event signified a general triumph. The *Constitution*'s editorial page echoed McGill's sentiments: "In doing honor to Dr. Martin Luther King . . . Atlanta also did honor to itself. . . . Progress in the past decade has come in many modes—by court order, by direct action demonstrations, by act of Congress and, most important, by individuals' examination of their own consciences." During the dinner, McGill heard his own persistent theme amplified—the summons to people of good conscience to express themselves—as King told the audience that the tragedy of the civil rights movement had been "the appalling silence and indifference of the good people. . . . Our generation will have to repent not only for the words and acts of the children of darkness, but also for the fears and apathy of the children of light. . . . This hour represents a great opportunity for white persons of good will, if they will only speak the truth, and suffer, if necessary, for what they know is right."[45]

19

Semper Fi

*The South Vietnamese soldiers, in number of about
200,000, are willing to fight and die for something they
see in their future. There has been no civilian counterpart.
How do people come into, and accept, a free society—
and be willing to defend and keep it strong?*
—RALPH MCGILL, 1965

*We are the richest and most powerful nation
in the world. We can eliminate the worst of the
poverty in this country. Indeed, we must do so
or see our wealth and power decline.*
—RALPH MCGILL, 1967

THE CIVIL RIGHTS ACT convulsed the political landscape of the South.
In the reconfigured alliances, as McGill feared, the South deserted the
Democratic Party in the 1964 presidential election for the first time in a
generation. In November, Barry Goldwater's campaign carried the "solid
South" but little else. Johnson's landslide gave him a mandate for
enforcement but not the necessary cooperative partners.

The election confirmed that McGill would have the same difficult
task of speaking to two audiences. In writing his syndicated column he
would take solace in the progress of justice without rejoicing overly in
the defeat of segregation. He would write with a nation in mind but a
region at heart. He would envision the fast-approaching New South while
remaining sympathetic to the Old South's burden of history and critical
of its fatuous demagogues.

Politically, the heights rising before the South seemed formidable to
a man now sixty-six years old. The emergence of a popular segregationist
candidate seeking the Democratic nomination for governor in Georgia

presented the party with a dilemma: how to lead the South into this new age without backsliding into lawlessness? After enjoying the relatively enlightened, at times liberal, regime of Governor Carl Sanders, the state faced the likelihood of either a racist Democrat or a Republican.

The Democratic nominee was Lester Maddox, the segregationist restaurateur craving a public pulpit in the wake of the Civil Rights Act. In the statewide Democratic primary election of 1966, Maddox prevailed. Facing former governor Ellis Arnall (McGill's choice), Maddox did well, especially among rural voters, because of his reputation as a gun-wielding defender of segregation. His confrontation with the black ministers outside his Atlanta restaurant, amplified by the media, projected a political persona attractive to agitated Georgians who revered segregation and a simplistic if violent approach. Maddox's icon was the axe handle, which his followers carried as emblems of resistance. The parallel to Nazi thugs was not lost on those who remembered recent history. As an unorthodox candidate without a high school diploma, Maddox had some "extra talents" that augmented his character, particularly the ability, often photographed, to ride a bicycle backward. Even so, he might not have won the Democratic primary without a large crossover vote—seventy-five thousand Republicans who voted in the Democratic primary because, McGill explained, "they thought he would easier for their nominee to defeat."[1]

Facing this prospect, all but avid "yellow dog" Democrats (who would vote for a yellow dog rather than a Republican) found the Republican attractive. Howard "Bo" Callaway was the West Georgia scion of the Callaway cotton-mill fortune who had served reasonably well in the state senate. Callaway appealed not only to the anti-Maddox crowd but also to livid segregationists who wanted to send a punitive message to the Democratic Party. He also drew voters because, unlike Maddox, he was not based in Atlanta, the city whose mayor had capitulated to the Civil Rights Act. In contrast to Maddox, Callaway projected the orthodoxy of an elite businessman and a stable, if bland, personality.

The election of 1966 confounded predictions. In the popular vote, Callaway surpassed Maddox, but only barely, and not with a majority. That meant that the Georgia legislature must choose the governor. Dominated by rural Democrats, the general assembly selected the proclaimed segregationist. To McGill's chagrin, Maddox in the state capitol, across the street from city hall and Mayor Ivan Allen, became a daily reminder of the contrast between Atlanta and the surrounding state—the reactionary resistance to the Civil Rights Act of 1964, the Voting Rights Act of 1965, and *Brown v. Board*. The city might lead, but the state did not have to follow, at least not for the present. It worried McGill's optimism about human nature and its adaptation to change.

Governor Maddox, as promised, aligned his race policies with those of segregationists. He combined the tired strategy of delay with the practice of making deals with the White House, a technique Henry Grady's contemporaries had used to negotiate the end of Reconstruction. In 1966, Senator Talmadge was among those leading the retreat from school desegregation. In 1967, a few months into Maddox's first year, news leaked that new governor was also meddling in Washington, meeting secretly with Vice President Hubert Humphrey and with federal officials who were reportedly anxious to bargain with southern Democrats. Although in Chicago and elsewhere similar bargains were being sought, Maddox got credit in Georgia for winning a concession in the enforcement of desegregation guidelines. By March 1966, the U.S. Office of Education was closing "legal loopholes" and urging school officials to triple the number of Negro students in previously all-white schools, from 4,240 to more than 12,000 by fall 1966. By May 1967 the federal government softened one of the more offensive aspects of enforcement—the authority to deprive a segregated school district of federal funds. That authority was transferred from the education commissioner and given to a Cabinet officer less offensive to Georgians.[2]

Alarms rang across the South as Democrats retreated from the national party or converted to the Republican side. McGill warned against taking refuge among southern Republicans as one would warn an unthinking child about a stranger offering candy. In Alabama in 1966, "the dilemma of the Democrats and the Republicans . . . is that with one exception all candidates are segregationists working the same side of the street." The Democrats who converted to the Republican Party were still men of the same stripe: "These men, angry with the leadership of their party, ignore the fact that the Republican national civil rights platform accepts everything the Democrats have stood for. The political development of the Republican party in the south is, in general, racist. It ignores the planks of the national party." Between the parties in the South "there is hardly a dime's worth of difference in principle or outlook."[3] By 1967, Maddox, while declining to support Johnson for reelection, positioned himself for a run at the presidency in 1968, warning the South that in the 1966 elections "pursuit of left-wing policy cost the Democratic Party 47 seats in the U.S. House of Representatives alone."[4]

Consumed by emotions over desegregation, neither the Right nor the Left in the South anticipated the impact on the 1968 election of the Vietnam "conflict." In early 1965, as fighting continued, news reports reflected a disheartening struggle among Vietnamese political and military leaders, with U.S. officials exerting increasing influence.[5] The political turmoil troubled McGill, who saw that American democracy "simply will not work" there. Nearly all the emerging nations of Asia and Africa faced numerous obstacles to democratic government—perhaps "a dozen rival chiefs seeking power, or which has an electorate unable to read or speak to the neighbors 50 miles away, or which has a handful of educated, trained men and no bureaucracy." He envisioned the persistence of "a semi-totalitarian or authoritarian" regime because it "comes easier to people who have never known any of the forms of a free society regulated by free ballots." In Vietnam, the north "produced a Communist leadership with a highly trained and competent leader: Ho Chi Minh. In a decade of war against the French colonial armies, largely foreign mercenaries, they developed a rather efficient army and an administration that was disciplined and tough." By contrast, "in the South there was no ready army. There was no leader. There is none now. But the South Vietnamese soldiers, in number of about 200,000, are willing to fight and die for something they see in their future. There has been no civilian counterpart. How do people come into, and accept, a free society—and be willing to defend and keep it strong?"[6]

By 1966, as more marines went to war, McGill's doubts diminished. Certainly his new support of the war stemmed in part from loyalty to the administration. Yet he also felt an abiding personal loyalty ("Semper Fi") to his fellow marines. Now, whatever the gloomy prospects for political democracy, he emphasized support for the military, differentiating himself from "the clamor of defeatists" demanding disengagement. He

berated the antiwar activists as ill-informed "pacifists." The public understood, he believed, that "Secretary of State [Dean] Rusk and his department are better informed and more competent to make a decision and a
judgment, than, let us say, a pacifist professor, however sincere the latter
may be." He criticized Senator William Fulbright of Arkansas for "scholarly ambiguities" and Senator Wayne Morse of Oregon for "irresponsible
caterwaulings." He labeled them as opportunists "seeking, in part at least,
to make political gains out of opposing the conduct of the *war*." To him,
indeed, it was no longer a *conflict,* the administration's term, but a war in
which cynicism at home "is beginning to gag all but the most callous."
At the end of the Senate debate over Vietnam in March 1996, Senators
approved 95 to 2 President Johnson's request for $4.8 billion to help
carry on the war. The House approved 392 to 4, with Representative Melvin
Laird of Michigan accusing the administration of distorting the record to
make it appear that combat there was forced upon the United States by
the commitments of earlier administrations. Following Johnson's insistence, McGill agreed that the war "is related to our national security and
self interests." In signing the military-aid bill, Johnson hoped that "the
leaders who provoked and the leaders who continue this aggression in
Viet Nam will finally abandon their hopeless attempts at conquest." McGill
adopted the same line, laying out clearly the political risk the administration was taking to bring the Communists to the bargaining table: "If
Charlie Cong [Vietcong] is hurt to the point where the Administration's
hopes for negotiations to produce a neutralize Southeast Asia are realized, the political profit will be on the side of those who made it possible.
The Doomsayers and defeatists may not at all have the last word."[7]

That March, after visiting his Washington contacts, McGill imagined for his syndicated audience an improvement in the Johnson
administration's "over-all position" in public opinion and in war. This
was also the administration's belief, or hope, expressed frequently until
1968. Increasing American military power, together with training of South
Vietnamese troops, was turning the tide, and the American public was
beginning to realize that "Charlie Cong is being hurt." In a further miscalculation, McGill accepted the military estimation that those well-trained
troops from North Vietnam "are being severely mauled. This is in part
because they don't know all the paths and trails through the jungle, the

tall grass, or the rice-paddy country as does Charlie Cong." McGill consistently ignored contradictions to his optimistic outlook. Just a few days later, however, United Press reported that North Vietnam was funneling men and supplies to the South over a new "Ho Chi Minh trail."[8]

McGill retained faith in "the American soldier's ability to adapt and improvise" in order to outlast the North Vietnamese and Charlie Cong. Adaptive techniques and new technology helped Americans cope with "the new kind of war" on several fronts. McGill noted how American troops in Vietnam adapted to the enemy's guerrilla warfare by creating their own ambush technique. U.S. troops slipped into the jungle, established a "kill zone" with high-tech firepower, waited until the enemy entered the zone, and saturated it with thousands of shells. Although McGill conceded that the Vietcong knew their own jungles better, he believed that American helicopters compensated for the multiple fronts and "surpassed Charlie Cong in mobility. . . . Helicopters fly supplies anywhere there is a need, in any direction there is a radio-code call for help."[9]

All this he wrote from afar, like most pundits of his era, a continent and an ocean away from the theater of the war. This nettled him, and he knew that he needed to go as soon as possible. Without personal experience of the war, he relied on press accounts, military contacts in the Pentagon, and historical precedents. Curiously, however, he used only facts and precedents which supported his a priori decision to support American involvement in the war. In recalling colonial warfare against Indians and the British army, he reminded that Americans knew well how to fight in ambush. Yet he failed to note that the colonists ultimately defeated the British in large part because of their belief in the cause—liberation in a war of national self-determination—and in large part because the colonists had more staying power than the British government which had to ship troops across an ocean, and the British public.

Early on, McGill recognized the need to continue pressing the argument that the Civil Rights Act of 1964 liberated the South economically. Acceptance of the end of segregation opened the South to normality for the first time in its slave-haunted history. In one stroke Congress and the president brought the South into line with national policy and with national economic development, eliminating the one distinction which had made the South a pariah, stigmatized everywhere by the specter of slavery and lynching. After July 1964 it was just a matter of time before the South would attract large-scale capital investment, improve commerce, and multiply employment beyond the vision of most southerners. These new jobs would exceed the expectations of Henry Grady, whose appeal to northern capitalists in the 1880s had offered rock-bottom wages for labor. The enterprises which populated McGill's New South after 1964 would be of a higher class, seeking a better educated work force, requiring higher education for southerners, and resulting in higher wages and greater prosperity. As before, McGill tried to persuade southerners of the legitimacy of the Civil Rights Act through economic evidence.

McGill found ample evidence of progress for anyone willing to leave behind the tired traditions of Dixie. In the world of sports, the dropping of color barriers eliminated segregated seating in stadiums and leagues, and opened up the South for expansion of major professional teams. In 1965 Atlanta was chosen as the South's first site for major league baseball *and* professional football. The owners of the Milwaukee Braves of the National League, seeking a new market, settled on Atlanta largely because it would pack a stadium with fans from the entire baseball-hungry region. The bitterness expressed by Milwaukee fans at the desertion of their city was matched by delirium in Atlanta. Possibly no other single event converted more southerners to acceptance of desegregation of public accommodations.

The religious establishment seemed more difficult to persuade. Whatever he might think about what he termed the "power of Episcopalianism," McGill felt utterly frustrated and even betrayed by the actions, and inaction, of his own and others' churches. While he was reared a Calvinist Presbyterian, he had been searching all his life, as he told Harold Martin, for a faith that did not limit the meaning of God. He suspected the sincerity of men who "speak with certitude from the pulpit, of the sure men who can cut out a faith for you and fit it to you as if it were a suit." In 1953, when the Episcopal Church seemed the best of all he had visited, he and Mary Elizabeth and their son were confirmed by the bishop and became active members of the congregation at the Cathedral of St.

Philip, Mary Elizabeth as a lecturer on herbs and raising flowers for the children's chapel, Ralph Jr. as an acolyte, carrying the cross and assisting at communion, and Ralph as a Sunday schoolteacher and later a member of the cathedral's governing body.[10]

Ten years later, McGill, citing hypocrisy, resigned. As a member of the St. Philip's governing body, he had voted to approve accepting responsibility for the private Lovett School. When the all-white Lovett School in 1963 refused to admit the son of Martin Luther King Jr. and two other black Episcopalians, McGill was stunned. The school maintained that it was not "officially" a church school. The decision stood. Harold Martin recalled how McGill "felt personally betrayed." Having voted to help the Lovett School, he had assumed the church would ameliorate its segregationist policies. On resigning, McGill moved the family to the Episcopal All Saints Church, which had social programs for the poor and the handicapped McGill could endorse and where the rector, Frank Ross, spoke courageously in and out of the pulpit.[11]

McGill's unequivocal condemnation of church hypocrisy in the post-*Brown* era came through clearly in his chapter on the "Agony of the Church" in *The South and the Southerner*. "The moral weight of the court's rule fell even more heavily on the Christian church and its clergy than on education," he wrote. "The Christian would not easily evade the moral issue so starkly raised by the judicial order." Yet the Christian church "has either been in retreat or standing afar off wringing its hands in an agony of spirit and guilt."[12] Occasionally there was cause for hope, when church assemblies and individuals refused to accept racial segregation. As early as 1955, one year after *Brown,* the Episcopal Church moved its general assembly from Houston to Honolulu after Houston officials could not assure integrated hotels and restaurants. In 1961, a group of black and white Episcopal priests made their own freedom ride on a Greyhound bus from New Orleans to Detroit. In 1965, when a Presbyterian church in Memphis refused to admit Negroes to its services, Presbyterian leaders moved their forthcoming general assembly meeting from Memphis to Montreat, North Carolina.[13]

In 1966, when investigators found that communities in the South engaged in secret intimidation campaigns to warn blacks against putting their children in the better, white schools, McGill cast much of the blame on clergymen: "Any community, where acts of intimidation have prevented carrying out the agreement of compliance, confesses that its local church leadership and the influence of its 'best people' are nonexistent. Such things cannot happen in communities where the minister, the local business and professional leadership say 'No.'"[14]

This protracted conflict playing out in southern pulpits, between evil and the soul of Christianity, challenged his wits. Considering it the ultimate hypocrisy, he imagined that by shaming the clergy he might at least nudge them toward a Christian stance, if not reform. He wished to shake them from the silence that condoned uncharitable and unjust acts. Acquiescence to discrimination placed them implicitly in league with the devil. This idea so compelled him that by the late 1960s he was planning a book on the failures and triumphs of the church, not just in the South, but nationally. In 1966, still inspired by his talk with W. E. B. DuBois in Nigeria, he wrote to Edward Weeks, "I have a vague idea about a book. I am interested in and disturbed by the church in the South and its attitude toward the great social changes of our day." His added note of caution—"I don't know whether this idea is any good or not"—was dispelled by Weeks's reply: "The answer is 'yes.' Damn the torpedoes! Full steam ahead!"[15]

McGill delayed, outlining the book in his head long before he jotted down the first paragraph. He told Harold Martin he would continue to focus on "the agony of the Christian church in a time of racial crisis," the failure of the church to act out the Christian creed in society, and, especially, the deadening silence of clergy who could have applied the teachings of Christ to the plight of black Americans. In 1965, Robert McNeill, the dismissed Columbus pastor who had broken the silence on race, told his story in a book for which McGill wrote a three-page introduction. "A shockingly high percentage of Southern churches was found utterly committed to the past and blind not merely to the future but to the present. Even more dismaying was the fact that so large a number of churches were forced to reveal themselves as putting material commitments first." The evidence, McGill wrote, "is plain that if the Christian church and the synagogues had moved into a position of quiet leadership, much of the violence, hate, fear, physical assaults, and murders that have strained so many areas in the South might well have been avoided.

Robert McNeill is one of the several magnificent exceptions of men who tried to provide that leadership. Almost every one of these men suffered." McGill understood that other young ministers in the South wanted to intervene, but church policy constrained them from speaking out or inviting blacks into their congregations. In such situations, courage evidenced itself when a minister simply refused to "preach segregation," as McGill had written earlier. Such a minister "developed a technique of survival, merely because he did not want to desert those in the congregation who depended on him and needed him. . . . So, silent on the subject, he stayed on. . . . Every minister with any shred of sensitiveness understands that just as the racial issue is the paramount political issue before the world today, so it is for Christianity."[16]

The crisis, springing from the rocks of the southern conflict, now faced the nation as a whole. The book would stress "the failure of the Christian church to speak out in all its authority in support of racial justice is the single most melancholy aspect of what has been called the moral decline of our time."[17]

Through the early 1960s, as he contested the insidious demon of discrimination, the "paramount political issue facing the world," he had been troubled by the serious issues in his personal life. The chronic illness and death of Mary Elizabeth had pained him, as did the failure of Ralph Jr. to finish at any of three universities. In time, as he conceded to Harold Martin, he accepted that his son's strengths were not in scholarship.

His own health was now troubling him. From 1964 on, he worried about his heart. The heartbeat had become so arhythmic (da-da/da-da-da/da-da) he could not ignore it. It was a daily reminder of mortality, that it was over for him. He might pass from the scene on the next heartbeat, or the treatment prescribed by Dr. Joe Wilbur might, as the doctor thought, prolong the inevitable for years. The heart condition was serious enough for him to give up drinking or slacken his intake. His old drinking buddies noticed his abstention at get-togethers, or his avoidance of the events. He had seldom written about alcoholism, but in the '60s he became an advocate of medical treatment for street vagrants on cheap wine, "lady alcoholics who keep hitting a sherry bottle or martinis all day," and "the man with a job who drinks himself out of it. . . . There is no pleasure or fun in such drinking. These alcoholics and the winos are close kin in some sort of sickness of spirit. If the court can cause society re-examine its procedures we will have done society a service."[18]

His public persona, as before, concealed private sorrows or disguised them to all but those who knew him well enough to read between the lines. His remedy for sorrow as before was to keep busy, and now he added to his workload by accepting more speaking invitations which served as distractions, solace, and inspiration. Yet the telltale heart in his chest haunted him, reminding him of his fragility. This ever-present reality contributed to an increasing tendency to repeat significant stories, even reprint old columns, and in general to write as though he were documenting the age and staking a claim to his role on the stage. Any event, any issue, anywhere, gave him a fresh opportunity to relive his experiences. His prodigious memory now spoke with the perspective of time passed and wisdom gained, as if lighting up the recesses, an aged sage addressing the populace. These columns would begin "Memory went back to . . ." or "A warm, fine memory stirs . . ." or "In the early spring of 1945 . . ." or "It has been a long hard road . . ." or "I never expected a solemn district court case to recall a speak-easy and a bum."[19]

Many of his readers in the '60s were a new breed who knew little of McGill's roots. The national audience had not read him in the '30s, when, fresh out of the sports department, he was finding his voice; nor in the '40s as he broke silence and attacked the "separate but equal" foundation of legal segregation; nor in the '50s as he stood with the Supreme Court against governors and neighbors. In Georgia, too, thousands of newcomers swelled the population of Atlanta in the 1960s as the city leaders, with new vigor and optimism, welcomed new industry, business, skyscrapers and major league sports. Apart from the new readers, however, there was a core of older, steadfast readers who recognized when McGill occasionally repeated some story about southern characters and hunting dogs he had met, or visited some memory he had shared before. By now these readers were accustomed to Ol' Ralph's storytelling and reminiscing as though he were on the front porch rocker, now telling a tale that coaxed tears or remorse, now one that produced a cackle. Many of the aging readers welcomed the storytelling, and understood it. They did it themselves.

Anyone reading McGill in the '60s learned that he had traveled the world, shared the company of great leaders, and witnessed history being made. When in 1966 rumors out of Hong Kong suggested that Mao Tse-tung's leadership was being "reassessed," Ol' Ralph took his readers back twenty-one years to 1945, when he was in Chungking with his ASNE companions Ackerman and Forrest, meeting Mao's rival Chiang Kai-shek. Without naming Ackerman, McGill poked the professor for hero worship: "It was true that one visiting VIP, a professor, turned to friends after an interview with Chiang and said, his face rapt, 'I feel as if I had been in the presence of a divinity.' Legend has it that the two men with the VIP were immediately sick." When Kwame Nkrumah was ousted as ruler of Ghana in 1966, McGill recalled his own "45-minute talk with him a few years ago. It was a pleasant, interesting experience. Yet, even then he seemed on a collision course with a political *coup d'état*. There were too many unhappy persons. Nkrumah seemed less and less 'The Redeemer.'" In the very next column he embellished the memory of walking past "the scarlet-coated guards" to meet Nkrumah, who had on his bookshelves Carl Sandburg's *Lincoln*. "Every African, I think," said the president, "has Lincoln among his list of great men who have served humanity well."[20]

His mind served as a time machine, traversing years at any prompting. This happened instantly when he learned that death had claimed another contemporary. On these occasions he eulogized the individual while conjuring up the bygone era and his own role in it. With Winston Churchill's death in 1965 McGill carried readers to Britain, when he was there on the Rosenwald grant. "It was my good luck to have seen Churchill when he was out of power in 1937 and 1938," he wrote, "warning a blind and smug government of what it meant to be so lacking in arms when Germany and Italy were so obviously prepared and moving toward war." Later, during the war, he and Ted Weeks, aboard the *Queen Mary* troop-ship off Scotland, learned that "Churchill was aboard with a large staff. Averell Harriman, U.S. Lend Lease representative, was with him. It was he who arranged a meeting—not an interview—with the great man. He sat deep in a comfortable chair, gray and weary. "He looked like an extinct volcano," said one of those who met him. He appeared a number of times, once reviewing British airmen going to Canada for advanced training." One afternoon

> the ship's amplifying system blew a call to attention. Down the stairway from his upper deck came Churchill and his staff. The Prime Minister wore a mustard-colored air force uniform. There was a deep respectful silence. Suddenly the Scottish girl's baby began to wave his chubby arms and cry. "Daddy, daddy, daddy." There was just the sign of a smile about Churchill's lips as the flustered mother sought to quiet her boy. That baby is now about 23 years old. I imagine the story of him crying out "Daddy" to Winston Churchill is a family legend.[21]

Eulogies carried him still further, to the ghostly world of the 1920s, imbued with nostalgia for the good times. Five days after the Churchill column, a legendary footballer from the "golden era of sports" died at sixty-three, and McGill dusted off his memories of Harry A. Stuhldreher and that era when "all heroes were great and good." "Granny" Rice had coined the phrase "the Four Horsemen" to describe Stuhldreher and the other three in the Notre Dame backfield coached by Knute Rockne. They scored again and again, outshining the traditional Ivy League power-houses. As sportswriters trumpeted their exploits, the Four Horsemen altered the emotional landscape of the sport and "produced a sort of social revolution. They brought the common man to football enthusiasm. The Four Horsemen brought to Notre Dame the fervent, prayerful support of literally millions who had never seen a football game. . . . All of a sudden here came 'The Irish of South Bend' beating all the long-time gridiron aristocrats. The Irish everywhere responded. Men who couldn't write much more than their name were fanatic cheerers-on for Rockne and Notre Dame."[22]

By 1965, his stubborn endurance and faith rewarded him with a respite from personal troubles and a glimpse of joy. Ralph Jr., after failing at scholarship, made his father proud by enlisting in the Marine Corps Reserve and heading off to the famed marine boot camp at Parris Island, South Carolina, where McGill had trained in 1919 for a war that ended before he could get there. In the reserve, Ralph Jr. would now be on call. Harold Martin, another faithful marine whose own son John was a private in Vietnam, saw Ralph Jr. when he came home from boot camp "lean, bronzed and self-assured," touting a rifle sharpshooter's medal. The "rough-tongued" Semper Fi marine drill instructors, Martin thought, "matured him in a way the scholarly professors at Wesleyan, Vanderbilt and Georgia State had not been able to do." Soon after, Ralph Jr. rooted himself into a career with advertising agencies in Atlanta. Between work and his social life, he saw a lot less of his father, especially after he began dating a young woman named Adelaide.[23]

McGill himself eased out of mourning slowly. His friends recalled one or two romantic interests before 1965. They assumed he would marry again, and for a time it was rumored he would marry the widow of an Atlanta physician. Whatever his interests in her, by 1965 he had fallen in love with a serious-minded woman twenty-two years younger than he, slender, with ash-blond hair and blue eyes. McGill and Mary Lynn Morgan knew each other casually from meeting at Christmas parties in the home of a mutual friend, Dr. James Steele, a specialist at the national Centers for Disease Control.

Mary Lynn was pleased to chat with the great Mr. McGill. She was a children's dentist who had been reading his columns for a quarter century since moving to Atlanta in 1940 at the age of twenty to go to the Southern Dental College. She realized that his opinions had helped her form her own. Studious and serious, she had come from Jacksonville intent on a career as a dentist. She combined this with her love of children and her realization that very few dentists concerned themselves with children's special needs. She got her degree, worked for a time as an assistant in an established practice, did advanced study and, in 1946, opened her own practice as a pedodontist. She devoted herself to the children and to the profession. Reticent and not much interested in dating—she did not dance, had few boyfriends and never thought of herself as pretty—she never married and by her forties had put the idea of marriage out of mind. By contrast, McGill was a man of the world, conqueror of the Talmadge machine, an intellectual icon to her, a voice without body. When she met the man at the Steeles' home she felt respect and awe, as for a revered sage. Apart from the Christmas parties McGill saw her only at All Saints Church, in the choir. Then in 1965 they ran into each other, by chance.[24]

The accidental meeting happened at the Atlanta airport. Everyone knew McGill didn't drive, though nobody could or would say exactly why—was it because he was so inept with machinery? At home, his driving history or lack of it "was a closed subject," according to Ralph Jr. Whatever the reason, McGill turned this peculiarity to his advantage. Always dependent on rides, he found himself observing people from the seat of a trolley or a bus, or being chauffeured in taxis, or by friends— once in the mid-1960s doubling up in the front seat with a fellow editor's wife sitting, unforgettably for her, on McGill's lap. It was natural then, when Mary Lynn saw him at the airport one day, to offer to drive him home. She chauffeured him as one would deliver a valuable cargo, safely, to its destination. During the ride, as he related to Harold Martin, they chatted freely and easily "about everything under the sun." For him at least, the relationship changed that day from casual to serious. Soon he invited her to lunch on a Saturday and they continued their conversations at a table in the Capital City Club, where earlier he had charmed George Biggers. She enjoyed their time together—"I never knew a mind like that," she later recalled—and they met there for lunch on more Saturdays and then more often, then daily, after work, for drinks at her apartment, then dinner, after which Mary Lynn would chauffeur him home.[25]

For months, McGill found himself in the awkward position of being too much the wise and old sage. Though he had fallen in love and was thinking about marriage, Mary Lynn lived on another emotional plane. "He loved me first," as she later put it. When at last he proposed, she was so unprepared that it stunned her.

"I'm in awe of you and you don't marry someone you're in awe of," she told him. "Maybe," he said thoughtfully, "You'll learn to love me."

With that in mind he kept courting her, reminding her how serious he was and occasionally mentioning marriage, talking about her as the "Paragon" and confessing his love in letters to her sister-in-law Helen in Boston. She made it clear to him that she cherished his companionship but that marriage wouldn't work. "I told him," she recalled, "that I loved going out to dinner with him, I loved talking to him, I loved just sitting with him at home not talking, or driving him somewhere in the car, but

I didn't love him. I just looked up to him as a father figure. And we couldn't build a marriage on that." His persistence paid off. While on vacation, away from McGill's loving attention, Mary Lynn realized how much she missed him and all the things they did together. It was all very mysterious as the man who understood the couple best explained it: "Somehow, her feelings changed. He was no longer a father figure, but her contemporary." When she returned, she told him she would marry him.[26]

His friends noticed an immediate swing in his emotional well being. "Nothing that had happened to McGill in many years had given him a deeper sense of happiness and fulfillment than this promise," Martin thought. "Pride in his city, pride in his son, joy in his own good fortune at having won, so late in life, the love of an attractive and intelligent woman, made McGill's mood almost euphoric."[27]

He took her to meet his mother, who was then weakened by cancer. Even from her sickbed, Mary Loula McGill projected a strong will. As matriarch, she had knit the family together during hard times, alone for twenty-six years since Ben's death. She was especially proud of Ralph. His luster outshone that of his three sisters in his mother's eyes, and to friends she continually cataloged his many accomplishments and travels. She had of course heard from Ralph of his rapture for his new love. Now she asked Mary Lynn to come closer to her bedside. She spoke in a whisper the sentence Mary Lynn treasured forever: "I just want you to know that we all love you very much." Shortly after, in August 1966, with Ralph by her bedside, his mother died at the age of eighty-eight. In his grieving, McGill told Martin how much he owed his mother; his mother's dominance was all the more evident by the absence of references to his father. To her he traced his bedrock faith in God and in the Presbyterian belief in predestination. Because of this, Martin thought, McGill "never spoke of any future plan without adding the provisional, 'God willing.'"[28]

McGill's outlook brightened shortly after, when Ralph Jr. announced that he and Adelaide Martin planned to marry. McGill and Mary Lynn agreed to hold off their wedding until after Ralph Jr. and Adelaide were wed in December 1966, with Ralph Sr. as best man. They set their own date for April 20. It would also allow McGill to make two trips he had delayed.

McGill had put off overseas journeys while his mother was gravely ill, but now he planned a trip to Vietnam. He always gained confidence from his own observations and conversations at the scene, and this trip was the missing ingredient he needed. His own critics argued that he did not know what was actually happening there. Eugene Patterson, the *Constitution* editor since 1960, when McGill became publisher, had gone to Vietnam in 1964. Now McGill, particularly as he supported the president's military escalation, could verify what he thought he already knew and, as always, mix with the real people and sense the reality of the war.

McGill's sojourn in Vietnam in September 1966 resembled the occasional "fact-finding" tours by emissaries from the Pentagon, the State Department, and the White House. He visited the troops in cities and in war zones, one visit including a happy evening with Harold Martin's son. But he found only facts which supported his a priori conclusion that the American military presence there stabilized the government until a peace could be negotiated, as in Korea. Nothing shook him from this belief, not the history of the triumph of the North Vietnamese over the French or the North's frequent, surprising successes, or the resurgence of Vietcong in villages around the South. In this frame of mind he was supportive of any measures the Johnson administration took to protect American soldiers, including the bombing of North Vietnam. He wrote fifteen columns concerning Vietnam, all of which were published during October. None of them supported serious doubts about American policy such as were then held by two of his closest associates.

During 1966 his old friend Harry Ashmore and McGill's protégé at the *Miami News,* Bill Baggs, discouraged by the escalation of the war and unsatisfied with the Johnson administration's attempts to end it, were planning a private peace initiative to Hanoi. It was an endeavor unthinkable to McGill because it conflicted with the administration's strategy to force a peace settlement. When McGill learned of it, it strained the relationship among the Brethren, who had banded together through the struggle for civil rights.

Ashmore was the principal protagonist, becoming as committed to the peace movement as he had been to civil rights. After winning the Pulitzer, he left journalism and continued his writing and advocacy with the Center for the Study of Democratic Institutions headed by Robert M. Hutchins in Santa Barbara, California. From 1965 on, he was at the heart of the peace movement as the center opened lines of communication with Hanoi. In June 1966, Ho Chi Minh replied to Hutchins's initiative: "The Vietnamese people cherish peace, genuine peace, peace in independence and freedom, not the sham peace of 'Johnson's brand.'" While the United States was "still expanding the criminal war, the convening of a conference to discuss a peaceful settlement of the Viet Nam problem, as suggested by you, is not yet appropriate." Nonetheless, the center proceeded with plans for a peace convocation in July in Geneva, with invitations especially to Asian delegates and a specific "unofficial" focus on Vietnam.[29]

Ashmore enlisted Baggs as the journalist who would document the effort for the mass media. In contrast to his mentor, McGill, Baggs was a far freer spirit, younger and less encumbered by loyalties to party and power brokers in Washington. With his Florida connections, he had become a darling of the Kennedy clan, conversing often with the president and Attorney General Robert Kennedy. Baggs's loyalties, however, did not carry over, as McGill's did, to Johnson and Johnson's war. Early on, while the so-called peaceniks had few converts even among the civil rights movement, Baggs acknowledged their antiwar arguments and believed that the escalation of hostilities was harmful to the nation's interests, if not futile. By 1965 Baggs was eager to join Ashmore in a radical, undercover scheme to initiate peace talks. Working confidentially through a middle man with access to Hanoi, Ashmore and Baggs arranged for a strictly "unofficial" peace initiative, an offer to begin a dialogue with Ho Chi Minh. In late November 1965, when the Johnson administration was planning to ask Congress for the massive military buildup, they had succeeded in breaking the ice. Baggs sent Ashmore a "personal and confidential" message saying he had advised Senator Fulbright of "our little pieces of business in world peace and Viet Nam. . . . I was quite candid with Bill and told him the whole story about our man in Hanoi and the reaction of Ho Chi Minh to the proposal. . . . I emphasized that we did not know whether we were dealing in fairy tales or facts at this point, but if it were true, a long season of silence with Ho has been broken. The Senator was enthusiastic."

In early 1966, after Fulbright questioned the president's military buildup, Baggs received cautionary advice from McGeorge Bundy in the White House. Ashmore's center was planning a general conference in Geneva to provide a peace forum for anyone, especially the Vietnamese. The conference, Bundy advised, should not appear to be "merely a condemnation" of White House Vietnam policy. "In other words," Baggs told Ashmore, "the less we can look like angry dissenters on the Viet policy, and the more we can look like concerned Americans, interested in examining all of the ingredients necessary for peace, the better off I think we are going to be."[30]

The center's "Pacem in Terris Convocation" in Geneva opened pathways for unofficial talks in Hanoi. In January 1967 Ashmore and Baggs traveled to Hanoi, photographed the devastation caused by American bombing, and spoke with top government officials. In 1968 they returned, and on March 24 met Ho Chi Minh and heard his prerequisite for opening peace talks. Ho was "lively and alert at 78, chain-smoking American cigarets" probably brought in by the Vietcong from U.S. bases in the South. "When the bombing stops," Ho said, "we can talk." The "long season of silence with Ho" was broken. but the State Department gave them both a chilly reception. Secretary of State Dean Rusk passed them in a corridor one day without a word and refused to meet with them, as they noted in their book chronicling the entire mission. Johnson's reaction to their visit, relayed by Senator Fulbright, was: "I'd like to see them, Bill, but you know I can't talk with everybody who's been over there talking with Ho Chi Minh." Up to then, Baggs and Ashmore were the only ones in that class.[31]

McGill was disappointed in them both, but particularly in Baggs. Ashmore had left journalism, but McGill looked upon Baggs as a protégé, bright, courageous, promising—one of his own making. He regarded their relationship as one of mutual respect. Now he felt rejection, if not betrayal, and spent hours on the phone sharing his laments with Johnny Popham, who had retired to Lookout Mountain, near Chattanooga. "Oh, yes, it troubled him so. He would call late at night and I would listen to him go on," Popham recalled.[32]

Baggs realized the futility of trying to justify or persuade. McGill's loyalty to the party and to the Johnson administration, and his allegiance to the flag and the marines in battle, precluded a reasonable dialogue. It was as though, when it came to war, McGill surrendered qualities which were a source of wisdom and strength—his lifelong moderation between extremes and his capability of gleaning truth from even those who disagreed with him. One evening, attending a party in the home of the *Atlanta Journal* city editor Harold Davis, McGill was accosted by an antiwar liberal. Davis watched as McGill, refusing to discuss the issue, immediately said goodbye and left. It was the same tactic McGill had used with rabid segregationists whose minds he knew he could not change. People who celebrated McGill's lifelong campaign for civil rights wondered at his intransigence on the war. Jack Tarver recalled an in-air conversation with Martin Luther King Jr. when they happened to be on the same flight.

"How can McGill be so right on race," King asked Tarver, "and so wrong about Vietnam?"

"Remember," Tarver told King, "Ralph McGill is an old Marine and he's going to follow that flag wherever it goes."[33]

By contrast, Baggs was a free thinker, a "maverick," as McGill called him—a characteristic McGill admired, usually. But Baggs was unwilling to give Johnson a blank check, although he admired the president's historic accomplishments for the disfranchised and underprivileged for whom Baggs cared deeply throughout his career. Referring to McGill's Medal of Freedom and devotion to the president, Baggs wrote to Ashmore that McGill "is assuming the ways of the man he most admires. . . . The cunning insight of Dr. McGill reminds me that no one of us is immune from imitating our heroes. For instance, lately I have noticed Dr. McGill lifting his little dog by the ears. . . . I think, Colonel, we must realize imitation has become a hallmark of our times and know that our beloved older brother in Atlanta is not wrong in style, it is just the substance he overlooked."[34]

Whenever Baggs brought up arguments against the war, McGill discounted them as capricious and dangerous, undermining American soldiers in battle and encouraging Hanoi that it could win by outlasting American public opinion. Nonetheless, McGill avoided a complete break with Baggs, resorting instead to humor laced with sarcasm. He suggested that Baggs and Ashmore commission self-commemorative garden statues of themselves, "done in the Greek manner." "Dr. Baggs has a nice garden, and in my mind's eye I can see a life statue of him in the nude except for the fig leaf, standing close by the old mango tree." On another occasion McGill jested that he would lend Baggs "a blanket and a sheet" if Baggs attended the Vietnam peace sleep-in at Atlanta's Piedmont Park. Tarver would lend a second blanket and Harold Martin a pillow. When in the aftermath of Arab-Israeli War in 1967 Baggs was honored with the Eleanor Roosevelt–Israel Humanities Award, McGill reminded that he had earlier received that award, as well as the Israeli Medal of Valor. McGill wrote that the honor raised a question about Baggs's new role as an Israeli hawk conflicting with his dovish stance on Vietnam. They had both been "ardent supporters in the war of Israel against the Arab states. I was not in favor of peace at that moment, but of victory in war by the valiant forces of the armies of Israel and the airforce. . . . I am a little puzzled by those who are for war in one part of the world and insistent on peace in another." He added that "all of us are happy to see you in the position of an Israeli hawk."[35]

Baggs's response to the dove-hawk quandary clarified the reality of the fissure that separated the Brethren. Baggs too preferred to aim for the jocular rather than the jugular. But now in candor he paraphrased one of Emerson's axioms, telling McGill that "man should not be a slave to consistency." Baggs said he championed Israel as "what is at least a promising democratic experiment." Reminding that he was a bomber pilot in World War II, he added, "Like you, I am a soldier, not so old, but aging, and am not horrified by war when it is necessary. My only argument about the war in Vietnam is that we are fighting on the wrong side. Any old Confederate, below or above the battalion level, can sniff and know if he is fighting on the wrong side. Have you tried sniffing lately, Doctor?" Offsetting the sarcasm, Baggs added, "know that I love you, and I will feel even more your brother wearing the badge of the new award."[36]

While he continued to make foreign and domestic troubles his own, McGill seemed much happier to all who knew him in 1967. Most attributed his improved outlook to Mary Lynn. Even before their marriage in April he was happy at the prospect of sharing everything with her. She was pleased to attend the wedding of Ralph Jr. and Adelaide. Well before her own wedding she was acclimating to the idea of marriage to this venerable, charming, nostalgic man whose work had become his life inextricably intertwined.

Early on, he had began the habit of asking Mary Lynn what she thought of his columns after they appeared in the paper to see if they made sense. Getting her opinion was no small concern at a time when events at home and overseas seemed to be changing at an accelerating rate and McGill found himself writing not only about a frustrating war, but about rioting in the cities and the emergence of new political forces— reactionaries seeking to turn the country back before 1964 and radicals articulating dissatisfaction with the slow implementation of civil rights. Because he was writing everyday, with so much to attend to, he usually wrote fast, "off the top of his head." As his fellow editorial writers knew, he would have some "off" days when his memory failed him or he didn't make the connections he hoped he had. And he knew his influence was diminishing with the increasing impact of television in showing foreign and domestic news. Beneath all this were his old insecurities dating back to when he made himself write seven days a week because he was "so fearful if he dropped out of sight they'd find someone else." His new sounding board, Mary Lynn, recalled the daily ritual: "He would read his column. Then he would have me read it. He would ask did I know what he meant? If I said no, he would say, 'Oh, my God, if you don't know.'"[37]

She was also getting used to his need to travel. Neither fear for his heart condition nor love for her could keep him from heading off restlessly, here and there. Visits to Washington to drop in on government and political sources had become a routine requirement for a national columnist. But on February 26, just two months before the wedding, he left the country, this time for another extensive tour of Africa that was expected to last six weeks. He was fulfilling a promise to the State Department that he would return to nations teetering toward communism and stress America's recent commitments to human rights for its own black citizens. When he asked Mary Lynn what she wanted from Africa, she replied, "A love letter." So, in addition to his daily columns, sent in batches of three for the newspaper, he also wrote her at length, describing the development of his "composite of love and affection" constructed "out of human experiences and out of oneself—ourselves, separately and together. So, I do not know in all its details why or how I love you, but I do."[38]

His second sojourn in Africa permitted McGill to renew acquaintances made in 1963 in West Africa and make new ones in the east. He went first to Ghana, then flew east to see Kenya for the first time, then Tanzania, Zambia, Rhodesia and, if he got a visa, South Africa. From Dar es Salaam on the Indian Ocean, his "Notes from Africa" column echoed President Kennedy's appeal to assist African progress: "If these new states and emerging peoples turn bitter in their taste of independence, then the reason will be that the Western powers, by their indifference or lack of imagination, have failed to see that it is their own future that is also at stake." McGill noted that President Johnson had also impressed the Africans at the signing of the Voting Rights Act with his declaration that, "It is not just (American) Negroes, but all of us, who must overcome the crippling legacy of bigotry and injustice." More recently in March, while McGill was in Africa, Johnson spoke at Howard University, giving what McGill interpreted as "a powerful commitment to unrelenting struggle against the powers of prejudice and ignorance."[39]

Given McGill's sentiments on racial injustice, it was not surprising when the apartheid South African government denied him a visa and the opportunity to make talks at several universities. The government gave no reason. In Washington, a State Department spokesman reported the refusal during a news conference, saying it was "regrettable." As early as 1947 he had been interviewing South African editors who visited Atlanta. That year, he was incredulous when an editor told him, "Our chief problem is not racial conflict but soil erosion and the inability to find more soil which can be cultivated. The problem is not the native problem but the survival of the white man's economy upon which the native economy depends." In 1955, after receiving the editor of the South African prime minister's newspaper, an "Afrikaner on tour," McGill filtered out the public relations messages and wrote caustically that "some 10,000,000 natives are deprived of even the most elemental rights under the very rigid form of separateness. There is, inevitably, a continuing crisis, fear and concern—and no solution. The population gulf widens, the pressures increase." Now in 1967, McGill was denied the chance to repay those visits. As news reports noted, he joined a "growing list of journalists and other Americans to be refused entry," including newsmen who in 1966 wanted to accompany Robert Kennedy, traveling as a U.S. senator from New York. The cancellation abbreviated McGill's tour, bringing him home two weeks earlier to Mary Lynn and the reality of getting married a second time.[40]

The wedding at All Saints Episcopal Church was grander than she had imagined, in part because they both approached the ceremony without fanfare. "We sent no invitations," she recalled. When someone suggested photographs, Mary Lynn agreed, "It would be nice to have some." McGill did invite people informally. At work, he posted a notice on the *Constitution* bulletin board inviting all colleagues. On the day, April 20, Mary Lynn went to her dentist's office in the morning. After noon, she arrived at the church surprised to see the police motorcycles out front. She had not expected the need. News photographers captured the joy of the event, and in North Carolina the ailing Carl Sandburg and his wife, Helga, saw the picture. "It made me quite giddy with delight to open the morning paper," Helga wrote the next day, "and see the lovely smiling face of your bride—and you looking so pleased." The other North Carolina member of the Brethren, Harry Golden, added, "Congratulations. And to you and Mary Lynn my best wishes for a long and happy life." His life was far happier, so thought his friends. As Margaret Tarver saw it, "She made his last years very happy."[41]

McGill's life habit of writing the column while on vacation extended to their honeymoon in New England. His "Notes Made in New England" chronicled their visit to Salem, Massachusetts, where the community leaders had condoned hanging women as witches, based on the "mean and fearful lies" of nine-year-old minister's daughter, Elizabeth Parris. The eighteenth-century girl provided a segue to criticize twentieth-century politicians who practiced witch hunting and dishonest or shallow-minded reporters who spread distortions. In the first camp Goldwater "conservatives" were "busy trying to make President Johnson and his administration out as communistic." In his own profession, "too much of today's journalism—on the radio and TV and newspapers is cheap, dishonest stuff—the distortion of truth by the use of lies, half truths and innuendoes. It has been a long time since 'witches' were hanged in Salem. But the neurotic Elizabeth Parrises are still around."[42]

The critics chiseling away at the monumental Civil Rights Act disturbed McGill as much as anything. Criticism came from the Left as well as the Right, from radicals as well as Stone Age reactionaries. While the old men defended segregation and the way things were, young men were rousing audiences for greater justice. The segregationists were as worrisome as fleas but easy to identify and swat. More indecipherable to McGill was the rising "black power" movement and the "New Left," appealing to those frustrated by delays of civil rights and joined by young blacks and whites. Many seemed willing to abandon Martin Luther King's formula of nonviolence and compromise that was visibly biracial. That formula had reached a mountaintop, as King imagined it would, but many now wanted speedy implementation of what they saw from that vista— civil rights *and* economic rights.

McGill walked another tightrope as he criticized disruptive agitators and demagogues without belittling the legitimate causes they espoused. He targeted Stokely Carmichael, the new head of a vehement Student Nonviolent Coordinating Committee, SNCC ("Snick" as almost everyone called it). The black power movement drew strength from polarization, rallying opposition to Johnson administration policies, domestic and foreign. McGill wrote of Carmichael's "coup" at SNCC as racist, in that he "ousted from it all its thousands of dedicated white supporters." McGill found that Carmichael shared a technique common to segregationist demagogues like Wallace, "a verbal shock technique that is carefully designed to anger and arouse the opposition, to delight their more avid followers, and to dismay the noncommitted or middle-of-the-roader, if there be any of the latter left in the seismic sixties." At opposite poles, these two "political extremists," the familiar white supremacist Wallace and the young, fiery Carmichael, differed mainly in approach: "Mr. Carmichael, the more erudite and better read, might be said to employ the rapier style, with slashes of stinging wit and blood-letting satire. Mr. Wallace uses the club of denunciation and castigation. He is not without wit, but it is that of the old-style Southern political demagogue and there is no style in it."[43]

At worst, McGill warned, radicals of the New Left aimed to increase resistance to the Vietnam war draft and foment riots in the cities the summer of 1967. With information supplied by "researchers" into the New Left, McGill noted that the Students for a Democratic Society "welcomes Communists to membership and hopes to remake them into activists in the new revolution. . . . 'Che' Guevara, who for a time was Fidel Castro's alter-ego, is one of the new heroes and/or idols of the New Left." Guevara was, "along with the late Malcolm X, a rough U.S. equivalent of Marx and Lenin for the New Left."[44]

Linking the New Left to the urban riots, McGill claimed to understand the underlying reasons for frustration in the slums of Los Angeles, Newark, and Detroit. Years of deprivation of basic economic, social, and political rights had created a tinderbox, and now, with rising expectations in the wake of the civil rights acts, the frustrated underclass was restless and ripe for exploitation. He pounded home the thesis he had maintained about racial problems, that they were not strictly southern. Injustice was general across the land.

He showed his continuing frustration with politicians. The reason Carmichael attracted audiences, he insisted, was because of the failure of political leaders at all levels to move ahead with nationally agreed-upon objectives, to simply "obey the law." "Who makes it possible for the Stokely Carmichaels to have ears ready to listen, emotional resentments ready to expand, bitterness ready to curdle into the acid of hatred and riots?" He traced despair and violence of the "long, hot summers" to "those congressmen who are seeking to 'water down' federal power to desegregate schools and give to all children the best possible system of education":

> Are the state officials, governors, superintendents, local politicians, and others who curse and denounce federal "interference" in schools giving aid and comfort to those whose profession is that of encouraging violence and resistance?
>
> Are these officials in substantial part as responsible for the incitement of lawlessness as Stokely Carmichael, whose "field work" is the recitation of their record? Could the Carmichaels tell their listeners who live with bitterness that white politicians never intend to satisfy the just claims of the

minorities if persons at congressional, state, and local levels moved to obey and implement law?

The answer is inescapable.

The nation had committed itself to civil rights and a war against poverty. "We are the richest and most powerful nation in the world," McGill wrote. "We can eliminate the worst of the poverty in this country. Indeed, we must do so or see our wealth and power decline."[45]

The basic flaw of the New Left, McGill concluded, was that it sought to destroy hated American "life" values while suffering from "a bankruptcy of replacement values." His composite caricature of New Left followers were pleasure seekers who "withdraw from society via the drugs of hallucination" and the "long-haired, bearded groups of varied interests and attachments" whose "rebellion of long hair and odd costumes is an identifying uniform" and whose "publications are verbose, but not communicatively articulate."[46]

His reference to New Left publications in 1967 was made several months before the first issue of the *Great Speckled Bird,* the alternative biweekly newspaper whose editors regularly castigated McGill. Given the Cox family monopoly on newspaper journalism in Atlanta, it was highly unusual to have the revered ancient sage of Atlanta raked over the coals as a senile fossil. Launched in Atlanta in March 1968, the *Bird* gave a voice to the antiwar movement. Its editors avowed in the first issue to "bitch and badger, carp and cry, and perhaps give Atlanta . . . a bit of honest and interesting and, we trust, even readable journalism." In the same statement, they portrayed McGill as hypocritic, senile, and either stupid or insane: "On one day peace demonstrators may be attacked by such men as Ralph McGill, publisher of the Atlanta Constitution, who the next day very rationally determines that the use of nuclear weapons in Vietnam may well become the only 'reasonable' and 'responsible' course for us to pursue! Insane? Obscene? And America." During 1968, as the antiwar movement gained adherents, the editors regularly targeted McGill in a "Dear Ralphie" column. In its very first issue, on page one, *Bird* columnist Don Speicher asked, "What's It All About, Ralphie?" and lamented in a fantasy obituary the death of the liberal McGill:

Died. Ralph McGill, editor, publisher, early civil rights advocate, pragmatic realist, manipulator and leading exponent of U.S. Imperialism and deception; of pronounced self-righteousness and senility, compounded by both the Red and Yellow perils; in Atlanta, Washington, Saigon, Newark, Hanoi, Detroit.

. . . Although a onetime supporter of progressive civil rights causes, albeit not unfalteringly, McGill later denounced these ties and began to redbait the progressive camp himself.

More recently, when his sense of southern guilt, sentimentality and maudlin self-preoccupation along with his credo of "objectivity" proved unable to cope with contemporary political realities, McGill withdrew to the nuclear powered, riot controlled tower of liberal reason and rationality, from whence he never returned.[47]

Speicher's main theme was that McGill and other "liberals born of the Cold War"—mired in the "rigid ideological and moral framework of cold war thought and power politics"—claimed a monopoly on reason while saying the unreasonable. "So it is that McGill can say that a great power must become involved in conflicts of power, without ever questioning the possibility that the great power may have initiated the conflict." On the use of nuclear weapons, he quoted McGill's hypothesis: "We are very close to the necessity to use the small strategic nuclear weapons. We cannot put massive armies to the task if the task comes." Again, claiming reason as the sole property of his camp, McGill, wrote Speicher, "can make the use of nuclear weapons seem reasonable, because after all, Vietnam is clearly a case of Chinese aggression and it's a guerrilla war and many soldiers are dying and large armies in that kind of war are not feasible and to make the world safe and rational again we might just have to drop a bomb or two or three or maybe more."[48]

While segregationists had for years declared open season on Ralph McGill, they had often fired with less articulation and accuracy (and more misspellings), as well as from a morally weak position doomed to erode in time. By contrast, the *Bird* shot from the *left* with a much sharper scope on the issues of morality, justice, and conscience upon which McGill had built his reputation. As the Democratic convention neared, the *Bird* sniped at McGill as being slavishly loyal to Vice President Hubert Humphrey. McGill had defended Humphrey's support of Johnson's war on the grounds that only a dishonorable man like the traitorous Aaron Burr would take the oath as vice president and then differ with the president. A regular reader, Tom O'Ware, wrote the "Dear Ralphie" column excoriating McGill for misrepresenting the history of American vice presidents from Thomas Jefferson to John C. Calhoun, Millard Fillmore, and John Nance Garner. In concluding, O'Ware spread the dishonor to McGill: "If Humphrey had the guts to stand up to Johnson, it would hardly have been a precedent. Humphrey may have set a precedent, however, in his utter subservience to LBJ. . . . No, Ralphie, the dishonorable man is . . . the veep who prostitutes his principles for a shot at his boss' job . . . and the journalist who perverts history to further that ambition."[49]

Whatever his critics might say, McGill still resonated prophecy and truth to his dear friend Carl Sandburg. In July 1967 came word of Sandburg's death at the age of eighty-nine. He had kept in touch with Sandburg through friends who carried his warm wishes and even the poet's favorite champagne to Connemara, particularly Harry Golden. "Carl was about the same on Christmas as he was on Thanksgiving Day. He gets out of bed for his meals but he still has the two nurses," Golden reported on January 7, 1966, the day after Sandburg's eighty-eighth birthday. "If I make 88, I'll go on to 99," Sandburg had predicted. Golden found "flashes of great lucidity and even brilliance. Like supplying the last line of an old IWW song I sang."[50]

McGill hastened to share the grief with Helga and attend the simple funeral service which brought together McGill and Golden, the family, and a few other friends. In a small church amid the pines, firs, poplars, and oaks, poems by Sandburg and Whitman were read from the pulpit, and the spirit of Stephen Vincent Benét was evoked in McGill's favorite poem. "Some few of us joined in a low singing of the old song ["John Brown's Body"] which Sandburg thought one of the most rousing tunes in American history," he wrote. "There was no eulogy, but the poems were eulogy enough. The minister read them well and those in the ancient church sat enchanted with a feeling of happiness and assurance that all was well with Carl Sandburg."[51]

20

A Legacy

*[Martin Luther] King ended his life as a disappointed, yet
ultimately faithful, Jeremiah, still pursuing and prophesy-
ing the final fulfillment of America's democratic promise.*
—DAVID HOWARD-PITNEY, *The Afro-American Jeremiad*

There is a New South, not yet here—but coming.
—RALPH McGILL, 1968

THE DEATH OF FRIENDS saddened McGill but did not drive him into a
morose sense of his own impending doom. With each departure he seemed
to work all the harder to rationalize his life and make sense of his world.
Despite his arrhythmic heart, he continued to work as a man who did
not intend to retire. Throughout 1968 his columns continued to pour
daily, chronicling the volatile national political scene, interspersed often
with personal reminiscences and history lessons for those who had not
had the experience of living so long as he, or of meeting the great men
who shaped the twentieth century. At the same time, he crowded his life
as he continued to write book reviews and prefaces to books, contribute
articles to national publications, and accept numerous invitations to make
public speeches. "The genius of McGill," Harold Martin would conclude
shortly afterward, "lay in the fact that everything turned him on, mentally and emotionally, and once the idea began to glow and shimmer in
his mind, there was nothing that could throw his thoughts off track." A
year later, another old friend would recall McGill's swirling activity as his
greatest shortcoming. "He always took on too much," Reb Gershon concluded. "He wore himself out."[1]

At bottom, he staved off any lapses into depression by taking comfort in his family. At Christmas he enjoyed spending time with his new
grandson, Ralph III, in Richmond, where Ralph Jr. had found a job with

an advertising agency. At home, McGill delighted in the hours he spent with Mary Lynn. "Marriage was very important to him," she said. He worked with her planting in the garden. He taught her to split logs. He loved splitting logs so much she worried aloud to his doctor. She worried about his heart and kept a supply of oxygen at hand. Listening to that irregular heartbeat, she would hear the ta duh ta duh—duh duh duh.

The politics of an election year always intrigued him, but 1968 disturbed him profoundly and seemed to threaten the fabric of the nation. The war was going badly. The Communists' Tet Offensive in February turned the war into a minefield for the political year: it was difficult enough to defend an unpopular war, though McGill remained faithful to Johnson and the American soldiers doing the fighting. More than ever, the defeats drove doves into the antiwar movement and incited hawks to demand that the United States do more to win. Realizing his no-win situation, Johnson on March 30 shocked his supporters by announcing his decision not to seek reelection, throwing the race for the presidency into complete disarray. McGill favored Vice President Hubert Humphrey over Senator Robert Kennedy.[2]

One shock followed another. On April 4, in Memphis, Martin Luther King was shot and killed during his campaign to assist the city's sanitation workers. The nation was plunged into days of gloom and anger. Many expressed their frustration by rioting, burning, and looting. Front-page photographs showed the destruction and, symbolic of civil unrest, the troops guarding the nation's Capitol.

The King funeral centered attention on Atlanta, bringing a host of admirers and political leaders from around the world. McGill mourned and eulogized. In a sense, King had done as much for whites as for his own people. King had helped free the "white slaves," the men and women who for generations had been so occupied with the systematic suppression of an entire race that their own energies had been wasted. "And at last the killer, slave to his own hatreds and guilt, destroyed the one prestigious voice that called for nonviolent action," McGill wrote a week later in the *Boston Globe*. "The loss is enormous." The riots warned of greater troubles. "Extremists see an opportunity to gain ground and power, especially if there are not other voices and personalities to come forward to fill the power vacuum before the violent bear it away."[3]

Among those paying last respects to King on the campus around Atlanta University was Senator Robert Kennedy, whose collaboration with King and the civil rights movement had been a source of political and personal strength. Only two months later, just after winning the California primary, Kennedy himself was the victim of an assassin. Though McGill had tilted politically away from Kennedy in favor of Johnson then Humphrey, he eulogized the former president's brother as one "who believed in human rights and justice; a man who took that belief to the people and imposed it upon their consciences."[4]

The summer's political conventions drew him magnetically, though their strangeness and hostility saddened him. At the Republican convention in Miami Beach, Nixon's nomination this time around seemed to bode ill for the pace of school desegregation and the accomplishments of the civil rights movement. This was underscored as Nixon gained support from South Carolina senator Strom Thurmond, who had converted to the Republican party during the Goldwater retreat from the Civil Rights Act. The Democratic convention in Chicago also lacked the joy of the prewar conventions when Democrats had been happier and McGill's associates were closer. As for the South, the old "Gothic" politics had changed radically in the '60s. To a betting man, the odds had changed. "The pre-1962 and 1964 molds," he wrote, "are already broken."[5]

These conventions were less joyful for personal reasons. Before his estrangement from Bill Baggs and Harry Ashmore, their happy nighttime cavorting at the conventions that nominated John F. Kennedy and Lyndon Johnson punctuated the day's political trading. Perhaps in an effort to make peace, McGill in March had gone out of his way to praise Ashmore ("Ashmore was at his superb rational best") on a domestic topic they both agreed on: Stokely Carmichael. After reading Ashmore's review of Carmichael's book, McGill wrote a long letter to *Center* magazine, recalling the time shared with Ashmore during the Little Rock crisis eleven years earlier, and refuting Carmichael's assertion that white society bestowed only "token" rights upon blacks: "Mr. Ashmore accurately argues that the presence of a brilliant lawyer, Thurgood Marshall, on the U.S. Supreme Court and the election of Negro mayors, legislators, and judges, plus the grass-roots election of some two hundred local officials in the Southern states, including two sheriffs, are not 'tokenism.' Nor is the job opportunity for educated and trained men and women tokenism."[6]

At the Chicago convention, the calling out of the national guard to maintain order distressed McGill and called forth more analysis of the New Left. "The one bright light was the nomination of Humphrey with the hope that he would be able to emerge victorious despite the stigma attached to his serving Johnson and the war," he wrote.

As the nation headed into the tumultuous general election campaign, McGill seemed to embody the contradictions in the country. He wavered constantly between lamenting the state of the nation and counting its blessings. When asked for his observations by editors at an African American newspaper, the *Atlanta Inquirer,* McGill wanted to side with optimism when looking back at the nearly forty years since he arrived in Atlanta. "I am almost awed by the changes that have come and by the progress made," he wrote. Thinking of his audience of black readers, he quickly added, "However, I am well aware that the progress has been largely in a few areas and that advances have not been general. . . . I can well understand the more militant demands for separatism, but I cannot see how separatism in any country is a workable concept or policy." With that exception, he suppressed the apocalyptic apparitions of Maddox, Nixon, Thurmond, and Wallace: "I have always had hope. And I now believe that much of the old inertia is dissipated and that there is a general forward movement. I am sure this forward advance will be of increased tempo." The whites and blacks of the South seemed in the situation "like that expressed in a wedding ceremony: We must go along together, for better or worse."[7]

To another audience, however, McGill gave a darker forecast. Asked to write a preface to the posthumous reprinting of Carl Sandburg's *Chicago Race Riots,* McGill concluded that people had learned "not much" in the half century since Sandburg wrote about the riots that began when a black boy "swam past an invisible line of segregation at one end of Chicago's public beaches" and ended after three days of riots with thirty-four men dead, twenty blacks and fourteen whites, hundreds injured, and several houses burned. "The lesson of 1919 and of later years has not been fully learned. There still is resistance to creating an unsegregated society in which the Negro is free to be his own self—not an imitation white man, but a Negro or black citizen of this country." He forecast "renewed attempts to thwart, delay or ignore the laws and the gains." But with a nod to optimism, he added, "They can hardly succeed."[8]

Ferment in the South in the '60s led to all manner of forecasts. McGill was never happier than when informing the public mind of his interpretation of events. When Time-Life Books was about to publish a book about the Old South, McGill accepted the opportunity to write an introduction which covered slavery to the '60s. He seemed like some Moses who on a high mount could see "there is a New South, not yet here—but coming. One sees it in the face of young Negro children in school singing lustily and confidently. . . . The New South is in the faces of students, white and black, and in the faces of the young executives, Southern trained and oriented." He quoted an optimistic Twentieth Century Fund study, which concluded that the South was undergoing "a slow moving social revolution of significant proportions" that needed increased education and upgraded training of its work force. "That," McGill noted, "will be done—it is being done." Asked to write about the South for the 1969 *Compton Yearbook,* McGill reckoned with the black militant who "scorns the progress made—and that is understandable." Yet he wanted even the militants to admit "the cumulative push" of the sacrifices and successes of the '50s and '60s: "The laws enacted, the violence and the nonviolent campaigns, the murders of civil rights workers in Mississippi and Alabama, the days and weeks spent in Southern jails, the beatings, the brutalizing by sheriffs and jailers. All these, plus successes, have given the old and young black people pride and determination, a pride the white people are sharing."[9]

After the election, he worried that Nixon would set back the clock on the arrival of a New South. Across the South voters gave Nixon 34.7 percent, Wallace 34.3 percent, and Humphrey 31 percent. Southerners seemed to be saying they preferred the dual school system, poor and segregated, that they had grown up with. The southerner, McGill concluded, does not "seem to understand what it has done to him and his children. 'The fabric' of his being, what he likes and what he has become accustomed to, was created in his youth. He will not give it up. He prefers for his children to have less opportunity than those of other regions if to have improvement means sharing it with the colored child."[10]

McGill suspected that Nixon's political debts to Thurmond and others would postpone or reverse progress on the racial issue, a swing of the pendulum backward, as when President Rutherford Hayes withdrew enforcement of gains made by the freed slaves. "'The New South'—so long prophesied—is on the way," he wrote. "It will come faster when, and if, the racial prejudices are ended and the state's educational and political institutions can function freely. Mr. Nixon, as president, can help it along if he refuses to deal with the more negative influences in the south." On the other hand, Nixon could arrest the South's progress by turning education over to local control which, in areas still resisting the *Brown* decision, means "the Segs."[11]

Even in the dismal defeat of Humphrey McGill found a silver lining in the fact that George Wallace, running on the issue of race, was a "bust" in forty states outside the South. True, Georgia (though not Atlanta) and four other Deep South states had chosen Wallace, and in doing so they had "placed themselves, their economies and social institutions under a national microscope." Nationally the "working class" rejected him. Why did he appeal to the Deep South? "Gentle reader," McGill wrote, "thou knowest the answer. Early in the campaign Mr. Wallace's Georgia manager said that when all the issues were considered they spelled 'N-I-G-G-E-R.'" McGill speculated that perhaps "there are enough around who find THE issue dominant in their lives and who will keep Mr. Wallace around for yet another run around the national track." More likely, Wallace Democrats would convert to Republicans.[12]

McGill worried all the more when he regarded the respect paid at the national level to right-wing reactionaries. To his mind, the John Birch Society subsumed the mantle of segregationists, amplifying the message coast to coast. Birchers claimed to be anti-Communists, intent on rooting out an invisible Communist conspiracy through which the Soviet Union was manipulating American political institutions. "The mind boggles at such beliefs so solemnly proclaimed," McGill wrote. "And yet there are men and women who say, 'Well, you've got to hand it to the Birchers—they are against communism.'" He saw beyond the anti-Communist cloak into an organization that wished to "deny the

American minorities the protection of the American Constitution—to impose military might for law, to remove civilian control of the military, to destroy the checks and balances of our Constitution. What's wrong with the Birchers? The answer seems plain enough."[13]

Amid the rhetoric for "black power," McGill acknowledged the importance of black pride and the persistence of racism in white southern traditions. "Today's understandable and commendable search for identity and origins by American Negroes finds a shift in word usage from Negro to Afro-American and black," he noted. At the same time, whites needed to consider the implications of even the songs they sang. "The South's fervent commitment to 'Dixie,'" he wrote, "is an example of the stubborn, tenacious hold of old prejudices and customs." Doing some research, he noted that "Dixie" was written in New York City in 1859, one of the popular "darky songs" of the minstrel shows that "featured, of course, white performers in exaggerated black-face makeup" and "pandered to the myth that slavery was really a benign institution and that all the slaves were happy, dancing, singing, simple souls who dearly loved the old plantation and Ol' Massa and Ol' Missus."[14]

McGill's habit of reading never abated, nor did his book reviews, often capsulated in a column, lavishly quoting the book. He delighted in setting the record straight whenever a good history was published, such as James Weinstein's *Decline of Socialism in America, 1912–1925*. McGill noted that the socialist movement in the early years of the century was a "necessary force for reform" but by 1922 had dwindled to almost nothing. All who blamed socialists for America's ills, McGill concluded, might consider "There are almost no 'Socialists' per se in America."[15]

His passion for books impressed those who knew him well. The only way he could read three books a week, his rate at his peak, was by devouring them. "I had never seen a mind like his," Mary Lynn said. Sitting at the table in the kitchen, he would "flip the pages. I thought he was just skimming. But he would tell me what was there word for word." Books extended his intellectual reach in every direction. His mind, as Harold Martin eulogized him, "ranged from the atom to the stars." His phenomenal memory always impressed Mary Lynn. "He could read an historical marker after he had gone by it."[16]

McGill's mind held a storehouse of information, but he also had habits of mind that empowered him to bring the right information to bear quickly on the matter at hand, whether it was slavery or Eastern Europe. Mary Lynn recalled the day they hosted a dinner guest from Czechoslovakia. "Ralph knew the name of every one in the government, when they'd been to Moscow. I asked him how. 'I just knew it,' he said. The same was true for Israel. He knew all the mountains and rivers. Same thing happened to us with a man from Outer Mongolia." He encouraged her to read more. "We were invited to a White House dinner and I was to sit at the same table with the President of Tunisia," she recalled. "I did not know much about Tunisia and I was nervous. Ralph said, 'Go read about Tunisia, get familiar.' I tell you I knew so much. That was his advice, and I thought it was so handy." One night McGill was invited to join a radio hookup to talk about civil rights by phone from their bedroom.

"Who is it?" Mary Lynn asked.

"I don't know," he said.

"What are you going to say?"

"I don't know yet."

"He was in his robe," she recalled, "and he expounded on civil rights as though he prepared a text."[17]

By virtue of the title of publisher, McGill was assumed by many to be in charge of the newspaper. There were times when he probably wished he were, but friends knew that he usually was happy that Eugene Patterson was in charge as editor and Jack Tarver ruled the business side. When McGill was named publisher, Reb Gershon remembered, she asked him what the new title meant. "It means," he replied, "that I'm going to have the time to do what I like best and can do best and not have to bother about the things I hate and don't do well." He was satisfied that he could ward off the nemesis of retirement by confining himself to writing. "Somebody may come into my office one of these days," he said weeks before his death, "and tell me that my working time is up, but I don't expect that. No, I'll probably not retire. I'm feeling good and working hard; I'm married to a fine, beautiful woman; I like what I'm doing for a living; and I'm not nearly finished with what I hope to get done." While the public may have assumed that the publisher ruled the realm, in actuality McGill controlled only his own column and sometimes, by persuasion, influenced the editorial board. He did not run the newsroom, as evidenced by the fact that the newsroom did not cover the civil rights marches in Selma and elsewhere, as McGill would have liked. After McGill's death, critics summing up his contributions generally noted his relegation of authority as a shortcoming.[18]

Nowhere was McGill more helpless than in mediating between his two friends, Patterson and Tarver, two strong and fiercely independent personalities. Biggers, not Tarver, had hired Patterson. "Jack never liked me," Patterson declared. Until 1960, Patterson was executive editor, overseeing the news operations of both the *Journal* and the *Constitution*. "Instead of firing me he sent me upstairs to be editor of the *Constitution* under Mr. McGill," Patterson recalled. "He told me, 'I'm doing you no favors. I'm asking you to play right field after Babe Ruth.'" The switch, Patterson thought, was for "mixed reasons. He knew I could write. He knew that I shared Mr. McGill's views on race and, being a native Georgian, that was a fairly rare thing. He knew I was a fairly conservative man. He figured he could use me to slow Mr. McGill down."[19]

The contrary happened. McGill emboldened Patterson, and the two developed a deep friendship. "He became the best friend I ever had. We were absolutely close for about 12 years," Patterson said. When they discussed subjects for their columns, "he was thinking mainly of right and wrong—and who's right and who's wrong. If that made a nationally syndicated column, that's fine. He was a uniquely idealistic and honorable man. He said what he thought, and he had the guts of a burglar. He taught all of us Southern editors to be bolder than we were. He broke the frozen silence and then gave us all the courage to go further than we thought we could. He didn't look on himself as any great courageous leader at all. He was combative, pugnacious—he had played football at Vanderbilt—and he had that great sense of humor. He'd say exactly what he thought. Taught me to be brave."[20]

The arrangement lasted for almost eight years, with occasional disagreements between Patterson and Tarver. In the summer of 1968, Patterson recalled a disagreement over news coverage which ended when Tarver leapt up and left Patterson's office, asking, "Why are you against everything I'm trying to do at this paper?" That September they had one final clash that attracted national attention to the management of the *Constitution* when Patterson resigned.

The triggering event was a satirical column. One of Patterson's young writers, B. J. Phillips, wrote a personal opinion column satirizing the Georgia Power Company for seeking a rate increase. Tarver was understandably upset. He had asked Patterson not to criticize Georgia Power because the *Constitution* itself was about to raise its own rates for advertising and subscriptions. "We're going to look hypocritical," Patterson recalled Tarver telling him over the phone. "I'm asking you to leave them alone on this." "I didn't feel good about it," Patterson said, but he agreed: "OK, we'll lay off it editorially. I went in the tank about it for Jack." Afterward, Phillips showed him her column. "She didn't know that I had this deal," Patterson said. "So she wrote a column, which is totally separate from the editorials, that asked, 'Wouldn't it be wonderful if *we* could pass along rate increases?' I read the column and I knew it was trouble. But all I promised Tarver was that the editorial policy of the *Atlanta Constitution* is not going to come down hard on Georgia Power. But columnists are independent. And here this kid had written a column that I thought was pretty good."

Tarver telephoned immediately on reading the column in the first edition. Patterson recalled that he was "just raging, just squealing with anger: 'I thought you told me that we weren't going to say anything.' I explained that this was a column separate from an editorial. And he went on." As Harold Martin told the story, Tarver "suggested, with considerable asperity, that Miss Phillips should confine herself to matters within her field of competence. Patterson responded that he had no intention of telling his columnists what they should or should not write, so long as they stayed within the boundaries of the libel laws and the canons of good taste." "My fuse had been getting shorter and shorter," Patterson recalled. "'That's enough,' I said. 'Get yourself another editor.'"[21]

Patterson's abrupt departure fed the rumor mill. McGill indicated afterward that Patterson would have left anyway, indicating that the Georgia Power incident merely provided the timing for the departure of an ambitious young man who had, the previous year, won the Pulitzer Prize for editorial writing when only forty-four (McGill won it at sixty-one), young enough to cash in the award's prestige and move on to a better opportunity. "Gene Patterson was neither forced out nor fired," McGill said, but instead needed to "find his best opportunity in life." Until then, however, Patterson seemed content enough and comfortable. He had considerable prestige and a satisfactory income, as Martin noted, with "stock options, though paid for laboriously out of the grocery money, in time would make him rich."[22]

In any case, McGill did not persuade him to stay, but helped him find a job. As Martin recalled, "He got on the phone instead to newspaper owners whose professionalism he respected, telling them that Patterson was available and what a tremendous man he was." McGill played down his own initiatives. "Well . . . my friend Ben Bradlee, who had just been named editor of the *Washington Post,* called me. He said he wanted to hire Gene Patterson as managing editor of the *Post.* . . . He had thought, he said, that he could handle both jobs but now felt the need for a strong managing editor. And he said, 'I want him now. We need him today.'" Katharine Graham, the publisher, knew of Patterson's "reputation for the kind of independent-minded, tough, straight editing we all admired." Patterson was in the Brown Hotel in Louisville, Kentucky, to talk with the Binghams, who owned the Louisville newspaper. "I get this call from Ben Bradlee in Washington. So I assumed that he talked either to Mr. McGill or Tom Winship at the *Boston Globe.* 'Hey you want to fly into Washington and well talk about being managing editor?'" So, as McGill noted, with "our consent and blessings, he left suddenly. I won't say there wasn't any acrimony—there always is on a newspaper." In a farewell column, McGill wrote, "Gene and I, despite the gap of years between us, had the rare gift of being able to talk with one another in the full meaning of that word. . . . Sometimes we wondered about it as we worked, as we said, to keep the light burning in editorial windows so that all wandering sinners might return and the Philistines be more able to see."[23]

Shortly after Patterson left, McGill while making the rounds in Washington visited him at the *Post.* Martin recorded Patterson's response. Patterson "looked up from his desk in the managing editor's glass cage to see Pappy, 'his wise-old-owl face breaking into a big laugh,' coming towards him, arms outstretched. They gave each other a big embrazo, the back-pounded bear hug with which McGill loved to greet his closest friends." McGill had Patterson introduce him around the newsroom, where his reputation had preceded him. "You've got a good managing editor here," McGill told them. At dinner, Patterson wondered if McGill had been disappointed in his leaving. "Gene, I never blamed you. I understood how you felt. If I had been your age, I think I would have done the same thing. But now, I am getting old. I am just playing out my string."[24]

Not long after, Patterson ran into McGill in Washington. "The last time I saw him alive," Patterson recalled, "Bradlee and Philip J. Lang, the editorial page editor, we decided to walk down to Lafayette Park in front of the White House. There had been some fighting with demonstrators, tear gas. We were almost to the end of the street and coming out of this great scrimmage of demonstrators and police, comes Ralph McGill with his hat sideways, and his overcoat open, grinning. 'Where have you guys been?' He had this wonderful mischievous sense of humor."[25]

In Miami, Baggs received from Tarver a copy of Patterson's farewell note to the staff. "I can only imagine there is a sense or resentment, if not insurrection, in the news room. Or at least, a surliness expressed or unexpressed. As I understand the particulars I will be damned if I know what you could have done in the circumstances," Baggs told Tarver, adding:

> When there is a sense of severe difference on policy, and it can't be satisfied by reason, then I believe Gene did the proper thing. As you know better than I know, he is a splendid Gutenberg type, committed, involved, and feisty without being offensive. But for God's sake don't let any of this gossip find a resting place in your subconscious. The Atlanta papers today are far superior to what they were when you took over from Biggers. . . . I am proud of the inky backbone of both the Constitution and the Journal and I know you as the steadying hand of the soapbox.

Somewhat sage about newspaper politics, Baggs predicted that "Eugene will find the challenge he seems to be looking for in Washington. He also is going to find, I suspect, less freedom to flail in the objects of his dissatisfaction than he did when he resided in Atlanta."[26]

In the *Constitution* newsroom, some recognized the end of an era. "Pappy" McGill at seventy could not be around for much longer, and the presumed heir to his tradition of reason, decency, and racial justice was gone. Would management avoid a recurrence of the episode by finding someone more manageable? In any case, the man chosen to succeed Patterson was the *Constitution*'s political columnist, Reg Murphy, who also left Atlanta a few years later for a new opportunity, in his case to take charge of the Hearst newspaper in San Francisco and, after that, the *Baltimore Sun*.

One heartfelt wish of McGill's in 1968 was to reconcile with his maverick protégé in Miami, Bill Baggs. Baggs was now seriously ill with a kidney disease that McGill could readily appreciate after Mary Elizabeth's more than thirty years of suffering. Baggs's illness seemed to mend relations all around. In September, McGill, Tarver, and another dear friend, John Griffin of Atlanta, telegrammed Baggs at the Miami Heart Institute, jesting, "While you are there please have them carefully examine your gall bladder. For years your friends have noticed you have an excess of gall." A month later, after speaking with Ashmore, McGill wrote to "Dear Dr. Baggs" in the banter of the pre-Hanoi days. "Dr. Ashmore and I have consulted about this, and we both agree that it is time you emulated him and me, along with some of your other friends and begin to show a certain maturity which enables a man to look after himself physically. My own limitations of alcoholic intake to a couple of glasses of red wine with dinner, the abstemiousness of Colonel [John] Popham . . . and others ought to be an example to you." As a medical precaution, he added, "These learned medical men observe that if a person begins to pour bloody Mary mixtures down his throat, beginning at breakfasttime and continuing into the evening, the combination of acids from tomato juice, Worcestershire sauce and vodka by a process of osmosis moves through the esophagus and sets up an irritation in the parathyroid and thyroid glands."[27]

Meanwhile, McGill kept in touch with Baggs's two boys, especially the elder, Craig, who had gone off to study at Proctor College in New Hampshire. In the last letter he wrote to Craig, after Baggs's death and a few days before his own, he advised the boy to remember his father "as a real fine, great fellow who made many, many valuable contributions to journalism and to his region."[28]

The peace negotiations that Baggs and Ashmore worked for were now within sight. Days before the November election, President Johnson stopped the bombing of North Vietnam, Hanoi's precondition for peace talks. McGill credited the U.S. negotiator in Paris, Averell Harriman, with gaining an agreement that talks would start soon after the bombing stopped, although the avenues opened by Baggs and Ashmore may have brought the Vietnamese into the Paris pre-talks. By late January, the talks were about to begin, with McGill explaining how the Vietnamese related the shape of the negotiation table to the issue of status. He quoted a diplomat who said, "He wants to sit down as an equal in pride—even though he is not equal in power." McGill asserted that history would "take very good care of President Johnson as it did to Harry Truman." In the last column he wrote about Vietnam, he alluded to the complexity of the Vietnam issue and wagered on the correctness of U.S. policy: "No man may now evaluate the war in Vietnam. It will be years before that may be done. And it is not improbable that evaluation may then show our involvement there as having been necessary to this nation's security and future at a critical time in the movement of events."[29]

On January 1, 1969, McGill's customary New Year's column looked backward and forward like the Roman god Janus. It was an overlong column, but rather than cut it to size, the layout editor found space for the overflow to page seven. Of 1968, McGill wrote, "Many ghosts shall crawl from its tomb to frighten us." The coming peace talks in Paris could be credited also to Mao Tse-tung's "out-of-control" Cultural Revolution in China and his possession of nuclear devices. "It was the Soviet confrontation with the puzzle and threat of China that led them to lend substantial pressure on North Vietnam in 1968 to begin negotiations about Vietnam." In the realm of domestic civil rights, a subject on which he was truly prophetic, he wrote one of his final pronouncements. The "dear, departed year" witnessed a rise in black political activity matched by a backlash in white racial folly. On the one hand there was a record number of five hundred black elected officials in the southern states. "But 1968 also was the peak year of militancy against the slowness with which Americans were moving to make their society a truly open one." Adding to the "ominous auguries" of 1968 in the murders of Kennedy and King were the fearful portents of 1969"—"the folly and blindness" in parts of the South where communities "fought to keep the Negro in the historic 'place' of inferiority and discrimination."[30]

Bill Baggs's death was an enormous loss. It came as a shock, although for two years he had seen Baggs's health steadily failing. "Bill died at six 0 five," a friend telegraphed on a Tuesday night in January. The official cause was viral pneumonia brought on by influenza, but the root cause was the kidney disease which had progressively weakened his body. "Ralph was very much grieved by Baggs' death," Tarver said, "because, as he said, it was so unnecessary."[31]

At his typewriter McGill immersed in the eulogy that would appear two days later, on the day before the funeral. Foremost, McGill remembered Baggs's "considerable joy of life," unconventional and preposterous as it sometimes seemed to an older man. "Life sang in him, though he had no voice for singing." The two shared an admiration for John Keats, whose flat in Rome at the foot of the Spanish Steps they had visited on separate occasions. Keats died at age twenty-five, and his gravestone read "Here lies one whose name was writ in water." Baggs was forty-six. "His name was etched deeply in the hearts of all who knew him and in the records of journalism that he had served so well and with so much honor." He "wrote a strong, fearless column when there was need for it. He was compassionate and kind. . . . He enjoyed poetry and good writing. He had a way with children and was devoted to his own." Courage was early on exemplified by his experiences flying B-24 bombers out of Italy in World War II. "Twice, as I recall, he and his crew had to bail out over Yugoslavia." Both times, Yugoslav partisans helped them avoid capture by the Germans. This was not a place to stir up their old differences over Vietnam, but McGill alluded to Baggs's personal sacrifice: "Two exhausting trips to Hanoi sapped much of his stamina. He was, like many persons, greatly taken with Jack Kennedy and Bobby Kennedy. Their deaths further eroded his spirit. But he kept working, planning, telephoning his friends, keeping in touch until the last illness and the terrible finality of death. He was not a conventional man."[32]

An unsigned *Constitution* editorial the same day expanded on the Vietnam issue. Baggs "agonized over the fact that there were no easy ways out, but he had the strength to follow his inquiring mind wherever it led. It led him into making two trips to Hanoi to observe the effects of U.S. bombing of North Vietnam, and it led him to coauthor a book which bitterly attacked the Johnson Administration for its involvement in the war."[33]

McGill's eulogy was almost lost in a stream of tributes he read and heard in the next two days. The funeral demonstrated how in twelve years as editor Baggs had won the admiration of readers in Miami and the nation. U.S. senator Edward Kennedy and former Florida governor LeRoy Collins walked as pallbearers with James M. Cox Jr. and *Miami News* reporter Howard Kleinberg. Vice President Hubert Humphrey sent a tribute that Baggs "wrote the truth as he saw it, and we are all better for his wisdom, his common sense and his great humanity." From the Paris peace talks, which now the press credited Baggs with helping to initiate, Ambassador Harriman recognized him as "a determined fighter for the principles in which he believed. His early stand for civil rights marks him as a man of clear vision and unflinching courage." The final edition of the *Miami News* with the front-page funeral story (written by another popular eccentric, Milt Sosin), also mentioned "Big John" Johnson, the "genial Bahamian Negro janitor of the old News Tower on Biscayne Boulevard with whom Baggs, as reporter, columnist and editor shared quips over the years" who sat "on middle aisle of the church, wiping away an occasional mistiness in his eyes." Joan Baggs remembered her husband had "the world's greatest charm, yet with so much intelligence behind it." Condolences came from "kings, princes and prime ministers who said 'he was my friend.' And I got one from the janitor." She knew the community owed much to his efforts to bring in rapid transit, to clean up slums, and to provide better housing for blacks. "Basically," she said, "he believed in fresh air and environment." One could conclude, as Jack Tarver did, that Baggs "was a real hero in Miami at that time." At the public service in Trinity Episcopal Church, the diocesan bishop proclaimed Baggs "a man with the courage to lay bare the hypocrisy and selfishness" of fellow men but who "believed in man's destiny to be cocreator with God."[34]

McGill went instead to a small, private service in the Episcopal chapel. With him was John Griffin, then executive director of the Southern Education Foundation, who had been among the first Georgians to fight the poll tax. "McGill followed the ceremony with a chubby little finger in the Episcopal prayer book. Afterwards we were all invited to Baggs' house and McGill wouldn't go. He simply wouldn't go. I was impressed that he wouldn't go. There was speculation that I think Harry Ashmore and I talked about, that somehow his death had suggested to McGill that his own might be coming one of these days."[35]

Rather than go to the house, McGill did what he did best. He spent time comforting Baggs's two sons, going for a long walk on the beach with Craig, and, two weeks later, a week before his own death, he wrote to him at college. "I was very proud of you when I was down in Miami," he wrote. "A very harsh destiny had made it necessary for you to play the role of a man at a very early age, but you certainly played it, and I know you will keep on doing it." He wanted the boy to know he himself had survived great loss. "I am getting to be an old-timer, Craig, and along the way I lost two children, one three days old and one five [years]. There have been other losses, but these I remember the most. I call tell you that the passing of time will help a lot. You will never forget and you would not want to forget, but time will dull some of the feeling of loss and resentment at the great inexplicable mystery of life and death." As was his custom, he slipped in a ten-dollar bill. Learning of McGill's death, Craig wrote to Mary Lynn, acknowledging him as "my best friend that I could always turn to" and returning consolation: "As Mr. McGill said to me, the passing of time will help a lot."[36]

Despite a hectic travel schedule, McGill accomplished one last memorial for his dear friend. On January 31, he wrote a longhand resolution, which Grace Lundy typed and sent to Jerry Anderson of the Southern Committee on Political Issues in Washington, an organization Baggs had helped found. "I am a little delayed in sending it as I have been out in Des Moines, Iowa," McGill noted. "I assume you will send copies to Mrs. Baggs and her two sons." In this final tribute McGill praised his friend's "long years of editorial service to political ethics in the South generally and his consistent contribution to all that motivated his region to identify and develop the best in its great potential for becoming a better South." One thing he never got around to, though, was fulfilling a request from one of Baggs's devoted readers: "Because you were such a friend of his, would you compile his editorials and columns into a book? Bill's wisdom and wit should be readily available to his friends and readers."[37]

Whatever the stresses, McGill found solace and satisfaction in his marriage. He told everyone how lucky he felt in having a beautiful and intelligent wife, and he showed it when he was with Mary Lynn. She understood that "marriage itself was a thing that was terribly important to him. He was a little bit old fashioned about it. It was very important that we do things together. He always made me feel beautiful and he thought I was smart. It was just fun every day." The farm instinct had stayed with him all his life, and he enjoyed growing things. They worked a home garden and had vegetables for the table. He also loved a wood fire. "He taught me how to split logs, by putting a wedge. It was important that you use only one wedge," she said. She worried, however, that log splitting was too strenuous for his heart. In case of emergencies she knew how to administer mouth-to-mouth resuscitation, and she kept oxygen on hand.[38]

During January he was busy traveling, writing his column and keeping up with correspondence. In Washington he devoted several columns to Nixon's inauguration. Back home, as a member of the Pulitzer Prize Advisory Committee, he was not pleased with the irony that the advisory committee had recommended a biography of William Randolph Hearst. In New York journalism in the 1890s Hearst had been anathema to Joseph Pulitzer, raiding Pulitzer's staff and luring away his best writers with bigger paychecks, then stampeding the press into the "yellow journalism" era of sensationalism. McGill agreed with the decision of the Pulitzer trustees to reject the recommendation. After all, McGill reasoned, Pulitzer's will insisted that a biography must "contribute to the American moral quality." To McGill, "the life of Mr. Hearst [who died in 1951] could not be said to have done that." He also found time to send a check for the Rev. Austin Ford's charity work downtown at the Emmaus House.[39]

Speaking requests streamed in. Duke University asked him to speak about the South and southern politics in March. Grace Lundy glanced at his March lineup and noted that he already had a conflict—"either Daytona or the John Hancock Awards in Boston." Although some of these were "important" engagements with influential audiences, he nonetheless enjoyed speaking to the next generation at high schools. On the last afternoon of his life, he addressed students at Booker T. Washington High School, telling them he wished he were as young as they and could see what they would see. In what may have been a Freudian slip, he told them he was born in 1998, caught himself, and said he *wished* he were so young. He was on his feet for "two hours and five minutes. They just kept on with the questions."[40]

That evening he and Mary Lynn were dinner guests in the home of a brilliant young teacher. John Lawhorn, a concert pianist with a master's degree from Columbia University, was introducing music to public school curriculum, believing that music could relieve tensions in city slums by giving children a meaningful skill. In the spring of 1968 he began with disadvantaged children in an Atlanta slum, then contacted McGill and persuaded him to visit the class of kids aged seven through nine. "Not merely were they learning," McGill wrote, "they were happy to be learning. It gave one a sense of achieving, especially since the teacher was thoughtful enough to commend accuracy in enunciation and beat, and to correct the few errors with a smile. 'Let's try that one again, we don't want to miss, do we?'" The fact that the teacher and students were black was not the issue. The issue was teaching and learning. McGill considered it unfair to label any child or group of children as "unable to learn" when perhaps it is the system that fails the child, or an unskilled or uninspired teacher. When he left that class, he was emotionally smitten, particularly as each child lined up to hug him. In addition to writing, McGill raised money for the project by contacting a foundation set up by southern business and professional men interested in helping the region.[41]

At dinner, the McGills joined John and Phyllis Lawhorn in celebrating the twelfth birthday of their son, Michael. Mary Lynn noticed that Ralph was quiet, listening to her rather than talking. At times he seemed to be checking his pulse. In the living room after dinner McGill was talking about how Lawhorn could raise money for a bus equipped as a traveling music school. "He was sitting, talking," Mary Lynn remembered, "and suddenly he faltered."

"Ralph, are you all right?" she asked.

"Yes, but I think we better go home."

Then, she said, "he got up and fell to the floor."

Lawhorn recalled catching him. "I grabbed him and caught him and laid him down gently on the floor."

His wife called Dr. Wilber while Mary Lynn got down on the floor, removed his dentures and breathed into his mouth and lungs. Wilber arrived and then an ambulance. "Joe gave him an injection into the heart muscle," she recalled. "I was so angry, You can do *something!* 'Mary Lynn, there's nothing we can do.' But he didn't give up until we got to the hospital." McGill was pronounced dead two days shy of his seventy-first birthday.[42]

Word of McGill's death reverberated through the community, beginning with those closest. At about 11:00 P.M. Jack Tarver called Grace Lundy. She went to the office and answered calls and requests for information until about 4:00 A.M. By dawn the phones would be ringing constantly.[43]

The *Constitution* newsroom devoted much of the next morning's front page to him. Reg Murphy, Patterson's successor, helped write the lead story, which continued on two more pages inside. "Ralph McGill Dies Here in 70th Year After Heart Attack; Stricken at Dinner at Friends' Home" was packaged with an oversized, flattering head-and-shoulders portrait of him in his chubbier prime, scanning outward with a wry smile hinting at the corners of his closed lips. In the right two columns was an editorial eulogizing him for his longevity, his appetite for knowledge, his range of experience and acquaintances, his inspiration for a generation of journalists, and his timely performance on the southern stage. "Ralph McGill spoke as the home-bred conscience of the South in an era of the emancipation of the spirit: the final unshackling, the paying of the final judgment."

Another front-page story quoted the tributes of local and state leaders, many of whom were now out of office. Among the politicians, former Atlanta mayor Ivan Allen Jr. credited McGill's accomplishments as "the mark of great leadership of this century in the United States." McGill's "courageous advocacy for racial justice had a profound effect and he has left his mark on the South," said Allen's predecessor, former Mayor Hartsfield. Former governor Carl Sanders said McGill "probably did as much to bring about some needed change in the South as any man I know." Former governor Arnall recalled how McGill "contributed most effectively to the advancement of Georgia." Former congressman Charles Weltner remarked that McGill's "interest and powers were not the least bit diminished by age or health. He was a battler and fighter right up until the end." (The governor in office, Maddox, was not quoted.) The southern director of the American Civil Liberties Union, Charles

Morgan, posed the irony that McGill "changed the world we live in, yet lived in the world he couldn't change."[44]

The black community was equally laudatory, if not more so. The former Atlanta chapter president of the NAACP, Albert M. Davis, stressed that McGill "was the force that changed the South. He interpreted the voice of all people who suffered, not only Negroes, but all people who wanted freedom. He was the only voice we had for 25 years. If anyone brought the South back into the Union it was Mr. McGill. We call Martin Luther King, Jr. a prophet, but McGill was a greater one because he didn't have to be." King's father, Martin Luther King Sr., said, "I have known no man more devoted to the ideals and principles for which he stood and lived."[45]

Speaking for fellow journalists, Patterson was most eloquent. From the *Post,* Patterson claimed McGill as "my brother. I loved him. I respected him, and he taught me what a man ought to be. He was loved by his friends and respected by his enemies because a Southerner always recognizes that a man who said what he thought was right, and stuck by it, was a man you had to respect. There never will be another one like him."[46]

The front page carried two more McGill items. One featured his "There Are Many Souths" theme from his autobiographical *South and the Southerner.* The other was his daily column, in the same place. He had written ahead as usual, thinking of course of the demands of his syndicate which now carried the column in about one hundred newspapers. The subject today was education, and he wanted the U.S. secretary of education to strengthen enforcement of the school desegregation, to protect black children and parents in small-town, rural-South districts from intimidation under so-called freedom of choice plans: "You may be assured, sir, that the freedom of choice plan is, in fact, neither real freedom nor a choice. It is discrimination." On the editorial page, Reg Murphy rushed to write a timely column in praise of the legendary McGill. Having succeeded Patterson and survived McGill, Murphy was now at center stage for the next act at the paper. After McGill had come back from Washington High, Murphy had been among the last to speak to him. "As he sat talking in his office Monday night, with the twilight of another winter day falling around him, in the city he loved, there was an air of resignation about him. I had not noticed it before."

"I hope nobody thinks I am in their way. I'm not trying to be," he said.

"The one thing this newspaper needs is you," answered a colleague.

"Oh, I don't know about that."

That evening, McGill advised Murphy to be a traveling editor, to get out into the South, to write about the hometowns of the people who had come to his city in the last few years.

"You certainly should be doing that," McGill said. "We need to have these people keep in touch with home, and we have to keep in touch with them."

In his column the next morning Murphy pledged he would do that, and in the process try to write a column from McGill's homeplace north of Chattanooga, the town called Soddy. Soon afterward someone probably informed Murphy that years before, in the electrification projects of the Tennessee Valley Authority, Soddy was covered by the water behind the hydroelectric dams.[47]

The funeral on Wednesday, February 5, McGill's birthday, attracted one of the most diverse audiences ever assembled in the pews of the All Saints Church. The Rev. Frank Ross, the rector, told Harold Martin he had never seen such a mix of humanity. "In the same pew with Hubert Humphrey," Martin noted, "sat Julia Johnson, gentle old Negro waitress, long retired, who for many years had served [McGill] lunch at a downtown tea room." Filing into the sanctuary were men of contrasting political profiles, among them Senator Herman Talmadge and the ACLU's Chuck Morgan. "Crowded into the pews and standing along the walls were a cross section of Atlanta and the South, black and white, rich and poor, old winos sitting hip to hip with millionaires. . . . There were many in whose lives he had been deeply involved[,] . . . youngsters he had helped and believed in." Reverend Ross himself had migrated to Atlanta from Louisiana partly because of the power of McGill's writing. To Martin, the crowd in the brownstone church reflected McGill's "great gift—that he could change the lives of strangers, influencing men and women whom he never knew to become more gentle, compassionate, kind and understanding, turning them into a bolder, better way despite their fears, their ingrained prejudices."[48]

For politicians, it was good company in which to *be seen*. Now that desegregation was increasingly accepted as law and publisher McGill was being canonized each day as a man of wisdom and grace, this was undoubtedly the right side. People great and small voted with their feet this day, marching to this church. If a funeral could function as a referendum, his did. McGill might have laughed wryly (but thankfully) at all the worthies who now agreed with him on what came to be known as the greatest moral issue of the twentieth century. His pallbearers included devoted colleagues from journalism—Tarver, Martin, Ashmore, and Patterson—plus the owner, James M. Cox Jr., who a month earlier in Miami had carried Baggs's coffin, his old friend John Griffin, with whom McGill had prayed at the Baggs memorial, and an old friend, Henry Troutman Sr. The eighth pallbearer was Murphy, who devoted the day's editorial page to an outpouring of staff remembrances of McGill. Remembrance was also the focus of columns by Celestine Sibley, Leo Aikman, Bruce Galphin, and Calvin Cox, and smaller "Tributes from the Staff" by Harold Martin and Jim Rankin, as well as an unsigned editorial and a cartoon by "Baldy," Cliff Baldowski, showing a pedestal and torch against the Atlanta skyline with the caption "The Torch Is Passed."[49]

McGill was laid to rest in Westview Cemetery next to the grave of Mary Elizabeth. Two small stones marked where they buried their two daughters in the 1930s. The honor guard was a troop of Boy Scouts from a storefront mission. Harold Martin bowed his head as Reverend Ross led the Lord's Prayer and "over the raw mound of earth at last was laid a blanket of flowers."

In the short history of Atlanta few men have been eulogized as thoroughly as Ralph McGill. For a week his memory was evoked in stories, reminiscences, and photographs, tracing him back to the hills of East Tennessee, and to his ancestors. More articles followed in the magazines. And Martin took up the task of writing the biography "put together mainly from my own memories of the man, of the memories of many others . . . and from McGill's own voluminous collection of papers, letters, speeches, and memos."[50]

After so many years of McGill and Patterson, it seemed to some that the thunder and lightning of righteousness to which they were accustomed had vanished too suddenly from print. Eight years later, Ralph McGill Jr. wrote a plaintive lament in an alternative weekly, the *Atlanta Gazette*, recalling the journalists of his father's era and mourning the death of a courageous "real newspaper." He addressed the column to Jack Tarver:

> I remember when you had a paper that had the guts to stand up and fight for what is right and to hell with the consequences. Remember when Rich's pulled out the advertising over the paper's stand on integrated lunch counters? I do.
>
> Remember when they set Reg Murphy's car on fire in his garage when he was political editor? I do.
>
> Remember when they burned crosses on the editor's lawn. And fired into his lighted windows? I certainly do.
>
> I wonder if the gutless wonders that run things at your shop would have the intestinal fortitude to stand up to the kind of financial and physical intimidating that the Jack Nelsons and Gene Pattersons and Ralph McGills had to face? I don't think so.[51]

In sum, two things were clear to McGill's close contemporaries. The first was that he spoke and wrote unfalteringly what he thought and felt "about everything under the sun." He had the poet's facility, the preacher's persistence, and the journalist's medium. Over the trail of years he gave ample evidence of what he held close, as articles of faith. Yet when new light persuaded him differently, he articulated his new insights and tried to persuade people to join him in the new dawn. Usually he was more correct about what was closest to his heart and soul, the South, and less accurate about the other worlds he reached out to—distant cultures where he was not a citizen but a sojourner. His autobiography was aptly titled. And this bond between truth and proximity helps to answer Martin Luther King Jr.'s question, posed to Jack Tarver on the plane trip: How could McGill be so right on race and so wrong on Vietnam? Time and again his ideas were right about his region, though often askew about other peoples' worlds. Usually, McGill was looking forward; always, he was searching within. In the last months of his life, as often before, he repeated a central article of faith that he did not expect to change, that "the desire for individual dignity and freedom . . . is in the genes of all mankind."[52]

The second reality was his bedrock intellectualism. From his mother in particular he received his reverence for The Book. His father bequeathed what he himself could not maintain—a never-ending energy and appetite for scholarship, what Jacques Barzun has called "a bias in favor of Intellect," that desire to ride on the streams of words flowing from the pens of men, fresh rivulets each day, feeding into the great body of knowledge from which intellect is nourished. Few public men in his day read so ravenously as McGill, nor understood as much and communicated it to such an audience, often unready, frequently hostile. McGill consciously employed his mind methodically, he developed habits which made him work his mind tirelessly, and he found the conditions which encouraged him to study, to write, and to publish. Once discovered, the discovery was never relinquished.[53]

Notes

INTRODUCTION

1. Great Britain, of course, is relatively free, but even it passed an Official Secrets Act in 1911.
2. In McGill's era, southern newspapers by their general silence on questions about racial segregation reinforced the institutions of segregation. In later research, Elisabeth Noelle-Neumann asserted, "The fact than an individual is aware that his or her opinion is supported by the media is an important factor in determining that person's willingness to speak out." She asserted that "the fear of isolation . . . makes most people willing to heed the opinion of others. . . . The fear of isolation seems to be the force that sets the spiral of silence in motion." Elisabeth Noelle-Neumann, *The Spiral of Silence: Public Opinion—Our Social Skin,* 2d ed. (Chicago: Univ. of Chicago Press, 1993), 6, 62, 201. Noelle-Neumann credits Alexis de Tocqueville with the nineteenth-century observation of the spiral of silence. Tocqueville wrote that "people dread isolation more than error." Alexis de Tocqueville, *Democracy in America,* ed. Phillips Bradley, trans. Henry Reeve, 2 vols. (New York: Alfred A. Knopf, 1948).
3. Walter Lippmann, *Public Opinion* (New York: Macmillan, 1922); Laura Ashley and Beth Olson, "Constructing Reality: Print Media's Framing of the Women's Movement, 1966–1986," *Journalism and Mass Communication Quarterly* 75, no. 2 (Summer 1998): 263.
4. Ralph McGill, "Once a Biscuit Is Opened," *Atlanta Constitution,* Apr. 1, 1956, p. 6.
5. Eugene Patterson, telephone interview by author, Jan. 5, 2000.
6. In *Plessy v. Ferguson,* as McGill noted, the court's "separate but equal" ruling related specifically to a railroad transportation case. In the South the concept was extended to sanction across-the-spectrum segregation. Ralph McGill, *The South and the Southerner* (Boston: Little, Brown, 1963), 20–21.
7. McGill, "Once a Biscuit."
8. Obituary, *New York Times,* Feb. 5, 1969, cited in Calvin McLeod Logue, ed., *Ralph McGill: Editor and Publisher* (Durham, N.C: Moore Publishing, 1969), vol. 1, frontispiece; Ralph McGill, *Atlanta Constitution,* July 8, 1946, p. 6; Ralph McGill, *Atlanta Constitution,* Oct. 2, 1962, p. 1; Logue, *Ralph McGill* 1:7.
9. Ralph McGill, *Atlanta Constitution,* Jan. 22, 1948, and Aug. 3, 1948.
10. Ibid.
11. Calvin McLeod Logue and Howard Dorgan, "Public Discourse in a Changing South," in *A New Diversity in Contemporary Southern Rhetoric,* ed. Calvin McLeod Logue and Howard Dorgan (Baton Rouge: Louisiana State Univ. Press, 1987), 14.

1. PROVINCIAL

1. The term *gink,* slang of unknown origin, was in use as early as 1910 to refer to "a person" or "a guy." McGill's use, to refer to a person with undesirable or lamentable habits, was unique.

2. Harold E. Davis, *Henry Grady's New South: Atlanta, a Brave and Beautiful City* (Tuscaloosa: Univ. of Alabama Press, 1990), 168, 173–74.
3. Ibid., 173.
4. William Anderson, *The Wild Man from Sugar Creek: The Political Career of Eugene Talmadge* (Baton Rouge: Louisiana State Univ. Press, 1975), 57–60.
5. Leonard Ray Teel, "W. A. Scott and the *Atlanta World*," *American Journalism* 6, no. 3 (July 1989): 158–78. For Davis's literary achievements, see John Edgar Tidwell, "Davis," in *Afro-American Writers,* vol. 51 of *Dictionary of Literary Biography* (Detroit: Gale Research Co., 1981), 60, 63–64. The year after leaving the *Atlanta Daily World* in 1934, Davis published his first volume of poetry, *Black Man's Verse* (Chicago: Black Cat Press, 1935). This gained him a grant from the Julius Rosenwald Foundation in 1937. Soon after, he published a second volume, *I Am the American Negro* (Chicago: Black Cat Press, 1937), followed by a special limited edition Christmas volume of four poems, *Through Sepia Eyes* (Chicago: Black Cat Press, 1938). His last book of poetry, including his Chicago poems, was *47th Street: Poems* (Prairie City, Ill.: Decker Press, 1948). See also Arthur P. Davis, *From the Dark Tower: Afro-American Writers, 1900–1960* (Washington, D.C.: Howard Univ. Press, 1974), 120–25; Abby Arthur Johnson and Ronald Maberry Johnson, *Propaganda and Aesthetics: The Literary Politics of Afro-American Magazines in the Twentieth Century* (Amherst: Univ. of Massachusetts Press, 1979), 43, 112, 116, 118, 133–34, 142, 152, 154–55; Dudley Randall, "An Interview with Frank Marshall Davis," *Black World* 23, no. 3 (1974): 37–48; and Benjamin Brawley, *The Negro Genius: A New Appraisal of the Achievement of the American Negro in Literature and the Fine Arts* (New York: Biblo and Tannen, 1966), 266–67. For Davis's journalistic achievements after leaving the *World,* see Lawrence D. Hogan, *A Black National News Service: The Associated Negro Press and Claude Barnett, 1919–1945* (London: Associated Univ. Presses, 1984), 65–66, 88, 129 (photo), 148, 206, 209. Roosevelt never supported a federal antilynching bill, mainly because of opposition by southern Democrats in the Senate who threatened to filibuster and whom he needed to pass his vital New Deal economic legislation.
6. Kenneth S. Lynn, *Hemingway* (New York: Simon and Schuster, 1987), 403–4, 406–7, 546; Ernest Hemingway, *Ernest Hemingway: Selected Letters, 1917–1961,* ed. Carlos Baker (New York: Charles Scribner's Sons, 1981), 389–95; Walker Evans to Carleton Beals, in Walker Evans, *Havana 1933,* with introduction by Gilles Mora, trans. by Christie McDonald (New York: Pantheon Books, 1989), 5, 8–23. As Evans's editor, Gilles Mora, wrote, Evans arrived in Havana in May 1933 to do a photographic essay in two weeks, to illustrate radical author Carleton Beals's polemic about to be published by Lippincott denouncing Cuban president Gerardo Machado and U.S. policy toward Cuba. Evans soon met Hemingway and they became friends. Besides their ages—Evans at twenty-nine was only four years younger—they had much to talk about while they drank. When Evans's expense account was gone and he was penniless, Hemingway paid for Evans's extra days in Havana, "desiring to retain the company of a partner equally qualified in literary conversation and drinking."
7. Ralph McGill to Louise Stevens, c. Aug. 25, Oct. 25, 26, 27, 1926, Ralph Emerson McGill Papers, Special Collections, Robert W. Woodruff Library, Emory Univ., Atlanta (hereafter cited as RMP); Harold Martin, *Ralph McGill: Reporter* (Boston: Little, Brown, 1973), 50, 56.
8. Frederick Lewis Allen, *Only Yesterday* (New York: Bantam Books, 1959), 132, 137–38; Freddie Russell, telephone interview by author, Sept. 10, 1993 (Russell

became sports editor of the *Nashville Banner* after McGill left for Atlanta); Ralph McGill to Louise Stevens, Dec. 27, 1927, RMP. Writing to his girlfriend from the Hotel Robert E. Lee in South Pittsburg, Tennessee, McGill shared his fleeting moods about his journalism: "This is funny work, a man near thirty sitting here at a desk in a small-town hotel lobby a few feet from where six men died—writing about it, digging up stuff where there isn't any from a story that is as stale as a cigaret that's left burning too long."

9.   Frances "Fannie" (Mrs. Brainard) Cheney, interview by author, Nashville Health Care Center, Nashville, Mar. 2, 1990; Ralph McGill to Louise Stevens, c. Aug. 1928, 1, RMP.

10.   Ralph McGill, "Sports Aerial," *Nashville Banner,* 1929, in McGill's personal scrapbooks, RMP; Ralph McGill to Louise Stevens, c. Dec. 22, 1928, RMP.

11.   Martin, *McGill,* 32–33.

12.   Ibid., 32.

13.   Traveling overseas at the military's expense was a time-honored tradition for other budding journalists, among them one of the prominent journalists at the time of McGill's birth, Joseph Pulitzer. During the American Civil War, Pulitzer, notwithstanding his poor eyesight, enlisted in the Union army when a Union recruiter came to Budapest. Pulitzer got free passage to Boston in 1864, collected a bounty for enlisting, and saw limited action with a New York regiment. Sam Kuczun, "Joseph Pulitzer," in *Biographical Dictionary of American Journalism* (New York: Greenwood Press, 1989), 562.

14.   Cheney interviews, Nashville Health Care Center, Mar. 2, 1990, Apr. 10, 1993; Martin, *McGill,* 30–31, 35–36.

15.   Ralph McGill, "Cuba Is Very Fond of Our National Game," *Atlanta Constitution,* Aug. 2, 1933, p. 16.

2. IN THE LABYRINTH

1.   Cheney interview, Mar. 2, 1990.

2.   McGill interview, "Dawn's Early Light: Ralph McGill and the Segregated South," produced and directed by Kathleen Dowdy and Jed Dannenbaum, Public Broadcasting System, 1989, transcript (subsequent page references are to the transcript).

3.   The general was Valeriano Weyler. Joseph Wisan, *The Cuban Crisis as Reflected in the New York Press* (New York: Octagon Books, 1965), 199; Hugh Thomas, *Cuba: The Pursuit of Freedom* (New York: Harper and Row, 1971), 336–37; Charles E. Chapman, *A History of the Cuban Republic: A Study in Hispanic American Politics* (New York: Octagon Books, 1969), 81.

4.   Martin, *McGill,* 46.

5.   Russell interview.

6.   "Floyd Collins," *Nashville Banner,* Feb. 4, 1925, p. 1;William Burke ("Skeets") Miller, "A Young Man Dies in a Cave," *Louisville Courier-Journal,* Feb. 3, 1925, reprinted in Calder M. Pickett, *Voice of the Past: Key Documents in the History of American Journalism* (New York: Macmillan, 1977), 268.

7.   Cheney interviews, Mar. 2, 1990, Apr. 10, 1993; Special Agent Jack D. Huguelet, Special Inquiry, Knoxville, Nov. 28, 1961, Bureau File 161-1745-17, p. 4.

8.   Ralph McGill, "Break of the Day!" *Atlanta Constitution,* Aug. 6, 1933, p. 2B.

9.   Ralph McGill, "One Word More," *Atlanta Constitution,* Feb. 5, 1941, p. 8A. McGill did not mention this suicide in his reports from Cuba in 1933. He cited

it in the 1941 column when reminiscing about the rise of the Fulgencio Batista regime. It was an image he returned to again. In 1952 he referred to the "young patriot. . . . I can yet see his body in the newly cleaned and starched white suit, the flamboyant flower in his free hand, the deadly pistol near the other, his head all bloody and messy with brains. A .45 Colt will do things to the human head." Ralph McGill, "I Remember Gerardo Machado," *Atlanta Constitution,* Apr. 8, 1952, p. 1.

10.   Ralph McGill, "One Word More," *Atlanta Constitution,* Apr. 3, 1939, p. 6; McGill recalled that Welles had been "cold and firm as ice" with "no wilt to his collar," in "One Word More," *Atlanta Constitution,* Oct. 2, 1938, p. 6.
11.   Sumner Welles to Cordell Hull, May 13, 1933, 837.00/3512, General Records of the State Department, Record Group 59, National Archives (hereafter cited as DS/RG 59), cited in C. Neale Ronning and Albert P. Vannuci, *Ambassadors in Foreign Policy: The Influence of Individuals on U.S.–Latin American Policy* (New York: Praeger, 1987), 34–36.
12.   Louis A. Perez Jr., *Cuba Under the Platt Amendment, 1902–1934* (Pittsburgh: Univ. of Pittsburgh Press, 1986), 308.
13.   Sumner Welles to President Roosevelt, July 17, 1933, 873.00/3579 1/2, DS/RG 59, cited in Perez, *Cuba Under the Platt Amendment,* 308–9.
14.   Associated Press, "Strike Paralyzes Cuban Commerce; 'Revolt' Is Seen; Machado Threatens to Declare Martial Law to Break Movement Regarded as Seditious," *Atlanta Constitution,* Aug. 5, 1933, p. 1; Luis E. Aguilar, *Cuba 1933* (Ithaca: Cornell Univ. Press, 1971), 144–45.
15.   Sumner Welles to Cordell Hull, Aug. 8, 1933, 837.00/3616, DS/RG 59, in Ronning and Vannuci, *Ambassadors in Foreign Policy,* 37.
16.   Thomas, *Cuba,* 612, 614.
17.   Ralph McGill, "McGill Lauds Sumner Welles for Brilliant Work in Cuba," *Atlanta Constitution,* Aug. 8, 1933, p. 1. McGill's account of the interview "when I sat in Sumner Welles' office last week" was published after McGill returned to Atlanta. Although the Welles interview occurred before the interview with Machado, it was published after the Machado interview, as the fourth in a series of front-page articles on the Cuban situation. Immediately after McGill's departure from Cuba, the political situation changed dramatically. Back in Atlanta, McGill kept current by reading the Associated Press and *New York Times* dispatches and updated his dispatches. He inserted into the second paragraph of the Welles interview story the latest news of August 8 of "a historical meeting at which it was agreed by political leaders that President Gerarado [*sic*] Machado, feared and hated as a tyrant by 90 per cent of Cuba's population, and followed as misguided and libeled patriot by the other 10 per cent, must resign. It was an inevitable course, hastened by the strike for passive revolution."
18.   Sumner Welles to Clark Howell, Aug. 26, 1933, Ser. 2, Box 3, Folder 1, RMP.
19.   Ralph McGill, "Ghosts of Many Martyrs Walk at Morro Castle," *Atlanta Constitution,* Aug. 4, 1933, p. 16.
20.   McGill, "Cuba Is Very Fond of Our National Game."
21.   Cheney interviews, Mar. 2, 1990, Apr. 10, 1993.
22.   Ibid.
23.   Ralph McGill, "McGill Finds Once Gay Cuba Has Become Isle of Bitterness; *Constitution* Staff Writer Reveals First-Hand Picture of Internal Strife and Discontent in Island Republic," *Atlanta Constitution,* Aug. 5, 1933, p. 1.
24.   McGill, "Ghosts of Many Martyrs."

25. Ibid.
26. McGill, "One Word More," Feb. 5, 1941; Ralph McGill, "Machado Receives McGill in Closely-Guarded Palace, Denies Ordering Gun Rule; *Constitution* Writer Finds Hated Cuban Ruler a Lonely Old Man Who Has Stayed Too Long at Tasks Beyond His Capabilities," *Atlanta Constitution*, Aug. 6, 1933, p. 11.
27. Luque's experience opened opportunities and hopes for other Cubans in baseball. He proved that light-skinned Cubans could pass the barrier of segregation by being presented as pure Castilians. In 1933, his eighteenth year in the majors, he was on the way toward compiling a record of eight wins, two losses, and a win in the last game of the World Series against the Washington Senators. His four innings of shutout ball persuaded the Senators to send a scout to Havana, who began stocking the Senators with light-skinned Cubans. When "Papa Joe" Cambria signed up Roberto Estalella, who was slightly darker, sports columnist Red Smith articulated the suspicion that "there was a Senegambian somewhere in the Cuban batpile where Senatorial lumber was seasoned." John Thorn and Pete Palmer, *Total Baseball* (New York: Warner Books, 1989), 129, 500, 607, 1093, 1809.
28. McGill, "Cuba Is Very Fond of Our National Game."
29. It was a tricky question because 1926 was an off-year for Burleigh "Ol' Stubblebeard" Grimes (1893–1985). Grimes was a hardy, middleweight (175 pounds) spitballer who had six shining seasons from 1920 to 1924 as the ace right-hander of the Brooklyn Dodgers. In those five years he won 105 games, leading the National League with 22 wins in 1921. In 1928 with the Pittsburgh Pirates he tied for first in most games won, 25. However, in 1926 he won only 12 and lost 13. Thorn and Palmer, *Total Baseball*, 1720–21.
30. McGill might have reason to know this one because Tyrus Raymond ("the Georgia Peach") Cobb was from the farming community of Narrows in northeastern Georgia. Cobb led the American League in hitting for ten seasons. His best average was .420 in 1911, when he was twenty-five. In 1926, at forty, he was still hitting an impressive .339 but well behind the league leaders. Thorn and Palmer, *Total Baseball*, 1028.
31. Another trick question, depending on who was termed an "all star." He acquired three key players in 1928, but Mack required a period of five years to build the Philadelphia Athletics team that won the World Series in 1929 and 1930 and the American League pennant in 1931. The Athletics became champs on the pitching of starters George Earnshaw (acquired in 1928) and Lefty Grove (1926), and the hitting of Jimmie Foxx (1928), Al Simmons (1924), Jimmy Dykes (1929), Mickey Cochrane (1925), and even Mule Haas (1928), who had his best year in 1929. Thorn and Palmer, *Total Baseball*, 139, 799, 2111.
32. McGill, "Break of the Day!" Matty was Christy Mathewson (1880–1925), the ace New York Giants pitcher with superb years from 1901 to 1914, including thirteen seasons with twenty or more wins. In 1905 he led the Giants to the championship by pitching three shutouts in the World Series. In 1908, at twenty-eight, he led the league with thirty-seven wins—thirty-four of them complete games, eleven of them shutouts. That year he led the league in strikeouts (259) and earned run average (1.43).
33. Cuba was the first center of baseball in the Caribbean. The first known game with local participation occurred in June 1866, when sailors of a U.S. ship taking on sugar invited Cuban longshoremen to play. Two years later, organized baseball began with Havana defeating Matanzas. Between 1898 and

1933, the era of U.S. "Big Stick" diplomacy, marines landed thirty-four times in ten different countries, which also served to advance baseball in Cuba, Puerto Rico, Mexico, Nicaragua, and the Dominican Republic. Thorn and Palmer, *Total Baseball*, 605–7.

34. McGill, "Cuba Is Very Fond of Our National Game." The article was datelined, or presumably written, on "Aug. 1" (Tuesday), was sent "by air mail," and was published in the Wednesday editions. McGill's concern for organized youth baseball was shared by others. The first official little league was founded in 1939 in Williamsport, Pennsylvania. American Legion baseball also expanded in the 1930s, and among its early teenaged stars was a boy from Donora, Pennsylvania, a Polish immigrant miner's son, Stan Musial, who by the time he was twenty in 1941 was ready to hit in the majors with the St. Louis Cardinals.

35. McGill, "Cuba Is Very Fond of our National Game."

36. Ralph McGill, "Hand of Mysterious A.B.C. Seen Behind Cuban Strike; McGill Reports Secret Society Is Working for a 'New Deal' for Island with Machado as Unpleasant Incident," *Atlanta Constitution*, Aug. 2, 1933, p. 1.

37. Thomas, *Cuba*, 594–95; Aguilar, *Cuba 1933*, 136–39.

38. McGill, "Hand of Mysterious A.B.C.," 1.

39. McGill, "One Word More," Feb. 5, 1941.

40. McGill, "McGill Lauds Sumner Welles," 4; McGill, "One Word More," Feb. 5, 1941, 6.

41. McGill, "Hand of Mysterious A.B.C.," 1.

42. McGill, "Hand of Mysterious A.B.C.," 1; "McGill Lauds Sumner Welles," 4.

43. McGill, "Hand of Mysterious A.B.C.," 1.

44. Ibid., 4.

45. McGill, "One Word More," Feb. 5, 1941.

46. On McGill's voyage to Cuba that week he had met three exiles returning to Cuba and he had seen that "great crowds greeted them." McGill, "Machado Receives McGill," 11.

47. McGill, "Hand of Mysterious A.B.C.," 4. Fliteras's notoriety was fleeting; histories of the 1933 revolution do not mention him.

48. Ibid.

49. Aguilar, *Cuba 1933*, 145.

50. Ralph McGill, "Machado, Batista, Fidel—," *Atlanta Constitution*, Oct. 9, 1968, p. 1.

51. McGill, "Break of the Day!"

52. Aguilar, *Cuba 1933*, 145.

53. McGill, "McGill Finds Once Gay Cuba," 1.

54. Charles A. Thompson, "The Cuban Revolution: Reform and Reaction," *Foreign Policy Reports* 11 (Jan. 1, 1936): 254, cited in Aguilar, *Cuba 1933*, 144; "Interview with Blas Castillo," *Pensamiento crítico* 38 (Apr. 1970): 197–99, cited in Aguilar, *Cuba 1933*, 145–46.

55. McGill, "Machado, Batista, Fidel—," 1.

56. Ibid.

57. Ibid.

58. Ibid.

59. McGill, "McGill Finds Once Gay Cuba," 1.

60. McGill, "Machado, Batista, Fidel—."

61. McGill, "Break of the Day!" This last column from Havana was a hastily composed hodgepodge. It included "the best chicken story of the year," told him by the captain of the *Florida,* an update on the Cuban strike, repetition

about Cubans' love of baseball, a visit to the touristy bar that become famous
because it was rarely wiped off (Sloppy Joe's), and the story of a persistent
broom vendor, evidence that "the American is the world's greatest sucker." In
the chicken story, intended for his sports readers' bawdier natures, McGill
showed he had not ignored Latin women. This was "not a story of the very
chic and beautiful young Cuban chickens whom one sees on the Prado or
around town." It was a about a harbor pilot who invested in chickens and one
"very fine rooster." Amid all the troubles in Cuba, the pilot discovered
someone had stolen all his chickens and left a note around the rooster's neck:
Desde midio noche yo soy solo (Since midnight I have been alone).

62. McGill, "Machado Receives McGill," 1.
63. McGill, "McGill Lauds Sumner Welles," 1.
64. Ibid.
65. John P. McKnight, "Machado to Resign Today as Cuban President; 26 Slain,
    150 Shot Down by Troops in Havana," *Atlanta Constitution,* Aug. 8, 1933, p. 1;
    Thomas, *Cuba,* 617.
66. Ralph McGill, "Machado Places Last Hopes in Trained, Well-Paid Army; McGill
    Believes President's Policy in Regard to Military Was Shrewdly Conceived
    Against Just Such Crisis as Now Prevails," *Atlanta Constitution,* Aug. 10, 1933,
    p. 1.
67. Ibid., 1, 6.
68. Lt. Col. T. N. Gimperling, "Causes of Recent Revolt of Armed Forces Against
    Machado," G-2 Report, Aug. 21, 1933, File 2012-133(7); also, records of the
    War Department, General and Special Staffs, RG 165, National Archives, as
    cited in Perez, *Cuba Under the Platt Amendment,* 316–17.
69. Thomas, *Cuba,* 617–24.

3. BREAKING WITH THE PAST

1. Russell interview. Russell was sports editor of the *Nashville Banner* after McGill
   left for Atlanta; Tom Clark, *The World of Damon Runyon* (New York: Harper and
   Row, 1978), 48.
2. Frederick Lewis Allen, *Only Yesterday* (New York: Bantam Books, 1959), 56,
   146–47, 253.
3. Clark, *Damon Runyon,* 49.
4. The *Georgian* had started publication in 1906. "Founded in 1906; 450 Employees Will Be Affected; Journal to Take Over Features and News Services of the
   Paper as 33-Year Career Ends," *Atlanta Constitution,* Dec. 17, 1939, p. 1.
5. See Fuzzy Woodruff, *History of Southern Football* (1929), cited in Morgan Blake,
   "Sportanic Eruptions," *Atlanta Journal,* Jan. 20, 1929, sports section front page.
6. According to the *Atlanta Journal-Constitution* business archives, the *Constitution*
   (founded in 1868) in 1929 led the *Journal* by about 8,000 in circulation daily,
   but the *Journal,* the younger paper (founded in 1881), had gone ahead on
   Sundays by about 5,000 and was closing the gap on daily circulation. From
   October 1929 to September 1930, the *Constitution*'s daily circulation (Monday
   through Saturday) averaged 93,236—and holding. The *Journal* had 90,584—
   and increasing. On Sundays, the *Constitution* had 131,635, but the *Journal* had
   136,504.
7. For comparison, see the Sunday sports pages of the *Atlanta Constitution* and
   Atlanta Journal, Jan. 20, 1929.
8. Ed Danforth, "Mawnin'!" *Atlanta Constitution,* July 20, 1929, p. 15.

9. Al Thomy, "Ed Danforth Dies in His Office Here," *Atlanta Constitution*, Dec. 6, 1962, p. 1; Russell interview.

10. Ralph McGill, "You Know How It Was, Ed," *Atlanta Constitution*, Dec. 6, 1962, p. 1; Don H. Doyle, *Nashville in the New South, 1880–1930* (Knoxville: Univ. of Tennessee Press, 1985), 165–67; Ralph McGill, "Drunk on the Street," *Atlanta Constitution*, Mar. 19, 1966, p. 1.

11. Martin, *McGill*, 27–28; Russell interview. To put McGill's $90 salary in perspective, when McGill in 1936 tried unsuccessfully to lure the *Banner's* Russell to Atlanta to be his assistant, McGill offered Russell only $47.50 a week. One variable was the Great Depression, which began six months after McGill was hired in 1929; McGill took three 10 percent pay cuts, reducing his $90 to $63 a week in the early '30s; Ralph McGill to Louise Stevens, Apr. 19, 1929, 1, 2, RMP.

12. Martin, *McGill*, 27–28.

13. McGill, *South and the Southerner*, 71–72, 76–77.

14. Ralph McGill, *Atlanta Constitution*, Aug. 6, 1947, p. 6; McGill, *South and the Southerner*, 72–75.

15. Ralph McGill, "Past Perfect: Four Teachers McGill Remembers Best," *Vanderbilt Alumnus*, Mar. 1952, 8.

16. Cheney interview, Mar. 2, 1990; Frances Cheney, interview by Beth Hill, Nov. 16, 1994; McGill, *South and the Southerner*, 86, 79.

17. McGill, *South and the Southerner*, 77, 79–80, 85; Carol Muske, "Laura Riding Roughshod," review of *In Extremis: The Life of Laura Riding*, by Deborah Baker, *New York Times Book Review*, Nov. 29, 1993, 14.

18. In the spring of 1920, he was listed on the *Hustler* masthead and in the yearbook, *Commodore*, as "Censored Editor." *Vanderbilt Hustler*, May 5, 1920, 4; "Hustler Staff, 1919–1920," *Commodore*, 291; McGill, *South and the Southerner*, 76.

19. Paul Keith Conkin, *Gone with the Ivy: A Biography of Vanderbilt University* (Knoxville: Univ. of Tennessee Press, 1985), 298. The *Jade's* sense of humor often poked fun at fraternities, studies, and dating. McGill's first issue carried this joke, signed by "Juggler": "I thought you said it was a case of love at first sight." "It was." "Well—why didn't you marry her?" "I saw her on several other occasions." "Once Too Often," *Jade* 1, no. 4 (June 5, 1920): 15.

20. McGill, *South and the Southerner*, 76.

21. Ralph McGill, "Review of Brainard Cheney's *This Is Adam*," *Atlanta Constitution*, in Ralph McGill, *No Place to Hide: The South and Human Rights*, ed. Calvin McLeod Logue (Macon, Ga.: Mercer Univ. Press, 1984), 1:257; Martin, *McGill*, 22. See Brainard Cheney, *This Is Adam* (New York: McDowell, Oblensky, 1958).

22. Ralph McGill, "Memories of Bellamy and FDR," reprinted from the *Atlanta Constitution*, Jan. 25, 1960, in McGill, *No Place to Hide* 1:312–13.

23. Martin, *McGill*, 21–22.

24. Cheney interview, Apr. 10, 1993; Russell interview.

25. Gilbert E. Govan and James W. Livingood, *The Chattanooga Country, 1540–1962: From Tomahawks to TVA* (Chapel Hill: Univ. of North Carolina Press, 1963), 336. The *Times's* daily circulation by 1886 was about four thousand.

26. McGill, *South and the Southerner*, 34; David N. McGill, father of Benjamin Franklin McGill and grandfather of Ralph McGill, died on September 15, 1896. Charles W. Lusk, "Hamilton County, Tennessee Cemeteries," unpublished manuscript, Chattanooga Public Library. The Chattanooga attorney was Ben McGill's uncle, Maj. M. L. (Moses) Clift, son of Col. William Clift, Ben McGill's maternal grandfather. Maj. Moses Clift fought for the Confederacy during the

Civil War despite the fact that his father the colonel fought for the Union. The successful criminal defense attorney in the family was a cousin, W. J. (Joe) Clift. John Wilson, *Hamilton County Pioneers* (Chelsea, Mich.: BookCrafters, 1998), 42; John Wilson, *Chattanooga's Story* (Chattanooga: Chattanooga News Free Press, 1980), 184–85. Scots-Irish Presbyterian farmers had come south to the Chattanooga region beginning in 1822. In 1826, Ralph McGill's great-grandfather, David McGill, bought two hundred acres to farm.

27. McGill, *South and the Southerner*, 40.

28. "Another Tragedy; A Student at the University Kills a Companion; J. C. Johnson and M. McGill Quarrel, and the Latter Crushes the Skull of the Former with a Base Ball Bat; Opprobrious Epithets the Cause; Johnson Lives Until 5 O'Clock in the Afternoon and Expires—The Slayer Escapes—Reward for His Arrest—The Coroner's Inquest," *Chattanooga Daily Times*, Feb. 23, 1888, p. 6; "Report of the Committee on the Case of Benj. F. McGill" (hand-written), Minutes of the Faculty of Chattanooga University, Apr. 1, 1888, 107–8, in Special Collections, Lupton Library, Univ. of Tennessee–Chattanooga; Harry M. Hays, "Who Killed James Johnson?" unpublished research paper, Aug. 15, 1990, 4–5, Special Collections, Lupton Library, Univ. of Tennessee–Chattanooga; "Academic Department," *Year-Book of Chattanooga University, 1887–88*, May 1888, 2:6–7, in Special Collections, Lupton Library, Univ. of Tennessee–Chattanooga.

29. "Another Tragedy," 6. The newspaper's identification of the assailant as "M. McGill" was one of several misspellings of the name during the course of the case. *Chattanooga Daily Times* reporters identified Benjamin Franklin McGill as "McGill," "Ben McGill," "B. F. McGill," "Magill," "B. F. Magill" and "D. F. Magill." He was also identified by residence, age, and family. His home was given as Igou's Ferry, near Soddy, Tennessee, his age as twenty-one, and his father as David McGill, "a wealthy farmer of that locality."

An autopsy showed the blow from the hickory baseball bat fractured the skull. The blow also ruptured an artery and filled the cranial cavity with blood, pressing the brain away from the skull "nearly an inch." Doctors concluded that no treatment could have saved Johnson's life. "The tragic death of Mr. Johnson" was recorded by classmates in the Minutes of the Demosthenean Literary Society, Mar. 2, 1888, 55, Special Collections, Lupton Library, Univ. of Tennessee–Chattanooga. The student newspaper, *University Outlook*, followed the progress of the murder case, noting in February that "the case of B.F. McGill will be called for trial February 11." *University Outlook*, Feb. 6, 1889, p. 9. On the popularity of baseball in the 1880s, see Edward L. Ayers, *The Promise of the New South: Life After Reconstruction* (New York: Oxford Univ. Press, 1992), 310–11.

30. "Gave Himself Up; McGill, Who Killed Young Johnson, Surrenders; A Pathetic and Touching Meeting Between the Unfortunate Young Man and His Father; Remains of the Dead Boy Carried Home," *Chattanooga Daily Times*, Feb. 24, 1888, p. 6; "M'Gill in Court; He Is Taken on a Warrant for Murder and Admitted to Bail," *Chattanooga Daily Times*, Feb. 25, 1888, p. 6.

31. Govan and Livingood, *Chattanooga Country*, 185–86; Wilson, *Hamilton County Pioneers*, 41–43. Col. William Clift was the great-grandfather of movie star Montgomery Clift.

32. "Circuit Court; Magill Murder Case Settled," *Chattanooga Times*, June 21, 1889, p. 6; *Ruling Book of the Circuit Court of Hamilton County, 1888*, unpublished; the *Year-Book of Chattanooga University* that year printed an asterisk after Benjamin F. McGill's name with the explanation "withdrawn under charges." The asterisk

after James C. Johnson's name told that he was "deceased." Johnson's tombstone declared, "Killed by a Schoolmate." *Year-Book of Chattanooga University, 1887–88,* 6–7; Hays, "James Johnson," cover page, 10–11. The day after Ben McGill's trial ended, Johnson's cousin, Sam Webster, sought to get the case reconsidered and swore out a warrant for murder, but nothing came of it.

33. McGill, *South and the Southerner,* 47.
34. Ibid., 36–38; Jack Tarver Jr., interview by author, Atlanta, Dec. 10, 1999.
35. The marriage of Ben F. McGill and Mary Louise Skillern on May 5, 1896, at the Soddy Presbyterian Church is listed in Lusk, "Hamilton County, Tennessee Cemeteries"; Wilson, *Hamilton County Pioneers,* 274–75; McGill, *South and the Southerner,* 37, 38–39.
36. McGill, *South and the Southerner,* 34, 36–38, 47–48.
37. Ibid., 33–35, 38; Martin, *McGill,* 8; Barbara Barksdale Clowse, *Ralph McGill: A Biography* (Macon, Ga.: Mercer Univ. Press, 1998), 9; "Last Rites Today for Ben F. McGill; Retired Businessman Died Monday Night—Had Lived Here for 36 Years," *Chattanooga Daily Times,* Aug. 7, 1940, p. 7.
38. McGill, *South and the Southerner,* 32–33. Years later he thought that the experience with his parents on the skiff occurred "when I was about four years old, before we had moved from the old farm on the Tennessee River."
39. Cheney interview, Mar. 2, 1990; Ralph McGill to Louise Stevens, c. Aug. 1926, 1, RMP. The vice of drinking, common among sports writers but not limited to them, was a problem Ring Lardner had to contend with in 1911 when, at twenty-six, he approached marriage to Ellis Abbott. Lardner tried abstaining with "water, tea and coffee" and asked her, "Why shouldn't I make a wonderful impression on your family?" Ring Lardner to Ellis Abbott, Jan. 20, 1911, in Clifford M. Caruthers, ed., *Letters from Ring* (Flint, Mich.: Walden Press, 1979), 93–94.
40. Doyle, *Nashville in the New South,* 97–98; Peter Taylor, "The Captain's Son," in *In the Miro District,* by Peter Taylor (New York: Carroll and Graf, 1987), 9; Taylor, *In the Miro District,* 161. Taylor was born in Trenton, Tennessee, in 1917 and attended Vanderbilt University. Taylor "has written, in elegantly unobtrusive style, of the bewilderments and aspirations of genteel, resourceful people, who weave the strands of tradition into the tensions of new times with grace and persistent responsibility." R. V. Cassill, ed., *The Norton Anthology of Short Fiction,* 2d ed. (New York: W. W. Norton, 1981), 1512.
41. Ralph McGill to Louise Stevens, c. Sept. 3, 1926, 1, 2, RMP; Ralph McGill to Louise Stevens, c. Oct. 26, 1926, 5–6, RMP; Beth Ann Hill, "'Love, Mac': An Analysis of Letters Written from Ralph McGill to Louise Stevens, 1926–1929" (Master's degree practicum, Georgia State Univ., Atlanta, 1995).
42. Ralph McGill to Louise Stevens, c. Oct. 26, 1926, 4, 5, RMP; McGill to Stevens, c. Oct. 27, 1926, 1, RMP.
43. Ralph McGill to Louise Stevens, Aug. 25, 1926, 3, RMP; McGill to Stevens, Oct. 26, 1926, 2–3, RMP; McGill to Stevens, c. Apr. 6, 1927, RMP.
44. Ralph McGill to Louise Stevens, Dec. 28, 1927, 3–5, RMP.
45. "McGill Brings Peace," *Vanderbilt Alumnus* 13, no. 4 (Mar.–Apr. 1928): 148. The Vanderbilt publication referred to McGill as being in the class of 1921.
46. Ralph McGill to Louise Stevens, May 12, 1928, 3–4, RMP.
47. Ralph McGill to Louise Stevens, May 12, 1928, 10, RMP; McGill to Stevens, c. Aug. 1927, 2, RMP; McGill to Stevens, c. Dec. 27, 1927, 2, RMP.
48. Ralph McGill to Louise Stevens, Sept. 7, 1926, RMP; McGill to Stevens, Sept. 3, 1926, RMP; Martin, *McGill,* 30.

49. After his marriage to Mary Elizabeth in 1929 and his first month in Atlanta, McGill wrote to Louise Stevens: "Steve honey, you know that I am your friend and will be as long as I live and could not be otherwise if I tried." Mary Elizabeth, staying in Nashville until Ralph found a place for them in Atlanta, had met Louise, perhaps at his urging: "Red wrote me that she had met you and liked you. And she did, too, because she went on to elaborate on it and she doesn't lie. She wondered at my king [*sic*] two people of such different types."

50. "Mrs. Ralph McGill Dies; Wife of Publisher of *Atlanta Constitution* Was 57," *New York Times*, Mar. 22, 1962, p. 35; "Mrs. Ralph McGill Is Dead; *Constitution* Publisher's Wife," *Atlanta Constitution*, Mar. 22, 1962, p. 1; George Evans, interview by author, Charlotte, N.C., Jan. 21, 1994; Evans interview; "Strong Constitution," *Time*, Sept. 14, 1942, p. 46; Cheney interview, Mar. 2, 1990; Ralph McGill to Louise Stevens, Apr. 19, 1929, 2, RMP.

51. Cheney interview, Mar. 2, 1990.

52. Ralph McGill, "Parham's Double Beats Barons in 9th, 13–12; 10 Pitchers See Action in Wild Tilt; Lead Changes Hands Five Times—Large Crowd Watches Game," *Atlanta Constitution*, July 20, 1929, p. 15.

53. Ibid.

54. Russell interview. Russell could, as Grantland Rice did, create heroics out of some routine event. At a lackluster football practice, Russell focused on Vanderbilt's injured captain. He had broken his wrist early in the season and now at practice was testing to see if he could play again. Russell conveyed the drama: "They went into a huddle out on McGugin field this afternoon—a huddle far more important than any that had occurred in a game." Freddie Russell, "'Mouse' Defies Docs; May Play Saturday; Broken Wrist Still Unhealed but Brace and Super-nerve Gives Vandy Star Chance," *Atlanta Constitution*, Oct. 30, 1931, p. 19, reprinted from the *Nashville Banner*.

55. Cheney interview, Mar. 2, 1990; Ralph McGill, "Peace, New Air of Hope Reign in Cuba—McGill," *Atlanta Constitution*, May 16, 1935, p. 1; other articles by McGill were "Story Behind New Cuba Is Batista, Says McGill," *Atlanta Constitution*, May 17, 1935, p. 1; "Batista, 'Man of Hour,' Brought About Peace; Ralph McGill Writes About How Sergeant Fulgencio Batista Took Command and Changed Chaos into Order," *Atlanta Constitution*, May 18, 1935, p. 1. McGill also wrote three "Break O' Day" columns from Havana published May 14–16; Martin, *McGill*, 49; John Patillo, telephone interview by author, Jan. 12, 2000. The one-and-a-half story Craftsman-style house, built around 1915, is now included in the Peachtree Highlands National Historic District.

56. Jack Troy wrote McGill's "Break O' Day" columns on January 9 and 10, 1936; Ralph McGill, "'See-My-Operation-Club' Fails Because of Inside Job," *Atlanta Constitution*, May 16, 1934, p. 14; Martin, *McGill*, 49.

57. Martin, *McGill*, 51–52. The article about Margaret Mitchell was first printed in *Red Barrel*, published by the Coca-Cola Company; *New York Times* published an expanded version.

58. Walter Lippmann, "Magical Prosperity," *New York Herald Tribune*, Sept. 8, 1931, in *Interpretations, 1931–1932*, ed. Allan Nevins (New York: Macmillan, 1932), 8.

59. John Kenneth Galbraith, *The Great Crash: 1929* (Boston: Houghton Mifflin, 1961), 74, 91–92.

60. Edward E. Scharff, *Worldly Power: The Making of the Wall Street Journal* (New York: Beaufort Books, 1986), reviewed by James L. Baughman, *Journalism Quarterly* 63 (Winter 1986): 863–64.

61. George Seldes, *Freedom of the Press* (Garden City, N.Y.: Garden City Publishing Co., Inc., 1937), 149.

62. Leo Rosten, *The Washington Correspondents* (New York: Harcourt Brace, 1937), 345.

63. Virginia Jean Rock, "The Making and Meaning of *I'll Take My Stand:* A Study in Utopian-Conservatism, 1925–1939" (Ph.D. diss., Univ. of Minnesota, 1961), 2–4; John Crowe Ransom, *I'll Take My Stand,* 21, 16, in Mark G. Malvasi, *The Unregenerate South: The Agrarian Thought of John Crowe Ransom, Allen Tate, and Donald Davidson* (Baton Rouge: Louisiana State Univ. Press, 1997), 47–49. For a critique of Malvasi, see Don Keck DuPree, "Newt and Jeff Shall Prevail," *Chattahoochee Review* 18, no. 4 (Summer 1998): 93–99.

64. Ralph McGill, "Agrarianism vs. Industrialism Question Skillfully Debated by Anderson and Dr. Ransom," *Atlanta Constitution,* Feb. 15, 1931, pp. 1, 5.

65. McGill, *South and the Southerner,* 81–82; Cheney interview, Mar. 2, 1990; the *McCallie Pennant,* 1916, 45, cited in Logue, *Ralph McGill* 1:26–27; Malvasi, *Unregenerate South,* 75.

66. McGill, *South and the Southerner,* 159–60.

67. Ibid., 166–67.

68. Ralph McGill, "Banks and Credit are Sound, Report Reserve Heads Here; Farm Tenancy and Farm Income Problems Must Be Solved by South Before Section Assumes Rightful Place in Nation, Say Officials," *Atlanta Constitution,* May 15, 1937, 1, 3.

69. Ibid., 3.

70. Ralph McGill, "This Is the Story of the Farmer Who Went to College, Added Hard Work to New Ideas and Won to Success; John Gunnels Finds Freedom, Stillness, and Calm Restoring Wornout, Eroded Acres of Farm He Manages," *Atlanta Constitution,* May 30, 1937, p. 1.

71. Ibid., 13.

72. Martin, *McGill,* 50, 56.

73. Ibid., 56–57.

4. Scandinavian Studies

1. Ralph McGill, "Card Scene Come to Life," *Atlanta Constitution,* Dec. 23, 1937, p. 18. Ten years earlier in Nashville, McGill had ridiculed the man who "must run places" to show off to the girls his "manly, running stride." Ralph McGill, "I'm the Gink," *Nashville Banner,* July 4, 1927, p. 1.

2. Editor's note, *Atlanta Constitution,* Dec. 17, 1937, p. 1; Ralph McGill, "Break O' Day!" *Atlanta Constitution,* Dec. 17, 1937, p. 26; Ralph McGill, "Break O' Day!" *Atlanta Constitution,* Dec. 21, 1937, p. 10; Ralph McGill, "Break O' Day! The Irish Won Out Because They Could Talk Louder," *Atlanta Constitution,* Dec. 18, 1937, p. 8.

3. McGill, "Break O' Day!" Dec. 18, 1937.

4. "The Press," *Time,* Sept. 14, 1942, 46. McGill's mini-columns were in excellent company; across the front page in the lower left corner was the syndicated short comment on current events, "Will Rogers Says." Years later *Time* magazine saw a connection, characterizing McGill's columns as "popular, Will Rogerish." McGill, however, remained anonymous.

5. Ralph McGill, "I'm the Gink," *Nashville Banner,* Nov. 23, 1928, p. 1.

6. Ralph McGill, "I'm the Gink," *Nashville Banner,* Nov. 23, 1928, p. 1; July 25, 1928, p. 1; Mar. 29, 1928, p. 1; Dec. 14, 1928, p. 1.

7. Ralph McGill, "I'm the Gink," *Nashville Banner,* Dec. 4, 1928, p. 1; Oct. 29, 1928; Oct. 22, 1928, p. 1; Apr. 5, 1928, p. 1; Mar. 27, 1928, p. 1; Nov. 7, 1928, p. 1; Mar. 22, 1928, p. 1.

8. Ralph McGill, "I'm the Gink," *Nashville Banner,* Dec. 16, 1928, p. 1; Oct. 24, 1928, p. 1; Aug. 15, 1927; Mar. 12, 1927, p. 1.

9. Ralph McGill, "I'm the Gink," *Nashville Banner,* Apr. 2, 1928, p. 1; Mar. 30, 1928, p. 1; Apr. 3, 1928, p. 1; Apr. 4, 1928, p. 1; Mar. 28, 1928, p. 1; Mar. 22, 1928, p. 1; Aug. 8, 1927, p. 1.

10. Ralph McGill, "I'm the Gink," *Nashville Banner,* Dec. 14, 1928, p. 1; Dec. 30, 1928, p. 1; Mar. 25, 1928, p. 1; Mar. 24, 1928, p. 1; Clowse, *McGill,* 20; Russell interview.

11. Ralph McGill, "I'm the Gink," *Nashville Banner,* Sept. 7, 1928, p. 1.

12. Ralph McGill, "Bob Scally, Farr's Sparmate, Is Adept at Handling Babies," *Atlanta Constitution,* Dec. 19, 1937, p. 2B; Ralph McGill, "Break O' Day!" *Atlanta Constitution,* Dec. 22, 1937, p. 8.

13. McGill, "Card Scene."

14. Ralph McGill, "Break O' Day! Sweden's Colors, Blue and Orange; Auburn Should Complain," *Atlanta Constitution,* Feb. 1, 1938, p. 10.

15. Ralph McGill, "Break O' Day! Viking Ships, Which Sailed 700 Years Before Columbus, Still Well Preserved," *Atlanta Constitution,* Feb. 9, 1938, p. 8.

16. Ralph McGill, "Scandinavian Studies: Norway's Sad Labor Affiliation with Moscow Proves Third International Exists Only for Itself and Intrigue, McGill Told," *Atlanta Constitution,* Feb. 27, 1938, p. 1; Kaare Strom and Lars Svasand, *Challenges to Political Parties: The Case of Norway* (Ann Arbor: Univ. of Michigan Press, 1997), 39; Henry Valen and Daniel Katz, *Political Parties in Norway: A Community Study* (London: Tavistock Publications), 26–30; Bjorn Gustavsen and Gerry Hunnius, *New Patterns of Work Reform: The Case of Norway* (Oslo: Universitetsforlaget, 1981), 17–18.

17. Ralph McGill, "Break O' Day!" *Atlanta Constitution,* Feb. 11, 1938, 23–24; "Break O' Day!: Birger Ruud Has Entered 200 Meets, Set 50 Records, Won 110 Times," *Atlanta Constitution,* Feb. 12, 1938, p. 9.

18. Ralph McGill, "Break O' Day! In America, a Journalist Is One Who Carries a Cane," *Atlanta Constitution,* Feb. 19, 1938, p. 8.

19. Ralph McGill, "One Word More," *Atlanta Constitution,* June 23, 1938, p. 8.

20. Frederick P. Keppel to Gunnar Myrdal, Aug. 12, 1937, quoted in Gunnar Myrdal, *An American Dilemma: The Negro Problem and Modern Democracy* (New York: Harper and Brothers, 1944), ix.

21. Guy B. Johnson, "Does the South Owe the Negro a New Deal?" *Social Forces* 13, no. 1 (Oct. 1934): 100–103; Arthur F. Raper, *The Tragedy of Lynching* (Chapel Hill: Univ. of North Carolina, 1933); Daniel Joseph Singal, *The War Within: From Victorian to Modernist Thought in the South, 1919–1945* (Chapel Hill: Univ. of North Carolina Press, 1982), 121, 143, 328; Myrdal, *American Dilemma,* 262, 449–50, 561.

22. Myrdal, *American Dilemma,* 1015.

23. The editor was Martin Tranmael, who led his faction of the Labor Party away from Moscow's domination and in 1938 was still influential as editor of *Arbeiderbladet,* one of Norway's leading newspapers. Tranmael was the "major theoretician and agitator" in the Norwegian Labor Party around 1920. "He was a socialist who believed in revolution as the vehicle for bringing the working class to power." McGill, "Scandinavian Studies: Norway's Sad Labor Affiliation," 4; Gustavsen and Hunnius, *New Patterns of Work Reform,* 17–18.

24. Ralph McGill, "Scandinavian Studies: Swedish Editor Queries Ralph McGill on New Pulp Mill Business in South Which Brings on Conservation Comparison," *Atlanta Constitution,* Feb. 28, 1938; McGill, "Scandinavian Studies: Norway's Sad Labor Affiliation"; "Union Bag and Paper Corporation," *Fortune* 16 (Aug. 1937): 122, 126, 132.
25. McGill, "Scandinavian Studies: Swedish Editor."
26. Ralph McGill, "Scandinavian Studies: McGill Delves into Social Law, Co-Operation and Farm Aid and Finds Them Good, but Not Suitable for Transplanting to U.S.," *Atlanta Constitution,* Mar. 1, 1938.
27. Ibid.
28. Ralph McGill, "Scandinavian Studies: A Strong Hotel Strike Reigns in Sweden, One in Which the Owners Close Down and 'Lockout' Their Workers," *Atlanta Constitution,* Mar. 2, 1938; Ralph McGill, "Scandinavian Studies: Examination Similar to One for Insurance Required Before Permit Is Granted to Purchase Liquor to Drink at Home in Sweden," *Atlanta Constitution,* Mar. 3, 1938.
29. McGill, "Scandinavian Studies: Examination Similar."
30. Ibid.
31. Ralph McGill, "Scandinavian Studies: Ralph McGill Observes Work of Swedish Liquor Control System that Stresses Education as Making of Temperate Country," *Atlanta Constitution,* Mar. 4, 1938; Harry S. Ashmore, interview by author, Friends of John Popham Seminar, Atlanta Airport Holiday Inn, Atlanta, June 20, 1993.

5. WITNESS TO TYRANNY

1. John Toland, *Adolf Hitler* (New York: Ballantine Books, 1976), 431, 433, 437; Ralph McGill, "How Fuehrer Sets Stage for Talk Told by McGill," *Atlanta Constitution,* Mar. 9, 1938, p. 3; Ralph McGill to Rebecca Mathis Gershon, Mar. 6, 1938, quoted in a 1969 interview with Gershon, in Ralph McGill, *Southern Encounters: Southerners of Note in Ralph McGill's South,* ed. Calvin McLeod Logue (Macon, Ga.: Mercer Univ. Press, 1983), 303.
2. McGill, "How Fuehrer Sets Stage," 3.
3. Anderson, *Wild Man,* 161–62.
4. McGill, "How Fuehrer Sets Stage," 1, 3.
5. William L. Shirer, *The Rise and Fall of the Third Reich: A History of Nazi Germany* (New York: Simon and Schuster, 1960), 332–33; Toland, *Hitler,* 437–38; McGill, "How Fuehrer Sets Stage," 3.
6. McGill, "How Fuehrer Sets Stage."
7. Ralph McGill, "Break O' Day! Youth Is Called to Arms in Germany's 'Olympic Village,'" *Atlanta Constitution,* Mar. 9, 1938, p. 10.
8. Ralph McGill, "Break O' Day: It Was the Kaiser's Desk—There He Signed the Mobilization Papers," *Atlanta Constitution,* Mar. 10, 1938, p. 16; McGill, *South and the Southerner,* 58.
9. Martin, *McGill,* 61; Shirer, *Third Reich,* 345, 347, 353.
10. Clark Howell [Jr.] to Ralph McGill, Mar. 24, 1938, Ser. 2, Box 3, Folder 1, RMP.
11. Francis W. Clarke, "The European Maelstrom," *Atlanta Constitution,* June 7, 1936, p. 14; June 8, 1936, p. 4; June 9, 1936, p. 4. At Berlin, Clarke had visited the Olympic Village before the Olympics and wrote ominously that "after the games are over [it] will become the permanent habitat of 30,000 soldiers."
12. Martin, *McGill,* 62–63. In Paris he did an errand for an old friend named Charlie, who had fought with the American Expeditionary Force in 1918.

Charlie wanted McGill to find a cute, petite French girl named Charmaine with whom he had gone on picnics. McGill found her and wrote that "she was more like a mastiff than a speckled pup, and as for being about as big as a minute—well, Charlie, she's about twenty minutes now. And she had a hard time remembering which one was you." The war had ended before McGill's marine unit could be sent, but he wanted to see the battlefields. He wrote one column about visiting the River Marne to which French troops hastened in taxicabs to halt the first German advance on Paris in 1914. Then he went to Château-Thierry, where in 1918 the Americans, in their first major battle, helped the French stop the kaiser's last big advance. There in a museum McGill found a prescient letter written by Edward Frank Graham of Rochester, New York, to his parents shortly before he was killed: "This trouble is not a thing to be finished in five years, or a decade, or a generation. The effort to rule the world by force and barbarism may go on for one hundred years, and the battle must begin now."

13. Ralph McGill, "McGill in Vienna: McGill Foils Nazi Terror to Aid Refugee; Writer Brings Memorized Message to Vienna Victims," *Atlanta Constitution,* May 2, 1938, p. 5.

14. Ibid.

15. Ibid.

16. Ralph McGill, unpublished manuscript, p. 5, Box 31, Folder 4, RMP. This manuscript, written between 1938 and 1945, noted that Robert Best later collaborated with the Nazis, or as McGill put it, "now has turned traitor in Vienna."

17. Ralph McGill, "McGill in Vienna: Orgy of Adulation Accorded Hitler, the 'Build-Up of Herr Goebbels Described in Dramatic Detail by Writer,'" *Atlanta Constitution,* Apr. 28, 1938, p. 1.

18. McGill, "Orgy of Adulation"; Ralph McGill, "McGill in London: Mention of Hard, Wooden Benches Again Appears, but He Hears of Taxation Problem from Austrian Girl," *Atlanta Constitution,* May 6, 1938, p. 1; Ralph McGill, "McGill in Vienna: Hitler Invests Salute to Viennese with Pompous Drama," *Atlanta Constitution,* Apr. 29, 1938, p. 1.

19. McGill, "Hitler Invests Salute."

20. Ibid. Ralph McGill, "McGill in Vienna: Only a Fool Will Deny Hitler Hasn't Done Much for Germany and Will Do Much for Austria, Writer Declares," *Atlanta Constitution,* May 4, 1938, p. 7.

21. McGill, "Only a Fool."

22. Ralph McGill, "There Is Time Yet: Freedom of the Press," *Atlantic Monthly* 174 (Sept. 1944): 61–62; Ralph McGill, "McGill in Vienna: McGill Says Businessmen Like Hitler Rule; Most of Them Are Doing Better than in Dark Days After War, Writer Declares at Vienna; Wages Are Low," *Atlanta Constitution,* May 5, 1938, p. 11.

23. McGill, "McGill Says Businessmen Like Hitler Rule," 11.

24. Shirer, *Third Reich,* 351–52. After the plebiscite, Shirer witnessed "an orgy of sadism" toward the Jews. Hundreds of men and women were stopped on the streets and forced to scrub Schuschnigg signs off sidewalks and clean gutters while troops watched them and crowds taunted them. Others cleaned public latrines and barracks toilets. Thousands were jailed and their possessions confiscated.

25. McGill, "McGill Foils Nazi Terror."

26. McGill, "McGill Says Businessmen Like Hitler Rule," 11.

27. Ralph McGill, "McGill in Vienna: People of Austria Were Skillfully Coerced Into Voting 'Ja' in Humorless Plebiscite with Fine Goebbels Touch," *Atlanta Constitution,* May 1, 1938, p. 9K.
28. Ralph McGill, "McGill in Vienna: Vienna Becomes Transformed into Center of Great Public Gatherings as Adolf Hitler Makes His Speech on Union," *Atlanta Constitution,* Apr. 30, 1938, 1.
29. McGill, "People of Austria."
30. McGill, "McGill Says Businessmen Like Hitler Rule."
31. McGill, "McGill Foils Nazi Terror"; Shirer, *Third Reich,* 351.
32. Eugene Patterson to author, July 30, 1995, 1.
33. McGill, "There Is Time Yet," 61–62.
34. The article wired from sea was published in the *Atlanta Constitution,* May 30, 1938, p. 12; McGill's last batch of "Break O' Day" columns from Europe included "Keats' Home at Hampstead Heath," May 1, 1938, p. 1B; "All Is Not Beer and Skittles in Skittles," May 2, 1938, p. 10; "Dot Kirby Caused an English Matron to Get Jabbed in the Ribs," May 2, 1938, p. 14; "Does Coach Alexander Need a Good 'Punting Coach?'" (Stratford-on-Avon), May 4, 1938, p. 10; "It Might Be Worth $25,000 (£5,000) to Get [Henry] Cotton in U.S. Winter Meets," May 5, 1938, p. 22; "Old Alex McKellar's Wife," May 6, 1938, p. 23; "Gridders Clad in 14th Century Togs Play for Hitler at Florence," May 7, 1938, p. 8; "'It Is Not Every Day Ye Can Buy Beauty,' Said the Flower Woman," May 12, 1938, p. 16; "There Is No Intensity in Ireland—Just a Brooding Quietness," May 13, 1938, p. 25.

6. Fleas on the Southern Body-Politic

1. "Friends Greet Ralph McGill," *Atlanta Constitution,* June 8, 1938, p. 1.
2. In addition to Howell, who bought into the paper in 1876, and Grady, who joined in 1880, other shareholders and directors in the early years included William A. Hemphill, the newspaper's key founder in 1868, and N. P. T. Finch, an associate editor since 1872. Davis, *Henry Grady's New South,* 22–23, 53–54, 66–71; Wallace B. Eberhard, "Clark Howell," in *Biographical Dictionary of American Journalism,* 355–56.
3. These unsigned editorials were "New Uses for Cotton," June 1, 1936, p. 6; "Ill-Advised Strike," June 3, 1936, p. 6; "A Worthily Bestowed Honor," June 4, 1936, p. 6; and "Social Security," June 7, 1936, p. 14.
4. "Tax Reduction," May 3, 1938, p. 6; "Constructive Spending," May 3, 1936, p. 6; "The Pay-Hour Bill," May 4, 1938, p. 6.
5. "Hear the Death Rattle," June 4, 1936, p. 6; "Law Must Be Modified," June 6, 1936, p. 6.
6. "To Purge Atlanta's Blue," May 1, 1938, p. 8; "Courtroom Circus," May 2, 1938, p. 4; "An Imperative Need," May 4, 1938, p. 6; "Bad Road Advances," June 1, 1936, p. 6.
7. "Worse than Cattle Shacks," June 1, 1936, p. 6; "The Mote and the Beam," June 4, 1936, p. 6.
8. "Ralph McGill Appointed to Executive Editorship; Ralph T. Jones Becomes Associate Editor in Promotions Announced by Major Clark Howell, Editor and Publisher of the Constitution," *Atlanta Constitution,* June 17, 1938, p. 1.
9. "Ralph McGill Appointed to Executive Editorship"; Jack Spalding, interview by author, Atlanta, Oct. 15, 1986. The sports writer whom McGill declined to fire stayed on the staff for several years, so that his wife "must have had five

children while he was there," recalled Spalding, who was hired at the *Constitution* by Francis Clarke in 1938 for fifteen dollars a week. Spalding later became editor of the *Atlanta Journal.*

10. Russell interview; Ralph McGill, "Break O' Day," *Atlanta Constitution,* June 17, 1938, p. 23.

11. McGill, "Break O' Day," June 17, 1938.

12. Through an oversight, Ralph Jones, the editorial director, neglected until the third day to tell readers that Pegler was on vacation, and then ran a small box under McGill's column.

13. Ralph McGill, "One Word More," *Atlanta Constitution,* June 20, 1938, p. 4; June 21, 1938, p. 4; June 22, 1938, p. 4; June 23, 1938, p. 8; June 25, 1938, p. 6; June 26, 1938, p. 4K.

14. "Ralph McGill Is Elected Member of Ten Club at Monthly Meeting," *Atlanta Constitution,* Nov. 23, 1938, p. 2. The newspaper published a photograph of McGill, smiling.

15. Anderson, *Wild Man,* 173–76.

16. Ralph McGill, "One Word More," *Atlanta Constitution,* Aug. 18, 1938, p. 12.

17. Ralph McGill, "One Word More," *Atlanta Constitution,* July 7, 1938, p. 6. McGill wrote that rabble-rousers merely dropped the names of Hill, Toombs, and Watson to audiences that had no real idea of their actual contributions. Sen. Benjamin H. Hill had opposed secession and after the Civil War was "the first to speak of the New South." McGill quoted one of Hill's "moving orations": "There was a South of slavery and secession—that South is dead. There is a South of union and freedom—that South, thank God, is living, breathing, growing every hour." McGill believed that "it was this sentiment of Hill's, one of Henry Grady's heroes, which so excited and thrilled the young editor . . . [that] Grady worked to make it come true." Ralph McGill, "My Georgia," manuscript, RMP, reprinted in McGill, *No Place to Hide* 1:65. The "great Robert Toombs almost became president" of the Confederacy, McGill noted; he served as secretary of state and as a general. McGill, "This Is Our Georgia," in *A Book of the South,* ed. John Temple Graves II et al., (Southern Editors Association: Jas. O. Jones, 1940), 54–56, reprinted in McGill, *No Place to Hide* 1:57. McGill traced many of Talmadge's tactics to "the ghost" of Tom Watson of Hickory Hill, who in his successful race for the U.S. Senate in 1920 "appealed to the prejudices much in the manner of the man from Sugar Creek [Talmadge]. . . . You may be sure the man from Sugar Creek has studied his Tom Watson." McGill, "One Word More," Aug. 18, 1938, 12.

18. McGill, "One Word More," July 7, 1938, 6.

19. Martin, *McGill,* 70–71; Anderson, *Wild Man,* 177–78; Ralph McGill, "One Word More," *Atlanta Constitution,* Aug. 19, 1938, p. 6.

20. John T. Kneebone, *Southern Liberal Journalists and the Issue of Race, 1920–1944* (Chapel Hill: Univ. of North Carolina Press, 1985), xiv.

21. Thomas Krueger, *And Promises to Keep: The Southern Conference for Human Welfare, 1938–1948* (Nashville: Vanderbilt Univ. Press, 1967), 22. Krueger, citing the Birmingham Proceedings of the Southern Conference, 24, listed as liberal participants: Sen. Lister Hill, Supreme Court Justice Hugo Black's replacement in the U.S. Senate; Cong. Luther Patrick of Birmingham; Democratic National Committeeman Brook Hays of Arkansas; historian Howard K. Beale; Gov. Bibb Graves of Alabama; Edwin A. Elliott of the National Labor Relations Board in Texas; University of North Carolina president Frank P. Graham; Mrs. Raymond Robbins, honorary president of the National Women's

Trade Union League; First Lady Eleanor Roosevelt; Cong. Claude Pepper of
Miami; and Aubrey Williams of the Works Progress Administration.

22. Krueger, *And Promises to Keep*, 22; Francis Pickens Miller Papers, Box 103,
Alderman Library, Univ. of Virginia–Charlottesville, cited in Kneebone,
Southern Liberal Journalists, 168; "Conference," *Birmingham Post*, Oct. 27, 1938,
p. 1; Special Agent James P. O'Connell, Special Inquiry, for the Joint Committee on Atomic Energy, Washington, D.C., Nov. 23, 1951, Bureau File 77-52062-
3X, pp. 1, 4. The FBI agent in Atlanta, John P. Slaydon, interviewed McGill on
November 8, 1951.

23. [Associated Press], "Urge U.S. Subsidy for Dixie Schools; Southern Welfare
Conference 'Answers' Report on No. 1 Problem," *Atlanta Constitution*, Nov. 21,
1938; National Emergency Council, Report on Economic Conditions, p. 1,
cited in Kneebone, *Southern Liberal Journalists*, 165–68.

24. "Welfare Conference Resolutions Touch on Variety of Questions," *Birmingham
News*, Nov. 24, 1938, p. 2.

25. "Medal for Work as Humanitarian Awarded Black; Justice Cites Early Efforts of
Jefferson for Underprivileged in Acceptance," *Birmingham News*, Nov. 24,
1938, 1–2; Kneebone, *Southern Liberal Journalists*, 169.

26. "Welfare Conference Resolutions," 2; Kneebone, *Southern Liberal Journalists*,
170; Rob Hall, "The Southern Conference for Human Welfare," *Communist*,
Jan. 1939, 60, 65, cited in Harvey Klehr, *The Heyday of American Communism:
The Depression Decade* (New York: Basic Books, 1984), 276–77. During the
1940s, McGill told one New Deal administrator who was at the Birmingham
sessions, Aubrey Williams, that the conference, whatever its aims, had "too
many Communists" in the membership. In 1946, when the conference
announced it would bestow its highest award on Georgia governor Ellis Arnall
for his courageous, liberal stance against the whites-only primary elections,
McGill advised Arnall not to go to New Orleans to accept the award because
Arnall's political enemies would attach guilt by association. Arnall disregarded
McGill's advice and collected the honor. Ralph McGill to Aubrey Williams,
Oct. 17, 1947, RMP; Ellis Gibbs Arnall, telephone interview by author, Mar. 11,
1987. Historian Krueger noted "six avowed members of the Communist party
and, so accusations have run, perhaps a score of covert members and con-
scious fellow-travelers from such organizations as the International Labor
Defense, the American League for Peace and Democracy, the Workers'
Alliance, and the American Youth Congress." Beyond this there were delegates
from suspect Negro associations, including the Southern Negro Youth
Congress. In addition, Krueger recorded, the Socialist Party sent twenty-seven
in various socialist factions: the Southern Tenant Farmers' Union, the
Southern Workers' Defense League, and the Southern branch of the Amalgam-
ated Clothing workers of America." Krueger, *And Promises to Keep*, 22–23.

27. O'Connell, Special Inquiry, 1.

28. Ralph McGill, "One Word More," *Atlanta Constitution*, Nov. 21, 1938, p. 4;
Nov. 23, 1938, p. 6; Nov. 24, 1938, p. 10B; Nov. 25, 1938, p. 6; Nov. 27, 1938,
p. 12. McGill did receive and file the Southern Conference on Human Welfare
"Report on Proceedings, Nov. 20–23, 1938," Box 67, Folder 22, RMP.

29. "Has the South Lagged Economically?" *Atlanta Constitution*, Nov. 30, 1938, p. 4.

30. On March 29, 1944, the House committee cited the SCHW as a Communist-
front organization. On June 12, 1947, the same committee stated that the
SCHW as a Communist front "seeks to attract Southern liberals on the basis of
its seeming interest in the problems of the South, [although its] professed

interest in Southern welfare is simply an expedient for larger aims serving the Soviet Union and its subservient Communist Party in the United States." O'Connell, Special Inquiry, 4.

31. Harold H. Martin, *William Berry Hartsfield: Mayor of Atlanta* (Athens: Univ. of Georgia Press, 1978), 12–19; Gary M. Pomerantz, *Where Peachtree Meets Sweet Auburn: The Saga of Two Families and the Making of Atlanta* (New York: Scribner, 1996), 96, 130.

32. Arnall interview, Mar. 11, 1987.

33. Anderson, *Wild Man,* 114–16.

34. "Ellis Arnall" (obituary), *Atlanta Constitution,* Dec. 14, 1992, p. 1; Ralph McGill, "One Word More," *Atlanta Constitution,* Sept. 1, 1939, p. 10.

35. Ralph McGill, "Leg Men," *Atlanta Constitution,* Dec. 19, 1939, p. 21.

36. The town in the study was Lavonia, Georgia, population 1,511. Ralph McGill, "One Word More," *Atlanta Constitution,* Mar. 1, 1939, p. 6; the legislature met the deficit by scaling down most payments to 74 percent. Teachers were paid in full. E. Merton Coulter, *Georgia: A Short History,* rev. ed. (Chapel Hill: Univ. of North Carolina Press, 1960), 440–41; Ralph McGill, "One Word More," *Atlanta Constitution,* Mar. 3, 1939, p. 10.

37. Ralph McGill, "One Word More," *Atlanta Constitution,* Mar. 31, 1939, p. 12; Coulter, *Georgia,* 442.

38. Ralph McGill, "One Word More," *Atlanta Constitution,* Mar. 5, 1939, p. 6K.

39. Ralph McGill, "One Word More," *Atlanta Constitution,* Mar. 12, 1939, p. 10M.

40. Ibid.

41. Jack Spalding, interview by author, Atlanta, July 18, 1994; Martin, *McGill,* 72.

42. McGill, "One Word More," Sept. 1, 1939, 10; Ralph McGill, "One Word More," *Atlanta Constitution,* Sept. 2, 1939, p. 6.

43. McGill, "One Word More," Sept. 2, 1939, 6.

44. Ibid.

45. Ralph McGill, "One Word More," *Atlanta Constitution,* Sept. 4, 1939, p. 4.

46. Ralph McGill, "One Word More," *Atlanta Constitution,* Sept. 5, 1939, p. 8.

47. McGill, "One Word More," Sept. 4, 1939; "We Do Not Have to Get in It" (editorial), *Atlanta Constitution,* Sept. 4, 1939, p. 4.

48. W. A. Swanberg, *Citizen Hearst: A Biography of William Randolph Hearst* (New York: Charles Scribner's, 1961), 476; "Georgian Marks Eighth Major Change in Chain," *Atlanta Constitution,* Dec. 17, 1939, p. 10. Between 1936 and 1939, Hearst's *New York American* merged with the *New York Journal,* the *Omaha Bee-News* was sold to the *Omaha World Herald,* the *Milwaukee News* consolidated with the *Milwaukee Sentinel,* the *Washington Herald* was leased to Eleanor M. Patterson of the McCormick-Patterson newspaper family, the *Syracuse Journal and Sunday American* was sold to the *Syracuse Herald,* the *Rochester Journal and Sunday American* was closed, and the *Chicago Herald and Examiner* merged with the Chicago *American;* in addition, the two Hearst wire services, International News Service and Universal Service, were consolidated in 1937. "Journal-Georgian Bill of Sale Filed; Deed Covers Transfer of Building, Machines and Other Equipment," *Atlanta Constitution,* Dec. 19, 1939, p. 5.

49. "Cox Files Application to Buy Station WSB," *Atlanta Constitution,* Dec. 12, 1939, p. 1; "Journal, WSB Sold to James M. Cox; New Owner of Paper Ex-Governor of Ohio; Divided Control Termed Factor by James R. Gray; Purchaser Was Democratic Nominee for President in 1920; Sale Effective Immediately," *Atlanta Constitution,* Dec. 13, 1939, p. 1; "'Miss Scarlett' Makes Triumphant Return to Atlanta Today as Stars, Film Dignitaries Start Arriving for Gala Fete;

Ann Rutherford to Be First of Stellar Deluge," *Atlanta Constitution,* Dec. 13, 1939, p. 1.

50. "Journal, WSB Sold," 1; "Price Announced in Journal Sale," *Atlanta Constitution,* Dec. 14, 1939, p. 1; James M. Cox, *Journey Through My Years* (New York: Simon and Schuster, 1946); Leonard Ray Teel, "How James Cox Bought Atlanta's Newspapers," *Georgia Trend* 2 (Dec. 1986): 87–90; "Reasons for Sale of Journal Cited; Cox Is Expected to Make Statement on Arrival in Atlanta Today," *Atlanta Constitution,* Dec. 13, 1939, 1, 11; In *Journey,* his autobiography, Cox said the purchase of the *Journal* "was the rounding out of a dream." An Atlanta newspaper and radio station would extend his media influence through "three climates and the 'air' from the Great Lakes on the north to Latin America on the south."

51. "George Harsh Confesses Local Killings and Implicates Richard G. Gallogly," *Atlanta Constitution,* Oct. 28, 1928, p. 1; "Jury Deadlocked in Gallogly Trial," *Atlanta Constitution,* Feb. 1, 1928, p. 1; "Gallogly Murder Case Ends in Mistrial," *Atlanta Constitution,* Feb. 2, 1929, p. 1; "Second Trial of Richard Gallogly," *Atlanta Constitution,* Mar. 20, 1929, p. 1; "Second Mistrial Ordered, New Date April 2," *Atlanta Constitution,* Mar. 24, 1929, p. 1; "Harsh, Gallogly Given Life Terms by Guilty Pleas," *Atlanta Constitution,* Apr. 2, 1929, p. 1.

52. Ellis Gibbs Arnall, telephone interview by author, Nov. 10, 1986; Spalding interview, Oct. 15, 1986. In January 1941, as one of his last acts as governor, E. D. Rivers pardoned several prisoners, among them Dick Gallogly.

53. "James M. Cox Asserts Journal 'To Remain Free,'" *Atlanta Constitution,* Dec. 19, 1939, p. 5; "Welcome, Governor Cox" (editorial), *Atlanta Constitution,* Dec. 20, 1939; advertisement, *Atlanta Constitution,* Dec. 14, 1939; McGill, "Leg Men."

54. "Founded in 1906," 1, 10; "The News Quits in Chattanooga," *Atlanta Constitution,* Dec. 17, 1939, 1, 10.

55. "Founded in 1906," 10; Tom Bennett, "Harold Martin, 83, Wrote for Newspaper, Magazine," *Atlanta Journal and Constitution,* July 11, 1994, p. 6B; Celestine Sibley, "A Man of Rare Goodness and Fun Passes On," *Atlanta Constitution,* July 11, 1994, p. 1C.

56. Ralph McGill, "One Word More," *Atlanta Constitution,* Dec. 17, 1939, p. 10B; Josephus Daniels, *Tar Heel Editor* (Chapel Hill: Univ. of North Carolina Press, 1939). On leaving the theater, McGill ran into golfer Bobby Jones, who told him, "I am worn out. Nothing has ever taken so much out of me as that picture." In one of the quirky responses to the movie, the critic for the Communist *Daily Worker,* Howard Rushmore, resigned rather than write a bad review. "Red Paper's Critic Scorns 'Pan GWTW' Order; Daily Worker's Reviewer Resigns Rather than Rewrite Story; Declares Board Told Him to Urge Boycott of Film," *Atlanta Constitution,* Dec. 22, 1939, p. 1.

57. Editorial, *Atlanta Constitution,* Dec. 17, 1939, p. 10B; Martin, *McGill,* 73.

58. "McGill, Virginia Colvin" (obituary), *Atlanta Constitution,* Dec. 20, 1939, p. 29; "Virginia M'Gill Dies After Long Illness; Rites for Daughter of *Constitution* Editor to Be Held Today," *Atlanta Constitution,* Dec. 20, 1939, p. 29. Virginia's birth date was given as February 4, 1936; Martin, *McGill,* 73; Celestine Sibley interview, "Dawn's Early Light," 31.

59. Ralph McGill, "One Word More," *Atlanta Constitution,* Dec. 29, 1939, p. 6; Dec. 28, 1939, p. 6; Dec. 27, 1939, p. 4.

7. TAKING ON THE TALMADGE MACHINE

1. Ralph McGill, "One Word More," *Atlanta Constitution,* Aug. 5, 1940, p. 4.
2. McGill, *South and the Southerner,* 39.
3. Ibid., 38–40.
4. Calvin McLeod Logue, "Ralph McGill's Moderate Campaign for Racial Reform," in Logue and Dorgan, *New Diversity in Contemporary Southern Rhetoric,* 92.
5. Martin, *McGill,* 84–85.
6. McGill, "One Word More," Aug. 5, 1940; McGill, "One Word More," *Atlanta Constitution,* Aug. 17, 1940, p. 4.
7. Ralph McGill, "One Word More," *Atlanta Constitution,* Aug. 13, 1940, p. 4; Aug. 11, 1940, p. 8B.
8. Ralph McGill, "One Word More," *Atlanta Constitution,* July 29, 1940, p. 4.
9. Ralph McGill, "One Word More," *Atlanta Constitution,* July 15, 1940, p. 4.
10. Ibid.
11. Ralph McGill, "Coming Events, and Shadows," *Atlanta Constitution,* July 31, 1947; Ralph McGill, "One Word More," *Atlanta Constitution,* Jan. 28, 1939; Ralph McGill, "Our Three Most Valuable Citizens," *Atlanta Constitution,* July 3, 1947, p. 10A; Robert L. Zangrando, *The NAACP Crusade Against Lynching, 1909–1950* (Philadelphia: Temple Univ. Press, 1980), 9. The numbers of lynchings had declined notably. From 1882, when the Tuskegee Institute began keeping records, until 1939, 4,697 lynchings were recorded in the forty-eight states. More than half (2,598) were in eight southern states, and 90 percent of the victims were Negroes. Since 1882 Georgia had been second only to Mississippi in the number of lynchings; each state had more than 500. Ralph McGill, "Meditations in a Hammock," *Atlanta Constitution,* June 7, 1949, p. 10A; Jessie Daniel Ames, *The Changing Character of Lynching: Review of Lynching, 1931–1941* (Atlanta: Commission on Interracial Cooperation, 1942), 2; McGill, "A Lynching and 'The Difference,'" *Atlanta Constitution,* June 1, 1949, p. 12A. See also Jacquelyn Dowd Hall, *Revolt Against Chivalry: Jessie Daniel Ames and the Women's Campaign Against Lynching* (New York: Columbia Univ. Press, 1979).
12. "Willkie Leading Roosevelt in Electoral Votes—Gallup," *Atlanta Constitution,* Aug. 4, 1940, p. 1. Gallup's prediction in 1938 was all the more remarkable because of the razor-thin margins in some counties, where as few as 20 votes tipped the balance. Anderson, in *Wild Man,* 181, notes that "a change of only 210 votes in right counties would have given Talmadge the election through the county-unit system." The migration from the farms to the medium and large cities had eroded Talmadge's base in the smaller counties.
13. McGill, "One Word More," *Atlanta Constitution,* July 1, 1940, p. 4. The county-unit system as decreed by the Neill Primary Act (1917) gave each of the 159 counties 2 votes for every representative it had in the general assembly. The 8 largest counties, no matter how large, were limited to 6 votes. The next 30 medium-sized counties each got 4 votes. The other 121 had 2 votes each. In this scheme, if large and medium counties combined—which was next to impossible—they had only 168 votes; the small counties as a bloc had 242. The system effectively disfranchised people who migrated to the cities, whites and blacks alike, and handicapped the cities that received them. Consolidation of smaller

counties, which McGill advocated, would have increased urban power; it never passed. There was no proper relief until the U.S. Supreme Court's "one man, one vote" ruling. Anderson, *Wild Man,* 16; see also Albert B. Saye, *Georgia's County Unit System of Election* (Athens, n.d.); John M. Greybeal, "The Georgia Primary Election System" (Master's thesis, Emory Univ., 1932); Lynwood M. Holland, "The Conduct of Elections in Georgia" (Master's thesis, Emory Univ., 1933); Alice Owens, "The County Unit System as an Integral Part of the Georgia Primary Election System" (Master's thesis, Emory Univ., 1934).

14. Ralph McGill, "One Word More," *Atlanta Constitution,* Aug. 4, 1940, p. 8B.

15. Ralph McGill, "One Word More," *Atlanta Constitution,* July 31, 1940, p. 4. Talmadge's rivals were Abit Nix, an Athens politician; Hugh Howell, Talmadge's former supporter; and Columbus Roberts, a former agriculture commissioner.

16. Anderson, *Wild Man,* 186–91; McGill, "One Word More," July 31, 1940; Herman E. Talmadge, with Mark Royden Winchell, *Talmadge: A Political Legacy, A Politician's Life: A Memoir* (Atlanta: Peachtree, 1987), 9.

17. McGill, "One Word More," July 31, 1940; Anderson, *Wild Man,* 191.

18. McGill, "One Word More," July 31, 1940; Talmadge and Winchell, *Talmadge,* 36. In 1936 there had been talk that the Republicans considered running Eugene Talmadge against Roosevelt, but that was "idle talk," said his son, Herman: "[The] overwhelming majority of Georgians at that time would have voted for an Abyssinian goat before they would a Republican." Anderson, *Wild Man,* 180.

19. McGill, "One Word More," July 31, 1940; Anderson, *Wild Man,* 191.

20. Ralph McGill, "One Word More," *Atlanta Constitution,* July 6, 1940, p. 4; Anderson, *Wild Man,* 191.

21. McGill, "One Word More," July 31, 1940; McGill, "One Word More," *Atlanta Constitution,* Aug. 18, 1940, p. 2D.

22. Georgia Official and Statistical Record (Atlanta, 1940), 501, and Ralph McGill, *Atlanta Constitution,* Sept. 13, Oct. 3, 1940, cited in Anderson, *Wild Man,* 192.

23. Ralph McGill, "One Word More," *Atlanta Constitution,* Nov. 13, 1940, p. 8; George B. Tindall, *The Emergence of the New South, 1913–1945* (Baton Rouge: Louisiana State Univ. Press, 1967), 639–40. The poll tax varied from one to twenty-five dollars. The other southern states with the tax were Alabama, Arkansas, Mississippi, South Carolina, and Tennessee.

24. McGill, "One Word More," Nov. 13, 1940. North Carolina's "Our Boy" Reynolds was the most consistent senator against lend-lease and rearmament; in Florida, repeal was backed by the Claude Pepper faction. Tindall, *New South,* 639, 690, 691.

25. Ibid. Ralph McGill, "One Word More," *Atlanta Constitution,* Nov. 17, 1940, p. 8. One repealer was the young editor of the *Cobb County Times,* Chess Abernathy, whose argument for abolishing the tax had triggered the debate at the Georgia League of Women Voters' conference. While lumping him with the idealists, McGill politely described him as an "able young editor."

26. McGill, "One Word More," Nov. 13, 1940; Nov. 17, 1940.

27. V. O. Key, *Southern Politics* (New York: Vintage Books, 1949), 599; J. Morgan Kousser, *The Shaping of Southern Politics: Suffrage Restriction and the Establishment of the One-Party South* (New Haven, Conn.: Yale Univ. Press), 65; John A. Griffin, interview by author, Atlanta, Apr. 20, 1987. Griffin was a leading Atlanta liberal voice who helped found the Southern Regional Council.

28. In Tennessee, Edward H. Crump delivered votes and patronage, in partnership with U.S. senator Kenneth McKellar; Crump is credited with seating governors

from 1930 to 1946. Tindall, *New South,* 639–40, 646. McGill, "One Word More," Nov. 13, 1940; Nov. 17, 1940.

29. McGill, "One Word More," Nov. 13, 1940.

30. Coulter, *Georgia,* 366–67. Among the thirty-seven Negroes elected to remake the Georgia Constitution in 1867, Coulter wrote, were "the vicious, the innocent, the ignorant, the illiterate." They included a convict from New York, a carpetbagger who had attempted to set up a government on St. Catherine's Island after the war, a future bishop in the African Methodist Church, and others who "were clay in the hands of their cunning and designing white friends." As ominous, said Coulter, were the "native white Georgians who had turned against the old traditions of their state and who were known under the despicable name of scalawags."

31. C. Vann Woodward, *Tom Watson: Agrarian Rebel* (New York, 1938), 370–71. Watson believed that fear prevented poor whites from uniting with poor blacks against economic forces which oppressed both races: "The white people dare not revolt so long as they can be intimidated by the fear of the negro vote." Without the "bugaboo of negro domination," he said, "every white man would act according to his own conscience and judgment in deciding how he shall vote." Watson, *Atlanta Journal,* July 27, 1906, and *Weekly Jeffersonian,* Mar. 24, 1910, cited in Woodward, *Tom Watson,* 371. In his resurgence as a white supremacist, Watson published *Watson's Jeffersonian Magazine* and *Watson's Jeffersonian Weekly.* In 1936, Talmadge supporters invited "Jeffersonian Democrats" to an anti–New Deal rally. Tindall, *New South,* 617.

32. Newspaper clippings in Governor's Unofficial Papers, State of Georgia Archives, Atlanta, cited in Anderson, *Wild Man,* 193–94.

33. Ralph McGill, "One Word More," *Atlanta Constitution,* Mar. 1, 1942, p. 6E.

34. Walter D. Cocking, "Report of the Study of Higher Education of Negroes in Georgia," in Special Collections, Univ. of Georgia Libraries, Athens, 1938, cited in Anderson, *Wild Man,* 196; Ralph McGill, "It Has Happened Here," *Survey Graphic,* Sept. 30, 1941, 449–453, reprinted in McGill, *No Place to Hide* 1:69.

35. Ralph McGill, "One Word More," *Atlanta Constitution,* Aug. 3, 1942, p. 8; McGill, "One Word More," *Atlanta Constitution,* Aug. 9, 1942, p. 8; Anderson, *Wild Man,* 194.

36. Anderson, *Wild Man,* 196; Ralph McGill, "One Word More," *Atlanta Constitution,* Sept. 6, 1942, p. 4B; Talmadge and Winchell, *Talmadge,* 76.

37. Talmadge and Winchell, *Talmadge,* 197–98; this is based on Anderson's interview with Jim Peters, June 12, 1970.

38. Talmadge and Winchell, *Talmadge,* 198–99.

39. Coulter, *Georgia,* 443.

40. Anderson, *Wild Man;* McGill, "One Word More," Aug. 9, 1942.

41. Arnall interview, Nov. 10, 1986.

42. Arnall interview, Mar. 11, 1987.

43. McGill, "One Word More," Sept. 6, 1942; Arnall interview, Mar. 11, 1987.

44. "Hitler in Georgia" (editorial), *American Press,* Aug. 2, 1941, p. 462, Box 3, Folder 1, RMP.

45. Arnall interview, Mar. 11, 1987; "Where Danger Lies" (editorial), *Atlanta Constitution,* Aug. 21, 1942, p. 4A; Rufus Jarmin, "Wool Hat Dictator," *Saturday Evening Post,* June 27, 1947, 111, cited in Anderson, *Wild Man,* 194.

46. McGill, *Southerner,* 90–92.

47. Ibid., 96–97, 100.

48. Ibid., 100.

49. Jack Spalding, interview by author, Atlanta, Dec. 7, 1994.

50. On the prison pardons issue, McGill claimed that Talmadge's people were creating false issues in part because they hoped "to divert attention away from the fact that the Governor pardoned more than 4,500 prisoners in four years when they were not needed for work and that there was a scandal in the fact that at least 4,000 of the pardons had to be worked through one man." Ralph McGill, "One Word More," *Atlanta Constitution,* Aug. 19, 1942, p. 8; Spalding interview, Dec. 7, 1994.

51. Lamar Q. Ball, "Talmadge Statement Denied by Victim of Tear Gas Plot," *Atlanta Constitution,* Aug. 2, 1942, 1, 9.

52. "Beaver Resigns from Regent Board; Protests Interference by Talmadge; Gainesville Educator Also Gives Up Post as Chief of Staff," *Atlanta Constitution,* Aug. 28, 1942, p. 1; Lamar Q. Ball, "Two Talmadge Stalwarts Join Arnall's Ranks," *Atlanta Constitution,* Aug. 17, 1942, p. 1.

53. "Caldwell Deplores Racial Charges Against University; Asserts It's His Duty to Inform People Properly on Issue," *Atlanta Constitution,* Aug. 2, 1942, p. 1; Ralph McGill, "One Word More," *Atlanta Constitution,* Sept. 3, 1942, p. 16.

54. Lamar Q. Ball, "Talmadge Is Accused of Selling State Jobs," *Atlanta Constitution,* Aug. 14, 1942, p. 1; Lamar Q. Ball, "Talmadge Shakedown of Publishers Charged; Firms Allowed to Up Price, Arnall Says," *Atlanta Constitution,* Aug. 12, 1942, p. 1.

55. Lamar Q. Ball, "Arnall Warns on 'Rosy' Promises for Talmadge Roads," *Atlanta Constitution,* Aug. 15, 1942, p. 2; Ball, "Talmadge Statement Denied."

56. Lamar Q. Ball, "'Regular Fellow,' Say Schoolmates of Ellis Arnall," *Atlanta Constitution,* Aug. 2, 1942, p. 3D; "U.S. Courts Uphold Ellis Arnall's Legal Opinions," *Atlanta Constitution,* Aug. 16, 1942, p. 3D.

57. "Arnall Leads, 2 to 1, in Peace Justices' Poll; Survey Covers All of Georgia; Never Wrong," *Atlanta Constitution,* Aug. 23, 1942, p. 1.

58. *Statesman,* July 2, 1940, p. 3, cited in McGill, *Constitution,* Aug. 13, 1942, p. 8; Talmadge bought the *Statesman* to emulate Tom Watson's *Jeffersonian,* the newspaper in which Watson published his views. The *Statesman* was founded in 1930 by a northerner named Frank Lawson. Around 1932, Talmadge became associate editor by lending Lawson one thousand dollars. The newspaper soon was hailing Talmadge as a reformer. On April 1, 1934, Talmadge bought 51 percent control for one thousand dollars. Lawson later told a friend that "Talmadge then began to discover . . . he could not . . . duplicate Tom Watson's *Jeffersonian* for the simple reason Gene CANNOT write." *Athens (Ga.) Banner Herald,* Sept. 13, 1934, and A. Dixon Adair III, "Eugene Talmadge of Georgia" (Master's thesis, Princeton Univ., 1936), 64, cited in Anderson, *Wild Man,* 109–10; Talmadge and Winchell, *Talmadge,* 37–38.

59. McGill, "One Word More," Aug. 9, 1942; Arnall interview, Mar. 11, 1987.

60. Lamar Q. Ball, "Will Vote for Arnall, Tom Linder Declares," *Atlanta Constitution,* Sept. 5, 1942, p. 1; Lamar Q. Ball, "Dublin Throng Hears Linder Predict Easy Win for Ellis Arnall," *Constitution,* Sept. 6, 1942, p. 1; Ralph McGill, "One Word More," *Atlanta Constitution,* Sept. 7, 1942, p. 16A; Lamar Q. Ball, "DeKalb Is Solid for Arnall, Last Rally Indicates," *Atlanta Constitution,* Sept. 9, 1942, p. 1. Two days before the election, the Arnall campaign paid for a full-page ad urging voters to "Wipe out all dictatorship!" and showing Talmadge with a whip in his left hand, his right hand holding a chain attached to

Georgia. "What is a dictator, American style? It is a governor, or other public
official, who seized power which rightfully does not go with his office."

61. Ralph McGill, interview by Calvin Kytle and James Mackay, transcript, Atlanta,
May 20, 1947, pp. 1–2, unpublished series of interviews by Kytle and Mackay
with seventy-five Georgia leaders in Calvin Kytle Papers, Chapel Hill, N.C.

62. "Arnall Runs Unit Margin to 261–149 as All Counties Complete Vote Count,"
Atlanta Constitution, Sept. 11, 1942, p. 1; "Talmadge Still Refuses to Concede
His Defeat; Palace Guard Urging Contest of Vote Count," *Atlanta Constitution*,
Sept. 13, 1942, 1, 13.

63. Ralph McGill, "One Word More," *Atlanta Constitution*, Sept. 11, 1942, p. 11.

64. Ibid.

65. Spalding interview, Dec. 7, 1994.

8. THE NATIONAL ARENA

1. Howland and McGill had met at Sand Cave, Kentucky, in 1925, when they
both covered the story of Floyd Collins, the cave explorer trapped underground. Ralph McGill, "One Word More," *Atlanta Constitution*, Mar. 13, 1943,
p. 14; "Strong Constitution," 46; "Constitution Amended," *Time*, Jan. 5, 1948,
p. 48. "In 1942," *Time* declared, "he [McGill] was a big help in keeping Gene
Talmadge out of the Governor's mansion and getting Ellis Arnall in."

2. Ralph McGill, "One Word More," *Atlanta Constitution*, Mar. 19, 1943, p. 8.

3. Ralph McGill, "One Word More," *Atlanta Constitution*, Mar. 4, 1943, p. 8.

4. McGill, "One Word More," Mar. 19, 1943, p. 8. Arnall was photographed
signing the state patrol bill, *Atlanta Constitution*, Mar. 4, 1943, p. 7.

5. Ralph McGill, "One Word More," *Atlanta Constitution*, Mar. 1, 1943, p. 8; Jack
Tarver (former publisher), interview, *Atlanta Constitution*, Dec. 12, 1994.

6. Arnall interview, Mar. 11, 1987; Claude Pepper to Ralph McGill II, Box 3,
Folder 2, RMP. After a national governor's conference at Mackinaw Island,
where Arnall spoke as the southerner on a panel with Harold Stassen of
Minnesota, Earl Warren of California, and Thomas Dewey of New York, *New
York Times* reporter James Reston confided that "Ellis Arnall is the smartest one
of those four." Of Dewey, Reston only said, "Did you notice how he always
keeps the left side of his face to the camera?" Jack Tarver, interview by author,
Atlanta, Dec. 13, 1994.

7. Ralph McGill, "One Word More," *Atlanta Constitution*, Mar. 30, 1943, p. 8.

8. Margaret Tarver, interview by author, Atlanta, Dec. 12, 1994.

9. Jack Tarver interview, Dec. 13, 1994; Margaret "Peggy" Mitchell to "Red"
McGill, Mar. 9, 1944, Box 3, Folder 2, RMP.

10. Ralph McGill, "One Word More," *Atlanta Constitution*, Mar. 29, 1943, p. 6;
McGill, "One Word More," *Atlanta Constitution*, Mar. 25, 1943, p. 20; McGill,
"One Word More," *Atlanta Constitution*, Mar. 27, 1943, p. 4.

11. McGill, "One Word More," Mar. 30, 1943; Arnall interview, Mar. 11, 1987.

12. McGill, "One Word More," Mar. 30, 1943.

13. Ibid.; Martin, *McGill*, 87.

14. "Edwin A. Peebles, 79, Author of Books," *Atlanta Constitution*, Dec. 17, 1994, p.
12B; Jack Tarver interview, Dec. 13, 1994.

15. Martin, *McGill*, 87–88.

16. Ralph McGill, "Seven Miles Is Not High Enough," *Atlanta Constitution*, Mar. 7,
1944, p. 14.

17. Martin, *McGill*, 92–94.
18. Ibid., 94; Ellis Gibbs Arnall, telephone interview by author, Sept. 8, 1987.
19. Jack Tarver interview, Dec. 13, 1994; "Synopsis of GWTW," in Harold Martin Papers, Atlanta History Center (hereafter cited as Martin Papers). Later, at a meeting of the Georgia Press Association, an editor of the *Macon News,* Susan Myrica, introduced Tarver to Margaret Mitchell. Mitchell immediately responded, "Oh, I know the sonofabitch." She had to pay a clipping service fifty cents for each copy of that column clipped from papers around the country.
20. Jack Tarver interview, Dec. 13, 1994; Margaret Tarver interview, Dec. 13, 1994.
21. Jack Tarver interview, Dec. 13, 1994.
22. Ibid.
23. Ibid.
24. Ralph McGill, "The Three Georgians Didn't Shadowbox," *Atlanta Constitution,* Mar. 5, 1944, p. 2D. The third Georgian was the president of Emory University, Dr. Goodrich White, who naturally emphasized the role of education.
25. Mark Ethridge to Ralph McGill, Sept. 7, 1944, Box 3, Folder 2, RMP; Jack Tarver interview, Dec. 13, 1994; Barry Bingham to Robert Worth Bingham, Apr. 9, 1936, and Bingham Diary, bk. 4, p. 4, Mar. 1936, in William E. Ellis, "The Bingham Papers: Passing the Torch in the 1930s" (paper presented to the American Journalism Historians Association national conference, Louisville, Ky., Oct. 22, 1998), 6; see also William E. Ellis, *Robert Worth Bingham and the Southern Mystique: From the Old South to the New South and Beyond* (Kent, Ohio: Kent State Univ. Press, 1997).
26. Mark Ethridge to Ralph McGill, Sept. 7, 1944.
27. Arnall interview, Mar. 11, 1987; Ellis Gibbs Arnall, *The Shore Dimly Seen* (1946; reprint, New York: Acclaim Publishing, 1966), 56–57, 315. Arnall calculated that the poll tax in Tennessee reduced the electorate from 72 percent to less than 30 percent; in North Carolina, removal of the tax caused an increase in voting of 18 percent, but a greater increase in registration.
28. Arnall interview, Mar. 11, 1987; Arnall, *Shore Dimly Seen,* 58.
29. Ibid. When the commission recommended repeal and the legislature complied in 1945, the national press hailed Georgia and one journalist recommended Arnall for a Cabinet post. The editor of *Collier's* weekly, Henry LaCossitt, was quoted in the *Constitution* as saying that he came to Georgia to "see what is going on in the New South. . . . Your governor speaks a language that the North understands. And it's so different from the language of other southerners like Bilbo of Mississippi and Cotton Ed Smith of South Carolina. Georgia's repeal of the poll tax was a light shining in the darkness." "Editor Says Cabinet Post Open to Arnall," *Atlanta Constitution,* Mar. 6, 1945, p. 2.
30. "Southern Reaction to Negro Voting Decision Record," *Atlanta Constitution,* Apr. 4, 1944, p. 1. Encouraged by the Court ruling, Negroes registered to vote in increasing numbers, paying poll taxes and passing literacy tests. In Miami, however, Negroes were allowed to register only as Republicans, eligible to vote only in the Republican primary. In Mobile, a deputy sheriff during the Tennessee primary election barred Negroes at one polling place, telling them, "This is a white primary. You can't vote here." In Georgia, Negroes registered and paid poll taxes in expectation of being able to vote. "Voting in the South," *Life,* May 18, 1944, 33–34.
31. Ralph McGill, "The Winners: Pepper, Hill and Common Sense," *Atlanta Constitution,* May 5, 1944, p. 6.

32. Ibid.
33. "Voting in the South," *Life*, May 18, 1944, p. 38.
34. John Temple Graves, *The Fighting South*, 120, in Tindall, *New South*, 718.
35. Ralph McGill, "One Word More," *Atlanta Constitution*, Mar. 17, 1943, p. 6.
36. Tindall, *New South*, 177–80, 719–21.
37. Griffin interview, Apr. 20, 1987. Griffin was closely associated with the SRC; Martin, *McGill*, 130–31.
38. Cason J. Callaway to Ralph McGill, 1944, Box 3, Folder 2, RMP; Mark F. Ethridge to Ralph McGill, Sept. 7, 1944, Box 3, Folder 2, RMP; Claude Pepper to Ralph McGill, Sept. 23, 1944, Box 3, Folder 2, RMP; Tindall, *New South*, 721.
39. Jack Tarver interview, Dec. 13, 1994.
40. Ibid.
41. Ralph McGill, "One Word More," *Atlanta Constitution*, Dec. 19, 1943, p. 8; Ralph McGill, "One Word More," *Atlanta Constitution*, Dec. 20, 1943, p. 8.
42. Eugene Talmadge to Ralph McGill, Dec. 20, 1943 (copy), Box 3, Folder 2, RMP.
43. Ibid.
44. Charles Whited, *Knight: A Publisher in the Tumultuous Century* (New York: E. P. Dutton, 1988), 96–97.
45. Whited, *Knight*, 95. See also Arthur Krock, "Why Our Newspapers Can't Tell the Truth," *Reader's Digest*, Nov. 1942, 75.
46. Whited, *Knight*, 105–9.
47. McGill, "There Is Time Yet," 61.
48. Ibid., 63, 65.
49. Ralph McGill to Carl W. Ackerman, Sept. 22, 1944, 1, Container 39, Carl W. Ackerman Papers, ASNE World Free Press Mission, Library of Congress (hereafter cited as Ackerman Papers).
50. Ibid., 2.
51. Ibid., 1.
52. Whited, *Knight*, 138; Wilbur Forrest, Carl W. Ackerman, and Ralph McGill, "Full Report of the ASNE Committee on Freedom of Information," *Editor and Publisher* (June 18, 1945), 3.
53. Dwight Young to John S. Knight, Oct. 12, 1944 (copy), John S. Knight Papers, Univ. of Akron, Akron, Ohio (hereafter cited as Knight Papers).

9. THE WORLD IN FLUX

1. John S. Knight to Dwight Young, Oct. 16, 1944 (copy), Knight Papers.
2. Martin, *McGill*, 98.
3. Margaret A. Blanchard, *Exporting the First Amendment: The Press-Government Crusade of 1945–1952* (New York: Longman, 1986), 22–24.
4. Whited, *Knight*, 128.
5. Forrest, Ackerman, and McGill, "Full Report," 3. See also James B. Reston, "American Nations Form an Alliance to Protect Peace: Act of Chapultepec, Accepted Unanimously, Guarantees Borders in Hemisphere," *New York Times*, Mar. 4, 1945, 1, 25.
6. Forrest, Ackerman, and McGill, "Full Report," 9; "'Feeling Pulse of Europe,' Touring McGill Asserts," *Atlanta Constitution*, Jan. 24, 1944, p. 1.
7. Ralph McGill, "Reflections on World News Freedom Following the ASNE Tour," *Journalism Quarterly* 22 (3) (Sept. 1945): 195; Forrest, Ackerman, and McGill, "Full Report," 3; Eduard Beneš to Wilbur Forrest, Jan. 23, 1945, in Forrest, Ackerman, and McGill, "Full Report," 6.

8. Forrest, Ackerman, and McGill, "Full Report," 3.
9. Ralph McGill, "A Sure Cure for the Drink Habit," *Atlanta Constitution,* Apr. 5, 1945, p. 8; Carl W. Ackerman to John S. Knight, Apr. 4, 1945, Container 38, Ackerman Papers; Carl W. Ackerman to Vandy Ackerman, Apr. 2, 1945, 13, Container 38, Ackerman Papers.
10. McGill, "Sure Cure for the Drink Habit."
11. McGill, *South and the Southerner,* 179–80.
12. Ibid., 179; Forrest, Ackerman, and McGill, "Full Report," 10, 12.
13. Forrest, Ackerman, and McGill, "Full Report," 14; Ralph McGill, "Roman Ruins Pose Question for Future," *Atlanta Constitution,* Mar. 5, 1945, p. 6. Because of delays in wartime mail, the column was published about five weeks after McGill was in Rome.
14. McGill, *South and the Southerner,* 180–81.
15. McGill, "Sure Cure for the Drink Habit."
16. Forrest, Ackerman, and McGill, "Full Report," 15–16; Ralph McGill, "German Sickness a Terrible Disease," *Atlanta Constitution,* Mar. 29, 1945, p. 8.
17. Ralph McGill, "You Don't Destroy People Like the Greeks," *Atlanta Constitution,* Mar. 8, 1945, 8.
18. Forrest, Ackerman, and McGill, "Full Report," 16–17.
19. McGill, "Reflections on World News Freedom," 194.
20. Carl W. Ackerman to Vandy Ackerman, Feb. 13, 1945, Container 37, 7, Ackerman Papers.
21. Martin, *McGill,* 106.
22. Patterson interview, Jan. 5, 2000.
23. Ackerman to Vandy Ackerman, Feb. 13, 1945.
24. Ibid.
25. McGill, "Reflections on World News Freedom," 194; Forrest, Ackerman, and McGill, "Full Report," 18; Zubeyda Shaply-Shamyl to Ralph McGill, Feb. 22, 1945, Box 3, Folder 2, RMP.
26. Forrest, Ackerman, and McGill, "Full Report," 18.
27. Ralph McGill, "Russia Really Isn't an Enigma," *Atlanta Constitution,* May 1, 1945, p. 6. McGill got the Russian's name wrong; the committee's final report (p. 17) referred to the Tass representative as Dr. Mikhail Korostovtsev.
28. Forrest, Ackerman, and McGill, "Full Report," 20–21.
29. Ackerman to Vandy Ackerman, Mar. 9, 1945, Container 37, 9, Ackerman Papers.
30. Ibid.
31. Ackerman to Vandy Ackerman, Apr. 2, 1945, Container 37, 9, 13, Ackerman Papers.
32. McGill, "Russia Really Isn't an Enigma."
33. Ralph McGill, "One Word More," *Atlanta Constitution,* Jan. 15, 1940; Ralph McGill, "One Word More," *Atlanta Constitution,* Dec. 1, 1942.
34. McGill, "Russia Really Isn't an Enigma."
35. Carl W. Ackerman, transcript of 1934 address, with ASNE Final Report (1945), Box 39, Ackerman Papers.
36. "American Editors' Failure to Contact A.I.N.E.C.," *Hindustan Times,* Apr. 19, 1945, n.p.
37. Ralph Block to S. A. Brelvi, Apr. 19, 1945 (copy), Box 3, Folder 2, RMP.
38. Ackerman to Knight, Apr. 4, 1945; Ackerman to Vandy Ackerman, Apr. 2, 1945, 13.
39. Ackerman to Knight, Apr. 4, 1945.

40. Ackerman to Vandy Ackerman, Apr. 2, 1945, 9, 13.
41. Barbara W. Tuchman, *Stilwell and the American Experience in China, 1911–1945* (New York: Macmillan, 1971), 511.
42. Ralph McGill, "The Curtain Falls on One War Theater," *Atlanta Constitution,* May 4, 1945, p. 8A.
43. Forrest, Ackerman, and McGill, "Full Report," 24; Martin, *McGill,* 107.
44. Ackerman to Vandy Ackerman, Apr. 2, 1944, 12–13.
45. Ibid.
46. Ackerman to Knight, Apr. 4, 1945.
47. Ibid.
48. Ibid.
49. Calvin Kytle to author, July 14, 1993, 3.
50. Martin, *McGill,* 107–8.
51. Forrest, Ackerman, and McGill, "Full Report," 26.
52. Harold E. Davis, interview by author, Atlanta, Dec. 14, 1992; Harold E. Davis to author, memorandum, Feb. 19, 1987. Davis was a reporter and editor for the *Atlanta Journal* from October 1951, becoming assistant city editor in 1953. "McGill and I talked a lot. He would come by the city desk," Davis recalled. "He seemed to like me. He said he believed Ackerman had kept him from getting the Pulitzer Prize. I knew who Ackerman was—the Pulitzer Prize man at Columbia. He was one of the personalities of American journalism."

10. A PORTABLE TYPEWRITER

1. Ralph McGill to Tom Chubb, cited in Martin, *McGill,* 109.
2. Martin, *McGill,* 110–11.
3. Ralph McGill, "The Death Rattle Sounds from Japan!" *Atlanta Constitution,* Aug. 9, 1945, 8.
4. Ibid. McGill repeated "one of Joseph Stalin's most quoted maxims" on leadership: "He who wishes to lead a movement must conduct a fight on two fronts—against those who lag behind and those who rush ahead."
5. Ralph McGill, "General Eisenhower and Soviet Friendship," *Atlanta Constitution,* Aug. 14, 1945, p. 5.
6. Ibid.
7. Swope was involved in the release to the Jews of arms embargoed in the United States and helped to get the partition plan passed. Dr. David Geffen, "Ralph McGill, Southern Editor and Zionist Enthusiast," unpublished manuscript, 10, McGill File, News Research Division, *Atlanta Journal-Constitution* Archives (hereafter cited as McGill File). Dr. Geffen, formerly of Atlanta, was living in Israel in 1988 (Stuart Lewengrub, Anti-Defamation League of B'nai Brith, to Tom Teepen, memorandum, May 16, 1988, McGill File). For more on Swope's roles, see Melvin Urofsky, *We Are One* (Garden City, N.Y.: Anchor Press/Doubleday, 1978), 144, 156; John Snetsinger, *Truman, the Jewish Vote and the Creation of Israel* (Stanford, Calif.: Hoover Institution Press, 1974), 66, 164; Richard Stevens, *American Zionism and U.S. Foreign Policy, 1942–1947* (New York: Pageant Press, 1970), 181–83; and Peter Grose, *Israel in the Mind of America* (New York: Afred Knopf, 1983), 178–81.
8. Zionists credited McGill with working "behind the scenes" in 1943 with Georgia state representative Helen Douglas Mankin to help win passage of a resolution citing "the need for a Jewish homeland for stricken and persecuted Jewish masses after the War." Geffen, "Ralph McGill," 10.

9. Herbert Bayard Swope to Ralph McGill, Nov. 28, 1945, Box 3, Folder 3, RMP. Swope (1882–1958) was a latter-day embodiment of the crusading spirit at the heart of Joseph Pulitzer's "new journalism."

10. The Overseas News Agency was created in 1940. With Jacob Landau, director of the Jewish Telegraphic Agency, as managing director, the agency provided stories about ethnic populations. A. J. Kahn, *The House of Swope* (New York, 1966), 433–36, cited in Geffen, "Ralph McGill," note 62.

11. Ibid.; Herbert Bayard Swope to Ralph McGill, Dec. 4, 1945, Box 3, Folder 3, RMP.

12. Shirer, *Third Reich*, 233.

13. William Benton to American Chiefs of Mission in Europe and the Near East [by hand], Jan. 16, 1946, Box 3, Folder 3, RMP; Ralph McGill, *Israel Revisited* (Atlanta: Tupper and Love, 1950), 7.

14. McGill, *Israel Revisited*, 7–8; Shirer, *Third Reich*, 4, 112, 145–46, 834–38, 848–49.

15. McGill, *Israel Revisited*, 8–9.

16. Martin, *McGill*, 114–16. Each year, McGill sent money, clothes, and food to Else and others in Heidelberg. When Else married a soccer player named Heinrich Volkwein, McGill had his background investigated and evidently found no problems. The couple named their first child Ralph Emerson Volkwein; McGill visited his godson, who early on, as Harold Martin was told, had "a reporter's inquiring mind."

17. McGill, *Israel Revisited*, 11.

18. Ibid., 2–3, 17; Martin, *McGill*, 112; Ralph McGill, "The Palestine Issue Reopened by Big 3," *Atlanta Constitution*, Mar. 15, 1945, p. 6A.

19. McGill, *Israel Revisited*, 12–14.

20. Ibid., 15–16.

21. Harry Levin had another job as "the secret announcer for the Haganah underground radio broadcasts." Geffen, "Ralph McGill," 25. See Harry Levin, *I Saw the Battle of Jerusalem* (New York, 1950), 23, 53, 153.

22. McGill, *Israel Revisited*, 17–18.

23. Ibid., 18–21, 23.

24. Ibid., 23–26.

25. Ibid., 2, 6.

26. Ibid., 35–39.

27. Ibid., 38–39. The industry statistics were supplied to McGill in Tel Aviv by the manager of an industrial exhibit, H. Bochko, whom McGill called "one of the best public relations men I ever met."

28. Geffen, "McGill," 23; Ralph McGill, "Report on Palestine," *Pageant* (Aug. 1946), 87–94.

29. Martin, *McGill*, 117; Anderson, *Wild Man*, 222.

30. "Supreme Court Rules Primary Open to Negro," *Atlanta Constitution*, Apr. 4, 1944, p. 1; "Negro Voting," *Constitution*, Apr. 4, 1944, p. 1; Arnall, *Shore Dimly Seen*, 60.

31. Ralph McGill, "How It Happened Down in Georgia," *New Republic*, Jan. 27, 1947, in McGill, *No Place to Hide* 1:90–91; Harry Ashmore, *Civil Rights and Wrongs: A Memoir of Race and Politics, 1944–1994* (New York: Pantheon Books, 1994), 58; Anderson, *Wild Man*, 236.

32. Keeler McCartney to Ralph McGill, manuscript, RMP; Ralph McGill, "Hate at Cut Rates," unpublished manuscript (written between July and Dec. 1946), RMP, printed posthumously in McGill, *No Place to Hide* 1:79–88.

33. McGill, *No Place to Hide* 1:79–88; McGill, "Winners: Pepper, Hill and Common Sense," 6.

34. John Egerton, *Speak Now Against the Day: The Generation Before the Civil Rights Movement in the South* (New York: Knopf, 1994), 385.
35. Ralph McGill, *Atlanta Constitution,* July 19, 1946, p. 8; Ralph McGill, "Konfessions Koncerning Klans," *Atlanta Constitution,* June 2, 1946, p. 14C; Ralph McGill, "The KKK's Candidate Plan," *Atlanta Constitution,* May 26, 1946, p. 2D.
36. Ames, *Changing Character of Lynching,* 2, 7, 174. Since 1882, Georgia had been second only to Mississippi in lynchings; each state had more than five hundred. In 1942, the Atlanta leader of the Association of Southern Women for the Prevention of Lynching noted that in 1940 "Mississippi dropped out of the regular lynching states, leaving only Georgia and Florida as 'regulars.'" McGill, "Coming Events, and Shadows," 8.
37. Jack Tarver, "Gene Wouldn't Have Won Anyway," *Atlanta Constitution,* June 2, 1946, 14C.
38. Martin, *McGill,* 117–18; McGill, *No Place to Hide* 1:li.
39. McGill, "How It Happened"; Anderson, *Wild Man,* 234–35.
40. McGill, "How It Happened"; Anderson, *Wild Man,* 235.
41. McGill, "How It Happened."
42. Martin, *McGill,* 120; Herman Talmadge, interview, Oct. 8, 1970, in Anderson, *Wild Man,* 235.
43. McGill, "How It Happened."
44. Ibid. Talmadge and Winchell, *Talmadge,* 87–89.
45. Martin, *McGill,* 121.
46. McGill, "How It Happened"; McGill, transcript of interview by Kytle and Mackay.
47. Ralph McGill, "So, the Russ Is on Us—Even Now!" *Atlanta Constitution,* Mar. 11, 1946, p. 8A.
48. Ibid.
49. Ibid.
50. Ralph McGill, "There Isn't Going to Be War," *Atlanta Constitution,* Mar. 15, 1946, p. 10A.
51. Ralph McGill, "Not Peace, but a Sword?" *Atlanta Constitution,* Aug. 25, 1946, p. 10.
52. Ralph McGill, "Russia Has Problems, Too," *Atlanta Constitution,* Mar. 17, 1947, p. 6A.
53. Ralph McGill, "The Commies Have Come to Town," *Atlanta Constitution,* Apr. 4, 1947, p. 4.
54. McGill, "It Has Happened Here."
55. McGill, transcript of interview by Kytle and Mackay. "Ralph McGill, Editor," 1.
56. Ibid., 2–3; McGill, "It Has Happened Here."
57. Bill Boring, "Milt, Here to Receive Law Degree, Recalls Art Days in High School; His Mr. Canyon Paying Off," *Atlanta Constitution,* May 21, 1947, pp. 1, 7.
58. Ibid., 3.
59. Ralph McGill, "The Political Platypuses," *Atlanta Constitution,* June 11, 1947, p. 8A.
60. Ibid.
61. Ibid.
62. Ibid.
63. Ralph McGill, "Bread and France," *Atlanta Constitution,* June 19, 1947, p. 10A.
64. Ralph McGill to Maj. Gen. F. L. Parks, U.S. Army Public Information Office, Nov. 13, 1947, Box 3, Folder 5, RMP.

65. Robert P. Patterson to Ralph McGill, telegram, Mar. 15, 1948, Box 3, Folder 6, RMP.
66. Ralph McGill, draft for telegrams, Mar. 15, 1948, Box 3, Folder 6, RMP.

11. POLITICAL STORMS

1. Ralph McGill, "Will the South Ditch Truman?" *Saturday Evening Post,* May 22, 1948, 15–17, 88–90.
2. Ibid.
3. Ibid.
4. McGill, "Will the South Ditch Truman?"; David McCullough, *Truman* (New York: Simon and Schuster, 1992), 586–87; J. William Fulbright to Herbert Thomas, Mar. 15, 1948, cited in Randall Bennett Woods, *Fulbright: A Biography* (New York: Cambridge Univ. Press, 1995), 148.
5. McGill, "Will the South Ditch Truman?"
6. Anne Rochelle, "Harold C. Fleming, 70, Veteran Civil Rights Leader and Ex-Atlantan, Dies," *Atlanta Constitution,* Sept. 6, 1992, p. 3H; Griffin interview, Apr. 20, 1987; Robert J. Norrell, "Next Steps to Democracy: The First Fifty Years of the Southern Regional Council," unpublished manuscript, 27–28, Southern Regional Council, Atlanta.
7. Norrell, "Next Steps to Democracy," 28–29.
8. John Popham, interview by author, Friends of John Popham Seminar, Atlanta Airport Holiday Inn, Atlanta, June 10, 1995.
9. Ibid.; McGill, "Will the South Ditch Truman?" 97.
10. McGill, "Will the South Ditch Truman?" 97.
11. Ralph McGill, "Let's Look at the Record," *Atlanta Constitution,* Aug. 25, 1948; Ralph McGill to Donald Dawson, Sept. 15, 1948, White House Central Files, Truman Papers, Truman Presidential Library, Independence, Mo. (hereafter cited as Truman Papers).
12. Leonard Ray Teel, "The African-American Press and the Campaign for a Federal Antilynching Law, 1933–34: Putting Civil Rights on the National Agenda," *American Journalism* 8, no. 2–3 (Spring–Summer 1991): 97–98, 104–5; McGill, *South and the Southerner,* 96.
13. McGill, "Meditations in a Hammock," 10A. The statistics were compiled by the Archives at Tuskegee Institute. Ames, *Changing Character of Lynching,* 2.
14. Ames, *Changing Character of Lynching,* 7, 174.
15. McGill, "Coming Events, and Shadows," 12.
16. Ibid.
17. Ralph McGill, "At the Threshold," *Confluence* (Harvard Univ. Summer School of Arts and Sciences) 3 (Mar. 1954): 93–100, reprinted in McGill, *No Place to Hide* 1:189.
18. Martin, *McGill,* 149–51; Eugene Patterson, McGill lecture, Atlanta Public Library, June 4, 1989.
19. Ralph McGill, "They Simply Do Not Trust Us," *Atlanta Constitution,* Mar. 4, 1948, p. 8A. Typical of some Georgians who saw nothing terrible about the Klan, one rural Georgian noted that he had "never known the Klan to take any action that the subject didn't deserve it, and more." J. B. Payne to the Editor, *Atlanta Constitution,* June 28, 1949, Box 4, Folder 6, RMP.
20. McGill, "Coming Events, and Shadows."
21. Ibid.

22. McGill, "They Simply Do Not Trust Us."
23. Ibid.
24. McGill, "Coming Events, and Shadows."
25. Ibid.
26. Woods, *Fulbright*, 118.
27. Robert L. Zangrando, *The NAACP Crusade Against Lynching, 1909–1950* (Philadelphia: Temple Univ. Press, 1980), 9; Kneebone, *Southern Liberal Journalists*, 82–83.
28. McGill, "Meditations in a Hammock," 10A; Martin, *McGill*, 151.
29. Wright Bryan and Ellen Bryan, interviews by author, Clemson, S.C., Nov. 26, 1987.
30. James M. Cox to Wright Bryan Sr., Feb. 13, 1940, in Bryan Family Papers, Clemson, S.C. Bryan was then managing editor of the *Journal*.
31. Jack Tarver interview, Dec. 13, 1994.
32. Wright Bryan and Ellen Bryan, interview, Clemson, S.C., Nov. 26, 1987.
33. Ibid.
34. Jack Tarver interview, Dec. 13, 1994.
35. Luke Moon to Ralph McGill, June 18, 1949, Box 4, Folder 6, RMP; Moon, among the few who identified themselves, said he worked at Atlantic Steel Company and had been a Klan member since 1906, when he was sixteen.
36. James Mackay, interview by author, Atlanta, Nov. 2, 1995.
37. Spalding interview, Oct. 15, 1986; Patterson, McGill lecture.
38. Ralph McGill, "Tom Watson: The People's Man," *New Republic*, Aug. 23, 1948, 16–20; Ralph McGill, "Reading, 'Riting, and Russia," *Saturday Review of Literature*, Aug. 28, 1948, 7–9; Ralph McGill, "What's Wrong with Southern Cooking?" *Saturday Evening Post*, Mar. 26, 1949, 38–39, 102–5; Ralph McGill, "They Stuck to the South," *Saturday Evening Post*, Apr. 30, 1949, 38–39, 59, 62, 64; Ralph McGill, "Demagoguery State by State," review of *Southern Politics*, by V. O. Key Jr., *Saturday Review of Literature*, Dec. 3, 1949, 32.
39. Ralph McGill, "She'll Talk Later," *Harper's Magazine*, Oct. 1947, 365–69; Emily M. Danton to McGill, Oct. 25, 1947, Box 3, Folder 5, RMP; Orrin C. Evans to McGill, Oct. 1947, Box 3, Folder 4, RMP; Ralph McGill to June Montgomery, Athens, W.Va., Nov. 5, 1947, RMP.
40. Egerton, *Speak Now*, 480–81.
41. McGill, "Let's Look at the Record," 8.
42. McGill, "Demagoguery State by State," 32.
43. Ralph McGill to President Truman, telegram, Nov. 3, 1948, PPF 200 Election Congratulations, Truman Papers; Harry S. Truman to Ralph McGill, Nov. 26, 1948, PPF 1109, Truman Papers.
44. "Negro Vote," *Atlantic Monthly*.
45. Jack Tarver interview, Dec. 13, 1994.
46. Ibid.; Martin, *McGill*, 121–22, 134.
47. Doris Lockerman interview, "Dawn's Early Light," 29–30; John Griffin interview, "Dawn's Early Light," 30; Jack Tarver interview, Dec. 13, 1994; Patterson interview, Jan. 5, 2000; Ralph McGill, *The Best of Ralph McGill: Selected Columns*, ed. Michael Strickland, Harry Davis, and Jeff Strickland (Atlanta: Cherokee Publishing, 1980). The five sections indicate McGill's range and pace: "The South," "People and American Life," "Civil Rights," "The Presidency," and "McGill on McGill."
48. Martin, *McGill*, 122.
49. Jack Tarver interview, Dec. 13, 1994.

12. ONE DAY IT WILL BE MONDAY

1. Martin, *McGill*, 143.
2. McGill, *Israel Revisited*, 1, 58, 60.
3. Ibid.
4. Harry S. Ashmore to Joseph B. Cumming Jr., Dec. 11, 1968, p. 2, Box 25, Folder 2, William C. Baggs Papers, Special Collections, Otto G. Richter Library, Univ. of Miami, Fla. (hereafter cited as Baggs Papers).
5. Special Agent Jack T. Beverstein to the FBI, U.S. Department of Justice, Nov. 29, 1961, FBI Field Office File 161-98, p. 10.
6. Margaret Tarver interview, Dec. 13, 1994.
7. "Pulitzer Prizes" (editorial), *Atlanta Constitution*, May 9, 1951, p. 12.
8. Fitzpatrick's subject was an analysis of constitutional law and treaties. See the transcript of the minutes of the Pulitzer board meeting, Apr. 17, 1951, in Container 136 (Pulitzer Prizes), Ackerman Papers; Arthur Krock to Dean Ackerman, Apr. 28, 1951 (copy), Collection 136, Ackerman Papers. At the same April 17 meeting, Krock in turn nominated Knight's newspaper, the *Miami Herald*, for a Pulitzer in public service, and the motion was seconded unanimously. Krock had been a board member since May 3, 1940; Knight joined the board on April 28, 1944, when he was ASNE president.
9. Stanley Frank, "Mr. Pulitzer's Prize Hair Pull," *Saturday Evening Post*, May 3, 1947. Quoted in Container 136 (Pulitzer Prizes), Ackerman Papers.
10. Transcripts of two letters from two journalists (names deleted) to Carl W. Ackerman, June 2 and June 11, 1951, Container 136 (Pulitzer Prizes), Ackerman Papers. (There was no indication who deleted the names.)
11. Ibid.
12. *Atlanta Constitution*, May 9, 1951. Unknown to McGill, biographies of Lincoln and Washington were excluded from candidacy for a prize by Joseph Pulitzer's original rules. Pulitzer intended to reward "the best American biography teaching patriotic and unselfish services to the people, illustrated by eminent example, excluding, as too obvious, the names of George Washington and Abraham Lincoln." In 1940, the board, at the urging of historian Arthur Schlesinger Sr., made an exception to honor Carl Sandburg for his two-volume biography of Lincoln. The rule was eliminated in the mid-1950s. John Hohenberg, *The Pulitzer Prizes: A History of the Awards in Books, Drama, Music, and Journalism, Based on the Private Files over Six Decades* (New York: Columbia Univ. Press, 1974), 19–20, 66, 159, 161.
13. "Watered-Down Pulitzers?" *Time*, May 21, 1951, p. 56.
14. Special Agent Alan G. Sentinella to FBI, Nov. 29, 1961; Special Agent Richard Hamilton, Nov. 27, 1961; FBI Field Office File 161-98, pp. 1, 14.
15. Harry S. Ashmore, interview by author, Popham Seminar, Atlanta, June 10, 1994.
16. Martin, *McGill*, 135.
17. Harry S. Ashmore interview, "Dawn's Early Light," 27.
18. Patterson to author, July 30, 1995, 1; Eugene Patterson, interview by author, Friends of John Popham Seminar, Athens, Georgia, June 8, 1996.
19. William Howland, "Live with the Change," *Time*, Dec. 14, 1953, 51.
20. Ralph McGill, "One Day It Will Be Monday," *Atlanta Constitution*, Apr. 9, 1953, reprinted in Strickland, *Best of McGill*, 108–9; Ellen Bryan, interview, Nov. 26, 1987.
21. Ibid.

22. Ralph McGill, "To Inform, Not Inflame," *Atlanta Constitution,* Dec. 11, 1953, p. 1.

23. Martin, *McGill,* 146; Ralph McGill, "University of Arkansas Commencement Address," Fayetteville, Ark., Jan. 30, 1954, in Logue, *McGill at Work,* 1:130, 141.

24. McGill, "One Day," in Strickland, *Best of McGill,* 110.

25. Ralph McGill, "Carl Sandburg Says: Don't Let Others Spend Your Time," *Atlanta Journal and Constitution Magazine,* Jan. 6, 1952, reprinted in McGill, *Southern Encounters,* 31, 33.

26. Carl Sandburg to Ralph McGill, June 25, 1952, Box 23, RMP.

27. McGill, "Carl Sandburg Says," 31.

28. Carl Sandburg to Ralph McGill, Aug. 21, 1953, Box 23, RMP.

29. Ralph McGill to Harry Golden, Jan. 6, 1958, Box 7, RMP.

30. Carl Sandburg to Ralph McGill, Mar. 14, 1954, Box 23, RMP.

31. Carl Sandburg to Ralph McGill, Apr. 3, 1954, Box 23, RMP.

32. Ralph McGill to Ann ["Eppie"] Landers, Mar. 27, 1959, Box 7, RMP. Landers, with the *Chicago Sun-Times* syndicate, was a friend also of Harry Ashmore.

33. Ralph McGill, "The Most Unforgettable Character I've Met," *Reader's Digest,* May 1954, 110.

34. Roberta D. Fleming to Carl Sandburg, Feb. 3, 1955, Box 23, RMP.

35. Carl Sandburg to Ralph McGill, Mar. 15, 1955, Box 23, RMP.

36. Carl Sandburg, *Abraham Lincoln: The Prairie Years* (New York: Harcourt, Brace, 1926), 1:134; Richard Crowder, *Carl Sandburg* (New Haven, Conn.: College and Univ. Press, 1964), 126–33.

37. Ralph McGill, review of *In the Land of Jim Crow,* by Ray Sprigle, *New York Times Book Review,* June 5, 1949.

38. McGill, "Demagoguery State by State," 32.

39. Ralph McGill, "Weighing a Dixie Dilemma: Review of Hodding Carter's *Southern Legacy,*" *Saturday Review,* Feb. 4, 1950, in McGill, *No Place to Hide* 1:144–46.

40. Ralph McGill, "Dwight D. Eisenhower," essay, July 1952, RMP.

41. Ashmore, *Civil Rights and Wrongs,* 72.

42. Martin, *McGill,* 137–38.

43. Arthur Krock, *New York Times,* Nov. 7, 1951, in McCullough, *Truman,* 887; Arthur Krock, *Memoirs: Sixty Years on the Firing Line* (New York: Funk and Wagnall's, 1968). The Eisenhower-Truman meeting occurred on November 5. Krock later said his source was Supreme Court Justice William O. Douglas.

44. Martin, *McGill,* 138.

45. Ralph McGill, "Not All Liars Are Communists," *Atlanta Constitution,* Dec. 14, 1950, p. 1.

46. McGill, "Not All Liars"; McCullough, *Truman,* 859.

47. McGill, "Not All Liars"; Ralph McGill, "One Word More," *Atlanta Constitution,* June 20, 1943, p. 10C.

48. McCullough, *Truman,* 860–61.

49. Ibid., 910–12; Martin, *McGill,* 139; Ralph McGill, "Report on Adlai Stevenson," *Atlanta Journal and Constitution Magazine,* Nov. 2, 1952.

50. Golden, *Right Time,* 280.

51. Ralph McGill, "Report on Adlai Stevenson," *Atlanta Journal and Constitution Magazine,* Nov. 2, 1952.

52. Ibid.

53. Ralph McGill, "How Adlai Stevenson Won Georgia's Heart All Over Again," *Atlanta Journal and Constitution Magazine,* Dec. 27, 1953.

54. Ralph McGill, "V-Bomb Attacks on This Nation?" *Atlanta Constitution,* Jan. 13, 1945, p. 4; Jack Lockhart to N. S. Noble, Jan. 15, 1945, in Record Group 216, File 012 D/4, Atom Smashing, Jan. 1945, National Archives, Washington, D.C.

55. FBI to Sen. Brien McMahon, Chair, Joint Committee on Atomic Energy, Nov. 9, 1951, Bureau File 77-52062-3; John P. Slayden to FBI, Special Inquiry for State Department, July 8, 1952, Bureau File 123-14255-11.

56. Slayden to FBI, July 8, 1952, 2.

57. Ibid., 1.

58. FBI to McMahon, 2. In 1943, in fact, McGill still supported segregation, largely because it was the law in Georgia. McGill advocated obedience to the law. After *Brown v. Board of Education* in 1954, he could rationalize desegregation of schools because that represented obedience to the new law of the land.

59. Ibid. The FBI also referred the senator to other articles by McGill collected by the bureau, including one on November 3, 1947, in Bureau File 100-3-A, one on February 10, 1950, in Bureau File 100-0-A, and one on September 24, 1948, in Bureau File 100-7801-A.

60. Memorandum, New York Research, Crime Records, to Director, FBI, and SAC, Atlanta, "Personal and Confidential," Feb. 21, 1955, FBI file 94-48048, originally filed as 62-21364-43.

13. The Brethren

1. Patterson interview, Jan. 5, 2000.

2. Ibid.

3. William O. Douglas, *The Court Years* (New York: Vintage Books, 1981); Ashmore, *Civil Rights and Wrongs,* 100–102.

4. Ashmore, *Hearts and Minds: A Personal Chronicle of Race in America,* rev. ed. (Cabin John, Md.: Seven Locks Press, 1988), 140.

5. McGill, *South and the Southerner,* 245.

6. McGill, "One Day."

7. Ibid.

8. Ashmore, *Civil Rights and Wrongs,* 102, 105. Ashmore, while editor of the *Arkansas Gazette* in Little Rock, directed a study of southern schools known "The Negro and the Schools." Funded by the Ford Foundation, the survey's suggestions influenced some Supreme Court justices during the 1954–55 term as they considered how to implement the *Brown* decision.

9. "America's Town Meeting of the Air," Nov. 3, 1954, reprinted in McGill, *No Place to Hide* 1:196, 200.

10. Jack Tarver interview, Dec. 13, 1994.

11. Ralph McGill, "The Angry South," *Atlantic Monthly* 197 (Apr. 1956): 31–34, reprinted in McGill, *No Place to Hide* 1:224, 227.

12. McGill, *South and the Southerner,* 228.

13. Ralph McGill, "The Harvest of Hate," *Atlanta Constitution,* June 7, 1968, p. 1.

14. Ralph McGill, "Men Who Shame Our State and Flag," *Atlanta Constitution,* Aug. 18, 1949, p. 8; Ashmore, *Civil Rights and Wrongs,* 112.

15. Harold Mixon, "The Rhetoric of States' Rights and White Supremacy," in Logue and Dorgan, *New Diversity in Contemporary Southern Rhetoric,* 175.

16. Ralph McGill, "A Southerner Talks with the South: A Review of Robert Penn Warren's *Segregation,*" *New York Times,* Sept. 6, 1956.

17. Ralph McGill, *The Fleas Come with the Dog* (New York: Abingdon Press, 1954), 5.

18. Carl Sandburg to Ralph McGill, c. 1954, RMP.

19. Ralph McGill to J. Edgar Hoover, May 12, 1954, Bureau File 94-48048-XI; J. Edgar Hoover to Ralph McGill, May 14, 1954, Bureau File 94-48048-XI.
20. McGill, *Fleas,* 47–48.
21. FBI memo, Apr. 19, 1955, Bureau File 123-14255-17.
22. [Name deleted] to J. Edgar Hoover, Feb. 2, 1954, Bureau File 94-48048-X.
23. Ralph McGill, "The Last Joke on John Lynn," *Atlanta Constitution,* June 6, 1953, p. 6.
24. Note to J. Edgar Hoover, Jan. 13, 1955, Bureau file 94-48048-2.
25. McGill to Hoover, Jan. 13, 1955, Bureau file 94-48048-2.
26. J. Edgar Hoover to Ralph McGill, Jan. 18, 1955, Bureau File 94-48048-2.
27. Atlanta SAC to Hoover, Jan. 6, 1955, Bureau file 94-48048-1; the FBI's approval date was written in: 1-17-55; Ralph McGill to David Lawrence, June 23, 1953, Box 5, RMP.
28. Atlanta SAC to Hoover, Jan. 6, 1955.
29. W. V. Cleveland, FBI, to Mr. Evans, U.S. State Department, Nov. 20, 1961, FBI Field Office File 161-1745-2, p. 1.
30. William C. Sullivan, with Bill Brown, *The Bureau: My Thirty Years in Hoover's FBI* (New York: W. W. Norton, 1979), 83–84.
31. Dirk Cameron Gibson, "Neither God nor Devil: Perspective on the Political Myths of J. Edgar Hoover" (Ph.D. diss., Indiana Univ., 1983), 252–59.
32. J. Edgar Hoover, "B-r-e-a-k-i-n-g the Communist Spell," *American Mercury,* Mar. 1954, 57–61; "Hoover Speaks Out on Spies After Years Chasing Them," *U.S. News,* Nov. 27, 1953, 35–38; Herbert Brownell Jr., "Success of FBI Is Outstanding," *U.S. News,* Apr. 16, 1954, 112–14; "Communists in the U.S. a Greater Menace Now," interview with Herbert Brownell Jr., *U.S. News,* Sept. 4, 1953, 49–50; "What and Why of the Files," interview with Herbert Brownell Jr., *Newsweek,* Apr. 6, 1953, 24–25; "FBI Unassisted Can Catch No Spies," *Saturday Evening Post,* Sept. 19, 1953, 10; B. Clark, "Let's Unshackle the FBI," *Reader's Digest,* Apr. 1954, 111–14; K. Detzer, "FBI Protects the Innocent; Crime Laboratory," *Reader's Digest,* Mar. 1954, 57–60; J. Wilson, "G-men Keep Their Shooting Irons and Corn Plasters Handy," *Look,* Oct. 6, 1953, 126.
33. Sullivan and Brown, *Bureau,* 93. One such reporter, according to Sullivan, was Miriam Ottenberg of the conservative *Washington Evening Star.* When in 1965 Hoover was accused by the vice president of Americans for Democratic Action of not enforcing the law to protect civil rights workers in the South, Hoover's public relations machine was put to work. An FBI memo assured that, "pursuant to Mr. Tolson's instructions, we are making immediate contact with Miriam Ottenberg at the Washington Star so that [Joseph L.] Rauh's charges can be answered in the press at the earliest possible time. We will prevail on her to get an article out if at all possible this weekend. Previously approved material is being furnished her for use in the article to combat Rauh's charges in accordance with the Director's instructions. We should also utilize other sources."
34. Martin, *McGill,* 248.
35. Ralph McGill, "Homecoming Games and Pain," *Atlanta Constitution,* Oct. 23, 1954, p. 8.
36. Ralph McGill, "The Derby Merry-Go-Round," *Atlanta Constitution,* May 7, 1955, p. 8.
37. Ibid.
38. Ralph McGill Jr., interview by author, Atlanta, Dec. 12, 1989.
39. Huguelet, Special Inquiry, 1–2; Mark B. Millen, Special Agent in Charge, Indianapolis, Indiana, Dec. 1, 1961, FBI Field Office File 161-1745-199, pp. 1–2.

40. Ralph McGill, "This Was It, This Very Room," *Atlanta Constitution*, Dec. 26, 1952, p. 8.
41. Ibid.
42. Carl Sandburg to Ralph McGill, n.d., Box 23, RMP.
43. Ralph McGill, "America, I Love You," *Atlanta Constitution*, June 4, 1956, p. 8.
44. Ralph McGill, "Dwight Eisenhower and the South," n.d. (after 1956), unpublished manuscript, RMP.
45. Ashmore, *Civil Rights and Wrongs*, 116, 122.
46. Ralph McGill, "Adlai Stevenson and the Democratic South," *New Republic*, June 27, 1957. Eisenhower won in a landslide, carrying even Stevenson's home state of Illinois. The popular vote was 35.5 million to 26 million; but Stevenson won only seven states for 73 electoral votes, compared to Ike's 457.
47. Sandburg to McGill, Jan. 23, 1956. McGill beamed when he spoke about his friendship during speeches. In Chicago to address the Hybrid Corn Conference, he reminded the delegates of "my great and good friend Carl Sandburg, who first came to national attention here." And then he read them an appropriate poem, "Laughing Corn." Ralph McGill, speech to Hybrid Corn Division, American Seed Trade Association, Dec. 4, 1958, in Logue, *Ralph McGill* 2:118. In delivering the Cooper Union Lincoln Day Address in New York City, McGill drew a parallel between the burden of desegregation and the travails of Lincoln. McGill noted that Lincoln, as Sandburg had discovered, "almost never had a choice between right on the one hand and wrong on the other. Most of the time, said Sandburg, Lincoln had to choose between what was partly right and partly wrong." Ralph McGill, "The Cooper Union Lincoln Day Address," New York, Feb. 12, 1960, reprinted in Logue, *Ralph McGill* 2:165–66.
48. Carl Sandburg to Ralph McGill, Mar. 17, 1956, Box 23, RMP.
49. Carl Sandburg to Ralph McGill, July 19, 1956, Box 23, RMP.
50. Carl Sandburg to Ralph McGill, Jan. 23, 1956, Box 23, RMP.
51. McGill to Golden, Jan. 6, 1958.
52. Carl Sandburg to Ralph McGill, Dec. 14, 1956, Box 23, RMP.
53. McGill to Golden, Jan. 6, 1958.
54. Harry Golden to William Targ, Dec. 30, 1957 (copy to Ralph McGill), Box 7, RMP. Targ, editor at the World Publishing Company in New York, was involved with publication of Golden's *Carl Sandburg*, which came out in 1961. For the context of Sandburg's remark, see Harry Golden, *The Right Time: An Autobiography of Harry Golden* (New York: G. P. Putnam's Sons, 1969), 321.
55. Carl Sandburg to Ralph McGill, Nov. 17, 1957, Box 23, RMP.
56. McGill to Golden, Jan. 6, 1958.

14. HARVEST OF HATE

1. Maurine Hoffman Beasley and Richard R. Harlow, *Voices of Change: Southern Pulitzer Winners* (McLean, Va.: Univ. Press of America, 1979), 49–52, 54.
2. Ibid., 53.
3. Ibid., 52, 55.
4. Ibid.; Ralph McGill, Atlanta Constitution, Feb. 7, 1956, in Logue, *McGill* 1:122. After winning the prize in May 1957, Boone was invited to join one of the Pulitzer juries in 1958, making recommendations to the board.
5. John Hohenberg, *The Pulitzer Diaries: Inside America's Greatest Prize* (Syracuse, N.Y.: Syracuse Univ. Press), 75, vi.
6. Harry S. Ashmore to author, June 27, 1997.

7. Ibid. Ralph McGill, "Editors View the South," speech at Emory University, Fall 1957, in Logue, *McGill* 1:162. During the eight-week course, eight editors spoke including Harry Ashmore, who said the Emory forum for rational discourse was unique at a time when tempers were flaring across the South.

8. Ralph McGill to Gertrude Barger, May 8, 1957, Box 6, Folder 8, RMP.

9. Martin, *McGill*, 156.

10. Jack Tarver interview, Dec. 13, 1994.

11. Martin, *McGill*, 156.

12. Ralph McGill to George C. Biggers Sr., memorandum, Feb. 14, 1957, Box 6, Folder 7, RMP. The memorandum was dictated to McGill's new secretary, Grace Lundy.

13. Martin, *McGill*, 297–98.

14. Drew Dowell, "Editorial and Critical Writing" (Master's research paper, Nov. 21, 1989), 2, 8–9, 11.

15. Egerton, *Speak Now*, 626.

16. Carl Sandburg to Ralph McGill, Nov. 17, 1957, Box 23, RMP; Harry Golden to William Targ, Dec. 30, 1957 (copy to Ralph McGill), Box 7, RMP. Targ, editor at the World Publishing Company in New York, was involved with publication of Golden's *Carl Sandburg*, which came out in 1961. On Sandburg's fondness for McGill see also Golden, *Right Time*, 321; Carl Sandburg, *The Sandburg Range* (New York: Harcourt, Brace and Company), 61–62.

17. Ashmore, *Hearts and Minds*, 255.

18. Roy Reed, *Faubus: The Life and Times of An American Prodigal* (Fayetteville: Univ. of Arkansas Press, 1997), 189–90.

19. Ashmore, *Hearts and Minds*, 256. The politician was U.S. Rep. Brooks Hays. See Ralph McGill, "Speaking for the South—and to It: Review of Brooks Hays's *A Southern Moderate Speaks*," *New York Times*, Mar. 15, 1959.

20. Ashmore, *Hearts and Minds*, 257–58.

21. Ibid., 258.

22. Ralph McGill, "Like World of Three Stages," *Atlanta Constitution*, Sept. 2, 1957, p. 1; Ralph McGill, "'Ozymandias' and the Reich," *Atlanta Constitution*, Sept. 3, 1957, p. 1.

23. Ralph McGill, "Poor Ad for Communism," *Atlanta Constitution*, Sept. 5, 1957, p. 1.

24. "Integration Problems Follow No Set Pattern," *Atlanta Constitution*, Sept. 4, 1957, p. 4.

25. "Rep. Davis Needs Rest, Shade and Light Diet" (editorial), *Atlanta Constitution*, Sept. 7, 1957, p. 4; "Ike Silent in Signing Rights Bill," *Atlanta Constitution*, Sept. 10, 1957, p. 1; William M. Bates, "Rights Bill Upset GOP's Plans in the South," *Atlanta Constitution*, Sept. 11, 1957, p. 7; Ralph McGill, "The Face of the South," *Atlanta Constitution*, Sept. 12, 1957, p. 1.

26. Bryce Miller (United Press), "Ike Appeals to Faubus to Stop Defiance of Little Rock Integration," *Atlanta Constitution*, Sept. 6, 1957, p. 1.

27. "Little Rock Crucial Test Moves Toward Climax" (editorial), *Atlanta Constitution*, Sept. 6, 1957, p. 4; Ralph McGill, "What Is Faubus' Role?" *Atlanta Constitution*, Sept. 26, 1957, p. 1; Reed, *Faubus*, 190; Logue, *McGill*, "Editor's View" 1:161.

28. "Birmingham Crowd Beats Negro Minister," *Atlanta Constitution*, Sept. 10, 1957, p. 1; "Bricks Fly in Nashville Boycott," *Atlanta Constitution*, Sept. 10, 1957, p. 1; "Nashville Dynamiters Raze Integrated School," *Atlanta Constitution*, Sept. 11, 1957, p. 1.

29. "The Mob Will Destroy All It Seeks to Protect" (editorial), *Atlanta Constitution*, Sept. 11, 1957, p. 4; "No Law Condones Rule by Violence" (editorial), *Atlanta*

Constitution, Sept. 12, 1957, p. 4; W. A. Cash, *The Mind of the South* (New York: Vintage Books, 1941), 382.

30. McGill, "Face of the South," 1.
31. "Griffin Sees Presidency Shut to Dixie," *Atlanta Constitution,* Sept. 12, 1957, p. 30.
32. Ralph McGill, "It Is Something Else," *Atlanta Constitution,* Sept. 25, 1957, p. 1.
33. Ralph McGill, "Prayers for Guidance," *Atlanta Constitution,* Sept. 16, 1957, p. 1; Ralph McGill, "Faubus" (editorial), *Atlanta Constitution,* Sept. 16, 1957, p. 4.
34. McGill, "Prayers for Guidance"; McGill, "Faubus," 4; Ralph McGill, "The Southern Moderates Are Still There," *New York Times Magazines,"* Sept. 21, 1958, in McGill, *No Place to Hide* 1:246; "1,000 Paratroopers Poured in to Force Little Rock Integration," *Atlanta Constitution,* Sept. 25, 1957, p. 1; W. H. Lawrence, "Ike Finds Peace Isn't Enforced," *Atlanta Constitution* (reprint from *New York Times*), Sept. 25, 1957, p. 1.
35. Ralph McGill, "Letter," *Center,* Mar. 1968.
36. Ibid.
37. Ibid.
38. McGill, "What Is Faubus' Role?"
39. McGill, "Prayers for Guidance"; Ralph McGill, "Reverence for the Law," in Ralph McGill, *A Church, A School* (New York: Abingdon Press, 1959), 29.
40. McGill, "Southern Moderates," *New York Times Magazine,* Sept. 21, 1958, in McGill, *No Place to Hide* 1:249.
41. Ralph McGill, "*Arkansas Gazette* Pulitzer Winners Speech," Little Rock, June 3, 1958, in Logue, *McGill* 2:103–7; see also *Arkansas Gazette,* June 4, 1958.
42. Logue, *McGill* 2, 108, 110–11.
43. Ibid., 104.
44. Ralph McGill to William P. Rogers, Mar. 25, 1958, in Ann Whitman files, Dwight D. Eisenhower Library (hereafter cited as DDEL), Abilene, Kan.; William P. Rogers to Ralph McGill, Apr. 10, 1958, Ann Whitman files, DDEL.
45. Ralph McGill to William P. Rogers, July 1, 1958; William P Rogers to Ralph McGill, July 24, 1968, both Ann Whitman files, DDEL
46. Ibid.; Harold Paulk Henderson, *Ernest Vandiver: Governor of Georgia* (Athens: Univ. of Georgia Press, 2000), 81.
47. Martin, *McGill,* 157.
48. Ralph McGill, "A Church, A School," *Atlanta Constitution,* Oct. 13, 1958, p. 1.
49. Melissa Fay Greene, *The Temple Bombing* (Reading, Mass.: Addison-Wesley Publishing, 1996), 1.
50. Ibid., 238–39.
51. Keeler McCartney and James Sheppard, "Jewish Temple on Peachtree Wrecked by Dynamite Blast," *Atlanta Constitution,* Oct. 13, 1958, p. 1.
52. McGill, "A Church, A School."
53. Jack Nelson, "Thousands of Spectators Stream by but See Little of Debris and Drama," *Atlanta Constitution,* Oct. 13, 1958, p. 6; "Godless Bombing Aimed at All Atlantans, a 'Sick at Heart' Rabbi Rothschild Asserts," *Atlanta Constitution,* Oct. 13, 1958, p. 6; Greene, *Temple Bombing,* 254–55.
54. McGill, "A Church, A School."
55. Ibid.
56. Ibid.
57. Ibid.
58. Ralph McGill, "Decision in Faubus Case," *Atlanta Constitution,* reprinted in McGill, *A Church, A School,* 38–39.
59. Ralph McGill, *Atlanta Constitution,* Oct. 14, 1958, p. 1.

60. Greene, *Temple Bombing,* 272–73, 370.
61. Miscellaneous File, RMP; Martin, *McGill,* 159.

15. WITH ALL DELIBERATE SPEED

1. Calvin Trillin, "Mississippi's State Sovereignty Commission," *New Yorker,* May 29, 1995, 55. In Mississippi in the early 1960s, a senior at the University of Mississippi, Billy Barton, seeking to become editor of the student newspaper, was smeared by his opponents as being "a protégé of Ralph McGill—an accusation that Barton, of course, vehemently denied. He said he had never met Ralph McGill . . . and he voluntarily took a lie detector test to confirm that statement."
2. Ralph McGill to Harry Ashmore, Bill Baggs, Harry Golden, and Sander Vanocur, Jan. 18, 1963, Box 12, Folder 10, RMP.
3. Ralph McGill, "Flight of the Beast," *Atlanta Constitution,* Jan. 3, 1959, p. 1.
4. "There'll Be No Primary in Cuba," *Atlanta Constitution,* Mar. 12, 1952, p. 8.
5. McGill, "I Remember Gerardo Machado," 1.
6. Ibid.
7. McGill, "Flight of the Beast."
8. McGill, "I Remember Gerardo Machado."
9. McGill, "Flight of the Beast."
10. Ralph McGill, "Pulitzer Memorial Address," Columbia University, May 29, 1959, in Logue, *McGill* 2:145. McGill saved the arm band and various mementos of his 1959 trip. Box 52, Folder 2, RMP.
11. A copy of the Cuban agrarian reform document was given to McGill. *Ley De Reforma Agraria,* Box 52, Folder 1, RMP.
12. Ralph McGill, "Castro and the Pageant," *Atlanta Constitution,* July 2, 1959, p. 1.
13. Ibid.
14. Ralph McGill, "Castro: No Cash in the Bank," *Atlanta Constitution,* Oct. 26, 1959, p. 1.
15. Ralph McGill, "An Old Story Retold," *Atlanta Constitution,* June 16, 1961, p. 1.
16. Ralph McGill, "Freedom and Responsibility in Broadcasting," Institute for Education By Radio and Television, Ohio State University, May 4, 1960, in Logue, *McGill* 2:168; Ralph McGill, "News and Propaganda," *Atlanta Constitution,* Apr. 21, 1961, p. 1.
17. Ralph McGill, "Moscow Reflections: Sitting in the Baptist Church in Moscow," *Atlanta Constitution,* Aug. 12, 1959; Martin, *McGill,* 163.
18. Martin, *McGill,* 163.
19. Edward Weeks, *Writers and Friends* (Boston: Little, Brown, 1981), 3, 50–51, 71–72, 80, 171, 173.
20. Peter Davison, interview by author, Houghton Mifflin, Boston, Aug. 8, 1991.
21. Weeks, *Writers and Friends,* 173.
22. McGill, *South and the Southerner,* 3–6.
23. W. J. Haley to Ralph McGill, Apr. 2, 1963, Box 12, Folder 4, RMP.
24. Jack Tarver interview, Dec. 13, 1994.
25. McGill Jr. interview.
26. Weeks, *Writers and Friends,* 173–74.
27. Ibid., 174.
28. Ralph McGill to President Dwight D. Eisenhower, Feb. 23, 1959, Ann Whitman files, DDEL.
29. Dwight D. Eisenhower to Ralph McGill, Feb. 26, 1959, Ann Whitman files, DDEL.

30. S. Ernest Vandiver, *Report to the People from the Governor*, Jan. 10, 1962, p. 8.
31. Ibid.
32. Marvin Griffin, *Progress Report by the Governor, Transmitted to the Members of the General Assembly*, State of Georgia, Nov. 1957, 10–11, 14; Harold E. Davis, interview by author, Atlanta, May 28, 1997; Henderson, *Vandiver*, 107.
33. Davis interview, May 28, 1997. Davis was Washington correspondent of the *Atlanta Journal* in January 1960.
34. "'Mr. Jim' Peters Warns the Politicians of Consequences of Closing Schools" (editorial), *Atlanta Constitution*, Jan. 18, 1960, p. 4.
35. "Integration Sure, Peters Predicts," *Atlanta Constitution*, Jan. 17, 1960, p. 1.
36. "Integration Sure, Peters Predicts," 1; "'Mr. Jim' Peters Warns," 4.
37. "Integration Sure, Peters Predicts," 1; Harold E. Davis, unpublished memoir, 99–100, Harold E. Davis Family Papers, Atlanta.
38. "Integration Sure, Peters Predicts"; Davis interview; Numan V. Bartley, *The New South, 1945–1980* (Baton Rouge: Louisiana State Univ. Press, 1995), 255–56.
39. Harold Fleming interview, "Dawn's Early Light."
40. Davis, unpublished memoir, 99–100.
41. Ibid.; "Integration Sure, Peters Predicts," 1.
42. Davis, unpublished memoir, 99–100.
43. Ibid. William R. Bowdoin was also a public figure. Educated in law at the University of Georgia, he prospered because the Trust Company wanted bank officers who were also concerned about public service. Gov. Herman Talmadge appointed Bowdoin as chair of the Georgia Ports Authority in 1953. In 1959, Bowdoin was named state supervisor of purchases. Harold H. Martin, *Three Strong Pillars: The Story of the Trust Company of Georgia*, 2d ed. (Atlanta: Trust Company of Georgia, 1981), 101.
44. Alexander Leidholdt, *Standing Before the Shouting Mob: Lenoir Chambers and Virginia's Massive Resistance to Public-School Integration* (Tuscaloosa: Univ. of Alabama Press, 1997), 91–92, 94, 120–21.
45. Ibid., 98, 111–12. In retrospect, Leidholdt concluded, the business community's fears "appear to have been unrealistic. Shortly after the reopening, Almond wrote to Senator [Harry F.] Byrd [Sr.], 'I have not been able to find any documented evidence that any industry has declined to locate in Virginia because of the pending school program. Throughout the struggle, our industries in Virginia have continued to expand and from 1950 to date, there has been a steady and substantial acquisition of new and stable industries not only in Virginia, but throughout the south.'"
46. Vandiver, *Report*, 8; Bruce Galphin, "Georgia Must Choose Integration or Grants, School Study Unit Told: Sibley Warns of Grave Duty," *Atlanta Constitution*, Feb. 18, 1960, p. 1.
47. Marion Gaines, "Segregation at All Costs Backed 5–1 at Moultrie Before Cheering Crowd; Sibley Unit Hears from 14 Counties," *Atlanta Constitution*, Mar. 22, 1960, p. 1; Bruce Galphin, "Open Schools Backed Overwhelmingly Here; 114 Testify at Sibley Hearing," *Atlanta Constitution*, Mar. 24, 1960, p. 1; "Local School Chiefs Back Local Option," *Atlanta Constitution*, Mar. 24, 1960, p. 4; Galphin, "Georgia Must Choose"; Vandiver, *Report*, 8.
48. Bruce Galphin, "Assembly Made History By Saving the Schools," *Atlanta Constitution*, Mar. 7, 1961, p. 1; Frank Wells, "Placement Left Up to Counties," *Atlanta Constitution*, Mar. 7, 1961, p. 1, 12.
49. Ralph McGill, oral history interview with Charles T. Morrissey for the John F. Kennedy Library, Jan. 6, 1966, in McGill, *No Place to Hide* 2:554–55; in 1963,

Dean of Men William Tate notified Holmes that he had been elected to Phi Beta Kappa; that fall he became the first black student at the Emory University Medical School and became an orthopedic surgeon. Howell Raines, *My Soul Is Rested: Movement Days in the Deep South Remembered* (New York: Putnam's Sons, 1977), 336.

50. David J. Garrow, *Bearing the Cross: Martin Luther King, Jr., and the Southern Christian Leadership Conference* (New York: William Morrow, 1999), 66–71, 75; Taylor Branch, *Parting the Waters: American in the King Years, 1954–63* (New York: Simon and Schuster, 1988), 199; Ralph McGill to Harry Ashmore, Dec. 15, 1959, Box 9, Folder 4, RMP.

51. McGill to Ashmore, Dec. 15, 1959.

52. Martin Luther King Sr., *Daddy King: An Autobiography,* with Clayton Riley (New York: William Morrow, 1980), 162, 134.

53. "Negro Collegians Fill All Seats at Cafe in Integration Sitdown," *Atlanta Constitution,* Mar. 4, 1960, p. 12; Vincent D. Fort, "The Atlanta Sit-In Movement, 1960–1961: An Oral Study," in *Atlanta, Georgia, 1960–1961: Sit-Ins and Student Activism,* ed. David J. Garrow (Brooklyn, N.Y.: Carlson Publishing, 1989), 129; Jack Walker, "Sit-Ins in Atlanta: A Study in the Negro Revolt," in Garrow, *Atlanta, Georgia,* 63; Branch, *Parting the Waters,* 271, 273; Steven Kasher, *The Civil Rights Movement: A Photographic History, 1954–68* (New York: Abbeville Press), 78.

54. Lonnie C. King Jr. interview, "Dawn's Early Light"; Walker, "Sit-Ins in Atlanta," 64.

55. Clarence N. Stone, *Regime Politics: Governing Atlanta, 1946–1988* (Lawrence: Univ. Press of Kansas, 1989), 54; Walker, "Sit-Ins in Atlanta," 64–65; Garrow, *Bearing the Cross,* 130; Fort, "Atlanta Sit-In Movement," 158.

56. Branch, *Parting the Waters,* 274–75, 279, 283; Kasher, *Photographic History,* 83. Between February 1960 and August 1961, 110 cities were affected by the student sit-in movement. Fort, "Atlanta Sit-In Movement," 129.

57. Raines, *My Soul Is Rested,* 352; Pomerantz, *Peachtree Meets Sweet Auburn,* 162–64; Clifford M. Kuhn, Harlon E. Joyce, and E. Bernard West, *Living Atlanta: An Oral History of the City, 1914–1948* (Athens: Univ. of Georgia Press, 1990), 340–44.

58. Raines, *My Soul Is Rested,* 353–54; Kuhn, Joyce, and West, *Living Atlanta,* 344.

59. Raines, *My Soul Is Rested,* 353.

60. Stone, *Regime Politics,* 54; Walker, "Sit-Ins in Atlanta," 65.

61. Walker, "Sit-Ins in Atlanta," 64–65.

62. Stone, *Regime Politics,* 54; Walker, "Sit-Ins in Atlanta," 66–67.

63. "77 Negroes Arrested in Student Sitdowns at 10 Eating Places Here; Act Jointly in Orderly Protests," *Atlanta Constitution,* Mar. 16, 1960, p. 1. On the same day, 1,000 black students demonstrated—and 350 were arrested—at Orangeburg, South Carolina; Ted Lippman, "No More Sitdowns Now, Students Say," *Atlanta Constitution,* Mar. 17, 1960, p. 1; "'Protest' Incidents Need No Repetition," *Atlanta Constitution,* Mar. 16, 1960, p. 4.

64. C. Eric Lincoln, "The Strategy of a Sit-In," in Garrow, *Atlanta, Georgia,* 99; Garrow, *Bearing the Cross,* 143–48.

65. "Atlanta C of C Supports Local Option on Schools," *Atlanta Constitution,* Mar. 24, 1960, p. 1; Eugene Patterson, "Ivan Allen Jr. and the Sit-Ins," *Atlanta Constitution,* Mar. 9, 1961, p. 4; Pomerantz, *Peachtree Meets Sweet Auburn,* 265–68.

66. Bruce Galphin, "Negroes Agree to End Sit-Ins," *Atlanta Constitution,* Mar. 8, 1961, p. 1; Stone, *Regime Politics,* 54; "Good Instincts, Wisely Applied," *Atlanta*

Constitution, Mar. 8, 1961, p. 4; Patterson, "Ivan Allen Jr.," *Atlanta Constitution,* Mar. 9, 1961; Fort, "Atlanta Sit-In Movement," 134, 139; Walker, "Sit-Ins in Atlanta," 87–90; Garrow, *Bearing the Cross,* 152.

67. "'Protest' Incidents," Mar. 16, 1960, 4.
68. McGill, *South and the Southerner,* 237; Dan Carter interview, "Dawn's Early Light."
69. McGill, *South and the Southerner,* 16.
70. Ibid., 16–17; "Dawn's Early Light."
71. Ralph McGill, "South Needs New Mood," *Atlanta Constitution,* Apr. 23, 1960.
72. Eugene Patterson interview, "Dawn's Early Light."
73. Patterson interview, Jan. 5, 2000; Martin, *McGill,* 166–67.
74. Patterson interview, Jan. 5, 2000; Pomerantz, *Peachtree Meets Sweet Auburn,* 287, 299.
75. Patterson interview, "Dawn's Early Light"; Patterson interview, Jan. 5, 2000.
76. Patterson interview, "Dawn's Early Light"; Patterson interview, Jan. 5, 2000; Pomerantz, *Peachtree Meets Sweet Auburn,* 269.
77. Patterson interview, "Dawn's Early Light."
78. Ashmore to author; Harry S. Ashmore, "A Place of the Heart," *Virginia Quarterly Review* (Summer 1963): 486.
79. Ashmore to author.
80. Martin, *McGill,* 170.
81. Eugene Patterson to author, July 2, 1989.
82. Ralph McGill, "New Frontiers by Fast Travel," *Atlanta Constitution,* July 18, 1960.
83. Ralph McGill to Carl Sandburg, *New York Times,* Box 10, RMP.
84. Ashmore, *Civil Rights and Wrongs,* 156; Martin, *McGill,* 212.
85. Ashmore interview, June 10, 1994; Martin, *McGill,* 212.
86. Patterson to author, July 2, 1989.
87. Theodore H. White, *The Making of the President, 1960* (New York: Atheneum, 1961), 202–5.
88. Ibid., 270–71, 268.
89. Ralph McGill, "Kennedy Believes in Future of U.S.," *Atlanta Constitution,* Oct. 20, 1960.
90. Ralph McGill, "In Dixie Land He Takes a Stand," *Atlanta Constitution,* Oct. 11, 1960; Ralph McGill, "Nixon—At His Best or Worst?" *Atlanta Constitution,* Oct. 14, 1960; Ralph McGill, "Kennedy-Nixon Campaign Far Cry from McKinley's," *Atlanta Constitution,* Oct. 17, 1960; Ralph McGill, "Democratic Heart Throbs in Florida," *Atlanta Constitution,* Oct. 19, 1960; McGill, "Kennedy Believes."
91. McGill, *No Place to Hide* 1:15. Editor Logue traced McGill's comments on politics to various columns in the *Constitution* in the mid- to late 1940s, during political wars against Talmadge and for Truman. See *Atlanta Constitution,* Feb. 27, June 29, Dec. 12, 1946; June 13, 1948; Jan. 28, 1949; July 19, 1946; and Feb. 27, 1946.
92. Ralph McGill, "Democrats Sense Chance at Victory," *Atlanta Constitution,* Oct. 22, 1960; Ralph McGill, "The 'New Nixon' Is on the Spot," *Atlanta Constitution,* Oct. 24, 1960.
93. Martin, *McGill,* 171.
94. McGill to Sandburg, Aug. 15, 1960.
95. Ralph McGill to Helga Sandburg [care of Mrs. Arthur D. Golby], Nov. 18, 1960, Box 23, RMP.
96. Martin, *McGill,* 172, photograph following 173.

16. Ambassador to Africa

1. Ashmore, "Place of the Heart," 489.
2. "'Protest' Incidents," *Atlanta Constitution*, Mar. 26, 1960, p. 4.
3. John Lewis, with Michael D'Orso, *Walking with the Wind: A Memoir of the Movement* (New York: Simon and Schuster, 1998), 142–47; Garrow, *Bearing the Cross*, 154–56.
4. Lamar Alexander, interview by author, Southeast Journalism Conference, Feb. 22, 1997; Lewis, *Walking with the Wind*, 104–17.
5. McGill, interview with Morrissey, in McGill, *No Place to Hide* 2:552.
6. McGill, "Pulitzer Memorial," in Logue, *McGill* 2:144.
7. M. A. Jones to Mr. [Cartha] DeLoach, Mar. 6, 1961, FBI File 94-48048-13; Worthington Smith, memo, Mar. 6, 1961, FBI File 94-48048-14; J. Edgar Hoover to Ralph McGill, Mar. 7, 1961, FBI File 94-48048-15.
8. In the FBI's surveillance of Martin Luther King Jr., Milton A. Jones wrote one of the first headquarters memos in February 1961 about King's reference in *Nation* magazine that the FBI employed too few blacks. David J. Garrow, *The FBI and Martin Luther King, Jr.: From 'Solo' to Memphis* (New York: W. W. Norton, 1981), 83.
9. M. A. Jones to Mr. [Cartha] DeLoach, Oct. 6, 1961, Oct. 12, 1961, FBI File 94-48048; J. Edgar Hoover to Ralph McGill, Jan. 30, 1962, FBI File 94-48048-16. The article was reprinted in newspapers. See "Publisher Puts Stark Questions to Modern Parents: Are You to Blame?" *Sacramento Bee*, Feb. 18, 1962.
10. Director, FBI, to Special Agent in Charge, Atlanta, Nov. 20, 1961, FBI Field Office File 161-1745, "Ralph Emerson McGill," p. 1.
11. Ibid., 1–2.
12. Special Agent Alan G. Sentinella to FBI, Nov. 29, 1961, FBI Field Office File 161-98 in Bureau File 161-1745, p. 2; Martin, *McGill*, 242–43; J. Edgar Hoover to Secretary of State, Dec. 12, 1961, Bureau File 161-1745.
13. Mark B. Millen to FBI, Dec. 1, 1961, Field Office File IP 161-199 in Bureau File 161-1745, pp. 1, 2.
14. W. V. Cleveland to Mr. Evans, Dec. 12, 1961, Bureau File 161-1745, p. 29.
15. Ibid.
16. Ibid. In early 1959, when McGill accepted an invitation to participate in a "Global Strategy Conference" at the Naval War College, the request for his FBI file was made by a rather low-ranking functionary, Chief Yeoman W. J. Carroll, Office of Naval Intelligence, who asked "for main subversive files only." The FBI response included nine enclosures "loaned for your use and is not to be disseminated outside of your agency." A. L. Flotman, Feb. 24, 1959, Bureau file 77-52062-7.
17. Eugene Patterson, "She Counted Sunny Hours," *Atlanta Constitution*, Mar. 22, 1962, p. 1; "Mrs. Ralph McGill Is Dead," 1, 8; "Mrs. Ralph McGill Dies," 35.
18. Martin, *McGill*, 184–85.
19. Ibid., 185.
20. Martin, *McGill*, 187–88; Ralph McGill to Harry Ashmore, May 25, 1962, Box 11, Item 20, RMP.
21. Martin, *McGill*, 189–90; Ralph McGill, "Thoughts After Climbing Mount Fuji," *Atlanta Constitution*, July 8, 1962, p. 1.
22. Harry Golden to Ambassador Adlai E. Stevenson, Aug. 17, 1962, Box 11, Item 22, RMP; Martin, *McGill*, 190–91.
23. Martin, *McGill*, 252.

24. Ralph McGill, "Dakar and History," *Atlanta Constitution,* Feb. 13, 1963, p. 1.
25. Ralph McGill, "Questions and Answers," *Atlanta Constitution,* Feb. 16, 1963, p. 1.
26. Ibid.
27. Ralph McGill, "A String of Beads," *Atlanta Constitution,* Feb. 24, 1963, p. 1.
28. Ralph McGill, "Uneasy Times for Presidents," *Atlanta Constitution,* Feb. 17, 1963, p. 1.
29. Ibid. Ralph McGill, "W. E. B. DuBois," *Atlantic Monthly* (November 1965), in David Levering Lewis, *W. E. B. DuBois: The Fight for Equality and the American Century, 1919–1963* (New York: Henry Holt, 2000), 569. DuBois died in 1963, shortly after McGill's visit.
30. McGill, interview with Morrissey, in McGill, *No Place to Hide* 2:537–38. King, on that March night in Accra in 1957, at the closing of the British parliament, was to be forever impressed by the sight of Nkrumah entering with his ministers, all of them in prison caps and coats—and with the sight of the great black leader at the state ball dancing with the Duchess of Kent—"dancing with the lord on an equal plane." Branch, *Parting the Waters,* 204, 214–15.
31. McGill, interview with Morrissey, in McGill, *No Place to Hide* 2:537–38.
32. Ibid., 2:539.
33. Cal M. Logue, "Ralph McGill: Convictions of a Southern Editor," *Journalism Quarterly* 45 (Winter 1968): 647–52.

17. Law of Compensation

1. Martin, *McGill,* 194–95, 208; Ralph McGill, "Harvests Come from Seeds," *Atlanta Constitution,* Sept. 17, 1963, p. 1.
2. Branch, *Parting the Waters,* 814–16, 822, 825; *New York Times,* June 13, 1963, p. 1; Harold C. Fleming, "The Federal Executive and Civil Rights, 1961–1965," *Daedalus,* Fall 1965, 942.
3. McGill, "Harvests Come from Seeds." The bomb that killed the girls in Sunday school was, according to author David Garrow, the "deadliest act of racial terrorism during the entire black freedom struggle." Garrow, interview with Gary M. Pomerantz, in "'63 Bombing Was Era's Worst Act of Terrorism," *Atlanta Constitution,* July 12, 1997, p. 2. The dynamite killed Denise McNair, eleven, Cynthia Wesley, fourteen, Addie Mae Collins, fourteen, and Carole Robertson, fourteen. Birmingham civil rights activists whose homes and churches had been targets of previous bombings included attorney Arthur Shoes and Rev. Fred Shuttlesworth.
4. McGill, "Harvests Come from Seeds."
5. Weeks, *Writers and Friends,* 174; Martin, *McGill,* 193–94. Appropriately, McGill dedicated the book to Weeks, Peter Davison, and Lundy, as well as to *Journal and Constitution* publisher, James M. Cox Jr. McGill's inscription inspired Schwartz to write a lengthy thank-you, acknowledging that "We actually have a smoother and wider road than did my father's and grandfather's generations. They had neither the quality not the quantity of effective leaders." William B. Schwartz III to Ralph McGill, Nov. 10, 1963, in William B. Schwartz III private papers, Atlanta; William B. Schwartz III, interview by author, Piedmont Driving Club, Atlanta, Apr. 12, 2000.
6. Week, *Friends and Writers,* 174; Harry Golden to Edward Weeks, Apr. 9, 1963, Box 12, Item 4, RMP.
7. Ashmore, "Place of the Heart," 486–87, 489. Ashmore's eloquence was revered by his friends. Johnny Popham eulogized him in 1998 as being "gifted with the

ability to write in a way people could understand, and not only understand but to accept that this was a new time in the history of this country." Popham Seminar, Univ. of Georgia, Athens, June 20, 1998.

8. McGill, *South and the Southerner,* 285, 17–18; Ashmore, "Place of the Heart," 489.
9. McGill, *South and the Southerner,* 224.
10. Branch, *Parting the Waters,* 598; McGill, *South and the Southerner,* 285.
11. McGill, *South and the Southerner,* 223, 284.
12. Ibid., 225, 286.
13. Ibid., 228; Robert McNeill, *God Wills Us Free: The Ordeal of a Southern Minister* (New York: Hill and Wang, 1965), 138–53.
14. Ibid. 225.
15. Ashmore, "Place of the Heart," 489.
16. McGill, *South and the Southerner,* 228.
17. Ibid.
18. Ibid., 227–28.
19. Ibid., 292–93.
20. Patterson interview, Jan. 5, 2000.
21. Ibid.; Martin, *McGill,* 208–9. The libel suits against the *Constitution* were settled out of court in 1968 after the U.S. Supreme ruled in favor of the press's right to criticize without malice public officials for public actions. See *New York Times v. Sullivan,* a lawsuit filed by Birmingham officials after the *Times*'s coverage of the Birmingham police use of dogs and cattle prods against civil rights demonstrators. In writing about the violence at Oxford, McGill had identified "a considerable number of armed men"—outsiders, as police called them, many of them Klan members from other southern states: "Some of them were quoted as saying they had come in response to General Edwin Walker's plea for supporters to join him there. Some of these men were found to have as many as three rifles in their cars." McGill, *South and the Southerner,* 293.
22. Patterson interview, Jan. 5, 2000; Martin, *McGill,* 208.
23. Patterson interview, Jan. 5, 2000; Johnny Popham, Popham Seminar, June 20, 1998.
24. Patterson interview, Jan. 5, 2000.
25. Ibid.
26. McGill, *South and the Southerner,* 296.
27. Ibid., 297.
28. Ibid.
29. McGill, *South and the Southerner,* 18.
30. Ashmore, "Place of the Heart," 489.
31. McGill, *South and the Southerner,* 18; Martin, *McGill,* 288–91.
32. Martin, *McGill,* 290.

18. To the Summit

1. Ralph McGill, "When the News Came in Flight," *Atlanta Journal and Constitution,* Nov. 24, 1963, p. 1.
2. Martin, *McGill,* 203.
3. McGill, "When the News Came in Flight."
4. "JFK Dixie Critics Voice Indignation," *Atlanta Constitution,* Nov. 24, 1963, p. 23.
5. Dan T. Carter, *The Politics of Rage: George Wallace, the Origins of the New Conservatism, and the Transformation of American Politics* (New York: Simon and

Schuster, 1995), 96–97. The aide was James Rowe, whose political seasoning dated from the Roosevelt administrations.

6. "Johnson Sees Top Aides, Decrees Monday Mourning; Cabinet Called, Ike Consulted," *Atlanta Constitution,* Nov. 24, 1963, p. 1; Jay G. Hayden, "Johnson Faces 2-Way Distrust; Southerner in the White House," *Atlanta Constitution,* Nov. 24, 1963, p. 25.

7. Ralph McGill, "Very Cautious Optimism," *Atlanta Constitution,* Jan. 1, 1964, p. 1; Dean Rusk, *As I Saw It* (New York: W. W. Norton, 1990), 337. Rusk, having gone through the Cuban Missile Crisis with both John and Robert Kennedy, agreed with Johnson: "I felt that Bobby lacked the personal qualifies, experience, maturity, depth of commitment, and ability to lead this country as president."

8. Ralph McGill, "Very Cautious Optimism," 1.

9. Ibid.

10. Ralph McGill, "The President Moves in 'Aid,'" *Atlanta Constitution,* Jan. 9, 1964, p. 1.

11. Ralph McGill, "A Ticket to Excite the Vote," *Atlanta Constitution,* Jan. 20, 1964, p. 1.

12. Paul K. Conkin, *Big Daddy from the Pedernales: Lyndon Baines Johnson* (Boston: Twayne, 1986), 121; Robert A. Caro, *The Years of Lyndon Johnson: Means of Ascent* (New York: Alfred A. Knopf, 1990), xvii–xviii.

13. Ralph McGill, "The Kennedy Magic," *Atlanta Constitution,* Mar. 25, 1964, p. 1; Michael R. Beschloss, *Taking Charge: The Johnson White House Tapes, 1963–1964* (New York: Simon and Schuster, 1997), 220, 236–37, 272.

14. Ralph McGill, "Dangerous Social Dynamite," *Atlanta Constitution,* Feb. 26, 1964, p. 1.

15. Ralph McGill, "Political Weather Fronts," *Atlanta Constitution,* Jan. 15, 1964, p. 1.

16. Ibid.

17. Ralph McGill, "Civil Rights: A Background," *Atlanta Constitution,* Feb. 25, 1964, p. 1.

18. Ralph McGill, "'Is the Thing Possible,'" *Atlanta Constitution,* Apr. 5, 1964, p. 1.

19. Griffin interview, Apr. 20, 1987; Martin, *McGill,* 210.

20. Martin, *McGill,* 220, 222; Mary Lynn Morgan, interview by author, Atlanta, Oct. 31, 1998.

21. Ralph McGill, "Extremists Aid Subversion," *Atlanta Constitution,* May 2, 1964, p. 1.

22. Ralph McGill, "Errors of Bloc Leadership," *Atlanta Constitution,* June 22, 1966, p. 1.

23. Ibid.

24. Ralph McGill to Lyndon Johnson, June 17, 1964, White House Tapes, WH6406.09, Program 13, Lyndon B. Johnson Library, Austin, Tex. (hereafter cited as LBJ Library).

25. Ralph McGill to Lyndon Johnson, June 22, 1964, White House Tapes, WH6406.12, Program 13, LBJ Library.

26. McGill to Johnson, June 22, 1964; Ralph McGill, "Proud Progress, or Paralysis?" *Atlanta Constitution,* June 29, 1964, p. 1; Taylor Branch, *Pillar of Fire: America in the King Years, 1963–65* (New York: Simon and Schuster, 1998), 36, 38, 337–40.

27. McGill, "Proud Progress," 1.

28. "Dixie's Politicians," *Atlanta Constitution,* June 20, 1964, p. 1; Peter Kihss, "Dixie Rights Attitude Mixed; Legal Steps Are Considered," *Atlanta Constitution,* June 22, 1964, p. 1.

29. "Sit-Ins Win 5 Cases in High Court," *Atlanta Constitution,* June 23, 1964, p. 1.

30. Ralph McGill, "Rights Car Found Burned; Dulles Sent to Mississippi," *Atlanta Constitution,* June 24, 1964, p. 1; "Searchers Losing Hope for 3 Rights Workers," *Atlanta Constitution,* June 25, 1964, p. 1. Ralph McGill, "Word from Mississippi," *Atlanta Constitution,* June 26, 1964, p. 1.
31. McGill, "Rights Car Found."
32. "Johnson Signs Civil Rights Act, Allen Urges All to Obey," *Atlanta Constitution,* July 3, 1964, p. 1; Joseph E. Mohbat, "U.S. Moves Slowly in Enforcing Law," *Atlanta Constitution,* July 3, 1964, p. 1.
33. "Must Comply with Law Now, Talmadge Advises," *Atlanta Constitution,* July 4, 1964, p. 1; "Maddox Holds Gun, Bars 3 Negroes," *Atlanta Constitution,* July 4, 1964, p. 1.
34. Gershon interview, in McGill, *Southern Encounters,* 300, 313.
35. Pomerantz, *Peachtree Meets Sweet Auburn,* 335; Ralph McGill, *Atlanta Constitution,* Oct. 16, 1964, p. 1.
36. Helen Bullard, interview, in Raines, *My Soul Is Rested,* 411; Ivan Allen Jr. with Paul Hemphill, *Mayor: Notes on the Sixties* (New York: Simon and Schuster, 1971); Eugene Patterson, telephone interview by author, Sept. 8, 1986; "Banquet to Honor Dr. King Sets Off Quiet Dispute Here," *Atlanta Constitution,* Dec. 29, 1964.
37. Bullard interview, in Raines, *My Soul Is Rested,* 412–13; "Banquet to Honor Dr. King"; "Ted Simmons, City's Leaders Express Cautious, Mixed Feeling," *Atlanta Constitution,* Dec. 29, 1964; "Archbishop, Rabbi Push King Banquet," *Atlanta Journal,* Dec. 30, 1964.
38. Patterson interview, Sept. 8, 1986; Raines, *My Soul Is Rested,* 368. Patterson said he reported the FBI agent's request to John Doar of the Justice Department during an airline flight, and Doar agreed he would tell Attorney General Robert Kennedy. But Doar "just continued to stare at the seat in front of him. . . . And all of a sudden it hit me like a thunderclap that Bobby Kennedy knew about it."
39. Garrow, *FBI and Martin Luther King, Jr.,* 121, 135.
40. Herbert Jenkins interview, in Raines, *My Soul Is Rested,* 353–54.
41. "The South: Rare Tribute," *Time,* Feb. 5, 1964, 24.
42. Pomerantz, *Peachtree Meets Sweet Auburn,* 336–77; Patterson interview, Sept. 8, 1986.
43. Patterson interview, Sept. 8, 1986; Mrs. Janice Blumberg (widow of Rabbi Rothschild), telephone interview by author, Sept. 9, 1986.
44. Paul Valentine, "Atlantans Pay Tribute to Dr. King," *Atlanta Journal,* Jan. 28, 1965; Bullard interview, in Raines, *My Soul Is Rested,* 414.
45. "The South: Rare Tribute," 24.

19. SEMPER FI

1. Ralph McGill, "The South's Glowing Horizon—IF," *Saturday Review,* Mar. 9, 1968, 115.
2. Remer Tyson, "Guidelines Fight Led by Talmadge," *Atlanta Constitution,* Mar. 30, 1966, p. 1; Joe Zellner, "Maddox Gets a Change on Compliance," *Atlanta Constitution,* May 12, 1967, p. 1; Joe Brown, "State Told to Triple Integration," *Atlanta Constitution,* Mar. 10, 1966, p. 1.
3. Ralph McGill, "Politics in Alabama," *Atlanta Constitution,* Mar. 11, 1966, p. 1.
4. "Is Maddox Out After Johnson?" *Atlanta Constitution,* May 12, 1967, p. 1.
5. "Viet Junta Yields to the U.S., Frees 20 Political Prisoners," *Atlanta Constitution,* Jan. 11, 1965, p. 1.

6. Ralph McGill, "History Teaches a Lesson," *Atlanta Constitution,* Jan. 15, 1965, p. 1.
7. Ralph McGill, "'Charlie Cong' and Politics," *Atlanta Constitution,* Mar. 15, 1966, p. 1; "President Pleads for Peace in Signing $4.8 Billion Arms Bill," *Atlanta Constitution,* Mar. 16, 1966, p. 1.
8. "Nation's Attitude on Vietnam War Is Improving, Says President Johnson," *Atlanta Constitution,* May 19, 1967, p. 2; McGill, "Charlie Cong"; Ray F. Herndon, "Viet Reds Regroup Via Neutral Zone," *Atlanta Constitution,* Mar. 19, 1966, p. 1.
9. McGill, "Charlie Cong"; Ralph McGill, "U.S. Soldiers Are Learning," *Atlanta Constitution,* Mar. 12, 1966, p. 1.
10. Martin, *McGill,* 146–47.
11. Ibid.
12. McGill, *South and the Southerner,* 270, 286.
13. David Sumner, *The Episcopal Church's History, 1945–1985* (Atlanta: Morehouse, 1987); "Race Dispute Moves Presbyterian Rally," *Atlanta Constitution,* Jan. 27, 1965, p. 1.
14. Ralph McGill, "Best School for Children," *Atlanta Constitution,* Mar. 3, 1966, p. 1.
15. Martin, *McGill,* 303.
16. Ibid., 301, 304; McNeill, *God Wills Us Free,* vii, ix. McGill, *South and the Southerner,* 280.
17. Martin, *McGill,* 304–5.
18. McGill, "Drunk on the Street," 1.
19. Ralph McGill, "Sublimity—Then Shock," *Atlanta Constitution,* May 16, 1967, p. 1; Ralph McGill, "Great Lady of the Sea," *Atlanta Constitution,* May 20, 1967, p. 1; Ralph McGill, "Old Women on Bound Feet," *Atlanta Constitution,* Mar. 28, 1966, p. 1; Ralph McGill, "Long Look at Consequences," *Atlanta Constitution,* Mar. 17, 1966, p. 1; McGill, "Drunk on the Street."
20. Ralph McGill, "China—Always the Enigma," *Atlanta Constitution,* Mar. 2, 1966, p. 1; Ralph McGill, "The Tale of Osagyefe," *Atlanta Constitution,* Mar. 4, 1966, p. 1; Ralph McGill, "A Memory of Nkrumah," *Atlanta Constitution,* Mar. 5, 1966, p. 1.
21. Ralph McGill, "The Warmest Memory," *Atlanta Constitution,* Jan. 25, 1965, 1, 8.
22. Ralph McGill, "Four Horsemen and Revolution," *Atlanta Constitution,* Jan. 30, 1965, p. 1.
23. Ibid., 224; Pfc. John Martin, twenty-four in 1966, was pictured on the front page of the *Atlanta Constitution* smiling and displaying between thumb and index finger the inch-long bullet removed from his left leg at a hospital in Tokyo after he was ambushed by the Vietcong on February 17, 1966. "Atlantan Shows Enemy Bullet," *Atlanta Constitution,* Mar. 2, 1966, p. 1.
24. Morgan interview.
25. Morgan interview; Martin, *McGill,* 222.
26. Morgan interview; Martin, *McGill,* 222–23.
27. Morgan interview; Martin, *McGill,* 224.
28. Morgan interview; Nancy Sneed (caretaker of McGill's mother), interview by author, Chattanooga, Tenn., Nov. 5, 1992; Martin, *McGill,* 224–25.
29. Ho Chi Minh to Robert M. Hutchins, June 1966, 1–2, Box 25, Baggs Papers.
30. William C. Baggs to Harry Ashmore, Nov. 23, 1965, Mar. 8, 1966, Box 1, Folder 8, Baggs Papers.

31. Harry S. Ashmore and William C. Baggs, *Mission to Hanoi: A Chronicle of Double-Dealing in High Places* (New York: Putnam Berkley Publishing Group, 1968). The book underscored the frustration of seeking peace without a government portfolio. One reviewer noted, "The two amateur diplomats are intensely conscious of their lack of influence in Washington and resent the way their reports and opinions were received. . . . Nevertheless, the evidence of executive mismanagement is sufficiently damning to place this book in the category of documents to be considered when an historical judgment is passed upon our involvement in Vietnam and particularly the part played by the Johnson Administration." E. J. Cutler, *Library Journal* 93 (Nov. 1, 1968): 4213. See also Lee Lockwood, *Nation* 208 (Mar. 24, 1969): 374, and *New Yorker* 44 (Dec. 7, 1968): 246.

32. Johnny Popham, interviews by author, Popham Seminars, Athens, Georgia, June 1997 and June 1998.

33. Harold E. Davis, interview by author, Atlanta, Oct. 6, 1987; Jack Tarver interview, Dec. 13, 1994.

34. William C. Baggs to Harry Scott Ashmore, Mar. 19, 1968, 1–2, Box 1, Folder 8, Baggs Papers.

35. Ralph McGill to Harry Ashmore and William Baggs, Mar. 24, 1966, p. 2, and Ralph McGill to William Baggs, Dec. 15, 1967, p. 1, Box 4, Folder 120, Baggs Papers; Ralph McGill to Bill Baggs, Aug. 3, 1967, 1–2, RMP.

36. Ralph McGill to William C. Baggs, Dec. 15, 1967, p. 1, Box 4, Folder 120, Baggs Papers; William C. Baggs to Ralph McGill, Dec. 20, 1967, p. 1, Box 4, Folder 120, Baggs Papers.

37. Morgan interview; Bill Shipp, lecture, Georgia State Univ., Oct. 22, 1987.

38. Martin, *McGill,* 226–27.

39. Ralph McGill, "Africa's Future Affects Us All," *Atlanta Constitution,* Mar. 25, 1967, p. 1.

40. "McGill Is Barred from South Africa," *Atlanta Constitution,* Mar. 24, 1967, p. 1; Ralph McGill, "A Visitor from South Africa," *Atlanta Constitution,* Oct. 3, 1947, p. 6; Ralph McGill, "An 'Afrikaner' on Tour," *Atlanta Constitution,* Oct. 26, 1955, p. 1.

41. Helga Sandburg to Ralph McGill, Apr. 21, 1967, and Harry Golden to Ralph McGill, Apr. 24, 1967, Box 16, Folder 8, RMP; Margaret Tarver interview, Dec. 13, 1994.

42. Ralph McGill, "Liz Parris Is Still Around," *Atlanta Constitution,* May 3, 1967, p. 1.

43. Ralph McGill, "Two Dixie 'Educators,'" *Atlanta Constitution,* May 15, 1967, p. 1.

44. McGill, "Two Dixie 'Educators'"; Ralph McGill, "The Pursuit of Pleasure," *Atlanta Constitution,* May 17, 1967, p. 1.

45. Ralph McGill, "Encouragement of Discontent," *Atlanta Constitution,* May 27, 1967, p. 1.

46. McGill, "Pursuit of Pleasure."

47. Don Speicher, "What's It All About, Ralphie?" *Great Speckled Bird* 1, no. 1 (Mar. 15, 1968): 1; Tom Coffin, "Chirp," *Great Speckled Bird* 1, no. 1 (Mar. 15, 1968): 1.

48. Speicher, "What's It All About, Ralphie?" 7.

49. Tom O'Ware, "DEAR RALPHIE: The Mis-Use of History," *Great Speckled Bird,* no. 10 (July 19, 1968), p. 4.

50. Harry Golden to Ralph McGill, Jan. 7, 1966, Box 15, RMP; *Atlanta Constitution* photographer Charles R. Pugh Jr. became a messenger and conduit between McGill and Sandburg. When Pugh visited his hometown in Erwin, Tennessee, he

often stopped at Connemara to see Sandburg. Once, Pugh carried champagne from McGill. "I have two bottles for you," he told Sandburg. "No, you don't. You have *one*," the poet replied. "Take that and give it to Mrs. Sandburg. Tell her you only brought one up here." The second bottle, Pugh recalled, Sandburg took immediately to his upstairs hideaway. Charles R. Pugh Jr., interview by author, Erwin, Tenn., Jan. 14, 2000.

51. Ralph McGill, "Man for All the World," *Atlanta Constitution,* July 25, 1967, p. 1. At Christmas 1967, Golden told McGill he paid his customary visit to Connemara "and sat in Carl's chair and after the Christmas dinner I recited some of Carl's poetry, among them 'Happiness.'" Harry Golden to Ralph McGill, Dec. 26, 1967, Box 17, RMP.

20. A Legacy

1. Martin, *McGill,* 296; Gershon interview, in McGill, *Southern Encounters,* 313.
2. Kennedy was elected to the Senate from New York in 1964.
3. Ralph McGill, "Martin Luther King, Jr.: 1929–1968," *Boston Globe,* Apr. 14, 1968, reprinted in McGill, *Southern Encounters,* 74.
4. McGill, "Harvest of Hate."
5. Ralph McGill, "The New Confederacy: Review of Robert Sherrill's *Gothic Politics in the Deep South,*" *New York Times,* Mar. 22, 1968, reprinted in McGill, *No Place to Hide* 2:610.
6. Ralph McGill to the Editor, *Center,* Mar. 1968, reprinted in McGill, *No Place to Hide* 2:619, 620, 621.
7. Ralph McGill, "We Must Go Along Together for Better or Worse," *Atlanta Inquirer,* Aug. 3, 1969, reprinted in McGill, *No Place to Hide* 2:625.
8. Ralph McGill, preface to Carl Sandburg, *The Chicago Race Riots* (New York: Harcourt, Brace and World, 1969).
9. Ralph McGill, introduction to *The Old South: Alabama, Florida, Georgia, Mississippi, South Carolina,* by John Osborne (New York: Time-Life Books, 1969); Ralph McGill, "The New South and a New America," *1969 Compton Yearbook* (Encyclopedia Britannica, 1969), reprinted in McGill, *No Place to Hide* 2:645–46.
10. Ralph McGill, ". . . The Fabric of Our Soul," *Atlanta Constitution,* Nov. 27 1968, p. 1.
11. Ralph McGill, "Old South? New South?" *Atlanta Constitution,* Nov. 23 1968, p. 1; Ralph McGill, "Mr. Nixon; His Own 'Aaron,'" *Atlanta Constitution,* Nov. 25 1968, p. 1.
12. Ralph McGill, "Mr. Wallace Bust! Bomb!" *Atlanta Constitution,* Nov. 20, 1968, p. 1.
13. Ralph McGill, "Now, Really! Now, Really!" *Atlanta Constitution,* Nov. 14, 1968, p. 1.
14. Ralph McGill, "Afro-American, Negro, Black—?" *Atlanta Constitution,* Nov. 16, 1968, p. 1; Ralph McGill, "Pandering to a Myth," *Atlanta Constitution,* Nov. 18, 1968, p. 1.
15. Ralph McGill, "The Story of U.S. Socialists," *Atlanta Constitution,* Nov. 19, 1968, p. 1.
16. Morgan interview; "State's Leaders Hail McGill," *Atlanta Constitution,* Feb. 4, 1969, p. 1.
17. Ibid.
18. Gershon interview, in McGill, *Southern Encounters,* 314; Ralph McGill, interviews with Calvin Logue, Nov. 27, 1968, and Jan. 1969, published as "A

Conversation with Ralph McGill," in McGill, *No Place to Hide* 2:658–59; *Time,* Feb. 14, 1969, 68; *Nation,* Feb. 17, 1969.

19. Patterson interview, Jan. 5, 2000.
20. Ibid.
21. Patterson interview, Jan. 5, 2000; McGill interviews, Nov. 27, 1968, and Jan. 1969, in McGill, *No Place to Hide* 2:650–51; Martin, *McGill,* 241, 242, 244. B. J. Phillips also resigned and went to work in Washington.
22. McGill interviews, Nov. 27, 1968, and Jan. 1969, in McGill, *No Place to Hide* 2:650–51; Martin, *McGill,* 241, 242, 244.
23. McGill interviews, Nov. 27, 1968, and Jan. 1969, in McGill, *No Place to Hide* 2:650–51; Martin, *McGill,* 241, 242, 244; Katharine Graham, *Personal History* (New York: Alfred A. Knopf, 1997), 411; Patterson interview, Jan. 5, 2000.
24. Martin, *McGill,* 245.
25. Patterson interview, Jan. 5, 2000.
26. Bill Baggs to Jack Tarver, Oct. 2, 1968, Box 7, Folder 205, Baggs Papers. Baggs correctly estimated both Patterson and the *Post.* Patterson stayed only three years before leaving the Washington scene for a quieter setting on the faculty of Duke University, and later to the *St. Petersburg Times,* where in 1978 he became chief executive officer, retiring in 1988. At the *Post,* Katharine Graham thought that "over a three-year period, a combination of mismatched temperaments, overlapping responsibilities, and newsroom politics convinced Ben [Bradlee] that things weren't working out. He aired his doubts to Gene and Gene resigned immediately. When he left the *Post,* Gene summed up his feelings by saying, 'Ben Bradlee needs a managing editor like a boar needs tits.' This was a quote that amused Ben vastly, but it accurately spelled out what Gene had long suspected: 'There was no job there.' Miraculously, we all stayed friends, a remarkable tribute to Gene's classy, lovely character." Graham, *Personal History,* 411.
27. John Griffin, Jack Tarver, and Ralph McGill, telegram, to Bill Baggs, Sept. 26, 1968, Box 20, Item 29, RMP; Ralph McGill to Bill Baggs, Oct. 29, 1968, pp. 1–2, Box 20, Item 40, RMP.
28. Ralph McGill to Craig Baggs, Jan. 27, 1969, Box 21, Item 41, RMP.
29. John W. Finney, "President Orders Cessation in the Bombing of N. Vietnam," *Atlanta Constitution,* Nov. 1, 1968, p. 1; Ralph McGill, "History Will Be Fair," *Atlanta Constitution,* Nov. 3, 1968, 1, 12; Ralph McGill, "The Shape of the Table," *Atlanta Constitution,* Jan. 27, 1968, p. 1; McGill, "History Will Be Fair," 1.
30. Ralph McGill, "One More Look Back to 1968," *Atlanta Constitution,* Jan. 1, 1969, 1, 7.
31. Jack Tarver interview, Oct. 8, 1992.
32. Ralph McGill, "Bill Baggs: In Memory," *Atlanta Constitution,* Jan. 9, 1969, 1, 12.
33. "The Man Who Searched for Answers" (editorial), *Atlanta Constitution,* Jan. 9, 1969.
34. Milt Sosin, "Miami Turns Out for Bill," *Miami News,* Jan. 10, 1969, p. 1; "HHH Joins Baggs' Tribute," *Atlanta Constitution,* Jan. 9, 1969; Jane Baggs, interview by author, Coral Gables, Fla., Feb. 24, 1990; Jack Tarver interview, Oct. 8, 1992.
35. John A. Griffin interview, June 19, 1992.
36. Ralph McGill to Craig Baggs, Jan. 27, 1969, Box 21, Item 111, RMP; Craig Baggs to Mary Lynn McGill, Feb. 1969, Box 22, Item 44, RMP.
37. Ralph McGill to Jerry Anderson, Jan. 31, 1969, Box 21, Item 46, RMP; Suzanne B. Spear to Ralph McGill, Jan. 9, 1969, Box 21, Item 43, RMP.
38. Morgan interview.

39. Ralph McGill to Mrs. Sylvan [Anne] Meyer, Jan. 22, 1969, Box 21, Item 3, RMP. She was the wife of the editor Sylvan Meyer, who succeeded Bill Baggs as editor; Austin Ford to Ralph McGill, Jan. 17, 1969, Box 21, File 3, RMP.

40. Reg Murphy, "The Man Who Loved the South," *Atlanta Constitution,* Feb. 4, 1969, p. 4.

41. Martin, *McGill,* 312–13.

42. Morgan interview.

43. Martin, *McGill,* 317.

44. Reg Murphy and Bob Hurt, "Ralph McGill Dies Here in 70th Year After Heart Attack; Stricken at Dinner at Friends' Home," *Atlanta Constitution,* Feb. 4, 1969, p. 1; "An Editorial," *Atlanta Constitution,* Feb. 4, 1969, p. 1; "State's Leaders Hail McGill," 1, 12.

45. "State's Leaders Hail McGill," 12.

46. Ibid.

47. Murphy, "Man Who Loved the South."

48. Martin, *McGill,* 319–20.

49. Celestine Sibley, "Ralph McGill Rites Today on Birthday," *Atlanta Constitution,* Feb. 5, 1969, p. 1; also in the *Atlanta Constitution,* Feb. 5, 1969, p. 4: Reg Murphy, "'Trust Instinct,' He Advised Us"; Celestine Sibley, "McGill: Earth Held No Higher Calling"; Leo Aikman, "He Practiced Kindness"; Bruce Galphin, "The Thunderer Behind the Print Was a Gentle, Generous Man"; Calvin Cox, "Watching the World"; "His Loss Diminishes Us All: Tributes from the Staff"; "Ralph Emerson McGill" (editorial); Baldy, "The Torch Is Passed."

50. Harold Martin to J. James McElveen, Feb. 18, 1977, 1, Martin Papers.

51. Ralph McGill [Jr.], "Getting It Off My Chest," *Atlanta Gazette,* Apr. 3, 1977, p. 7.

52. McGill, "Now, Really! Now, Really!"

53. Jacques Barzun, *The House of Intellect* (New York: Harper, 1959), 3.

Bibliography

Primary Sources

Books by Ralph McGill
The Best of Ralph McGill: Selected Columns. Edited by Michael Strickland, Harry
    Davis, and Jeff Strickland. Atlanta: Cherokee Publishing, 1980.
A Church, A School. New York: Abingdon Press, 1959.
The Fleas Come with the Dog. New York: Abingdon Press, 1954.
Israel Revisited. Atlanta: Tupper and Love, 1950.
No Place to Hide: The South and Human Rights. 2 vols. Edited by Calvin M. Logue.
    Atlanta: Mercer Univ. Press, 1984.
Ralph McGill: Editor and Publisher. 2 vols. Edited by Calvin M. Logue. Durham,
    N.C.: Moore Publishing, 1969.
The South and the Southerner. Boston: Little, Brown, 1963.
Southern Encounters: Southerners of Note in Ralph McGill's South. Edited by Calvin
    M. Logue. Macon, Ga.: Mercer Univ. Press, 1983.

Book Reviews by Ralph McGill
Review of *In the Land of Jim Crow,* by Ray Sprigle. *New York Times Book Review,*
    June 5, 1949.
"Speaking for the South—and to It: Review of Brooks Hays's *A Southern Moderate
    Speaks.*" *New York Times,* Mar. 15, 1959.

Libraries and Archives
Ackerman, Carl W. Papers. Library of Congress.
Baggs, William C. [Bill]. Papers. Special Collections, Otto G. Richter Library, Univ.
    of Miami, Fla.
Bryan, Wright. Papers. Privately held, heirs of Wright Bryan, Clemson, S.C.
Davis, Harold E. Papers. Privately held, Priscilla Davis, Atlanta.
Eisenhower, Dwight David. Papers. Dwight D. Eisenhower Library, Abilene, Kan.
Howell, Clark. File. Atlanta Newspapers Archives. Atlanta Journal-Constitution
    Building, 72 Marietta St. N.W., Atlanta.
Johnson, Lyndon B. Papers. White House Tapes, Lyndon B. Johnson Library,
    Austin, Tex.
Knight, John S. Papers. Univ. of Akron, Akron, Ohio.
Kytle, Calvin. Papers. Privately held, Calvin Kytle, Chapel Hill, N.C.
Martin, Harold. Papers. Atlanta History Center.
McGill, Ralph Emerson. Papers. Special Collections, Robert W. Woodruff Library,
    Emory Univ., Atlanta. (RMP)
McGill, Ralph. File. Atlanta Newspapers Archives.
Rogers, William P. Papers. Dwight D. Eisenhower Library, Abilene, Kan.
Tarver, Jack. Papers. Mercer Univ., Macon, Ga.
Truman, Harry S. Papers. Truman Library, Independence, Mo.

INTERVIEWS AND LECTURES

Alexander, Lamar. Interview by author. Southeast Journalism Conference, Feb. 22, 1997.

Arnall, Ellis Gibbs. Telephone interview by author. Nov. 10, 1986, Mar. 11, 1987, Sept. 8, 1987.

Ashmore, Harry S. Interview by author. Friends of John Popham Seminar, Atlanta Airport Holiday Inn, June 20, 1993; Popham Seminar, Atlanta, June 10, 1994; Popham Seminar, Univ. of Georgia–Athens, June 8, 1996.

Baggs, Joan. Interview by author. Coral Gables, Fla., Feb. 24, 1990.

Blumberg, Janice. Telephone interview by author. Atlanta, Sept. 9, 1986.

Bryan, Ellen. Interview by author. Clemson, S.C., Nov. 26, 1987.

Bryan, Wright. Interview by author. Clemson, S.C., Nov. 26, 1987.

Cheney, Frances "Fannie" [Mrs. Brainard]. Telephone interview by author. Nashville Health Care Center, Nashville, Mar. 2, 1990, Apr. 10, 1993.

Davis, Harold E. Interview by author. Atlanta, Oct. 6, 1987, Dec. 14, 1992, May 28, 1997.

Davison, Peter. Interview by author. Houghton Mifflin, Boston, Aug. 8, 1991.

Evans, George. Interview by author. Charlotte, N.C., Jan. 21, 1994.

Griffin, John A. Interview by author. Atlanta, Apr. 20, 1987. Griffin, who helped found the Southern Regional Council, was a leading liberal voice in Atlanta.

Mackay, James. Interview by author. Atlanta, Nov. 2, 1995.

Martin, Harold. Interview by author. Atlanta, Mar. 12, 1987.

McGill, Ralph. Interview by Calvin Kytle. Transcript. Atlanta, May 20, 1947. Calvin Kytle Papers, Carolina Meadows, Villa 130, Chapel Hill, N.C.

McGill, Ralph, Jr. Interview by author. Atlanta, Dec. 12, 1989.

Morgan, Mary Lynn. Interview by author. Atlanta, Oct. 31, 1998.

Patillo, John. Interview by author. Atlanta, Jan. 12, 2000.

Patterson, Eugene. Telephone interview by author. Sept. 8, 1986; interview by author, Friends of John Popham Seminar, Univ. of Georgia, Athens, June 8, 1997, telephone interview by author. Jan. 5, 2000.

———. McGill lecture. Twentieth Anniversary Commemoration, Atlanta Public Library, June 4, 1989.

Popham, John. Interview by author. Friends of John Popham Seminar, Atlanta Airport Holiday Inn, June 10, 1995; Popham Seminars, Univ. of Georgia–Athens, June 1997, June 1998.

Pugh, Charles R., Jr. Interview by author. Erwin, Tenn., Jan. 14, 2000.

Russell, Freddie. Telephone interview by author. Sept. 10, 1993. Russell became sports editor of the *Nashville Banner* after McGill left for Atlanta.

Schwartz, William B., III. Interview by author. Atlanta, Apr. 12, 2000.

Shipp, Bill. Lecture. Journalism class, Georgia State Univ., Oct. 22, 1987.

Sibley, Celestine. Interview. "Dawn's Early Light: Ralph McGill and the Segregated South." Produced and directed by Kathleen Dowdey and Jed Dannenbaum. Public Broadcasting System, 1989. Transcript of videocassette.

Sneed, Nancy. Interview by author. Old McGill house, Chattanooga, Tenn., Nov. 5, 1992. Ms. Sneed was a caretaker of McGill's mother.

Spalding, Jack. Interview by author. Atlanta, Oct. 15, 1986, July 18, 1994, Dec. 7, 1994.

Tarver, Jack. Interview by author. Atlanta, Dec. 13, 1994.

Tarver, Jack Jr. Interview by author. Atlanta, Dec. 10, 1999.
Tarver, Margaret. Interview by author. Atlanta, Dec. 12, 1994.

NEWSPAPER COLUMNS AND ARTICLES BY RALPH MCGILL

"Africa's Future Affects Us All." *Atlanta Constitution,* Mar. 25, 1967, p. 1.
"An 'Afrikaner' on Tour." *Atlanta Constitution,* Oct. 26, 1955, p. 1.
"Afro-American, Negro, Black—?" *Atlanta Constitution,* Nov. 16, 1968, p. 1.
"Agrarianism vs. Industrialism Question Skillfully Debated by Anderson and Dr. Ransom." *Atlanta Constitution,* Feb. 15, 1931, pp. 1, 5.
"America, I Love You." *Atlanta Constitution,* June 4, 1956, p. 8.
"Banks and Credit are Sound, Report Reserve Heads Here; Farm Tenancy and Farm Income Problems Must Be Solved by South Before Section Assumes Rightful Place in Nation, Say Officials." *Atlanta Constitution,* May 15, 1937, pp. 1, 3.
"Batista, 'Man of Hour,' Brought About Peace; Ralph McGill Writes About How Sergeant Fulgencio Batista Took Command and Changed Chaos into Order." *Atlanta Constitution,* May 18, 1935, p. 1.
"Best School for Children." *Atlanta Constitution,* Mar. 3, 1966, p. 1.
"Bill Baggs: In Memory." *Atlanta Constitution,* Jan. 9, 1969, pp. 1, 12.
"Bob Scally, Farr's Sparmate, Is Adept at Handling Babies." *Atlanta Constitution,* Dec. 19, 1937, p. 2B.
"Bread and France." *Atlanta Constitution,* June 19, 1947, p. 10A.
"Break O' Day!" A regular column in the *Atlanta Constitution.* Ran from 1931 to 1938.
"Card Scene Come to Life." *Atlanta Constitution,* Dec. 23, 1937, p. 18.
"Castro and the Pageant." *Atlanta Constitution,* July 2, 1959, p. 1.
"Castro: No Cash in the Bank." *Atlanta Constitution,* Oct. 26, 1959, p. 1.
"'Charlie Cong' and Politics." *Atlanta Constitution,* Mar. 15, 1966, p. 1.
"China—Always the Enigma." *Atlanta Constitution,* Mar. 2, 1966, p. 1.
"A Church, A School." *Atlanta Constitution,* Oct. 13, 1958, p. 1.
"Civil Rights: A Background." *Atlanta Constitution,* Feb. 25, 1964, p. 1.
"Coming Events, and Shadows." *Atlanta Constitution,* July 31, 1947, p. 12.
"The Commies Have Come to Town." *Atlanta Constitution,* Apr. 4, 1947, p. 4.
"Cuba Is Very Fond of Our National Game." *Atlanta Constitution,* Aug. 2, 1933, p. 16.
"The Curtain Falls on One War Theater." *Atlanta Constitution,* May 4, 1945, p. 8A.
"Dakar and History." *Atlanta Constitution,* Feb. 13, 1963, p. 1.
"Dangerous Social Dynamite." *Atlanta Constitution,* Feb. 26, 1964, p. 1.
"The Death Rattle Sounds from Japan!" *Atlanta Constitution,* Aug. 9, 1945, p. 8.
"Democratic Heart Throbs in Florida." *Atlanta Constitution,* Oct. 19, 1960, p. 1.
"Democrats Sense Chance at Victory." *Atlanta Constitution,* Oct. 22, 1960, p. 1.
"The Derby Merry-Go-Round." *Atlanta Constitution,* May 7, 1955, p. 8.
"Drunk on the Street." *Atlanta Constitution,* Mar. 19, 1966, p. 1.
"Encouragement of Discontent." *Atlanta Constitution,* May 27, 1967, p. 1.
"Errors of Bloc Leadership." *Atlanta Constitution,* June 22, 1966, p. 1.
"Extremists Aid Subversion." *Atlanta Constitution,* May 2, 1964, p. 1.
". . . The Fabric of Our Soul." *Atlanta Constitution,* Nov. 27, 1968, p. 1.
"The Face of the South." *Atlanta Constitution,* Sept. 12, 1957, p. 1.
"'Feeling Pulse of Europe,' Touring McGill Asserts." *Atlanta Constitution,* Jan. 24, 1944, p. 1.
"Flight of the Beast." *Atlanta Constitution,* Jan. 3, 1959, p. 1.

"Four Horsemen and Revolution." *Atlanta Constitution,* Jan. 30, 1965, p. 1.

"General Eisenhower and Soviet Friendship." *Atlanta Constitution,* Aug. 14, 1945, p. 5.

"German Sickness a Terrible Disease." *Atlanta Constitution,* Mar. 29, 1945, p. 8.

"Ghosts of Many Martyrs Walk at Morro Castle." *Atlanta Constitution,* Aug. 4, 1933, p. 16.

"Great Lady of the Sea." *Atlanta Constitution,* May 20, 1967, p. 1.

"Hand of Mysterious A.B.C. Seen Behind Cuban Strike; McGill Reports Secret Society Is Working for a 'New Deal' for Island with Machado as Unpleasant Incident." *Atlanta Constitution,* Aug. 2, 1933, pp. 1, 4.

"Harvests Come from Seeds." *Atlanta Constitution,* Sept. 17, 1963, p. 1.

"The Harvest of Hate." *Atlanta Constitution,* June 7, 1968, p. 1.

"History Teaches a Lesson." *Atlanta Constitution,* Jan. 15, 1965, p. 1.

"History Will Be Fair." *Atlanta Constitution,* Nov. 3, 1968, pp. 1, 12.

"Homecoming Games and Pain." *Atlanta Constitution,* Oct. 23, 1954, p. 8.

"How Fuehrer Sets Stage for Talk Told by McGill." *Atlanta Constitution,* Mar. 9, 1938, p. 3.

"I Remember Gerardo Machado." *Atlanta Constitution,* Apr. 8, 1952, p. 1.

"I'm the Gink." A regular column in the *Nashville Banner.* Ran from 1927 to 1928.

"In Dixie Land He Takes a Stand." *Atlanta Constitution,* Oct. 11, 1960, p. 1.

"Is the Thing Possible." *Atlanta Constitution,* Apr. 5, 1964, p. 1.

"It Is Something Else." *Atlanta Constitution,* Sept. 25, 1957, p. 1.

"Kennedy Believes in Future of U.S." *Atlanta Constitution,* Oct. 20, 1960, p. 1.

"The Kennedy Magic." *Atlanta Constitution,* Mar. 25, 1964, p. 1.

"Kennedy-Nixon Campaign Far Cry from McKinley's." *Atlanta Constitution,* Oct. 17, 1960, p. 1.

"The KKK's Candidate Plan." *Atlanta Constitution,* May 26, 1946, p. 2D.

"Konfessions Koncerning Klans." *Atlanta Constitution,* June 2, 1946, p. 14C.

"The Last Joke on John Lynn." *Atlanta Constitution,* June 6, 1953, p. 6.

"Leg Men." *Atlanta Constitution,* Dec. 19, 1939, p. 21.

"Let's Look at the Record." *Atlanta Constitution,* Aug. 25, 1948, p. 8.

"Like World of Three Stages." *Atlanta Constitution,* Sept. 2, 1957, p. 1.

"Liz Parris Is Still Around." *Atlanta Constitution,* May 3, 1967, p. 1.

"Long Look at Consequences." *Atlanta Constitution,* Mar. 17, 1966, p. 1.

"A Lynching and 'The Difference.'" *Atlanta Constitution,* June 1, 1949, p. 12A.

"Machado, Batista, Fidel—." *Atlanta Constitution,* Oct. 9, 1968, p. 1.

"Machado Places Last Hopes in Trained, Well-Paid Army; McGill Believes President's Policy in Regard to Military Was Shrewdly Conceived Against Just Such Crisis as Now Prevails." *Atlanta Constitution,* Aug. 10, 1933, p. 1.

"Machado Receives McGill in Closely-Guarded Palace, Denies Ordering Gun Rule; *Constitution* Writer Finds Hated Cuban Ruler a Lonely Old Man Who Has Stayed Too Long at Tasks Beyond His Capabilities." *Atlanta Constitution,* Aug. 6, 1933, pp. 1, 11.

"Man for All the World." *Atlanta Constitution,* July 25, 1967, p. 1.

"McGill Finds Once Gay Cuba Has Become Isle of Bitterness; *Constitution* Staff Writer Reveals First-Hand Picture of Internal Strife and Discontent in Island Republic." *Atlanta Constitution,* Aug. 5, 1933, p. 1.

"McGill Foils Nazi Terror to Aid Refugee; Writer Brings Memorized Message to Vienna Victims." *Atlanta Constitution,* May 2, 1938, p. 5.

"McGill in London: Mention of Hard, Wooden Benches Again Appears, but He Hears of Taxation Problem from Austrian Girl." *Atlanta Constitution,* May 6, 1938, p. 1.

"McGill in Vienna: Hitler Invests Salute to Viennese with Pompous Drama." *Atlanta Constitution,* Apr. 29, 1938, p. 1.
"McGill in Vienna: Only a Fool Will Deny Hitler Hasn't Done Much for Germany and Will Do Much for Austria, Writer Declares." *Atlanta Constitution,* May 4, 1938, p. 7.
"McGill in Vienna: Orgy of Adulation Accorded Hitler, the 'Build-Up of Herr Goebbels Described in Dramatic Detail by Writer." *Atlanta Constitution,* Apr. 28, 1938, p. 1.
"McGill in Vienna: People of Austria Were Skillfully Coerced Into Voting 'Ja' in Humorless Plebiscite with Fine Goebbels Touch." *Atlanta Constitution,* May 1, 1938, p. 9K.
"McGill in Vienna: Vienna Becomes Transformed into Center of Great Public Gatherings As Adolf Hitler Makes His Speech on Union." *Atlanta Constitution,* Apr. 30, 1938, p. 1.
"McGill Lauds Sumner Welles for Brilliant Work in Cuba." *Atlanta Constitution,* Aug. 8, 1933, pp. 1, 4.
"McGill Says Businessmen Like Hitler Rule; Most of Them Are Doing Better than in Dark Days After War, Writer Declares at Vienna; Wages Are Low." *Atlanta Constitution,* May 5, 1938, p. 11.
"Meditations in a Hammock." *Atlanta Constitution,* June 7, 1949, p. 10A.
"A Memory of Nkrumah." *Atlanta Constitution,* Mar. 5, 1966, p. 1.
"Men Who Shame Our State and Flag." *Atlanta Constitution,* Aug. 18, 1949, p. 8.
"Moscow Reflections: Sitting in the Baptist Church in Moscow." *Atlanta Constitution,* Aug. 12, 1959.
"Mr. Nixon; His Own 'Aaron.'" *Atlanta Constitution,* Nov. 25 1968, p. 1.
"Mr. Wallace Bust! Bomb!" *Atlanta Constitution,* Nov. 20, 1968, p. 1.
"New Frontiers by Fast Travel." *Atlanta Constitution,* July 18, 1960.
"The 'New Nixon' Is on the Spot." *Atlanta Constitution,* Oct. 24, 1960, p. 1.
"News and Propaganda." *Atlanta Constitution,* Apr. 21, 1961, p. 1.
"Nixon—At His Best or Worst?" *Atlanta Constitution,* Oct. 14, 1960, p. 1.
"Not All Liars Are Communists." *Atlanta Constitution,* Dec. 14, 1950, p. 1.
"Not Peace, But a Sword?" *Atlanta Constitution,* Aug. 25, 1946, p. 10.
"Now, Really! Now, Really!" *Atlanta Constitution,* Nov. 14, 1968, p. 1.
"Old South? New South?" *Atlanta Constitution,* Nov. 23 1968, p. 1.
"An Old Story Retold." *Atlanta Constitution,* June 16, 1961, p. 1.
"Old Women on Bound Feet." *Atlanta Constitution,* Mar. 28, 1966, p. 1.
"One Day It Will Be Monday." *Atlanta Constitution,* Apr. 9, 1953, p. 1.
"One More Look Back to 1968." *Atlanta Constitution,* Jan. 1, 1969, pp. 1, 7.
"One Word More." Regular column in the *Atlanta Constitution.* Ran from 1938 to 1942.
"Our Three Most Valuable Citizens." Atlanta Constitution, July 3, 1947, p. 10A.
"'Ozymandias' and the Reich." *Atlanta Constitution,* Sept. 3, 1957, p. 1.
"Palestine Issue Reopened by Big 3." *Atlanta Constitution,* Mar. 16, 1945, p. 6A.
"Pandering to a Myth." *Atlanta Constitution,* Nov. 18, 1968, p. 1.
"Parham's Double Beats Barons in 9th, 13–12; 10 Pitchers See Action in Wild Tilt; Lead Changes Hands Five Times—Large Crowd Watches Game." *Atlanta Constitution,* July 20, 1929, p. 15.
"Peace, New Air of Hope Reign in Cuba—McGill." *Atlanta Constitution,* May 16, 1935, p. 1.
"The Political Platypuses." *Atlanta Constitution,* June 11, 1947, p. 8A.
"Political Weather Fronts." *Atlanta Constitution,* Jan. 15, 1964, p. 1.
"Politics in Alabama." *Atlanta Constitution,* Mar. 11, 1966, p. 1.

"Poor Ad for Communism." *Atlanta Constitution,* Sept. 5, 1957, p. 1.

"Prayers for Guidance." *Atlanta Constitution,* Sept. 16, 1957, p. 1.

"The President Moves in 'Aid.'" *Atlanta Constitution,* Jan. 9, 1964, p. 1.

"Proud Progress, or Paralysis?" *Atlanta Constitution,* June 29, 1964, p. 1.

"The Pursuit of Pleasure." *Atlanta Constitution,* May 17, 1967, p. 1.

"Questions and Answers." *Atlanta Constitution,* Feb. 16, 1963, p. 1.

"Rights Car Found Burned; Dulles Sent to Mississippi." *Atlanta Constitution,* June 24, 1964, p. 1.

"Roman Ruins Pose Question for Future." *Atlanta Constitution,* Mar. 5, 1945, p. 6.

"Russia Has Problems, Too." *Atlanta Constitution,* Mar. 17, 1947, p. 6A.

"Russia Really Isn't an Enigma." *Atlanta Constitution,* May 1, 1945, p. 6.

"Scandinavian Studies: Examination Similar to One for Insurance Required Before Permit Is Granted to Purchase Liquor to Drink at Home in Sweden." *Atlanta Constitution,* Mar. 3, 1938.

"Scandinavian Studies: McGill Delves into Social Law, Co-Operation and Farm Aid and Finds Them Good, but Not Suitable for Transplanting to U.S." *Atlanta Constitution,* Mar. 1, 1938.

"Scandinavian Studies: Norway's Sad Labor Affiliation with Moscow Proves Third International Exists Only for Itself and Intrigue, McGill Told." *Atlanta Constitution,* Feb. 27, 1938, p. 1.

"Scandinavian Studies: Ralph McGill Observes Work of Swedish Liquor Control System that Stresses Education as Making of Temperate Country." *Atlanta Constitution,* Mar. 4, 1938.

"Scandinavian Studies: A Strong Hotel Strike Reigns in Sweden, One in Which the Owners Close Down and 'Lockout' Their Workers." *Atlanta Constitution,* Mar. 2, 1938.

"Scandinavian Studies: Swedish Editor Queries Ralph McGill on New Pulp Mill Business in South Which Brings on Conservation Comparison." *Atlanta Constitution,* Feb. 28, 1938.

"'See-My-Operation-Club' Fails because of Inside Job." *Atlanta Constitution,* May 16, 1934, p. 14.

"Seven Miles Is Not High Enough." *Atlanta Constitution,* Mar. 7, 1944, p. 14.

"The Shape of the Table." *Atlanta Constitution,* Jan. 27, 1968, p. 1.

"So, the Russ Is on Us—Even Now!" *Atlanta Constitution,* Mar. 11, 1946, p. 8A.

"South Needs New Mood." *Atlanta Constitution,* Apr. 23, 1960.

"Sports Aerial." *Nashville Banner* [1929?]. McGill's personal scrapbooks.

"Story Behind New Cuba Is Batista, Says McGill." *Atlanta Constitution,* May 17, 1935, p. 1.

"The Story of U.S. Socialists." *Atlanta Constitution,* Nov. 19, 1968, p. 1.

"A String of Beads." *Atlanta Constitution,* Feb. 24, 1963, p. 1.

"Sublimity—Then Shock." *Atlanta Constitution,* May 16, 1967, p. 1.

"A Sure Cure for the Drink Habit." *Atlanta Constitution,* Apr. 5, 1945, p. 8.

"The Tale of Osagyefe." *Atlanta Constitution,* Mar. 4, 1966, p. 1.

"There Isn't Going to Be War." *Atlanta Constitution,* Mar. 15, 1946, p. 10A.

"They Simply Do Not Trust Us." *Atlanta Constitution,* Mar. 4, 1948, p. 8A.

"This Is the Story of the Farmer Who Went to College, Added Hard Work to New Ideas and Won to Success; John Gunnels Finds Freedom, Stillness, and Calm Restoring Wornout, Eroded Acres of Farm He Manages." *Atlanta Constitution,* May 30, 1937, p. 1.

"This Was It, This Very Room." *Atlanta Constitution,* Dec. 26, 1952, p. 8.

"Thoughts After Climbing Mount Fuji." *Atlanta Constitution,* July 8, 1962, p. 1.

"The Three Georgians Didn't Shadowbox." *Atlanta Constitution,* Mar. 5, 1944, p. 2D.
"A Ticket to Excite the Vote." *Atlanta Constitution,* Jan. 20, 1964, p. 1.
"To Inform, Not Inflame." *Atlanta Constitution,* Dec. 11, 1953, p. 1.
"Two Dixie 'Educators.'" *Atlanta Constitution,* May 15, 1967, p. 1.
"Uneasy Times for Presidents." *Atlanta Constitution,* Feb. 17, 1963, p. 1.
"U.S. Soldiers Are Learning." *Atlanta Constitution,* Mar. 12, 1966, p. 1.
"V-Bomb Attacks on This Nation?" *Atlanta Constitution,* Jan. 13, 1945, p. 4.
"Very Cautious Optimism." *Atlanta Constitution,* Jan. 1, 1964, p. 1.
"A Visitor from South Africa." *Atlanta Constitution,* Oct. 3, 1947, p. 6.
"The Warmest Memory." *Atlanta Constitution,* Jan. 25, 1965, pp. 1,8.
"What Is Faubus' Role?" *Atlanta Constitution,* Sept. 26, 1957, p. 1.
"When the News Came in Flight." *Atlanta Journal and Constitution,* Nov. 24, 1963, p. 1.
"The Winners: Pepper, Hill and Common Sense." *Atlanta Constitution,* May 5, 1944, p. 6.
"Word from Mississippi." *Atlanta Constitution,* June 26, 1964, p. 1.
"You Don't Destroy People Like the Greeks." *Atlanta Constitution,* Mar. 8, 1945, p. 8.
"You Know How It Was, Ed." *Atlanta Constitution,* Dec. 6, 1962, p. 1.

OTHER PERIODICAL ARTICLES BY RALPH MCGILL

"Adlai Stevenson and the Democratic South." *New Republic,* June 27, 1957.
"Demagoguery State by State." Review of *Southern Politics,* by V. O. Key Jr. *Saturday Review of Literature,* Dec. 3, 1949, 32.
"Dwight D. Eisenhower." Essay. July 1952, RMP.
"Dwight Eisenhower and the South." Unpublished manuscript. N.d. (after 1956), RMP.
"How Adlai Stevenson Won Georgia's Heart All Over Again." *Atlanta Journal and Constitution Magazine,* Dec. 27, 1953.
"It Has Happened Here." *Survey Graphic,* Sept. 30, 1941, 449–53.
"The Most Unforgettable Character I've Met." *Reader's Digest,* May 1954, 110.
"Past Perfect: Four Teachers McGill Remembers Best." *Vanderbilt Alumnus,* Mar. 1952, 8.
"Reading, 'Riting, and Russia." *Saturday Review of Literature,* Aug. 28, 1948, 7–9.
"Reflections on World News Freedom Following the ASNE Tour." *Journalism Quarterly* 22 (31) (Sept. 1945): 193.
"Report on Adlai Stevenson." *Atlanta Journal and Constitution Magazine,* Nov. 2, 1952.
"She'll Talk Later." *Harper's Magazine,* Oct. 1947, 365–69.
"A Southerner Talks with the South: A Review of Robert Penn Warren's *Segregation.*" *New York Times,* Sept. 6, 1956.
"The South's Glowing Horizon—IF." *Saturday Review,* Mar. 9, 1968, 115.
"There Is Time Yet: Freedom of the Press." *Atlantic* 174 (Sept. 1944): 61–62.
"They Stuck to the South." *Saturday Evening Post,* Apr. 30, 1949, 38–39, 59, 62, 64.
"Tom Watson: The People's Man." *New Republic,* Aug. 23, 1948, 16–20.
"Union Bag and Paper Corporation." *Fortune* 16 (Aug. 1937): 122, 126, 132.
Unpublished manuscript. Box 31, Folder 4, RMP.
"What's Wrong with Southern Cooking?" *Saturday Evening Post,* Mar. 26, 1949, 38–39, 102–5.
"Will the South Ditch Truman?" *Saturday Evening Post,* May 22, 1948, 15–17, 88–90.

OTHER NEWSPAPER ARTICLES

"77 Negroes Arrested in Student Sitdowns at 10 Eating Places Here; Act Jointly in Orderly Protests." *Atlanta Constitution,* Mar. 16, 1960, p. 1.

"1,000 Paratroopers Poured in to Force Little Rock Integration." *Atlanta Constitution,* Sept. 25, 1957, p. 1.

Aikman, Leo. "He Practiced Kindness." *Atlanta Constitution,* Feb. 5, 1969, p. 4.

"American Editors' Failure to Contact A.I.N.E.C." *Hindustan Times,* Apr. 19, 1945, n.p.

"Another Tragedy; A Student at the University Kills a Companion; J. C. Johnson and M. McGill Quarrel, and the Latter Crushes the Skull of the Former with a Base Ball Bat; Opprobrious Epithets the Cause; Johnson Lives Until 5 O'Clock in the Afternoon and Expires—The Slayer Escapes—Reward for His Arrest—The Coroner's Inquest." *Chattanooga Daily Times,* Feb. 23, 1888, p. 6.

"Arnall Leads, 2 to 1, in Peace Justices' Poll; Survey Covers All of Georgia; Never Wrong." *Atlanta Constitution,* Aug. 23, 1942, p. 1.

"Arnall Runs Unit Margin to 261–149 as All Counties Complete Vote Count." *Atlanta Constitution,* Sept. 11, 1942, p. 1.

Associated Press. "Strike Paralyzes Cuban Commerce; 'Revolt' Is Seen; Machado Threatens to Declare Martial Law to Break Movement Regarded as Seditious." *Atlanta Constitution,* Aug. 5, 1933, p. 1.

"Atlanta C of C Supports Local Option on Schools." *Atlanta Constitution,* Mar. 24, 1960, p. 1.

"Atlantan Shows Enemy Bullet." *Atlanta Constitution,* Mar. 2, 1966, p. 1.

"Bad Road Advances." *Atlanta Constitution,* June 1, 1936, p. 6.

Ball, Lamar Q. "Arnall Warns on 'Rosy' Promises for Talmadge Roads." *Atlanta Constitution,* Aug. 15, 1942, p. 2.

———. "DeKalb Is Solid for Arnall, Last Rally Indicates." *Atlanta Constitution,* Sept. 9, 1942, p. 1.

———. "Dublin Throng Hears Linder Predict Easy Win for Ellis Arnall." *Constitution,* Sept. 6, 1942, p. 1.

———. "'Regular Fellow,' Say Schoolmates of Ellis Arnall." *Atlanta Constitution,* Aug. 2, 1942, p. 3D.

———. "Talmadge Is Accused of Selling State Jobs." *Atlanta Constitution,* Aug. 14, 1942, p. 1.

———. "Talmadge Shakedown of Publishers Charged; Firms Allowed to Up Price, Arnall Says." *Atlanta Constitution,* Aug. 12, 1942, p. 1.

———. "Talmadge Statement Denied by Victim of Tear Gas Plot." *Atlanta Constitution,* Aug. 2, 1942, pp. 1, 9.

———. "Two Talmadge Stalwarts Join Arnall's Ranks." *Atlanta Constitution,* Aug. 17, 1942, p. 1.

———. "Will Vote for Arnall, Tom Linder Declares." *Atlanta Constitution,* Sept. 5, 1942, p. 1.

"Beaver Resigns from Regent Board; Protests Interference by Talmadge; Gainesville Educator Also Gives Up Post as Chief of Staff." *Atlanta Constitution,* Aug. 28, 1942, p. 1.

Bennett, Tom. "Harold Martin, 83, Wrote for Newspaper, Magazine." *Atlanta Journal and Constitution,* July 11, 1994, p. 6B.

"Birmingham Crowd Beats Negro Minister." *Atlanta Constitution,* Sept. 10, 1957, p. 1.

Blake, Morgan. "Sportanic Eruptions." *Atlanta Journal,* Jan. 20, 1929, sports front page.

Boring, Bill. "Milt [Caniff], Here to Receive Law Degree, Recalls Art Days in High School; His Mr. Canyon Paying Off." *Atlanta Constitution,* May 21, 1947, pp. 1,7.

"Bricks Fly in Nashville Boycott." *Atlanta Constitution,* Sept. 10, 1957, p. 1.

"Caldwell Deplores Racial Charges Against University; Asserts It's His Duty to Inform People Properly on Issue." *Atlanta Constitution,* Aug. 2, 1942, p. 1.

"Circuit Court; Magill Murder Case Settled." *Chattanooga Times,* June 21, 1889, p. 6.

Clarke, Francis W. "The European Maelstrom." *Atlanta Constitution,* June 7, 1936, p. 14.

———. "The European Maelstrom." *Atlanta Constitution,* June 8, 1936, p. 4.

———. "The European Maelstrom." *Atlanta Constitution,* June 9, 1936, p. 4.

Coffin, Tom. "Chirp." *Great Speckled Bird* 1, no. 1 (Mar. 15, 1968): 1.

"Conference." *Birmingham Post,* Oct. 27, 1938, p. 1.

"Constructive Spending." *Atlanta Constitution,* May 3, 1936, p. 6.

"Courtroom Circus." *Atlanta Constitution,* May 2, 1938, p. 4.

Cox, Calvin. "Watching the World." *Atlanta Constitution,* Feb. 5, 1969, p. 4.

"Cox Files Application to Buy Station WSB." *Atlanta Constitution,* Dec. 12, 1939, p. 1.

Cox Is Expected to Make Statement on Arrival in Atlanta Today." *Atlanta Constitution,* Dec. 13, 1939, pp. 1, 11.

"Cuba Warns Castro About Communism." *Atlanta Constitution,* Feb. 6, 1960, p. 4.

Danforth, Ed. "Mawnin'!" *Atlanta Constitution,* July 20, 1929, p. 15.

"Dixie's Politicians." *Atlanta Constitution,* June 20, 1964, p. 1.

Editorial. *Atlanta Constitution,* Dec. 17, 1939, p. 10B.

"An Editorial." *Atlanta Constitution,* Feb. 4, 1969, p. 1.

"Editor Says Cabinet Post Open to Arnall." *Atlanta Constitution,* Mar. 6, 1945, p. 2.

Editor's note. *Atlanta Constitution,* Dec. 17, 1937, p. 1.

"Edwin A. Peebles, 79, author of books." *Atlanta Constitution,* Dec. 17, 1994, p. 12B.

"Ellis Arnall." Obituary. *Atlanta Constitution,* Dec. 14, 1992, p. 1.

"Faubus." *Atlanta Constitution,* Sept. 16, 1957, p. 4.

Finney, John W. "President Orders Cessation in the Bombing of N. Vietnam." *Atlanta Constitution,* Nov. 1, 1968, p. 1.

"Floyd Collins." *Nashville Banner,* Feb. 4, 1925, p. 1.

"Founded in 1906; 450 Employees Will Be Affected; Journal to Take Over Features and News Services of the Paper as 33-Year Career Ends." *Atlanta Constitution,* Dec. 17, 1939, p. 1.

"Friends Greet Ralph McGill." *Atlanta Constitution,* June 8, 1938, p. 1.

Gaines, Marion. "Segregation at All Costs Backed 5–1 at Moultrie Before Cheering Crowd; Sibley Unit Hears from 14 Counties." *Atlanta Constitution,* Mar. 22, 1960, p. 1.

"Gallogly Murder Case Ends in Mistrial." *Atlanta Constitution,* Feb. 2, 1929, p. 1.

Galphin, Bruce. "Assembly Made History by Saving the Schools." *Atlanta Constitution,* Mar. 7, 1968, p. 1.

———. "Georgia Must Choose Integration or Grants, School Study Unit Told: Sibley Warns of Grave Duty." *Atlanta Constitution,* Feb. 18, 1960, p. 1.

———. "Negroes Agree to End Sit-Ins." *Atlanta Constitution,* Mar. 8, 1961, p. 1.

———. "Open Schools Backed Overwhelmingly Here; 114 Testify at Sibley Hearing." *Atlanta Constitution,* Mar. 24, 1960, p. 1.

———. "The Thunderer Behind the Print Was a Gentle, Generous Man." *Atlanta Constitution,* Feb. 5, 1969, p. 4.

"Gave Himself Up; McGill, Who Killed Young Johnson, Surrenders; A Pathetic and Touching Meeting Between the Unfortunate Young Man and His Father; Remains of the Dead Boy Carried Home." *Chattanooga Daily Times,* Feb. 24, 1888, p. 6.

"George Harsh Confesses Local Killings and Implicates Richard G. Gallogly." *Atlanta Constitution,* Oct. 28, 1928, p. 1.

"Georgian Marks Eighth Major Change in Chain." *Atlanta Constitution,* Dec. 17, 1939, p. 10.

"Godless Bombing Aimed at All Atlantans, a 'Sick at Heart' Rabbi Rothschild Asserts." *Atlanta Constitution,* Oct. 13, 1958, p. 6.

"Good Instincts, Wisely Applied." *Atlanta Constitution,* Mar. 8, 1961, p. 4.

"Griffin Sees Presidency Shut to Dixie." *Atlanta Constitution,* Sept. 12, 1957, p. 30.

"Harsh, Gallogly Given Life Terms by Guilty Pleas." *Atlanta Constitution,* Apr. 2, 1929, p. 1.

"Has the South Lagged Economically?" *Atlanta Constitution,* Nov. 30, 1938, p. 4.

Hayden, Jay G. "Johnson Faces 2-Way Distrust; Southerner in the White House." *Atlanta Constitution,* Nov. 24, 1963, p. 25.

"Hear the Death Rattle." *Atlanta Constitution,* June 4, 1936, p. 6.

Herndon, Ray F. "Viet Reds Regroup Via Neutral Zone." *Atlanta Constitution,* Mar. 19, 1966, p. 1.

"HHH Joins Baggs' Tribute." *Atlanta Constitution,* Jan. 9, 1969, p. 1.

"His Loss Diminishes Us All: Tributes from the Staff." *Atlanta Constitution,* Feb. 5, 1969, p. 4.

"Ike Silent in Signing Rights Bill." *Atlanta Constitution,* Sept. 10, 1957, p. 1.

"Ill-Advised Strike." *Atlanta Constitution,* June 3, 1936, p. 6.

"An Imperative Need." *Atlanta Constitution,* May 4, 1938, p. 6.

"Integration Problems Follow No Set Pattern." *Atlanta Constitution,* Sept. 4, 1957, p. 4.

"Integration Sure, Peters Predicts." *Atlanta Constitution,* Jan. 17, 1960, p. 1.

"Is Maddox Out After Johnson?" *Atlanta Constitution,* May 12, 1967, p. 1.

"James M. Cox Asserts Journal 'To Remain Free.'" *Atlanta Constitution,* Dec. 19, 1939, p. 5.

"JFK Dixie Critics Voice Indignation." *Atlanta Constitution,* Nov. 24, 1963, p. 23.

"Jim Peters Survived Lions' Dean Admirably." *Atlanta Constitution,* Feb. 11, 1960, p. 4.

"Johnson Sees Top Aides, Decrees Monday Mourning; Cabinet Called, Ike Consulted." *Atlanta Constitution,* Nov. 24, 1963, p. 1.

"Johnson Signs Civil Rights Act, Allen Urges All to Obey." *Atlanta Constitution,* July 3, 1964, p. 1.

"Journal-Georgian Bill of Sale Filed; Deed Covers Transfer of Building, Machines and Other Equipment." *Atlanta Constitution,* Dec. 19, 1939, p. 5.

"Journal, WSB Sold to James M. Cox; New Owner of Paper Ex-Governor of Ohio; Divided Control Termed Factor by James R. Gray; Purchaser Was Democratic Nominee for President in 1920; Sale Effective Immediately." *Atlanta Constitution,* Dec. 13, 1939, p. 5.

"Jury Deadlocked in Gallogly Trial." *Atlanta Constitution,* Feb. 1, 1928, p. 1.

Kihss, Peter. "Dixie Rights Attitude Mixed; Legal Steps Are Considered." *Atlanta Constitution,* June 22, 1964, p. 1.

Krock, Arthur. "Why Our Newspapers Can't Tell the Truth." *Reader's Digest,* Nov. 1942, 75.

"Last Rites Today for Ben F. McGill; Retired Businessman Died Monday Night— Had Lived Here for 36 Years." *Chattanooga Daily Times,* Aug. 7, 1940, p. 7.

"Law Must Be Modified." *Atlanta Constitution,* June 6, 1936, p. 6.

Lawrence, W. H. "Ike Finds Peace Isn't Enforced." *Atlanta Constitution,* reprint from *New York Times,* Sept. 25, 1957, p. 1.

"Little Rock Crucial Test Moves Toward Climax." *Atlanta Constitution,* Sept. 6, 1957, p. 4.

Lippman, Ted. "No More Sitdowns Now, Students Say." *Atlanta Constitution,* Mar. 17, 1960, p. 1.

Lippmann, Walter. "Magical Prosperity." *New York Herald Tribune,* Sept. 8, 1931. In *Interpretations, 1931–1932,* edited by Allan Nevins. New York: Macmillan, 1932.

"Local School Chiefs Back Local Option." *Atlanta Constitution,* Mar. 24, 1960, p. 4.

"Maddox Holds Gun, Bars 3 Negroes." *Atlanta Constitution,* July 4, 1964, p. 1.

"The Man Who Searched for Answers." Editorial. *Atlanta Constitution,* Jan. 9, 1969.

McCartney, Keeler, and James Sheppard. "Jewish Temple on Peachtree Wrecked by Dynamite Blast." *Atlanta Constitution,* Oct. 13, 1958, p. 1.

"McGill Is Barred from South Africa." *Atlanta Constitution,* Mar. 24, 1967, p. 1.

"McGill, Virginia Colvin." Obituary. *Atlanta Constitution,* Dec. 20, 1939, p. 29.

McKnight, John P. "Machado to Resign Today as Cuban President; 26 Slain, 150 Shot Down by Troops in Havana." *Atlanta Constitution,* Aug. 8, 1933, p. 1.

"Medal for Work as Humanitarian Awarded Black; Justice Cites Early Efforts of Jefferson for Underprivileged in Acceptance." *Birmingham News,* Nov. 24, 1938, pp. 1–2.

Miller, Bryce. "Ike Appeals to Faubus to Stop Defiance of Little Rock Integration." *Atlanta Constitution,* Sept. 6, 1957, p. 1.

"'Miss Scarlett' Makes Triumphant Return to Atlanta Today as Stars, Film Dignitaries Start Arriving for Gala Fete; Ann Rutherford to be First of Stellar Deluge." *Atlanta Constitution,* Dec. 13, 1939, p. 1.

"The Mob Will Destroy All It Seeks to Protect." *Atlanta Constitution,* Sept. 11, 1957, p. 4.

Mohbat, Joseph E. "U.S. Moves Slowly in Enforcing Law." *Atlanta Constitution,* July 3, 1964, p. 1.

"The Mote and the Beam." *Atlanta Constitution,* June 4, 1936, p. 6.

"'Mr. Jim' Peters Warns the Politicians of Consequences of Closing Schools." *Atlanta Constitution,* Jan. 18, 1960, p. 4.

"Mrs. Ralph McGill Dies; Wife of Publisher of *Atlanta Constitution* Was 57." *New York Times,* Mar. 22, 1962, p. 35.

"Mrs. Ralph McGill Is Dead; *Constitution* Publisher's Wife." *Atlanta Constitution,* Mar. 22, 1962, pp. 1, 8.

Murphy, Reg. "The Man Who Loved the South." *Atlanta Constitution,* Feb. 4, 1969, p. 4.

———. "'Trust Instinct,' He Advised Us." *Atlanta Constitution,* Feb. 5, 1969, p. 4.

Murphy, Reg, and Bob Hurt. "Ralph McGill Dies Here in 70th Year After Heart Attack; Stricken at Dinner at Friends' Home." *Atlanta Constitution,* Feb. 4, 1969, p. 1.

"Must Comply with Law Now, Talmadge Advises." *Atlanta Constitution,* July 4, 1964, p. 1.

"Nashville Dynamiters Raze Integrated School." *Atlanta Constitution,* Sept. 11, 1957, p. 1.

"Nation's Attitude on Vietnam War Is Improving, Says President Johnson." *Atlanta Constitution,* May 19, 1967, p. 2.

"Negro Collegians Fill All Seats at Cafe in Integration Sitdown." *Atlanta Constitution,* Feb. 4, 1960, p. 12.

Nelson, Jack. "Thousands of Spectators Stream by but See Little of Debris and Drama." *Atlanta Constitution,* Oct. 13, 1958, p. 6.

"The News Quits in Chattanooga." *Atlanta Constitution,* Dec. 17, 1939, pp. 1, 10.

"New Uses for Cotton." *Atlanta Constitution,* June 1, 1936, p. 6.

"No Law Condones Rule by Violence." *Atlanta Constitution,* Sept. 12, 1957, p. 4.

O'Ware, Tom. "DEAR RALPHIE: The Mis-Use of History." *Great Speckled Bird,* no. 10 (July 19, 1968), p. 4.

Patterson, Eugene. "Ivan Allen Jr. and the Sit-Ins." *Atlanta Constitution,* Mar. 9, 1961, p. 4.

————. "She Counted Sunny Hours." *Atlanta Constitution,* Mar. 22, 1962, p. 1.

"The Pay-Hour Bill." *Atlanta Constitution,* May 4, 1938, p. 6.

Pomerantz, Gary M. "'63 Bombing Was Era's Worst Act of Terrorism." *Atlanta Constitution,* July 12, 1997, p. 2.

"Pre-Letter Conference Reported Between Peters and Talmadge." *Atlanta Constitution,* Feb. 8, 1960, p. 1.

"President Pleads for Peace in Signing $4.8 Billion Arms Bill." *Atlanta Constitution,* Mar. 16, 1966, p. 1.

"The Press." *Time,* Sept. 14, 1942, 46.

"Price Announced in Journal Sale." *Atlanta Constitution,* Dec. 14, 1939, p. 1.

"'Protest' Incidents Need No Repetition." *Atlanta Constitution,* Mar. 16, 1960, p. 4.

"Pulitzer Prizes." Editorial. *Atlanta Constitution,* May 9, 1951, p. 12.

"Race Dispute Moves Presbyterian Rally." *Atlanta Constitution,* Jan. 27, 1965, p. 1.

"Ralph Emerson McGill." Editorial. *Atlanta Constitution,* Feb. 5, 1969, p. 4.

"Ralph McGill Appointed to Executive Editorship; Ralph T. Jones Becomes Associate Editor in Promotions Announced by Major Clark Howell, Editor and Publisher of the Constitution." *Atlanta Constitution,* June 17, 1938, p. 1.

"Ralph McGill Is Elected Member of Ten Club at Monthly Meeting." *Atlanta Constitution,* Nov. 23, 1938, p. 2.

"Red Paper's Critic Scorns 'Pan GWTW' Order; Daily Worker's Reviewer Resigns Rather than Rewrite Story; Declares Board Told Him to Urge Boycott of Film." *Atlanta Constitution,* Dec. 22, 1939, p. 1.

"Rep. Davis Needs Rest, Shade and Light Diet." *Atlanta Constitution,* Sept. 7, 1957, p. 4.

Reston, James B. "American Nations Form an Alliance to Protect Peace: Act of Chapultepec, Accepted Unanimously, Guarantees Borders in Hemisphere." *New York Times,* Mar. 4, 1945, pp. 1, 25.

Rochelle, Anne. "Harold C. Fleming, 70, Veteran Civil Rights Leader and ex-Atlantan, Dies." *Atlanta Constitution,* Sept. 6, 1992, p. 3H.

Russell, Freddie. "'Mouse' Defies Docs; May Play Saturday; Broken Wrist Still Unhealed but Brace and Super-nerve Gives Vandy Star Chance." *Atlanta Constitution,* Oct. 30, 1931, p. 19. Reprinted from the *Nashville Banner.*

"Searchers Losing Hope for 3 Rights Workers." *Atlanta Constitution,* June 25, 1964, p. 1.

"Second Mistrial Ordered, New Date Apr. 2." *Atlanta Constitution,* Mar. 24, 1929, p. 1.

"Second Trial of Richard Gallogly." *Atlanta Constitution,* Mar. 20, 1929, p. 1.

Sibley, Celestine. "A Man of Rare Goodness and Fun Passes On." *Atlanta Constitution,* July 11, 1994, p. 1C.

————. "McGill: Earth Held No Higher Calling." *Atlanta Constitution,* Feb. 5, 1969, p. 4.

———. "Ralph McGill Rites Today on Birthday." *Atlanta Constitution,* Feb. 5, 1969, p. 1.

"Sit-Ins Win 5 Cases in High Court." *Atlanta Constitution,* June 23, 1964, p. 1.

"Social Security." *Atlanta Constitution,* June 7, 1936, p. 14.

Sosin, Milt. "Miami Turns Out for Bill." *Miami News,* Jan. 10, 1969, p. 1.

"Southern Reaction to Negro Voting Decision Record." *Atlanta Constitution,* Apr. 4, 1944, p. 1.

Speicher, Don. "What's It All About, Ralphie?" *Great Speckled Bird* 1, no. 1 (Mar. 15, 1968): 1.

"State's Leaders Hail McGill." *Atlanta Constitution,* Feb. 4, 1969, pp. 1, 12.

"Supreme Court Rules Primary Open to Negro." *Atlanta Constitution,* Apr. 4, 1944, p. 1.

"Talmadge Still Refuses to Concede His Defeat; Palace Guard Urging Contest of Vote Count." *Atlanta Constitution,* Sept. 13, 1942, pp. 1, 13.

Tarver, Jack. "Gene Wouldn't Have Won Anyway." *Atlanta Constitution,* June 2, 1946, p. 14C.

"Tax Reduction." *Atlanta Constitution,* May 3, 1938, p. 6.

"There'll Be No Primary in Cuba." *Atlanta Constitution,* Mar. 12, 1952, p. 8.

Thomy, Al. "Ed Danforth Dies in His Office Here." *Atlanta Constitution,* Dec. 6, 1962, p. 1.

"To Purge Atlanta's Blue." *Atlanta Constitution,* May 1, 1938, p. 8.

Tyson, Remer. "Guidelines Fight Led by Talmadge." *Atlanta Constitution,* Mar. 30, 1966, p. 1.

"U.S. Courts Uphold Ellis Arnall's Legal Opinions." *Atlanta Constitution,* Aug. 16, 1942, p. 3D.

"Viet Junta Yields to the U.S., Frees 20 Political Prisoners." *Atlanta Constitution,* Jan. 11, 1965, p. 1.

"Virginia M'Gill Dies After Long Illness; Rites for Daughter of *Constitution* Editor to Be Held Today." *Atlanta Constitution,* Dec. 20, 1939, p. 29.

"We Do Not Have to Get in It." Editorial. *Atlanta Constitution,* Sept. 4, 1939, p. 4.

"Welcome, Governor Cox." Editorial. *Atlanta Constitution,* Dec. 20, 1939.

"Welfare Conference Resolutions Touch on Variety of Questions." *Birmingham News,* Nov. 24, 1938, p. 2.

Wells, Frank. "Placement Left Up to Counties." *Atlanta Constitution,* Mar. 7, 1961, pp. 1, 12.

"Where Danger Lies." Editorial. *Atlanta Constitution,* Aug. 21, 1942, p. 4A.

William M. Bates. "Rights Bill Upset GOP's Plans in the South." *Atlanta Constitution,* Sept. 11, 1957, p. 7.

"Willkie Leading Roosevelt in Electoral Votes—Gallup." *Atlanta Constitution,* Aug. 4, 1940, p. 1.

"Worse than Cattle Shacks." *Atlanta Constitution,* June 1, 1936, p. 6.

"A Worthily Bestowed Honor." *Atlanta Constitution,* June 4, 1936, p. 6.

Zellner, Joe. "Maddox Gets a Change on Compliance." *Atlanta Constitution,* May 12, 1967, p. 1.

OFFICIAL RECORDS AND GOVERNMENT DOCUMENTS

Federal Bureau of Investigation. Special Inquiry. Nov. 28, 1961. Bureau File 161-1745-17.

———. Special Inquiry, for the Joint Congressional Committee on Atomic Energy. Washington, D.C., Nov. 23, 1951. Bureau File 77-52062-3X.

Georgia Official and Statistical Record. Atlanta, 1940.

Griffin, Marvin. *Progress Report by the Governor, Transmitted to the Members of the General Assembly.* State of Georgia. Nov. 1957.
South Conference on Human Welfare. "Report on Proceedings, Nov. 20–23, 1938." Box 67, Folder 22, RMP.
Vandiver, S. Ernest. "Report to the People from the Governor." State of Georgia. Jan. 10, 1962.

OTHER MAGAZINE ARTICLES
Brownell, Herbert, Jr. "Success of FBI Is Outstanding." *U.S. News,* Apr. 16, 1954, 112–14.
Clark, B. "Let's Unshackle the FBI." *Reader's Digest,* Apr. 1954, 111–14.
"Communists in the U.S. a Greater Menace Now." Interview with Herbert Brownell Jr. *U.S. News,* Sept. 4, 1953, 49–50.
"Constitution Amended." *Time,* Jan. 5, 1948, 48.
Detzer, K. "FBI Protects the Innocent; Crime Laboratory." *Reader's Digest,* Mar. 1954, 57–60.
"FBI Unassisted Can Catch No Spies." *Saturday Evening Post,* Sept. 19, 1953, 10.
Hoover, J. Edgar. "B-r-e-a-k-i-n-g the Communist Spell." *American Mercury,* Mar. 1954, 57–61.
"Hoover Speaks Out on Spies After Years Chasing Them." *U.S. News,* Nov. 27, 1953, 35–38.
Howland, William. "Live with the Change." *Time,* Dec. 14, 1953, 51.
Jarmin, Rufus. "Wool Hat Dictator." *Saturday Evening Post,* June 27, 1947, 111.
"Strong Constitution." *Time,* Sept. 14, 1942, 46.
Teel, Leonard Ray. "How James Cox Bought Atlanta's Newspapers." *Georgia Trend* 2 (Dec. 1986): 87–90.
Trillin, Calvin. "Mississippi's State Sovereignty Commission." *New Yorker,* May 29, 1995, 55.
"Voting in the South." *Life,* May 18, 1944, 33–34.
"Watered-Down Pulitzers?" *Time,* May 21, 1951, 56.
"What and Why of the Files." Interview with Herbert Brownell Jr. *Newsweek,* Apr. 6, 1953, 24–25.
Wilson, J. "G-men Keep Their Shooting Irons and Corn Plasters Handy." *Look,* Oct. 6, 1953, 126.

MISCELLANEOUS PUBLICATIONS, PRESENTATIONS, AND FILMS
"Censored Editor." *Vanderbilt Hustler,* May 5, 1920, 4.
"Dawn's Early Light: Ralph McGill and the Segregated South." Produced and directed by Kathleen Dowdey and Jed Dannenbaum. Center for Contemporary Media, 1989. Videocassette.
Forrest, Wilbur, Carl W. Ackerman, and Ralph McGill. "Full Report of the ASNE Committee on Freedom of Information." *Editor and Publisher,* June 18, 1945, 3.
"Hitler in Georgia." Editorial. *American Press,* Aug. 2, 1941, 462.
"McGill Brings Peace." *Vanderbilt Alumnus* 13, no. 4 (Mar.–Apr. 1928): 148.
"Once Too Often." *Jade* (Vanderbilt Univ.) 1, no. 4 (June 5, 1920): 15.
Year-Book of Chattanooga University, 1887–88. Special Collections, Lupton Library, Univ. of Tennessee–Chattanooga.

General Reference Works

Eberhard, Wallace B. "Clark Howell." In *Biographical Dictionary of American Journalism,* 355–56. New York: Greenwood Press, 1989.

Kuczun, Sam. "Joseph Pulitzer." In *Biographical Dictionary of American Journalism,* 562.

Miller, William Burke ("Skeets"). "A Young Man Dies in a Cave." *Louisville Courier-Journal,* Feb. 3, 1925. Reprinted in Calder M. Pickett, *Voice of the Past: Key Documents in the History of American Journalism.* New York: Macmillan, 1977.

Tidwell, John Edgar. "Davis." *Afro-American Writers.* Vol. 51, *Dictionary of Literary Biography.* Detroit: Gale Research Co., 1987. Pp. 60, 63–64.

Secondary Sources

Books

Aguilar, Luis E. *Cuba 1933.* Ithaca: Cornell Univ. Press, 1971.

Allen, Frederick Lewis. *Only Yesterday.* New York: Bantam Books, 1959.

Ames, Jessie Daniel. *The Changing Character of Lynching: Review of Lynching, 1931–1941.* Atlanta: Commission on Interracial Cooperation, 1942.

Anderson, William. *The Wild Man from Sugar Creek: The Political Career of Eugene Talmadge.* Baton Rouge: Louisiana State Univ. Press, 1975.

Arnall, Ellis Gibbs. *The Shore Dimly Seen.* 1946. Reprint, New York: Acclaim Publishing, 1966.

Ashmore, Harry S. *Civil Rights and Wrongs: A Memoir of Race and Politics, 1944–1994.* New York: Pantheon Books, 1994.

———. *Hearts and Minds: A Personal Chronicle of Race in America.* Rev. ed. Cabin John, Md.: Seven Locks Press, 1988.

Ashmore, Harry S., and William C. Baggs. *Mission to Hanoi: A Chronicle of Double-Dealing in High Places.* New York: Putnam Berkley Publishing Group, 1968.

Ayers, Edward L. *The Promise of the New South: Life After Reconstruction.* New York: Oxford Univ. Press, 1992.

Bartley, Numan V. *The New South, 1945–1980.* Baton Rouge: Louisiana State Univ. Press, 1995.

Barzun, Jacques. *The House of Intellect.* New York: Harper, 1959.

Beasley, Maurine Hoffman, and Richard R. Harlow. *Voices of Change: Southern Pulitzer Winners.* McLean, Va.: Univ. Press of America, 1979.

Benét, Stephen Vincent. *John Brown's Body.* Garden City, N.Y.: Country Life Press, 1928.

Beschloss, Michael R. *Taking Charge: The Johnson White House Tapes, 1963–1964.* New York: Simon and Schuster, 1997.

Blanchard, Margaret A. *Exporting the First Amendment: The Press-Government Crusade of 1945–1952.* New York: Longman, 1986.

Branch, Taylor. *Parting the Waters: American in the King Years, 1954–63.* New York: Simon and Schuster, 1988.

———. *Pillar of Fire: America in the King Years, 1963–65.* New York: Simon and Schuster, 1998.

Brawley, Benjamin. *The Negro Genius: A New Appraisal of the Achievement of the American Negro in Literature and the Fine Arts.* New York: Biblo and Tannen, 1966.

Caro, Robert A. *The Years of Lyndon Johnson: Means of Ascent.* New York: Alfred A. Knopf, 1990.

Carter, Dan T. *The Politics of Rage: George Wallace, the Origins of the New Conservatism, and the Transformation of American Politics.* New York: Simon and Schuster, 1995.

Caruthers, Clifford M., ed. *Letters from Ring.* Flint, Mich.: Walden Press, 1979.

Cash, W. A. *The Mind of the South.* New York: Vintage Books, 1941.

Cassill, R. V., ed. *The Norton Anthology of Short Fiction.* 2d ed. New York: W. W. Norton, 1981.

Chapman, Charles E. *A History of the Cuban Republic: A Study in Hispanic American Politics.* New York: Octagon Books, 1969.

Cheney, Brainard. *This Is Adam.* New York: McDowell, Oblensky, 1958.

Conkin, Paul Keith. *Gone with the Ivy: A Biography of Vanderbilt University.* Knoxville: Univ. of Tennessee Press, 1985.

Coulter, E. Merton. *Georgia: A Short History.* Rev. ed. Chapel Hill: Univ. of North Carolina Press, 1960.

Conkin, Paul K. *Big Daddy from the Pedernales: Lyndon Baines Johnson.* Boston: Twayne, 1986.

Cox, James M. *Journey Through My Years.* New York: Simon and Schuster, 1946.

Crowder, Richard. *Carl Sandburg.* New Haven, Conn.: College and Univ. Press, 1964.

Daniels, Josephus. *Tar Heel Editor.* Chapel Hill: Univ. of North Carolina Press, 1939.

Davis, Arthur P. *From the Dark Tower: Afro-American Writers, 1900–1960.* Washington, D.C.: Howard Univ. Press, 1974.

Davis, Frank Marshall. *47th Street: Poems.* Prairie City, Ill.: Decker Press, 1948.

———. *Black Man's Verse.* Chicago: Black Cat Press, 1935.

———. *I Am the American Negro.* Chicago: Black Cat Press, 1937.

———. *Through Sepia Eyes.* Chicago: Black Cat Press, 1938.

Davis, Harold E. *Henry Grady's New South: Atlanta, a Brave and Beautiful City.* Tuscaloosa: Univ. of Alabama Press, 1990.

Douglas, William O. *The Court Years.* New York: Vintage Books, 1981.

Doyle, Don H. *Nashville in the New South, 1880–1930.* Knoxville: Univ. of Tennessee Press, 1985.

Egerton, John. *Speak Now Against the Day: The Generation Before the Civil Rights Movement in the South.* New York: Knopf, 1994.

Ellis, William E. *Robert Worth Bingham and the Southern Mystique: From the Old South to the New South and Beyond.* Kent, Ohio: Kent State Univ. Press, 1997.

Evans, Walker. *Havana 1933.* Introduction by Gilles Mora, translated by Christie McDonald. New York: Pantheon Books, 1989.

Galbraith, John Kenneth. *The Great Crash: 1929.* Boston: Houghton Mifflin, 1961.

Garrow, David J., ed. *Atlanta, Georgia, 1960–1961: Sit-Ins and Student Activism.* Brooklyn, N.Y.: Carlson Publishing, 1989.

———. *Bearing the Cross: Martin Luther King, Jr., and the Southern Christian Leadership Conference.* New York: William Morrow, 1999.

———. *The FBI and Martin Luther King, Jr.: From 'Solo' to Memphis.* New York: W. W. Norton, 1981.

Golden, Harry. *The Right Time: An Autobiography of Harry Golden.* New York: G. P. Putnam's Sons, 1969.

Govan, Gilbert E., and James W. Livingood. *The Chattanooga Country, 1540–1962: From Tomahawks to TVA.* Chapel Hill: Univ. of North Carolina Press, 1963.

———. *The University of Chattanooga: Sixty Years.* Chattanooga: Univ. of Chattanooga, 1947.

Toland, John. *Adolf Hitler.* New York: Ballantine Books, 1976.

Tuchman, Barbara W. *Stilwell and the American Experience in China, 1911–1945.* New York: Macmillan, 1971.

Weeks, Edward. *Writers and Friends.* Boston: Little, Brown, 1981.

White, Theodore H. *The Making of the President, 1960.* New York: Atheneum, 1961.

Whited, Charles. *Knight: A Publisher in the Tumultuous Century.* New York: E. P. Dutton, 1988.

Wilson, John. *Chattanooga's Story.* Chattanooga: Chattanooga News Free Press, 1980.

———. *Hamilton County Pioneers.* Chelsea, Mich.: BookCrafters, 1998.

Wisan, Joseph. *The Cuban Crisis as Reflected in the New York Press.* New York: Octagon Books, 1965.

Woods, Randall Bennett. *Fulbright: A Biography.* New York: Cambridge Univ. Press, 1995.

Woodward, C. Vann. *Tom Watson: Agrarian Rebel.* New York, 1938.

Zangrando, Robert L. *The NAACP Crusade Against Lynching, 1909–1950.* Philadelphia: Temple Univ. Press, 1980.

JOURNAL ARTICLES

Fleming, Harold C. "The Federal Executive and Civil Rights, 1961–1965." *Daedalus,* Fall 1965, 942.

Johnson, Guy B. "Does the South Owe the Negro a New Deal?" *Social Forces* 13, no. 1 (Oct. 1934): 100–103.

Logue, Calvin McLeod. "Ralph McGill: Convictions of a Southern Editor." *Journalism Quarterly* 45 (Winter 1968): 647–52.

Randall, Dudley. "An Interview with Frank Marshall Davis." *Black World* 23, no. 3 (1974): 37–48.

Teel, Leonard Ray. "The African-American Press and the Campaign for a Federal Antilynching Law, 1933–34: Putting Civil Rights on the National Agenda." *American Journalism* 8, no. 2–3 (Spring–Summer 1991): 97–98, 104–5.

———. "W. A. Scott and the Atlanta World." *American Journalism* 6, no. 3 (July 1989): 158–78.

BOOK REVIEWS

Ashmore, Harry S. "A Place of the Heart." *Virginia Quarterly Review* (Summer 1963): 486.

Baughman, James L. Review of *Worldly Power: The Making of the Wall Street Journal,* by Edward E. Scharff. *Journalism Quarterly* (Winter 1986): 863–64.

Cutler, E. J. Review of *Mission to Hanoi: A Chronicle of Double-Dealing in High Places,* by Harry S. Ashmore and William C. Baggs. *Library Journal* 93 (Nov. 1, 1968): 4213.

DuPree, Don Keck. "Newt and Jeff Shall Prevail." Review of *The Unregenerate South: The Agrarian Thought of John Crowe Ransom, Allen Tate, and Donald Davidson,* by Mark G. Malvasi. *Chattahoochee Review* 18, no. 4 (Summer 1998): 93–99.

Lockwood, Lee. Review of *Mission to Hanoi: A Chronicle of Double-Dealing in High Places,* by Harry S. Ashmore and William C. Baggs. *Nation* 208 (Mar. 24, 1969): 374.

Muske, Carol. "Laura Riding Roughshod." Review of *In Extremis: The Life of Laura Riding,* by Deborah Baker. *New York Times Book Review,* Nov. 29, 1993, 14.

Review of *Mission to Hanoi: A Chronicle of Double-Dealing in High Places,* by Harry
    S. Ashmore and William C. Baggs. *New Yorker* 44 (Dec. 7, 1968): 246.

DISSERTATIONS, THESES, AND MANUSCRIPTS

Adair, A. Dixon, III. "Eugene Talmadge of Georgia." Master's thesis, Princeton
    Univ., 1936.
Dowell, Drew. "Editorial and Critical Writing." Master's research paper, Nov. 21,
    1989.
Ellis, William E. "The Bingham Papers: Passing the Torch in the 1930s." Paper
    presented to the American Journalism Historians Association national
    conference, Louisville, Ky., Oct. 22, 1998.
Gibson, Dirk Cameron. "Neither God nor Devil: Perspective on the Political
    Myths of J. Edgar Hoover." Ph.D. diss., Indiana Univ., 1983.
Greybeal, John M. "The Georgia Primary Election System." Master's thesis, Emory
    Univ., 1932.
Hays, Harry M. "Who Killed James Johnson?" Unpublished research paper, Aug.
    15, 1990. Special Collections, Lupton Library, Univ. of Tennessee-
    Chattanooga.
Holland, Lynwood M. "The Conduct of Elections in Georgia." Master's thesis,
    Emory Univ., 1933.
Lusk, Charles W. "Hamilton County." Unpublished manuscript, Chattanooga
    Public Library.
Norrell, Robert J. "Next Steps to Democracy: The First Fifty Years of the Southern
    Regional Council." Unpublished manuscript. Southern Regional Council,
    Atlanta.
Owens, Alice. "The County Unit System as an Integral Part of the Georgia
    Primary Election System." Master's thesis, Emory Univ., 1934.
Rock, Virginia Jean. "The Making and Meaning of *I'll Take My Stand:* A Study in
    Utopian-Conservatism, 1925–1939." Ph.D. diss., Univ. of Minnesota, 1961.

Index

Ralph Emerson McGill was designed and typeset on a Macintosh computer system using PageMaker software. The text and chapter openings are set in Stone Serif. This book was designed by Vernon Boes, typeset by Kimberly Scarbrough, and manufactured by Thomson-Shore, Inc. The paper used in this book is designed for an effective life of at least three hundred years.